Private Law and Social Inequality
in the Industrial Age

STUDIES OF THE GERMAN
HISTORICAL INSTITUTE LONDON

GENERAL EDITOR: Peter Wende

Private Law and Social Inequality in the Industrial Age

Comparing Legal Cultures in
Britain, France, Germany, and
the United States

EDITED BY
WILLIBALD STEINMETZ

THE GERMAN HISTORICAL
INSTITUTE LONDON

OXFORD
UNIVERSITY PRESS

OXFORD
UNIVERSITY PRESS

Great Clarendon Street, Oxford OX2 6DP

Oxford University Press is a department of the University of Oxford.
It furthers the University's objective of excellence in research, scholarship,
and education by publishing worldwide in

Oxford New York

Athens Auckland Bangkok Bogotá Buenos Aires Calcutta
Cape Town Chennai Dar es Salaam Delhi Florence Hong Kong Istanbul
Karachi Kuala Lumpur Madrid Melbourne Mexico City Mumbai
Nairobi Paris Sao Paulo Singapore Taipei Tokyo Toronto Warsaw

with associated companies in Berlin Ibadan

Oxford is registered trade mark of Oxford University Press
in the UK and in certain other countries

Published in the United States
by Oxford University Press Inc., New York

© The German Historical Institute, London 2000

The moral rights of the author have been asserted
Database right Oxford University Press (maker)

First published 2000

British Library Cataloguing in Publication Data
Data available
Library of Congress Cataloging in Publication Data
Data applied for

ISBN 0-19-920236-2

1 3 5 7 9 10 8 6 4 2

Typeset in Baskerville
by Best-set Typesetter Ltd, Hong Kong
Printed in Great Britain
on acid-free paper by
Biddles Ltd, www.biddles.co.uk

Foreword

The present volume grew out of an international and interdisciplinary conference held at the German Historical Institute London in December 1995. Bringing together social historians and legal historians from four major industrialized countries, the conference aimed to set in motion a dialogue on cross-country comparisons of legal cultures. The leading idea was to investigate the significance of private law in central areas of social conflict: rural production, family relations, work, housing, and debt. During the nineteenth and early twentieth centuries unequal treatment by the law and unequal chances of making use of the law characterized these areas in all four countries observed. Basic types of dispute were in many respects similar in Britain, France, Germany, and the United States. This is what makes comparisons possible. On the other hand, the way in which legislators and judges intervened in social relations were different, as were the capacity and willingness of people to appeal to courts of law in order to solve their conflicts. To explain such differences in the patterns of juridification is what makes comparisons a rewarding task.

This volume is one of the first to explore the intermediate territory between formal legal provisions and actual judicial proceedings from a historical perspective and on a comparative basis. Research on these topics is only just starting, and has followed different paths in Britain, continental Europe, and the United States. The contributions assembled here reflect this diversity of approach. Historians generally have long neglected private law and tended to concentrate on matters such as criminal justice and the genesis of the welfare state. Doctrinal legal history has been mostly concerned with the evolution of theories of legislation and rules elaborated by the superior courts. The views of those who used the law and the reality of judicial proceedings, especially in lower courts of civil jurisdiction and special tribunals, have been largely ignored. This unsatisfactory situation is beginning to change and attempts are being made in many countries to close the gap between the two disciplines. None the less, most of these studies are still undertaken in isolation from each other. The conference in London provided one of the first occasions for exchanging results and methods across disciplinary and national boundaries, and this collection of essays deriving from the conference will provide materials to be built upon for other studies and theoretical analyses in this rapidly growing field.

The German Historical Institute owes thanks to many individuals and institutions. A number of people gave expert advice during the planning phase and helped to establish contacts. We should like to mention especially Professor Alfons Bürge, Dr Albrecht Cordes, Professor Lawrence M. Friedman, Professor Paul Johnson, Professor Norbert Olszak, Professor Joachim Rückert, Dr Peter Schöttler, Professor Hannes Siegrist, Dr Francine Soubiran-Paillet, and Professor David Sugarman. Special thanks are due to the Gerda Henkel Foundation, which generously supported the conference. During the conference Dr Lynn Abrams, Professor Martin Daunton, Professor Robert Gray, Dr Michael Lobban, and Professor Janet M. Neeson chaired the discussions with great discretion. We are also grateful to those who, like Professor Morton J. Horwitz, Professor Kjell A. Modéer, Dr Ute Schneider, and Professor David Sugarman, stimulated the debate during the conference. The difficult task of translating the French and some of the German essays into English was undertaken by Dr Angela Davies, Jane Rafferty, and Jim Underwood. In addition, Angela Davies helped in editing the volume. Many thanks to her. Critical comments by Professor Jörg Fisch, Professor Reinhart Koselleck, Oliver Müller MA, Dr Johannes Paulmann, and Dr Benedikt Stuchtey were very helpful. The main credit, however, for conceiving and organizing the conference, as well as for editing the present volume, must go to Dr Willibald Steinmetz, and I should like to take this opportunity to express my thanks to him.

Peter Wende

London, October 1998

Contents

List of Figures

List of Abbreviations

English and American law reports and collections of statutes are cited by the references currently in use.

ABGB *(Österreichisches) Allgemeines Bürgerliches Gesetzbuch* (Austrian Civil Code of 1811)

ALR *Allgemeines Landrecht für die Preussischen Staaten* (Prussian General Code of 1794)

art. article

BGB *Bürgerliches Gesetzbuch* (German Civil Code of 1900)

BVerfGE *Entscheidungen des Bundesverfassungsgerichts* (Decisions of the German Constitutional Court)

C. Codex Iustinianus

Cass. *Cour de Cassation*

CC *Code civil* (French Civil Code of 1804)

CGT Confédération Générale du Travail

Civ. *Cour de cassation, Chambre Civile*

CN *Collection nouvelle* (L. M. Devilleneuve and A. A. Carette, *Recueil général des lois et arrêts . . . rédigé à partir de l'ancien Recueil général des lois et des arrêts fondé par M. Sirey, 1791–1830, revu et complété, 1840–1843*)

COS Charity Organization Society

D. Digesta Iustiniani

DP D. Dalloz, *Recueil périodique et critique de jurisprudence, de législation et de doctrine (1825–1940)*

JP justice of the peace

Jur. gén. D. Dalloz, *Répertoire méthodique et alphabétique de législation, de doctrine et de jurisprudence (1846–70)*

NS new series

OLG *Oberlandesgericht* (German Higher Regional Court)

PP *Parliamentary Papers*

PRO Public Record Office

QC Queen's Counsel

RdNr. Randnummer (marginal note)

Req. *Cour de Cassation, Chambre de requêtes*

RGZ   *Entscheidungen des Reichsgerichts in Zivilsachen* (Decisions
             of the German Imperial Court in civil matters)
RO   Record Office
S.   J.-B. Sirey, *Recueil général des lois et arrêts*
SächsBGB   *Bürgerliches Gesetzbuch für das Königreich Sachsen* (Saxon
             Civil Code of 1863)
SP Dom.   State Papers Domestic
StGB   *Strafgesetzbuch* (German Penal Code of 1871)

I

Introduction
Towards a Comparative History of Legal Cultures, 1750–1950

WILLIBALD STEINMETZ

'Equality . . . is the soul of justice.' One would not expect a court of law to use such poetic language. Yet it appeared in a judgment on a question of civil procedure delivered in 1980 by the German Constitutional Court.[1] Similar statements pervade the Western tradition of social and legal philosophy from the ancient Greeks to our own times. Perhaps they may even be found in cultures where the law is based on custom or religious beliefs. There seems to be universal agreement that justice and equality are related to each other. In abstract terms justice should consist in treating equal facts and persons equally, and unequal facts and persons unequally. As a guideline for practice, however, this rule of 'equal' treatment is no more than an empty formula. It is evident that notions of equality have changed over time and vary between political communities.[2] Accordingly different constructions of that golden rule of justice will be found as we move on from Antiquity to the present or as we cross boundaries.[3] Aristotle for

[1] *BVerfGE*, 54 (1981), 296. The judges even referred back to the Bible: 'Denn im Bereich des Normvollzugs ist die Gleichheit der Rechtsanwendung die Seele der Gerechtigkeit. Und dies seit den Anfängen unseres Rechtsdenkens (vgl. 3 Mose 19, 15).'

[2] For the history of the concept from Antiquity to the late 19th century see Otto Dann, 'Gleichheit', in Otto Brunner, Werner Conze, and Reinhart Koselleck (eds.), *Geschichtliche Grundbegriffe: Historisches Lexikon zur politisch-sozialen Sprache in Deutschland*, vol. ii (Stuttgart, 1975), 997–1046; and Otto Dann, *Gleichheit und Gleichberechtigung: Das Gleichheitspostulat in der alteuropäischen Ordnung und in Deutschland bis zum ausgehenden 19. Jahrhundert* (Berlin, 1980). For a survey on contemporary attitudes towards social inequality in ten Western and Eastern European countries see Max Haller, Bogdan Mach, and Heinrich Zwicky, 'Egalitarismus und Antiegalitarismus zwischen gesellschaftlichen Interessen und kulturellen Leitbildern: Ergebnisse eines internationalen Vergleichs', in Hans-Peter Müller and Bernd Wegener (eds.), *Soziale Ungleichheit und soziale Gerechtigkeit* (Opladen, 1995), 221–64.

[3] Cf. Chaim Perelman, 'Equality and Justice', in id., *Justice, Law, and Argument: Essays on Moral and Legal Reasoning* (Dordrecht, 1980), 83–7; Isaiah Berlin, 'Equality', in id., *Concepts*

example could easily exclude slaves, non-Greeks, and women from any consideration of equal treatment by the legislator or the citizens themselves. Nor did he have any objections to honours and goods being distributed unequally among male citizens depending on how 'worthy' they were.[4] Yet he recognized that the criteria for 'worthiness' were not the same in all polities and that material justice would differ widely, for example between oligarchies and democracies in ancient Greece.[5] In other words Aristotle knew about the relativity of justice which followed from a (limited) variety of patterns to assert equality.

While in theory the connection between justice and equality is well established, there is less certainty with regard to the relation between justice and the reality of the law. Does a legal system have to be just? Is it necessary that norms and jurisdiction conform to that golden rule of equal treatment? 'Of course,' will be the answer of almost anyone who has not spent much time on the question. 'No, not necessarily,' reply many lawyers, sociologists, and historians. 'It is usually more important that a rule of law be settled than that it be settled right.' This was written by Justice Brandeis (1856–1941) whose reputation was certainly not that of a cynic but of a progressive lawyer.[6] Sociologists' thoughts go in the same direction when they contend that the essential function of the law is to stabilize expectations by adopting certain and predictable rules. People need to know, it is argued, what to expect when they turn to litigation or defend themselves in court. That need is served by a legal system which draws its own distinctions between 'just' and 'unjust' and applies them consistently. Whether these distinctions match the moral judgements prevailing in society is of secondary importance for the proper functioning of the system.[7] Arguing along similar lines, historians point to the

and Categories: Philosophical Essays, ed. Henry Hardy (Oxford, 1980), 81–102 (1st pub. in Proceedings of the Aristotelian Society, ns 56 (1956), 281–326).

  [4] Aristotle, Nic. Eth. 5. 1130^{b}30ff. and 1131^{a}22ff.

  [5] Aristotle, Pol. 6. 1317^{b}1ff., 1318^{a}5ff.

  [6] The phrase was part of a dissenting opinion by Brandeis in the case Di Santo v. Pennsylvania, 273 US, 34, 42 (1927). The problem at issue was the adjustment between state and federal legislation. Cf. The Social and Economic Views of Mr. Justice Brandeis, collected, with introductory notes by Alfred Lief (New York, 1930), 328–33 (quotation on 332). See also Melvin I. Urofsky, A Mind of One Piece: Brandeis and American Reform (New York, 1971), 139f.; and Philippa Strum, Brandeis: Beyond Progressivism (Lawrence, Kan., 1993).

  [7] For an example of this line of argument see Niklas Luhmann, Das Recht der Gesellschaft (Frankfurt am Main, 1993).

fact that legal institutions and judicial practices often continued to exist or indeed even thrived, while at the same time they were regarded as unfair by significant groups, perhaps even a majority of the societies concerned.

The nineteenth century provides plenty of examples of a growing distance between people's sense of justice and the reality of the law. Many of the individuals and groups who figure as subjects in this volume—agricultural labourers, women, workers, tenants, consumers—experienced unequal treatment by the law or the courts, while they regarded themselves as the equals of their landlords, husbands, masters, or contractual partners. Yet, despite all demands for substantive justice, legal systems often remained unaffected. Law and popular ideas of fairness were dissociated for long periods of time. However, as the contributions to this volume also demonstrate, this is not the whole story. Law never developed in complete isolation from the needs of society. Legislators and judges had to take into account what those who used or criticized the legal system considered to be 'just'. Where this did not happen or where it happened too late, the legal system lost part of its legitimacy and people turned to alternative means for solving their disputes: negotiation, arbitration, collective action, or violence. In the long run, then, it is not sufficient that rules of law be settled regardless of justice; they must be settled right or they will no longer be accepted. Any legal system therefore, unless it serves a tyranny, will sooner or later have to respond to inequalities which a majority in society has defined as 'unjust'.

I

This volume seeks to give a new impetus to comparative research on relations between law and society in the industrial age. The aim is historical explanation, not legal philosophy or practical jurisprudence. Comparisons are made not in order to find better solutions for the future, but to help account for differences and similarities between legal cultures in the past. The comparative history of legal cultures is not traditional lawyers' legal history as it is not restricted to the inner life of the legal system—norms, doctrines, institutions, and professions. The notion of 'legal culture' comprises more. It includes the attitudes and practical experience of laymen and laywomen who became involved with the law. What has to be investigated is the mutual interference, as well as the distance between a legal system and those who appealed to it or were drawn into it.[8] In order to achieve this, contributors have been asked to focus on two questions which are closely linked to each other. On the one hand, it is asked how jurisdiction and legislation shaped or eliminated social inequalities. On the other hand, it is explored to what extent people of unequal standing in society could use or challenge private law and courts of civil jurisdiction.

The restriction to private law should not be taken too strictly. 'Private law' is itself a historical category, the boundaries of which have changed over time and have been drawn differently in the countries under observation here: Britain, France, Germany, and the United States.[9] Nevertheless, in all four countries private law was regarded as the core of the legal order for most of the time-span with which this volume is concerned—the industrial age, broadly speaking the period from the end of the eighteenth to the middle of the twentieth century. The legal historian Franz Wieacker has pointed to the fact that the social vision (*Sozialmodell*) inherent in nineteenth-century law codes and legal doctrine was congenial to a bourgeois society composed of individuals

---

[8] For a critical discussion of the term 'legal culture' see Roger Cotterrell, 'The Concept of Legal Culture', in David Nelken (ed.), *Comparing Legal Cultures* (Aldershot, 1997), 13–31. Cotterrell argues that the term is too vague to define a meaningful research strategy. Against this cf. Lawrence M. Friedman, 'The Concept of Legal Culture: A Reply', ibid. 33–9. With Friedman I would like to insist on the utility of the term for defining a field of research distinct from traditional legal history. This does not necessarily include the claim that legal culture is 'an essential intervening variable' in the process of producing legal change (ibid. 34). As I use the term here it serves to delineate spaces or spheres within which changes occurred through constant interferences between the legal system and the social system.

[9] Much has been written on the changing political significance of the distinction between public law and private law in the four countries. For Britain see J. W. F. Allison, *A Continental Distinction in the Common Law: A Historical and Comparative Perspective on English Public Law* (Oxford, 1996); cf. also the essay by Raymond Cocks in this volume. For France cf. Jean-Louis Halpérin, *Histoire du droit privé français depuis 1804* (Paris, 1996), 10 ff. For Germany see Dieter Grimm, 'Zur politischen Funktion der Trennung von öffentlichem und privatem Recht in Deutschland', in id., *Recht und Staat der bürgerlichen Gesellschaft* (Frankfurt am Main, 1987), 84–103. For the United States cf. Joan Williams, 'The Development of the Public/Private Distinction in American Law', *Texas Law Review*, 64 (1985), 225–50; Morton J. Horwitz, 'The History of the Public/Private Distinction', *University of Pennsylvania Law Review*, 130 (1982), 1423–8; Duncan Kennedy, 'The Stages of the Decline of the Public/Private Distinction', *University of Pennsylvania Law Review*, 130 (1982), 1349–57.

which were conceived of as autonomous (male) producers.[10] Appropriately the society of the nineteenth century has been called a *Privatrechtsgesellschaft*.[11] During that period private law provided key categories to be used when individuals and groups positioned themselves or were positioned in society. Private law was thus one of the main battlegrounds for struggles to defend or to reverse existing social inequalities.

The topic of social inequality has been chosen because it lies at the heart of the social system as well as the legal system. Not every 'real' inequality, however, is perceived as unjust, and not every 'unjust' inequality, as we have seen, immediately becomes a problem for the law. So long as distinctions are taken for granted and result from shared convictions of a whole community they may not even need the sanction of the law. They are reproduced in practice and tend to be seen as natural or given by God.[12] Inequalities like these, although they may bring about 'real' differences, for example in material wealth or opportunities, which can be made the subject of historical research, will usually not constitute a challenge to legal systems and are of little relevance for the volume. The focus here is on those distinctions and discriminations which have given offence and caused frequent conflicts.

Modern society, it can be argued, has witnessed a growing intolerance of social inequalities of all kinds, whether founded on natural features such as sex, age, and colour of skin, or on acquired features such as wealth, occupation, and lifestyle, or on imagined and ascribed categories such as nationality, 'estate',[13]

---

[10] Franz Wieacker, 'Das Sozialmodell der klassischen Privatrechtsgesetzbücher und die Entwicklung der modernen Gesellschaft' (1953), repr. in id., *Industriegesellschaft und Privatrechtsordnung* (Frankfurt am Main, 1974), 9–35; id., 'Pandektenwissenschaft und Industrielle Revolution' (1966), repr. ibid. 55–78.

[11] Cf. Dieter Grimm, 'Bürgerlichkeit im Recht', in id., *Recht und Staat der bürgerlichen Gesellschaft* (Frankfurt am Main, 1987), 11–50, 27 ff.

[12] G.o.d. = Generator of diversity. I take this note from Luhmann, *Recht der Gesellschaft*, 222.

[13] This word may serve here as an admittedly inadequate translation for the French terms *état* and *ordre* and the German term *Stand*. No exact equivalents are available in English. In pre-revolutionary continental Europe *Stände* or *ordres* were social groups constituted by specific rights, liberties, honours, and obligations. Distinctions by *Stand* or *état* were more than hierarchical visions of society; they had above all a legal quality which permeated all aspects of daily life. For the complex and intermingled history of the German terms *Stand* and *Klasse* see now Otto Gerhard Oexle, Werner Conze, and Rudolf Walther, 'Stand, Klasse', in Otto Brunner, Werner Conze, and Reinhart Koselleck (eds.), *Geschichtliche Grundbegriffe*, vol. vi (Stuttgart, 1990), 155–284.

gender, race, class, and religion. The area of undisputed inequalities between human beings has shrunk. Ever more inequalities are disputed and have become the subject of legislation and lawsuits. Several factors have contributed to this development. First of all the promise of equality laid down in revolutionary declarations of rights, enlightened law codes, and implied in the common law ideal of the rule of law, opened up new expectations for those who felt underprivileged and oppressed, and simultaneously erected new burdens of proof for those who wanted to exclude others from being treated in the same way as themselves.

The explosive force of this promise was immense, even if, at first, it meant no more than equality before the law, especially in criminal procedures and matters pertaining to public law.[14] Women, black slave labourers, members of religious minorities, and generally all those who were subject to special laws or police ordinances made for certain 'estates' or occupations could appeal to this principle. Thus fragmentation of public law had to give way to uniformity. But the principle could be stretched further to include private law. In this case it could even justify legislative measures which would make it possible for the poor in fact to enjoy what was promised in the theory of a *Privatrechtsgesellschaft*: equal freedom for all individuals to contract and to compete in the marketplace. That demand was to lead, for instance, to a more extensive interpretation of protection clauses contained in constitutions or private law and eventually to the introduction of new special legislation for 'weak' groups or classes. Paradoxically then, the demand for equal treatment could result in 'unequal' legislation. It is this 'flippability of the argument'[15] which seems to have been characteristic of social and legal conflicts in the industrial age.

On a less theoretical level industrialization itself caused material inequalities to grow in many places[16] and created instances

---

[14] In 19th-century legal doctrine assertions of equal treatment in catalogues of basic rights and constitutions aimed primarily at those areas in which the state was competent to act, whereas private law constituted a sphere in which individuals were free to act according to their own dispositions. Cf. Grimm, 'Bürgerlichkeit im Recht', 12f., 29; id., 'Funktion', 99.

[15] Morton J. Horwitz used this expression during the conference which led to this volume.

[16] This is the result of a comparative survey based on data concerning inequalities in wealth, salaries, education, housing, and health in West European countries: Hartmut

where these inequalities would be felt more acutely than before. Population growth exacerbated the tensions between rich and poor, especially in the countryside. Increased mobility facilitated opportunities for contact and allowed more individuals to compare their own situation with that of others. Industrial forms of production created new forms of dependence and new types of conflict between employers and employed. As more people moved into big cities for work, they found themselves dependent on landlords for accommodation and on dealers and companies for goods and services. Anonymous market forces increasingly governed work, housing, and consumption and let the life situation of many appear arbitrary. These developments generally affected women in different ways from men and thus added another dimension of inequality cutting across class lines. Towards the end of the nineteenth century the replacement of individual entrepreneurs by large corporations and the corresponding proliferation of mass organizations 'bred both interdependence and insecurity'; compared to these fundamental changes in society traditional legal rules were seen as inadequate and demands for a new 'social interpretation of the law' (Laski) arose.[17] All this added to the tension between the promise of equal treatment and real-life experience.

No less important than these demographic, economic, and psychological factors were developments at the level of ideology and discourse. Here too, as everyone knows, the industrial age produced two innovations: liberalism and socialism. They had a major impact on the way in which inequalities were perceived and they offered languages with which existing social relations could be challenged or stabilized. Law was affected by those 'external' languages, but it was also a language of its own, the impact of which on self-descriptions of society has not yet been properly understood. It is neither true, as a majority of lawyers tended to think, that law developed autonomously and could only respond to its own problems, nor is it plausible as radical and Marxist

Kaelble, *Industrialisierung und soziale Ungleichheit: Europa im 19. Jahrhundert: Eine Bilanz* (Göttingen, 1983), 217. Kaelble sees an attenuation of material inequalities beginning at the end of the 19th century. Inequalities before the law are mentioned by Kaelble as one among other problems deserving further study (p. 16).

[17] William Fisher III, Morton J. Horwitz, and Thomas A. Reed (eds.), *American Legal Realism* (New York, 1993), 132 f.

critics claimed that law was nothing but a reflection of the political and social ideology of the governing class put into technical vocabulary. If the historical essays assembled here show anything it is that there was constant interference, constant communication between the language of the law and the languages dominant in society. This interference happened in political struggles for new legislation, in legal doctrine, in public controversies between lawyers and their critics, in lawyers' offices and—perhaps most importantly—in the courtrooms themselves.

II

The contributions to this volume concentrate on some of the most prominent inequalities with which the legal community and society at large have been concerned during the industrial age. Since the late eighteenth century for the reasons just mentioned legal distinctions in civil and criminal proceedings between individuals born into a different 'estate' or status came to be regarded everywhere as in need of justification. But this did not mean that all former discriminations suddenly disappeared. Even where this process went a long way, as in the United States or in France, the existence of black slave labourers in the South or the colonies reminded everyone that equality before the law had not been fully achieved. In England too, although the common law took no notice of 'estates' (except in the political sense of King, Lords, and Commons), the relations between landowners, tenants, and agricultural labourers, especially with regard to property and crime, still bore characteristics of a 'feudal' dependency. Social and legal distinctions by 'estate', however, proved to be most persistent in large parts of Germany, again particularly in the countryside, where special jurisdictions existed until 1848 and special laws for agricultural servants stayed in force until as late as 1918.[18] For the emerging industrial societies the countryside was a perpetual reminder of a situation in which labour had been unfree and the

[18] Cf. Reinhart Koselleck, 'Die Auflösung des Hauses als ständischer Herrschaftseinheit: Anmerkungen zum Rechtswandel von Haus, Familie und Gesinde in Preußen zwischen der Französischen Revolution und 1848', in Neithard Bulst, Joseph Goy, and Jochen Hoock (eds.), *Familie zwischen Tradition und Moderne: Studien zur Geschichte der Familie in Deutschland und Frankreich vom 16. bis zum 20. Jahrhundert* (Göttingen, 1981), 109–24; Thomas Vormbaum, *Politik und Gesinderecht im 19. Jahrhundert (vornehmlich in Preußen 1810–1918)* (Berlin, 1980).

use of property encumbered by all sorts of unequal legal provisions. To include this vision which counters the bourgeois ideal of
a society composed of equally free individuals the volume starts
with a chapter on judicial conflicts between lords, peasants, and
labourers in England and Germany.[19]

The so-called legal 'disabilities' or 'incapacities' of women constituted another permanent challenge to those who claimed that
with the advent of constitutions and liberal legislation all individuals had gained equal freedom to manage their own affairs. Why
so many men, whether of noble, bourgeois, or working-class
origin, instinctively excluded women and especially married
women from considerations of equal treatment remains unclear.
The fact is that the free individuals spoken of in declarations of
rights and law codes were almost always conceived of as males.
The principle of equal freedom was primarily applied to the
sphere of production where men were in the majority and held
the dominant position. By contrast the sphere of reproduction in
which women played a more prominent role remained a separate
'domain' or an 'enclave' within the *Privatrechtsgesellschaft* until at
least the end of the nineteenth century.[20] Whereas women's campaigns for the right to vote and other political rights are generally
well researched by historians, their legal situation in 'private'
matters such as the right to inherit and alienate property, the capability to enter into contracts, or the right to adopt children and
the procedures leading to divorce remain less studied, except on
a doctrinal level. It is as if historians for a long time had accepted
the metaphorical English term for the legal status of married
women, 'coverture', as a sufficient ground for neglecting further
enquiry into women's experiences with private law. Only in recent

---

[19] Essays by Monika Wienfort and Raymond Cocks. Cf. the contribution by Douglas
Hay who also deals with agricultural labourers. For England see in addition Peter King,
'Gleaners, Farmers and the Failure of Legal Sanctions in England 1750–1850', *Past and
Present*, 125 (1989), 116–50; id., 'Customary Rights and Women's Earnings: The Importance
of Gleaning to the Rural Labouring Poor, 1750–1850', *Economic History Review*, 44 (1991),
461–76; Janet M. Neeson, *Commoners, Common Right, Enclosure and Social Change in England,
1700–1820* (Cambridge, 1993).
[20] See the essay by Ursula Vogel in this volume. See also Ute Gerhard, *Gleichheit ohne
Angleichung: Frauen im Recht* (Munich, 1990); ead., *Verhältnisse und Verhinderungen: Frauenarbeit,
Familie und Rechte der Frauen im 19. Jahrhundert* (Frankfurt am Main, 1978). The expression
'enclave' is from Grimm, 'Bürgerlichkeit im Recht', 33 f. The expression 'domain' is used
by Karen Orren in her analysis of American master–servant relations in this volume. It is
also applicable to relations within the family.

years have scholars picked up some of the issues mentioned.[21] They are looked at more closely in the second section of the volume.[22]

The next three sections deal with inequalities between individuals or groups whose opportunities were predominantly the result of market forces: employers and employees, landlords and tenants, producers and consumers. From the late eighteenth century onwards, somewhat earlier in Britain and North America, somewhat later in many parts of Germany, their relations were governed by the central figure of private law—contract. Such at least was the situation in theory. For manual workers, however, or 'servants' as they were called in contemporary English parlance until the last quarter of the nineteenth century, special legislation remained in place everywhere, denying them (or restraining) among other things one essential freedom which other citizens had, namely the right to form associations in order to improve their own bargaining power by collective action.[23] In addition to this, all sorts of other regulations deriving from the police power of the states intervened into employment relations, mainly in continental Europe, but also in England and to a lesser degree in the

---

[21] Divorce has received particular attention. Cf. the study by Lawrence Stone, *Road to Divorce: England 1530–1987* (Oxford, 1990). For Germany see Dirk Blasius, *Ehescheidung in Deutschland im 19. und 20. Jahrhundert* (2nd rev. edn., Frankfurt am Main, 1992). For France cf. Bernard Schnapper, 'Autorité domestique et partis politiques de Napoléon à de Gaulle', in Heinz Mohnhaupt (ed.), *Zur Geschichte des Familien- und Erbrechts: Politische Implikationen und Perspektiven* (Frankfurt am Main, 1987), 177–219; Irène Théry and Christian Biet (eds.), *La Famille, la loi, l'état de la Révolution au Code civil* (Paris, 1989); Anne Lefebvre-Teillard, *Introduction historique au droit des personnes et de la famille* (Paris, 1996). For married women's property see Ursula Vogel, 'Patriarchale Herrschaft, bürgerliches Recht, bürgerliche Utopie: Eigentumsrechte der Frauen in Deutschland und England', in Jürgen Kocka (ed.), *Bürgertum im 19. Jahrhundert: Deutschland im europäischen Vergleich*, 3 vols. (Munich, 1988), i. 406–38; Ute Gerhard, 'Die Rechtsstellung der Frau in der bürgerlichen Gesellschaft des 19. Jahrhunderts: Frankreich und Deutschland im Vergleich', ibid. 439–68; Norma Basch, *In the Eyes of the Law: Women, Marriage and Property in Nineteenth-Century New York* (Ithaca, NY, 1982); Reva B. Siegel, 'Home as Work: The First Woman's Rights Claims Concerning Wives' Household Labor, 1850–1880', *Yale Law Journal*, 103 (1994), 1073–217; Margot Finn, 'Women, Consumption and Coverture in England, c. 1760–1860', *Historical Journal*, 39 (1996), 703–22.

[22] Essays by Ursula Vogel, Jean-Louis Halpérin, Ute Gerhard, and Lawrence M. Friedman.

[23] The history of trade union rights is generally well studied: Cf. John Breuilly, 'Civil Society and the Labour Movement, Class Relations and the Law: A Comparison between Germany and England', in id., *Labour and Liberalism in Nineteenth-Century Europe: Essays in Comparative History* (Manchester, 1992), 160–96; John V. Orth, *Combination and Conspiracy: A Legal History of Trade Unionism, 1721–1906* (Oxford, 1991); Francine Soubiran-Paillet, 'Dépé-

United States.[24] Not all of this was detrimental to workers' interests. The borderline between policing and welfare legislation was always fluid. Such well-meaning legislation however was mostly directed at protecting particular groups of the workforce— children, women, male workers in certain dangerous occupations. A new fragmentation of the legal order was the consequence, and sometimes those who were meant to profit from these measures saw them more as a burden than as an advantage.[25] What has to be kept in mind generally is that as far as labour relations were concerned, private law was continuously counteracted by public law. This served to readjust the balance, one way or the other, between employers and employees. This can also be taken as an indication that legislators themselves did not fully subscribe to the private law doctrine of equal freedom to contract. The movement to re-regulate and restrict the scope of individual labour contracts followed a broadly similar pattern in all four countries.[26] None the less, solutions differed with regard to timing and institutional outlook. In practice this led to remarkable national differences in the ability of individual employees to resort to courts of law for achieving satisfactory settlements with their employers.[27]

nalisation, association professionnelle et personne morale au 19e siècle en droit français', *Revue interdisciplinaire d'études juridiques*, 35 (1995), 95–116; Gerd Bender, 'Die schwierige Koalitionsfreiheit: Eine Studie zu Rechtsprechung und Gesetzgebung im Jahrzehnt der Reichsgründung', in Heinz Mohnhaupt (ed.), *Rechtsgeschichte in den beiden deutschen Staaten (1988–1990): Beispiele, Parallelen, Positionen* (Frankfurt am Main, 1991), 466–90; Christopher L. Tomlins, *The State and the Unions: Labor Relations, Law, and the Organized Labor Movement in America, 1880–1960* (Cambridge, 1985).

[24] Cf. for the French case Alfons Bürge, 'Vom polizeilichen Ordnungsdenken zum Liberalismus: Entwicklungslinien des französischen Arbeitsrechts in der ersten Hälfte des 19. Jahrhunderts', *Archiv für Sozialgeschichte*, 31 (1991), 1–25; Vincent Viet, *Les Voltigeurs de la République: L'Inspection du travail en France jusqu'en 1914*, 2 vols. (Paris, 1994); Heinz-Gerhard Haupt, 'Sozialpolitik und ihre gesellschaftlichen Grenzen in Frankreich vor 1914', *Jahrbuch für Wirtschaftsgeschichte* (1995), 1: 171–91. On Germany see Karl Heinrich Kaufhold, 'Die Diskussion um die Neugestaltung des Arbeitsrechts im Deutschen Reich 1890 und die Novelle zur Reichsgewerbeordnung 1891', *Zeitschrift für Arbeitsrecht*, 22 (1991), 277–322. On England see Robert Gray, *The Factory Question and Industrial England, 1830–1860* (Cambridge, 1996).

[25] The case of working women is of particular interest. See the comparative collection by Ulla Wikander, Alice Kessler-Harris, and Jane Lewis (eds.), *Protecting Women: Labor Legislation in Europe, the United States, and Australia, 1880–1920* (Urbana, Ill., 1995).

[26] Cf. the contribution by Spiros Simitis. See also id., 'Zur Verrechtlichung der Arbeitsbeziehungen', in Friedrich Kübler (ed.), *Verrechtlichung von Wirtschaft, Arbeit und sozialer Solidarität: Vergleichende Analysen* (Frankfurt am Main, 1985), 73–165.

[27] Cf. the essays by Douglas Hay, Alain Cottereau, Willibald Steinmetz, and Karen Orren. Cf. also the comparative study by Ralf Rogowski and Adam Tooze, 'Individuelle

A constant tension between freedom of contract and public law intervention can also be observed with regard to the other two relations which form the subject of the volume's fourth and fifth sections: the relations between landlords and tenants, and producers and consumers. During the nineteenth century the markets for rented accommodation in cities and for the exchange of goods, money, and services were certainly less regulated than the employment relation. But the taking of excessive interest time and again gave rise to demands for laws on 'usury' which found some resonance especially in France and Germany.[28] And abuses by landlords combined with housing shortages led to the introduction of rent controls and public housing programmes in all European countries around the First World War.[29] In the United States legislative and administrative regulation of rent relations set in later and did not reach a comparable intensity before the 1960s.[30] Below the level of public activism private law itself did not always turn a blind eye to social inequalities between partners to a renting agreement or other contracts as the case of the German civil law code, the *Bürgerliches Gesetzbuch* of 1900, illustrates.[31] On the other hand, legal and institutional arrangements could also reinforce inequalities, as is shown for example by the unequal treatment of big commercial and small individual debtors in England and France.[32]

The general rule in all contract matters however, whether of

Arbeitskonfliktlösung und liberaler Korporatismus: Gewerbe- und Arbeitsgerichte in Frankreich, Großbritannien und Deutschland im historischen Vergleich', in Heinz Mohnhaupt and Dieter Simon (eds.), *Vorträge zur Justizforschung*, vol. i (Frankfurt am Main, 1992), 317–86.

[28] See the contributions by Fabien Valente and Martin Geyer. On the debate on usury in the United States see Morton J. Horwitz, *The Transformation of American Law, 1780–1860* (1st pub. 1977; 2nd edn., Oxford, 1992), 237–45.

[29] Essays by David Englander and Susanna Magri. For Germany cf. Karl Christian Führer, *Mieter, Hausbesitzer, Staat und Wohnungsmarkt: Wohnungsmangel und Wohnungszwangswirtschaft in Deutschland 1914–1960* (Stuttgart, 1995). See also the comparative studies in Martin J. Daunton (ed.), *Housing the Workers: A Comparative Perspective, 1850–1914* (Leicester, 1990); and Susanna Magri, 'Housing', in Jay Winter and Jean-Louis Robert (eds.), *Capital Cities at War: Paris, London, Berlin 1914–1919* (Cambridge, 1997), 374–417.

[30] Contribution by Richard Chused.

[31] Cf. the contribution by Tilman Repgen.

[32] Essays by Paul Johnson and Fabien Valente. For England see also: Gerry R. Rubin, 'Law, Poverty and Imprisonment for Debt, 1869–1914', in Gerry R. Rubin and David Sugarman (eds.), *Law, Economy and Society, 1750–1914* (Abingdon, 1984), 241–99; V. Markham Lester, *Victorian Insolvency: Bankruptcy, Imprisonment for Debt, and Company Winding-up in Nineteenth-Century England* (Oxford, 1995).

rent, moneylending, sale of goods, or hire of services, was the supposed equal freedom of all (male) adults to make agreements as they liked. The neutrality of the law thus gave market forces their full weight. For reasons too obvious to be recapitulated here these turned out in most cases, though not necessarily for all individuals, to be disadvantageous to employees, tenants, and consumers, and among them usually more disadvantageous to women than men. To these groups therefore the law would appear as unjust and discriminatory, in short as 'class law'. This term could be applied to denounce unfair distinctions on several levels: first of course in the norms themselves, second in institutions and procedures, third in access to legal advice and adequate legal aid, and fourth in the underlying social and moral assumptions which guided the practice of 'bourgeois' judges and lawyers. As a consequence a more or less pronounced alienation between the poorer classes and the law—private as well as criminal—can be observed in all industrialized countries around the turn of the nineteenth to the twentieth century. Private law came to be seen as essentially 'bourgeois' law, perhaps most persistently in Germany where even the terms could be fused in the one notion of *bürgerliches Recht.*[33]

Those on the weaker side had two basic options for coping with this situation. First, they could try to improve their legal position by bringing the state to legislate in their favour. Thus new distinctions were put into the law to compensate for inequalities in the marketplace. Such demands to correct socio-economic inequalities by protective legislation were a major driving force for the process known as juridification.[34] The result has also been described as a movement back from contract to status. It has led

---

[33] Perhaps the most famous critic of German 'bourgeois' law is Anton Menger, *Das bürgerliche Recht und die besitzlosen Volksklassen* (Tübingen, 1890). His criticisms were further developed and radicalized by Josef Karner [i.e. Karl Renner], 'Die soziale Funktion der Rechtsinstitute', in Max Adler and Rudolf Hilferding (eds.), *Marx-Studien*, vol. i (Vienna, 1904; repr. Glashütten im Taunus, 1971), 63–192. Renner's work has been translated into English: id., *The Institutions of Private Law and their Social Functions*, ed. Otto Kahn-Freund (London, 1949). See also Ernst Fraenkel, *Zur Soziologie der Klassenjustiz* (Berlin, 1927), repr. in id., *Zur Soziologie der Klassenjustiz und Aufsätze zur Verfassungskrise 1931–32* (Darmstadt, 1968), 1–41.

[34] Cf. Kübler (ed.), *Verrechtlichung.* Gunther Teubner (ed.), *Juridification of Social Spheres: A Comparative Analysis in the Areas of Labor, Corporate, Antitrust and Social Welfare Law* (Berlin, 1987). This collection contains shortened versions in English of the essays in the earlier German volume, and these are complemented by essays by English, French, Italian, and American scholars.

everywhere to an expansion of public welfare law at the expense of private law. Second, the disadvantaged groups could try to bypass the law and improve their economic and social position directly, thereby hoping to realize equality of bargaining powers. The means to achieve this was collective action, mainly unionism and strikes. In its pure form this strategy demanded the retreat of the legislator, the judiciary, and public administration from contractual relations altogether. The classic case coming closest to this was that of Britain's labour relations between 1906 and the 1960s, which have been described as 'collective laissez-faire'.[35] On the European continent a hybrid form prevailed in which the state participated actively in giving the sanction of the law to the agreements reached by collective actors. This has been named 'corporatism', with Germany usually being cited as the classic case.[36]

Both strategies, the legal-political as well as the socio-economic, required a capacity to act collectively—through trade unions, tenants' and consumers' associations, women's movements, or political parties. Indirectly and in the long run, even those who did not or could not take part in these movements profited from their achievements. But there were situations where no protective law or publicly administered insurance system or collective self-help organization was available to compensate for the weakness of the individual who had been harmed. In that case private law litigation with all its deficiencies remained the only resort. As the example of victims of railway accidents in America shows this very often resulted in weaker individuals being pressurized to renounce even those rights which they would have had if they had been able—economically and psychologically—to bring their cases to court.[37] This example also directs attention to an area of

[35] This expression was coined by Otto Kahn-Freund, 'Labour Law', in M. Ginsberg (ed.), *Law and Opinion in England in the Twentieth Century* (London, 1959), 215–63, 224. On the applicability of the juridification-paradigm to contemporary British labour relations see Jon Clark and Lord Wedderburn, 'Juridification—a Universal Trend? The British Experience in Labor Law', in Teubner (ed.), *Juridification of Social Spheres*, 163–90; and Paul Davies and Mark Freedland, *Labour Legislation and Public Policy* (Oxford, 1993), 411 ff.

[36] For useful short summaries see V. R. Berghahn, 'Corporatism in Germany in Historical Perspective', in Andrew Cox and Noel O'Sullivan (eds.), *The Corporate State: Corporatism and the State Tradition in Western Europe* (Aldershot, 1988), 104–22; and Hans-Ulrich Wehler, *Deutsche Gesellschaftsgeschichte*, iii: *Von der 'Deutschen Doppelrevolution' bis zum Beginn des Ersten Weltkrieges 1849–1914* (Munich, 1995), 662–80.

[37] See the contribution by Edward A. Purcell, Jr. Cf. also Barbara Y. Welke, 'Unreasonable Women: Gender and the Law of Accidental Injury, 1870–1920', *Law and Social*

legal-historical research which has hardly been touched upon because it is so difficult to explore: the grey area of legal proceedings before a case reached the courts. Many potentially 'good' cases probably never reached the courts at all because the costs seemed too high or the necessary knowledge and support were unavailable. Perhaps this has to be seen as the harshest and most unjust inequality before the law.

III

Juridification, collective *laissez-faire*, and corporatism were options which were pursued successively or simultaneously in all industrialized countries. After a more liberal period which reached its peak in the decades between 1850 and 1890 these strategies have characterized legal politics since the turn of the century. But although the problem was basically the same everywhere— economic and social inequalities ignored by private law—there were considerable national differences in the timing as well as the degree to which these solutions were tried. Especially for the first half of the twentieth century the dissimilarities between the British and the American legal cultures on the one hand, the German and French ones on the other, seem to outweigh the similarities. Some reasons for this are obvious. Among these the different traditions of state interventionism, much stronger in Germany and France than in Britain and in the United States (despite all recent 'revisionist' writing on this topic), were no doubt important.[38] Another reason, mirroring the different conceptions of the state, was the greater propensity towards self-help and voluntary organization in the Anglo-American world.

It is less clear whether, and if so how, differences in the legal

---

Inquiry, 19 (1994), 369–403. For further reflections on the asymmetric relationship between individual consumers and large companies as litigants see Edward E. Purcell, Jr., *Litigation and Inequality: Federal Diversity Jurisdiction in Industrial America, 1870–1958* (New York, 1992).

[38] For a sympathetic survey of 'revisionist' writings claiming that the English state of the 18th and 19th centuries, as compared to Germany for example, was much stronger than traditionally assumed see Eckhart Hellmuth and John Brewer, 'Introduction', in eid. (eds.), *Rethinking Leviathan: The Eighteenth-Century State in Britain and Germany* (Oxford, 1998), 1–21. The traditional belief that in the United States no such thing as a welfare state existed before the 1930s is challenged by Theda Skocpol, *Protecting Soldiers and Mothers: The Political Origins of Social Policy in the United States* (Cambridge, Mass., 1992).

systems themselves led those social groups who wanted to escape from their unfavourable position in private law to adopt different strategies. Most contributions to this volume do not address this question directly as they are concerned with one country alone. But even the mere juxtaposition of single-country studies provides materials which give rise to speculation. It could be argued that the British and American system, because of the rivalry between (at least) two separate bodies of law, a more 'liberal' common law and a more 'collectivist' statute law, the one deriving its legitimacy from tradition, the other from a democratically elected legislator, brought about situations in which the common law judges, out of sympathy or in order to defend their own identity as common lawyers, sided with the powerful against the legislator whose statutes had been made to protect the less powerful. If in these situations the powerful (employers, landlords, large companies) won their cases more often and the purposes of protective legislation were thus frequently defeated, the less powerful (employees, tenants, consumers) might turn away from the law as a solution for social problems altogether and find it more profitable to rely on their own collective strength rather than legislation. This could be one explanation for the somewhat slower process of juridification, for example of employment relations, in Britain and the United States, and it could also help to explain the more reluctant adoption of corporatist strategies by trade unions in both countries.

Yet, one should be careful not to exaggerate the differences between systems based on a codified law which aspired to be all-encompassing and those dual systems where a common law continued to coexist and compete with a growing body of statute law. As far as practical solutions were concerned, differences were mostly of degree, of sooner or later, as is shown by the fact that by the 1960s and 1970s similar developments took place in many areas of law in all four countries. This applies to family law, labour relations, rent controls, as well as consumer protection. Legislative *and* judicial activism then worked together in favour of women, employees, tenants, and consumers. From the perspective of the early twentieth century, the 1960s and 1970s appear as a period of convergence between the Western legal cultures.

Whether this convergence will continue is open to doubt. There are signs that Reagonomics and Thatcherism will have lasting effects on legal arrangements for weaker social groups in the USA and Great Britain, whereas the deregulating tendency has been generally less pronounced in continental Europe. Perhaps, again this will only prove to be a question of sooner or later, this time the other way round, so that Germany and France will have to follow the trend towards scaling down the process of juridification and dismantling corporatist structures. Whether this will happen or not, one thing seems certain: private law is already regaining some of its former significance. Even in the most perfectly organized welfare states new inequalities, for example between age cohorts and the sexes, have been created by the (unintended) consequences of distributional rules.[39] Other exclusions are the result of purposeful changes in the criteria determining the right to benefits or to be included under protective legislation. The issue of social inequality in the more traditional form of conflicts over distribution is thus not dead, as was hastily proclaimed by some sociologists in the mid-1980s.[40] The same can be said for private law as an alternative to public law solutions. For all those who can neither mobilize strong interest groups to defend existing protective legislation, nor have sufficient economic strength to defend themselves as a group in the marketplace, the individual use of private law has again become an important or indeed the only possible resort against the more powerful. This is another reason why the history of private law and social inequality should be further studied.

IV

It is an aspiration of this book to bring legal and social history closer together. This requires an interdisciplinary approach.[41] The

---

[39] See Christoph Conrad, 'Gewinner und Verlierer im Wohlfahrtsstaat: Deutsche und internationale Tendenzen im 20. Jahrhundert', *Archiv für Sozialgeschichte*, 30 (1990), 297–326; Birgit Geissler, 'Netz oder Sieb? Generationenkonflikt und Geschlechterkonflikt in der aktuellen Krise des Sozialstaats', *Kritische Justiz*, 30 (1997), 1–14.

[40] Cf. Reinhard Kreckel, *Politische Soziologie der sozialen Ungleichheit* (Frankfurt am Main, 1992), arguing against Ulrich Beck and others. See also John Westergaard, *Who Gets What? The Hardening of Class Inequality in the Late Twentieth Century* (Cambridge, 1995).

[41] There are only a few examples of interdisciplinary work on topics related to those treated here. See Norbert Horn and Jürgen Kocka (eds.), *Recht und Entwicklung der Großunternehmen im 19. und frühen 20. Jahrhundert: Wirtschafts-, sozial- und rechtshistorische Untersuchungen zur Industrialisierung in Deutschland, Frankreich, England und den USA* (=Law and the Formation of Big Enterprises in the 19th and Early 20th Centuries) (Göttingen, 1979) (contains articles in English and German with summaries); John Brewer and Susan Staves (eds.), *Early Modern Conceptions of Property* (London, 1995).

essays have been written either by lawyers specializing in one or more fields of legal history, or by historians and historical sociologists who are interested in law as a social factor. As a consequence specific disciplinary as well as national perspectives are discernible in each contribution. Readers of both disciplines may see this as an advantage. The multiplicity of perspectives helps to identify questions and materials which have been neglected and thereby opens up new fields of research for lawyers and historians alike. Moreover, readers belonging to the same discipline might profit from the findings of their colleagues who are looking at similar problems elsewhere.

Studies on law and society have been guided by different theoretical and methodological assumptions in each of the countries observed *and* in each discipline. It is difficult to give a satisfactory survey of all research activities which may be relevant.[42] Yet it is possible to recall a few master narratives which have transcended national and disciplinary boundaries and may still serve as a common ground for future research. Furthermore some advantages and deficiencies peculiar to individual national or scholarly traditions can be mentioned as examples of promising or less promising avenues to pursue.

Several keywords referring to master narratives have already been touched upon in the preceding remarks. Perhaps the most enduring short formula summing up a secular process of socio-legal change was Sir Henry Maine's famous dictum that the progress of societies had in general been marked by 'a movement from Status to Contract'.[43] This phrase was coined in 1861 when liberal individualism reached its apogee. Already at that time Maine found it necessary to qualify his statement by adding an

[42] For an overview with further bibliographical references especially on trends in British and American historiography see David Sugarman, 'Introduction: Histories of Law and Society', in id. (ed.), *Law in History: Histories of Law and Society*, 2 vols. (Aldershot, 1996), i, pp. xi–xxx. This useful collection contains reprints of seminal essays and research reports, mostly written in the 1980s and early 1990s.

[43] Henry Sumner Maine, *Ancient Law: Its Connection with the Early History of Society, and its Relation to Modern Ideas* (London, 1861), 170. The full quotation reads: 'If then we employ Status, agreeably with the usage of the best writers, to signify these personal conditions only, and avoid applying the term to such conditions as are the immediate or remote result of agreement, we may say that the movement of the progressive societies has hitherto been a movement *from Status to Contract*.' Cf. also ibid. 304 ff. For further appearances of this formula in Maine's work and the interpretations it has received by later scholars see: Raymond C. J. Cocks, *Sir Henry Maine: A Study in Victorian Jurisprudence* (Cambridge, 1988), 60 ff. and 169–80.

inconspicuous 'hitherto'. Cautious scepticism turned into pessimism among liberal lawyers around the turn of the century. Albert Venn Dicey expressed fears shared by many of his colleagues when he questioned the capacity of a common law order based on the notion of freedom of contract to stem the growing tide of what he defined as 'collectivism'.[44] Under that term he subsumed various forms of legislative and administrative regulation which in his opinion undermined 'individualism' by singling out groups supposedly too weak to know their own interests and giving them protection or rights which others did not need. Modern scholars particularly in Britain and America, whether they shared Dicey's critical view of welfare state measures or not, generally interpreted their expansion as a movement back from contract to status. This now quite familiar narrative is reflected for example in the title of Patrick Atiyah's book on 'The Rise and Fall of Freedom of Contract'.[45] The 1870s appear as the major watershed in this as well as some other works on law and society in England.[46] As Atiyah is mainly interested in the relationship between legal doctrine and ideology, he does not go deeper into the question of whether 'status' is really an adequate word to describe the new social structures resulting from the demise of contractual individualism. In an illuminating note which is often quoted, but apparently not always fully appreciated, Otto Kahn-Freund has pointed out that Maine himself had a much more restricted concept of 'status' than his modern interpreters. He only had in mind legal differentiations between categories of

[44] Cf. A. V. Dicey, *Lectures on the Relation between Law and Public Opinion in England during the Nineteenth Century* (London, 1905), esp. 63–9, 258–301.

[45] Patrick S. Atiyah, *The Rise and Fall of Freedom of Contract* (Oxford, 1979).

[46] W. R. Cornish and G. de N. Clark, *Law and Society in England, 1750–1950* (London, 1989), divide most of their chapters into two periods taking years between 1850 and 1890 as turning points. Institutional as well as ideological reasons are given as reasons for these periodizations. In criminal policy too Martin Wiener, *Reconstructing the Criminal: Culture, Law, and Policy in England, 1830–1914* (Cambridge, 1990), recognizes a shift away from the assumption that individuals are responsible for their actions in the 1890s. Similarly, for France, Halpérin, *Histoire du droit privé*, 171, sees the 1880s as a turning point in legal policy and private law doctrine. In America the heyday of 'Classical Legal Thought' with freedom of contract as its centrepiece lasted somewhat longer than in Britain and France. The 'progressive' attack only set in around the turn of the century. The case of *Lochner v. New York*, 198 US 45 (1905), in which a state regulation concerning maximum working hours was invalidated, served as a focal point. See Morton J. Horwitz, *The Transformation of American Law, 1870–1960: The Crisis of Legal Orthodoxy* (New York, 1992), chs. 1 and 2. See also the paper by Richard Chused in this volume (pp. 430–1).

persons following from the accident of birth or alleged physical incapacity.[47] Examples are slaves in ancient Rome, non-nobles in Europe's *anciens régimes*, or aliens, infants, and the mentally ill in modern societies. All these are treated differently without any foregoing act of will of their own. Held against that strict sense of the term the creation of classes of benefit recipients in the welfare state or the regulation of the substance of contracts by imperative norms (*ius cogens*), for example in labour law, could not be described as generating new forms of 'status'. To describe them as such would be inadequate, because the original freedom of the individual to act (or not to act) is left untouched.

Kahn-Freund attributed the pejorative use of the term 'status' for the consequences of modern legislation to a peculiar misunderstanding and a dislike among English lawyers for what they considered an illicit intrusion by the state into the common law of contract. A similar story could be told for some French jurists during the Third Republic and liberal-conservative German law professors during the period from the late Kaiserreich to the early Federal Republic. They too could hardly conceal their aversion for what they described as an erosion or creeping euthanasia of private law by a benevolent and over-patronizing, and at times indeed authoritarian state.[48] Freedom of contract was the central value in both stories. Common lawyers and private law jurists considered themselves its defenders, opposing a danger which came from the attempt to equalize material conditions through legislation. One important difference, however, between the two versions of this master narrative lies in the generally more widespread acceptance by continental European lawyers of *ius cogens* as a legitimate instrument to introduce considerations of social policy into private law. Examples of this can be found in this volume.[49] By contrast most English common lawyers, and to a lesser degree the Americans too, were unfamiliar with the notion of *ius cogens* and therefore rejected out of hand any determination of the

---

[47] Otto Kahn-Freund, 'A Note on Status and Contract in British Labour Law', *Modern Law Review*, 30 (1967), 635–44.

[48] Cf. Halpérin, *Histoire du droit privé*, 175–81, 186 ff.; Wieacker, 'Sozialmodell', 26 ff. and id., 'Das bürgerliche Recht im Wandel der Gesellschaftsordnungen', in id., *Industriegesellschaft*, 36–54, 38 ff.; Christian Joerges, 'Die Wissenschaft vom Privatrecht und der Nationalstaat', in Dieter Simon (ed.), *Rechtswissenschaft in der Bonner Republik: Studien zur Wissenschaftsgeschichte der Jurisprudenz* (Frankfurt am Main, 1994), 311–63, 313 f. and 338 ff.

[49] See the essays by Vogel (pp. 100, 120), Magri (pp. 374, 376), Repgen (pp. 396, 399–400), Valente (p. 445), and Geyer (pp. 477–8).

substance of contracts by imperative norms. Compared to this long-lasting difference in legal thinking other divergences seem of a more temporary nature. But they were of course not unimportant for contemporaries themselves. One case in point which should be mentioned here is the idea, still alive though less overtly put forward in recent years, that there was a special German path (*Sonderweg*) which was characterized among other things by a shorter period of bourgeois-liberal dominance. Studies on freedom of contract in nineteenth-century Germany seem to lend support to this idea: the 'rise' of freedom of contract set in later and its 'fall' began earlier than in the Anglo-American world.[50]

If one accepts Kahn-Freund's semantic observations on 'status', there is still some validity in Sir Henry Maine's optimistic narrative. Legal distinctions based on the purely accidental ground of birth or on supposed incapacity of will are, if anything, regarded more critically today than they were at the time when Maine and Dicey wrote their treatises or even in the 1950s. This is shown for example by laws giving more weight to the will of children or the mentally disabled against parents or guardians. In that sense there has certainly been no movement back to status.

Modernization theories as well as theories of justice which were in vogue from the 1950s to the late 1970s have also taken a more positive stance towards social legislation aiming at an 'equalization of conditions'.[51] For theorists like T. H. Marshall or Reinhard Bendix the guarantee of social rights and participation in cultural resources is the necessary and final step towards realizing the bourgeois ideal of equal freedom for all.[52] For them, equality before the civil and criminal law marked only the beginning of modernization. The achievement of political rights first for men, then for women, was the next step. But the full realization only

---

[50] Dieter Grimm, 'Soziale, wirtschaftliche und politische Voraussetzungen der Vertragsfreiheit', in id., *Recht und Staat der bürgerlichen Gesellschaft*, 165–91; Joachim Rückert, ' "Frei" und "sozial": Arbeitsvertrags-Konzeptionen um 1900 zwischen Liberalismen und Sozialismen', *Zeitschrift für Arbeitsrecht*, 23 (1992), 225–94; cf. also Michael John, 'The Peculiarities of the German State: Bourgeois Law and Society in the Imperial Era', *Past and Present*, 119 (1988), 105–31.

[51] Chaim Perelman, 'Liberty, Equality and Public Interest', in *Equality and Freedom: Past, Present and Future*, Archiv für Rechts- und Sozialphilosophie, Supplement, NS 10 (Wiesbaden, 1977), 1–7, 3.

[52] T. H. Marshall, *Citizenship and Social Class—and Other Essays* (Cambridge, 1950); Reinhard Bendix, *Nation-Building and Citizenship: Studies of our Changing Social Order* (2nd rev. edn., Berkeley, 1977).

came with legally enforceable social rights. As Richard Tawney had asserted earlier: 'equality of opportunity is not simply a matter of legal equality. Its existence depends, not merely on the absence of disabilities, but on the presence of abilities.'[53] In this view the welfare state stood at the end of a process which had started with Condorcet's forecast of a future 'progrès de l'éga-lité'.[54] The 'ingredients' of the modernization narrative are basi-cally the same as in the common lawyers' or the private law jurists' story, except that the underlying pattern is not one of 'rise and fall' but of linear or wavelike progress. The central positive value is not freedom of contract but equality, and the climax is not reached in the 1870s but in the 1970s.

Elements of both narratives are present in the essays assembled here and they are by no means distributed along disciplinary lines, in the sense that historians and sociologists might be thought generally to follow the more optimistic modernization theory whereas lawyers might be expected to keep to the more defensive, anti-welfare state line. This now definitely seems to be an opposi-tion of the past. In many contributions there is instead a strong sense of ambivalence. While much sympathy is shown for legisla-tive as well as judicial efforts to remove obvious injustices to the weak, attention is also directed to the incompleteness of such at-tempts. Some essays uncover unforeseen or artfully disguised con-sequences of legal reforms, others expose new or recurring forms of exclusion and fragmentation. Observations like these partly result from an enlargement of focus. It has already been said that historical studies of 'legal culture' as proposed here are no longer limited to what legal professionals thought or did, but include the actions and experiences of those who used and abused the law or indeed avoided it whenever they could.

This change in perspective has perhaps been informed, if only in an indirect way, by the current debate on a third, more recent master narrative which can conveniently be labelled 'juridification'. Although the word and the reality which it describes may be ugly, evoking images of bureaucracy gone mad and occupied with regulating every aspect of human and even vegetable life (the shape of tomatoes and the like), it is neverthe-

[53] Richard Tawney, *Equality* (2nd rev. edn., London, 1931), 139.
[54] J. A. Condorcet, *Esquisse d'un tableau historique des progrès de l'esprit humain* (1793), ed. Monique et François Hincker (Paris, 1971), 253.

less true that 'juridification' is a phenomenon which has characterized the legal development of all industrialized countries in the
last hundred years.[55] If a short definition of this complex process
may be allowed one could call 'juridification' the pretension to
engineer and control social change through law. Jürgen Habermas
sees a 'colonization' of the lifeworld by law.[56] Taking a more
neutral stance one could speak of an increasing penetration of
legal rules and procedures into all walks of life. The link with the
emergence of the welfare state is obvious. But the process by
which the law has become ubiquitous seems also to be driven by
a growing expectation of individuals to have their own freedom
of choice guaranteed and to make others liable for physical or
imagined torts.[57]

The debate on juridification started in the early 1980s, a time
when confidence that engineering social change through law
could be achieved was severely shaken.[58] Confidence has never
recovered since. That was also the time when 'deregulation' and
'delegalization' came to be advocated as proper ways for the state
to shed some of its self-imposed tasks which politicians felt could
be no longer fulfilled.[59] Alternatives to law as a means for solving
disputes were also discussed in this context.[60] The debate on

[55] The best introduction to this debate is Gunther Teubner, 'Juridification: Concepts,
Aspects, Limits, Solutions', in id. (ed.), *Juridification of Social Spheres*, 3–48.
[56] Jürgen Habermas, *The Theory of Communicative Action*, ii: *Life World and System*, trans.
Thomas McCarthy (Boston, 1987), 356–73. See also Jürgen Habermas, *Between Facts and
Norms: Contributions to a Discourse Theory of Law and Democracy*, trans. William Rehg (Cambridge, 1996), 404–9 and 427–30. (German original: *Faktizität und Geltung: Beiträge zur Diskurs-
theorie des Rechts und des demokratischen Rechtsstaats* (Frankfurt am Main, 1992), 487–93 and
516–19.)
[57] Cf. Lawrence Friedman, *The Republic of Choice: Law, Authority, and Culture* (Cambridge,
Mass., 1990), esp. 13–17, 60–87. Whether a litigation mania really exists and how the figures
of litigation in various countries can be compared remains an open question. Cf. Basil S.
Markesinis, 'Litigation-Mania in England, Germany and the USA: Are We So Very Different?', *Cambridge Law Journal*, 49/2 (1990), 233–76.
[58] Cf. Gerd Bender, 'Rechtssoziologie in der alten Bundesrepublik: Prozesse, Kontexte,
Zäsuren', in Simon (ed.), *Rechtswissenschaft in der Bonner Republik*, 100–44, 136–41.
[59] Dieter Grimm, 'Der Wandel der Staatsaufgaben und die Krise des Rechtsstaats', in
id. (ed.), *Wachsende Staatsaufgaben—sinkende Steuerungsfähigkeit des Rechts* (Baden-Baden, 1990),
291–306.
[60] Cf. for example: Erhard Blankenburg et al. (eds.), *Alternative Rechtsformen und Alterna-
tiven zum Recht*, Jahrbuch für Rechtssoziologie und Rechtstheorie 6 (Opladen, 1980), which
contains some contributions in English; Rüdiger Voigt (ed.), *Gegentendenzen zur Verrechtlichung*,
Jahrbuch für Rechtssoziologie und Rechtstheorie 9 (Opladen, 1983); Michael Freeman
(ed.), *Alternative Dispute Resolution* (Aldershot, 1995), a collection of essays ranging from the
1960s to the early 1990s.

juridification has thus from the beginning been guided by strong
political and normative concerns and was heavily geared towards
contemporary issues. It is therefore no wonder that so far mainly
lawyers and sociologists have been involved; social historians have
tended to stand aside. Yet it is time that historians too begin to
take part in the debate, because the concept of juridification, as
well as the criticisms levelled against it, opens up questions which
can be posed in a more empirical fashion and projected back into
earlier periods, particularly into the nineteenth century. The
ambivalent story of juridification offers a good frame of reference
for comparative historical studies on the use of the law and on its
avoidance by potential litigants. Research on 'legal pluralism'[61] or
on alternative forms of settling conflicts may also be positioned
within that narrative, even if such studies concern only shorter
periods or one special type of conflict. This volume by no means
claims to accomplish the research programme outlined here.
What it can reasonably aspire to however is to present a range of
possible ways to historicize the problems raised by juridification
and its counterpart, the absence or unavailability of law in certain
situations or for certain groups of people.

Below the level of big theories much empirical research by legal
and social historians has shed light on the topics addressed in this
book. Not all of this can be reviewed here. Only a few trends will
be mentioned. To begin with social historians, over the last ten or
twenty years they seem to have been much more reluctant than
their predecessors to inscribe their findings into one of the grand
narratives, be it modernization theory or a softened version of
Marxism or the Weberian thesis of progressive rationalization.
Textbooks and syntheses of social history which still subscribe
to these models, for example Hans-Ulrich Wehler's *Deutsche
Gesellschaftsgeschichte*, accord little space to law, except in the form
of legislation which is treated as part of the political struggle
between parties and interest groups.[62] Collective enterprises like
the *Cambridge Social History of Britain* contain essays on all aspects

---

[61] H. W. Arthurs, *'Without the Law': Administrative Justice and Legal Pluralism in Nineteenth-Century England* (Toronto, 1985); S. E. Merry, 'Legal Pluralism', *Law and Society Review*, 22 (1988), 869–96.

[62] H.-U. Wehler, *Deutsche Gesellschaftsgeschichte*, vols. i and ii (Munich, 1987), vol. iii (Munich, 1995).

of social policy. Here again, legislation is the one mode in which law becomes an important topic. There is, however, one additional feature here, a chapter on crime and police, which reflects the great achievements of British scholars in this particular field.[63] A similarly selective occupation with law is apparent in French and American syntheses of nineteenth- and twentieth-century social history. In all four countries the interest of social historians in law seems to have been restricted to two aspects: first, legislation centred around the emergence of the welfare state, and second, law enforcement against criminals and the lower classes. Private law and courts of civil jurisdiction are rarely looked at, with the notable exception of gender history. But even here, as in other fields of social history, law is primarily envisaged as something imposed on people 'from above'. The underlying model very often conforms to that of nineteenth-century radical, socialist, or feminist critics of 'class justice'. Law and the courts are seen as machinery in the hands of the rich, the powerful, and the state to discipline and oppress the poor and the weak. The slow emancipation of the latter mainly happened through collective action, exercise of the vote, and public pressure on the legislator.

Such a view may not be wrong and will indeed correspond to the perceptions of those who felt that they were ill treated by judges, public authorities, and police forces. But research should not stop there. Much more is to be said on the relationship between law and society. This is made clear by a growing number of historical case studies about the actual working of particular courts of justice, especially at the lower levels in the hierarchy. These studies now cover an ever larger variety of judicial and quasi-judicial institutions such as English magistrates' courts,[64]

[63] V. A. C. Gatrell, 'Crime, Authority and the Policeman-State', in F. M. L. Thompson (ed.), *The Cambridge Social History of Britain 1750–1950*, 3 vols. (Cambridge, 1990), iii. 243–310. Cf. also the following research reports: Joanna Innes and John Styles, 'The Crime Wave: Recent Writing on Crime and Criminal Justice in Eighteenth-Century England', *Journal of British Studies*, 25 (1986), 380–435; R. B. Shoemaker, 'The "Crime Wave" Revisited: Crime, Law Enforcement and Punishment in Britain, 1650–1900', *Historical Journal*, 34 (1991), 763–68; A. W. B. Simpson, 'Law, Crime, and the Victorians', *Journal of British Studies*, 32 (1993), 83–8; David Cohen, 'Crime, Prosecution, and Punishment in Early Modern England', *Ius Commune*, 21 (1994), 267–79.

[64] See for example Jennifer Davis, 'A Poor Man's System of Justice: The London Police Courts in the Second Half of the Nineteenth Century', *Historical Journal*, 27 (1984), 309–35; Carolyn A. Conley, *The Unwritten Law: Criminal Justice in Victorian Kent* (Oxford, 1991).

small debts courts,[65] county and district courts,[66] consistory and other church courts,[67] munitions tribunals,[68] the French *conseils de prud'hommes* and German factory courts,[69] Prussian patrimonial courts,[70] French and Rhenish justices of the peace,[71] and so on.[72] Opinions and obsessions of individual judges and lawyers as well as the history of legal professions and legal aid schemes are now also explored within that context.[73] Crime, sexuality, moral issues,

[65] See for example Margot Finn, 'Debt and Credit in Bath's Court of Requests, 1829–39', *Urban History*, 21 (1994), 211–36; Paul Johnson, 'Small Debts and Economic Distress in England and Wales, 1857–1913', *Economic History Review*, 46/1 (1993), 65–87.

[66] See, for example, Pat Polden, 'Judicial Independence and Executive Responsibilities: The Lord Chancellor's Department and the County Court Judges, 1846–1971', *Anglo-American Law Review*, 25 (1996), 1–38 and 133–62; Paul Johnson, 'Class Law in Victorian England', *Past and Present*, 141 (1993), 147–69; Gerry R. Rubin, 'The County Courts and the Tally Trade, 1846–1914', in id. and David Sugarman (eds.), *Law, Economy and Society, 1750–1914* (Abingdon, 1984), 321–48; Regina Schulte, *Das Dorf im Verhör: Brandstifter, Kindsmörderinnen und Wilderer vor den Schranken des bürgerlichen Gerichts: Oberbayern 1848–1910* (Reinbek, 1989).

[67] Stone, *Road to Divorce*, is largely based on records of consistory courts. For another example see Robert von Friedeburg, *Sündenzucht und sozialer Wandel: Earls Colne (England), Ipswich und Springfield (Neuengland) c. 1524–1690 im Vergleich* (Stuttgart, 1993).

[68] Gerry R. Rubin, *War, Law, and Labour: The Munitions Acts, State Regulation, and the Unions, 1915–1921* (Oxford, 1987).

[69] Alain Cottereau, 'L'Embauche et la vie normative des métiers durant les deux premiers tiers du XIXe siècle français', *Les Cahiers des relations professionelles*, 10 (1995), 47–71; id., 'Justice et injustice ordinaire sur les lieux de travail d'après les audiences prud'homales (1806–1866)', *Le Mouvement social*, 141 (Oct.–Dec. 1987), 25–59; Heinz-Gerhard Haupt, 'Les Employés lyonnais devant le conseil de prud'hommes du commerce (1910–1914)', *Le Mouvement social*, 141 (Oct.–Dec. 1987), 81–99; Peter Schöttler, 'Die rheinischen Fabrikengerichte im Vormärz und in der Revolution von 1848/49', *Zeitschrift für Neuere Rechtsgeschichte*, 7 (1985), 160–80; id., 'Zur Mikrogeschichte der Arbeitsgerichtsbarkeit am Beispiel der rheinischen Fabrikengerichte im Vormärz und in der Revolution von 1848', *Rechtshistorisches Journal*, 9 (1990), 127–42.

[70] Monika Wienfort, 'Preußische Patrimonialrichter im Vormärz: Bildungsbürgertum auf dem Lande zwischen staatlichem Einfluß und gutsherrlichen Interessen', in Klaus Tenfelde and Hans-Ulrich Wehler (eds.), *Wege zur Geschichte des Bürgertums* (Göttingen, 1994), 57–77.

[71] Marcel Erkens, *Die französische Friedensgerichtsbarkeit 1789–1814 unter besonderer Berücksichtigung der vier rheinischen Departements* (Cologne, 1994); Ute Schneider, 'Vom Notabelnamt zur Amtsprofession: Die Herkunft, Karrieren und der Rechtsalltag rheinischer Friedensrichter im 19. Jahrhundert', in Guillaume Métairie, *Le Monde des juges de paix de Paris (1790–1838)* (Paris, 1995).

[72] For further references about Germany and France cf. the research report by Barbara Dölemeyer, 'Justizforschung in Frankreich und Deutschland', *Zeitschrift für Neuere Rechtsgeschichte*, 18 (1996), 288–99. For Britain and the United States see the research reports by Sugarman (n. 42 above) and Friedman (n. 81 below).

[73] Martin H. Geyer, 'Recht, Gerechtigkeit und Gesetze: Reichsgerichtsrat Zeiler und die Inflation', *Zeitschrift für Neuere Rechtsgeschichte*, 16 (1994), 349–72; Joachim Rückert, 'Richtertum als Organ des Rechtsgeistes: Die Weimarer Erfüllung einer alten Versuchung', in Knut

civil rights, social control, and conflicts at the workplace have been the main topics of interest so far, but civil matters such as property rights, inheritance, marriage and divorce, debts, and accidents are also beginning to be looked at. Such work concentrates strongly upon the early modern period up to about 1850. Much less is known about the later periods with which this book is in large parts concerned.

These case studies, although increasing in number, are as yet not well connected with each other, but they have features in common. The methods used are often those of micro-history, history of everyday life (*Alltagsgeschichte*), or history 'from below'.[74] In some cases these are combined with analysis of language and symbols. More often however the social and administrative history of these lower courts has to be the main focus as so little is known about them. Materials are court records, judicial statistics, newspaper reports, and a wide range of other sources. These are interpreted in various imaginative ways. Some authors aggregate long series of data, counting for example caseloads or success rates of plaintiffs along gender and class lines. Others pick out only one or a few individual cases and make them the object of 'thick descriptions', confronting the expectations and experiences of all participants in the disputes. Combinations of quantitative and qualitative interpretation are also possible. Whenever court proceedings have been looked at 'from below', the crucial finding has almost invariably been that law and legal institutions could be resorted to for many purposes never contemplated by the legislator. Courts were appealed to, for example, to defend local or trade

---

Wolfgang Nörr, Bertram Schefold, and Friedrich Tenbruck (eds.), *Geisteswissenschaften zwischen Kaiserreich und Republik: Zur Entwicklung von Nationalökonomie, Rechtswissenschaft und Sozialwissenschaft im 20. Jahrhundert* (Stuttgart, 1994), 267–313; Raymond Cocks, *Foundations of the Modern Bar* (London, 1983); R. I. Morgan, 'The Introduction of Civil Legal Aid in England and Wales, 1914–1949', *Twentieth Century British History*, 5 (1994), 38–76; David Sugarman, 'Simple Images and Complex Realities: English Lawyers and their Relationship to Business and Politics, 1750–1950', *Law and History Review*, 11 (1993), 257–301; Jean-Louis Halpérin (ed.), *Avocats et notaires en Europe: Les Professions judiciaires et juridiques dans l'histoire contemporaine* (Paris, 1996); Hannes Siegrist, *Advokat, Bürger und Staat: Eine vergleichende Geschichte der Rechtsanwälte in Deutschland, Italien und der Schweiz, 18.–20. Jahrhundert* (Frankfurt am Main, 1996). Most studies on legal professions concentrate on institutional aspects and sociopolitical strategies; the actual work of lawyers in and out of court still remains a largely unexplored field, except in the United States. See the essay by Edward E. Purcell, Jr. in this volume.

[74] On *Alltagsgeschichte* see Alf Lüdtke (ed.), *The History of Everyday Life: Reconstructing Historical Experiences and Ways of Life*, trans. William Templer (Princeton, 1995).

customs, to sanction private arrangements, to put blame on outsiders, to expose certain issues to the public, or to get advice in a
difficult situation. For the lower classes a case fought by one of
their fellows often was an opportunity for social protest. Even if
an individual case was lost, a moral victory achieved in the local
community or by reports in the press could still lead to satisfaction. Taken together, what emerges from all these case studies is
a much more differentiated picture of what law could mean for
different social groups.[75] This does not necessarily challenge
everything which can be learnt from traditional legal and social
history, but crude statements on 'class justice' on the one hand,
neutrality or autonomy of the law on the other, will no longer
be acceptable.

Historical research on 'law in action'[76] has advanced differently
in the four countries compared here. It is obvious that among
historians of the eighteenth and nineteenth centuries British
scholars have taken the lead in the field. This may partly be due
to an extraordinary richness of sources, partly also to an exceptionally good understanding between legal historians and historians of modern social history in Britain. But the most important
factor is perhaps the influence of certain inspiring figures, including, to name a few, E. P. Thompson, Lawrence Stone, David Sugarman, and Douglas Hay. On the European continent historical
work on judicial practice is as yet much more sporadic, at least as
far as the modern age is concerned. In France the late *ancien régime*
and the revolutionary period absorb the attention of almost all
scholars working in the field.[77] The arid language of French court
judgments which do not disclose anything about the 'facts' of
cases is a serious obstacle to any study of legal culture. In
Germany interest is more widespread, with the first half of the
nineteenth century and (with a different objective) the Nazi period

[75] The work of E. P. Thompson has anticipated many of these findings; see in particular his essays assembled in id., *Customs in Common* (1st pub. 1991; Harmondsworth, 1993).

[76] As opposed to 'law in the books'. This distinction goes back to Roscoe Pound, who
was Professor of Law at Harvard from 1910 to 1936. Cf. id., 'Law in Books and Law in
Action', *American Law Review*, 44 (1910), 12–36.

[77] Apart from the works already mentioned see Michael Sonenscher, *Work and Wages:
Natural Law, Politics and the Eighteenth-Century French Trades* (Cambridge, 1989); id., 'Journey-
men, the Courts and the French Trades 1781–1791', *Past and Present*, 114 (1987), 77–109;
Bernard Schnapper, *Voies nouvelles en histoire du droit: La Justice, la famille, la répression pénale
(XVIème–XXème siècles)* (Paris, 1991).

being focal points.[78] The extreme diversity of the laws in force in various parts of Germany until the end of the nineteenth century makes it difficult to generalize. One way to deal with this complexity has been to concentrate first on legislation, institutions, and legal thinking. The study of judicial reality has suffered from this order of priority. Moreover, in continental European countries barriers between lawyers and historians are higher than in Britain. Legal historians in German and French law faculties often feel more bound by contemporary normative issues and by doctrinal questions; both are of little interest to social historians. With regard to the subject of this book, private law, communication between the disciplines is also rendered difficult by the fact that the *Code civil* and the *Bürgerliches Gesetzbuch* (*BGB*) are the laws actually in force. Until recently historicizing judicial practice under those codes consistently seems to have been a methodical problem for lawyers. In France this problem even reached back to the nineteenth century,[79] whereas in Germany extensive research projects on private law before the introduction of the *BGB* in 1900 have been undertaken since the 1970s.[80] Despite recent progress it will probably be many years before a handbook on 'law and society' comparable to that by Cornish and Clark on England between 1750 and 1950 is published for France and Germany.

The situation is completely different again in the United States. Here the law schools have almost monopolized the field of

[78] For the earlier periods see the literature mentioned above (n. 69–72). For private law jurisdiction under the Nazi regime see Bernd Rüthers, *Die unbegrenzte Auslegung: Zum Wandel der Privatrechtsordnung im Nationalsozialismus* (1st pub. 1968; 4th edn., Heidelberg, 1991); Rainer Schröder, '. . . aber im Zivilrecht sind die Richter standhaft geblieben': Die Urteile des OLG Celle aus dem Dritten Reich* (Baden-Baden, 1988). For labour law: Marc Linder, *The Supreme Labor Court in Nazi Germany: A Jurisprudential Analysis* (Frankfurt am Main, 1987).

[79] Cf. the remarks by Halpérin, *Histoire du droit privé*, 9 f.

[80] The starting point for these enterprises was Franz Wieacker's *Privatrechtsgeschichte der Neuzeit* which first appeared in 1952 and had a 2nd edn. in 1967. This work is now available in an English translation: Franz Wieacker, *A History of Private Law in Europe, with Particular Reference to Germany*, trans. Tony Weir, foreword Reinhard Zimmermann (Oxford, 1995). Wieacker's work has been taken up and expanded by Helmut Coing and the research groups at the Max-Planck Institut für Europäische Rechtsgeschichte in Frankfurt am Main. Their most notable achievement (and an indispensable resource not only for German legal history) is the *Handbuch der Quellen und Literatur der neueren europäischen Privatrechtsgeschichte*, ed. Helmut Coing, vol. i, vol. ii in 2 parts, vol. iii in 5 parts (Munich, 1973–88). The history of private law in the 20th century is now also receiving more attention: Knut Wolfgang Nörr, *Zwischen den Mühlsteinen: Eine Privatrechtsgeschichte der Weimarer Republik* (Tübingen, 1988); and more generally Karl Kroeschell, *Rechtsgeschichte Deutschlands im 20. Jahrhundert* (Göttingen, 1992).

historical studies on law and modern society. If disciplinary
boundaries are transgressed and methods exchanged, this
happens mainly between lawyers and social scientists; historians
are rarely involved in their debates. Since the 1950s the Wisconsin school of legal realism founded by Willard Hurst has produced
countless local studies on the practice of lower courts, most of
them of a quantitative nature.[81] This work was guided by the
hypothesis that legal development by and large had to follow social
demands and that the lower courts were the first point at which
legal professionals were confronted with those demands. On the
basis of this extensive work on judicial practice, which was done
at a time when legal history in Europe was still mostly doctrinal,
American legal history could reach out into new fields. Thus the
interdependence between legal thought and the growth of capitalism was explored,[82] several new legal histories of employment
relations were written,[83] theoretical models from various other disciplines including discourse analysis and system theory are applied
to the law under the general label of 'Critical Legal Studies',[84]
and much attention was of course paid to the equal protection
jurisdiction concerning women, African Americans, and other
minorities.[85] This research now covers all periods of American

[81] Cf. the overview by Lawrence M. Friedman, 'Opening the Time Capsule: A Progress
Report on Studies of Courts over Time', *Law and Society Review*, 24 (1990), 229–40.
[82] Robert W. Gordon, 'Legal Thought and Legal Practice in the Age of American
Enterprise, 1870–1920', in Gerald L. Geison (ed.), *Professions and Professional Ideologies in
America* (Chapel Hill, NC, 1983); Herbert Hovencamp, *Enterprise and American Law, 1836–1937*
(Cambridge, Mass., 1991); Horwitz, *Transformation of American Law, 1780–1860*.
[83] Karen Orren, *Belated Feudalism: Labor, the Law, and Liberal Development in the United States*
(Cambridge, 1991); Robert J. Steinfeld, *The Invention of Free Labor: The Employment Relation in
English and American Law and Culture, 1350–1870* (Chapel Hill, NC, 1991); William E. Forbath,
Law and the Shaping of the American Labor Movement (Cambridge, Mass., 1991); Christopher
Tomlins and Andrew J. King (eds.), *Labor Law in America: Historical and Critical Essays*
(Baltimore, 1992); Christopher Tomlins, 'How Who Rides Whom: Recent "New" Histo-
ries of American Labour Law and What They May Signify', *Social History*, 20 (1995), 1–21.
[84] See the critical review articles by Peter Goodrich, 'Sleeping with the Enemy: An Essay
on the Politics of Critical Legal Studies in America', *New York University Law Review*, 68
(1993), 389–425, and Daniel R. Ernst, 'The Critical Tradition in the Writing of American
Legal History', *Yale Law Journal*, 102 (1993), 1019–76.
[85] For a recent example (with further references) see the special issue of the *American
Historical Review*, 102 (1997): Elizabeth Dale, ' "Social Equality Does Not Exist among
Themselves, nor among Us": *Baylies* vs. *Curry* and Civil Rights in Chicago, 1888', *American
Historical Review*, 102 (1997), 311–39; Beth Tompkins Bates, 'A New Crowd Challenges the
Agenda of the Old Guard in the NAACP 1933–1941', *American Historical Review*, 102 (1997),
340–77; Kevin Gaines, 'Rethinking Race and Class in African-American Struggles for
Equality, 1885–1941', *American Historical Review*, 102 (1997), 378–87.

history and all levels of jurisdiction from the Supreme Court down to district courts.

It is hard to sum up an already much too brief survey of four national research traditions each divided into two disciplines and many subdisciplines. There is a notable asymmetry between the United States on the one hand, where innovations in modern legal history have primarily emanated from law schools, and the situation in Europe on the other, where lawyers as well as historians have made important contributions to the field. Within Europe again there is a difference between Britain, where legal and social historians tend to work with similar methods and on similar topics, and continental Europe, where the gap between the two disciplines is wide. It is inevitable that an interdisciplinary and comparative collection of essays reflects this asymmetry. However, there is sufficient common ground to start a meaningful discussion between research traditions which until now have worked too isolated from each other.

V

Academic study of comparative law began on a grand scale in the last decades of the nineteenth century.[86] All over Europe learned societies devoted to comparisons were founded almost simultaneously. Some of them were interdisciplinary, attracting not only lawyers but also economists and social scientists.[87] These societies often had their own journals or publication series and corresponded with each other. Conferences were also held to increase mutual understanding. All these undertakings were guided by a spirit of internationalism. There was a common desire, if not to work towards a unification of European legal systems, then at least to avoid further national divergence and confrontation and, perhaps, to construct a common legal science. To acquire knowledge about foreign legal systems and to compare the solutions they

---

[86] Cf. Konrad Zweigert and Hein Kötz, *Introduction to Comparative Law*, 2nd rev. edn., trans. Tony Weir (Oxford, 1987; repr. 1992), 57 f. In the new German edition: id., *Einführung in die Rechtsvergleichung auf dem Gebiete des Privatrechts* (3rd rev. edn., Tübingen, 1996), 56 ff.

[87] A truly international and interdisciplinary association was the Internationale Vereinigung für Vergleichende Rechtswissenschaft und Volkswirtschaftslehre, founded 1894 in Berlin.

had found with those found in one's own legal tradition was seen as the first step towards that end. *Historical* research about the 'other' was an integral part of that programme. Yet within that context the aim was usually to prove that, in the end, past differences in thought and practice could be overcome. The 'otherness' of the other was often not taken seriously enough.

The First World War was a brutal setback for this kind of comparative legal study, one from which it has never fully recovered. In a way, though it may sound odd, this is not to be regretted, at least as far as comparative legal *history* is concerned. For the aim of historical comparisons, whether of law or anything else, is to arrive at a balanced assessment of similarities *and* differences.[88] The 'phenomenon of alienation' which a comparatist encounters may indeed be a result just as valuable as the experience of proximity.[89] However, neither the one nor the other should be made the starting point for comparative historical research. Historians should neither set out to prove that things evolved in so irreconcilably different a way that conflict and disaster were inevitable nor pass over past divergences in order to show that everything can be reconciled and harmonized in the present. For instance, whether a further integration of European legal systems is possible now, or whether a worldwide co-ordination of fundamental legal standards can be achieved in future, are questions which should not directly be linked with historical research.

As the purpose of this volume is historical explanation only, not practical jurisprudence, the 'contemplative' approach adopted here differs somewhat from that 'historical legal science' which some, mostly German, lawyers have proposed in recent years with a view to promoting and better preparing the elaboration of a future European private law.[90] This is not to say that scholars

[88] Much has been written on the use and abuse of comparisons in social history. Good surveys are John Breuilly, 'Introduction: Making Comparisons in History', in id., *Labour and Liberalism in Nineteenth-Century Europe: Essays in Comparative History* (Manchester, 1992), 1–25; Heinz Gerhard Haupt and Jürgen Kocka (eds.), *Geschichte und Vergleich: Ansätze und Ergebnisse international vergleichender Geschichtsschreibung* (Frankfurt am Main, 1996); Johannes Paulmann, 'Internationaler Vergleich und interkultureller Transfer: Zwei Forschungsansätze zur Europäischen Geschichte des 18. bis 20. Jahrhunderts', *Historische Zeitschrift*, 267 (1998), 649–85.

[89] Pierre Legrand, 'Comparative Legal Studies and Commitment to Theory', *Modern Law Review*, 58 (1995), 262–73, 262. He even considers the achievement of this effect the 'heart of the comparative enterprise'.

[90] Reinhard Zimmermann, 'Savigny's Legacy: Legal History, Comparative Law, and the Emergence of a European Legal Science', *Law Quarterly Review*, 112 (1996), 576–605, 587;

working on that or similar projects could not profit from reading this book. The single-country studies and comparative essays assembled here indeed show that private law legislation and jurisdiction in Europe, as well as the United States, followed similar paths in essential fields. This happened even at times when these nations went to war against each other. The 'nationalization' of legal cultures which was expressed in the American and French constitutions, in the great codifications of continental Europe, and in the persistence of the English common law (in spite of various efforts to transform it into a code and thereby destroy its identity) never went so far as to exclude transfers and cross-fertilization. On the other hand, one should not brush aside the differences between the legal cultures. During the nineteenth century in particular, these differences were substantial and deeply affected the significance of the law in the four national societies observed.

Comparative history of legal cultures is not identical with traditional comparative law. The latter usually takes as its starting point certain norms, legal remedies, figures of judicial argument, or institutions, and then goes on to search for functional equivalents in other legal systems. Objects for such studies could be, for example, the contract for the benefit of third parties, the action for liability in case of accidents, the definition of 'public policy', or the jurisdiction of constitutional courts. Adding up the findings may ultimately result in defining 'families' of law according to their distance or proximity in solving certain juridical problems.[91]

To compare legal cultures demands a start from a different angle. Here, basic societal problems, in our case inequalities, provide the primary reference frame. It is then asked how (and when) these social problems were transformed into juridical ones. Once a legal response has been given, however, the direction of enquiry can also turn the other way round. Legal arrangements may then be taken as a starting point, and the question will be to what extent the arrangements and institutions 'offered' by the legal system were accepted or rejected by those for whom they

Reiner Schulze, 'European Legal History: A New Field of Research in Germany', *Journal of Legal History*, 13 (1992), 270–95.

[91] This 'functional' approach is dominant in Zweigert and Kötz, *Introduction to Comparative Law*. For a critical survey of various methods in comparing (contemporary) legal systems in their societal context see: Ralf Rogowski, 'The Art of Mirroring: Comparative Law and Social Theory', in id. and G. Wilson (eds.), *Challenges to European Legal Scholarship* (Aldershot, 1996), 217–33.

were designed. Ideally then, research on legal cultures would have to follow the continuous movements back and forth between social demands, legal reactions, and social counter-reactions. To compare legal cultures would mean identifying similarities and differences in those movements. As this requires a long-term perspective a historical approach seems to be a meaningful way in which legal cultures can be compared. 'Juridification' may be one possible way to describe such a long-term process of reaction and counter-reaction, but it will have become evident by now that this paradigm is too heavily geared towards the 'supply side' of the law (if that expression may be borrowed from economics) and pays too little attention to the behaviour and attitudes of those who are supposed to make use of the infrastructure 'offered' by the law.[92] The ultimate goal of a comparative history of legal cultures would be to describe various patterns of socio-legal change and to identify the variables which turned the process into one or the other direction.

This collection does not claim to come anywhere near achieving that aim. Given the present state of research even a full comparison between two national legal cultures would go far beyond the capacity of one scholar. What could reasonably be requested from the authors was either single-country studies guided by the same set of questions or outlines of comparisons limited to certain aspects. The concentration on just a handful of basic social relations and typical disputes arising out of them should help to make the results comparable. The volume will thus do no more, but also no less, than supply materials and first attempts at conceptualization for future comparisons. The findings will enable readers to put theories they may have about the evolution of their own or a foreign legal culture, or differences between them, to a test.

It may be asked whether nation-states are really the proper units to be compared. Is it not rather the case that legal cultures often transcended state boundaries, if one considers for example the application of English case law in America and the British Empire, or the validity of the French *Code civil* in Belgium and in Germany left of the Rhine until 1900? On the other hand, it could

---

[92] A 'supply-side' theory of legal behaviour, partly based on comparative data, is advocated by Erhard Blankenburg, *Mobilisierung des Rechts: Eine Einführung in die Rechtssoziologie* (Berlin, 1995).

as well be argued with some force that legal cultures are neither national nor transnational phenomena, but should rather be studied and compared on the level of local or group-specific communities. If judicial practice and the significance of law for various segments of society is the prime concern (instead of legislation and systems of norms as in traditional comparative law), then it might indeed be more profitable to compare smaller units than nation-states, for example agricultural regions, big cities, or coal and iron districts. This is in part what the volume does in some sections, for example when landlord–tenant relations in London, Paris, New York, and a few big German cities are treated side by side, or when examples of judicial conflicts in rural southern England are held up against the proceedings before Prussian patrimonial courts east of the River Elbe. In other sections, however, those on husbands and wives, employers and employees, and producers and consumers, the authors have clearly chosen nation-states as units for their observations to be put into a comparative perspective.

There are good reasons for doing so, at least for the period with which the volume is concerned. For it cannot be denied that law, from the late eighteenth century onwards, became increasingly 'nationalized'—as has been said—through constitutions, codifications, and the persistence of the English common law. Nationalization did not necessarily mean more and more differences in the *substance* of norms, but it was first and foremost a process which concerned the *legitimacy* of the law in the eyes of the public and the political rulers themselves. Since the late eighteenth century certain notions distinguishing one's own legal order from those of other countries have become revered national symbols. Thus, Englishmen (and women), although at times badly treated by their local magistrates or judges, were proud of the common law and certain procedural elements, such as trial by jury, because these were seen as a guarantee against being subject to an absolutist tyranny like people on the European continent.[93] The same was true for colonial America, where after independence the constitution came to symbolize unity against foreign intruders and freedom against local usurpers of

---

[93] On the 'Englishness' of the common law in legal discourse see Peter Goodrich, 'Poor Illiterate Reason: History, Nationalism and Common Law', *Social and Legal Studies*, 1 (1992), 7–28.

power.[94] Again, in France the Napoleonic codes derived their legitimacy from encapsulating and preserving as a legacy certain achievements of the French Revolution, first of all liberty of property and equality before the law, against all internal or external attempts to put the clock back.[95] Finally, even in Germany, where the written law in force before the period of legal unification ending with the introduction of the *BGB* in 1900 was extremely diverse, the notion of a *Rechtsstaat*,[96] founded on a common legal science in which all practising lawyers had to be trained, was considered a unique and unifying feature of German legal culture as compared with all others.[97] In short, in all four countries the law had acquired additional or indeed an entirely new legitimacy by being linked with the process of nation-building and democratization.[98] As a consequence, conflicts about the malpractice of

[94] The gradual transformation of the colonial common law mind into American constitutionalism is described by Bernard Bailyn, *The Ideological Origins of the American Revolution* (Cambridge, Mass., 1967), 175–98. Michael Kammen, *A Machine That Would Go of Itself: The Constitution in American Culture* (New York, 1986).

[95] Cf. Jean Carbonnier, 'Le Code civil', in Pierre Nora (ed.), *Les Lieux de mémoire*, ii: *La Nation* (Paris, 1986), 293–315. Alfons Bürge, *Das französische Privatrecht im 19. Jahrhundert: Zwischen Tradition und Pandektenwissenschaft, Liberalismus und Etatismus* (Frankfurt am Main, 1991), convincingly argues that the draftsmen of the code, as well as Napoleon himself and his successors in government, were primarily motivated by an *étatist* vision which was partly paternalist, partly authoritarian. They regarded and used the code as one instrument among others of administrative regulation. Going further Bürge claims that the liberal *Privatrechtsgesellschaft* was no legacy of the Revolution at all (p. 494), but was only achieved in the middle decades of the 19th century through prolonged attempts at reinterpretation in legal literature and jurisdiction. The influence of the German Historical School is regarded as a crucial factor in this development. However, all this does not invalidate the view that the *Code Napoléon* from the start possessed a legitimacy with contemporaries, in France as well as in parts of Germany, which was derived from the idea—whether erroneous or not—that the code *as a text* preserved revolutionary achievements. Compared with other laws in force in continental Europe it did so indeed, especially with regard to equal treatment of (male, Christian) citizens, and that was one reason why the Germans on the left bank of the Rhine wanted to keep the French law.

[96] On the uses of this German concept, in comparison with the French equivalent *état de droit* and the English idea of 'rule of law', see R. C. van Caenegem, 'The "Rechtsstaat" in Historical Perspective', in id., *Legal History: A European Perspective* (London, 1991), 185–99. Cf. also Ernst-Wolfgang Böckenförde, 'Entstehung und Wandel des Rechtsstaatsbegriffs', in id., *Staat, Gesellschaft, Freiheit: Studien zur Staatstheorie und zum Verfassungsrecht* (Frankfurt am Main, 1976), 65–92.

[97] On legal unification as an achievement of German liberal nationalism see Michael John, *Politics and the Law in Late Nineteenth-Century Germany: The Origins of the Civil Code* (Oxford, 1989).

[98] This aspect is ignored by Zimmermann, 'Savigny's Legacy'. In his desire to revitalize the pre-modern European *ius commune* and an 'organically progressive' legal science in the style of the German Pandektists (p. 605) Zimmermann gives short shrift to the essential innovation brought about by the constitutions and codifications of continental Europe.

jurisdiction or demands for a change in important areas of law often came to be articulated at a national level, even if they had originated in local disputes. Legal cultures in the nineteenth and twentieth centuries thus had local as well as national dimensions, and both can be made the object of comparisons.

But what about the transnational dimension of legal cultures? Is it not true that Roman civil law in the shape it had received in the treatises of learned jurists from the twelfth century onwards formed a European *ius commune* from which even England, despite the 'noble isolation' of its common law, was never completely cut off?[99] Was not the period of 'nationalization' only a short interval in the history of European law, perhaps even in the legal history of the Western world? These are questions that reach beyond the scope of the present volume. None the less, readers might find the following essays stimulating enough to rethink one problem which has puzzled scholars for centuries, that is, the question of convergence and divergence between the common law and the civil law worlds.

'Comparisons, indeed . . . , are reputed odious, and so I am not fond of making them but you will be able to gather more effectively whether both of these laws are of equal merit, or whether one more richly deserves praise than the other.' Thus Sir John Fortescue (*c*.1395–*c*.1477) introduced his observations on the 'manner in which the character of the civil and the English laws can be discerned'.[100] That was written in the fifteenth century. Since then, legions of scholars on both sides of the English Channel have made comparisons, mostly in order to prove the superiority of their own and the inferiority of the other legal order. It was more rare, though it happened too, that laws on the other side were studied out of a desire to prove that one's own

---

This innovation consisted in the establishment of the primacy of legislation driven by a *political* will over the continuum of judge-made law. In today's democracies it seems highly unlikely (and indeed undesirable) that the task of elaborating new law should be left to legal professionals alone. Even in the semi-authoritarian German Kaiserreich the new *BGB*—although drafted mainly by experts—would not have been accepted without the public and parliamentary debates preceding its introduction.

[99] John H. Baker, *An Introduction to English Legal History* (3rd edn., London, 1990), 35 (quotation). Against the 'isolationist' view of the common law: Reinhard Zimmermann, 'Der europäische Charakter des englischen Rechts: Historische Verbindungen zwischen Civil Law und Common Law', *Zeitschrift für Europäisches Privatrecht*, 1 (1993), 4–51.

[100] Sir John Fortescue, *On the Laws and Governance of England*, ed. Shelley Lockwood, Cambridge Texts in the History of Political Thought (Cambridge, 1997), 28 f.

legal-political system was in bad shape and needed reform. Montesquieu's famous chapter on the English constitution,[101] Bentham's critique of the absurdities of English common and statute law,[102] Rudolf Gneist's idealized picture of English self-governing institutions,[103] and Maitland's friendly review of the successful termination in 1900 of the German codification movement[104]—all these were examples of explicit or implicit comparisons with a view to highlighting domestic deficiencies.

The acquisition of knowledge about foreign legal systems thus nearly always took place under political auspices, either of reform or of resistance to reform. Transfers of legal ideas or practices could end up in the appropriation of the 'other', but also in its rejection. Moreover, even the appropriation of certain elements of a foreign system could be undertaken out of the desire to make the domestic system immune to more radical change. Thus, if English common lawyers like Blackstone or Lord Mansfield or Austin used categories of Roman civil law to systematize the common law, it does not follow that these lawyers were working towards an assimilation of the two legal orders. Rather, the contrary is true. By making the common law appear more systematic they backed up those English lawyers and politicians of the nineteenth century who argued against the necessity of codification in the continental style.[105] Again, if English and American lawyers of the nineteenth century translated and read Savigny, this does

[101] Montesquieu, *De l'esprit des lois*, XI. 6.

[102] On Bentham as critic of English law see Michael Lobban, *The Common Law and English Jurisprudence 1760–1850* (Oxford, 1991), chs. 5 and 6. Lobban's conclusion that Bentham 'remained a common law revisionist' (p. 145) seems to underestimate his principled opposition to judge-made law. Cf. *Edinburgh Review*, 29 (1817–18), 217–37 ('Bentham on Codification'), and John R. Dinwiddy, 'Bentham's Transition to Political Radicalism, 1809–10', in id., *Radicalism and Reform in Britain 1780–1850* (London, 1992), 271–90, 278.

[103] On Gneist's vision of English self-government see Hans-Christof Kraus, 'Die deutsche Rezeption und Darstellung der englischen Verfassung im neunzehnten Jahrhundert', in Rudolf Muhs, Johannes Paulmann, and Willibald Steinmetz (eds.), *Aneignung und Abwehr: Interkultureller Transfer zwischen Deutschland und Großbritannien im 19. Jahrhundert* (1998), 89–126, 113 ff.

[104] Frederic William Maitland, 'A Survey of the Century (1901)', in *The Collected Papers of Frederic William Maitland*, ed. H. A. L. Fisher (Cambridge, 1911), iii. 432–39, id. 'The Making of the German Civil Code (1906)', ibid. 474–88.

[105] Lobban, *Common Law*, 13. On Blackstone cf. also David Lieberman, *The Province of Legislation Determined: Legal Theory in Eighteenth-Century Britain* (Cambridge, 1989). On intellectual cross-currents between the continental European and English debates on codification see John R. Dinwiddy, 'Early Nineteenth-Century Reactions to Benthamism', in id., *Radicalism and Reform in Britain 1780–1850*, 339–61, 345–52.

not mean that they really accepted the ideas of the German His-torical School.[106] These reflections may sound trivial, but they are apparently not always kept in mind when mutual 'influences' between legal cultures are examined. 'Influence' itself is a rather loose term which is best avoided when transfers are described. Speaking of 'influences' suggests proximity and a quest for con-vergence where in fact the opposite might have happened. Knowl-edge about the 'other' might as well have been acquired with a view to rejecting any further rapprochement and to insisting on the essential distance between cultures.[107] During the nineteenth century this was indeed often the principal motive behind trans-fers of legal thought from the Roman civil law to the common law world.

Some notable differences between the Anglo-American and the continental European legal cultures have already been touched upon. German and French jurists accepted mandatory law (*ius cogens*) whereas the concept itself came to be regarded as alien by Anglo-American lawyers from the beginning of the nineteenth century. On the European continent the old 'common laws' of Roman or ethnic origin were supplanted by codes or statutes. Once a code had been passed, common law ceased to exist as a separate body of rules for all matters regulated by the code. It was different in Britain and America where common law continued to be applicable besides (and sometimes effectively turned against) statutes and constitutions.[108] This of course had consequences for the outward appearance of the law and for the style of judicial argument. In the Anglo-American world law appeared primarily as case law, and legal thinking was centred around actions. In con-tinental Europe law was primarily thought of as an authoritative

[106] The rather selective use which American lawyers made of German sources is studied by Mathias Reimann, *Historische Schule und Common Law: Die deutsche Rechtswissenschaft des 19. Jahrhunderts im amerikanischen Rechtsdenken* (Berlin, 1993). Cf. also the contributions in id. (ed.), *The Reception of Continental Ideas in the Common Law World 1820–1920* (Berlin, 1993).

[107] Cf. Rudolf Muhs, 'Geisteswehen: Rahmenbedingungen des deutsch-britischen Kul-turaustauschs im 19. Jahrhundert', in id., Paulmann, and Steinmetz (eds.), *Aneignung und Abwehr*, 44–70.

[108] Which sources are recognized as giving legitimacy to a legal system, whether case law or statutes or both, is not just a question of judicial technique or style. This is stressed by R. C. van Caenegem, *An Historical Introduction to Private Law* (Cambridge, 1988), 170: 'the use of these sources is not random or accidental; they are the basic options open to society when faced with the phenomenon of the law. And if law is an instrument of social control, then it matters who controls the sources of law.'

text from which all other rules and doctrines governing judicial practice had ultimately to be deduced.

Perhaps even more important than these obvious differences of form and style were their consequences for the potential utility of the law in the eyes of the public. It could be argued that in Britain and America, where the law itself appeared divided into separate and equally legitimate bodies, it was easier for people to form the idea that legal change could be set in motion by actions in court rather than by political pressure on the legislator. This at least seems to be a finding of this volume if one compares the contributions dealing with common law countries with those on civil law countries. Authors writing on France and Germany tend to start by exposing a given legal situation as defined by the text of laws, then go on to describe judicial interpretation and its perceived injustices or deficiencies. They usually end by pointing to some legal change achieved either through political action or through self-criticism within the academic legal community. Authors writing on Britain and the United States prefer to start with an exposition of circumstances which brought people of various social backgrounds to mobilize lawyers and courts for their purposes. Driven by continuous challenges inside and outside the courtrooms, legal change often appears as the result of adjustments or negotiations between social demands and practising lawyers rather than of legislation. One might wonder whether the apparent differences in methods and results between Anglo-American and continental European historians are not themselves an expression of the fact that they are part of the legal cultures they describe. In a way, this volume itself could be seen as an experiment. Contributors were asked to respond to the same set of questions, yet the kinds of answers given to these questions differ significantly, not only between national legal cultures but also between the wider legal cultures of the common law and the civil law worlds.

Should we conclude from this that legal cultures are mental prisons from which there is no escape? This would mean overemphasizing the dividing power of barriers to communication.[109] Just as in the past transfers and interferences have been possible, so in

---

[109] Among these the problem of translating juridical concepts is perhaps the most difficult to solve. Cf. the sceptical (and humorous) remarks of one of the most experienced translators of German legal studies into English: Tony Weir, 'Die Sprachen des europäi-

the present encounters between legal and social historians of different national and cultural backgrounds may help to upset fixed opinions about the other. By making comparisons between legal cultures easier, this volume hopes to encourage this process.

schen Rechts: Eine skeptische Betrachtung', *Zeitschrift für Europäisches Privatrecht*, 3 (1995), 368–74.

Part I

LANDOWNERS, PEASANTS, AND LABOURERS

2

The Private Use of Public Rights

Law and Social Conflict in Nineteenth-Century Rural England

RAYMOND COCKS

Between 1800 and 1900 there were many forms of social conflict in the English countryside. Episodes of widespread violence, such as the Swing Riots of 1830–2, may be contrasted with minor breaches of the law by poor people engaged in poaching or other small but sustained infringements upon the rights of landowners.[1] The role of law in all of these events varied greatly with time and place but two legal themes emerge with clarity and will be considered in this article.

First, in respect of the civil provisions relating to property, the social impact of the law was often important but, at the same time, indirect. Usually it was not worth suing a poor person in, say, trespass. A landowner was unlikely to recover his costs, still less any possible damages. Rather, with some notable exceptions, the role of the civil law was to provide the setting for the use of the criminal law. Proof in civil terms that a farmer owned a

I am grateful to Kathy de Gama for permission to read drafts of her research on private prosecutions.

[1] The sources on law and rural life in England at this time include the following. In respect of the legal framework used by those who were fortunate enough to own property see: J. Habakkuk, *Marriage, Debt and the Estates System: English Land Ownership 1650–1950* (Oxford, 1994). Habakkuk's notes between pp. 705 and 759 contain numerous references to detailed sources of information. For current debates on changes in the structure of land-holdings at this time, see F. M. L. Thompson (ed.), *Landowners, Capitalists, and Entrepreneurs* (Oxford, 1994). For an analysis of the social context of land law see W. R. Cornish and G. de N. Clark, *Law and Society in England, 1750–1950* (London, 1989); in particular, ch. 2, 'Land'. For the role of lawyers in changes in the legal structure of landholding see J. Stuart Anderson, *Lawyers and the Making of English Land Law, 1832–1940* (Oxford, 1992). For the social role of the law there is much to be said for starting with major 18th-century studies such as: E. P. Thompson, *Whigs and Hunters: The Origin of the Black Act* (Harmondsworth, 1975); D. Hay et al., *Albion's Fatal Tree: Crime and Society in Eighteenth-Century England* (New

machine could serve as the foundation for a criminal prosecution against agricultural labourers who had deliberately destroyed the machine: they had damaged private property. Given the poverty in which the labourers lived there was little point in suing them for the value of the machine. Such civil litigation was likely to be as futile as bringing an action in trespass. Civil law provided the property rights which the criminal law was designed to protect.

Secondly, when there was recourse to the criminal law, it was put to use by landowners in a way which may be contrasted with that found in continental Europe and most parts of the United States of America. The central point here is that there was no public prosecutor in England until 1879 when the office of Director of Public Prosecutions was created by statute. In the words of Hay and Snyder, 'England was almost unique among nations . . . in not having a bureaucracy staffed by lawyers with the responsibility to charge and proceed against those accused of crimes.'[2] Even after this innovation the new public official had a very restricted role and was chiefly concerned with especially serious and difficult cases. For all practical purposes, prosecutions in nineteenth-century rural England were under the control of individuals and this often meant, in reality, that they were under the control of the local gentry. In the course of this essay it will be suggested that this turned the public law of crime into something

York, 1975). Two helpful sources on the earlier part of the 19th century are: E. J. Hobsbawm and George Rudé, *Captain Swing* (Harmondsworth, 1968 and 1985); and P. B. Munsche, *Gentlemen and Poachers: The English Game Laws 1671–1831* (Cambridge, 1981). For later years two studies are useful in themselves and provide extensive guidance for further reading: A. Howkins, *Reshaping Rural England: A Social History, 1850–1925* (London, 1992); and id., *Poor Labouring Men: Rural Radicalism in Norfolk 1870–1923* (London, 1985). See, too, D. Philips, *Crime and Authority in Victorian England: The Black Country, 1835–1880* (London, 1977). There is potential for drawing interesting contrasts between the role of law in rural society and its place in industrial development: see, by way of contrast, R. W. Kostal, *Law and English Railway Capitalism, 1825–1875* (Oxford, 1994). Beyond modern works such as these there is a very extensive literature on rural life, and this includes, for example, J. L. Hammond and B. Hammond, *The Village Labourer, 1760–1832* (London, 1948). In respect of prosecutions the excellent and invaluable study is D. Hay and F. Snyder (eds.), *Policing and Prosecution in Britain, 1750–1850* (Oxford, 1989). Note, for example, the introduction by the editors: 'Using the Criminal Law, 1750–1850: Policing, Private Prosecution, and the State', 3–55; and also, for present purposes, R. D. Storch, 'Policing Rural Southern England before the Police: Opinion and Practice, 1830–1856', 211–66. The present article is a tiny addition to a great body of work on 19th-century crime in England.

[2] Hay and Snyder (eds.), *Policing*, 3–4, and see Cornish and Clark, *Law and Society*, 606.

like a private asset at the disposal of those with the time and the money to launch prosecutions. Belief in the desirability of such an approach was so strong amongst the gentry that it influenced Victorian thought on important constitutional issues and has to be explained against a background of the general role of the law—both civil and criminal—in rural life. This combination of private and public elements is what is most distinctive about the role of law in the context of nineteenth-century English rural conflict.

The poor and the civil law

At the start of the nineteenth century there was well-established bitterness amongst the poor about enclosure. Enclosure was the process whereby an Act of Parliament could be used to destroy the rights of minor landowners. Sometimes it could be used to bring to an end the rights of the landless poor to use large areas of common land for the purposes of grazing animals or taking firewood and the like. Where it was possible to prove the existence of pre-existing rights the dispossessed could obtain compensation; but, obviously, this was no consolation in cases where such rights were believed to exist and their existence could not be proved. Even where compensation was obtained it might well be felt that temporary financial relief was a poor substitute for the loss of ancient rights.[3]

In the eighteenth century the enclosure process had given rise to major disputes both in and outside of the courts. In the nineteenth century it could produce intense feeling but it had become even more difficult for the poor to make significant use of the law to assert their rights. For property holders seeking to enclose land the relevant procedures were greatly simplified by legislation of 1801 in

---

[3] For a recent guide to the literature on 18th- and 19th-century enclosure see: E. P. Thompson, *Customs in Common* (Harmondsworth, 1993). Important observations on the methods of 18th-century enclosure may be found in J. M. Neeson, 'The Opponents of Enclosure in Eighteenth-Century Northamptonshire', *Past and Present*, 105 (1984), 114–39. More generally see J. D. Chambers and G. E. Mingay, *The Agricultural Revolution 1750–1880* (London, 1996). For a late Victorian and early Edwardian perspective see G. Shaw-Lefevre, *English Commons and Forests* (1894), later revised under the name Lord Eversley (as Shaw-Lefevre became), *Commons, Forests and Footpaths* (London, 1910). The law on enclosure is explored in Cornish and Clark, *Law and Society*, 137–41.

the form of 'A General Act for Consolidating the Provisions Requisite in Acts of Inclosure' (41 Geo. III c. 109). In the course of the century these procedures came to be dominated by experts rather than by Parliament. In 1836 a new Act allowed a two-thirds majority of the landowners involved (by value) to appoint commissioners without resort to Parliament. A seven-eighths majority of landowners by value could proceed without even a commission. The award was ratified simply by being enrolled at quarter sessions with the clerk of the peace.[4] Cornish has emphasized the importance of these changes and pointed out that in 1845 a permanent bureaucracy was created. This took the form of a three-man Enclosure Commission which worked with the assistance of experts in the management of land.[5] By the middle of the century, the systematic and efficient approach to enclosures made it less and less likely that the poor would be able to use procedures effectively to assert what they took to be their rights.

The creation of enclosures did give rise to Victorian litigation but it was not usually the poor who were involved. Recently Getzler has pointed out that 'legal battles over hunting privileges in 19th century England were one embodiment of a three way conflict between traditional landed elites, commercial farming interests, and a labouring class over property rights in rural society'.[6] He observes that enclosures had an impact on the customary property rights of the rich as well as the poor and that, in respect of hunting, this might produce severe legal problems. Could landowners who had benefited from enclosure awards subsequently restrict the hunting rights of even more wealthy landowners who claimed the privilege of crossing their land? To what extent would the common law permit antisocial uses of land in defence of established privileges? In cases such as *Deane* v. *Clayton* and *Ewart* v. *Graham* the court sought to resolve issues which could be deeply puzzling to the nineteenth-century legal mind.[7]

[4] Cornish and Clark, *Law and Society*, 137–41, and 6 and 7 Wm. IV. c. 115 s. 2.

[5] Cornish and Clark, *Law and Society*, 137–41, and 8 and 9 Vic., c. 118.

[6] J. Getzler, 'Judges and Hunters: Law and Economic Conflict in the English Countryside, 1800–1860'. This is taken from a summary of a paper given to the Twelfth Legal History Conference, University of Durham, 19–22 July 1995. See, too, J. Getzler, 'Judges and Hunters: Law and Economic Conflict in the English Countryside, 1800–60', in C. W. Brooks and M. Lobban (eds.), *Communities and Courts in Britain 1150–1900* (London, 1997), 199–299.

[7] *Deane* v. *Clayton*, 1817, 7 Taunt 489; *Ewart* v. *Graham*, 1859, 7 HLC 331.

In *Dean* v. *Clayton* the court asked the general question: is one who finds game on his own ground justified in pursuing it into the land of another? In *Ewart* v. *Graham* the court assessed whether or not a particular Inclosure Act destroyed or preserved pre-existing rights to hunt. Notions of absolute and traditional property rights could easily conflict with social and utilitarian concepts of property. Eventually, it became apparent that in this context the protection of property, even the old property of the landed élite, was compatible with the liberal capitalist ethic. The poor could only take wry consolation in the fact that the comparatively wealthy users of the land which had been enclosed were now incapable of sorting out their respective property rights without recourse to expensive litigation.

This should not be taken to suggest that the poor were entirely helpless in the face of landowners asserting proprietary rights. There were areas where they were both adroit and successful in advancing their own interests, although they might do so in ways which were indirect. To take one example, the Ashdown Forest in Sussex is a stretch of heath and woodland of about 2,500 hectares. The quality of the land is very poor but throughout the nineteenth century there were sustained disputes about the precise nature of the various private rights which subsisted in and over the land. The earls De La Warr were lords of the local manor of Duddleswell and in this capacity owned the soil in the forest area. However, they had only restricted rights in respect of the surface of the land. Commoners were entitled to graze cattle and other animals and asserted additional rights, particularly in the form of an entitlement to cut bracken, take it away, and use it on surrounding farms. There were numerous possible points of conflict between such a lord of the manor and commoners; for example, at one stage, in the Ashdown Forest, the lord of the manor set out to plant fir trees across the forest and this was seen as a threat to the right to graze animals. The result was a series of detailed and acrimonious disputes in the Court of Chancery, and even in the Court of Appeal, about the precise nature of the relevant rights over the common and the possible role of the doctrine of prescription.[8]

---

[8] See, generally, Raymond Cocks, 'The Great Ashdown Forest Case', in T. G. Watkin (ed.), *The Legal Record and Historical Reality*, Proceedings of the Eighth British Legal History Conference, 1987 (London, 1989), 175–99.

Many of the commoners were wealthy farmers who owned
land in surrounding areas. Some of them were major national
landowners such as the Duke of Norfolk. The fact that such men
were prepared to dispute the nature of the rights with the lord of
the manor was of considerable importance to the poor who lived
in the area. It has long been recognized by local historians that
the forest provided the poor with a source of income and a place
to live when alternatives failed.[9] At times of harvest and prosperity the poor in Sussex had little difficulty in finding work but
during bad weather, particularly during the winter, they might be
forced to retreat to the forest. There they were able to benefit from
the legal dispute sustained by the landowners. Because of the
uncertainty about the relevant private proprietary rights it was
possible for the poor to act in an independent way and without
too much regard for local landed authority. They could practise a
sort of subsistence agriculture and graze their own animals. More
profitably, they could quarry stone and take away the soil. It is
probable that large quantities of the forest's peaty soil were trans-
ported north and laid out in London's gardens at a time when the
capital's suburbs were expanding rapidly. Attempts to introduce a
more ordered regime of forest life, particularly on the part of
the earls De La Warr and their agents, were met with subversion,
disorder, and occasionally even arson. Uncertainty as to private
rights in property gave the poor important social opportunities. It
was as if they had an interstitial role: they could live and
work within a framework of laws created and controlled by
others.[10]

There is evidence to suggest that similar situations existed elsewhere in the country; and there is also evidence that towards the
end of the century such opportunities became more restricted.
This arose chiefly because of the powerful move to create access
for the public to open spaces.[11] This was often done through legislation, which had considerable public support, for the creation
of access to areas which had previously been subject to a bewil-
dering variety of private rights. In this connection one can think
of, for example, Hampstead Heath and Epping Forest. In respect

---

[9] See B. M. Short, 'The Changing Rural Society and Economy of Sussex, 1750–1945',
in id. (ed.), *Sussex: Environment, Landscape and Society* (London, 1983), 154.

[10] Cocks, 'The Great Ashdown Forest Case', 193.

[11] See, generally, Shaw-Lefevre, *English Commons and Forests*. See, too, n. 3.

of the Ashdown Forest most of the rights had been clarified by the late 1880s and, in the course of the 1890s, public access was guaranteed both by local agreements and by private Acts of Parliament. This brought with it a much more efficient regime for the management of the forest and increasing difficulty for the poor in using it for their own purposes. In effect, the earlier uncertainty about private rights had been more use to the poor than the later public rights of the community as a whole asserted through statute.

For the most part, the weakness of the poor in the face of rural rights in land possessed by major landowners was striking. In his recent study *Marriage, Debt and the Estates System*, Professor Habakkuk has shown why, in law, it was so clearly the case that England had no peasantry.[12] Historians continue to debate the number of small farms that existed in one part of the country or another, but they are generally agreed that there was nothing like an indigenous peasantry with significant rights in the land.[13] In rural society, it was a century of the landless labourer and his family with large estates exercising a decisive influence over many people's lives.

It is important to recognize that the ascendancy of large landowners was in part a legal victory. As Habakkuk shows, their creation of trusts in land enabled them to establish a flexible and enduring system of private rights. Often, they could avoid the dangers of absolute ownership with its associated risks. Where there were trusts it was that much more difficult for a profligate or rebellious son to alienate land or to jeopardize it through taking out mortgages. When the poor sought to assert their rights it was not just that they had to take on any particular set of major landowners. In reality they had to take on a system which allowed for considerable legal flexibility and which did almost all that could be done in law to ensure the perpetuation of family interests and the preservation of estates. Ultimately, the success of the gentry in preserving their estates and power served to make a national issue of rights in land. Liberals and radicals set out to

---

[12] Habakkuk, *Marriage*. This is a monumental study.

[13] See the recent collection of essays in F. M. L. Thompson (ed.), *Landowners, Capitalists and Entrepreneurs* (Oxford, 1994). Note in particular the study by J. V. Beckett, 'The Decline of the Small Landowner in England and Wales 1650–1900', and the piece by F. M. L. Thompson, 'Business and Landed Elites in the 19th Century'.

attack the traditional system of preserving family interests. To take but one instance, the introduction of estate duty in 1894 contained great potential for the break-up of large units. But this late reform served only to emphasize the extent to which, during the greater part of the century, there was an effective legal regime for the regulation and preservation of private rights in land. For the poor of the nineteenth-century English countryside the civil law did much to determine the context of their lives but offered them only limited opportunities for participation in the legal system.

The poor and the criminal law

In considering private rights in land we have hardly mentioned physical violence. Predictably, when there were outbursts of disorder, even of insurrection, it was the criminal law which came to the fore. Criminal offences had an obvious public aspect; serious prosecutions were associated with all the ceremony of the very public assize system. But we have seen that when criminal offences took place, even offences involving public disorder, there was until towards the end of the century no public prosecutor who could instigate proceedings. Anyone who has read the studies of eighteenth- and nineteenth-century English law by Douglas Hay and others would have been surprised if it had been otherwise.[14] The great majority of prosecutions, even prosecutions for indictable offences, were initiated by the victim or his or her agent. Then, and later, there was widespread reliance on private citizens to lay informations, produce witnesses, and steer proceedings through the grand jury and the criminal trial. The details of criminal procedure are intricate and of interest in their own right, particularly in so far as they forced even policemen to bring prosecutions in their capacity as private citizens. But the social reality was clear to everyone. The bringing of prosecutions was largely a private matter.

[14] For example, Hay et al., *Albion's Fatal Tree*; J. M. Beattie, *Crime and the Courts in England: 1660–1800* (Oxford, 1986); D. Hay, 'War, Dearth and Theft in the Eighteenth Century: The Record of the English Courts', *Past and Present*, 95 (1982), 117–60. There have been lively debates about the 18th-century law and its application. For 19th-century studies see, for example, Philips, *Crime and Authority*; V. Bailey (ed.), *Policing and Punishment in 19th Century Britain* (London, 1981); and C. Emsley, *Crime and Society in England, 1750–1900* (London, 1987). Again, the most useful authority on prosecutions is Hay and Snyder (eds.), *Policing*.

In the age of Benthamite reform there were predictable protests about this state of affairs. When a police force came to be created reformers such as Colquhoun, Chadwick, Peel, and Bentham sought public prosecutors. Fear of central executive power had produced strong opposition to prevent such an innovation. But the demands for reform were forceful and increasingly convincing; for example, the 1839 Royal Commission on the Constabulary Force had questioned the power of individual prosecutors and revealed numerous abuses. Later, successive parliamentary committees were to enquire into sustained allegations of corruption associated with private prosecutions.[15] But, again and again, nothing was done to introduce a public official with a duty to prosecute in all cases. In almost all instances prosecutions were public events instigated by private individuals. It follows that the law's response to English rural crime during these years cannot be approached by looking first at the actions of central government. The exercise of the criminal law was likely to be predominantly a local matter.

Riots, rick-burning, and machine-breaking

Some acts of rural violence were so severe as to threaten the general enforcement of the law. The violence of 1831 in parts of England was without comparison in the breadth of the areas it covered and the intensity of feeling and action which it generated. The events concerned have been analysed by Hobsbawm and Rudé in their famous and controversial book *Captain Swing*.[16] They do something to reveal the extent of the misery in rural life in the late 1820s. Over a quarter of a million men had been demobilized after the Napoleonic wars and, in later years, they had

[15] Cornish and Clark, *Law and Society*, 606. 'After 1850, there would be a stream of bills to secure public prosecutors. But they made no progress until eventually in 1879 the office of Director of Public Prosecutions was set up on a small scale, restricted to specially serious and difficult cases.' The authors add: 'In the way of any whole-scale system stood the old attachment to private prosecution and the interests of the legal professions in a preserve of private practice. Equally there was the tradition that it was the justices who supervised the police.'

[16] Hobsbawm and Rudé, *Captain Swing*. For an analysis of contemporary rural responses to crime see Storch, 'Policing Rural Southern England before Police'. This has the advantage of placing 'Swing' in the context of later events such as reactions to the reformed Poor Law.

experienced acute difficulties in finding employment. The last years of the 1820s were marred by bad weather, bad harvests, and controversies about the administration of poor relief. The latter was of particular importance because at this time there were numerous villages where up to 60 per cent of the parish was dependent upon relief for survival. The misery was at its most intense in those parts of the country where arable rather than pastoral farming predominated. It was also given a political focus which it would otherwise have lacked by the current unrest over the possible reform of the parliamentary franchise; and the sense of political instability was further sharpened by a knowledge of what was happening in France and Belgium at the time.[17] Yet even the labourers who were driven to desperation could hardly be called revolutionaries. As Hobsbawm and Rudé constantly emphasize, the labourers sought the opportunity to earn a living in ways which they regarded as traditional.[18] Certainly, there were some unexpected alliances. In some areas labourers protesting against the payment of tithes were supported by farmers, particularly Nonconformist farmers, who found paying taxes to the established Church onerous and unjustifiable.

The first act of protest occurred on 28 August 1830. A threshing machine was destroyed near Canterbury.[19] Thereafter there was further destruction of machines, burning of barns, sending of threatening letters, attacks on justices, and, in some instances, riots. The first trial took place on 22 October 1830 in Canterbury.[20] The presiding magistrate, Sir Edward Knatchbull, considered the cases against seven prisoners charged with offences relating to machine-breaking. He decided to discharge all of them with a mere caution and a three-day prison sentence. This restraint alarmed the government in London and after disturbances had spread to other areas it responded by establishing special commissions for five counties where there was particularly sustained trouble.[21] Clearly, the government believed that there were risks in leaving local gentlemen who sat as magistrates to respond to what the government felt was becoming a national problem. A few very large landowners set out to alarm the government with stories of general insurrection. For example, the Duke of Buck-

---

[17] See, generally, Hobsbawm and Rudé, *Captain Swing*, pt. 1: 'Before Swing'.
[18] e.g. ibid. 211.   [19] Ibid. 71.   [20] Ibid. 75.   [21] Ibid. 220.

ingham expressed concern about the spread of 'outrages'.[22] But it has to be said that the role of the military was for the most part slight. There was such a shortage of troops and cavalry that almost inevitably they arrived long after the event.[23] In parts of Wiltshire the local yeomanry was active in repressing disturbances but it seems that their work engendered at least as much resentment as it repressed. More typical was the occasion on which Viscount Gage met local protesters in the village of Ringmer in Sussex with a view to mutual discussions on the need for calm and some measures of reform.[24] For landowners who were less sympathetic it was possible to divide the ranks of the poor. The Duke of Richmond, responding to difficulties in the eastern part of Hampshire, used local tradespeople and the more settled labourers to oppose those who were roaming the countryside.[25] As often as not, the nature of the protests reflected very local conditions. There were disturbances in parts of Surrey and Essex for example but none of them gave rise to difficulties in London. It seems that labourers on farms in areas immediately surrounding the capital were comparatively prosperous because of the strength of the local market for farm produce and they had little or no interest in protest.

Eventually the nature of the law's response became clear to contemporaries. By the last of the court hearings in 1832, 1,976 prisoners had been tried by 90 courts sitting in 34 counties. Of these, 800 prisoners were bound over or acquitted. One was whipped and 7 were fined. Six hundred and forty-four were imprisoned. Five hundred and five were sentenced to transportation of which 481 actually sailed. Two hundred and fifty-two were sentenced to death and, of these, 233 had their sentences commuted to transportation or prison. Only 19 were executed. (Note that in interpreting these figures it is necessary to keep in mind that, for example, the same person could be sentenced to transportation and prison.[26])

The disturbances of these years have rightly been called the Last Labourers' Rising.[27] In later years there were isolated events

---

[22] Ibid. 114.   [23] Ibid. 216.   [24] Ibid. 196.

[25] Ibid. 218. For the Duke of Richmond's thoughtful ideas about police reform see Storch, 'Policing Rural Southern England before Police'.

[26] Hobsbawm and Rudé, *Captain Swing*, 224.

[27] But Hobsbawm and Rudé point out that it was certainly not the last act of revolt on the part of labourers. See ibid. 241–2. There were isolated protests in later years.

of arson and the like but significant social protest and associated breaches of the criminal law were to shift to the cities, particularly with the coming of Chartism. In the late 1830s Parliament had sufficient confidence to reduce the penalties associated with a number of agricultural crimes; although in 1844, some of the rigour of the law was restored in the Act on the Law as to Burning of Farm Buildings.[28]

These events have much to tell us about the role of the law in the regulation of social conflict in rural society. Special commissions stood out as exceptions to the rule. The normal arrangements gave local gentry immense discretion in deciding whether or not to launch prosecutions. And even where prosecutions had been commenced, and convictions had been obtained, it was possible for the gentry to influence sentence and thereby to exhibit their capacity for mercy. In substance it is difficult to regard their use of the criminal law as other than the exercise of an essentially private right in response to a threat to private property.

Lesser criminal offences

At common law there was no property in wild animals. In other words there were no proprietary rights in game. It was Blackstone who had written that 'all mankind had by the original grant of the Creator a right to pursue and take any fowl or insect of the air, any fish or inhabitant of the waters and any beast or reptile of the field; and this natural right still continues in every individual, unless where it is restrained by the civil laws of the country'.[29] In practice this meant that statute law created property in game and, as Cornish has pointed out, Blackstone was sarcastic about these 'questionable' crimes which the 'sportsmen of England seem to think of the highest importance'.[30]

The story of the creation of property rights in game, and the associated development of criminal offences for poaching, is an intricate one.[31] The law, and the changes in the law, have to be

---

[28] 7 and 8 Vict. c. 62.
[29] Sir William Blackstone, *Commentaries on the Laws of England* (15th edn. London, 1809), ii. 403.
[30] Cornish and Clark, *Law and Society*, 547 referring to *Commentaries*, iv. 174–5, 409.
[31] See, generally, Munsche, *Gentlemen and Poachers*.

seen against a background of intensely felt social beliefs. As deer, rabbits, and game birds came to be 'enclosed' it was all the easier for the landed gentry to treat them as a species of private property. Amongst the poor there was a very different tradition. It was common to quote biblical authority for saying that no property rights could exist in wild animals. There was a passionate belief in ancient rights allowing the poor to take such animals at times of necessity. During winter, feelings about a natural entitlement to game were all but overwhelming in their strength.

Gradually, however, these social beliefs were overlaid by a network of detailed laws. For example, in 1671 it became a summary offence under certain circumstances for a person to hunt game if he was not a substantial landholder, heir to a person of 'higher degree' or owner of a chase or park.[32] Munsche has stressed how in the course of the eighteenth century it became an offence to possess hunting equipment, or to deal in game as a trader, and the penalties for hunting at night became very severe.[33] Despite this, poaching was an established part of rural life at the start of the nineteenth century, and it became still more important to the poor in the difficult years following the Napoleonic wars. There were numerous expressions of concern on behalf of the gentry and, in 1828, there was a systematic consolidation and clarification of the old law. This assisted the process of further reform and, in an Act of 1831, twenty-eight statutes concerned with game offences were repealed.[34] Amongst other things the new legislation gave the right to certified persons to kill game subject to the laws of trespass and reserved the right of shooting game to the owner and his appointees. The attempt to locate property rights in game provided Victorian lawyers with a good living and numerous legal problems. The full implications of the reform of 1831 only became clear in later case law.[35] Yet the Act of 1831 introduced the principle which became of central importance to any understanding of Victorian laws regulating poaching. In the view of Sir James Fitzjames Stephen, it was the statute of 1831 which ensured that the right to game became an incident to the

[32] 22 and 23 Car. II c. 25: see, also, Thompson, *Whigs and Hunters*, 58–60.

[33] Munsche, *Gentlemen and Poachers*. Admittedly, this oversimplifies Munsche's analysis which reveals that all generalizations in this area require qualification: see, for example, ch. 7.

[34] 9 Geo. IV c. 69 and the Game Act 1 and 2 Wm. IV c. 32.

[35] Howkins, *Reshaping Rural England*, 120–35.

ownership or possession of land.[36] It was as though there was a shifting frontier in the application of law in rural life. The gentry were never totally united amongst themselves with some major landowners always believing that an ancient order of rural life had been disturbed by the intrusion of new notions of proprietary rights. For example, the ageing Earl of Abingdon opposed the reform of the game laws in 1828 and 1831 on the ground that the old laws had proved their value through withstanding the test of time.[37] But such views were now exceptional. Conventions which had provided guidance as to what the poor might or might not do in any particular area were gradually being ironed out by a process of national legal reform. It was as if the law had become as disruptive as the spread of the railways.

Having secured proprietary rights in game landowners increasingly turned their attention to the practical problems associated with achieving poaching convictions. This produced many and sustained difficulties for the gentry. The poor had lost in the debates about the reform of the substantive law, but procedural disputes offered them important opportunities. After thirty years of frustration, Parliament passed the Poaching Prevention Act of 1862 which drew the police into the role of gamekeeper. In an important reform the Act gave the police the power to stop and search anyone who a policeman believed had been on enclosed ground in search of game.[38]

Yet this was to impose upon the police a responsibility which many of them did not seek. Within a few years senior policemen were expressing concern about the extent to which the new law made their relations with the poor very difficult. It even produced outbreaks of communal violence. In Worcestershire in 1876, at Blockley, a particularly zealous policeman who had been attempting to enforce the law was chased to his house by ten men. They broke the windows, dragged him into the street, beat him, threw

---

[36] Sir James Fitzjames Stephen, *A History of the Criminal Law of England*, 3 vols. (London, 1888), 282. Stephen argued that: 'the old system was swept away, and a new one was substituted for it, by which the right to game became an incident of the ownership or right to possession (as might be arranged between the owner and occupier) of land, and game itself was allowed to be sold like any other produce of the soil, subject to a few restrictions of no interest.'

[37] Howkins, *Reshaping Rural England*, 121.

[38] Howkins, ibid., points out at p. 125 that 'the Poaching Prevention Act of 1862 extended to the police the role of gamekeeper'.

him into a stream, and his life was only saved by other villagers fearful of prosecutions for murder. Sensing the extent of social resentment, the response of the authorities was cautious and only four men were sentenced to a mere eighteen months in jail. The caution was well advised for when the men eventually returned to their village they were hailed as heroes.[39]

For the gentry the effective enforcement of the law also became that much more difficult as notions of reform became increasingly politically respectable. An Anti-Game Law League came into existence in the 1840s and in later decades of the century it was supported by Joseph Arch's National Agricultural Labourers' Union. Yet the ultimate result of attempts at reform was of little legal significance to the poor. The Ground Game Act of 1880 advanced the interest of tenants who now, for example, had the right of ownership of hares and rabbits on their land.[40] But, emphatically, tenant farmers were not part of the rural poor. Of course they were not owners of land, but they had increasing rights in land and their incomes put them in a completely different social group from that of the labourers who worked on their farms.

In the last two decades of the century poaching became less of an issue in rural life. In some parts of the country the standard of living for the rural poor underwent a slight improvement and thereby reduced pressure on local game. More importantly, after the creation of universal voting rights for adult males in 1884, working-class politicians and trade unionists representing industrial areas hardly wished their movement for social reform to be associated with something as antiquated and subversive as 'poaching' rights. The National Agricultural Labourers Union was in no position to challenge this at a time when its primary concern lay in responding to the difficulties produced by cheap imports of grain from the United States and Canada. It appears that the conventions and hopes of the rural poor were becoming marginalized by political change and technological progress.[41]

With the benefit of hindsight, nineteenth-century poaching can hardly be interpreted as a systematic challenge to rural social order. It never threatened the social or economic position of the gentry, not even those elements in the gentry which had made themselves conspicuous through seeking radical legal reform. The

---

[39] Ibid. 126–7. [40] Ibid. 129–30 (Ground Game Act 43 and 44 Vic. c. 47).
[41] Howkins, *Reshaping Rural England*, ch. 5.

poor had an impossible task; in order to advance their rights to take game they had to assert ancient traditions which were, in the public mind, most easily identified with the very gentry who were themselves seeking to deprive the poor of any sort of rights. It was the reforming gentry who were the radicals. The legal changes they engineered produced both novel and powerful elements in private and public law. By creating new private rights in game they provided a platform for the assertion of public rights within the general structure of the criminal law.

The creation of new offences in poaching did nothing to reduce the control of the landed gentry over the discretion to prosecute. The creation of new private rights in game went hand in hand with the maintenance of the established capacity for private individuals to control the prosecution process. A manual such as Dickinson's *Guide to the Quarter Sessions, and Other Sessions of the Peace, Adapted to the Use of Young Magistrates, and Professional Gentlemen at the Commencement of their Practice* contained, by 1841, twenty-eight entries relating to game.[42] Such entries should be read alongside those relating to prosecutors which, in the above example, include the simple statement 'Prosecutor . . . any person may become'.[43] New private rights in game had created new forms of criminal offence but the prosecution of alleged crimes was as much under the discretionary control of the gentry as it had ever been. Once again, it becomes clear that in the rural life of the time private discretion was at the heart of public power.

Social ideals and the merging of private and public functions in English legal theory

The distinction between public and private legal roles had become an issue by the end of the nineteenth century but, before then, the capacity effortlessly to integrate these categories was at the centre of the gentry's legal powers. Sometimes this was obvious, as when private rights were created in game and then associated with criminal offences in respect of which prosecutions were begun and sustained by private individuals in the very public

[42] 5th edn., 'Revised and corrected with great additions' by T. N. Talfourd (London, 1841), index, 1058–9.
[43] Ibid. 1088.

arena of the courts with their capacity to enforce public sanctions. Sometimes it was less obvious, but no less important, as when the gentry exerted or withdrew influence over matters of sentence or of mercy.

Admittedly, there is a danger that taking this approach could overemphasize the extent to which the law was exclusively in the hands of those who owned land. Willibald Steinmetz has found evidence of agricultural labourers using the county courts after their creation in 1847.[44] It seems that in some rural counties at least these courts were used by labourers suing farmers for wages owed. More generally, many landowners of the day took it for granted that there were restraints upon their own capacity to use the law to their advantage. For example, if they were to seek the wholesale eviction of entire rural communities they at least would have to use the procedures required by special commissioners charged with carrying out the laws relating to enclosures. In fundamental respects they were not above the law. But this restraint had its limits. Given sufficient time and money they could usually apply the law so as to further their interests. In other words, they could use their private control over public rights to enforce social inequality.

For a full picture of how different groups used the law it would have to be placed in a much larger context than the events considered above. It is noticeable that most studies of rural history give little attention to the law itself. Alun Howkins, in *Reshaping Rural England: A Social History, 1850–1925* reveals the extent to which society was also changed and regulated through other agencies. Technological improvements reduced the demand for labour. Urban expansion, and opportunities for emigration to the United States and Australia, provided alternative forms of work for families who had previously been entirely reliant upon the land. One of the most sustained and forceful sources of both action and restraint on the part of the poor was religion. The significance of Dissent, and in particular of the various forms of Methodism, was a recurrent theme. It gave the poor an identity and sense of worth which both strengthened their capacity for protest and, at the same time, directed such protests into lawful action rather than mere riot and theft. The link between Methodism and the

---

[44] See the contribution by Willibald Steinmetz in this volume.

attempts of labourers to advance their various interests through forming rural trade unions is beyond dispute. Gradual improvements in diet and health were also important, and the widening of a franchise may have contributed to a greater concern for what was often called respectable conduct. Towards the end of the century much rural resentment on the part of the poor was mitigated by the belief that voting Liberal would bring about significant improvements in their everyday lives. Clearly, law and the awareness of law were only part—and often a small part—of these various changes in rural life.[45]

But in some ways these major social changes can reinforce what has been said above about the gentry and the rule of law. For example, Howkins emphasizes the extent to which, in any particular case, these developments have to be understood in their precise local context. So often, social conflict was local conflict. 'The labourer, both in his work place and in his social and cultural life, inhabited a local world. Strikes like everything else including hours, wages and conditions, were local, seldom the same even within one county.'[46] The importance of local feelings, of local conventions, and even of local personalities, was often decisive in shaping the response to national developments and, at times of extreme pressure, in determining whether or not there would be recourse to the criminal law. The fact that prosecutions were almost always the result of private initiative strengthened the importance of local life. It was local people, albeit local landowners, who made the important decisions.

The English capacity for private control over the bringing of prosecutions was both distinctive and important. In most continental jurisdictions state officials were given control of prosecutions. Scotland and many of the jurisdictions in the United States of America had public officials of various description performing the role of prosecutor. Yet the English approach was no strange accident: it was not a historical anachronism tolerated as some quaint custom. We have seen that when reformers such as Colquhoun and Bentham had called for a public prosecutor the opposition they encountered was both strong and predictable. For their critics, placing the power to bring prosecutions in the hands

---

[45] For further references to recent research into non-legal aspects of social change in the countryside, see G. E. Mingay, *Land and Society in England, 1750–1980* (London, 1994).

[46] Howkins, *Poor Labouring Men*, 78–9.

of officials was to transfer important powers from the citizen to the state. Nor was this assertion a matter of mere self-interest on the part of the landed gentry. It was part of the English tradition of thought concerned with the liberty of the individual.[47] The failure to distinguish between the public and the private limited the extent to which public powers could, as it were, develop a life of their own and become part of an overtly oppressive state apparatus.

Within this tradition it was of the first importance that the citizen should be able to hold anyone, including state officials, to account for their conduct. De Lolme, the Geneva-born commentator on the English constitution, wrote about eighteenth-century England and was much quoted by landowners in the nineteenth century in the course of political debate. In the language of Disraeli the author of the *Constitution of England* had become the English Montesquieu.[48] An 1822 edition of de Lolme's work could refer, for example, to the following distinctive procedures:

Indeed, to such a degree of impartiality has the administration of public justice been brought in England, that it is saying nothing beyond the exact truth, to affirm that any violation of the laws, though perpetrated by men of the most extensive influence—nay, though committed by the special direction of the very first servants of the crown—will be publicly and completely redressed. And the very lowest of subjects will obtain such redress, if he has but spirit enough to stand forth, and appeal to the laws of his country—most extraordinary circumstances these![49]

In the middle of the nineteenth century such sentiments were a matter of common observation. In his *History of England*, Macaulay celebrated the courage of the obscure John Hampden who, in 1638, had been prepared to challenge the King's powers

---

[47] Hay and Snyder (eds.), *Policing*, 35. They point out that 'It is important to grasp how important such a division of functions between policing and prosecuting, and between prosecutors and triers, was to 19th century English gentlemen. To confer special prosecutorial powers on government was for all of the 18th century and the first half of the 19th century an unacceptable innovation in the constitution.'

[48] See entry for de Lolme in *Dictionary of National Biography*.

[49] J. L. de Lolme, *The Constitution of England; or an Account of the English Government; in which it is Compared both with the Republican form of Government, and the Other Monarchies in Europe*, A New Edition, with Supplemental Notes and a Preface Biographical and Critical (London, 1822), 320.

in the courts.[50] It was precisely the capacity for English law to reflect interests other than the state which, for him, made it into an instrument of evolutionary change in the direction of 'the liberties of the nation'.

Arguments in favour of placing further powers in the hands of an executive could scarcely be expected to flourish in the context of English legal debate during the Victorian years. Traditional views were given a role of central importance in Dicey's *Law of the Constitution*, first published in 1885.[51] Even into the twentieth century he maintained his view that it was in the general public interest to use private initiative, and if possible private legal rights, as a foundation for securing the effective and just enforcement of the law. For Dicey 'the law of the constitution is little else than a generalisation of the rights which the courts secure to individuals'.[52] In particular the rule of law 'excludes the idea of any exemption of officials or others from the duty of obedience to the law which governs other systems or from the jurisdiction of the ordinary tribunals'.[53] For Dicey, the common law, being largely the product of private disputes between citizens over the centuries, had come to reflect the realities of beneficial social experiences and had enabled England to avoid the pitfalls of grand and abstract declarations of the sort to be found in foreign constitutions. The law of habeas corpus had initially been a parliamentary invention, but it needed to be understood in terms of the case law which secured English liberty as a whole.[54] Like independent prosecutions, it could be used by the private citizen. Dicey vigorously attacked French law for what he saw as its conferment of exemptions upon officials carrying out functions on behalf of the state. Dicey was emphatic about the importance of the individual discretion to bring a prosecution against anybody.

Suppose that in 1725 Voltaire had at the instigation of an English Lord been treated in London as he was treated in Paris. He would not have needed to depend for redress upon the goodwill of his friends or upon the favour of the Ministry. He could have pursued one of two courses.

---

[50] Lord Macaulay, *The History of England: From the Accession of James II*, vol. i (London, 1848; repr. 1885), 94. John Hampden soon ceased to be obscure but, in so far as his reputation was based on his challenge to the legality of royal conduct, this served to strengthen the views of those who argued that the right to bring private actions was of central constitutional importance.

[51] A. V. Dicey, *Law of the Constitution* (London, 1885).   [52] Ibid. (6th edn., 1902), 192.
[53] Ibid. 198.   [54] Ibid. 197–8.

He could by taking the proper steps have caused all his assailants to be brought to trial as criminals. He could, if he had preferred it, have brought an action against each and all of them: he could have sued the nobleman who caused him to be thrashed, the footman who thrashed him, the policeman who threw him into gaol and the jailer or lieutenant who kept him there. Notice particularly that the action for trespass to which Voltaire would have had recourse, can be brought, or, as the technical expression goes, 'lies' against every person throughout the realm. It can and has been brought against governors of colonies, against secretaries of state, against officers who have tried by courts marshall persons not subject to military law, against every kind of official high or low. Here then we come across another aspect of the 'rule of law'. No one of Voltaire's enemies would, if he had been injured in England, have been able to escape from responsibility on the plea of acting in an official character or in obedience to his official superiors. Nor would any one of them have been able to say that because he was a government officer he must be tried by an official court. Voltaire, to keep to our example, would have been able in England to have brought each and all of his assailants, including the officials who kept him in prison, before an ordinary court, and therefore before judges and jurymen who were not at all likely to think that official zeal or the orders of official superiors were either a legal or a moral excuse for breaking the law.[55]

In recent years there has been increasing interest in the role of public and private elements in Victorian legal thought. The emergence of a distinction between the two provided particularly clear challenges to traditional professional life. The bar was, of course, a very public institution but it was structured in such a way that its professional work was largely regulated through private conventions and private meetings. Many of the most effective sanctions for professional misconduct involved social discrimination rather than formal tribunals and expulsion from the profession. But Victorian public opinion, often influenced by crude notions of Benthamite radicalism, stood largely in opposition to this. For many journals and newspapers the Inns of Court were an anachronism; they allowed the public regulation of the profession to be conducted through essentially private processes. Dicey was aware of this and considered professional issues in various articles and then made them a theme of his study of the constitution.[56]

---

[55] Ibid. 205–6.
[56] See, for example, Raymond Cocks, *Foundations of the Modern Bar* (London, 1983), ch. 9 and on associated attitudes to legal practice 'Victorian Barristers, Judges and Taxation: A Study in the Expansion of Legal Work', in G. R. Rubin and D. Sugarman (eds.),

In effect he sought to show how a private, self-regulating profession largely immune from public scrutiny could produce beneficial results both in the development of the law and in the maintenance of constitutional values. For him the bar was to be both autonomous and a part of public life.

This is a theme capable of almost infinite enlargement. The literary and poetic vision of the late Victorian countryside was in part inspired by the belief that there had been a world which had functioned in some sense naturally. The natural order of rural life had been destroyed by the intrusion of very public and national changes.[57] The influence of London, the growth of national urban politics, and a statute book increasingly full of national regulations had produced a yearning for the ideal of smaller, self-regulating and, in a sense, private communities.

On an even more general level, a concern for preserving a powerful role for private initiative may, surely, be seen as one of the themes which came to the fore when Englishmen sought to contrast their laws and way of life with continental and American examples. This went far beyond Dicey's belief that English state officials were effectively regulated by the common law, and that French officials enjoyed dubious exemptions from the laws applicable to other French citizens. It might be compared with the attempt of Sir Henry Maine in *Popular Government* to show that the virtues of the American constitution lay not in the constitution itself but, strikingly, in the extent to which the constitution could be used to circumscribe the potential scope of law, by providing legal safeguards for entrepreneurial and business activity.[58] Public laws could defend a world of private initiative; they could restrict

Law, Economy and Society, 1750–1914: Essays in the History of English Law (Abingdon, 1984), 445–70.

[57] For some suggestive comments see Mingay, *Land and Society in England*, 272. See also S. Collini, *Public Moralists: Political Thought and Intellectual Life in Britain, 1850–1930* (Oxford, 1991), ch. 9, 'The Whig Interpretation of English Literature: Literary History and National Identity'.

[58] *Popular Government* (London, 1885), essay 4, 'The Constitution of the United States', reprinted in Liberty Classics series (New York, 1976): see, for example, pp. 236–9 and 243, discussed in Raymond Cocks, *Sir Henry Maine: A Study in Victorian Jurisprudence* (Cambridge, 1988), 131–3. Cf. James Bryce, *The American Commonwealth*, vol. iii (1888), ch. XCII, 'Laissez Faire'. The study of the growth in the English use of the terms public and private is now a lively area of research; see, for example, the interesting recent work by J. W. F. Allison, *A Continental Distinction in the Common Law: A Historical and Comparative Perspective on English Public Law* (Oxford, 1996).

the scope of public interference by the state. Such arguments may seem controversial today but at the time they had considerable historical resonance. Twentieth-century English lawyers were to react to the distinction between public and private legal roles in a more sceptical fashion, but this, obviously, is another story which is likely to be characterized by less self-confidence in English assumptions and, perhaps, greater and more detailed interest in foreign ideas.

3
Administration of Private Law or Private Jurisdiction?

The Prussian Patrimonial Courts 1820–1848

MONIKA WIENFORT

During the first half of the nineteenth century political discussion of law and civil rights was intense in most German states. Much of this discourse revolved round the concept of *Rechtsstaat*. The term itself was first used by Robert Mohl in 1829. Before the revolution of 1848 *Rechtsstaat* essentially meant that state action should be confined to ensuring the liberty and security of the individual. Later in the century the term took on a more specific meaning, now being applied primarily to the judicial control of administrative authority (*Verwaltungsgerichtsbarkeit*).[1] In Prussia, which until 1848 lacked parliamentary representation (the provincial diets established in 1823 were no equivalent), the fight for a *Rechtsstaat* acquired additional political significance: the *Rechtsstaat*, which would safeguard civil liberties against the 'despotism' of the monarchical state, was often seen as a substitute for the missing political representation of the middle classes. All over Germany the catalogue of liberal demands aiming for the establishment of a *Rechtsstaat* was more or less the same. Its main points were trial by jury, judicial proceedings to be held in public, and to be conducted orally, and the simplification of legal language. Another item which formed part of the catalogue and appeared time and again was the abolition of all remaining forms of judicial privilege. The most important of these were the patrimonial courts, that is, private jurisdictions of estate owners, which still existed in

---

[1] E.-W. Böckenförde, 'Entstehung und Wandel des Rechtsstaatsbegriffs', in id., *Recht, Staat, Freiheit* (Frankfurt am Main, 1991), 143–69, 145.

many parts of Germany. The demand to abolish these courts was less pronounced in the more liberal, south-western parts of Germany, where they no longer existed, or played a less prominent role. Here, other reforms, in particular, the legal unification of the whole of Germany, were considered more urgent, as stated, for example, in the *Staatslexikon* by the leading liberals Rotteck and Welcker.[2] However, in the eastern parts of Germany, particularly in Prussia and Saxony, the removal of the patrimonial courts was a crucial element in the campaign by liberals and parts of the state bureaucracy against the privileges of the traditional élites. The liberals considered the institution 'feudal', and for them this made opposing it a matter of course. For the Prussian bureaucracy the patrimonial courts symbolized the 'private' domination by the nobility of an essentially public function, jurisdiction, and starting from the Prussian Reform era this no longer seemed acceptable.[3]

This essay will not concentrate on the political debate about the patrimonial courts, which is well known,[4] but will look at the working of the institution itself. After briefly outlining the basic features of these courts, their composition, competence, procedures, and case load, this essay will go on to ask how the patrimonial courts were used by the social groups in rural Germany east of the River Elbe. Three types of cases will be examined more thoroughly: first, conflicts about property rights, duties, and services between landlords and those living in 'their' jurisdictional

[2] [Beck], 'Patrimonialgerichtsbarkeit', in C. von Rotteck and C. Welcker (eds.), *Staatslexikon oder Encyclopädie der Staatswissenschaften*, vol. xii (Altona, 1841), 379–86, 382 f.: 'We recognize the great challenges of our time concerning the administration of justice and the legal system. But the first thing we think of is not abolition of patrimonial jurisdiction, but judicial proceedings to be held in public, simple, German and popular law codes, or, to be more precise, one simple, universal German law code and the restoration of a high court for all Germany.'

[3] Concerning the history of the Prussian 'Junkers' see H. Rosenberg, *Bureaucracy, Aristocracy, and Autocracy: The Prussian Experience 1660–1815* (Cambridge, Mass., 1958); F. L. Carsten, *Geschichte der preußischen Junker* (Frankfurt am Main, 1988); E. Melton, 'The Prussian Junkers, 1600–1786', in H. M. Scott (ed.), *The European Nobilities in the Seventeenth and Eighteenth Centuries* (London, 1995), ii. 71–109; R. Koselleck, *Preußen zwischen Reform und Revolution* (Stuttgart, 1987); H. Schissler, *Preußische Agrargesellschaft im Wandel: Wirtschaftliche, gesellschaftliche und politische Transformationsprozesse 1763–1847* (Göttingen, 1978); R. M. Berdahl, *The Politics of the Prussian Nobility 1770–1848* (Princeton, 1988).

[4] W. Neugebauer, *Politischer Wandel im Osten* (Stuttgart, 1992), 267–70, 358–61; M. Wienfort, 'Ostpreußischer "Gutsbesitzerliberalismus" und märkischer "Adelskonservatismus"', in K. Adamy and K. Hübener (eds.), *Adel und Selbstverwaltung in Brandenburg im 19. und 20. Jahrhundert* (Berlin, 1996), 305–23.

districts; second, cases of typical petty crimes in the country, such as wood theft or poaching of small animals; and finally, summonses arising out of insubordination by peasants and farm labourers. This study is based on the archives of a number of estates in the Prussian provinces of Brandenburg, Silesia, and Saxony. In the light of this research the conventional view that the patrimonial courts were nothing but instruments in the hands of noble and non-noble estate owners who used them to 'oppress' the peasants and farm labourers living in their jurisdictional districts has to be corrected. It will be shown that at least the local élites of middling peasants were successful in securing their own property rights in these courts, whether against the landlord himself or—more often—against the lesser peasants and their own farm labourers.

The institution

During the first half of the nineteenth century, patrimonial courts seemed to many observers to be a strange relic of feudal Europe. In England, manorial courts had ceased to play an important role in the administration of rural justice, and in France, the revolution of 1789 had completely abolished them.[5] In fact, the Prussian patrimonial courts could not be called 'feudal' in the sense that the estate owners themselves administered the law and sat in judgment upon the inhabitants of their districts. The function of estate owners in that jurisdiction was reduced to financial responsibility for the court as a concern of the estate, and the right to appoint a trained jurist, who had studied at a university and passed a state examination, to sit as judge. Although this judge was privately employed by the estate owner, he could not be removed except for gross misbehaviour which had to be established by the highest Prussian court, the *Obertribunal*. Patrimonial

---

[5] Concerning the English and French legal systems in the 18th century see D. Hay et al., *Albion's Fatal Tree: Crime and Society in Eighteenth-Century England* (New York, 1975); D. Hay and F. Snyder (eds.), *Policing and Prosecution in Britain, 1750–1850* (Oxford, 1989); E. A. Moir, *The Justice of the Peace* (Harmondsworth, 1969); J. S. Cockburn and T. A. Green (eds.), *Twelve Good Men and True: The Criminal Trial Jury in England, 1200–1800* (Princeton, 1988); S. G. Reinhardt, *Justice in the Sarladais 1770–1790* (Baton Rouge, La., 1991); J. R. Ruff, *Crime, Justice and Public Order in Old Regime France: The Senechaussees of Libourne and Bazas, 1696–1789* (London, 1984).

judges had to apply the law of the state and were placed under the supervision of the higher courts, the *Oberlandesgerichte*, which also served as courts of appeal. In some German states, notably the kingdom of Saxony, the powers of landowners with regard to the judges were significantly stronger than in Prussia. Many German legal reformers admired the English model of a lower jurisdiction administered by lay justices of the peace. There was much sympathy with a system of laymen, which is not surprising given that the resentment against lawyers so prevalent in other legal cultures also affected the judges of patrimonial courts.[6]

Whereas in Prussia and Saxony the patrimonial jurisdictions could be acquired, together with the estate, by nobles as well as non-nobles, west of the River Elbe the situation was different. Here, the possession of jurisdictional rights was tied to noble privileged estates alone. But with the reforms in the states of the Confederation of the Rhine after 1800, noble estate owners in Baden, Württemberg, and Bavaria had trouble keeping their 'ancient' rights. The states' administrations tried hard to make the possession of jurisdictional powers ever more costly and thus unattractive. For this reason many owners were inclined to renounce their privileges. In Baden, most of the nobility renounced their jurisdictional rights in return for substantial compensation from state revenues.[7]

For much of the rural population, the patrimonial court was the place where they most frequently came into contact with the law. In Prussia, in 1837, 3.28 million people were subject to these courts in the first instance. In the kingdom of Saxony, more than half of the population had to be sued in a patrimonial court in all civil actions. The percentage of the population living in 'private' jurisdictional districts also differed *within* Prussia. In the eastern provinces of Silesia and Pomerania, more than 60 per cent and 44 per cent of the population respectively were subject to

[6] For an example, see the ideas of the Prussian reformer Vincke: H. Conrad, 'Vincke und der Adel', in H.-J. Behr and J. Kloosterhuis (eds.), *Ludwig Freiherr Vincke* (Münster, 1994), 241–64; D. Blasius, 'Der Kampf um die Geschworenengerichte im Vormärz', in H.-U. Wehler (ed.), *Sozialgeschichte Heute* (Göttingen, 1974), 148–61.

[7] See E. Fehrenbach, 'Das Erbe der Rheinbundzeit: Macht- und Privilegienschwund des badischen Adels zwischen Restauration und Vormärz', *Archiv für Sozialgeschichte*, 23 (1983), 99–122; E. Fehrenbach, 'Das Scheitern der Adelsrestauration in Baden', in E. Weis (ed.), *Reformen im rheinbündischen Deutschland* (Munich, 1984), 251–64; H. H. Hofmann, *Adelige Herrschaft und souveräner Staat* (Munich, 1962); W. Demel, *Der bayerische Staatsabsolutismus 1806/08–1817* (Munich, 1983).

'private' jurisdiction. For densely populated Silesia, in particular, this figure made abundantly clear to the Prussian bureaucracy that many Prussians were subject only to the manorial lord. On the other hand, the Rhine Province retained its own law code, the French *Code civil*, which was totally opposed to traditional privilege and, of course, to patrimonial courts. The Rhenish institutions of justices of the peace and juries were seen as the model of a 'civil society', a *bürgerliche Gesellschaft* not dominated by nobles and privileges of birth.[8] The tension between different law codes and different legal systems, and between industrializing and agricultural regions in Prussia during the *Vormärz*, encouraged the politicization of the 'legal' question. Much the same thing happened in the kingdom of Saxony, where the bourgeoisie of a highly commercialized society had to deal with a legal system even more 'old-fashioned' than Prussia's.[9]

The competence of patrimonial courts also differed between regions. In Prussia west of the River Elbe, patrimonial courts were restricted to civil jurisdiction, whereas east of the Elbe, they could also decide minor criminal cases. But in any case, the bulk of their work was dealing with non-litigious matters, that is, contracts, wills, leases, sales, mortgages, and guardianships. By contrast, *litigation* in civil matters was quantitatively less important, but patrimonial courts frequently acted in debt cases and tried paternity and defamation suits.[10] The owners of the jurisdictions had to pay all the expenses of the courts, but they also received the jurisdictional fees as a source of private income. In general, civil jurisdiction was quite profitable, especially where certain taxes were included. Criminal jurisdiction, by contrast, only cost money. The estate owners were obliged by law to bear jurisdictional fees if the

---

[8] See W. Schubert, *Französisches Recht in Deutschland zu Beginn des 19. Jahrhunderts: Zivilrecht, Gerichtsverfassungsrecht und Zivilprozeßrecht* (Cologne, 1977).

[9] P. Körner, *Der Kampf um die Aufhebung der gutsherrlichen Gerichtsbarkeit im Königreich Sachsen bis zum Revolutionskampf 1848*, Ph.D. thesis (Dresden, 1935); M. Reißner, 'Bauer und Advokat im spätfeudalen Kursachsen', in H. Harnisch and G. Heitz (eds.), *Deutsche Agrargeschichte des Spätfeudalismus* (Berlin, 1986), 245–59; M. Wienfort, 'Ländliche Rechtsverfassung und bürgerliche Gesellschaft: Patrimonialgerichtsbarkeit in den deutschen Staaten 1800 bis 1855', *Der Staat*, 33 (1994), 207–39.

[10] In 1837 the patrimonial court of Count Hochberg in Fürstenstein (Silesia) had to deal with 355 civil litigation matters, 501 non-litigious civil matters, 1,587 actions concerning guardianships, but only 62 actions in criminal cases; see W. F. C. Starke, *Beiträge zur Kenntnis der bestehenden Gerichtsverfassung*, pt. 2: *Justiz-Verwaltungs-Statistik des preußischen Staats* (Berlin, 1839), 343.

defendants were unable to pay. Although many estate owners shared the burdens of criminal jurisdiction by founding associations to pay these costs, they constantly complained. The provincial diets of the eastern provinces several times demanded that other proprietors or the Prussian state should take over the costs of criminal proceedings.[11] After Napoleon's defeat, the criminal jurisdiction of patrimonial courts was limited to minor offences or not restored at all. Thus the Prussian state assumed the bulk of responsibility for criminal law, which was of course part of the public law, but it hesitated to intrude into private law both institutionally and materially. This is also illustrated by the fact that the private law sections of the *Allgemeines Landrecht* (Prussian General Code of 1794) existed only as a subsidiary law code, which was subordinate to the different provincial and even local laws.[12]

After 1830, the merits and disadvantages of patrimonial justice were increasingly debated in public. This was part of a growing concern with legal affairs generally. Especially in the Prussian Rhine Province, the struggle for the *Rheinisches Recht* enjoyed great popularity among German liberals. The liberals fought in alliance with the defenders of the state's sovereignty, who were interested in abolishing all but state courts. The arguments most often heard against patrimonial jurisdiction initially sounded convincing. First a couple of technical objections were raised. The jurisdictional districts were highly splintered, making justice slow and expensive, because many cases could be handled only by sending documents back and forth from one court to another. This claim was obviously well founded. With more than 6,500 patrimonial court districts, the Prussian postal service profited handsomely from the stream of documents exchanged by the courts. But the general assumption of higher costs was not justified. Many deeds, the routine business of the courts, were dealt with rather efficiently. Peasants could save the expense and the time, especially during harvest, of travelling to the nearest town.[13]

---

[11] *Petition der Stände des Königreichs Preußen, 27.2.1827, Landtags-Verhandlungen der Provinzial-Stände in der preußischen Monarchie*, ed. J. D. F. Rumpf (Berlin, 1828), iv. 160 f.; *Verhandlungen des Zweiten Provinziallandtages der Mark Brandenburg und des Markgraftums Niederlausitz* (Berlin, 1828), 22.

[12] See Koselleck, *Preußen*, 35–46.

[13] See *Vorschläge zur möglichsten Beseitigung der Nachteile der Patrimonialgerichtsbarkeit* (Berlin, 1842).

A second complaint related to the persons of the judges, who were widely seen as less highly qualified jurists. Since the late eighteenth century, estate owners had been required to make a contract with a trained jurist who would act as a judge, but in fact, most proprietors had done so long before. The Prussian state would check the contract according to the provisions of the law and then approve it. As a consequence of the reception of Roman law in Germany during the early modern period, the administration of justice developed—in contrast to the justice of the peace system in England and the United States—as a monopoly of the jurists, which in general facilitated state control. Usually, the judge lived in the nearest market town, and he was either a state judge, who took on extra work as a patrimonial judge, or he administered a number of patrimonial districts. This system was often called 'itinerant justice', because the judge would visit the estate only once a month to hold a court day.[14]

The last and in many respects most important criticism of patrimonial courts concerned the relationship between the estate owner and judge as employer and employee. Although the judicial bureaucracy never grew weary of pronouncing the rule of law for the whole of Prussia, the rural population and the public shared mistrust of a judge who would earn his salary, fixed in a free contract, and eat at his master's table on court day. In contrast to the ideal of the judge's independence so crucial to the concept of the German *Rechtsstaat*, the patrimonial judge was perceived as dependent on a private person.

In spite of this contemporary critique it is possible to argue that in Prussia the development towards a 'civil society' in the sense of a guarantee of legal equality began not only in state-controlled jurisdictions, but also *within* the traditional legal system. During the 1830s and 1840s, liberal critics who demanded the abolition of patrimonial courts did not realize that these jurisdictions had already adapted to a changing society: patrimonial courts dealt with the most important business of property matters quite effectively, and often less expensively than state courts. In conflicts over

---

[14] See G. Dilcher, 'Die preußischen Juristen und die Staatsprüfungen: Zur Entwicklung der juristischen Professionalisierung im 18. Jahrhundert', in Karl Kroeschell (ed.), *Festschrift für Hans Thieme zu seinem 80. Geburtstag* (Sigmaringen, 1986), 295–305; M. Wienfort, 'Preußische Patrimonialrichter im Vormärz: Bildungsbürgertum auf dem Lande zwischen staatlichem Einfluß und gutsherrlichen Interessen', in K. Tenfelde and H.-U. Wehler (eds.), *Wege zur Geschichte des Bürgertums* (Göttingen, 1994), 57–77.

property involving peasants, they generally decided according to
the law and without undue bias. In fact, they often functioned as
defenders of the interests of richer peasants.[15]

But there was still at least one element of patrimonial jurisdiction which was believed to hinder effective 'modernization': the
court's right to hear cases of estate owners against the inhabitants
of their own jurisdictional districts. This provision, which made it
possible for estate owners to use their courts as a means of enforcing their own 'feudal' rights, was constantly discussed—the debate
in Prussia during the 1840s closely resembled the debate on *justice
seigneuriale* in France during the eighteenth century.[16]

The next part of this essay will concentrate on this quantitatively rather small, but crucial point for the legitimacy of the patrimonial courts. Obviously, these cases do not convey a complete
picture of the administration of patrimonial jurisdiction. Whereas
paternity suits and defamation suits, in which women were frequently involved, accounted for a significant proportion of total
cases, women were clearly underrepresented in cases concerning
conflicts with estate owners. While many convicted thieves were
young and poor, the men resisting the estate owner's demands
were generally older and often members of the propertied classes
in the country.

Litigation about property rights between estate owners and peasants

Since the beginning of judicial reforms in Prussia in the eighteenth century, complaints against patrimonial jurisdiction had
always made the point that estate owners could sue their peasants
in their own courts.[17] In 1840, a report of the *Oberlandesgericht*
Stettin insisted that 'the estate owner should not be allowed to sue
a peasant or tenant in his own court' ('daß der Gutsherr keinen
seiner Gerichts-Eingesessenen, wenigstens keinen mit Grund-

---

[15] See J. G. Gagliardo, *From Pariah to Patriot: The Changing Image of the German Peasant
1770–1840* (Lexington, K., 1969); R. J. Evans and W. R. Lee (eds.), *The German Peasantry:
Conflict and Community in Rural Society from the Eighteenth to the Twentieth Centuries* (London, 1986).

[16] See J. Mackrell, 'Criticism of Seigniorial Justice in Eighteenth Century France', in
J. F. Bosher (ed.), *French Government and Society 1500–1850* (London, 1973), 123–44.

[17] See *Vossische Zeitung*, 27 Oct. 1808, Talk between an Earl and a Baron about the
Abolition of Patrimonial Jurisdiction.

eigentum versehen, und keinen Pächter des ganzen Gutes oder eines Teils desselben, bei seinem Patrimonialgerichte verklagen darf').[18] In Silesia and the province of Prussia, such a provision did not become law until 1844, while in Brandenburg and Pomerania, the right of estate owners to sue their peasants in their own courts survived until the revolution of 1848.

Lawsuits between lords and peasants had a long tradition. Recent research on the jurisdiction of the *Reichskammergericht*, which lasted until the end of the Holy Roman Empire in 1806, has shed more light on the ways in which German peasants sought to defend their 'common rights' against lords who attempted to raise working obligations or dues. It has become especially clear that even in the early modern period peasants often chose to go to law rather than to react by rioting. The juridification (*Verrechtlichung*) of conflicts between lords and peasants now seems to be a constant motif in the historiography of the German peasantry.[19] But Prussian peasants could not appeal to the *Reichskammergericht*, since the *privilegia de non appellando* gave Prussia and some other German states exclusive jurisdictions.[20]

In contrast both to French seigneurial courts during the *ancien régime* and to English court organization, where plaintiffs could sometimes choose the court that best suited their interests, the German concept of *Gerichtsstand* was extremely strict. Anybody who wanted to sue someone had to turn to the court competent for that person. Which court was competent depended both on that person's place of residence and the social order (*Stand*) to which he or she belonged. There was virtually no chance to *choose*

---

[18] RO Berlin-Dahlem, Rep. 84a, Justizministerium, No. 736, fo. 14.

[19] M. Schimke and M. Hörner, 'Prozesse zwischen Untertanen und ihren Herrschaften vor dem Reichskammergericht in der zweiten Hälfte des 18. Jahrhunderts: Auseinandersetzungen um Fronen und Besitzwechselabgaben im Hochstift Würzburg', in D. Albrecht et al. (eds.), *Europa im Umbruch* (Munich, 1995), 279–303; W. Trossbach, *Bauern 1648–1806* (Munich, 1993). On often violent conflicts between peasants and lords see S. Göttsch, *'Alle für einen Mann': Leibeigene und Widerständigkeit in Schleswig-Holstein im 18. Jahrhundert* (Neumünster, 1991). For a comparison with France: W. Schmale, *Bäuerlicher Widerstand, Gerichte und Rechtsentwicklung in Frankreich: Untersuchungen zu Prozessen zwischen Bauern und Seigneurs vor dem Parlament von Paris (16.-18. Jahrhundert)* (Frankfurt am Main, 1986).

[20] U. Eisenhardt, *Die kaiserlichen privilegia de non appellando* (Cologne, 1980); F. Battenberg and F. Ranieri (eds.), *Geschichte der Zentraljustiz in Mitteleuropa* (Cologne, 1994). On the strategies which Prussian and Saxon peasants used against their lords in early modern times see J. Peters (ed.), *Konflikte und Kontrolle in Gutsherrschaftsgesellschaften: Über Resistenz- und Herrschaftsverhalten in ländlichen Sozialgebilden der frühen Neuzeit* (Göttingen, 1995); id. (ed.), *Gutsherrschaft als soziales Modell* (Munich, 1995).

a court according to one's own interests. From a judicial point of view Prussian subjects were divided into two groups. More than 90 per cent of the population belonged to the jurisdictional district of a *Stadt- und Landgericht* (a lower state court) or a patrimonial court. The rest of the population, namely the nobility, civil servants, the clergy—and their families—were exempt (*eximiert*), and their *Gerichtsstand* was with the *Oberlandesgericht*, a higher state court, where fees were substantially higher than in lower courts. The Prussian General Code, which adopted a strict concept of *Gerichtsstand* even in cases where the estate owner was the plaintiff, thus reinforced the principle of status inequality against the competing idea of legal equality.[21]

The most important type of legal conflict between estate owners and inhabitants of manorial districts concerned domanial rights, that is, manorial duties and services, or communal rights. More than half of the cases in my sample were of these types. A report by the Silesian *Justizrat* Krause in 1839 stated 'that the number of conflicts concerning rights and dues of lords and peasants is constantly rising' ('daß die Streitigkeiten über das, was der Dorfbewohner dem Gutsherrn zu tun, zu geben und zu leisten verbunden ist, und was er andererseits von diesem zu fordern hat . . . sich bedeutend vermehrt haben').[22] Starting in the late eighteenth century, both the legal discourse and the politics of the German states transformed traditional rights of dominion into private property rights, which became part of private rather than public law. For patrimonial jurisdiction in general the consequences of this distinction became quite complicated. German law codes guaranteed jurisdictional rights as legally acquired rights (*wohlerworbene Rechte*), as private property rights which were not to be violated by the state unless the 'common good' was severely endangered. But a competing interpretation by many law professors and philosophers saw the jurisdiction as a part of the state's sovereignty, which could never be legally alienated from the state. Especially in Prussia, state policy tried to find a compromise between the two opinions. Financial aspects of the jurisdiction, that is, the dues of the subjects, jurisdictional fees, and the salary

---

[21] See Koselleck, *Preußen*, 52–115.
[22] RO Berlin-Dahlem, Rep. 84a, No. 728, fo. 40. For an overview see W. Schulze, 'Die Entwicklung des "teutschen Bauernrechts" in der frühen Neuzeit', *Zeitschrift für Neuere Rechtsgeschichte*, 12 (1990), 127–63.

of the judge, were to be part of private law, and were thus the private property of the estate owner, or subject to a contract. But the administration of justice and the organization of the courts were part of public law, to be regulated by the state.[23]

Any patrimonial court in Prussia could deal with a suit brought by the estate owner against an individual peasant or worker concerning civil matters. But cases concerning peasants' duties were sometimes also treated in other courts. The 'general commissions' decided on the regulations governing lord–peasant relationships, and suits between a whole community (*Gemeinde*) and its lord on peasant obligations were usually treated in an *Oberlandesgericht*.[24]

Concerning the relationship between lords and peasants, manorial duties, and services, etc., provincial laws were extremely important, although often quite difficult to work with. In the late eighteenth century, the Prussian bureaucracy tried to collect provincial statutes, but without much success. Provincial law, especially Silesian provincial law, was notorious for being favourable to estate owners, and provincial diets with their noble majority often asked the state to strengthen provincial law against a *Landrecht* intended to impose uniformity.[25]

In Silesia, a local tax on property transfers (*Laudemien*), commonly 5 to 10 per cent of the value of the property, was one of the heaviest burdens on the rural 'propertied classes'. Traditionally, these duties had been imposed to keep the peasants tied to the estate and to make it impossible for them to move. After the publication of the *Octoberedict* in 1807, which abolished servitude (*Untertänigkeit*), many Silesian peasants expected these duties to be removed too. They often refused to pay, and the estate owners appealed to the law. No patrimonial court denied the estate owner's right to this tax. They confirmed the customary right (*Gewohnheitsrecht*), not reflecting that the original purpose of this

---

[23] See D. Grimm, 'Zur politischen Funktion der Trennung von öffentlichem und privatem Recht in Deutschland', in W. Wilhelm (ed.), *Studien zur europäischen Rechtsgeschichte* (Frankfurt am Main, 1972), 224–42; G. Lübbe-Wolff, 'Das wohlerworbene Recht als Grenze der Gesetzgebung im 19. Jahrhundert', *Zeitschrift der Savigny-Stiftung für Rechtsgeschichte, Germanist. Abteilung*, 103 (1986), 104–39.
[24] See RO Magdeburg, Rep. C 125 OLG Naumburg, No. 11–20; RO Wroclaw, Mittelwalde, No. 2355, fos. 1–5 (1846), the case of the inhabitants of Schoenthal v. the estate owner concerning the obligations confirmed by an *Urbar*. The decisions of the General Commission, the Prussian *Obertribunal*, and the Ministry of Justice went against the plaintiffs.
[25] See J. Ziekursch, *Hundert Jahre schlesische Agrargeschichte: Vom Hubertusburger Frieden bis zum Abschluß der Bauernbefreiung* (Breslau, 1915).

right had been to prevent the population from buying and selling property and that this was no longer appropriate in a commercial society. By 1807, the *Laudemien* had become a significant source of income for estate owners.[26]

Another duty, the protection tax (*Schutzgeld*), affected the poorer part of the population which did not own land or houses. Every head of a household—including women, if they ranked as independent persons—had to pay between 7 *Silbergroschen* and 2 *Taler* per annum (the average yearly income of a farm labourer was about 40 *Taler*) to help pay the expenses of the estate owner's courts.[27] During the 1820s and 1830s, the inhabitants of small towns within the jurisdiction of noblemen complained bitterly to the King about this tax. In Lübbenau, Lower Lusatia (Lausitz), Count Hermann Rochus Lynar levied a *Schutzgeld* of 1 *Taler* 7.5 *Silbergroschen* per annum on labourers, and 2 *Taler* on artisans. This amounted to more than the state tax (*Klassensteuer*), but only for the inhabitants of lower status, who nevertheless had to pay taxes like the burghers. During the 1840s, the inhabitants of Lübbenau sued Count Lynar in the higher court, the *Oberlandesgericht*, but in the summer of 1848 (during the revolution) they lost their case. Lynar graciously decided to pay the jurisdictional fees of 70 *Taler*.[28] In other parts of Brandenburg and Silesia, many estate owners 'invented'—often successfully—an obligation to pay *Schutzgeld*.

Peasants and day labourers could hope to win cases on duties only if they could prove that this duty had never existed or was no longer 'customary'. After 1840, higher courts sometimes found a way to side with the rural population. When Count Magnis of Ullersdorf in Silesia sued a miller for not paying a 'confirmation tax' for the acquisition of a mill, the patrimonial court found for the estate owner, but the *Oberlandesgericht* reversed the decision.

---

[26] On conflicts concerning *Laudemien* see H. Bleiber, 'Die Haltung von Gutsherren, Behörden und Bürgertum zur revolutionären Bewegung der schlesischen Bauern und Landarbeiter', *Jahrbuch für Geschichte*, 21 (1980), 103–46; C. v. Hodenberg, *Die Partei der Unparteiischen* (Göttingen, 1996), 199–214.

[27] See RO Berlin-Dahlem, Zivilkabinett 2.2.1, No. 16939 on the obligation of the inhabitants of Lübbenau, Niederlausitz, to pay *Schutzgeld*. Concerning wages see a list in L. Wiatrowski, 'Zur Entwicklung des schlesischen Dorfes in der ersten Hälfte des 19. Jahrhunderts', *Jahrbuch für Wirtschaftsgeschichte* (1970), 253–68, 266.

[28] RO (Brandenburgisches Landeshauptarchiv) Potsdam, Pr. Br. Rep. 37, Lübbenau, 3038; RO Berlin-Dahlem, Zivilkabinett 2.2.1, No. 16939.

The miller referred to a document of 1785 (*Urbar*) in which the 'confirmation tax' was called a 'jurisdictional fee', and jurisdictional fees had been abolished by law in 1815.[29] The other way to improve the legal status of the rural population was quite simple, but rarely chosen. In 1832, a new law specified the criteria for *Laudemien* and in general made it more difficult for estate owners to prove their titles. In a case concerning the inheritance of an innkeeper, following the introduction of the new law, the patrimonial court and the *Oberlandesgericht*, by ignoring the legislation, sided with the estate owner. But the *Obertribunal*, the highest Prussian court, finally found for the innkeeper's children, not without solemnly declaring that in Silesia, as everywhere, a legal presumption of the freedom of property from duties existed.[30]

During the period before 1848, many peasants in Prussia still had to render services to the estate. Traditionally, in many parts of East Elbia these services were not exactly defined (*ungemessen*). As late as 1839, the Silesian provincial law stated bluntly: 'In Silesia, all labour obligations so long as not exactly defined by *Urbarien* or tradition, are as a rule *ungemessen* ('Sämtliche Hand- und Spanndienste in Schlesien sind in der Regel und wo nicht durch Urbarien, Verträge, Judikate oder Gewohnheit seit rechtsverjährter Zeit gemessene Dienste eingeführt worden, ungemessen').[31] But even if an *Urbar* existed, it often specified enormous service obligations, with the result that peasants were frequently inclined to sue even if they did not see a reasonable chance of success.

In 1820 the estate management of Waldenburg in Silesia sued peasants in seven communities for not rendering services to the manorial brewery. The estate management wrote a report on the services which were fixed by a written contract (*Urbar*). The peasants wanted to commute the services into cash payments, but the

---

[29] That seemed to be a clear shift in favour of the peasants, RO Wroclaw, Magnisow, Nos. 6092, 6272, fo. 31 (1845). Cf. a decision of the 'old type', Magnisow, No. 6272, fo. 21 (OLG Breslau, 13 Jan. 1837).

[30] Cf. *Schlesisches Archiv für die praktische Rechtswissenschaft*, 4 (1842), 283–9; 309. Cf. the case of a miller who did not pay a *Laudemium* in 1843. Whereas the patrimonial court found for the estate owner, *Oberlandesgericht* and *Obertribunal* found for the miller: *Entscheidungen des Geheimen Obertribunals*, ed. Seligo, Kuhlmeyer, and Willke, vol. xviii (Berlin, 1850), 256–63.

[31] *Das jetzt bestehende Provinzial-Recht des Herzogtums Schlesien und der Grafschaft Glatz*, ed. A. Wentzel (Breslau, 1839), 16.

Waldenburg managers still preferred work obligations. In its judgment Count Hochberg's patrimonial court wrote: 'It is unbeliev-
able that peasants had the idea of contesting their duties' ('es sei
gar nicht zu glauben, daß die Bauerschaften auf den Einfall
kommen sollten, ihre Schuldigkeit in Zweifel ziehen und bestrei-
ten zu wollen'). As in this case, patrimonial courts were at least
partly successful in convincing the peasants to give in, telling them
that the law was with the proprietors. The peasants of four communities decided to fulfil their contested obligations; the others
awaited attachment proceedings.[32]

In general, both patrimonial and state courts conformed to the
jurisdiction of the Prussian *Obertribunal*, the state's highest court,
which interpreted most of the rights and duties in question as
manorial (*grundherrlich*), meaning that they were still in existence.
Many claims against the rural population went to appeal, and
although higher courts were traditionally and in general inclined
to defend the property rights of the big landowners, they increasingly found for the property rights of the peasants. During the
1840s, the Prussian *Obertribunal* gave some judgments which called
Bauernlegen (enclosures)—under certain circumstances—illegal.
After 1820, patrimonial jurisdiction was less important for suits
which contested rights and services *on principle*; most cases of this
type went to appeal. But in conflicts on the *performance* of services,
which often resulted in insubordination cases, patrimonial courts
were all the more involved.

Petty crime in the countryside

The second type of cases involved small crimes against property.
Of course, theft was a problem for many propertied people in the
countryside. The surviving records show that in most cases of theft
the victim was a member of the village community, and very often
the person who committed the crime was a neighbour who was
aware of the existence of valuable goods and of opportunities. As
far as the estates were concerned, thefts were almost always of
agricultural products such as grain, wood, and grass. Thefts of
crops and wood were subject to special legislation, which gave pat-

---

[32] Cf. RO Wroclaw, Hochberg VII, No. 1884.

rimonial courts precise instructions.[33] While aggravated thefts were treated by state tribunals, many small cases fell under police jurisdiction, which could be exercised by the estate owner himself, but was most often administered within the system of patrimonial justice. Small peasants, farmhands, and day labourers, many of them economically deprived, were brought to court for these thefts. But sometimes millers and peasants, who were among the better-off, were charged with stealing wood, so essential to life in the countryside.[34]

But many cases in patrimonial courts did not result in a verdict—for example, the case against a worker's daughter named Johanna Bartsch, who was accused of stealing grass worth 6 *Pfennig*. The same held true for a case of the office of Count Magnis against a day labourer and an industrial worker concerning the theft of corn in 1846. The reasons for the striking out of cases from the court registers are often unclear, but this time it was obvious that the court in Ullersdorf was not prepared to take responsibility for the costs of the prosecution. The two workers therefore went free, because even in cases concerning the estate itself, criminal prosecution did not always take place.[35] Rising court costs indeed became a big problem. More and more workers were unable to pay the fees if convicted. In 1846, the bailiff of the Magnis estate reported an attempt to execute court costs concerning a theft of wood. The weaver sentenced for the theft possessed only two looms, a bed, some clothes, and old household items. The bailiff went away without taking anything.[36] The estate therefore had to pay, and it is understandable that under these circumstances owners were not eager to prosecute crime.

Documents from the estate archives support the criticism made by the Prussian Ministry of Justice during the 1830s and 1840s that patrimonial courts were not prosecuting petty crime as harshly as the state wanted. But this was true only of agricultural thefts where the victim was the estate itself. In other cases, where

[33] See RO Wroclaw, Magnisow, No. 6272, fo. 46; J. Mooser, ' "Furcht bewahrt das Holz": Holzdiebstahl und sozialer Konflikt in der ländlichen Gesellschaft 1800–1850 an westfälischen Beispielen', in H. Reif (ed.), *Räuber, Volk und Obrigkeit: Studien zur Geschichte der Kriminalität in Deutschland seit dem 18. Jahrhundert* (Frankfurt am Main, 1984), 43–99.

[34] See RO Wroclaw, Mittelwalde, No. 2352; 2354.

[35] Cf. RO Wroclaw, Mittelwalde, No. 2356; Magnisow, No. 4558.

[36] Cf. RO Wroclaw, Magnisow, No. 6272.

another patrimonial or state court was involved, patrimonial courts were not free to drop cases so easily. Thus, the unsystematic practice of patrimonial courts worked in favour of the pauperized inhabitants of the countryside. It is not clear whether the estate had other means to punish these offenders, but it looks as if many small crimes remained without consequences.

In 1825, the Prussian conservative Friedrich von der Marwitz of Friedersdorf had to deal with a wood theft committed by several of his labourers. The labourers knew their pious and paternalistic lord all too well. They argued, 'our eyes were blind, but now as we are caught, our eyes are open, and as we are sentenced we beg you to lighten our punishment, because we found out about the 7th commandment only after we committed the theft' ('unsere Augen waren geblendet, da wir aber dabei ertappt worden, sind unsere Augen geöffnet und zur Strafe verurteilt, bitten wir den Herrn General die Strafe uns zu erleichtern, denn erst nachher fanden wir im 7. Gebot das wir einem jeden sein Gut und Nahrung haben lassen und behüten sollen').[37] The records do not show whether Marwitz decided to reduce the fine, which was by law pegged at four times the value of the stolen wood. But Marwitz did wonder why Christian people discovered their consciences so late. His interest in the administration of justice cannot be described as typical of all Prussian estate owners. Rather, it belonged to an 'estate culture' in which the owner managed the estate himself. Interest in the administration of justice was only one element of working and living as social superiors in the countryside. But whereas Marwitz, as the bearer of an ancient noble name, derived his authority from a 'holy' bond between estate owner and peasants, the rising group of *homines novi* had to manage without this traditional means.

More typical than Marwitz's anxious thoughts were the unsentimental decisions of the patrimonial court of Mittelwalde. Here convicted thieves were sentenced to a fine. If they were unable to pay, they were imprisoned for some days or even weeks as a substitute. During the 1840s, a 3 *Taler* fine was equivalent to four days' imprisonment.[38] In Lower Silesia, corporal punishment was rare, in contrast to many Brandenburg estates, where whipping was still

---

[37] RO Potsdam, Pr. Br. Rep. 37, Friedersdorf, No. 139, fo. 94.
[38] See RO Wroclaw, Mittelwalde, No. 2352.

practised.[39] The difference, which reflected the latitude of the Prussian General Code, probably had to do with different types of 'estate culture'. In Silesia, where big landowners were often absent from their estates, the administration favoured fines. Obviously the estate owners were more interested in the profitability of their property, whereas noble estate owners in Brandenburg, like von der Marwitz or von Rochow, who constantly lived on their estates, tried to keep up authority by corporal punishment, which was thus more important than profitability. Here, as in many other respects, the administration of patrimonial jurisdiction revealed huge regional differences, which militated against the state's aim to make jurisdiction more uniform.[40]

Disciplining farm labourers

The last and in many respects most interesting type of conflict between lords and members of rural society to be discussed in this essay concerns insubordination and defamation suits. Insubordination of farmhands must have been a fairly frequent occurrence. In 1838, the bourgeois estate owner Leo of Dahnsdorf in Brandenburg complained of disciplinary problems with his farmhands. They had left the estate without his permission, which was a clear violation of the *Gesindeordnung* (law regulating relations between agricultural labourers and servants, and their masters). The very same day, Leo wrote an angry letter to his patrimonial judge, urging him to imprison the farmhands for at least twenty-four hours. The records show only that the court imposed a fine and costs, and that both sums had been paid. It seems that the judge had avoided imprisoning the farmhands. In this case, the judge resisted the demand of the estate owner, but the peasants always feared, not without reason, that the judge would comply with the wishes of the landlord.[41]

The surviving records show that middle-class owners, tenants,

---

[39] See verdicts concerning wood theft: RO Wroclaw, Magnisow, No. 6272; RO Potsdam, Pr. Br. Rep. 37, Branitz, No. 24; whipping for theft: RO Berlin-Dahlem, XVIII. HA Sachsen A, No. 151; see Koselleck, *Preußen*, 641–59.

[40] See H. Hattenhauer (ed.), *Allgemeines Landrecht für die Preußischen Staaten von 1794* (Frankfurt am Main, 1970), 710.

[41] See RO Potsdam, Pr. Br. Rep. 37, Dahnsdorf, No. 247.

and estate managers often fought against the obstinacy (*Wider-spenstigkeit*) of peasants and labourers with the help of patrimonial courts. In 1821, the tenant of Branitz in Brandenburg, an estate of Count Pückler-Muskau, wrote a letter to the judge of the estate. The tenant, Siepmann, complained that the peasants, or the farmhands sent by the peasants, performed their labour duties very badly or did not work at all. This plea for help was substantiated by the warning that the tenant would not be able to pay his rent if the patrimonial judge refused to do something. 'I urge you to do something against this nuisance and make these people see that there is somebody above them, who could bring them to the obedience they owe. Really, my threat to sue them does not have any impact on them' ('Ew Hochwohlgeboren ersuche ich recht dringend diesem Unwesen zu steuern und den Leuten einmal ernstlich zu beweisen, daß noch jemand über ihnen ist, der sie zum schuldigen Gehorsam zu führen weiß. Ehrlich gestanden sie fürchten sich vor der Drohung, man werde es dem Gerichtshalter anzeigen, ganz und gar nicht').[42] Siepmann was not convinced that the court could help. But only ten days later, the judge summoned the peasants to question them about their behaviour. The peasants admitted that their farmhands had come to work too late and declared their willingness to perform their duties from now on, thereby avoiding a heavier fine. They paid only 2 *Taler*.

Although the judge imposed a fine, it is doubtful whether the verdict helped to solve the tenant's problem. Forced labour had many disadvantages, and the element of 'force' exerted by the court seemed inappropriate to improve labour relations. Patrimonial courts were often asked to defend the interests of the estate owners or their tenants against peasants and workers. Obviously, many patrimonial judges did their best, but in general they were not prepared to sentence peasants and workers as harshly as the Prussian General Code allowed.[43]

Bourgeois groups living in the country successfully employed the patrimonial courts to defend not only their property but also their honour. In 1843, the manager of the Silesian estate of Mittelwalde, Anton Reichart, sued the peasant Peregrin Heinrich for defamation. During a conference on the commutation of services

---

[42] RO Potsdam, Pr. Br. Rep. 37, Branitz, No. 24.

[43] See the case of the administrator of the Gneisenau estate v. a gardener, in: RO Magdeburg, Wernigerode, Rep. H Sommerschenburg, No. 1039.

(*Dienstablösungen*) Heinrich had asked Reichart when the drudgery (*Schinderei*) would stop, and had cried: 'You want our utter destruction.'[44] The patrimonial judge sentenced Heinrich to fourteen days in jail plus court costs. The verdict was justified as follows: 'because the parties are of different estates (*Stände*).' Whereas the plaintiff was a member of the *Höherer Bürgerstand* (higher middle class), the defendant was a peasant, and as such inferior to the representative of the estate owner. The Prussian General Code even assigned a penalty of four weeks to three months in jail for defamation of persons belonging to a higher estate. The judges often settled for lower sentences than the law prescribed, but in this case, the verdict was harsh enough. Heinrich wrote a petition, urging the court to reverse the verdict. As a *Schulze* (village mayor) and proprietor of a significant farm, Heinrich argued that 'a difference of estate between me and Mr Reichart is not to be found'. The patrimonial court changed the decision. Heinrich had to pay only the court costs. Nevertheless, the case went to appeal, and the *Oberlandesgericht* Breslau upheld the second verdict.

The verdict of the *Oberlandesgericht* upheld the perception of 'different estates'. The judges only wanted to show mildness to an ignorant peasant. Both courts, the 'feudal' patrimonial court and the state court, had found for the middle-class honour of the manager. This case is a good example of the ambiguous role of patrimonial courts in Prussia before 1848. Alliances between the judges, who were eager to demonstrate their membership of the professional middle classes, and the growing 'bourgeois' class of estate tenants or managers did not seem to be rare. On the other hand, this could also be interpreted as intensifying social control by contrast to the eighteenth century, when the traditional, noble élites had not been inclined to defend their honour in court against individual obstinate peasants.

In the case of the peasants, the question was more complex. During the first decades of the nineteenth century, social inequality in the countryside was rapidly growing. Well-to-do innkeepers, millers, and peasants, who were involved in many legal actions, valued the proximity of a court. Even if they generally preferred state courts, they accepted the 'private' courts of the landowners because of their proximity. This acceptance was encouraged by

---

[44] RO Wroclaw, Mittelwalde, No. 2376, fo. 2.

the fact that in many ways the performance of private courts was not inferior to that of state courts. Civil litigation in which both plaintiff and defendant were peasants, for example, trespass or debt cases, was usually treated by the judge with 'impartiality'. It seems as if the peasants accepted the patrimonial judges in cases concerning conflicts among themselves. But in cases concerning estate owners or their tenants, the picture is less clear. For the propertied rural population, legal equality was still far away, and for the propertyless, 'equal rights' could mean only due process or criminal prosecutions not always being strictly pursued.

On the other hand estate owners, whether middle class or noble, did not simply administer their own arbitrary law. As one would expect, in Prussia the state played a significant role. Whereas in the United States and in England the scope of the ruling élites acting as justices of the peace was limited by the publicity of many proceedings, in Prussia state officials continually interfered with the administration of rural justice. They influenced the patrimonial judges, who were often obliging to the estate owners, but were generally not prepared to pervert justice. While justices of the peace in England were inclined to avoid harsh punishments by understating the value of stolen goods, Prussian estate owners and their judges were lenient for economic reasons. In the last decades before the 1848 revolution there was thus no 'private' law in Prussia in the sense of an arbitrary jurisdiction, but private law existed in the sense of civil law-dominated relationships between estate owners and the rural population.

As the connection between the nobility and 'property' in the first half of the nineteenth century was partly dissolved, members of other propertied classes could increasingly profit from the traditional legal system. In any case, the represented interests could no longer be identified as 'feudal' or 'noble'. The 'society of estates' waned *within* the traditional institutions. In 1848 a modern civil society, consisting of differing social, economic, and political interests, had already conquered large parts of the countryside. In this respect the abolition of patrimonial jurisdiction in 1849 was not the sharp break with a feudal past which contemporary liberals and historians praised, but a continuation of the transition to a civil society in Prussia.

Part II

HUSBANDS AND WIVES

4

Fictions of Community

Property Relations in Marriage in European and American Legal Systems of the Nineteenth Century

URSULA VOGEL

Introduction

The idea of property played a role of strategic importance in the constitution of modern private law. The *Privatrechtsgesellschaft* that emerged from the revolutionary and evolutionary transformations at the beginning of the nineteenth century defined itself above all as a society of individual proprietors, that is, of owners of private property.[1] Leaving aside the manifold differences between the legal cultures of Europe and the complexity and immense variety of property rules within each of them, we can characterize the individualization of property as a process in which ownership became detached from community. Unlike today, the meanings of private property in that period were still entangled with the political opposition to those older practices—epitomized in the remnants of 'feudal' land tenure—which delimited an individual's rights to property by his ascriptive status and his relationship with others in a hierarchically ordered community. Hence the emphasis upon exclusive control over one's property as the necessary guarantee of personal independence and as the symbolic representation of moral agency and citizen equality.

This essay examines the normative foundations of matrimonial property in nineteenth-century Europe and America, taking account of the wider moral and political meanings of ownership referred to above. More precisely, I shall consider how the dominant legal discourses in a period that ranges from the codifications

---

[1] Cf. D. Grimm, 'Bürgerlichkeit im Recht', in id., *Recht und Staat der bürgerlichen Gesellschaft* (Frankfurt am Main, 1987), 11–52.

of the Enlightenment to the reforms of the late nineteenth century constructed the property relations of marriage. In many respects, a wide-ranging comparison of this kind will run the risk of yielding superficial generalizations. The civil law systems of continental Europe, on the one hand, and the English and American common law, on the other, evolved out of very different legal traditions which are manifest on the level of legal doctrine and, even more, on the plane of legislative and judicial practice.[2] These disparities are further compounded by the regional and local fragmentation of the law. And the latter was nowhere more in evidence than in the domain of matrimonial property.[3] Nothing but carefully confined local studies would enable the comparative legal historian to confront the question of how matrimonial property affected the position of husband and wife. A broader comparative sweep might, however, be possible if we locate the question in the terrain of normative legal discourse, by trying to derive the distinctive features of gender inequality in marriage from the general principles that were used at this time to explain and justify the law of husband and wife. Looked at from this perspective, it is clear that, in contrast with other paradigmatic cases which are investigated in this book, the relationship between husbands and wives is not primarily one of 'social' inequality. We are not dealing with patterns of unequal resources and unequal power between individuals who enjoy the same formal standing as legal subjects. (The relation between employer and formally free wage labourer might serve as an example here.) For until the end of the nineteenth century European laws treated marriage as an association between two individuals whose rights and obligations derived from a fundamental difference and asymmetry in personal status. This distinctive feature of the marriage bond can best be conveyed by reference to the common formula of the 'husband's right to the person and property of the wife'. With its origins in medieval conceptions of ownership and lordship, the formula still served as the guiding maxim in the *Code Napoléon* (art. 1388). It was confirmed as late as

---

[2] See F. Wieacker, *Privatrechtsgeschichte der Neuzeit* (2nd edn., Göttingen, 1967), 496–500; W. Friedman, *Legal Theory* (5th edn., London, 1967), 515–55; O. Kahn-Freund, 'Matrimonial Property Law in England', in id., *Selected Writings* (London, 1978), 163–95, esp. 196–9.

[3] See U. Gerhard, *Gleichheit ohne Angleichung: Frauen im Recht* (Munich, 1990), 144–8. See also her contribution to this volume.

1886 by the German Imperial Court in a judgment on the property implications of the husband's guardianship.[4] The last residual effects of this causal link between the husband's control over the wife's property and his prerogatives of personal dominion (*Herrschaft*) did not disappear until the reforms of the marriage law which took place in the 1970s and 1980s in Western Europe and America.[5] Only since then has the private law given full effect to the constitutive norms of modern liberal societies—by recognizing husband and wife as two independent legal subjects both of whom are entitled to the same rights and held to the same obligations.

It is not surprising that virtually all historical accounts of matrimonial property in the nineteenth century should remark upon the peculiar 'backwardness' of marriage. Dicey's comment on the lateness of the Married Women's Property Acts (in a political environment generally favourable to liberal reforms) highlights a puzzle that is widely echoed in the literature: 'What was it which delayed till nigh the end of the Benthamite era a reform which must, one would have thought, have approved itself to every Liberal?'[6] Why did it take so long to bring marriage into the modern era? More pointedly, why did inequality in the form of one individual's right to another's person and property remain entrenched in the institution of marriage long after this kind of relationship had disappeared from other domains of the private law?

It is difficult to think of any one conclusive answer to this question. Social historians and anthropologists whose studies have focused on household economies in largely agrarian communities have claimed that the lived experience of property among peasant and artisan populations bore little relation to, and was hardly affected by, the abstract, individualistic, and formalistic categories of bourgeois private law.[7] Marriage strategies in the nineteenth

---

[4] See C. Damm, *Die Stellung der Ehefrau und Mutter nach Urteilen des Reichsgerichts von 1879 bis 1914*, dissertation (Marburg, 1983), 37.

[5] Cf. J. Gernhuber, *Lehrbuch des Familienrechts* (3rd edn., Munich, 1980), 170–9; M. Ferid, *Das französische Familienrecht* (2nd edn., Heidelberg, 1987), iii. 115–202; L. Kanowitz, *Women and the Law: The Unfinished Revolution* (Albuquerque, N. Mex., 1969), 40–68.

[6] A. V. Dicey, *Lectures on the Relation between Law and Public Opinion in England during the Nineteenth Century* (London, 1930), 382.

[7] Cf. H. Medick and D. Sabean, *Emotionen und materielle Interessen: Sozialanthropologische und historische Beiträge zur Familienforschung* (Göttingen, 1984); P. Bourdieu, 'Marriage Strategies as Strategies of Social Reproduction', in R. Forster and O. Ranum (eds.), *Family and Society* (Baltimore, 1973), 117–44.

and still in the twentieth century remained geared not to the promotion of individual rights and choices, but to the collective,
familial interest of preserving the patrimony over successive generations. Although male supremacy was an integral part of those
strategies, women could wield considerable informal power in the
management of household property. Seen from this perspective,
the emphasis upon the formal legal inequality of husbands and
wives would give us little purchase on how the law worked in the
everyday lives of married couples. Other scholars have pointed to
the functional adequacy of spousal inequality by, for example,
emphasizing the vital role which the husband's exclusive powers
over matrimonial property played for the accumulation and
investment strategies of early capitalism.[8] Along more general
lines, theorists of modernization processes have argued that the
industrial market society of the nineteenth century displayed from
its very inception the pattern of a divided modernity (*halbierte
Moderne*). It was driven by the dynamic of individualization
processes which required the entrenchment of an ascribed hierarchy of gender relations.[9]

Such approaches and explanatory models have one feature in
common: they give little attention to the normative and political
dimensions of legal history. Law appears as the auxiliary of economic and social processes or as a mere bystander in the practices
of everyday life. However, the history of marriage in the nineteenth century is a good example to show that the key concepts,
images, and fictions in which an institution is represented in the
normative language of the law will significantly shape the perceptions not only of legislators and judges but also of a wider lay
public.[10] And the nature of these perceptions—for instance,
whether marriage is understood as primarily a contractual association, as a relation akin to protective guardianship, or as an
indivisible ethical community—will in turn have an impact on

[8] See O. Kahn-Freund, 'Matrimonial Property: Where do we Go from Here?', in id.,
Selected Writings, at 211–13; C. Shammas, 'Early American Women and Control over
Capital', in R. Hoffman and P. J. Albert (eds.), *Women in the Age of the American Revolution*
(Charlottesville, Va., 1989), 150–60.

[9] See U. Beck and E. Beck-Gernsheim, *Das ganz normale Chaos der Liebe* (Frankfurt am
Main, 1990), 38–43.

[10] See N. Basch, *In the Eyes of the Law: Women, Marriage and Property in Nineteenth-Century
New York* (Ithaca, NY, 1982), 230–3.

defining and demarcating the range of political and judicial choices.

As regards the 'backwardness' of marriage in the history of modern private law, it is true that on the surface the relationship between husband and wife hardly changed between the late Middle Ages and the end of the nineteenth century. What did change, however, were the discursive frameworks that established the political meanings and legitimizations of gender inequality. By focusing on the domain of legal discourses—on successive public debates occasioned by the need to reinterpret the traditional nexus of *Herrschaft* and subordination—we can get a perspective on the discontinuities and fractures that characterize the modern history of marriage as much as its more visible links with the past.

I shall begin by sketching a general profile of matrimonial property regimes in European legal systems (in Germany, Austria, France, England, and America) at the end of the eighteenth century. The intention is not to give a detailed account of the relevant rules of the positive law, but to highlight comparable structures and the general assumptions that underpinned the distribution of property in marriage. The next section will examine debates about matrimonial property which evolved in connection with the civil law codifications of the Enlightenment period. Neither the Prussian General Code of 1794 nor the Austrian Civil Code of 1811 and, least of all, the post-revolutionary Napoleonic Code of 1804 effected substantive changes in the existing marriage law. However, we shall see that the need to rationalize its purposes in the then dominant language of contractual individualism imposed noticeable strains upon the vindication of its hierarchical structures. The third part shows how the fictions of marital unity and community which dominated nineteenth-century legal thought rendered those contradictions invisible and the language of equality obsolete. While the community discourses did not preclude reforms that conceded to the married woman some measure of independent agency with regard to her property, they did erect effective conceptual and political barriers against any changes which would have entailed the legal equality of husband and wife. The conclusion suggests that the seemingly undisrupted continuity of gender inequality in marriage is best understood as a history of prevented equality.

*Common patterns of matrimonial property regimes in nineteenth-century
private law*[11]

In terms of their universally shared features, matrimonial property arrangements at this time can be described as complex
systems of exchange which regulated the transfer of material
goods, of benefits, and of personal services between the marriage
partners. In determining what belonged to whom and who was
responsible for the management and liabilities of property the
law had to mediate between a variety of potentially conflicting
interests. It had to reconcile the claims of husband and wife, of
their children, and their families of origin; it had to ensure the
rights of third parties in the commercial world (traders and
creditors) and—a point that is often forgotten—to safeguard the
interests that the state might pursue with regard to marriage. The
right to determine the place of domicile and to direct the affairs
of the household, as well as the correlative obligations of providing the matrimonial home and of maintaining wife and children,
at that time lay exclusively with the husband whom the law
addressed as the guardian and ruler of his wife. He had to bear
the costs of administering her property and of acting on behalf
of her interests both in ordinary commercial transactions and in
court. In most systems the range of his liabilities for debts covered
her actions under the so-called *Schlüsselgewalt*, or *mandat tacite*,
which allowed her to act as his agent and pledge his credit in the
purchase of necessary household goods. In some cases, as under
the English common law, he was liable even for her pre-nuptial
debts. In return for financial burdens and extensive responsibilities the husband acquired usufructuary as well as full ownership rights in the property that the wife brought into marriage.
For her part, a married woman was obliged to perform the

[11] For the material discussed in this section cf. for Germany and Austria: W. Brauneder,
Die Entwicklung des Ehegüterrechts in Österreich (Salzburg, 1973); U. Gerhard, *Verhältnisse und Verhinderungen: Frauenarbeit, Familie und Rechte der Frauen im 19. Jahrhundert* (Frankfurt am Main,
1978); U. Vogel, 'Property Rights and the Status of Women in Germany and England', in
J. Kocka and A. Mitchell (eds.), *Bourgeois Society in Nineteenth-Century Europe* (Oxford, 1993),
241–69; for France: E. Holthöfer, 'Frankreich', in H. Coing (ed.), *Handbuch der Quellen und
Literatur der neueren europäischen Privatrechtsgeschichte*, vol. iii, pt. 1 (Munich, 1982), 863–1068,
esp. 906–76; for England and America: Basch, *In the Eyes of the Law*; L. Holcombe, *Wives
and Property: Reform of the Married Woman's Property Act* (Toronto, 1983); Kahn-Freund, 'Matrimonial Property Law in England'; M. Salmon, *Women and the Law of Property in Early
America* (Chapel Hill, NC, 1986).

necessary domestic labour and to assist her husband in his work
or business.

All regimes of matrimonial property—and that is the salient
point for my argument—distinguished between rights of nominal
ownership, on the one hand, and dispositive rights over property,
on the other. While the latter assigned powers of management
and actual control for the duration of marriage, the former
defined each spouse's formal entitlements, mainly in anticipation
of the division of assets that would become necessary at its dissolution by death or separation.

As regards the entitlements and obligations of nominal ownership, European regimes of matrimonial property followed one of
two basic models. The first stipulated separate ownership, the
second a community of goods. Under the first system, the title to
any asset was vested in either the husband or the wife; nothing
was owned in common. The dotal regime of the classical Roman
law represented the model in its purest form. Its legacies, albeit in
patterns significantly modified by Germanic influences, prevailed
in France in the provinces of the *droit écrit* and in the regions of
Germany governed by the *ius commune* (*Gemeinrecht*). Further variants of the separation of goods were to be found in the dominant
regime of the Austrian Civil Code of 1811, in the German administrative community (*Verwaltungsgemeinschaft*: the statutory regime of
the Prussian General Code of 1794 as of its successor, the German
Civil Code of 1900), and in the provisions of the English and
American common law. The German *Verwaltungsgemeinschaft* was
one example of the distributive rules which governed this system.
Of the goods that a wife brought into marriage she would retain
the title to—but not control over—her real estate, and to capital
sums registered in her name. This meant that the substance of
such property had to be kept intact—it could not be alienated or
burdened with debts without her consent—and returned to her,
her heirs, or her family of origin at the dissolution of marriage.
However, the income from such assets (rents and interests) became
the husband's personal property over which he could dispose at
will and which was available to his creditors. He similarly acquired
full ownership rights to her moveables and—significantly—to any
returns from her work. This last point needs to be emphasized to
counter the common misunderstanding that matrimonial property laws were of relevance only to the propertied classes. A

husband's rights to the wife's moveables and earnings would have been of minor importance in a predominantly agrarian society. But the effect of these provisions broadened to the extent that money became the main form of property. For the rules of 'expropriation' not only included all funds, however small, which women would have saved up before marriage or which they acquired through the extension of domestic work (for example, by taking in lodgers), but by striking at gainful occupations of any kind the law also affected the growing number of married women who were to enter the labour market in the second half of the nineteenth century.

According to the rules which governed the community of goods all (or a substantial portion) of the assets that were brought into, and acquired during, marriage were joined into a single mass of which husband and wife were co-owners in equal parts. Both spouses had equal claims on the gains of marriage and both shared in its losses. When the marriage ended, both partners (or their respective heirs) took out their portion. Under this system a wife was entitled to a share in what had been acquired through her own labour. By the same token, however, all her property was liable for both the community's and the husband's personal debts. In the form of a community of moveables and acquests, this system acted as the statutory regime of the French Civil Code. It was also at home in many parts of Germany (especially among the artisans and merchants of the towns) and in some western and southern parts of the United States, such as California and Louisiana.

If we were to judge the matrimonial property arrangements outlined so far by their capacity to cater for the interests and needs of the marriage partners and for the common purposes of family life, we would be hard put to draw up a neat balance sheet of gains and losses. Whether the husband or the wife—or, of course, both—stood to benefit from the exchange of property would depend on a great number of concrete circumstances, such as the amount and type of assets that each brought to the marriage, the success or failure of efficient management, and the relationship between household economy and economic production. As regards the position of women within the system of exchange, there is little doubt that in return for submission to the extensive powers of husbands they received tangible benefits of material support and security for the future. At a time when marriage was their main source of livelihood, when the number of working wives was still relatively small and divorce rare, the distribution of property might well have worked in favour of most women's material interests.

If, on the other hand, we consider property ownership as the condition and guarantee of independent agency, the picture will change. It is here that the normative principles of matrimonial property deviate most clearly from the individual liberties and powers associated with modern bourgeois property. Moreover, in this regard the two systems hardly differed. Irrespective of whether property was owned in common or separately, a husband would acquire near-absolute control over the wife's property. What women lost as a consequence of marriage was the right to act with regard to their own property. Like a child or a minor under guardianship, a married woman could not perform legally valid actions without the authorization of her husband. In her own right, that is, she was incapable of making binding contracts, of assuming liabilities towards creditors, of suing or being sued in court. Two points need to be stressed in this context. First, the law did not assume, as it did in the case of minors, a natural incompetence on the part of all women. In most legal systems the single woman enjoyed property rights largely on a par with men. Rather, a wife's legal incapacity was premissed solely upon the husband's prerogatives of personal *Herrschaft*. The crucial link between his powers over her property and his quasi-proprietary rights in her person is evident in those rules that made him the owner not only of her earnings (that is, of the fruits of her labour), but of her labour itself. For it stood in his power to decide whether she could take up paid employment or establish a business of her own. In the language of liberal principles, a wife lacked the most fundamental of all property rights—the right of self-ownership. As the Prussian General Code of 1794 put it, a wife could not enter into any obligations towards others that would 'impair the rights on her person'.[12]

The husband's power to veto his wife's occupation outside the home was confirmed 100 years later in the German Civil Code of 1900. She could not, in the words of one commentator, act in such

---

[12] II. 1, §§ 195–6 *ALR*. *ALR* = H. Hattenhauer (ed.), *Allgemeines Landrecht für die preußischen Staaten von 1794: Textausgabe* (Frankfurt am Main, 1970).

matters on her own, 'just as a non-owner cannot dispose over alien property without the permission of its owner'.[13] Although fenced against abuse and probably not applied very much in practice, the rule as such remained on the statute books until the 1970s (in France until 1966). The second point to remember is that the prerogatives of personal rule and the corresponding duties of subservience belonged in the category of a *ius cogens*: they were not negotiable and not open to modification even with the agreement of both partners.

However, most regimes of matrimonial property allowed, to a greater or lesser degree, for institutional devices (usually in the form of special contracts) by means of which a married woman could attain some degree of control over her property. No modern system could in this respect compare with the classical Roman law according to which marriage had no effect upon the independent status of both women and men as property owners. But the dotal regime in both France and Germany recognized a married woman's capacity for contractual undertakings and her liabilities for debts. The Austrian *Gütertrennung* left the concrete administrative arrangements to contractual negotiations between the spouses. With regard to her property, a wife retained the powers of agency that had been hers before marriage. Other systems allowed for such powers in the form of special exceptions to the general rule. Into this category belonged the reserved estate (*Vorbehaltsgut*) of the Prussian General Code and, in England and America, the device of the married woman's separate estate under Equity. It was to be of considerable significance for the direction of future reforms that all these historical precedents for the wife's independence were associated with the separation of goods. This will explain why for the women's movements as for the liberal reformers of the nineteenth century gender equality became virtually synonymous with the rights of separate property (despite the material disadvantages that this system entailed for the great number of women who had no property of their own at the beginning of marriage and, if they were homemakers, no chance of acquiring any).

We can thus establish the peculiar kind of inequality that we have observed in the property relations of marriage only if we

---

[13] W. Schubert (ed.), *Materialien zum BGB* (Frankfurt am Main, 1985), iii. 301.

take account of the primacy of the husband's personal rights. The heart of the matter was not a difference in entitlements and access to assets of property; it was the difference between domination and subjection. The assumptions on which European laws construed marriage as a particular form of *Herrschaft* were derived from different legal traditions. Within each of them, however, the order of marriage reflected the structures of a social order that belonged to the early stages of European history. The identity fiction of the English common law—according to Blackstone's canonical interpretation of practices that went back to the feudal society of the thirteenth century—postulated a relationship in which the wife's legal persona was suspended—submerged and 'covered' by the persona of 'her baron, or lord'.[14] The marital guardianship of German law (*eheliche Vormundschaft*)[15] pointed to medieval notions of stewardship and association (*Genossenschaft*) and, further back still, to the ancient *mundium* and the judicial and disciplinary powers of the houselord over all members of the extended family. Similarly, the *puissance maritale* and the *incapacité de la femme mariée* under French law (as defined by the *Code civil*) encapsulated both the vestiges of the Roman *patria potestas* and the feudal connotations of a relationship of *protection* and *obéissance*.[16]

To recall these historical origins of the marriage law is not to suggest that in the nineteenth century husbands and wives perceived their relationship and went about the business of married life according to the precepts of a remote past. What matters is that this was still the official language of the law, preserved and reiterated in statutes and codes, in legal commentaries and court judgments. As will be shown below, all attempts at reforming matrimonial property had to contend with the resilience and the powerful symbolic resonance of a language in which the very unity of the marriage bond was staked upon a nexus of rule and dependence.

In the codification debates in Prussia, France, and Austria, to which we shall now turn, the connection between ownership, independent agency, and equality came into view precisely in those contexts where legislators addressed themselves to the

[14] W. Blackstone, *Commentaries on the Laws of England* (Oxford, 1765), i. 430.
[15] See Gerhard, *Gleichheit ohne Angleichung*, 142–67.
[16] See L. A. Warnkönig, *Geschichte der Rechtsquellen und des Privatrechts*, Französische Staats- und Rechtsgeschichte, vol. ii (Basle, 1875; repr. Aalen, 1968), 224–89.

consequences and the permissible extent of the married woman's separate property. These were not philosophical debates. But they did, if often unintentionally, shed light upon the uncertain legitimacy of traditional patterns of inequality within a discourse that sought to deduce all forms of authority from the principles of contract and individual consent.

Contract and hierarchical order: matrimonial property
in the codification debates of the Enlightenment

As regards their intellectual foundations, the codification projects in Prussia, Austria, and France owed much to the natural law doctrines of the seventeenth and eighteenth centuries.[17] Due to its dominance in many European universities, natural jurisprudence in the tradition of Grotius, Pufendorf, and Wolff shaped the orientations of a whole generation of civil servants, academic jurists, and professional lawyers who were to play a prominent role in drafting the new codes—among them Suarez and Klein in Prussia, Zeiller, the redactor of the Austrian law, and Portalis, the expositeur of the Napoleonic Code. The influence of natural law reasoning manifested itself above all in the architectonic intention to transform the chaotic plurality and local fragmentation of existing statutes and customs into a coherent, rational, and publicly accessible body of law that would serve as an effective instrument of centralized political rule and at the same time strengthen the loyalty of citizens towards their state. The formal unity and moral legitimacy of the codified law rested on the claim that all particular institutions and legal rules could, in principle, be shown to conform to the uniform dictates of nature and reason. While the hypothesis of the natural liberty and equality of all individuals supplied the initial premiss for all such deductions, the contract served as the paradigmatic figure

---

[17] See Wieacker, *Privatrechtsgeschichte*, 247–322; H. Hattenhauer, 'Einführung in die Geschichte des Preußischen Allgemeinen Landrechts', in id. (ed.), *Allgemeines Landrecht*, 11–22; E. Hellmuth, *Naturrechtsphilosophie und bürokratischer Werthorizont* (Göttingen, 1985); H. Mohnhaupt, 'Zeiller's Rechtsquellenverständnis', in W. Selb and H. Hofmeister (eds.), *Forschungsband Franz von Zeiller (1751–1828)* (Vienna, 1980), 167–79; A. J. Arnaud, 'La référence à l'école du droit moderne: les lectures des auteurs du Code civil français', in I. Théry and C. Biet (eds.), *La Famille, la loi, l'état de la Révolution au Code civil* (Paris, 1989), 3–10.

to explain and justify their rights and obligations under the civil law.

The place of marriage within this system can be summarized in three points.[18] First, like all other associations of civil society, marriage presupposed the original equality of the associated individuals. This meant, secondly, that the specific rights and obligations of husband and wife had to be construed from a constitutive act of mutual consent. The consent principle itself was, of course, not a novel idea. It had a long history in Christian doctrines and in the canon law. However, its distinctive emphasis in modern natural law doctrines—that is the third point—derived from the claim that marriage was nothing but a civil contract. As far as the law was concerned, marriage could not lay claim to the special status of a divinely ordained, sacramental institution; it shared the same normative properties as all other 'contractual societies'. In the concrete application of these principles to the relation of husband and wife the natural lawyers did little to challenge the hierarchical order that they found enshrined in the positive laws of their time. But they did place this order under new imperatives of legitimization. Because it had to accord with the a priori assumption of women's and men's natural equality, the subordination of the wife to the husband's rule could only be rendered legitimate by the device of a voluntary contract of submission.[19] The end result was the same. But the reasoning process necessary to vindicate the patriarchal marriage left its mark. Equality figured as a residual reference point which had to be modified, or circumvented, by additional rational principles. The following examples drawn from the deliberative contexts of the codifications show that this residual equality played a not insignificant role in the controversies about matrimonial property. What was the normative origin of the husband's power over the wife's property? How much scope was the enlightened lawgiver to concede to the contractual freedom of husband and wife to make their own arrangements? And, if as a consequence of mutual agreements

---

[18] Cf. D. Schwab, 'Die Familie als Vertragsgesellschaft im Naturrecht der Aufklärung', *Quaderni Fiorentini per la storia del pensiero giuridico moderno*, 1 (1972), 357–76; U. Vogel, 'Gleichheit und Herrschaft in der ehelichen Vertragsgesellschaft: Widersprüche der Aufklärung', in U. Gerhard (ed.), *Frauen in der Geschichte des Rechts: Von der Frühen Neuzeit bis zur Gegenwart* (Munich, 1997), 265–92.

[19] Samuel Pufendorf, *Herrn Samuels Freiherrn von Pufendorffs Acht Bücher vom Natur- und Völkerrecht* (Frankfurt, 1711), VI. i. 12.

the wife's property was to be released from the husband's control, what would be the implications for the order of marriage as of society at large?

The contrast between the principles of preordained hierarchy and of contractual equality is most sharply profiled in Zeiller's commentary on the Austrian Civil Code of 1811.[20] Uniquely among the civil law systems of modern Europe, Austrian law recognized the full dispositive rights of ownership not only in the single woman, but also in the wife.[21] In respect of property, marriage had no effect upon a woman's legal capacities. This meant, Zeiller explained, that it was to be left to the discretion of bride and groom whether, and to what extent, a woman's assets should be settled upon the husband in form of a dowry which would come under his administrative and usufructuary powers.[22] It meant further that the lawgiver would issue no binding prescriptions as to who should administer the goods that were not tied up by special agreements: 'Both spouses (husband or wife) are free to administer their separate property. It follows, however, that in such a case neither is liable for the debts of the other.'[23] Zeiller did not deny that common practice operated on the presumption that a woman would upon marriage transfer the control of her goods to her husband. And there is little doubt that he deemed this to be the most reasonable and beneficial arrangement. As a matter of principle, however, he insisted that customary presumptions of this kind did not constitute an incontrovertible right in favour of the husband's legal stewardship. A wife who was 'entitled to administer her own property' could 'choose another *Machthaber*' (curator) to take care of her interests, or act in her own person.[24]

The most unequivocal assertion of a married woman's equal legal capacity can be found in the deliberations on the rules of intercession and in Zeiller's determination to lift the age-old prohibition which prevented women from using their property to guarantee another person's credit obligations (*Bürgschaftsrecht*).[25]

---

[20] Franz Edler von Zeiller, *Commentar über das Allgemeine Bürgerliche Gesetzbuch für die gesammten deutschen Erbländer der oesterreichischen Monarchie*, 4 vols. (Vienna, 1811).

[21] Cf. Brauneder, *Entwicklung*, 360–8.

[22] Zeiller, *Commentar*, iii. 582 f.   [23] Ibid. 614.

[24] Ibid., i. 252; J. Ofner (ed.), *Der Ur-Entwurf und die Beratungsprotokolle des österreichischen Allgemeinen Bürgerlichen Gesetzbuches* (Vienna, 1889; repr. Glashütten, 1976), i. 72 f.

[25] Cf. Ofner, *Ur-Entwurf*, ii. 213–15; Zeiller, *Commentar*, iv. 10–14.

The defenders of the status quo pleaded the natural incompetence of the female sex and—not unrealistically—a wife's vulnerability to the husband's superior powers of manipulation. Zeiller argued that, like all other owners of property, married women had to be included in the strict correlation of rights and liabilities and, furthermore, that in an age of general enlightenment they could be trusted with the knowledge required in such transactions. The case has little to do with benevolent intentions towards women. On the contrary, in his prior concern with the security of credit relations Zeiller targeted what he considered to be typical instances of female irresponsibility (that is, of pleading legal incapacity in order to avoid liability): the price of independence was loss of special legal protection. The example shows, however, that where it suited political purposes all the conceptual ingredients for a recognition of equality were in place.

While recognizing a wife's independent agency in the domain of property Zeiller affirmed her obligation to follow and obey her husband in all other matters of conjugal and familial life. Given his generally patriarchal preconceptions about the nature of men and women,[26] it is not hard to see why he should have endorsed the privileges of the superior sex. However, equality asserted itself, albeit negatively and against the grain, in the visible failure to reconcile the husband's prerogatives with the natural lawyers' claim (emphasized especially in the Wolffian tradition) that in virtue of its contractual origins marriage must count as an association of 'two powerholders'. The gap of legitimacy was closed by reasons of sexual psychology, pragmatic wisdom, and state interest. Yet, by his own admission such reasons did not amount to a stringent normative principle, 'because neither his natural superiority nor the purpose of marriage can confer upon a husband the right to dominate his wife'.[27]

The marriage law of the Prussian General Code of 1794 introduced a contractual option which enabled a married woman, by means of a special contract with her husband, to reserve an unspecified part of her property for her own use and disposition.[28]

---

[26] Cf. U. Flossmann, 'Die beschränkte Grundrechtssubjektivität der Frau: Ein Beitrag zum österreichischen Gleichheitsdiskurs', in Gerhard (ed.), *Frauen in der Geschichte des Rechts*, 293–324.

[27] Zeiller, *Commentar*, i. 249 f.

[28] II. 1, §§ 205–8 *ALR*.

Without precedent in the tradition of German law, the married woman's reserved property (*Vorbehaltsgut*) was from the outset a subject of numerous controversies, both among the members of the commission and in the general public.[29] Judged by the relatively small number of women who stood to benefit from it, the provision was probably of limited practical importance. Yet, as a challenge to the traditional law of marriage it had, especially for the defenders of the status quo, much wider and disturbing implications: it confounded conventional gender roles by introducing a type of property in relation to which a wife had the status of a *pater familias*; indeed, in the eyes of the law she was 'not at all a woman but a legal subject, just as if she were a man'.[30] Conservatives dwelt on the incompatibility between a wife's personal independence as an owner of separate property, on the one hand, and the institute of marital guardianship, that is, the very essence of marriage, on the other. Commentators at the other end of the political spectrum claimed that by the law of nature all of a woman's property should be reserved to her and that the normal case of the husband's administrative and usufructuary rights was built upon the relics of archaic force and servitude: 'Our women are free and so should be their property.'[31] Moderate defenders of the wife's reserved property, like Suarez, had no inclination to challenge the rights of marital supremacy. But in order to argue an exception to the rule they had to step outside tradition. It is in this specific context that the equality premiss of natural law would come into play—in references to the 'natural liberty of the spouses' to manage their property according to rules of their own choice, and to 'the natural freedom [of all women] to dispose over the assets thus reserved to them'.[32]

Similar controversies surrounded the norm which classified the returns from a wife's gainful occupation as the husband's personal property: 'What a wife acquires [through her labour] during mar-

---

[29] For a detailed discussion of the largely unpublished material of these debates, see S. Weber-Will, *Die rechtliche Stellung der Frau im Privatrecht des Preußischen Allgemeinen Landrechts von 1794* (Frankfurt am Main etc., 1983), 90–109; further references under '(Revisor), Gesetz-Revision Pensum XV: Motive zu dem vom Revisor vorgelegten Entwurf des Tit. I, Th. II des Allgemeinen Landrechts' (Berlin, 1830), in Gerhard, *Verhältnisse*, 413–19.

[30] Quoted in Weber-Will, *Rechtliche Stellung*, 96 f.

[31] Quoted ibid. 108.

[32] Suarez, quoted ibid. 93; and in Gerhard, *Verhältnisse*, 413.

riage she acquires, as a rule, for her husband.'[33] Traditional legal reasoning included a married woman's work—domestic labour as well as her co-operation in the husband's trade and, by analogy, independent work undertaken on her own account—among the personal obligations and services that the wife owed to the husband as head or ruler of the marriage relation. It was difficult to reconcile this kind of property right, which, as critics commented, reduced the wife to the status of a serf or servant,[34] with the self-images of an age of reason. To exclude a wife from even a share in what she had contributed to the assets or savings of the household was to deny her 'the most incontestible property of a human being'—'that which one has acquired through talents, skills and the work of one's hands'.[35]

Although without much impact on the final form of the law, the critical references to the rational foundations of property had the effect of drawing attention to the real foundations of the husband's prerogatives. They existed, Suarez pointed out, not for the benefit of women and on grounds of their natural weakness; they were instituted in the interest of men and by means of the law's necessary partiality for those interests.[36] Given the preponderance of this alignment, it could do 'no harm if the legislator occasionally restores the natural equality of the sexes'.[37] As Klein saw it, the state could pursue its own goals—numerous, fertile, and stable marriages—only by modifying the equality principle presumed in the marriage contract and swinging the law behind the husband's interests. At the same time—a typical dilemma of Enlightenment reasoning—the modern legislator had to be aware of the profound 'contradiction between a situation of female slavery and the general improvement of the nation'.[38]

Candid admissions that 'the public magistrate has several good reasons for elevating [the husband's] wishes into law'[39] are not uncommon in the codification debates. The interests of the state as the ultimate arbiter would typically be invoked where the constitutive norms of private law came into conflict with the precepts of

[33] II. 1, § 211 *ALR*.   [34] (Revisor), in Gerhard, *Verhältnisse*, 415.   [35] Ibid. 414.
[36] Cf. Weber-Will, *Rechtliche Stellung*, 99 f.   [37] Suarez, quoted ibid. 89.
[38] E. F. Klein, *System des preußischen Civilrechts*, rev. F. von Rönne, 2 vols. (Halle, 1830), i. 2.
[39] Zeiller, *Commentar*, i. 328.

marriage law. Thus the *Code Napoléon* placed the rules of matrimonial property under the general norm that 'the law does not reign over marriage as far as the goods of property are concerned' (art. 1387). This meant that pre-nuptial contracts could establish options other than the statutory regime of the community of goods. A couple might choose the dotal regime or the separation of goods, both of which allowed the wife some control over her property. Triggered by the controversial issue of whether a wife should be in a position to alienate her real estate without the husband's permission, the debates in the commission[40] focused on the most extreme amongst the conceivable outcomes of contractual choice—a world turned upside down where control over all property had passed to the wife and where, as a consequence, the husband's personal authority was bound to wither away. To forestall the unacceptable possibilities of such a property contract the code issued the strict prohibition that 'the spouses cannot derogate the rights which are inherent in the husband's power over the person of wife and children and which pertain to him as chief' (art. 1388). The restriction was justified, and inequality entrenched beyond challenge, by aligning the husband's right to person and property of the wife directly with the superior interests of the 'ordre public'.[41]

The extent to which conceptions of political order, even under the very different circumstances of a successful democratic revolution, remained anchored in deeply gendered assumptions is conveyed by a Massachusetts court case of 1805.[42] A dispute over inheritance claims to a wife's dower (the widow's share in part of her husband's real estate) compelled the court to clarify the nature of a married woman's membership in the republican polity. The issue was whether a woman who had fled the country with her husband could be implicated in the criminal act of treason and held liable to suffer the consequences—the confiscation of loyalist property. The majority of judges insisted upon the disabilities of the *feme covert* under the common law and on the presumption that criminal offences of this kind were committed under marital coercion. A wife was no more a member of the state than an alien

---

[40] Cf. *Conférence du Code civil avec la discussion particulière du Conseil d'État et du Tribunat, avant la rédaction définitive de chaque projet de loi*, par un jurisconsulte (Paris, 1805), v. 209–24.

[41] Ibid., v. 215, 219.

[42] See L. A. Kerber, 'The Paradox of Women's Citizenship in the Early Republic: The Case of *Martin* vs. *Massachusetts*, 1805', *American Historical Review*, 97 (1992), 349–78.

and thus not held to the loyalty demanded of citizens. Opponents countered the presumption by the precepts of natural law which included all individuals in the obligations derived from the human capacity for reason and moral judgement. Moreover, if patriarchy had been rejected in the polity, it could no longer hold sway in marriage either. The significance of the case, Kerber argues, did not lie in the substance of the final decision, but in the process of confrontation and in the texture of the arguments that it brought forth. What decided the case was not simple traditionalism, the mere affirmation of custom in the absence of alternative modes of conceptualizing the place of women in marriage and society. It was a political choice which affirmed a wife's legal incapacity— and, ironically, saved her property for her heir.

The debates and controversies which we have reviewed posed no radical challenge to the traditional order of marriage. However, while enlightened legislators on the whole endorsed the husband's domestic empire as the arrangement most conducive to the public good, they also acknowledged that property contracts could legitimately establish enclaves of women's independence. The dual track of reasoning which runs through their arguments conveys two important insights: that marriage had to be understood as an association whose members have separate interests and conflicting claims as well as common purposes; and that the existing inequalities did not reflect a natural order of unequal capacities, but were an effect of the coercive rules of the law itself. The move from Enlightenment rationalism to the 'reactionary' marriage discourses of the nineteenth century thus does not signal the loss of a positive model of gender equality. What was lost was the transparence of inequality.

*Reaction, reform, and retrenchment: matrimonial property
in the community discourses of the nineteenth century*

In nineteenth-century Europe—and the same holds for the United States—the private law acted as the major driving force of economic and social transformation.[43] It developed and refined

---

[43] Cf. H. Coing, *Europäisches Privatrecht*, ii: *19. Jahrhundert: Überblick über die Entwicklung des Privatrechts in den ehemals gemeinrechtlichen Ländern* (Munich, 1989), 70–92, 284–302; M. J. Horwitz, *The Transformation of American Law, 1780–1860* (Cambridge, Mass., 1977).

the law of contract for the purpose of commercial expansion, improved the security of credit transactions, and freed land and labour from the encumbrances of feudal land tenure, from guild restrictions, and from the divides of hereditary rank and hierarchies based on 'estates' (*Stände*). Status differentiations between individuals gave way to a condition of formal equality based upon the universal and uniform capacity for rights (*allgemeine Rechtsfähigkeit*): 'All individuals had, in principle, equal access to the institutes of private law.'[44] Marriage by contrast, remained enclosed in forms that bore the imprint of medieval institutions. Its legal order—epitomized in the husband's right to the person and property of the wife—carried into the modern world the very kind of inequality which an age of revolution and reform seemed to have consigned to historical memory.

After around 1850 reforms of matrimonial property began to make inroads into the patriarchal marriage law, first in the United States, then in England, and at the turn of the century in Germany and France. The reforms were not aimed at, nor did they bring about, legal equality between husband and wife. Indeed, on the ideological level at least, they acted as vehicles to pre-empt demands for full equality. This section examines the ways in which fictions of community shaped the discourse on marriage in different national contexts. The aim obviously cannot be to give a complete account of the complex and increasingly diverse developments of legal doctrine in the nineteenth century. I shall confine myself, again, to a few representative examples that can illuminate the significant shift which transformed the normative orientations of the debates on marriage. The shift is threefold—from abstract equality to essential difference and natural complementarity as regards the relation between the sexes; from contract to institution in the general definition of marriage; from private to public in the emphasis on its special relationship to the state. In focusing on the fiction of spousal identity and marital unity in the American context, on the attempts to decontractualize the marriage contract in post-revolutionary France, and on the impact of the notion of *sittliche Gemeinschaft* (ethical community) in the deliberations on the German Civil Code (*BGB*) we can identify a process in which marriage was rendered imper-

---

[44] Coing, *Europäisches Privatrecht*, ii. 284.

meable to the language of individual rights and, as a consequence, to the demand for equality.

The political revolution that had led to the independence of the former American colonies from the imperial power of England did not challenge the rule of the English common law in the domain of private legal relations. Embedded in this common heritage and unaffected by the rhetoric of republican citizenship, learned exegesis and popular legal textbooks alike continued to convey the relation between husband and wife in the Blackstonian language of 'baron and feme'.[45] The fiction of marital unity according to which the husband alone represented the marriage in the eyes of the law implied that a married woman was altogether incapable of acting in her own right and on her own responsibility. In practice, of course, there were numerous ways, especially where husband and wife co-operated in the pursuit of a common interest, to circumvent the strictures of legal disability.[46] But the identity principle would commonly assert itself when disputed claims reached the courts. Pressure for reform[47] arose from the increasingly felt inadequacies of these arrangements under conditions of rapid commercial development. Both the need to clarify and stabilize debtor–creditor relations and—in periods of economic instability which after the 1830s triggered a spate of bankruptcies—to protect some family assets against the impact of the husband's failed business ventures pointed in the direction of equipping the wife with some control over her own property. A model of the required changes was available in the married woman's separate estate which English lawyers had developed since the sixteenth century under the trust provisions of Equity in order to circumvent the rigidities of the common law. Originally designed to protect a daughter's landed wealth against the husband and his creditors and in reach only of a small élite, the equitable trust formed the basis of the Married Women's Property Acts that were passed in various states of the American republic from the mid-century onwards. The Acts declared the

[45] See Basch, *In the Eyes of the Law*, ch. 2.
[46] See M. R. Beard, *Women as a Force in History: A Study in Tradition and Realities* (New York, 1946); Basch, *In the Eyes of the Law*, ch. 3.
[47] Cf. P. A. Rabkin, *Fathers to Daughters: The Legal Foundations of Female Emancipation* (Westport, Conn., 1980); P. Lucie, 'Marriage and Law Reform in Nineteenth-Century America', in E. M. Craik (ed.), *Marriage and Property* (Aberdeen, 1984), 138–58.

assets that a woman brought into marriage and which she
acquired subsequently by inheritance to be her own separate
property over which she could dispose at will. Further amendments extended these rights to her earnings from paid employment, to life insurance policies, and to deposits in saving banks.
With regard to all these assets of her separate property she
acquired the same rights and obligations 'as if she were a single
female'.[48]

The Married Women's Property Acts in both America and
England[49] were promoted on grounds of equity, not equality.
Characteristically, the reforms made the married woman an equal
of the single woman, not of her husband. The latter's powers
over her person (his rights to the wife's services) remained intact.
She acquired contractual and litigational capacities only with
regard to, and to the extent of, her separate property. Indeed, the
reformist discourse itself was tempered by pervasive fears that
separate interests would jeopardize the indivisible nexus of 'one
flesh, one legal person, one property'.[50]

Throughout the nineteenth century, as Basch has shown for
New York, Blackstone's formulation of the single identity of the
married couple remained the dominant paradigm through which
lawyers as well as broad sections of the lay public perceived the
nature of the marriage bond. A legal construct whose origins lay
in the thirteenth century remained effective 600 years later
because it proved flexible enough to accommodate new experiences and changed circumstances. Similarly, it had a broad public
resonance because it did not demand recourse to technical legal
constructions or abstract philosophical principle, but could be
taken as the felicitous, timeless expression of common sentiment.
By the nineteenth century the idea of marital unity had shed its
erstwhile feudal connotations which were no longer compatible
with democratic sensibilities. The focus shifted from a unity
secured through domination and obedience towards a moral and
spiritual community. In this form, the idea had absorbed both the
quest for the companionate marriage and the new evaluation of

---

[48] Laws of New York, 1848, ch. 200, quoted in Basch, *In the Eyes of the Law*, 233.
[49] Cf. L. Holcombe, *Wives and Property: Reform of the Married Women's Property Law in Nineteenth-Century England* (Oxford, 1983); Kahn-Freund, 'Matrimonial Property Law in England', 169–79.
[50] Holcombe, *Wives and Property*, 90.

women's domestic role and its unique contribution to republican virtue. Due to the blurred boundaries between legal and non-legal meanings and to the prevalence of sentimental connotations, this rhetoric obscured that the unity of marriage was and remained anchored in a relationship of unequal right and unequal power. As regards the practice of the law, the fiction bore upon the restrictive interpretations of the reform statutes by the judiciary who habitually limited what was to count as a married woman's separate property and what she could do with it.[51] 'Judicial patri- archy'—the tendency of nineteenth-century courts to curtail a wife's statutory rights through increasingly narrow interpreta- tion—has also been observed in other national contexts.[52] Unless she could offer tangible documentary evidence that she had pur- chased certain goods with the resources of her separate property, or that she had reserved the administration of certain assets to herself, judges used the presumption of marital unity to place the assets in question under the husband's control.

The French *Code civil* owed its reputation as an exemplary system of modern private law to the homogeneous application of the principles of bourgeois liberty and formal equality. These goods were guaranteed to all citizens of the nation (to 'even the hum- blest individual') in the right to the unconstrained use and enjoy- ment of their *propriété*—'the fundamental right which sustains all institutions of the community and which is as precious to the indi- vidual as life itself'.[53] The marriage law of the code, by contrast, defined property by reference to the relation of seigneur and sub- ordinate:[54] 'because the husband is the master of the wife he con- trols her property, just as if it were part of his own.'[55] Although most of the code's provisions stemmed from the customary law of the *ancien régime*, the 'continuity' of the past, across more than two decades of revolutionary change, must be understood as the result of a comprehensive political and intellectual reaction. As regards its specific focus, the reaction was aimed against the civil

[51] Cf. Basch, *In the Eyes of the Law*, 201–22.

[52] Cf. Gerhard, *Verhältnisse*, 166 f.; Brauneder, *Entwicklung*, 363–8.

[53] J. E. M. Portalis, 'Exposé des motifs du projet de loi sur la propriété', in id., *Écrits et discours juridiques et politiques* (Aix, 1988), 127.

[54] See N. Arnaud-Duc, 'Le Droit et les comportements, la genèse du titre V du livre III du Code civil: Les Régimes matrimoniaux', in Théry and Biet (eds.), *La Famille*, 183–95.

[55] K. S. Zachariä, *Handbuch des französischen Zivilrechts* (Heidelberg, 1811), iii. 214.

legislation of the Revolution, in particular against the divorce by mutual consent. In its wider ramifications it reinforced the vision of subversion and social disorder which were widely perceived to be the inevitable consequence of women's greater freedom and the decline of the husband's and father's undisputed authority.[56]

In order to legitimize the reinforcement of patterns of domination and subjection in marriage the framers of the code did not, on the whole, resort to traditionalist arguments. They recast the meanings of *puissance maritale* and *incapacité*, of contract and communal property in ways that responded to contemporary experiences and sensibilities. The rhetorical modernization of anachronistic institutional forms relied on various strategies which, most notably in Portalis's representation, combined to form a highly effective discourse of reaction.[57] The first strategy drew heavily on Rousseau's influence—on his conception of marriage as a pre-legal, pre-political union, formed in nature and inaccessible to the will of the legislator, and on his idea of the beneficent natural complementarity of the sexes. Taken together, these notions endowed the hierarchical marriage of the positive law with an aura of naturalness and sentimental unity in relation to which individual property rights and legal equality could appear as singularly inappropriate. A second strategy, which aimed above all to undermine the legitimacy of the consensual divorce, divested the marriage contract of its individualist and voluntarist elements. Dissociated from both the sacrament of the theologians and the contract of the jurists, marriage was to receive permanence and secular sanctity from 'a higher political viewpoint'.[58] As a *contrat perpétuel* it stood above the arbitrary disposition and transient interests of the individual and outside the reach of legislative manipulation.[59] The third strategy (which has already been referred to above) moved the boundaries between private and public law. It

---

[56] Cf. D. Blasius, 'Bürgerliche Rechtsgleichheit und die Ungleichheit der Geschlechter: Das Scheidungsrecht im historischen Vergleich', in U. Frevert (ed.), *Bürgerinnen und Bürger: Geschlechterverhältnisse im 19. Jahrhundert* (Göttingen, 1988), 67–84; L. Hunt, *The Family Romance of the French Revolution* (Berkeley and Los Angeles, 1992); U. Vogel, 'The Fear of Public Disorder: Marriage between Revolution and Reaction', in D. Castiglione and L. Sharpe (eds.), *Shifting the Boundaries: Transformation of the Languages of Public and Private in the Eighteenth Century* (Exeter, 1995), 71–88.

[57] Cf. I. Théry and C. Biet, 'Portalis ou l'esprit des siècles: La Rhétorique du mariage dans le Discours préliminaire au projet du Code civil', in eid. (eds.), *La Famille*, 104–21.

[58] Portalis, 'Discours préliminaire sur le projet du Code civil', in id., *Écrits et discours*, 39.

[59] Ibid, 38, 43.

denied the competence of the former for the core domain of conjugal rights and placed the husband's prerogatives as *seigneur* of the
wife and *maître* of the common property under the imperatives of
the public order.

What these legitimatory strategies have in common is the
appeal to metajuridical principles and the intention to disconnect
the essential core of marriage from the norms that govern ordinary contracts under the civil law. As a special institution which
was constituted by a permanent contract and absorbed into the
ordre public, the association of husband and wife was effectively
insulated against the language of individual rights and separate
property. Indeed, in this construction the interests of property had
become marginal to the essence of the marriage bond. It needs
to be stressed, here too, that the strategies of seemingly non-legal
reasoning served to defend and entrench a particular institution
of the positive law and that the hierarchical order of gender was
built into the very foundations of what was presented as an indivisible community of a higher order.

As was the case in Germany, political debates in nineteenth-
century France saw conservatives and liberals divided on the question of divorce but in basic agreement on the need to preserve the
inner unity of marriage.[60] Challenges to the husband's exclusive
control of the common property first came with a decree of 1883
giving married women independent access to their saving bank
accounts and with the concession of the *libre salaire* (control over
earnings) in 1907. Like the corresponding measures in America,
England, and Germany, these changes were not meant to open
the door to the legal emancipation of the married woman. They
were owed to the acknowledgement by the state that its own interest in the material well-being and the pacification of the working
classes depended to a large extent on the labour, good household
management, and thrift of the wife and mother. In order to
perform those functions effectively, she had to be capable of managing the property derived from her own work.[61] *Puissance maritale*
and *incapacité de la femme mariée* did not disappear until the end of

---

[60] Cf. Coing, *Europäisches Privatrecht*, ii. 304 f.; B. Schnapper, 'Autorité domestique et partis
politiques, de Napoléon à de Gaulle', in H. Mohnhaupt (ed.), *Zur Geschichte des Familien-
und Erbrechts* (Frankfurt am Main, 1988), 177–220.

[61] See L. Balbo, 'Family, Women and the State: Notes toward a Typology of Family
Roles and Public Intervention', in C. S. Maier (ed.), *Changing Boundaries of the Political* (Cambridge, Mass., 1987), 201–20, esp. 204–7.

the Second World War, the husband's position as *maître* of the community of goods not until the reforms of 1966 and 1985. Only from then on was it possible in France to say: 'Liberté et égalité, devise du ménage comme de la République.'[62]

In Germany, matrimonial property became an issue of legislative attention and wider public debate in the decades that preceded the enactment of the new Civil Code (*BGB*, 1896/1900). There was, first of all, a pressing need to rationalize and simplify the prevailing plurality and fragmentation of the existing law. Secondly and as elsewhere, legislators had to address new economic exigencies, such as the increased participation of married women in the labour market and the commercial disadvantages inherent in the ambiguous status of a wife's liabilities. In what must be considered the most significant innovation, the new code established the married woman's earnings from paid employment or an independent business as her reserved property over which she was to hold full dispositive rights (*BGB*, original version of 1900, § 1367). However, under the statutory regime of the *Verwaltungsgemeinschaft* the husband continued to hold the administrative and usufructuary rights in all other property assets of the wife (*BGB*, original version of 1900, § 1363). Moreover, although it was generally acknowledged that marriage did not impair a woman's legal capacity and although the letter of the law no longer referred to a husband's guardianship and status as head of the marriage relation, the code reaffirmed these powers in all but name. In all matters affecting the conjugal community the prerogative of ultimate decision was vested in him (*BGB*, original version of 1900, § 1354). This meant, in particular, that he retained that right to her person which allowed him to revoke contracts of personal obligations towards third parties if he deemed them incompatible with her domestic duties (*BGB*, original version of 1900, § 1358). Even the *Schlüsselgewalt* (power of the keys)—acclaimed by conservative jurists like Gierke as the authentic expression of the German wife's dignified status[63]—confirmed her dependence. It gave her the power to act in representation of her husband in the pursuit of her household responsibilities. But it was a

---

[62] Schnapper, 'Autorité domestique', 177.

[63] O. Gierke, *Der Entwurf eines Bürgerlichen Gesetzbuches und das deutsche Recht* (Leipzig, 1889), 404 f.

power based on the presumption that all such transactions were his.

In the course of the deliberations on the first draft proposals in the 1870s and 1880s the representatives of the main women's organization had demanded that the new law should adopt the separation of goods, in the form of the Roman dotal regime, as the statutory regime.[64] Gottlieb Planck, the redactor of the family law, conceded that no other regime of matrimonial property gave to the wife as much independence as the provisions of the Roman law. However, since according to the German and Christian understanding of law matrimonial property should be true to the essential purpose of marriage, the code had to uphold the preponderant position of the husband. As Planck put it in response to a similar demand of the Social Democrats for strict spousal equality: the institution of marriage was to rank above the independence of the wife.[65]

Like a magic formula, the invocation of marriage as an institution—as an ethical community independent of the will of the spouses—served as the ultimate arbiter in virtually all discussions of the draft propositions of the new code.[66] The wide appeal of this language reflected the profound reorientations of German legal and political thought since 1815.[67] As in France, the paradigm shift from contract to institution in legal doctrine was in many ways connected with the political and ideological conflicts of the time. Initially, in the 1830s and 1840s, it sustained the conservative backlash against the liberal divorce provisions of the Prussian code. In the eyes of critics, like Savigny, divorce by mutual consent—and the increasing number of cases that came to the courts, most of them initiated by women—demonstrated the fundamental flaws inherent in the contractual conception of marriage and attested to the inadequacies of the amoral

[64] L. Otto, *Einige deutsche Gesetzesparagraphen* (Leipzig, 1876); S. Buchholz, 'Das Bürgerliche Gesetzbuch und die Frauen: Zur Kritik des Ehegüterrechts', in Gerhard (ed.), *Frauen in der Geschichte des Rechts*, 670–82.

[65] See J. P. Schäfer, *Die Entstehung der Vorschriften des BGB über das persönliche Eherecht* (Frankfurt am Main, 1983), 221 f.; B. Dölemeyer, 'Frau und Familie im Privatrecht des 19. Jahrhunderts', in Gerhard (ed.), *Frauen in der Geschichte des Rechts*, 633–58.

[66] Cf. B. Harms-Ziegler, *Illegitimität und Ehe: Illegitimität als Reflex des Ehediskurses in Preußen im 18. und 19. Jahrhundert* (Berlin, 1991), 249–63; Karina Kroj, *Die Abhängigkeit der Frau in Eherechtformen des Mittelalters und der Neuzeit als Ausdruck eines gesellschaftlichen Leitbilds von Ehe und Familie*, dissertation (Mainz, 1988), 258–65.

[67] Cf. Gerhard, *Verhältnisse*, 167–79.

foundations of eighteenth-century rationalism.[68] By the 1870s
marriage and the family had become a major catalyst for the critique of modern society and the ubiquitous reference point in
diverse conceptualizations of social order, state cohesion, and
national identity.

The recasting of the marriage discourse evolved in many different variants. The notions of institution and ethical community—
distinct concepts, though often used interchangeably—might
draw upon the philosophical heritage of Fichte and Hegel; they
might associate themselves with the romantic cult of intimate
unity born from love and spiritual affinity, or with the quest for a
return to Christian values. Germanistic jurisprudence derived the
communal character of marriage from the model of the medieval
Genossenschaft and the institute of the *mundium* or, more diffusely,
from the claim to a uniquely German understanding of the law.

How did the demands of institution and ethical community
bear upon the position of husband and wife and, in particular,
upon the question of their property rights? Without claiming to
do justice to the diversity of legal arguments, we can summarize
the implications in the following points. First, the insistence on the
ethical foundations of marriage entailed the claim that its essence
was not in any significant way constituted by the law and thus
could not be judged by the formal criteria of merely juridical relationships. While this claim placed the essential core of the marriage bond out of reach of legislative interference, by the same
token, it entrenched the existing laws as sacrosanct. Secondly,
'community' postulated the epistemological and moral primacy of
the whole over the parts, of the institution over the individual participants, of collective over individual purposes. Whereas the contractual marriage of the eighteenth century was an association
constructed from the rights and obligations of individuals, the
community stipulated a *Gesamtpersönlichkeit*—a single collective
person of the spouses. Because they took unity as their starting
point, such arguments left no epistemological space for consider-

---

[68] F. C. v. Savigny, 'Darstellung der in den preußischen Gesetzen über Ehescheidung
unternommenen Reform', in id., *Vermischte Schriften* (Berlin, 1850), v. 222–343; D. Blasius,
'Reform gegen die Frau: Das preussische Scheidungsrecht im frühen 19. Jahrhundert', in
Gerhard (ed.), *Frauen in der Geschichte des Rechts*, 659–69; U. Vogel, 'Whose Property? The
Double Standard of Adultery in Nineteenth Century Law', in C. Smart (ed.), *Regulating
Womanhood: Historical Essays on Marriage, Motherhood and Sexuality* (London, 1991), 147–65.

ing husband and wife as independent persons and for judging the law in terms of their individual interests. Nor was it possible to define the 'essence' of marriage by reference to specific public purposes (whether of population increase, economic utility, or social peace). The essence of marriage was intertwined with the metaphysical essence of the state in a closed circle of mutual substitution which did not allow for political reasoning of the kind that had characterized debates in the forum of Enlightenment rationalism.

Thirdly, the strictures against individualist and contractual principles had significant implications for the arguments about matrimonial property. As regards their preference for particular arrangements, liberals and conservatives differed. The latter associated the ethical imperatives of marriage with the general community of goods because it gave effect to the personal unity of husband and wife and because it alone could impart to the new code the elements of a genuinely social law (*Sozialrecht*) necessary to combat the atomistic tendencies of modern private law.[69] Liberals, on the other hand, endorsed the administrative community, on the grounds that the separation of goods safeguarded the principle of individual property rights and took care to protect the wife's entitlements against the husband's irresponsible dealings or misfortunes.[70] But such differences paled against the common emphasis that the concentration of dispositive powers in the hands of the husband had to be preserved at all costs. Whether this was justified by reference to the *mundium* and the husband's status 'as the born representative of his wife',[71] or by sentimental analogies, widely deployed in the second half of the century, with the nature of sexual love (whereby a woman's capacity for selfless devotion (*Hingabe*) was made out to relate to both her body and her property),[72] the effect was the same. Marital prerogatives were projected as the faithful expression of the essential wholeness of the marriage bond. Most importantly, the husband's administrative and usufructuary rights continued to be classified as 'an eminently

---

[69] See Gierke, *Entwurf*, 393, 407–26.
[70] See Buchholz, 'Das Bürgerliche Gesetzbuch und die Frauen', 672–5.
[71] Gierke, *Entwurf*, 403.
[72] For an earlier example of a romanticized legal language see C. F. von Gerber, 'Betrachtungen über das Güterrecht der Ehegatten nach deutschem Rechte', *Iherings Jahrbücher*, 1 (1857), 257.

personal right'.[73] Planck's proposal to delimit those powers by
bringing them under the general constraints of usufructuary property was rejected. In contrast to the normal provisions of the
private law, it was argued, a husband's usufruct 'expressed the
totality of his legal relationships to his wife and was valid even if
the latter, at any given point in time, had no property of her
own'.[74]

Fourthly, the exceptional character of the husband's personal
and property rights was reinforced by the claim that by virtue of
its essential attributes marriage belonged properly to the public
rather than the private law. Apart from the marginal domain governed by contractual dealings over goods, marriage constituted a
relationship of rule over persons and as such came under the *ius
cogens* of the public law. Although practical proposals to this effect,
namely to exclude marriage altogether from the Civil Code, did
not in the end meet with sufficient agreement, the underlying
reasons did, and they were effectively used as barriers against the
equality norms of the private law.

Inequality between husband and wife was thus built into the
basic design of institution and ethical community, but in a form
that no longer relied on outdated notions of female inferiority.
After the gradual disappearance of the institute of sex guardianship (*Geschlechtsvormundschaft*) in most German states marital
guardianship could only be justified by amalgamating it with the
essence of marriage. It was further reinforced by a discourse that
emphasized the complementarity and equal worth of the sexes.
Gleichwertigkeit, went the dominant opinion, expressed the true
meaning of spousal equality in the husband's privilege of domestic rule.

Whatever their particular ideological focus, the community
discourses of the nineteenth century did not aim to challenge
the power relationship sanctioned by the positive law. They
entrenched that power in two ways—by postulating a specific historical form as the essence of marriage, and by placing the relation of husband and wife under incommensurable moral and legal
norms. 'Community' presupposed inequality but filtered out the

---

[73] Planck, quoted in Buchholz, 'Das Bürgerliche Gesetzbuch und die Frauen', 674.

[74] Schubert, *Materialien*, 380 f.; see also K. Heinsheimer, *Das Recht des Mannes am Vermö-
gen der Frau bei dem ordentlichen gesetzlichen Güterstand des BGB für das Deutsche Reich* (Jena, 1903),
81–4.

meanings of exclusion and denied rights. An enduring legacy of these discourses for the twentieth century was their capacity to block the comparison of the marriage relationship with the universal postulates of modern private law.

Conclusion: the prevention of equality

This essay has asked what eighteenth- and nineteenth-century debates about matrimonial property can tell us about the inequality between husbands and wives. Unlike most textbooks of family law, which separate matrimonial property from the personal rights of the spouses, these debates show how property was constituted by, and in turn cemented, a relation of *Herrschaft* and subordination. It is this nexus, rather than the unequal or inequitable distribution of material resources, which in the nineteenth century distinguished marriage from other forms of social inequality. I have argued that the enduring presence of seemingly 'feudal' patterns of ownership and rule in bourgeois private law cannot be explained by the common connotations of 'backwardness' or by the functional necessities of economic and social modernization. At least, we should not assume that alternatives to the hierarchical order of marriage were not considered or could not have been envisaged before the twentieth century. The codification debates in Austria and Prussia, the civil legislation of the French Revolution, and the Massachusetts court case provide proof to the contrary. It *was* possible for the contemporaries of that period to conceive of the equality of husband and wife. To put it differently, enormous effort was undertaken to suppress that possibility and to continue to deny women's capacity for independent agency and citizenship.[75] The fictions of community and marital unity, in which nineteenth-century legal discourses projected marriage as an institution *sui generis* and an enclave of special rules within the private law, did not belong in the intellectual universe of premodern society. As a reaction against the egalitarian possibilities of Enlightenment universalism, they embodied distinctly modern modes of thinking and specific political intentions. The history of inequality, to use Ute Gerhard's felicitous phrase, entails the

---

[75] See Kerber, 'Women's Citizenship', 354.

'prevention' of equality.[76] It is a history of controversy and conflict over the meanings of the law, of political choices and their
legitimization. The judges of Massachusetts chose the prescriptions of the common law over the principles of natural law.
Similarly, the framers of the German Civil Code chose a property regime of marital prerogative over the egalitarian implications of separate property.

As a result of legal changes since the Second World War,
Western democracies today recognize the equality of the marriage
partners as legal subjects and citizens. These changes were not
owed to reform impulses internal to the private law; they came
about under the pressure of democratic citizenship (and, in countries like West Germany, from the constitutional entrenchment of
equal human rights). Programmatic declarations of the principle
of gender equality as such were not a novelty. General statements
to this effect go back as far as the codifications of the eighteenth
century. The truly radical break with tradition occurred in the
recognition that a citizen's basic rights also apply to the marriage
relation and must trump any claims made on behalf of its special
institutional purposes. If for nineteenth-century legislators the
institution of marriage ranked above the independence of the
wife, today the independence of both wife and husband ranks
above the institution.

---

[76] See the title of Gerhard's study of women's rights in the 19th century: *Verhältnisse und
Verhinderungen*.

5
Husbands, Wives, and Judges in Nineteenth-Century France

Jean-Louis Halpérin

On 29 October 1904, during the solemn celebration of the cen-
tenary of the passing of the Civil Code in the great amphitheatre
of the Sorbonne in Paris, a feminist militant interjected: 'The
Code oppresses women.' The heckler was immediately expelled,
but several of her fellow feminists demonstrated in front of the
Colonne Vendôme and tried to burn a copy of the Civil Code.[1]
This provocation did not surprise the French professors of law.
Although they were all men, they were all aware of the unfairness
of the Napoleonic Code towards women in general, and married
women in particular. While the Civil Code submitted unmarried
women to few prohibitions,[2] it literally put wives into tutelage. It
considered them as minors or infants, as Balzac wrote.[3] According to article 1124 of the Civil Code, minors, people declared to
be mentally disordered, and married women lacked the capacity
to contract in the instances expressed by law.

Owing 'obedience to her husband' (art. 213 CC), obliged to live
in the home chosen by him and to follow him anywhere he judged
fit to reside (art. 214), the wife was struck with a general civil
incompetence: she could not sue, alienate property, or acquire it
without the special authorization of her spouse (arts. 215 and 217).
Whatever matrimonial property regime the spouses may have
chosen, the husband 'administers all, he surveys all, his partner's

---

[1] G. Fraisse and M. Perrot (eds.), *A History of Women in the West* (Cambridge, Mass., 1993),
iv. 504; M. Ozouf, *Les Mots des femmes: Essai sur la singularité française* (Paris, 1995), 203. In
subsequent notes, *S.* stands for J.-B. Sirey, *Recueil général des lois et arrêts*; *DP* stands for D.
Dalloz, *Recueil périodique et critique de jurisprudence, de législation et de doctrine (1825–1940); Jur. gén.*
stands for D. Dalloz, *Répertoire méthodique et alphabétique de législation, de doctrine et de jurisprudence*, 44 vols. (Paris, 1846–70).

[2] According to the Napoleonic Code (arts. 37 and 980), a woman could not act as a
witness for the registration of births, deaths, and marriages, or for wills.

[3] H. de Balzac, *Le Contrat de mariage* (Paris, 1966), 59.

property and morals',[4] as Portalis put it. In particular, under the community property regime, he could alienate it alone and practically do as he liked with it.[5] Civil and penal sanctions for adultery also reflected a deep inequality between husbands and wives.[6]

This subjection of the wife was justified at great length by the drafters of the Civil Code, who had clear ideas about 'the preferential treatment or equality of the sexes'. The family, like society, needed a government and this government needed a head who acted alone.[7] The incapacity of the married woman was therefore a logical consequence of the husband's marital authority. This concept also included the idea that the wife was weak and inexperienced by nature and therefore in need of her husband's protection. Strength and audacity were seen as male qualities, whereas shyness and prudence were regarded as female qualities.[8] Nineteenth-century lawyers, who annotated the Napoleonic Code, shared these ideas.[9]

This incapacity was not abolished in principle until 1938, and its effects were felt in matrimonial property regimes until 1942.[10] Complete equality between husbands and wives was not fully established until 1985.[11] In 1904, the movement for the emancipation of married women was only twenty years old, encouraged by changes in statute law. When the republicans came to power, married women received the right to open a savings account in their own names (Law of 9 April 1881), before obtaining free access to the fruits of their labour (Law of 13 July 1907). Divorce

---

[4] F. Ewald (ed.), *Naissance du Code civil* (Paris, 1989), 73.

[5] Except for gifts of immoveable property.

[6] M. Bordeaux, 'Le Maître et l'infidèle', in I. Théry and C. Biet (eds.), *La Famille, la loi, l'état de la Révolution au Code civil* (Paris, 1989), 432–46.

[7] X. Martin, 'L'Individualisme libéral en France autour de 1800: Essai de spectroscopie', *Revue d'histoire des facultés de droit et de la science juridique*, 4 (1987), 122.

[8] Ewald, *Naissance du Code civil*, 370 (quotation of Portalis).

[9] R. T. Troplong, *Du contrat de mariage* (Paris, 1857), i, no. 2; C. Demolombe, *Traité du mariage et de la séparation de corps* (Paris, 1880), ii. 137. For unusual opinions in favour of women, see P. Gide, *Étude sur la condition privée de la femme* (Paris, 1867) and E. Acollas, *Manuel de droit civil* (Paris, 1869).

[10] The Law of 18 February 1938 abolished the marital authority of the husband and the Law of 22 September 1942 reformed matrimonial regimes accordingly. This can be compared with the situation in England where married women gained the full power to acquire and dispose of property in 1882: W. R. Cornish and G. de N. Clark, *Law and Society in England, 1750–1950* (London, 1989), 401.

[11] The Law of 13 July 1965 expanded the powers of married women considerably and the Law of 23 December 1985 established a perfect equality between wives and husbands.

was re-established in 1884,[12] and women separated from their husbands gained full civil rights in 1893. These developments were seen to be a consequence of the growth in women's education and employment, and of a change in morals.[13]

Limited and late as this legislative process was, it could not obliterate the memory of three-quarters of a century of oppression by the Napoleonic Code, reinforced by the abolition of divorce in 1816. On the evening of 29 October 1904, the French Minister of Justice replied to the feminists thus: 'Ladies, it is about you that I wish to speak . . . Bypassing the harsh law imposed by men, you have been able to bring about a judicial interpretation which reverses, to your advantage and to our comfort, old-fashioned legal texts in which one had the stupid pretension of making you subject to your husbands.'[14] The Minister suggested that the courts could have helped married women during the nineteenth century. At first sight, the idea of judges being in favour of married women seems anachronistic. Judges, all men, most of them husbands and fathers, would have been unlikely to assist victims of male marital authority. Wives could not sue without the permission of their husbands except to obtain a separation, and access to civil courts was difficult for poor litigants, even after the legal aid law of 1851.[15] Composed of wealthy judges who resisted democratic ideas and held traditional views of the family, the French judiciary does not appear as a natural supporter of the feminists.[16]

However, even French judges were not blind and deaf to the development of ideas, mentalities, and social changes, and over a century they must have changed their position. This essay will present the results of a limited research project on the judicial

---

[12] Divorce provisions of the Napoleonic Code were repealed in 1816. With the law of 1884 (linked with the anticlerical battle of the Third Republic), civil equality was established between male and female adultery.

[13] A. Colin and H. Capitant, *Cours élémentaire de droit civil français* (Paris, 1914), i. 605.

[14] *Le Code civil 1804–1904: Livre du Centenaire* (Paris, 1904), ii. 64: 'C'est de vous, Mesdames, que je veux parler . . . à côté de la loi si dure de l'homme, vous avez su instituer une jurisprudence qui renverse avantageusement pour vous, agréablement pour nous, les textes aujourd'hui démodés par lesquels on avait eu la sotte prétention de vous asservir à vos maris.' The French word 'jurisprudence' is ambiguous: as a technical term, it means judicial decisions, but here it can be understood as customs or manners.

[15] B. Schnapper, 'De la charité à la solidarité: L'Assistance judiciaire française 1851–1972', in id., *Voies nouvelles en histoire du droit* (Paris, 1991), 435–89.

[16] J. P. Royer, *Histoire de la justice en France* (Paris, 1995), 493–94.

decisions published in the nineteenth century. It can only make suggestions about judges' behaviour towards married women. I have tried to classify these decisions according to whether or not they improved the status of married women by comparison with the Civil Code.

Despite its apparent precision, the Napoleonic Code was not explicit about many details of the status of married women. What were the limits of the obedience they owed to their husbands? How was the legal incapacity of married women justified? Judges often answered these questions by reinforcing the authority of married men: case law increased the dependence of married women in respect of their persons and all matters relating to property.

According to Napoleon, a husband could say to his wife: 'Madam, you will not go out, you will not go to the theatre, you will not meet Mr So-and-So.'[17] In such matters, judicial action was exceptional. In general it was used only to obtain a separation. Should the husband have the right to open his wife's letters? French and Belgian judges answered this question in favour of the 'head of the family' in the late nineteenth century.[18] But in the early twentieth century the powers of husbands were cut back on this issue.[19]

Courts allowed husbands to use force in dealing with their wives; however, violence could be a reason for obtaining a separation.[20] In the 1870s the court of Chambéry speaks of the husband's 'duty strongly but affectionately to lead his young wife, to complete her moral education using the necessary means'.[21] The majority of lawyers, however, did not seem to agree that the husband had the right to chastise his wife, defended by traditionalist judges.[22]

In few cases did French judges in the nineteenth century pro-

---

[17] A. Dansette, *Napoléon: Pensées politiques et sociales* (Paris, 1969), 133.

[18] Brussels, 28 Apr. 1875, *S.* 1877, ii. 161.

[19] Colin and Capitant, *Cours élémentaire*, i. 613.

[20] *Jur. gén.* 1858, vol. xxxix, V° Séparation de corps, 967 about the distinction between forceful action and violence.

[21] Chambéry, 4 May 1872, *DP* 1873, ii. 129.

[22] This judgment can perhaps be explained in terms of the atmosphere of the 1870s (with the so-called *Ordre moral*), or by the Catholic and traditionalist ideas which were predominant in Savoy.

nounce judgment on the issue of sexual relations between spouses. In 1841, the court of Rennes claimed not to interfere with the secrets of conjugal life; however, judges denied that insistent caresses by the husband were an injury to his wife.[23] According to the judges, it was in the husband's interest to respect his wife's decency. The wife could also take legal action for the restitution of conjugal rights, but only if she wanted to give birth to a child.[24] Here again reciprocity of obligations did not mean equality of the partners.

Most judicial decisions concerning the obedience of married women dealt with the means a husband could legitimately use in case of desertion by his wife. Courts allowed the husband to exert financial pressure, for example, by seizing the income of his wife's property. According to the judges a wealthy woman living outside the matrimonial home could not be tolerated. Such licence, they said, would 'injure the holiness of marriage and crush the most sacred principles'.[25]

Recourse to police force was discussed in greater depth. From the beginning of the nineteenth century, this idea offended the sensibilities of those judges who wished to differentiate between the old and the new law.[26] A few decisions rejected use of seizure of the person of the wife, on moral grounds.[27] But it seems that most judges did accept this recourse to police force in the case of a recalcitrant spouse. They gave several reasons: the need to respect the law 'equally', the need to give due consideration to the wife's voluntary engagements, and the utility of thus establishing disobedience to obtain a separation afterwards.[28] Above all, judges rejected the possibility of the independence of married women, an idea that they associated with instability and sheer fancy.[29]

To all appearances, these judgments concerned the upper classes, perhaps because desertion by the wife was a greater scandal for them, and the use of violence less frequent than among the working classes. Decisions dating from the beginning

---

[23] Rennes, 13 Dec. 1841, *Jur. gén.* 1858, vol. xxxix, V° Séparation de corps, 904–5.
[24] Metz, 25 May 1869, *DP* 1869, ii. 202.
[25] Nîmes, 11 June 1806, *Jur. gén.* 1854, vol. xxxix, V° Mariage, 378.
[26] Colmar, 4 Jan. 1817, ibid. 380.
[27] Bourges, 15 July 1811, Colmar, 10 July 1833, ibid. 380.
[28] Req. 9 Aug. 1826, Dijon, 25 July 1840, ibid. 337.
[29] Pau, 12 Apr. 1810, ibid. 337.

of the twentieth century still allow recourse to police force. But at this time most lawyers found this way of proceeding inefficient: husbands could not shut away their wives.[30] Judges had to choose the most appropriate means to deal with the situation.[31] The marital authority of the husband was not reduced as a result of this search for efficiency.

On the civil incompetence of wives, judges were often more rigorous than the terse text of the Civil Code. To begin with, judges did not accept any exceptions from the rule that wives who wanted to sue had to have their husband's permission, except when suing for a separation. Even if a wife sued her husband for the purpose of disposing of her own property, she had to obtain his authorization! Secondly, judges extended the scope of the incapacity of married women to enter into contracts: although the Napoleonic Code said nothing on this matter, married women could not contract debts. If a wife wanted to guarantee her husband's debts, some judges deemed a judicial authorization necessary. Under pretence of protecting the wife, a few decisions supported the concept of women's 'fragility'.[32] Most judges held excessively traditional ideas about how specific this marital authorization had to be. The Civil Code had only prohibited general authorization, and some lawyers asserted that a single authorization concerning property was sufficient. Judges rejected this interpretation: in 1840 the Court of Cassation required a specific authorization for every transaction.[33] Most courts also refused to ratify a contract entered into by a married woman even if her husband had subsequently given his authorization.[34]

If judges thought in this way, we can imagine how rarely courts gave the wife an authorization refused by her husband, a possibility provided for by article 219 of the Civil Code. The lack of precedents relating to the abuse of male marital authority suggests that this was only a theoretical case.[35] Judges could compel

---

[30] Colin and Capitant, *Cours élémentaire*, 611–12.

[31] Req. 26 June 1878, *DP* 1879, i. 80.

[32] Turin, 17 Dec. 1808, *Jur. gén.* 1854, vol. xxxix, V° Mariage, 400; *contra* Nîmes, 9 Feb. 1842. The opinion of Demolombe, *Traité du mariage*, ii, no. 117 was ambiguous: *de lege lata*, he thought that the civil incompetence of married women was based on marital authority, but he considered their inexperience as 'the most ordinary fact'.

[33] Req. 18 Mar. 1840, *Jur. gén.* 1854, vol. xxxix, V° Mariage, 411–13.

[34] Grenoble, 26 July 1828, ibid. 415.

[35] H. Basset, *Le Rôle de la femme mariée dans la gestion des intérêts pécuniaires de l'association conjugale*, dissertation (Paris, 1896), 47.

a wife to wait for her husband's return in order to obtain his authorization, even if he was absent for a long time.[36]

The same bias can be found in the discussion of married women engaging in professional activities. Judges had to apply civil and commercial law which gave women conducting a separate business the right to enter into contracts.[37] But they added that authorization, necessary for a married woman to engage in trade, could be retracted at any time. The husband could prevent his wife (duly authorized to be a pork-butcher) from forming a company with other people.[38]

Judges were even more suspicious of women as independent as actresses. In principle, a married woman needed her husband's authorization for every engagement.[39] This authorization could be tacit: in this way judges did not secure the liberty of women but prevented actresses from claiming that a contract was null and void by arguing that there had been no marital authorization.[40] Sometimes judges confirmed a husband's veto by pleading the risks of this profession and family interest.[41] The situation of working women who could not enter into contracts of employment or retain the fruits of their labour (before the Law of July 1907) did not seem to trouble the courts: there was no real way in which a wife could sue for her wages without her husband's permission.

Did married women obtain property rights as a result of marriage settlements? Whereas the legal regime gave the husband full power over joint property and the right to administer his wife's property, the incapacity of married women seemed less absolute when property was divided (by settlement or judgment), or under the dowry system. In the case of division of property, the wife had the power to alienate her moveable property (art. 1449 *CC*). Under the dowry system, the wife herself could administer real or personal assets that were not included in the dowry (called *paraphernaux*).

---

[36] Colmar, 31 July 1810, *Jur. gén.* 1854, xxxi. 420.

[37] *Jur. gén.* 1847, vol. viii, V° Commerçant, 518. It can be compared with the English situation: Cornish and Clark, *Law and Society*, 367–8 (an English married woman could sue when engaged in a trade, whereas a French one could not).

[38] *Jur. gén.* 1847, vol. viii, V° Commerçant, 522.

[39] Paris, 4 May 1852, *DP* 1853, ii. 95.

[40] Paris, 23 Aug. 1851, *DP* 1852, ii. 10: this judgment is particularly contemptuous of the 'independent' married woman.

[41] Paris, 3 Jan. 1868, *S.* 1868, ii. 65.

In these situations (which were relatively rare[42]), judges rather tended to increase the wife's incapacity. At the beginning of the nineteenth century, judges tolerated the fact that a woman separated from her husband could borrow money guaranteed by her moveable property.[43] In the 1820s, however, courts nullified agreements that were not related to the administration of this moveable property. Although the Napoleonic Code said nothing about this situation, a woman separated from her husband was no longer able to contract debts without her husband's permission. Judges invoked Roman law (the *senatusconsultum Velleianum*) and spoke of the risks of a wife causing her family's ruin. Not seeing the danger, the wife might be too eager to borrow, and her imprudence could be a threat to the whole family. According to the judiciary, article 1449 was an exceptional rule to be interpreted with restrictions; civil incompetence remained the natural state for married women.[44] Judges used the literary image of the thriftless woman to restrain wealthy wives. They did not seem aware of the danger of a wife remaining dependent on her husband's authorization after a sentence of separation.[45]

French judges put women married under the dowry regime into an even more unfortunate situation.[46] The drafters of the Civil Code revived the Roman dowry system: they thought that wives would bring real estate to the marriage which their husbands would administer without power of alienation. From the beginning of the nineteenth century, this model was frequently overturned in practice. Dowries more often consisted of moveable property and were given in small amounts.[47] Was it possible to alienate this moveable property? The Napoleonic Code had nothing to say on this question, and judges and lawyers argued at great length about it.

There was no problem for the husband: he administered the dowry and could therefore alienate moveable property. For the

---

[42] The dowry system, used in the south of France and Normandy, declined during the 19th century. Division of property by settlement was exceptional.

[43] Req. 16 Mar. 1813, Civ. 18 May 1819, *Jur. gén.* 1852, vol. xiii, V° Contrat de mariage, 411.

[44] Civ. 5 May 1829, Paris, 7 Aug. 1820, Paris, 1 June 1824, ibid. 412–15.

[45] Troplong, *Du contrat de mariage*, no. 1417, approved this case law.

[46] Basset, *Le Rôle de la femme mariée*, 5.

[47] Nicole Arnaud-Duc, *Droit, mentalités et changement social en Provence occidentale* (Aix-en-Provence, 1985), 475.

wife the question was whether she could directly or indirectly alienate the dowry with her husband's consent, at the same time renouncing her right to recover the dowry. Most of the commentators on the Civil Code answered yes.[48] But in 1819, the Court of Cassation found that the wife could not alienate her moveable dowry. Judges invoked Roman law (*fragilitas sexus*), the customs of the south of France under the *Ancien Régime*, and the need to protect the wife against her own weakness. Above all, the dowry had to remain intact for family and children.[49]

Courts gave the same decision on similar cases not only in the 1840s, but also in the 1880s.[50] Judicial practice prevented the wife from borrowing money or giving guarantees to secure her husband's loans. Judges said that they would not restore the *senatusconsultum Velleianum*: wives could borrow money using their other assets (*biens paraphernaux*) as security.[51] But many married women did not have any assets, and even if they did, they could not use their credit to help their husbands. It had the same result as the *senatusconsultum Velleianum*: the wife was condemned to passive idleness.[52]

Because it was more severe than the Napoleonic Code and ran counter to the opinions of most lawyers, this case law was the keystone of the judges' opposition to the emancipation of married women. It cannot be dismissed merely as the resistance of southern courts, or as the reactionary attitude of Restoration judges towards the Napoleonic Code. These decisions were made by judges from the whole of France, throughout the entire nineteenth century, and, in some respects, made things worse than under the *Ancien Régime*.[53] Judges remained traditionalists at heart: they rejected the idea that married women could be independent, have a separate home, pursue a profession, and manage their assets freely. French judges claimed to be protecting married women when they used the paradigm of the housewife as a good

---

[48] *Jur. gén.* 1853, vol. xiv, V° Contrat de mariage, 81.
[49] Civ. 1 Feb. 1819, S. 1819, i. 146.
[50] *Jur. gén.* 1853, xiv. 79–80 and *Supplément du Répertoire Dalloz* 1889, iv. 213.
[51] Paris, 1 Feb. 1809, Req. 28 June 1810, *Jur. gén.* 1853, xiv. 87–8.
[52] Troplong, *Du contrat de mariage*, iv. 300–25; Gide, *Étude sur la condition privée*, 547–53; Basset, *Le Rôle de la femme mariée*, 414.
[53] Fraisse and Perrot (eds.), *History of Women*, 107–8. Under the *Ancien Régime* the wife could alienate the *biens paraphernaux*: Arnaud-Duc, *Droit*, 237. In Italy (Civil Code of 1865), the wife could borrow money with a judicial authorization using her dowry as security.

housekeeper. Paradoxically, this paternalistic attitude also explains the judicial decisions which favoured married women.

To demonstrate that things had improved for wives, nineteenth-century French lawyers first invoked the theory of *mandat tacite*, which could be compared with the 'agency of necessity' in England, or the *Schlüsselgewalt* in Germanic countries.[54] According to this theory, a married woman could buy necessary goods such as food, clothes, furniture, medicine without her husband's authorization. In these cases, the wife acted with an implicit power of attorney because her husband was too busy to attend to the mundane details of housekeeping. For necessary goods and services, the wife could also borrow against her husband's property, or against property held in common under the community property regime.

In some respects, this case law seems to fit the facts and to favour married women. It was also daring, because the Napoleonic Code said nothing of this power of attorney. Futhermore, judges recognized this *mandat tacite* even if the husband was absent (for instance, as the master of an ocean-going ship) or had deserted the matrimonial home.[55] The theory was stretched to fiction. Lastly, it was difficult for the husband to revoke this power, requiring adequate notice and a public announcement.[56]

On the other hand, this theory of *mandat tacite* was not a sign of women's emancipation, even if working-class wives were often described as the family banker.[57] This case law was created not by nineteenth-century judges, but by *Ancien Régime* courts.[58] The idea was revived by Restoration judges and 'old-world' lawyers such as Merlin or Toullier. Later, judges intended to obtain the payment of tradesmen who had acted in good faith, and could reduce expenses deemed excessive.[59] It was not possible for married

[54] Cornish and Clark, *Law and Society*, 367; R. Ganghofer and J. M. Poughon, 'Le Droit de la femme dans le Code civil et l'ALR', in B. Dölemeyer and H. Mohnhaupt (eds.), *200 Jahre Allgemeines Landrecht für die preußischen Staaten* (Frankfurt am Main, 1995), 361; P. Binet, *La femme dans le ménage*, dissertation (Nancy, 1904), 143–52.

[55] Bordeaux, 29 Mar. 1838, *Jur. gén.* 1852, xiii. 220; Civ. 6 Aug. 1878, *DP* 1879, i. 400.

[56] Req. 30 Nov. 1868, *DP* 1869, i. 132.

[57] P. Ariès and G. Duby (eds.), *Histoire de la vie privée* (Paris, 1987), iv. 124.

[58] Binet, *La Femme*, 29–30; I. A. Merlin, *Répertoire universel et raisonné de jurisprudence* (Paris, 1827), vol. i, V° Autorisation maritale, 590.

[59] *Jur. gén.* 1852, vol. xiii, V° Contrat de mariage, 225; C. B. M. Toullier, *Le Droit civil français suivant l'ordre du Code* (Paris, 1826), xii. 398–400.

women to take decisions beyond everyday domestic life.[60] The
mandat tacite was not a legal and clearly defined institution such as
the German *Schlüsselgewalt*. The social consequences of this case law are also open to question. Judicial decisions almost exclusively concerned wealthy
women, in particular, noble or high-society wives, buying luxuries.[61] Judges took into account not only the income of the household but also the status of the family. Only late nineteenth-century
lawyers could imagine applying this theory to poor people. Case
law, made for middle- or upper-class women, was merely a model
for the 1881 law about savings accounts for working women.
Finally, this theory reinforced the traditional view of women's abilities: the role of married women was domestic and subordinate,
and big business was not for women.[62]

It was a different matter with another body of case law concerning legal mortgages taken out for the benefit of married
women. According to the Napoleonic Code (art. 2135), the
husband's immoveable property had to be mortgaged as a form
of security for the wife's rights. According to the practice established by notaries at the beginning of the nineteenth century,
wives would renounce their claim in favour of outsiders contracting with their husbands. Judges validated this practice,[63]
before it was definitely confirmed by a Law of 25 March 1855.
Under the community property system, the husband needed his
wife's co-operation to sell or borrow.[64] For wealthy women who
were interested in their husbands' business, this provided a good
opportunity. Whereas wives married under the dowry system
could not renounce their mortgage, the majority of women, who
married under the community property system, could participate
in contracts with their spouses and help their husbands to obtain
credit.

[60] For instance, a married woman could not rent a flat alone: Civ. 15 June 1842, *Jur. gén.*
1852, xiii. 226.

[61] Binet, *La Femme*, 81.

[62] Toullier, *Le Droit civil*, 388; Binet, *La femme*, 491; D. Godineau, 'Qu'y a-t-il de commun
entre vous et nous? Enjeux et discours opposés de la différence des sexes pendant la Révolution française (1789–1793)', in Théry and Biet (eds.), *La Famille*, 79.

[63] Civ. 12 Feb. 1811, *S.* 1809–11, i. 292; *Jur. gén.* 1858, vol. xxxvii, V° Privilèges et
hypothèques, 263 and 270. Judges extended this mortgage in regard to immoveable assets
acquired during the marriage.

[64] Gide, *Étude sur la condition privée*, 544, approved this case law; *contra* Dalloz, *Jur. gén.*,
xxxvii. 264.

In all these cases concerning property, the courts merely followed the practice, and actions were mostly initiated by husbands or outsiders. Judicial separation was the only civil proceeding (from 1816 to 1884 when divorce was impossible) in which judges could truly meet the demands of married women. The grounds for judicial separation were the same as those for divorce before 1816: adultery, assault, cruelty, or severe injury (*injures graves*). Simple adultery was a matrimonial offence by the wife, but adultery by the husband had to be 'aggravated' by the fact of maintaining the mistress in the matrimonial home. Although most lawyers approved of this double standard until 1884,[65] judges were rather less rigorous in their interpretation of the Napoleonic Code. From the 1830s courts deemed that adultery by the husband could be a severe injury to his wife: for instance, when it was 'aggravated' by notoriety or a scandalous attitude on the part of the mistress. In 1836, the Court of Cassation admitted judicial separation in favour of a wife whose husband had committed adultery with a farmer's daughter with the knowledge of the whole household.[66] This case could be called 'Lord Bruyère de Sussac's mistress', a century before 'Lady Chatterley's lover'! There was no doubt that beaten wives could obtain a judicial separation for assault and cruelty. Husbands could appeal against such judgments by taking the case to the Court of Cassation. In fact, the Court of Cassation took few decisions in such cases because violent husbands probably did not dare to use this remedy for fear of publicity.[67]

Judges could also define more precisely what behaviour implied a severe injury. Courts considered judicial separation appropriate when the husband charged his wife wrongly and publicly with adultery. Such an accusation was the 'most severe injury' in the presence of children or servants.[68] The reputation of the mother and housekeeper had to be preserved. Another kind of severe injury happened if the husband wrote seriously insulting letters to

[65] *Jur. gén.* 1858, vol. xxxix, V° Séparation de corps, 916. A double standard was used too in England: Cornish and Clark, *Law and Society*, 380–96.

[66] Req. 14 June 1836, *Jur. gén.* 1858, vol. xxxix, V° Séparation de corps, 920.

[67] B. Schnapper, 'La Séparation de corps de 1837 à 1914: Essai de sociologie juridique', in id., *Voies nouvelles*, 449: more beaten wives than deceived wives obtained a separation, but judges had an unlimited authority about questions of fact.

[68] Metz, 7 May 1807, Bordeaux, 10 Apr. 1826, *Jur. gén.* 1858, vol. xxxix, V° Séparation de corps, 904.

his wife (or sometimes to another member of the family).[69] To use vocabulary that was not appropriate to married people wounded decency. According to judges, words as well as facts could constitute a severe injury. In the mid-nineteenth century, courts might order separation if the husband deserted his wife, refused to maintain her in the matrimonial home, or tolerated his wife being insulted by servants.[70] Public scandal and offences against good manners were decisive arguments; yet judges hesitated if a husband knowingly transmitted syphilis to his wife.[71]

In the early nineteenth century, case law took the social status of the married couple into account. For example, an injury which was considered serious for a high-society woman (supposed to be delicate and sensitive)[72] could be of no importance at a lower social level.[73] Almost always demanded by the woman (in more than 80 per cent of claims), judicial separation was an unusual remedy at this time. It was not reserved for the aristocracy and middle classes, but the costs involved made it very difficult for working women to contemplate.[74] However, this changed after the Legal Aid Act of 30 January 1851. Judgments of separation suddenly increased (from 1,000 each year in 1840, to 3,000 in 1868) and almost half of the petitions came from the working class.[75] In this field judges could satisfy a social need. Can this be taken as an indication that the judges were becoming more receptive towards the liberty of partners within marriage and the revolution in feelings disseminated by literature? It is more likely that they extended the rules created for the upper classes to the whole of society. In any case, this case law prepared the way for the restoration of divorce, which demonstrates that divorce law was not a class privilege.[76]

---

[69] Poitiers, 29 July 1806, Nîmes, 30 Apr. 1834, Poitiers, 13 Jan. 1843, ibid. 907.

[70] Aix, 28 Apr. 1843, Bordeaux, 5 Apr. 1848, Req. 19 Apr. 1825, ibid. 910–13.

[71] Some judges rejected this reason for separation: Toulouse, 30 Jan. 1821, Lyon, 4 Apr. 1818, ibid. 911.

[72] Toulouse, 30 Jan. 1821, Rouen, 30 Dec. 1840, Poitiers, 13 Jan. 1843, ibid. 907, 911, and 913.

[73] Bourges, 4 Jan. 1825 (about an ill-educated forester), ibid. 908.

[74] Schnapper, 'La Séparation', 500–2.

[75] Ibid. 496–502. At the same time in England, divorce was very difficult for the poor, but working women could obtain a separation from magistrates: Cornish and Clark, *Law and Society*, 391.

[76] C. S. Kselman, 'The Modernization of Family Law: the Politics and Ideology of Family Reform in Third Republic France', Ph.D. thesis (University of Michigan, 1980), 55–6.

In conclusion, it can be pointed out that case law concerning married women was settled in the early nineteenth century and did not change until the twentieth century. I suggest, as a hypothesis, that nineteenth-century French judges continued to believe in a family model based on middle-class marriage, which implied the inequality of the sexes and divided the roles accordingly.[77]

---

[77] A. M. Sohn, 'Les Rôles féminins dans la vie privée: Approche méthodologique et bilan de recherches', *Revue d'histoire moderne et contemporaine*, 28 (1981), 597–623. The opinion of some judges about the access of women to the bar in the late 19th century was significant: C. Fillon, 'La profession d'avocat et son image dans l'entre-deux-guerres', Ph.D. thesis (University of Lyon III, 1995), 329.

6

Legal Particularism and the Complexity of Women's Rights in Nineteenth-Century Germany

UTE GERHARD

Evaluating nineteenth-century German law from any perspective—in this case from a gender perspective—is difficult because before the introduction of the Civil Code in 1900, private law was multifaceted, complex, and fragmented into different legal sources, jurisdictions, and geographical regions which did not coincide with state boundaries. Comparative legal studies generally restrict themselves to comparing the major codifications, these being the Prussian General Code (*ALR*) of 1794, the French *Code civil* of 1804, and the Austrian General Civil Code of 1811 (*ABGB*).[1] Others deal mainly with the Prussian *ALR* as a pioneering example for German law.[2] But from this perspective German legal conditions might appear in too positive a light as rather favourable to women. Despite the importance of the Prussian code for the construction of civil law and its practice in Germany before the enactment of the Civil Code (*BGB*) in 1900, its multiplicity, complexity, and therefore uncertainty stand out. The particularism of small states, whose borders were constantly shifting and regimes changing, contributed to the fact that 'positive law' was splintered into individual laws and statutes, and based on various sources. Above all, legislation dealing with marriage and property rights was weighed down by local

---

[1] For example H. Conrad, 'Die Rechtsstellung der Ehefrau in der Privatrechtsgesetzgebung', in J. Engel and H. M. Klingenberg (eds.), *Aus Mittelalter und Neuzeit: Gerhard Kallen zum 70. Geburtstag* (Bonn, 1957), 253–70; H. Dörner, *Industrialisierung und Familienrecht: Die Auswirkungen des sozialen Wandels dargestellt an den Familienmodellen des ALR, BGB und des französischen Code civil* (Berlin, 1974); H. Coing (ed.), *Handbuch der Quellen und Literatur der neueren europäischen Privatrechtsgeschichte*, vol. iii, pts. 1 and 2 (Munich, 1982); M. Weber, *Ehefrau und Mutter in der Rechtsentwicklung: Eine Einführung* (1st pub. Tübingen, 1907; repr. Aalen, 1971).

[2] U. Gerhard, *Verhältnisse und Verhinderungen: Frauenarbeit, Familie und Rechte der Frauen im 19. Jahrhundert* (Frankfurt am Main, 1978); S. Weber-Will, *Die rechtliche Stellung der Frau im Privatrecht des Preußischen Allgemeinen Landrechts von 1794* (Frankfurt am Main, 1983).

statutes, customs, particularist privileges, and laws pertaining to traditional 'estates' (*Stände*). Not only did the chequered legal map make the preparation of the Civil Code (*BGB*) a national 'thankless work of detail'[3]—the 100 different legal systems of marital property regimes to be surveyed were often mentioned—but the lack of legal unity was ultimately construed as a failure of 'national culture'. Contemporaries experienced this as a lack of state legality, if not as legal insecurity.[4]

Until now in nearly all German states differing laws [concerning the legal state of German women] have existed, whose flexibility and old-fashioned phraseology lead to very different applications. Thus the intentions and understanding of individual judges determine how the law will be applied. This is one of the main reasons why to know the law remains such a challenge, not only for individual citizens but also for lawyers and even more so for us as women, wanting to achieve an overview.[5]

Louise Otto wrote this in her foreword to a petition published by the General German Women's Association in 1876. The petition had been addressed to the first preliminary commission for the new Civil Code (which had been meeting since 1874). This petition demanded that 'when changes are made to the civil code, women's rights, particularly relating to marriage and guardianship, should be taken into account'.[6]

Thus the legal landscape in Germany before 1900 is to be imagined as a multicoloured patchwork whose patterns were partially faded but none the less interwoven with each other. And as is usual for lawyers, those concerned saw the legal situation as controversial in itself. Often a preliminary procedure would be required to determine which legal system and which particular norms had to be applied. The plaintiff's place of residence was usually decisive. If marriage partners were involved, the husband's residence was relevant, creating legal conditions plaintiffs often experienced as arbitrary.[7]

[3] Franz Wieacker, *A History of Private Law in Europe, with Particular Reference to Germany*, trans. Tony Weir (Oxford, 1995), 373; German original, F. Wieacker, *Privatrechtsgeschichte der Neuzeit* (Göttingen, 1967), 473: 'entsagungsvollen Kleinarbeit.'
[4] See the quotations, cited by H. Coing, 'Einleitung', in J. v. Staudinger, *Kommentar zum Bürgerlichen Gesetzbuch* (12th edn., Berlin, 1980), RdNr. 19–22.
[5] L. Otto, Preliminary to *Einige deutsche Gesetzesparagraphen über die Stellung der Frau*, ed. Allgemeiner Deutscher Frauen-Verein (Leipzig, 1876), 3.
[6] Ibid.
[7] v. Staudinger, *Kommentar*, RdNr. 25.

This survey of the legal situation of women in nineteenth-century Germany is limited to the four most important legal regions according to an 1896 map of jurisdictions: 42.6 per cent of the population lived under the jurisdiction of the Prussian *ALR*;[8] 29.2 per cent were subjected to the Roman common law; 16.6 per cent were governed by French law (*Code civil*); and 10.9 per cent were under Saxon law (Saxon Civil Code of 1863).[9] Based on these main sources of 'law in action', this essay first gives a short overview of legal conditions with regard to women's rights. It goes on to deal with specific legal questions concerning women that were discussed in jurisprudence and jurisdiction, and finally, considers the role that the women's movement played in the struggle for equal rights in the Civil Code. Each of these three points would be worth an essay in itself, as a legal history of gender would have to deal with much more fundamental issues. The usual periodization in particular would have to be re-examined under a gender perspective.

Patchwork of women's rights

1. *The Prussian ALR*. In the early nineteenth century legal scholars tended to be extremely critical of the Prussian *ALR* of 1794, despite its status as a 'model for enlightened state planning' and the art of codification,[10] because it aimed to be exhaustive and it contained authoritative regulations which were intended to restrict the influence of judges and of jurisdiction. One of the most cited examples of a paternalistic type of rule was the directive on how long a mother was to breastfeed her child.[11] None the less, the 'spirit of well-meaning paternalism and nannying the subject',[12] intended 'to secure and promote the personal happiness of each citizen of the state',[13] benefited women. Indeed, some

---

[8] Without doubt this region was bigger at the end of the 19th century than at the beginning, when the *ALR* even in Prussia was implemented only subsidiarily. For the areas of application just before 1900 see E. Kempin, *Die Stellung der Frau nach den zur Zeit in Deutschland gültigen Gesetzesbestimmungen* (Leipzig, 1892), 9 f.

[9] v. Staudinger, *Kommentar*, RdNr. 24.

[10] R. Koselleck, *Preußen zwischen Reform und Revolution* (Stuttgart, 1975), 23 f.

[11] See II. 2, §§ 67 ff. Prussian *ALR*.

[12] Wieacker, *History of Private Law*, 264. German original, Wieacker, *Privatrechtsgeschichte*, 332: 'Grundstimmung wohlmeinender Gängelung und Beglückung des Untertanen.'

[13] 'Patent wegen Publication des neuen allgemeinen Gesetzbuches für die preußischen Staaten', in *Allgemeines Landrecht für die preußischen Staaten* (Berlin, 1794), 1.

regulations were so unreservedly favourable to women—for instance, according property rights to wives and granting unmarried mothers a claim to maintenance for the support of their illegitimate children—that an early commentator expressed his fear that the *ALR* would soon make Prussia a true paradise for women.[14]

In fact, the *ALR* fulfilled a transitional purpose. The influence of Enlightenment philosophy, in particular, of Christian Wolff's natural rights school, has often been noted.[15] Thus part I, title 1, § 24 of the *ALR* explicitly affirms that 'the rights of both sexes are the same'. Yet the principle of equality was manipulated to allow so many exceptions, especially in regard to marriage, that the result was often to privilege inequality. Christian Wolff and, after him, Johann G. Fichte in his *Theory of Natural Law*, in the chapter 'Deductions Concerning Marriage',[16] interpreted the freedom to enter contracts assigned to both sexes in favour of the man. In order to maintain the principle of equality it was supposed that the woman, through her 'freedom' to enter into a contract of marriage, 'had silently approved what custom brings'; however, custom meant 'male dominance', with the result that 'the woman ended up subordinate to the man'.[17] Despite the principle of equality, the *ALR* explicitly designated the male as 'the head of the conjugal union', 'with final decision-making power in marital affairs' (I. 1, § 184 *ALR*). The husband, for instance, dictated the place of residence as well as the family name and its status. And although a married woman was required to run the household, she could not engage in business or sign a labour contract without his permission, with the exception of a tradeswoman whose husband had agreed. Consequently, the man alone had the right of administration and usufruct of matrimonial property. Yet the wife remained at least in part free to sign business contracts and acquire goods in order to facilitate the smooth functioning of her household (known as the 'power of the keys'). Only if her prop-

[14] J. G. Schlosser, *Briefe über die Gesetzgebung überhaupt und den Entwurf des preußischen Gesetzbuchs insbesondere* (1st pub. 1789; repr. Glashütten, 1970), 279.

[15] See Conrad, 'Die Rechtsstellung der Ehefrau', 260.

[16] J. G. Fichte, *Grundlage des Naturrechts nach Prinzipien der Wissenschaftslehre* (1st pub. 1796; Hamburg, 1960), 298 ff.

[17] C. Wolff, *Grundzüge des Natur- und Völkerrechts, worin alle Verbindlichkeiten und alle Rechte aus der Natur des Menschen in einem beständigen Zusammenhang hergeleitet werden können* (1st pub. 1754; Meisenheim, 1980), 638.

erty was explicitly recognized through addenda to the marital contract as 'reserved property' was she recognized as an independent legal subject in respect of that property. This extraordinary concession, in particular, was the reason for the description of the Prussian *ALR* as favourable to women.

2. *The Roman common law.* The Roman common law, which had grown out of multiple receptions of Roman law in Germany, was treated as customary law and was invoked whenever specific legislation had not explicitly replaced it. Thus the 'common German private law' was a mixture of layers of Roman law and Germanic legal traditions, dividing jurisprudence into two camps, Germanic and Roman, depending on which historical legitimization was given preference. However, it is remarkable that the common law of marriage preserved some provisions favourable to women. The only exceptions were the rights of parents and children. Because of the father's patriarchal rights, even relating to custody, women's parental rights were wholly denied.

By comparison with the other laws in force, Roman common law, because of the way in which it regulated marital property, appears astonishingly liberal, especially in the sense that it conferred legal capacity to own or alienate property, as it can be said that the individual is 'free inasmuch as he is proprietor of his person and capacities'.[18] In marriage law, the Roman legal influence on female status proved favourable to women, because in the late Roman 'free union', marriage had no impact on the legal status and the property relations of the spouses.[19] A peculiarity of Roman marriage law was the dowry system, by which the woman fulfilled her obligation to shoulder 'conjugal burdens' by paying a dowry which was transferred to the man's property, although it was to be paid back in case of divorce or the husband's death. Apart from these regulations concerning the dowry, separation of property was the rule, so that the married woman, like the unmarried, could enter into contracts, administer her fortune independently, and work outside the household. An opinion penned by Georg Puchta, denouncing his colleagues' 'vain attempts to cite Roman law in support of enforcing performance of the

[18] C. B. Macpherson, *The Political Theory of Possessive Individualism: Hobbes to Locke* (Oxford, 1964), 3.
[19] See J. F. L. Göschen, *Vorlesungen über das gemeine Recht* (Göttingen, 1839), iii. 38–41; see also G. Puchta, *Pandekten* (8th edn., Leipzig, 1856), 586.

wife's household duties',[20] appears to be remarkably free of prejudice.

And yet, rights so comparatively favourable to women[21] were in many ways being transformed to favour men by local and customary deviations from common law principles. This occurred not only where Roman law applied subsidiarily, but also where it applied directly. For instance, in the Hanseatic city-states[22]—Lübeck's statutes were typical—a traditional regime of community of property was in operation. This allowed the businessman husband speedy access to his wife's property even without her consent. Another indication of the very close connection between law and social needs that shaped the 'reality of law' can be seen in the different marital property regimes under common law in Hesse, where the Roman dowry system held sway for 'the nobility, the well-educated, and government employees', while for the petty bourgeoisie and the peasants a special form of community of property was usual, which applied only to the property acquired during marriage.[23] This came close to what nowadays is called a 'community of surplus'.

3. *Saxon law*. Saxon law, whose scope included the kingdom of Saxony as well as Thüringia and Schleswig-Holstein (which belonged to Prussia), retained Germanic legal traditions in their purest form. Its principal sources were medieval legal texts, especially the legal code known as the *Sachsenspiegel*.[24] The Saxon Civil Code of 1863, passed in the teeth of mounting pressure for legal and political unification of Germany, represented a determined effort to replace the law developed by academics with state-derived legislation.[25] Marriage laws were a characteristic feature of the Saxon legal tradition which seemed to be totally unaffected

---

[20] Puchta, *Pandekten*, 586.

[21] This was why in their legal rights campaigns the organizations of the women's movement argued for the marital property system of the Roman common law. See *Schriften des Bundes deutscher Frauenvereine, Petition und Begleitschrift betreffend das Familienrecht* (Leipzig, n.d. [1895]).

[22] Among the countries under Roman common law we find many of the former independent city-states such as Lübeck, Bremen, Hamburg, and Frankfurt, but also Brunswick, Hanover, Hesse, Württemberg, and the duchy of Oldenburg.

[23] See Otto, *Gesetzesparagraphen*, 17.

[24] See C. G. Haubold, *Lehrbuch des Königlich-Sächsischen Privat-Rechts* (3rd edn., Leipzig, 1847), 1, § 7.

[25] Cf. Wieacker, *History of Private Law*, 363; German original: *Privatrechtsgeschichte*, 459.

by any natural law or Enlightenment thinking.[26] In the Saxon Civil Code, traditional and unmodified patriarchy ruled, placing the married woman under male tutelage. In other words, without her husband's 'support' a married woman could not appear before a court of law. Nor could she act without his permission in business dealings, except those 'in which she merely acquired goods' (§ 1640 of Saxon Civil Code). This meant that Saxon law preserved in its purity the Germanic institution of gender tutelage that did not wholly deny to women all possibility of entering into contracts, but limited them to the status of minors. The man's privileges, however, which were justified in terms of women's need for protection because of 'their ignorance and weakness', in reality preserved male access to property and women's labour power.[27] In 1838 when this legal concept of gender tutelage was recognized as antiquated by bourgeois public opinion and abolished by statute for single women, it was expressly confirmed for married women in the form of marital guardianship.[28] In order to prevent any doubt arising concerning male dominance, the lawmakers in 1863 confirmed in § 1634 of the new Saxon Civil Code that: 'The husband has the right to his wife's obedience, including housekeeping services and professional assistance'. This 'marital dominance' or 'guardianship in marriage' corresponded to a property law which permitted the woman to own property, but in all cases transferred to the husband the right to manage and enjoy the fruits of the wife's property.

4. *French Code civil.* During Napoleonic hegemony the French *Code civil* was in force in many parts of Germany, mainly on the left bank of the Rhine (in Rhineland and the Pfalz), but also in the kingdom of Westphalia and the grand duchy of Berg, in Frankfurt as well as Aremberg and Anhalt-Köthen, two tiny states whose rulers admired Napoleon. In the grand duchy of Baden, the *Code civil* of 1810, in German translation and with

---

[26] S. Buchholz, 'Deutschland, Einzelgesetzgebung', in Coing (ed.), *Handbuch*, vol. iii, pt. 2, 1626–773, 1639.

[27] For gender tutelage see Wilhelm T. Kraut, *Die Vormundschaft nach den Grundsätzen des gemeinen deutschen Rechts*, 3 vols. (Göttingen, 1835, 1847, 1859), vol. ii (1847), 267 f., 320; Ute Gerhard, *Gleichheit ohne Angleichung: Frauen im Recht* (Munich, 1990), 142 f.

[28] See Haubold, *Lehrbuch*, § 153 and § 154. Cf. also the 1st edn. (Leipzig, 1820).

modifications and addenda, was pronounced the 'General Law of Baden'.[29] It remained in force there, as well as in the Prussian Rhine Province, and in Berg until 1900.[30] It is interesting to note exactly which aspects of this foreign law had to be adapted, in particular with regard to marriage and property law, 'given their deep meaning for civil life'.[31]

Given the pre-modern and particularistic legal conditions in the countries surrounding France, the Code civil, dating from 1804, which first introduced liberal principles into private law, appeared quite splendid, especially because of its unifying, systematic, and clearly formulated regulations. Thus the French Code civil was generally viewed as the 'chef d'œuvre of the art of legislation'.[32] Its unity and systematic approach, its clarity of diction and linguistic elegance were generally admired. To support this view, Stendhal, who was said to have begun each writing day by reading the Code civil 'to get the tone', would be constantly invoked.[33] The paragraph Stendhal referred to as an illustration was the one in which the full contradictions in bourgeois women's legal rights are reflected, article 213. Until 1938 it read: 'The man owes his wife protection; the wife owes her husband obedience.'

In comparative legal-historical perspective the Code civil was renowned for its contradictions concerning women's rights and its rigid patriarchalism. According to French law the wife was able to own property, but she had no legal capacity to manage it. Thus, in contrast to Roman common law or the Prussian ALR, which at least allowed her to enter into legally advantageous business relationships, under the French Code civil married women were subjugated absolutely to the man and in each individual case needed the husband's permission to enter into contracts. Nor could a married woman turn to a court of law—not even as a

---

[29] W. Andreas, 'Die Einführung des Code Napoléon in Baden', Zeitschrift der Savigny-Stiftung für Rechtsgeschichte, Germanist. Abt., 31 (1910), 182–234; E. Fehrenbach, Traditionale Gesellschaft und revolutionäres Recht (Göttingen, 1978), 26; E. Fehrenbach, Der Kampf um die Einführung des Code Napoléon in den Rheinbundstaaten (Wiesbaden, 1973), 9 and 15.

[30] See Wieacker, History of Private Law, 272, 274 f.; German original, Privatrechtsgeschichte, 342, 345 f.

[31] J. N. F. Brauer, quoted in Andreas, 'Einführung', 223; see J. N. F. Brauer, Erläuterungen über den Code Napoléon und die Großherzoglich Badische bürgerliche Gesetzgebung, 6 vols. (Karlsruhe, 1809–12).

[32] E. Holthöfer, 'Frankreich', in Coing (ed.), Handbuch, vol. iii, pt. 1, 863–1068, 884.

[33] See M. Ferid, Das französische Zivilrecht (Frankfurt am Main, 1971), vol. i, RdNr. 1 A 50, n. 76.

tradeswoman—and even if separation of property had been agreed upon, she could neither give away, sell, nor acquire anything without her husband's authorization (arts. 215 to 217 *CC*). As liberal as the code may have appeared in terms of property rights, giving spouses a choice between various regimes of matrimonial property and respecting the principle of contractual freedom, it none the less expressly forbade any contractual opting-out or renunciation of the husband's authority (art. 1388 *CC*). As Ernst Holthöfer comments on the French law and its unequal legal relations governing women: 'freedom and equality went only as far as the *pater familias*.' As Holthöfer puts it, 'within the family the monarchical principle reigned as *royaute domestique*'.[34] This assessment agrees with a devastating criticism made by Marianne Weber in her 1907 history of women's and mothers' rights, which is still worth reading today. She held that with regard to women, the Napoleonic Code was essentially a systematization of customary law of the French Middle Ages. She argued that, like other codifications of that time, it prolonged 'those medieval statutes which preserved medieval patriarchalism in all its purity and longevity'.[35]

In sum, although they guaranteed property rights, the liberal and bourgeois statutes concerning marriage and gender relations in the nineteenth century retained the principle of dominance and hierarchy. They secured this principle at two levels: by requiring the woman's obedience and subordination to the husband's 'right of command', and by her economic dependence, anchored in the husband's right to administer her property and the earnings of her work. Emma Oekinghaus, one of the first German female sociologists of law, analysed the structural principles of patriarchal law in Weberian terms. Following Max Weber's typology of different forms of domination, she characterized patriarchy as a system in which the 'dominance of the *pater familias*' is secured under the pretence of protection and 'by confiscating the fortune and the labour force of women'.[36]

---

[34] Holthöfer, 'Frankreich', 906.
[35] Weber, *Ehefrau und Mutter*, 318 f.
[36] E. Oekinghaus, *Die gesellschaftliche und rechtliche Stellung der deutschen Frau* (Jena, 1925), 7 f.; see also E. Manheim, 'Beiträge zu einer Geschichte der autoritären Familie', in Ernst Fromm et al., *Studien über Autorität und Familie* (Paris, 1936), ii. 523 ff.; M. Weber, *Wirtschaft und Gesellschaft*, ed. J. Winckelmann (5th rev. edn., Tübingen, 1976), 133 f., 580 ff.

*Specific legal questions: examples of jurisprudence
and judicial decisions*

The multiplicity and complexity of legal systems meant that nineteenth-century jurisprudence was of extreme practical importance before the passing of the German Civil Code. The historical school of law, in its programme for renewing jurisprudence as a science of positive law,[37] aimed to 'consolidate the entire field of German law in its historical and scientific context',[38] in order to systematize the Latin and Germanic sources, the various receptions of Roman common law, and particularist and national law. Yet the law regarding women was to a large extent excluded from these efforts of systematization, or else, as pre-modern law, subsumed under the heading of 'a special case'.

Carl F. v. Gerber's standard textbook, *System des deutschen Privatrechts* (system of German private law), which went through numerous editions, is a prime example of this inconsistency. In his introduction Gerber complained about the imperfection of German law because of its lack of legal abstraction, the limitations it placed on 'free will', and the multiplicity of 'exceptional circumstances' it recognized. Yet with regard to women he himself defended the restrictions placed on them by reference to the 'influence of particular circumstances on the legal relations between persons'; he called these 'natural circumstances'. Undermining his own claim to be systematizing and abstracting from specific circumstances, he explained in § 222: 'I suppose that the special character of parental custody, the father's rights, the marital relations and the superiority of the male in today's legal system are derived for the most part from that deeper attitude toward the family and that special moral power with which the German folk spirit infuses that natural bond.'[39]

Gerber was not alone in making so open a claim for the superiority of the man in the household. On the contrary, he stands for an entire branch of Germanists and legal traditionalists offering opinions about family law. Again and again, the 'attitude

---

[37] Wieacker, *History of Private Law*, 283: 'context of a renewal of the study of positive law'; German original, Wieacker, *Privatrechtsgeschichte*, 353: 'Programm einer Erneuerung der Wissenschaft vom *positiven* Recht.'

[38] K. F. Eichhorn, *Einleitung in das deutsche Privatrecht mit Einschluß des Lehensrechts* (5th edn., Göttingen, 1845), p. vii.

[39] C. F. v. Gerber, *System des deutschen Privatrechts* (Jena, 1863), 81 f. and 573.

toward marriage so characteristic of our people' will be used to justify systematic contradiction. Thus in his *System des gemeinen deutschen Privatrechts* (system of common German private law), first published 1847, Georg Beseler writes: 'the marital union not only constitutes a legal person in the technical meaning of the word, but also a legal community, a union of the utmost solidity . . . German marriage law achieves its aim in that in most relations it recognizes *equality of marriage partners* while at the same time leaving room for *male predominance*.'[40]

Equality of marriage partners to be compatible with the husband's predominance—the contradiction could hardly be expressed more clearly. But the main area of dispute and lawsuits in the nineteenth century concerned with women's legal rights was not dominance or power of decision, but marital property. Courts rarely addressed the question of a wife's legal capacity as a matter of principle, but most often in relation to property disputes. Even the *Reichsgericht*, the Supreme Court of the German Reich, used contradictory arguments in cases brought before it, never attempting to harmonize the differing legal systems in force in Germany until 1900. Christiana Damm explains this reluctance by suggesting that 'ironing out the contradictions might well have worked to women's advantage, a consequence which this court wished to avoid at all costs'.[41] A few examples will be chosen from Damm's analysis of the *Reichsgericht*'s judgments to illustrate the contradictory legal background as well as the pervasive patriarchal leitmotif in lawyers' arguments. Many examples could be drawn from legal arguments concerning the 'power of the keys' or the position of women as mothers, especially unmarried mothers. However, this essay will deal only with a few basic decisions concerning the 'action to restore conjugal life' (*Klage auf Herstellung des ehelichen Lebens*), and the 'legal capacity to contract'.

At the beginning of a jurisdiction for the whole of the German Empire in 1871 quite a large number of court cases already addressed the question of whether the wife was constrained to share her husband's place of residence. The female plaintiffs objected that the husband lacked adequate accommodation, or was living with relatives, or in one particular case that he lived in

[40] G. Beseler, *System des gemeinen deutschen Privatrechts* (1st pub. 1847; Berlin, 1873), 480–1.

[41] C. Damm, *Die Stellung der Ehefrau und Mutter nach Urteilen des Reichsgerichts von 1879 bis 1914*, dissertation (Marburg, 1983), 37 and 46.

the same house as his adulterous lover. Judgments handed down all appealed to Roman common law,[42] and to those unwritten rules concerning the right to bring a suit which remained in force even after the Civil Code was introduced.[43] Although Roman common law was outstanding, as we have seen, for its lack of influence on the wife's legal status, the courts usually allowed specific actions to restore conjugal life, and in their judgments generally found that the wife was obliged to be obedient and to follow her husband regarding place of residence and other marital duties. The arguments in this context are revealing. In no case were the woman's objections accepted, despite solid reasons why it was impossible for her to carry out her marital obligations. Instead, the *Reichsgericht*'s decisions were likely to read: 'Judgment is based . . . on the unconditional right of the husband to have his wife reside with him, and his complaint rests on the fact that she refuses.'[44] Thus, the burden of evidence was shifted to the wife. How unprotected her legal situation then became, and how difficult it was for her to separate from her husband, became clear in a case in 1881, in which the wife objected 'that she had to put up with continual abuse by her husband' (*RGZ*, vi. 149). The Bavarian Higher Regional Court had refused to hear this case, arguing that the abuse was 'not severe enough', but lay within the legal punitive rights of the husband which no court had the authority to limit so long as no lasting damage to health resulted. Basing the judgment on the Bavarian Civil Code (I. VI, § 12 nos. 2 and 3), the arguments read as follows: 'In particular, since the husband is respected as the head of the household, his wife has to submit not only with regard to domestic affairs but is also constrained to exercise the usual and customary personal and housewifely duties, toward which end she can be coerced by her husband and, when necessary, chastised with moderation.'[45] None the less, the *Reichsgericht* overruled this decision of the Bavarian court and, with great care, suggested that 'particularly grievous maltreatment . . . on the part of the man can give the wife the right to refuse to return to the conjugal home'.[46] But the

---

[42] *Entscheidungen des Reichsgerichts in Zivilsachen (RGZ)*, v. 166 f.; *RGZ* xv. 188 f.; *RGZ* xxiii. 162 f.; see Damm, *Stellung der Ehefrau*, 3 f.

[43] *RGZ* li. 182; quoted by Damm, *Stellung der Ehefrau*, 17.

[44] *RGZ* xxiii. 163; quoted by Damm, *Stellung der Ehefrau*, 10.

[45] Bavarian Higher Regional Court, v. 146, quoted by Damm, *Stellung der Ehefrau*, 15.

[46] *RGZ* vi. 149, quoted by Damm, *Stellung der Ehefrau*, 12.

degree of maltreatment a wife had to accept from her husband was not specified.

The decisions of the *Reichsgericht* concerning women's property rights show that the same court, given the same facts, could produce different results based on the differing systems of law in Germany before 1900. This patchwork of laws could already have been replaced by a uniform rule potentially to be derived from § 102 of a special law of guardianship dating from 1875.[47] But this paragraph was not applied by the courts with respect to married women. Instead the courts continued to apply family law according to the various systems in force. Cases continually came to court in which spouses, sometimes with a third party, initiated suits to determine whether the wife was entitled to administer her marital property to her own advantage. As a basic principle, the *Reichsgericht* found that the special law of guardianship mentioned above did not apply to marital law and hence did not affect the husband's relation to his wife's property, since 'marital guardianship remains to this day characterized by the husband's prerogative, his right to dispose of the person and property of the wife'.[48]

None the less, in a decision based on Roman common law the same court affirmed that marriage had no influence on the status of either spouse in relation to their own property. Thus, in principle, the right of the wife to manage and administer her property could not be limited, only her right to dispose of it. Yet in this case the husband was excused from responsibility for covering her debts out of his marital property. In this particular case, the creditor was able to retrieve what was owed to him from the wife's dowry after its return to her upon dissolution of the marriage.[49]

The decision in a case dealt with under the rules of the *ALR* was more explicit. Here the issue of the wife's legal capacity was linked to the regime of marital property which had been chosen. Only in regard to reserved property could she be held legally responsible (II. 1, §§ 206, 221 ff. *ALR*). By contrast, the husband in general had the right to administer and use marital property (II. 1, § 320 *ALR*) as an 'effect of the personal predominance of the

---

[47] 'Vormundschaftsverordnung vom 5. Juli 1875', *Gesetz-Sammlung für die königlichen preußischen Staaten* (1875), 431–54, 454.

[48] *RGZ* xvi. 149 f.; see Damm, *Stellung der Ehefrau*, 27, 33, 34.

[49] See Damm, *Stellung der Ehefrau*, 37 f.

husband over the wife'.[50] For this reason, the *Reichsgericht* decided
time and again that all contracts signed by the wife without her
husband's permission were invalid (except where the power of the
keys and emergency administration were invoked).[51]

Even more striking is a decision concerning the jurisdiction
of the French *Code civil* in which the court stubbornly and unreservedly defended the husband's interests. According to French
law, the wife had property rights but was completely disenfran-
chised when it came to managing property or signing contracts,
except in individual cases 'authorized' by the husband. Thus, in
its 1889 decision the *Reichsgericht* issued the following judgment:
'The legal empowerment [of the woman] . . . must be applied to
each individual contract. Male predominance can only be assured
if in each case the husband conscientiously determines whether a
particular action serves the couple's interests.'[52]

The drafting commissions of the German Civil Code (*BGB*)
explicitly acknowledged in their justifications attached to the
relevant paragraphs that the couple's interests were identical to
the husband's, and that they should remain so. They continually
emphasized that in all matters concerning marital property,
its administration, and usufruct, priority should be given to the
husband. In fact, although the draftsmen of the code had more
than 100 legal and customary property relations from which to
choose, they selected solutions which privileged the husband as
the legal and usual administrator of marital property, quite openly,
in order 'to protect the interests of the man'.[53]

The struggle for rights in the first women's movement: a 'militia' against the Civil Code (BGB)

'Women learn to bear the burden of the law, they don't learn
law,' remarked Louise Otto, organizer of the first German women's
movement, toward the end of a long struggle for women's rights.[54]

---

[50] See Weber, *Ehefrau und Mutter*, 333.   [51] See Damm, *Stellung der Ehefrau*, 43 f.
[52] *RGZ* xxiv. 341, quoted by Damm, *Stellung der Ehefrau*, 54.
[53] See B. Mugdan, *Die gesamten Materialien zum Bürgerlichen Gesetzbuch für das deutsche Reich*, iv: *Familienrecht* (Berlin, 1899), 225, and Damm, *Stellung der Ehefrau*, 24.
[54] L. Otto-Peters, *Das erste Vierteljahrhundert des Allgemeinen Deutschen Frauenvereins* (Leipzig, 1890), 64.

The petition already mentioned above, prepared by the General German Women's Association (founded 1865), was inspired by Charlotte Pape's 1875 lecture on the occasion of a 'women's conference' in Gotha. Pape considered 'the rights of the mother to custody of her children' and described in detail a case in which a court had condemned a mother, after a divorce in which she was the innocent party, to release all six of her children into their father's custody. By depriving the mother of all rights in the raising of her children, this decision ignited the women's rage and strengthened the resolution of the General German Women's Association to work out a petition in order 'to emphasize in discussions of the women's question not only educational and professional rights, but also the question of rights in general, in order to highlight the demands of justice before the law'.[55] The association's newsletter, *Neue Bahnen*, then asked repeatedly for readers, women's organizations, and practising attorneys to share information on the legal status of women in the various German states. The call evoked an unexpected response. 'The evidence of female martyrdom was vast enough to fill several tomes,' Louise Otto wrote in the foreword to the petition, yet her 'feminine feeling of delicacy resisted exposing an unhappy marriage and family life given the women correspondents' fear and terror of provoking their estranged husbands' ire and revenge'.[56]

For today's legal scholars of women's history, the suppression of this evidence is regrettable. What legal historical material might we have had! Instead the General German Women's Association restricted itself to a rather sober compilation of legal regulations in force in Germany at that time concerning marriage and guardianship rules that governed women's lives. However, there proved to be great demand for this compilation, and it was already in its second edition in 1892, when it served as the basis for the campaign for rights initiated in the 1890s.[57] Literally at the last minute, between the first and third readings of the Civil Code Bill, a much mocked but striking movement succeeded in mobilizing a women's militia (the *Frauenlandsturm*) against the proposed version of marriage and family law. In numerous information

[55] Otto, *Gesetzesparagraphen*, 2.   [56] Ibid. 3.
[57] E. Kempin, *Die Stellung der Frau nach den zur Zeit gültigen Gesetzesbestimmungen sowie nach dem Entwurf eines Bürgerlichen Gesetzbuches für das deutsche Reich: Herausgegeben im Auftrag des Allgemeinen Deutschen Frauenvereins* (Leipzig, 1892).

brochures and propaganda leaflets distributed to members of the
Reichstag and the *Reichsrat*, the women's association subjected the
1895 bill to a detailed critique and made their wishes clear. 'What
had been up to that point handled in a highly theoretical and
abstract way was now, thanks to the women's mobilization and
input, dealt with precisely and concretely, becoming a question of
contemporary importance.'[58]

The major points of criticism, explaining women's unanimous
opposition to the bill, were first, that the legal guardianship of the
wife and mother implied in the man's right to decide in 'all matters
affecting the communal life of the couple' was continued (§ 1354
BGB). The second criticism was that even the newly won right
of women to enter into business and labour contracts, attributed
to the changed economic conditions, would only be of limited
significance because the man's right to 'end his wife's labour contract without giving any notice' was affirmed (§ 1358 *BGB*). Third,
women objected to the expropriation of women by means of
a marital property law replacing the myriad different statutes
valid in the nineteenth century, granting the husband exclusive
rights to manage marital property by means of the so-called
administration and usufruct regulations. The fourth point was that
although 'parental authority' was the term used, with regard to
children in reality it meant only the authority of the father. (This
regulation confirming paternal authority managed to survive
even the equal rights legislation in 1953. Not until 1959 did the
West German Supreme Court declare it unconstitutional.) Fifth,
the women protested against the new regulation governing the
status of illegitimate children, which in their opinion sanctioned
the 'outmoded double standard' and 'made a mockery of all
humane feeling'. The innovation in the Civil Code made the
status of unmarried mothers and their children worse by comparison not only with the Prussian *ALR*, but also with Saxon law,
by introducing the *exceptio plurium*, that is, a defence which men
could bring forward in paternity actions: any unmarried father
could avoid paying child support by suggesting the possibility of

[58] M. Stritt, *Das Bürgerliche Gesetzbuch und die Frauenfrage* (Hamburg, 1898), 4; see also M.
Stritt, 'Die Agitation der deutschen Frauenbewegung gegen das Familienrecht im Entwurf
des Bürgerlichen Gesetzbuches', in H. Lange and G. Bäumer (eds.), *Handbuch der Frauenbewegung* (Berlin, 1901), ii. 134 f.; for the context see U. Gerhard, *Unerhört: Die Geschichte der
deutschen Frauenbewegung* (Reinbek, 1990).

multiple sexual partners. And finally, the women sharply criticized the limitation of grounds for divorce for 'moral' reasons, because at that time, too, most divorces were sought by the wife.

Yet so much activity on the part of the women's movement amounted almost to nothing. With the exception of a few small concessions, such as allowing women to be their children's guardians, family law as part IV of the Civil Code was passed despite the opposition of the Social Democratic Party. Leaders of the women's movement commented on the debate in the *Reichstag*: 'An entire day of very stormy negotiations, reserved for consultation on family law, was instead devoted to the noteworthy "rabbit debate" concerning reparations for unexpected damage caused by hunters . . . whereas the discussion of family law and the most important questions governing the lives of half the population had to wait another two days and then were dealt with very superficially, with the usual emphasis on "ideal situations", the "God-given order of things" . . . and accompanied by the usual exaggerated "silliness".'[59]

None the less, legal and historical studies celebrate the German Civil Code of 1900 as a 'manifesto of bourgeois legal culture' which gave 'the German nation not only formal standardization of private legal relations but also justice and well-being'.[60] In reality, however, all the progressive legislation concerning women in today's Civil Code, and the major reforms of family law from 1953–7 and 1977, are no more than instalments of what the women's movement had claimed at the turn of the century.

More questions than conclusions

The question still is whether the contradictions between the principles of equality and autonomy, and the legal and social inequality between husbands and wives, are to be characterized only as a lack of modernity, a matter of a time-lag, or whether a gender hierarchy should be seen as a constitutive and indispensable element of modern society. If the latter is true, then perhaps only in a post-modern society can equality of rights for women be enforced. But this assessment of the significance of private law

[59] Stritt, 'Agitation', 145.
[60] R. Huber, *Deutsche Verfassungsgeschichte* (2nd edn., Stuttgart, 1982), iv. 275.

would be too negative and one-sided. The legal reforms and general laws, based on the principles and promises of liberty and equality, were a fundamental precondition for equal participation and equal citizenship. This presupposed a recognition of equality despite physical or other differences.

Family and marriage law continues to be a basis of the public/private dichotomy which structures modern societies and forms the core of liberal political theory. Since the French Revolution family policy has been at the heart of liberal state policies, the so-called crisis of the family having always been a public matter. Although in civil societies privacy, that is, the family, has been appreciated and defended as a realm of freedom against the state, to the present day the state has maintained a deep interest in family law and a particular order of the family which maintains hierarchical relationships. It would be too simple to explain this interference in terms only of a coalition or even complicity between legislators, politicians, civil servants, and men as husbands and fathers. Yet despite women's formal equality, family law has not yet solved the problems associated with women's participation in the public realm and the division of labour within the family.

Thus, once again, the social history of family law reveals the dialectical character of the law. For laws do not only reflect a social reality and its power relations, nor is the law only an instrument of oppression. In modern times it also functions as a means of social reform and liberation. Like other social movements, the women's movement has played a significant role in drawing attention to experiences of injustice and changing the law in favour of increased freedom and equality of both men and women. But because the law is two-sided in that it is an instrument of oppression as well as liberation, it has the potential to change unjust conditions. That is why it is so important to look at the law in both past and present.

7

A Moving Target

Class, Gender, and Family Law in the Nineteenth-Century United States

Lawrence M. Friedman

When one thinks of 'social inequality', particularly in the industrial age, what comes to mind most obviously is the gap between rich and poor, between workers and bosses. Certainly, these inequalities were vitally important in society; and were at the root of a good deal of social unrest in the nineteenth and twentieth centuries.

But there are other forms of social inequality—inequality that cuts across income and class lines. There are, for example, social inequalities within institutions or in certain settings—inequalities between students and teachers, for example, in schools or universities, even if both groups come from the same social class. More to our particular point, within families, children, women, the mentally ill, and the very old have historically been disadvantaged. It was adult men in the prime of life who acted as 'heads' of family, in terms of power and assets or access to assets and power. These forms of inequality—family and institutional—have become more salient in the contemporary world, to the point, perhaps, where they almost overshadow the classic inequalities of wealth and power. The nineteenth century, for example, would not have understood the very concept of 'student rights'. And some aspects of modern feminism would have bewildered and horrified the leading minds of the time.

This essay is about family law; how family law evolved in the nineteenth and twentieth centuries and how that evolution reflected what was happening in the larger society. At the beginning of the nineteenth century—more or less our starting point—men were (as far as family law was concerned) definitely in the

I want to thank Teresa Derichsweiler and Stanley Mallison for their help with the research on this essay.

saddle. When a man married, he scooped into his legal power all of his wife's property—all of it, that is, that was not somehow buttoned down through trusts or otherwise—and from then on, during the marriage, the power and the title were his. The husband and wife, in Blackstone's famous phrase, were 'one person in law: that is, the very being or legal existence of the woman is suspended during the marriage'.[1] The husband was, in law and social fact, the ruler of the little family kingdom. Divorce was rare and difficult (in England, virtually impossible).[2] But if the marriage should dissolve, the husband had the right to custody of his children. This, at any rate, is the state of the law as far as treatises were concerned, and it is also the doctrine enunciated in the (scanty) case law.

A century later, the law looked very different. Married women in America had gained full property rights. In custody cases, fathers were no longer granted a strong preference. Rather, custody followed the 'best interests' of the child and that meant, for younger children at least, that they belonged in the tender, loving arms of their mothers. Divorce had become quite common—not by today's standards, to be sure, but common enough to alarm respectable people in, say, 1900. Most divorces were granted to women. Divorce was not easy to get, again by today's standards; but compared to a century before, it was simple, plastic, and routine.

How can we explain these shifts in legal doctrine? If we look only at doctrine itself, the changes are simply incoherent. The study of doctrine in isolation is inherently static. At any given point in time, a good jurist can expound doctrine in such a way as to force it to make sense. But a given state of doctrine is like the price of a stock on the stock exchange: it can change in either direction, or stay as it is, but whether it will go up or down or sideways or in some other direction is impossible to predict or explain.

Any sensible legal history, then, will avoid explaining doctrine in terms of other doctrine. Legal history cannot account for change or evolution or destruction of doctrine through appealing to some sort of inherent logic in the prior state of the rules. One classical form of doctrinal analysis, which should be dead but

---

[1] William Blackstone, *Commentaries on the Law of England* (Oxford, 1765), bk. 1, ch. 15.

[2] That is, divorce in the modern sense: legal separation ('divorce from bed and board') existed, and so too did annulment.

probably is not, did in fact assume a kind of evolutionary progress in the law; we simply became smarter and smarter, or more and more civilized, or more and more modern, as the years went by; and doctrine was reformed accordingly.

No serious historian, I hope, adheres to this mode of writing legal history; some fossils probably linger on in the law schools. The plain fact is this: doctrines do not grow, like plants or animals. People in society make them, for some good and sufficient reason; and then unmake or remake them. One job of the legal historian is to look for these reasons; and for some social principles to explain evolution and change.

Legal historians have, for example, been much concerned with changing conceptions of the family, such as shifting gender roles, and have sought explanations of doctrinal change in terms of the evolution, not of legal concepts, but of concepts of family and gender. One prominent figure among legal historians is Michael Grossberg, who published a history of nineteenth-century American family law. The colonial (American) household, according to Grossberg, had been 'hierarchical' and 'patriarchal'. Women and children were 'subordinates and dependents' both in the family and in the community'.[3] In the nineteenth century, a new and more 'republican' family developed. Male authority remained 'supreme', but its scope narrowed. 'Egalitarianism encouraged the decline of deference to all social superiors, even patriarchs.' Self-government 'intensified intimate relations and encouraged greater reciprocity. Finally, affection began to replace status as the cement of domestic bonds.' Marriage became more 'contractual'; home became a woman's sphere and domain.[4]

This account certainly makes a good deal of sense; but seems (to me at least) to be somewhat incomplete. Incomplete because it places too much emphasis on *conceptions* of the family, and leaves out the actual, living issues that agitated legislatures and litigants. If we make the primitive but plausible assumption that concrete problems dictate the legislative agenda, and that men and women sue each other not for intellectual exercise but to get control of something they value, then we must broaden the account somewhat.

[3] Michael Grossberg, *Governing the Hearth: Law and the Family in Nineteenth-Century America* (Chapel Hill, NC, 1985), 5.
[4] Ibid. 7.

This is not to say that changing conceptions of the family do not play a role in the story; they most certainly do. A truly patriarchal family, with truly subservient wives, would generate no statutes and lawsuits. The family in the nineteenth century was most definitely evolving. This evolution laid the basis for a new legal dynamic. Still, we have to analyse legal changes in terms of who stands to gain or to lose—whose ox, in short, is gored.

The simple research methodology one follows, then, is not the same as the methodology one would use to ferret out changing 'conceptions' of the family. That is, we cannot merely look at learned treatises, and at the doctrines expressed in case law. We have to look at trial court cases (if we can), or at the very least, at the facts of the appellate cases. We do this to see (for example) *who* was suing, and for what, and what the cases seemed actually to be about. When we do this, we might find that some aspects both of gender and class come rather strikingly to the foreground. I will begin with some remarks about child custody.

Custody. Here the decisional progression seems quite clear-cut. Originally, American law, according to Grossberg, 'granted fathers an almost unlimited right to the custody of their minor children'.[5] This was, of course, the English rule as well—indeed, the English rule was the source of the (official) American rule.[6] In the course of the nineteenth century, however, this right softened, as we have mentioned, and was replaced by a new standard: the child's 'best interests'. This was to be the guiding star of any custody decision; and in practice, it meant a definite tilt toward the rights of the mother.

The father-preference rule was certainly 'patriarchal', without quibbling about the meaning of the word. But, in addition, it is hard to avoid the idea that it had a profoundly upper-class odour about it. It is a rule which most comfortably fits members of the upper class, or at least men wealthy enough to have servants. In other words, the father-preference rule was never based on an assumption that the men in question would be the care-givers, literally speaking—helping little children blow their noses, feeding

[5] Grossberg, *Governing the Hearth*, 235.

[6] On the English rule, see Blackstone, *Commentaries*, bk. 1, ch. 16; *King* v. *De Manneville*, 5 East 221 (1804); an American case enunciating the doctrine is *People* v. *Mercein*, 3 Hill 399 (NY 1842).

them, changing their clothes. It was always the assumption that some *woman* would do these basic things; to be precise, one or more of the maids, nannies, and governesses that abounded in the households of the gentry.

This was, I believe, the situation in England; and although custody cases seem quite rare before the later nineteenth century, the same assumptions might be made about the few American cases from early in that period—cases in which courts continued, dutifully, to mouth words about the absolute rights of the father.

But American law became, more and more, law for and about the middle class: small farmers, skilled workmen, men who owned village stores. Even in the late colonial period, when there were few divorces, and few custody disputes, the cases give off much less of the intense upper-class flavour that one finds in the British cases.[7] In a farm family, or the family of a craftsman or shop-keeper, there was nothing like the army of servants to be found in the great English household; and very early on, the American courts, despite the persistence of father-preference language, also sounded tones that reflected the actual class-composition of their cases.

The result was at first a kind of ambivalence. In *Miner* v. *Miner*, an Illinois case of 1849,[8] Laura Miner sued her husband Martin for divorce. Martin did not contest the divorce, but he did want custody of his only daughter Charlotte. The father had proposed to employ 'a housekeeper' to take care of the child; but the trial court disapproved of his choice—the housekeeper was an 'igno-rant' woman, 'wholly unfit to have the charge or care of children'. The appeal court, in its discussion of the issues, recognized the 'legal right of the father to the custody and control of his chil-dren'. The father kept this right, according to the court, unless he had 'forfeited, waived or lost it' through some form of miscon-duct. But a court of chancery, though it 'may not disregard the natural rights of parents', must consult 'primarily' the 'best inter-est of the child'; and on this consideration 'an infant of tender years is generally left with the mother'. The court was explicit about the reasons: 'If left with the father, the child must, to a great extent, be entrusted to the superintendence of others'; and the

---

[7] Merril D. Smith, *Breaking the Bonds: Marital Discord in Pennsylvania, 1730–1830* (New York, 1991), 34.

[8] 11 Ill. 43 (1849).

father's 'occupations' will 'doubtless prevent that constant watch-
fulness over her, so essential to her proper cultivation', which a
'vigilant and tender mother' would contribute.

This emerging doctrine, in short, was one which corresponded
more closely with the real life-situations of most of the litigants.
In these cases, the mother's image was the image of a woman in
the domestic sphere, whose main job was the care of children.
The man was the breadwinner. He worked, he ruled the family
(when the family was intact); but the care of children was certainly
not his primary business.[9]

By the end of the century the trend toward mother-custody had
become much more pronounced. Divorce cases were themselves
by now rather common, hence custody disputes were more
common as well. Divorce was no longer an upper-class matter.
Indeed there were thousands of divorces among working-class
people. The cases slid steadily down the social scale, and as they
did so, the father-custody rule slid into oblivion. When custody
disputes had arisen primarily among members of a landed gentry
class, the question was essentially one of brute legal power, as
between upper-class husband and upper-class wife. In 1900,
however, courts instead asked themselves which of these two *people*
was best able to care for the child. To most judges, the answer
seemed obvious: little children needed a mother's care.

I suspect that the shift took place *first* at the trial court level; and
percolated only slowly into formal doctrine. Most cases of course
were not appealed, and we lack studies of custody cases at the trial
court level. But even in the few reported decisions, if we read
between the lines, we can see the shift taking place. In a Kentucky
case (1866), a father appealed from a decision giving his ex-wife
custody of his daughter. 'As a general rule', said the court, the
father was entitled to custody; but it refused to disturb the lower
court verdict, since the judge there was in the best position to

[9] Some courts continued to talk about father-preference; and some statutes continued
to do so as well. In one interesting case, *Umlauf* v. *Umlauf*, 128 Ill. 378, 21 NE 600 (1889),
there were two children, Arthur, a boy of 9, and Oscar, a boy of 6. Arthur was lame and
'delicate'. The mother had custody after a divorce; but the father sought, successfully, to
get custody of Arthur. The father had 'two daughters by a former marriage, who keep
house for him'. The mother was a 'good woman . . . But she is a dress-maker by trade, and
pursues that business . . . Being thus actively engaged, she cannot devote to both of her
boys as much time and attention as she would be able to give them if she were differently
situated.' The court conceded that 'no other person can feel for a boy, or show to him the
love and affection which he receives from his mother'. But the 'right of the father is superior to that of every other person'.

examine 'the relative habits and situations of the two parents' and decide what was 'most beneficial to the child'.[10]

A Massachusetts case from 1890 is even more striking. John Haskell sued his wife Mary for divorce, accusing her of adultery and bigamy. He won his divorce, but not custody of his two sons, who were 5 and 6 years old. The divorce judge gave them to the mother, at least 'during their tender years'. John appealed; but the upper court refused to disturb the verdict; there was no 'absolute rule of law' in favour of a father, even when his wife had done the dirty deeds Mary was accused of.[11]

In a case from Wisconsin, in 1921, the trial court 'found' that both father and mother were 'morally fit and financially able to care for' the children. The two older children were with the father, but the youngest child, Eugene, was with the mother. The report does not give us Eugene's age, except that he was a child of 'tender years'. The trial court awarded Eugene to the father, but the Supreme Court of the state reversed. For a boy of 'tender years' nothing could be an 'adequate substitute for mother love—for that constant ministration required during the period of nurture that only a mother can give because in her alone is duty swallowed up in desire; in her alone is service expressed in terms of love. She alone has the patience and sympathy required to mold and soothe the infant mind . . . The difference between fatherhood and motherhood in this respect is fundamental.'[12]

This reads like a straightforward description of Victorian gender roles, as they were, and as they persisted until about a generation or so ago. Indeed, the tender years idea, according to Grossberg, basically 'institutionalized Victorian gender commitments'.[13] But the difference between the later American cases, and the English cases which established father-preference, is not only, or not even primarily, a matter of gender stereotypes; it is also an issue of social facts. In an upper-class household, a mother's role does not need to be described in terms of 'constant ministration' or 'patience and sympathy'. Maidservants, governesses, and others were the ones condemned to a life of 'constant ministration' and 'patience'.[14]

[10] *McBride* v. *McBride*, 64 Ky. 15 (1866).
[11] *Haskell* v. *Haskell*, 152 Mass. 16, 24 NE 859 (1890).
[12] *Jenkins* v. *Jenkins*, 173 Wis. 592 (1921).　　[13] Grossberg, *Governing the Hearth*, 248.
[14] And, in the American South, in the period before the Civil War, the messier aspects of child-rearing were often handed over to black slaves.

This point is both simple and plausible; though it is easily missed if one does not pay close attention to the facts of the cases and the courts' reaction to those facts. The actual life-situations of the parties shaped doctrine; these life-situations may or may not be typical of the range of transactions in the social field in question. The law certainly responded as conceptions of the family altered; but the different mix of social classes in the actual litigation also played a vital role in stimulating the evolution of doctrine.

Adoption. Adoption was, as such, unknown to the common law. Credit for introducing adoption as a legal status is often given to a statute passed in 1851 in Massachusetts.[15] There were, however, precursors of one sort or another. Very notably, a number of legislatures passed 'private Acts' to change the legal names of certain persons. Sometimes these laws were what they said they were: name changes, and nothing else. But here and there we find a 'name change' law that was, in essence, a private adoption statute. So, for example, in Missouri in the 1840s, the legislature changed the name of Maria Coffee to Maria McCoy, and she was 'hereby made and declared sole heir at law of James McCoy . . . and the property, real, personal and mixed, of said James McCoy shall descend to and be inherited by said Maria McCoy as such heir'.[16] A Vermont statute—one of many—of another type, passed in 1847, 'constituted' one Norman H. Eddy 'heir at law of Amos Eddy'.[17]

Of course, long before there were adoption statutes, there were thousands of people who raised somebody else's children. In fact, this was a period awash with wards and orphans. Mothers and fathers died young depressingly often, leaving their children emotionally stranded. Many households harboured children of dead relatives; but without the benefit of formal adoption. Nothing, of course, prevented aunts and uncles from raising an orphaned niece, for example, whether or not they 'adopted' the child. On the other hand, adoption laws seemed to fill a real need. The

---

[15] An Act to Provide for the Adoption of Children, 1851 Laws Mass. ch. 324.

[16] Laws Mo. 1844–5, p. 230, Act of 12 Feb. 1845. Sometimes a name change statute expressed a different function. The same Missouri legislature changed the name of Mary Jane Howard and her son back to her maiden name of Poore. She had married a bounder named Washington Howard, who 'represented himself as an unmarried man'; he had a wife, in fact, and soon left Mary (who later bore young Ferdinand). Ibid.

[17] Laws Vt. 1847, No. 48, p. 120.

idea—and its statutory basis—spread rapidly among the states after 1850.[18]

What was the engine behind this legal change? Inheritance law was a crucial factor, beyond a doubt. In a society like eighteenth-century England, inheritance law was basically law for a small and narrow élite, the landed gentry. But in the United States, the first society to be basically dominated numerically by the middle class, millions of families owned at least a bit of land—a farm, a lot or two in the county seat, a store, a vacant plot of land. Of course, it was no problem to leave money to a orphaned ward, if that is what was desired; after all, in the United States, primogeniture was extinct, and there was no equivalent (outside of Louisiana),[19] of the forced share for (legitimate) children, in the law of inheritance. A man was free to leave his money and land as he saw fit.

Still, for whatever reason, most men in fact died intestate;[20] and the elaborate system of trusts and settlements which had developed in England, and was used there by rich landowners, had no resonance whatsoever among (say) Illinois farmers. These devices were too expensive and too difficult to be used for what we would now call estate planning. The adoption procedure was a way to regularize property arrangements, a way to create a *legal* family, one which would work for all purposes, very notably inheritance; and, one supposes, relatively cheap and relatively fast.

Married women's property. A somewhat similar point can be made about the married women's property laws, which were so prominent an innovation in the late nineteenth century.[21] American law,

---

[18] See, for example, Rev. Code of Mississippi, 1857, p. 484, art. 41, giving circuit courts power, on petition, to change names, legitimize children, and make them heirs; 'any person who may desire to adopt any infant, and to change the name of such infant', was allowed to petition as well. In the petition, the adopting parent was to state 'what gifts, grants, bequests, or benefits he proposes to make or confer upon such infant'. If the court felt the 'interest and welfare' of the child would be 'promoted by such adoption', it could so decree; and could also confer on the infant 'all the benefits proposed by the petition'.

[19] La. Civ. Code art. 1621 (1889) listed ten grounds for disinheritance; otherwise, by art. 1493, a quarter of the estate was reserved if the testator had one legitimate child, one-half if he had two such children, two-thirds if he had three or more children.

[20] For data on this point, see Carole Shammas, Marylynn Salmon, and Michel Dahlin, *Inheritance in America: From Colonial Times to the Present* (New Brunswick, NJ, 1987), 16–17.

[21] There is a sizeable literature on the subject. See, notably, Norma Basch, *In the Eyes of the Law: Women, Marriage and Property in Nineteenth-Century New York* (Ithaca, NY, 1982); Peggy Rabkin, *Fathers to Daughters: The Legal Foundations of Female Emancipation* (Westport, Conn., 1980); Richard H. Chused, 'Married Women's Property Law: 1800–1850', *Georgetown Law Journal*, 71 (1983), 1359–425.

like English law, recognized that husband and wife were merged (legally speaking) into a single flesh; but this flesh belonged to the husband. As a leading treatise put it, in 1846, the husband, 'by marriage acquires an absolute title to all the personal property of the wife'; and, as to real estate, his marriage gave him the 'usufruct of all the freehold estate of the wife'; that is, the right to manage it, practically speaking, and to collect whatever income it produced.[22]

Certainly, the wife's disability was a major concern to many women; it was a crucial source of power imbalance within the family. But what is less often recognized is that the old law was also a problem for *men*. From the standpoint of a father or other male relative, the legal status of married women could be a major annoyance. If a woman had money or land, or was given money or land, her husband gained title or control when she married. If he went bankrupt, the property was lost. If he deserted his wife, it was hard for her to deal with their marital assets. This could be a problem for creditors or buyers of land.

Of course, there were ways around these legal disabilities; and these detours were very well worked out in English law. There, a legal practice had developed with a distinctive upper-class flavour. Among the American rich, too, there were similar devices—trusts, for example, of various sorts.[23] But for our prototypical Illinois farmer, elaborate trusts and suchlike were really out of the question, as we have already noted. The devices were too expensive, and required too much in the way of scarce lawyering skills.

We do, however, find occasional private Acts which attack the problem one person at a time. Some of these laws give a particular married woman the right to act as if she was a 'feme sole'. Thus, a private Act, passed in Tennessee in 1822, gave Martha Ann Dyer, the wife of William H. Dyer, the right 'to have and hold property by descent or otherwise in her own name, to sue and be sued, and in all respects to act and manage for herself as a *feme sole*'.[24] This probably solved Ms Dyer's problem; but such

[22] Tapping Reeve, *The Law of Baron and Feme* (2nd edn., New York, 1846), 1, 27.
[23] See Lawrence M. Friedman, 'The Dynastic Trust', *Yale Law Journal*, 73 (1964), 547–92.
[24] The property was to be 'free from all liability for . . . the debts of said William'. The Act extended the same privileges to three other women. Laws Tenn. 1822, ch. 134, p. 112 (22 Aug. 1822); see also Marylynn Salmon, *Women and the Law of Property in Early America* (Chapel Hill, NC, 1986), 55–6.

statutes were too piecemeal and sporadic to attack the general issue. Only the married women's property laws could offer a consistent way to untangle the knots of land titles, solve riddles of creditors' rights, and support (as the nineteenth century saw it) a vigorous real estate market.

The married women's property laws, then, reflected the interests of *men*, primarily, rather than the interests of women; and the men whose interests they represented were, by and large, men of the middling sort. Indeed, the reported cases deal mostly with such issues as creditors' rights, and have little or nothing to do with the social or economic status of women. These laws, then, are congruent with the laws about adoption, child custody, and indeed family law in general. They reflect the realities of a society in which a large middle-class mass owned property, especially land.

The first married women's property law saw the light of day in Mississippi, of all places, in 1839.[25] This early law attacked the problem in a somewhat piecemeal way, which was characteristic of the early statutes.[26] But the tide ran strong. The New York law of 1848 was a particularly important statutory landmark;[27] and by 1850, about seventeen states had granted married women some sort of legal capacity to deal with property. From then on, there was steady progress in the 'liberal disposition' of the law to bring the married woman 'nearer to the plane of manhood, and advance her condition from obedient wife to something like co-equal marriage partner',[28] at least as far as property was concerned. Indeed, by the end of the century, the rights of married women were, for all practical purposes, equal to those of single women, and, formally at least, equal to the rights of men. Here, too, it seems likely that demographic and social change

[25] See Elizabeth G. Brown, 'Husband and Wife: Memorandum on the Mississippi Woman's Law of 1839', *Michigan Law Review*, 42 (1944), 1110–21.

[26] See, for example, Laws Vt. 1847, p. 26, Act No. 37, 15 Nov. 1847: the 'rents, issues and profits of the real estate of any married woman, and the interest of her husband in her right in any real estate', which she had before marriage, or acquired during it, were made 'exempt from attachment or levy of execution, for the sole debts of her husband'. The statute also gave married women the right to devise their 'lands, tenements, and hereditaments' by will.

[27] Laws NY 1848, ch. 200, p. 307 (Act of 7 Apr. 1848).

[28] James Schouler, *A Treatise on the Law of Husband and Wife* (Boston, 1882), 230. 'Man makes the concessions, step by step, out of deference to woman's wishes', not to mention 'that love of justice and individual liberty which always characterized our Saxon race'. Ibid.

interacted. This was a middle-class society, with middle-class values and changing conceptions of family roles. It was also a society which had a felt need for the kind of regularity and certainty in the land market that married women's property rights were best able to advance.

Divorce. Divorce has had a tangled and complex history in the United States—a history far more complex than any other aspect of American family law.[29] Absolute divorce was rare in the colonial period; separation agreements a little more common.[30] After Independence, in the southern states, a system of legislative divorce prevailed; that is, a couple could divorce only through an act of the state legislature. These statutes are not very revealing; they consist usually of the bland statement that 'bonds of matrimony' between a man and a wife were thereby dissolved. Occasionally, these laws went into the whys and wherefores: William Owen of Missouri deserted his wife Milly 'without good cause', for six years; and Elizabeth Warden, also of Missouri, refused to live with her husband Congreve, swore she never would, and asserted that their marriage was nothing but 'a jest'.[31]

The northern states took a different approach to divorce. Divorce became available in court, through a regular proceeding ('judicial divorce'); Pennsylvania passed a divorce law of this kind in 1785,[32] and Massachusetts took the step a year later.[33] A divorce action was, in form, an adversary lawsuit. The plaintiff sued as a wronged and innocent party, alleging that the other partner had committed one or more offences against the marriage contract. These 'grounds' for divorce were listed in the local statute; they varied from state to state, but typically included desertion, adul-

---

[29] There is a considerable literature on the history of divorce; for example, Nelson Blake, *The Road to Reno: A History of Divorce in the United States* (New York, 1962); Elaine Tyler May, *Great Expectations: Marriage and Divorce in Post-Victorian America* (Chicago, 1980); Glenda Riley, *Divorce: An American Tradition* (New York, 1991); Lynne Carol Halem, *Divorce Reform: Changing Legal and Social Perspectives* (New York, 1980), among others.

[30] On the colonial situation, see Salmon, *Women and the Law of Property*, ch. 4. Legal separation continued to be available in the republican era, of course; thus, in New York, where adultery was practically speaking the only grounds for divorce, separation was available, for example, in cases of cruelty, abandonment, and neglect. NY Code Civ. Pro. s. 1762 (1896).

[31] These two examples come from Laws Mo. 1844–5, pp. 93–4, Acts of 24 Jan. 1845.

[32] Acts of 19 Sept. 1785, ch. MCLXXXVII, 1785 Pa. Laws, p. 94.

[33] An Act for Regulating Marriage and Divorce (16 Mar. 1786), repr. in J. Cushing, *The First Laws of the Commonwealth of Massachusetts* (Wilmington, Del., 1981), 256–8.

tery, and some version of 'cruelty'.[34] In Rhode Island, divorce was available for 'gross misbehaviour and wickedness in either of the parties'.[35] In New Hampshire, it was grounds for divorce if either party joined the Shakers, a sect which had no truck with sexual intercourse.[36]

During the course of the century, judicial divorce spread to the southern states as well. Tennessee was an early convert.[37] There was one conspicuous hold-out, however: South Carolina, which did not allow absolute divorce at all until later in the twentieth century. The reform of divorce law was of a piece with the other changes in family law. Again, the widespread ownership of land must have had an influence on legislation. If a man walked out on his wife, the woman was left in a state of legal limbo. She could not remarry; and, in addition, her property rights were a hopeless tangle (especially before the Married Women's Property Acts were fully implemented). Access to divorce was one way to help this situation. Access to divorce was also essential for both men and women whose marriages had collapsed, and who wanted to start, in a legitimate way, a new relationship.

Divorce, however, was much more controversial than adoption, and more controversial, too, than married women's property laws. There was always a strong undercurrent of moral disapproval: the President of Yale, Timothy Dwight, considered divorces 'dreadful beyond conception'; a rising divorce rate threatened to convert his state (he said) into 'one vast Brothel'.[38] At the same time, there was enormous pressure *for* divorce, and the pressure rose dramatically in the course of the nineteenth century. So did the number of divorces. The divorce rate in 1870 was 1.5 per 1,000 marriages; in 1900, 4 per thousand marriages, and in 1920, 7.7 per thousand.[39]

But the formal laws were in essence frozen; there was a kind of stalemate between the nay-sayers and those who demanded divorce. The increased demand for divorce did not result in significant loosening of the *formal* rules. Indeed, there was a

[34] See, for example, Ohio Rev. Code, ch. 37, s. 1 (1854); Ky. Rev. Stats. Ann., ch. 47, art. 3 (1852).
[35] RI Gen. Stats., ch. 153 (1872).
[36] See *Dyer* v. *Dyer*, 5 NH 271 (1830); NH Comp. Stat. ch. 157, s. 3 (1853).
[37] Code of Tenn. Sec. 2448 *et seq.* (1858).
[38] See Lawrence M. Friedman, *A History of American Law* (New York, 1985), 206.
[39] Table on marriage and divorce rates, in Tyler May, *Great Expectations*, 167.

certain amount of movement in the opposite direction; a number of states, faced with a rising divorce rate, tightened their laws at the end of the century.[40]

This, of course, had no effect whatsoever on the demand for divorce. Consequently, a number of detours developed around the formal law. The most significant was the collusive divorce, which grew like a weed after 1870. By the end of the century, it was clear that most divorces were in fact collusions. Any real battle between husband and wife ended before anybody entered the courtroom door. The parties had already decided on a divorce, for whatever reason, and whether reluctantly or not. At that point, one party, usually the wife,[41] would file suit for divorce, accusing her husband of violating the marriage in one or more ways that were listed in the statute. The husband would simply fail to answer or show up, and divorce would be awarded by default. Thus the 'battle' in court was essentially a sham.

Collusion was rampant, ubiquitous; most judges winked at it; but officially it was not in the least bit acceptable. Statutes and case law explicitly forbade it. Evidence of collusion vitiated any right to a divorce. For example, an Illinois statute, from the 1880s,[42] stated that 'no divorce' was to be 'decreed' if the court felt that 'the injury complained of was occasioned by collusion of the parties, or done with the assent of the complainant for the purpose of obtaining a divorce'. As one treatise-writer put it, a 'promise of a defendant in a divorce suit . . . to make no defense, is void as against public policy'. Collusive agreements 'between husband and wife to procure a divorce, when no real ground exists', are a 'fraud upon the court'.[43]

On this point, the rather skimpy case law was in full agreement. In other words, if the collusion, for some reason, came to public view; or if the judge was one of the few stubborn moralists who did not like the system, or who disapproved of divorce itself, the divorce

[40] Often by making residency requirements more stringent; thus South Dakota put a six-month residency requirement in place in 1893, Laws S. Dak. 1893, ch. 75, p. 97 (Act of 1 Mar. 1893). Indiana had enacted a statute requiring a one-year residency in 1859, Laws Ind. 1859, ch. 6, p. 108 (Act of 4 Mar. 1859); this was increased to two years in 1873, Laws Ind. 1873, ch. 43, p. 107 (Act of 10 Mar. 1873).

[41] See Lawrence M. Friedman and Robert V. Percival, 'Who Sues for Divorce? From Fault through Fiction to Freedom', *Journal of Legal Studies*, 5 (1976), 61–82.

[42] Rev. Stats. Ill. 1881, p. 546; see Neb. Rev. Stats. ch. 16, s. 9 (1866).

[43] Schouler, *Treatise*, 527.

might possibly be denied; and there are cases of precisely this nature on record. The evil of collusion was also regularly denounced by respectable society; an editorial in the *New York Times*, in 1899, condemned collusion as a 'peculiarly insidious and dangerous form of evasion . . . of the law'; it 'converts the marriage relation into a sort of veiled concubinage, which is more injurious to society in some regards than open concubinage would be'.[44]

The precise form of the collusion depended on what needed to be colluded about—that is, it depended on what the law said was needed to get a divorce. Legal literature talks about 'bargaining in the shadow of the law';[45] but here one has to talk about 'cheating in the shadow of the law'. In California, cruelty was grounds for divorce, and obviously the most malleable and useful; hence collusive divorces tended to allege cruelty. A study of San Francisco divorce suits in 1921[46] found that the single most common ground of divorce, when women filed, was cruelty (40 per cent); for men, the most common ground was desertion (62 per cent). About 70 per cent of the cases were brought by the wife.

On the surface, the situation appears quite peculiar. Surely men deserted women far more often than women deserted men. Probably most of the cases brought by men were non-collusive—that is, the grounds they alleged were real, not fictional. For women, it was the converse. Most of these cases were collusive. If the parties agreed to a divorce, it was on the whole better for the woman to bring the action. It was less stigmatic; and it was easier to claim child custody (which the men on the whole probably did not want anyway) and perhaps alimony, than if the lawsuit were brought the other way around.[47] In California, the default divorce was overwhelmingly common by the end of the century. Susan Wadsworth's was a typical case. In 1896, she complained that her husband Isaac, father of her many children, neglected to provide

[44] *New York Times*, 14 July 1899, p. 6.

[45] The phrase comes from the article by Robert H. Mnookin and Lewis Kornhauser, 'Bargaining in the Shadow of the Law: The Case of Divorce', *Yale Law Journal*, 88 (1979), 950–97.

[46] Sam B. Warner, 'San Francisco Divorce Suits', *California Law Review*, 9 (1921), 175–85.

[47] Friedman and Percival, 'Who Sues'; Robert Griswold, *Family and Divorce in California, 1850–1890: Victorian Illusions and Everyday Realities* (Albany, NY, 1982), 30, thinks that the high percentage of female plaintiffs in 19th-century California divorce cases suggests that women were moving 'toward self-assertion and a sense of personal efficacy'. But this ignores the many technical and structural reasons why a couple would choose to cast the woman in the role of plaintiff, in a collusive divorce.

her with 'the common necessaries of life by reason of idleness and dissipation'; and also that he was a habitual drunkard, which inflicted 'mental anguish' on Susan and her family. The divorce was granted, upon plaintiff's complaint, which was 'taken as confessed' by the defendant, 'whose default for failure to appear or answer . . . has been duly and regularly entered'.[48]

In New York, divorce was available, practically speaking, only for adultery.[49] The formal law was immovable; the forces opposed to divorce were far too powerful. Collusion was therefore the norm in New York as it was in other states. Under our general principle of cheating in the shadow of the law, collusive adultery developed—perhaps the most accurate term would be soft-core adultery. This involved a little charade in a hotel; the cast of characters included a woman (generally a blonde) hired for the occasion, and (of course) a photographer. The woman's fee was usually $50. The flavour of what went on is well captured in the title of a magazine article from 1934: 'I Was the Unknown Blonde in 100 New York Divorces.'[50] This rather sordid business, naturally, provided endless food for scandal; there were constant exposés and promises to clean up the situation. An occasional divorce fell through in New York, too, when an unusually hard-nosed judge confronted the parties. This happened, for example, to poor Mrs Lottie Longley, in 1901; the judge actually investigated the case, found the circumstances decidedly fishy, and threw the divorce out of court.[51]

Collusion was by far the most popular, and practical, way around the overly rigid statutes. The federal system opened the door to another possibility—the migratory divorce. In the course of the nineteenth century, a number of states hit on the happy idea of providing cheap and easy divorce as a way of attracting out-of-state business. Indiana was an early divorce mill; it was followed by South Dakota, otherwise a rather bleak and forbidding place to go. South Dakota was described in 1891 as 'a great state for divorces'. There was a big 'colony' of divorce-seekers in Sioux Falls, South Dakota, including 'prominent people' from New York

[48] Sup. Ct. Alameda Cnty., No. 11679, 1896.

[49] New York allowed divorce for narrow lack-of-consent reasons and for adultery. However, the state did allow separation on other grounds, such as cruel and inhuman treatment, abandonment, or neglect. NY Code Civ. Pro. Sec. 1762 (1896).

[50] Note, 'Collusive and Consensual Divorce and the New York Anomaly', *Columbia Law Review*, 36 (1936), 1121–31, at 1131 n.

[51] *New York Times*, 13 June 1901, p. 16.

City. These people 'live at the best hotels . . . they take things easy, going to baseball games regularly in the Summer'. The women, too, are 'as a rule, from good families'.[52] South Dakota was attractive as a divorce mill mainly in the warmer months; winters were much too cold for comfort.

The divorce mills of the nineteenth century tended to be unstable; they rose and fell. What ultimately drove them out of business was the opposition of the clergy and the respectable elements of society, who united in opposition to this odious practice and demanded an end to easy divorce.[53] Divorce was evil, immoral, a sign of social decay; and lax laws were evil because they encouraged divorce.[54] As other states fell by the wayside, Nevada became the ultimate, rather permanent divorce mill—a barren and underpopulated state, today the national gambling capital, where the 'respectable elements' have been historically a rather muted voice.[55] In 1911, it was reported that there were, at any given time, more than 200 'happiness-seeking, ill-mated' people from the East in Reno, Nevada, most of them 'well-to-do', and spending money 'with a free hand'.[56]

Divorce law thus had become what we might call a *dual system*. By this we mean a situation in which there is a radical disjuncture between the official law, and the operating law—the law in action, the law as it was lived in the lower courts. Of course, all fields of law are, to a degree, dual systems; but we can apply the term to cases where the disjuncture is extreme, or where the operating law directly contradicts the official law. A system of fairly widespread

[52] Ibid. 26 July 1891, p. 20. But soon there were signs of a crackdown, ibid. 31 July 1891, p. 1, when a circuit judge decided that only bona fide residents of the state were entitled to make use of its divorce law, ibid. 23 Aug. 1991, p. 1. The state raised the residence requirement from three to six months, and the torch passed to Oklahoma Territory, ibid. 7 Jan. 1894, p. 4.

[53] And an occasional moralizing judge; see above, n. 52.

[54] For a typical statement of this view: W. T. Lafferty, Dean of the College of Law, University of Kentucky, in 'Divorce Evils and the Remedy', *Kentucky Law Journal*, 8 (1920), 20–9. Lafferty took it for granted that 'easy' divorce laws were an unmitigated evil—in Kentucky the laws provided 'for fourteen causes for divorce, several of which are exceedingly trivial, thereby making it easy for any dissatisfied spouse to pave the way to divorcement'. His remedy: amend the law to restrict divorce to adultery and bigamy. Few voices spoke on the other side; but see Evans Holbrook, 'Divorce Laws and the Increase of Divorce', *Michigan Law Review*, 8 (1910), 386–95.

[55] See Gilman M. Ostrander, *Nevada: The Great Rotten Borough, 1859–1964* (New York, 1966).

[56] *New York Times*, 8 January 1911, p. 24.

tax avoidance and evasion does not necessarily constitute a dual system. Prostitution in the nineteenth- and early- twentieth-century United States was, on the other hand, a true dual system. This was especially true in cities where the police regulated prostitution, with formal rules and regulations for red light districts and brothels—that is, regulated the conduct and scope of a business which was totally illegal, as far as official law was concerned.[57]

The question is, what brings dual systems about? The case of prostitution gives us a clue to understanding divorce as well. Prostitution was officially proscribed, denounced from the pulpits, fulminated against with great regularity: but still it survived. It survived because there was a genuine demand for these sexual services.[58] For obvious reasons, the customers found it difficult to express themselves openly—there was never an active lobby pressing for legalization of the sex business, or demanding more and better prostitution.[59] Similarly, the anti-divorce forces of the nineteenth century occupied the moral high ground. In the nineteenth century, marriage was supposed to be a lifetime union, sacred and permanent. This was certainly the view of the clergy, by and large; and it was probably also the general view of respectable people.

In short, divorce was definitely not, as it is today, a routine method for getting out of a failed marriage. It was a public remedy for a social problem: a marriage withered and blasted by the immorality or crime of one of the parties.[60] It was definitely conceived of as a last resort—as an exceptional practice, to be avoided and discouraged if at all possible.

The actual demand for divorce was, on the whole, subdued and sub rosa—like the demand for prostitution, pornography, and gambling. Of course, divorce was not illegal, as these others were; but there was certainly no organized pro-divorce movement. But though the pressure for divorce was muted, it was most certainly

---

[57] Lawrence M. Friedman, *Crime and Punishment in American History* (New York, 1993), 329.

[58] John C. Burnham, *Bad Habits* (New York, 1993), 177, argues also that: 'Respectable people tended to tolerate the red-light district in part because the presence of the area and the labeling of the people there helped shore up understanding of what was good and proper elsewhere in society.'

[59] Nevada, of course, is once again an exception—prostitution is legal in Nevada, at least on a county-option basis, that is, each county can decide whether it wishes to have legal prostitution within its borders.

[60] Hendrik Hartog, 'Marital Exits and Marital Expectations in Nineteenth Century America', *Georgetown Law Journal*, 80 (1991), 95–129, at 114.

there. Moreover, as we noted when we discussed child custody, the demand for divorce embraced all classes of society. Indeed, studies of divorce at the end of the nineteenth and early twentieth centuries showed that divorce was not an upper-class habit at all. It was definitely as strong, if not stronger, in middle- and working-class families: people like David Taylor, a house painter, who sued for divorce in Alameda County, California, in 1898, were quite typical.[61] A survey of California divorce, for the late nineteenth century, reported that 24 per cent of the husbands were labourers, 9 per cent unskilled tradesmen, 14 per cent farmers, 17 per cent middle class, and 17 per cent upper class.[62] Divorce had gone very democratic.

What brought about this development? There were, to begin with, changes in the nature of marriage itself: or, more accurately, changes in the way ordinary people hoped for or conceived of their marriages; and the way they practised the business of being a husband or wife. Marriage had become, in a way, more sacred and significant, though not in the religious sense. It had become, ideally, a deeper, more intense relationship. Until this period, there had been an implicit theory of marriage in society; marriage was a binding arrangement between a man and a woman, for the basic purposes of making a home, having children, and carrying on the species. This concept, of course, left no room for romantic love or self-realization, and as these became, for more and more people, the ultimate point of marriage, fragile marriages simply could not bear the weight.[63]

Paradoxically, then, divorce thrived because of this new, sharper, and more demanding sense of marriage. Those who denounced divorce emphasized that marriage was, and had to be, sacred; but what did sacred mean? Divorce, as William O'Neill has argued, was not 'antithetical' to what became the 'dominant ideology of marriage'; but was rather 'a literal interpretation of its texts'.[64] And when a marriage broke down, for whatever reason, only through divorce could a man and woman try and try again. Only through divorce could a couple legitimize a second union,

---

[61] *Taylor* v. *Taylor*, Sup. Ct. Alameda Cnty., No. 13204 (1898).
[62] See Griswold, *Family and Divorce*. Tyler May, *Great Expectations*, 171, presents similar figures for Los Angeles in 1880: 21% of the husbands were 'unskilled' or 'semiskilled'; 23% were skilled workers; 36% were 'low white collar', and 20% 'high white collar'.
[63] See, on this point, Tyler May, *Great Expectations*.
[64] William O'Neill, *Divorce in the Progressive Era* (New Haven, 1967), 12.

and thus avoid immorality, in an age which judged cohabitation very severely. Thus the popularity of divorce was one more sign of a subtle change in the moral constitution of society, in which bourgeois morality became, as it were, more democratic. Or perhaps a better way of putting it is that bourgeois morality began to trickle down from the high middle class.

The result of these tensions was the dual system, in which the official law remained pure and stern, while the operating law was warped in the shape of the social demand. The forces of respectability exhausted themselves in occasional crackdowns and moral crusades; but these ultimately failed. A kind of uneasy equilibrium developed, which lasted, in one form or another, about 100 years.

Under the dual system, to be sure, divorce was more available to the rich than to the poor. Only the rich could afford migratory divorce—the wife of an average worker could hardly quit a job and move to South Dakota or Nevada. Nevertheless, the record shows plainly that divorce *was* available to ordinary people. The cost, in a way, amounted to a kind of regressive tax, but thousands of workers, plumbers, carpenters, and day labourers—or their wives—were none the less willing to pay. The system was, as we said, substantially 'democratized' by the turn of the century.

Perhaps a word is in order about the implications of the history of divorce—and the history of dual systems in general—for the theory and methodology of legal history. It is by now common-place that appellate cases, the normal fodder of legal research, have to be used with extreme care. These cases tend to be exceptions and anomalies. They may give a distorted and even down-right false picture of the working legal system. Nor can we assume that what we read in a statute is what is applied where the knuckle of the law meets flesh. These points are obviously true, but hardly go far enough.

We sometimes hear a claim made for the importance of appellate cases, learned treatises, and statutes, on quite another basis. These texts are crucially important, we are told, because they are clues to legal *ideology*; and, it is said, no function of the law is as important as its ideological function. The law both reflects and promotes a dominant ideology. As I see it, this means that the legal system shapes common understandings of what is right and indeed what simply *is*; it helps to convince us that what is, is right and natural; and in so doing, it acts as an essential prop of the social order. This thesis has been applied, often with great brilliance, to this or that aspect of legal history.[65]

Where I may part company with some of these scholars is in so far as they insist that the key to ideology and the ideological function lies in the study of the 'law discourse', to be found mainly, or exclusively, in appellate cases, treatises, statutes, and other 'mandarin' sources. To me, this cannot be right. Ideology after all has been defined as beliefs and world-views that serve to buttress a particular social structure. The assumption thus *has* to be that ideology has behavioural and instrumental consequences, otherwise it would be nothing but empty talk. But as soon as one admits this fairly obvious point, then the study of ideology is at best flawed and at worst meaningless without attention to a much broader range of data and evidence—broader, that is, than the official sources I have mentioned. One must look at what the relevant public is actually thinking and doing, what the working norms of the legal system are, and what they mean to the people who use them or are used by them. This is not to say that treatises, case law, and official norms are insignificant; but only that they cannot be understood even in their own terms unless we know if they are, or were, effective, or even if the relevant public had any idea that the official norms were there in the first place.

Consider, for example, the ultimate fate of American divorce law. The old dual system totally collapsed, and with blazing speed, in 1970 and thereafter. California led the way, when it enacted a no-fault law; and in very short order, in one way or another, almost every other state followed suit.[66] The speed and sweep of the change astonished everybody; the states seemed to fall into line like ten-pins. Of course, divorce law was ripe for reform. It was rotten to the core, and everyone knew it. There were scholars and jurists who worked for reform in California; but they proceeded, on the whole, somewhat gingerly. They did not, for example, really advocate no-fault divorce—not openly, at any rate. They were arguing, rather, for consensual divorce—for getting rid of the

---

[65] Very notably, for example, Douglas Hay, 'Property, Authority and the Criminal Law,' in id. et al., *Albion's Fatal Tree: Crime and Society in Eighteenth-Century England* (New York, 1976), 17; see Robert Gordon, 'Critical Legal Histories', *Stanford Law Review*, 36 (1984), 57–125.

[66] See Herbert Jacob, *Silent Revolution: The Transformation of Divorce Law in the United States* (Chicago, 1988), ch. 6.

fakery, and allowing couples that wanted a divorce to get one, without charades and collusion and such flummery.

What actually happened, however, was something nobody had really dared advocate: divorce for either party, more or less at will. This went far beyond consensual divorce. It was, in fact, unilateral divorce—divorce whenever anybody wanted it, with the other party totally helpless to resist or complain. Under no-fault law, there is no such thing as a defence to a petition for divorce ('dissolution of marriage', as the new euphemism has it). If you want to get out of your marriage, no one can stop you—not your partner, and certainly not the state.[67]

What brought about this revolutionary change? There are, in fact, a number of puzzling aspects to the history of no-fault, and I cannot honestly say the whole process is well understood.[68] But in retrospect it is clear that there were incredibly strong *social* forces undermining the old system, and affecting the nature of marriage itself.

What these forces were cannot be discovered from the case law, or the statutes, or from the reform jurists. They can only be detected—though not easily—from a study of social change, a study of how people thought and acted in society. A long-run levelling effect seemed to be taking place, in which class came to matter less and less in the working law of divorce. What began as purely upper class (around 1800), had become working class and middle class by 1900; the demand for cheap, easy divorce became more and more irresistible.

But it was, in fact, resisted; by the churches, very notably. What finally defeated the resistance, perhaps, was the so-called sexual revolution, which fatally undermined ideas that had been propping up the image of divorce as inherently immoral. I believe, too, that the process was profoundly influenced by the social emphasis on expressive individualism; on personal growth; on making your own way in the world; carving out your own style and form of intimate life.[69] An unhappy marriage—an unfulfilling marriage—is completely incompatible with this kind of 'personal growth'. Divorce lost both its stigma and its sting; and 'easy

[67] Lynn D. Wardle, 'No-Fault Divorce and the Divorce Conundrum', *Brigham Young University Law Review*, (1991), 79–142.

[68] See Jacob, *Silent Revolution*.

[69] On this theme more generally, see Lawrence M. Friedman, *The Republic of Choice: Law, Authority, and Culture* (Cambridge, Mass., 1990).

divorce' was no longer a bugaboo.[70] In hindsight, it is easy to see that the system was quietly rotting away—and was destined to collapse in a way of its own dead weight. Nor was the process of change exclusively American; perhaps the United States carried it to an extreme, but the trend toward no-fault is European as well.[71] There may be differences of detail; but the underlying forces are common to the whole of Western society.

Gender, class, and family law. If one had to describe what happened in the nineteenth century to American family law, in one short sentence, perhaps the best one could do would be to say that it became more democratic. By this I mean that it concerned itself more and more with the interests and problems of ordinary people. On the surface, the law moved away from a rigid patriarchy, and toward a nuclear family of autonomous individuals. Behind this change, however, was a change in the identity of users of the law: more and more, these users were plain, ordinary people, who farmed and worked, who bore and adopted children, and who wanted freedom to do so and to divorce and remarry at will. The law bent to meet the needs of this crowded mass of ordinary people. Where the surface of the law was unyielding, for one reason or another—divorce is the outstanding case—legal practice developed elaborate detours around it.

What of the social inequalities within classes? The most important of these, for our purposes, is gender inequality. Of course much has changed since the nineteenth century. Women vote; they have rights in the workplace that would have seemed revolutionary a century ago. Still, gender inequality is very much still with us. It is far from clear that the 'reforms' of this century have been totally a blessing to most women; the impact of no-fault divorce, for example, is much disputed.[72] But plainly here too there has been a critical levelling effect.

[70] Though there has been at least a certain amount of backlash from social conservatives; in early 1996, Michigan was at least considering a return to a fault system. *New York Times*, 12 Feb. 1996, p. A10.

[71] See Mary Ann Glendon, *The New Family and the New Property* (Toronto, 1981), 33–4; ead., *The Transformation of Family Law: State, Law and Family in the United States and Western Europe* (Chicago, 1989), 149–88.

[72] See Lenore Weitzman, *The Divorce Revolution: The Unexpected Social and Economic Consequences for Women and Children in America* (New York, 1985), 323; ead., 'The Economics of Divorce: Social and Economic Consequences of Property, Alimony and Child Support Awards', *U.C.L.A. Law Review*, 28 (1981), 1181–268.

Part III

EMPLOYERS AND EMPLOYEES

8

The Case of the Employment Relationship

Elements of a Comparison

SPIROS SIMITIS

I

In late 1836 the court of appeals in Lyon had to decide a case in which an employer had been sued by a worker injured by a fellow employee while performing his duties.[1] The court rejected the claim. The reasoning was short and clear: anyone who engages in a paid occupation knows and accepts its risks and has, therefore, to bear them, all the more so as any such danger is compensated for by the payment offered for the particular kind of work. Nearly a century later the United States Supreme Court was confronted with the question of whether the state of New York, by imposing a maximum number of hours of work, had exceeded its constitutional powers.[2] Justice Peckham pointed to the state's police power and outlined its limits.[3] State interference must be strictly limited to situations in which 'safety, health, morals and general welfare of the public' were challenged. 'Clean and wholesome bread', however, both in his and in the court's view 'does not depend upon whether the baker works but ten hours a day or only sixty hours a week'.[4] 'In our judgment', he therefore concluded, 'it is not possible in fact to discover the connection between the number of hours a baker may work in the bakery and the healthful quality of the bread made by the workman.' And as if to dissipate all doubts on the only relevant legal principle determining

[1] *Cour d'Appel de Lyon*, 29 Dec. 1836, *Dalloz périodique* (1837), 2: 161.
[2] *Lochner* v. *New York*, 198 US 45 (1905). For a critical analysis, see esp. O. Fiss, *Troubled Beginnings of the Modern State*, History of the Supreme Court of the United States 8 (New York, 1993), 155 f.
[3] *Lochner* v. *New York*, 198 US 45 (1905), 53.
[4] Ibid. 57.

the hours of work Justice Peckham added: 'There is no contention that bakers as a class are not equal in intelligence and capacity to men in other trades or manual occupations, or that they are not able to assert their rights and care for themselves without the protecting arm of the State, interfering with their independence of judgment and of action. They are in no sense wards of the State.'[5]

In sum, both the Lyon court of appeals and the United States Supreme Court made it perfectly clear that the sole rule governing employer–employee relations had to be the liberty of contract and that therefore, in the words of the French Civil Code (art. 1134) as well as of the *Cour de Cassation*, 'agreements which have been reached, taking into account what the law prescribes, by contractual parties are considered to be the law for these parties'.[6]

II

The reference to the liberty of contract explains and justifies the terse reactions of both legislators and courts. It is the contractual parties' primary duty to speak up and the legislator's foremost obligation to remain in silence. His function, no less than the task of the courts, is clearly supportive. The parties define the aim and the content of the intended rules, while legislators and courts secure the conditions in which the intentions laid down in the contract can be fulfilled without hindrance. Their attitude is therefore one of deliberate passivity. They are guardians of rules established by those who seek an agreement and governed by their interests.

The consequence is twofold. First, legislative intervention is manifestly minimal. Even the few provisions to which legislators confine themselves are largely mere proposals addressed to the contractual parties, thus leaving them at liberty ultimately to

---

[5] *Lochner* v. *New York*, 198 US 45 (1905), 57.

[6] 'Les conventions légalement formées tiennent lieu de loi à ceux qui les ont faites.' *Chambres Civiles*, 17 June 1896, *Dalloz périodique* (1899), 1, 159. For a discussion of the regulatory concepts leading to an equation of the parties' agreement with a legislative decision, see V. Ranouil, *L'Autonomie de la volonté: Naissance et évolution d'un concept* (Paris, 1980), 27 f.; A. Bürge, *Das französische Privatrecht im 19. Jahrhundert*, Ius Commune 52 (Frankfurt am Main, 1991), 64 f.

choose the approach they regard as the best. Secondly, there is a clear split between the technical details of the various transactions, and the economic and social background of the actors. While the technical details are carefully fitted into a system of norms outlining general principles as well as specific expectations with regard to a series of particular transactions, the economic and social background of individuals is resolutely ignored. Hence the perception of the actors is strictly determined by the demands of the individual transaction. All the law can do is to establish a regulatory framework that ensures the correct performance of these roles. Any attempt to lift the veil of the abstract assignment of a role defined in an equally abstract way and to restore the social and economic context of the parties' activities would thus contravene the very function of the law. The repression of the social substratum and the implicit depersonalization of the parties radically restricts external interference and stabilizes the supremacy of the actors.

It is therefore hardly surprising that the *Code civil* dedicates just two brief articles to the employment contract. The first (art. 1780) explicitly declares that services can be provided only for a particular time or purpose. The second (art. 1781) states that in case of a controversy over the exact sum of the payment due, the master must be trusted.[7] Not all legislators were so reticent. But the premisses of the *Code civil* were never really questioned. Even the 'late-born child of liberalism',[8] the 1900 German Civil Code, adhered to them. Despite the fact that the final version contained more than twice as many provisions as the eight in the first bill, the legislator never abandoned the position that the 'contract of services' should be governed by the general rules applicable to all contractual agreements. For precisely this reason, it should be put on the same level as, for instance, the contract of sale. Anton Menger, one of the German Civil Code's most prominent critics, therefore bitterly complained that like vendors who must simply hand over the pair of shoes they have sold, and buyers who have to pay the

---

[7] For the origins and the implications of this provision, see esp. A. Castaldo, 'L'Histoire juridique de l'article 1781 du Code civil: "Le maître est cru sur son affirmation"', *Revue historique de droit français et étranger*, 55 (1988), 211–37, 211 f.

[8] F. Wieacker, *Das Sozialmodell der klassischen Privatrechtsgesetzbücher und die Entwicklung der modernen Gesellschaft* (Karlsruhe, 1953), 9; see also id., *Privatrechtsgeschichte der Neuzeit* (2nd edn., Göttingen, 1967), 620.

price agreed, masters are expected only to pay for the services rendered.[9]

However, despite the manifest intention to situate the legal mechanisms in a reality-prone world, the social context was never ignored. On the contrary, both the minimalist intervention and consequent depersonalization of the parties were means intended to restructure the social substratum. The demonstrative passivity built into a legal system characterized by a degree of abstraction that apparently severs all relations with a particular social situation and establishes a logically impeccable, timeless regulation conceals the attempt to revise the formative elements of social, political, and economic development. The seemingly most 'non-activist' state was, in fact, paradoxical as it may sound, no less 'activist' than the much discussed genuine or the post-welfare state. Different as the concepts of the legislator's as well as of the government's responsibilities may be, the state of society, its structure as well as its future, have never been irrelevant. Legislative projects, administrative policies, and court decisions have at all times been governed by maxims only understandable and applicable against the background of a specific perception of society and its evolution.

Civil codes and the ensuing court decisions were nevertheless based on an oxymoron. It embodies a resolute criticism of the past, an open neglect of the present, and a clear vision of the future. Its premises are at the same time a rejection of past experiences and the foundations of a future society immune to these very experiences. Thus, the predominance of rules shaped by parties acting on their own will within a legal framework primarily determined by their expectations illustrates first and foremost the break with a society marked by hypostasized social distinctions and privileges. In exactly this spirit, the French National Assembly on 3 August 1789 had not only proclaimed the irrevocable end of the feudal regime but also, a few days later, on 26 August 1789, declared unequivocally: 'There will no longer be any privilege for any section of the nation, or for any individual.'[10] And in order

---

[9] A. Menger, *Das bürgerliche Recht und die besitzlosen Volksklassen* (4th edn., Tübingen, 1908), 168; but see also J. Rückert, ' "Frei" und "sozial": Arbeitsvertrags-Konzeptionen um 1900 zwischen Liberalismen und Sozialismen', *Zeitschrift für Arbeitsrecht*, 23 (1992), 225–94, 245f.; and M. Becker, *Arbeitsvertrag und Arbeitsverhältnis in Deutschland*, Ius Commune 76 (Frankfurt am Main, 1995), 162, 219f.

[10] 'Il n'y a plus pour aucune partie de la nation, ni pour aucun individu, aucun privilège.' See L. Blanc, *Histoire de la Révolution française* (repr. Paris, 1878), iii. 319f.

to exclude all doubts on the range of the quest for a society freed from all barriers preventing individuals from pursuing their specific interests the Assemblée Nationale made it clear on the same day that 'neither guilds, nor corporations of professions, arts, and other trades' would in future exist.[11] The consequences were drawn by Le Chapelier in his report on the law named after him.[12] The vote took place on 14 June 1791, aiming at the 'abolition of all kinds of corporations where the members belong to one and the same estate or profession' (art. 1). 'There are no longer any corporations within the state; there are only the particular interests of each individual, and the general interest.'[13]

The privileges of the few were replaced by a universal right of self-determination emerging out of two closely interconnected and truly interdependent elements: the freedom of industry and the liberty of contract. Only so long as both are combined and guaranteed can the individual, primarily perceived as a *homo oeconomicus*, determine and defend his interests and thus set the conditions for his development. The freedom of industry is his key to a market characterized by free as well as constant competition, the liberty of contract his main tool for the consistent use of his market chances. The right freely to choose the contractual partner and equally freely to define the object as well as the content of the contract, acknowledged by norms such as article 1134 of the *Code civil*, presupposes a readiness to accept and implement the 'liberté du commerce et de l'industrie' as sanctioned by the French law of March 1791, or the *Gewerbefreiheit* (freedom of trade) as acknowledged by the Prussian edict on the finances of the state and the new arrangements concerning tax of October 1810.[14]

The freedom of industry clears the market of traditional state or corporative privileges distorting competition, and prevents

---

[11] Ibid.

[12] For a detailed discussion, see S. Simitis, 'Die Loi le Chapelier: Bemerkungen zur Geschichte und möglichen Wiederentdeckung des Individuums', *Kritische Justiz*, 22 (1989), 157–75, 157 f.

[13] *Archives parlementaires*, ser. 1, vol. xxvii (Paris, 1889), 210: 'anéantissement de toutes espèces de corporations des citoyens du même état et profession' (art. 1). 'Il n'y a plus de corporation dans l'Etat; il n'y a plus que l'intérêt particulier de chaque individu et l'interêt général.'

[14] See esp. D. Willoweit, 'Gewerbeprivileg und "natürliche" Gewerbefreiheit', in id. and K. O. Scherner (eds.), *Vom Gewerbe zum Unternehmen* (Darmstadt, 1982), 60–111, 60 f.; H. Steindl, 'Die Einführung der Gewerbefreiheit', in H. Coing (ed.), *Handbuch der Quellen und Literatur der neueren europäischen Privatrechtsgeschichte*, vol. iii, pt. 3 (Munich, 1986), 3527–628, 3527 f.

individuals from restoring similar restraints through their agreements. To this extent it is not only an unmistakable rejection of all intervention both by the state and intermediary powers, however 'natural', 'historically justified', or 'well founded' they may appear, but also a restriction of individual activities, motivated and legitimized, however, by the need to safeguard open access to the market in the very interests of potential competitors. To demand unlimited *Gewerbefreiheit* thus does not include the readiness to tolerate its 'abuses'. In the words of the early nineteenth-century commentators: *Gewerbefreiheit* must end where *Gewerbefrechheit* (impudence of trade) begins.[15] The 'Kampf um die Gewerbefreiheit' (the struggle surrounding the freedom of trade), slightly to alter Rudolf von Jhering's famous formula, is therefore a fight both against the remnants of the *ancien régime* and all attempts to undermine the *nouveau régime* by new, no less dangerous trade barriers. Schäffle's remark in Bluntschli's *Staatswörterbuch*, 'Die Gewerbefreiheit schliesst nicht aus die Gewerbeordnung' (The freedom of trade does not exclude the regulation of trade),[16] confirms a readiness to accept restrictions. But it also illustrates the ambivalence of an *Ordnung* that, as the long and cumbersome discussions preceding the German *Gewerbeordnung* of 1869 and the decisions of the *Reichsgericht* show,[17] quickly proved to be a welcome opportunity to preserve old prerogatives and to ignore practices which, as in the case of cartels, openly dismantled the fundamental conditions of unhindered competition.

'Freedom of industry' has a wider range than terms such as *Gewerbefreiheit* seem to suggest. The *Constituante* was far more explicit than later regulations in Germany. In the law voted in March 1791 it spoke of the 'liberté du travail, du commerce et de l'industrie'. The *rapporteur* d'Allarde had insisted particularly on the need also to address the issue of work. 'The ability to work' is in his view 'one of the first rights of man. This right is his prop-

---

[15] See Jacob and Wilhelm Grimm, *Deutsches Wörterbuch*, vol. vi (1911 edn. by H. Wunderlich; repr. Munich, 1984), entry 'Gewerbe-, Gewerb-, Gewerbsfreiheit'.

[16] J. C. Bluntschli and K. Brater (eds.), *Deutsches Staatswörterbuch* (Stuttgart, 1857–70), iv. 320.

[17] *Entscheidungen des Reichsgerichts in Zivilsachen (RGZ)*, vol. xxviii (1890), 238; vol. xxxviii (1897), 155; see F. Böhm, 'Das Reichsgericht und die Kartelle', *Ordo*, i (1948), 197–235, 197; B. Grossfeld, 'Zur Kartellrechtsdiskussion vor dem Ersten Weltkrieg', in H. Coing and W. Wilhelm (eds.), *Wissenschaft und Kodifikation des Privatrechts im 19. Jahrhundert*, vol. iv (Frankfurt am Main, 1979), 255–96, 255.

erty and it is without doubt . . . the first and most sacred property which cannot be invalidated by prescriptions.'[18] The reason for the broader approach is more or less obvious. If the market is to be accessible to everyone, all individuals must be able to rely upon their particular abilities and to exercise them freely. The inclusion of work universalizes access to the market and at the same time stresses the common denominator of all competitors. Behind the merchants, artisans, or workers there is always a *citoyen-propriétaire*. In each of these cases property is seen as the foundation of the individual actor's independence, the motive for his activities, and the incentive for economically rational behaviour. But in order to equate workers with merchants or artisans, labour had to be commodified. Commodification is in fact a prerequisite for the transformation of the freedom of industry into a genuine 'liberté générale'. It is exactly for this reason that d'Allarde qualifies the 'faculté de travailler', in the words of Adam Smith,[19] as the 'première propriété, la plus sacrée'. The Grimm brothers later defined *Arbeitskraft* (labour power) simply as follows: 'Individuals with their labour power are seen as a commodity whose price rises and falls in line with supply and demand.'[20]

Commodification marks the step from status to contract. Once work is seen and treated like any other commodity, a relationship that simply subjects the workmen to the master's power is no longer tolerable. The *domesticité* (relation of servitude within the household) must give way to a relationship characterized by the offer and the payment of services.[21] This modified understanding of work therefore requires a change in the legal framework. As in all other cases, the elements of this framework are determined by the abolition of the old privileges and the freedom of industry. Society is henceforth to be governed by its own law reflecting the activities and aspirations of independent individuals defined on the basis of their discourse as well as of their mutual rights and duties. The 'nouvelle société juridique'[22] is therefore first and

[18] *Archives parlementaires*, ser. 1, vol. xxvii (Paris, 1889), 199.
[19] A. Smith, *The Wealth of Nations* (repr. London, 1960), i. 199: 'the original foundation of all other Property', 'the most sacred and inviolable'.
[20] J. and W. Grimm, *Deutsches Wörterbuch*, vol. i (Leipzig, 1854; repr. Munich, 1984), entry 'Arbeitskraft': 'man betrachtet den menschen mit seiner arbeitskraft wie eine waare, deren preis mit der menge des angebots und der nachfrage danach steigt und fällt.'
[21] See art. 1, No. 18 of the constitution of 24 June 1793.
[22] F. Furet, *La Révolution* (Paris, 1988), 88.

foremost a *Privatrechtsgesellschaft*, a society ruled by a 'civil law' establishing both the supremacy of a universally applicable law and the predominance of individual agreements. In their deliberations on the necessity and the principles of a civil code the *Constituante* and the *Consulat* argued along exactly these lines, despite all the political changes that had taken place.[23] And while Georg Friedrich Puchta[24] spoke of the civil law as the foundation of all the other parts of the law, Rudolf Sohm went even further, and, in the parliamentary debates on the first bill for the *BGB*, did not hesitate to qualify the German Civil Code as the Magna Carta of the public liberties.[25]

Workers thus exchange the specific status of servants for the anonymity of a contractual relationship. They no longer belong to a clearly specified group of persons subjected to equally specified rules but to an unidentified number of individuals who are perfectly free to decide when and under what conditions to negotiate their goods. Both the abstraction and the scarcity of rules are thus a tribute to self-regulation. The insistence on paternalistic rules and not the lack of binding legal provisions appears as the real source of oppression and, in the view of Adam Smith[26] as well as of the United States Supreme Court,[27] as a true act of 'impertinence'. The *Code civil* essentially limits itself therefore to one provision (art. 1780) the sole purpose of which is to inhibit all attempts to falsify the market by lifelong commitments, a preoccupation shared by the *BGB* (§ 624) according to which any contract for a period longer than five years can be terminated once that time has expired. For all other eventualities workmen, like tenants or buyers, are referred to the general principles regulating contractual relationships.

For precisely this reason child labour created no more problems than, for instance, the selling of a house belonging to a child. Each of these cases affected the child's property, his immoveables, and his commodified capacity to work. The child was, in other words, bestowed with the same 'sacred and inviolable' piece of property

---

[23] See also A. Tissier, 'Le Code civil et les classes ouvrières', in *Le Code civil: Livre du Centenaire*, vol. i (Paris, 1904) 71–94, 71 f.

[24] G. F. Puchta, *Das Gewohnheitsrecht*, vol. ii (Erlangen, 1837), 224.

[25] B. Mugdan (ed.), *Die gesamten Materialien zum Bürgerlichen Gesetzbuch* (Leipzig, 1894–9), i. 109.

[26] Smith, *Wealth of Nations*, i. 110.

[27] Justice Peckham in *Lochner* v. *New York*, 198 US 45 (1905) 57, 60–4.

as any adult, but, unlike adults, was not entitled to act personally. Minority subjected children unconditionally to the *patria potestas* and thus transferred their decision-making power into the hands of their 'natural agents', their parents, and primarily the husband and father. It was hence left to him to determine the uses of his children's property irrespective of the items of which it was constituted. There were very few limits on the father's administrative powers, especially with regard to risky transactions, such as, for example, the acquisition of shares, and these limits never questioned his right to dispose of the child's labour capacity. On the contrary, his authority was doubly protected: by the 'man-made' general agency rules and the 'natural' principles establishing and guaranteeing the *patria potestas*. Therefore even if the legislator attempted to modify the provisions normally governing transactions, he would have to respect the supremacy of 'natural' prerogatives. And indeed, it was the unique combination of a canonized freedom of contract and an equally holy parental authority that was the argument repeatedly invoked against all efforts to restrict children's hours of work, irrespective of whether they were working in German, Belgian, or French industry, and particularly in the coal mines.[28] In the words of a Belgian MP, 'as a worker, one is also a father', a statement that quickly led him to the conclusion: 'There is no doubt that the state, in the public interest, can regulate certain professions, such as, for instance, the art of healing, or the art of producing medicines; the state can protect birds that eat insects to ensure that they are not killed, and domestic animals so that they are not mistreated. But there is one being which the state cannot touch without touching ourselves, and that is the being that is united with us through all the fibres of our souls, that is, our child.'[29] In a similar way the liberal MP Frère-Orban had already in 1868 criticized the intention to regulate child labour by saying: 'This is a law which deprives the fathers of working-class families of the natural and legitimate

---

[28] See esp. L. François, *Introduction au droit social* (Liège, 1974), 71 f.

[29] *Annales parlementaires de la Chambre des représentants* (1877–8), 404 (de Moreau): 'Pour être ouvrier, on n'en est pas moins père.' 'Sans doute l'État, dans l'intérêt de la société publique, peut réglementer certaines professions, comme l'art de guérir, l'art de composer des médicaments, il peut protéger les oiseaux insectivores, pour qu'on ne les tue point, les animaux domestiques pour qu'on les frappe point. Mais il est un être auquel il ne peut toucher, sans toucher à nous-mêmes, un être qui nous est uni par toutes les fibres de notre âme, et cet être, c'est notre enfant.'

tutelage they exert over their children . . . this is a law which pro-
claims that in the working classes fathers are heartless and mothers
lack an instinctive love for their children.'[30]
    The insistence on fathers' rights is, however, significant in more
than one respect. It certainly confirms that the commodification
of labour power and the ensuing offer of labour on a market committed to the freedom of industry as well as to the liberty of contract aim at what has significantly been called the 'Entfesselung
der Arbeitskraft'[31] in both its literal and figurative sense. Commodification unchains labour power from its prior restrictions and
unleashes it in anticipation of the needs of the imminent industrialization process. But it is the *Arbeitskraft* and not the *Arbeiter*
(worker) that is set free. The emancipation of the worker is only
the potential result of the use of his specific property. The fathers'
right also illustrates, however, that the same 'nouvel ordre
juridique' that claims unconditionally to respect and further the
interests of the individual tolerates and reinforces a strictly hierarchical order within the family. Status was abolished in the case
of the servant but rigidly conserved with regard to the family. The
pater familias is the incarnation and perpetuation of the master.
Condorcet's passionate pleading for the equality of men and
women and Cambacérès's daring words were quickly forgotten:
'The imperious voice of reason has made itself heard. It has said:
paternal power no longer exists; it would be misleading nature to
establish rights by constraints.'[32] The *Constituante*[33] may have
declared as emphatically as the Kentucky court of appeal a few
years later[34] that 'marriage is nothing but a contract', but the influence of the contractual principles remained extremely limited.
The conclusion of marriage and to a certain extent marital prop-

---

[30] Ibid. (1868–9), 284: 'c'est une loi qui destitue en masse de la tutelle naturelle et
légitime de leurs enfants, les pères de famille des classes laborieuses; . . . c'est une loi qui
proclame qu'au sein des classes laborieuses, les pères sont sans cœur et les mères sans
entrailles.'
    [31] See esp. H. Steindl, 'Entfesselung der Arbeitskraft', in id. (ed.), *Wege zur Arbeitsrechts-
geschichte*, Ius Commune 20 (Frankfurt am Main, 1984), 29–136, 29f.
    [32] J. A. Condorcet, *Esquisse d'un tableau historique des progrès de l'esprit humain* (1793), Xème
époque (Paris, 1822), 23: 'La voix impérieuse de la raison s'est fait entendre; elle a dit: Il n'y
a plus de puissance paternelle, c'est tromper la nature que d'établir des droits par la
contrainte'; J. J. Cambacérès, in *Recueil complet des Travaux préparatoires du Code civil*, vol. ix
(Paris, 1836), 65.
    [33] See J. E. M. Portalis, in *Recueil*, above n. 32, 4.
    [34] *Dumaresly v. Fischly* (1821), 3 A. K. Marsh 368.

erty were their sole domain. Neither the English courts[35] nor the continental civil codes[36] left the slightest doubt that submission and obedience were the laws governing family relationships. To respect one's father only because of his obvious intelligence is, hence, no less an act of blasphemy than to contest the husband's right to decide whether his wife is to be allowed to cross the 'natural' boundaries of his house. Irrespective, therefore, of whether the labour capacity of his children or of his wife is at stake, he is the unsupervised, in fact, unsupervisable administrator and trustee of their property.

But however obvious the contradiction between the proclaimed liberation of the individual and the identification of the interests of the wife and the children with the wishes of the husband and father—the freedom of industry remains the guiding maxim and the liberty of contract its principal instrument. The degradation of wives and children within the family does not affect the principles regulating external transactions. The *pater familias* may act for the other family members, but he nevertheless remains a perfectly normal contracting party, fully subject to the few rules applicable to all contracts and in all other areas exposed to a bargaining process governed by the self-interest of the parties. Thus irrespective of whether, as in the Lyon case,[37] the allocation of risks, or as in Lochner,[38] the restriction of hours of work, was brought before an American, a British, a French, a German, or an Italian court, and despite the unquestionable differences between the laws involved, the judges' reactions would first and foremost be determined by the belief that 'men of full age and competent understanding shall', in the words Sir George Jessel, 'have the utmost liberty of contracting and that their contracts, when entered freely and voluntarily, shall be held sacred and shall be enforced by courts of justice'.[39] The courts are neither expected nor authorized to consider the social and economic context of the agreement and *a fortiori* not allowed to reallocate risks and burdens according to their appreciation of the parties' opportunities to

---

[35] 'By the laws of England, by the laws of christianity, and by the constitution of society, when there is a difference of opinion between husband and wife, it is the duty of the wife to submit to her husband', *Agar Ellis* v. *Lassalle*, 10 Ch. D. 4 (1878) at 55.

[36] See, for instance, arts. 213 and 234 of the French Civil Code and art. 160 of the Swiss Civil Code.

[37] Above, n. 1.   [38] Above, n. 2.

[39] In *Printing and Numerical Registering Co.* v. *Sampson* (1875), LR 19 Eq. 462, at 465.

express and defend their interests. They have only to ensure that the bargain made by 'honest men' is respected. The language may vary, but the conviction is both unanimous and universal: it is the contracting parties' agreement that both triggers and delimits judicial activity. Reflections on the structure and the implications of social reality are therefore not within the remit of the courts. Their exclusive domain is an artificial construct created by the contract. Hence Justice Peckham's words[40] no more reflect a particular American rule than the remarks of Sir George Jessel articulate a specific English maxim,[41] or the statement of the *Cour de Cassation* expresses a typically French principle.[42]

III

The dismantling of the supremacy of contractual agreements was as universal as its acknowledgement had been. The methods applied and the means used were once again strikingly similar. Deregulation and decorporation had signalled the transition to the liberty of contract; reregulation and recorporation mark its decline.

The deliberate inactivity of the legislator is replaced by an equally intentional legislative activism leading to a growing fragmentation and juridification of the contractual relationships. The commodification of labour capacity had been the last and decisive move in realizing a universalized freedom of contract; it also marked the beginning of a continuous erosion of the predominance of contractual agreements. The step from the proclamation to the application of the liberty of contract was in fact a step back into a social reality characterized by profound disparities between the various proprietors and not by their assumed equality. Therefore instead of improving the workers' chances to influence their employment conditions, contractual agreements simply sanctioned regulations as one-sided as the old masters' privileges had been.

It is certainly correct that workers were not treated the same everywhere.[43] Weavers and miners were, for instance, mostly in a

---

[40] Above, n. 3.   [41] Above, n. 39.   [42] Above, n. 6.

[43] See, for instance, J. Kocka, 'Situation am Arbeitsplatz: Einführung und Auswertung', in W. Conze and U. Engelhardt (eds.), *Arbeiter im Industrialisierungsprozess* (Stuttgart, 1979),

worse position than workers in the printing or the tobacco industries. Even within one industry both opportunities for training and deskilling processes often differed substantially. Besides, work in a factory was in many cases a clear improvement. But industrialization not only centralized and mechanized work; it also maximized the adaptation of the workers' behaviour to the demands of an efficient production process laid down in uniform rules dictated by the employer. Krupp's complaint that workers understand neither the importance of diligence nor the disastrous consequences that even a five-minute break can have for the production process[44] illustrates the entrepreneur's main concern: to force workers to comply with the exigencies of a production process requiring strict observance of equally strictly standardized behaviour essentially determined by the use of the machines. The work process was therefore not regulated by individual contracts taking into account the particular interests of the workers, but by factory rules that intentionally de-individualized the relationship between employers and employees and attempted to establish and secure discipline by both prescribing and closely controlling the behaviour of the workers. Hence factory rules both broke with past habits and paved the way for a radical change in the work process.[45] The striking combination of provisions not only, for example, imposing rigid time schedules but also prohibiting workers from cooking, sleeping, or drinking during work, or leaving their workplace to smoke a pipe, and the establishment of a system of controls including, for instance in the case of the Krupp works, regular inspection of the toilets in order to chase back to work those who were there for too long, exemplifies each of these aims.[46] Not the individually negotiated agreement but standardized factory-related provisions thus became the regulatory model for a society in which mass production and mass consumption determined the structure and the pace of economic

228–36, 228 f.; id., *Lohnarbeit und Klassenbildung* (Berlin, 1983), 71 f.; id., *Arbeitsverhältnisse und Arbeiterexistenzen* (Bonn, 1990), 373 f.

[44] See C. Deutschmann, *Der Weg zum Normalarbeitstag* (Frankfurt am Main, 1985), 91.

[45] See, for instance, S. Pollard, 'Die Fabrikdisziplin in der industriellen Revolution', in W. Fischer and G. Bajor (eds.), *Die soziale Frage* (Stuttgart, 1967), 159–85, 159 f.; Deutschmann, *Weg*, 76 f.

[46] See A. Lüdtke, 'Arbeitsbeginn, Arbeitspausen, Arbeitsende: Skizzen zur Bedürfnisbefriedigung und Industriearbeit im 19. und frühen 20. Jahrhundert', in G. Huck (ed.), *Sozialgeschichte der Freizeit. Untersuchungen zum Wandel der Alltagskultur in Deutschland* (Wuppertal, 1980), 95–122, 105; L. Machtan, 'Zum Innenleben deutscher Fabriken im 19. Jahrhundert', *Archiv für Sozialgeschichte*, 21 (1981), 179–236, 179.

development. The factory rules are thus the predecessors of what later would be called standardized conditions of work, as well as of the long list of equally standardized provisions inserted into all consumer contracts.

However, the more an entrepreneurial policy dictated by the factory owner's expectations and backed by his economic and social advantages produced regulations based exclusively on his interests as well as a restructuring of the workforce aiming at reducing the costs and consequently marked by the recruitment of children and women, the more the consciousness of the long-term perils of the degradation and exploitation of workers for the sake of economic development and political stability grew. The 'unchaining' of labour power may have promoted industrialization, but at the same time it threatened the very existence of the society that saw in the commodification of labour a condition crucial for the fulfilment of its political and economic purposes. In other words: the average working day of ten to thirteen hours as well as the increasing employment of children endangered the physical existence of the workers concerned. Above all, however, it also placed in question the continued existence of a society dependent on the use of 'human capital'. Thus the legislator could no longer remain passive once it became evident that the collapse of the individual negotiating process legitimized by the expectation of a balance of interests threatened to lead to a breakdown of the societal and political order.[47] The response to factory rules was therefore the adoption of Factory Acts.

Their range and content may have differed from country to country.[48] While, for instance, the need for both a restriction of

[47] See T. Ramm, 'Laissez-faire and State Protection of Workers', in B. Hepple (ed.), *The Making of Labour Law in Europe* (London, 1986), 73–113, 89 f.; L. Machtan, 'Der Arbeiterschutz als sozialpolitisches Problem im Zeitalter der Industrialisierung', in H. Pohl (ed.), *Staatliche, städtische, betriebliche und kirchliche Sozialpolitik vom Mittelalter bis zur Gegenwart*, Vierteljahresschrift für Sozial- und Wirtschaftsgeschichte, suppl. 95 (Stuttgart, 1991), 111–36, 136 f.
[48] See Ramm, 'Laissez-faire', 77 f.; Lord Wedderburn, *The Worker and the Law* (3rd edn., Harmondsworth, 1986), 385 f.; B. Hepple, 'Individual Labour Law', in G. Sayers Bain, *Industrial Relations in Britain* (Oxford, 1983), 393–418, 404 f.; P. W. J. Bartrip and P. T. Fenn, 'The Evolution of the Regulatory Style in the 19th Century: British Factory Inspectorate', *Journal of Law and Society*, 10 (1983), 201–22, 201 f.; François, *Introduction*, 70 f.; K. H. Kaufhold, '150 Jahre Arbeitsschutz in Deutschland: Das preußische Regulativ von 1839 und die weitere Entwicklung bis 1914', *Arbeit und Recht*, 37 (1989), 225–32, 225 f.

the hours of work of children and women and at least a few elementary safety standards was accepted everywhere, the regulations adopted were by no means identical. On the contrary, they reflect, among other things, specific national experiences, as well as the varying political impact of the supporters or opponents of legislative intervention. Factory Acts nevertheless have four features in common.[49]

First, intervention was always focused on specific issues. The aim of legislators was to deal with a particular problem and not to develop an overall policy. What they therefore addressed was child labour, truck practices, women's work, sanitation requirements, sources of accidents, and the allocation of clearly delimited risks, but never working conditions in general.

Secondly, the result placed limits on the liberty of contract and set in motion a growing juridification of the employment relationship. The minimum standards fixed by Factory Acts expressed a minimum of binding expectations. Employers and workers had to comply with the legislator's demands. The decision over any part of the agreement's content was hence no longer left to the parties but taken directly by the legislator.[50] Alternatives were not tolerated, unless and to the degree to which they had been explicitly accepted by the particular statute. The parties' liberty to regulate their relationship was *nota bene* never openly questioned. The interference was carefully concealed in provisions inserted either into the criminal or into the police law. They as a rule imposed certain obligations on the employer. But each of these duties inevitably reduced the employer's regulatory options and thus restricted the range of the application of a potential contractual agreement. To this extent the liberty of contract henceforth was conceived as a revokable concession and not, as originally assumed, as a genuine, 'natural' right of the parties. Thus industrialization reversed the seemingly incontestable premises of the legal order. Instead of affirming the sovereignty of the parties, it restored the supremacy of rules announced and imposed by the state. The consequence was a gradual regression from contract to status.

[49] See also S. Simitis, 'Juridification of Labor Relations', in G. Teubner (ed.), *Juridification of Social Spheres* (Berlin, 1987) 113–61, 114 f.
[50] See also J. T. Ward, *The Factory Movement* (London, 1962), 483: 'factory legislation was the mortal blow to the laissez-faire concept.'

Thirdly, juridification generated the establishment of government agencies whose task was to ensure that the demands made by the Acts were fulfilled. Consequently the intervention did not end with the adoption of a few rules. The state was not prepared to trust the goodwill of the employers. Their reactions were monitored in order to prevent both infractions and any continuation of the practices condemned by the Acts. The Acts thus operated on two levels. Mandatory requests to the employers were complemented by an organizational infrastructure consisting of 'inspectorates' created and run by the state. Their establishment marked the beginning of a progressively expanding bureaucracy which would ultimately transcend the limits of mere supervision and attempt to steer the labour market.

Fourthly, this intervention produced a fragmentation of once uniform rules. The accent was no longer on the contractual relationship as such but on the particular agreement and its specific modalities. The general rules might still have been in place. Behind their façade, however, a new regulatory system developed that deliberately abandoned the original level of abstraction and differentiated instead between the various types of contract. Workers, just like tenants at a later stage, were singled out and subjected to rules triggered by conflicts characteristic of their position and therefore confined to their agreements. The fragmentation of the substantive provisions was supplemented by a similar process on the procedural level. The *conseils de prud'hommes* led the way, and the *Gewerbegerichte* (German industrial courts) confirmed and emphasized the tendency towards reserving cases which were already increasingly subject to rules specifically designed for them to being heard in equally specialized tribunals.[51]

While the juridification of the employment relationship challenged the liberty of contract, the growing readiness of the workers to organize themselves in more and more professionalized associations led to a re-corporation and therefore no less clearly defied the abolition of intermediary powers. The first collective activities mostly developed on the margins of a political and economic system in whose view only individuals could legit-

---

[51] See esp. A. Cottereau, 'Justice et injustice ordinaire sur les lieux de travail d'après les audiences prud'homales (1806–1866)', *Le Mouvement social*, 141 (1987), 25–59, 25 f.; R. Rogowski and A. Tooze, 'Individuelle Arbeitskonfliktlösung und liberaler Korporatismus', in H. Mohnhaupt and D. Simon (eds.), *Vorträge zur Justizforschung*, vol. i (Frankfurt am Main, 1992), 317–86, 318 f.

imately express and promote their interests and thus those of society. Certainly, associations whose aim was either mutual help by insuring their members against professional risks or furthering their education[52] to enable them better to protect their own interests were hardly compatible with rigid individualism. But since they relied solely on the initiatives of their members and reflected their efforts to make up for the unleashing of labour capacity in a fully atomized society they were considered at least tolerable, all the more because they were regarded as means intended to correct a temporary malfunctioning of market mechanisms.

The early forms of association, however, were gradually replaced by organizations which, like the various 'combinations' and 'coalitions', concentrated their activities on the conditions of work and considered collective actions as the principal if not only way to counterbalance the entrepreneurs' power and to force them to accept changes ameliorating the workers' situation.[53] Their negotiations and accords were an early form of the 'collective bargaining' that became the distinctive mark of the 'new model' trade unions.[54] Both efforts to establish a collective representation of the workers and claims to influence the conditions of work with the help of instruments stressing no less clearly the collective approach were, however, unmistakable signs of a re-corporation. The 'new model' unions not only clearly rejected interventions by the state with the exception of protective measures in the interests of especially disadvantaged groups, unable to react by themselves, for instance, women and children, but, above all, openly questioned the regulatory monopoly assigned to the individual worker and thus defied the structural principles of the employment relationship. Hence the reaction could hardly be the same as in the case of the earlier associations.

IV

The response to the at first hesitant but then obviously quickening process of re-regulation and to the no less clearly expanding

[52] See, for instance, U. Engelhardt, 'Gewerkschaftliches Organisationsverhalten in der ersten Industrialisierungsphase', in Conze and Engelhardt (eds.), *Arbeiter im Industrialisierungsprozess*, 372–402, 374 f.

[53] See esp. A. Jacobs, 'Collective Self-Regulation', in Hepple (ed.), *Making of Labour Law in Europe*, 193–241, 193 f.

[54] Sydney and Beatrice Webb, *Industrial Democracy* (London, 1914 edn.), 842.

re-corporation was a laborious effort to preserve at least formally the coherence of a regulatory system relying in particular on the liberty of contract. This was achieved by attenuating the obvious contradiction to its premises with the help of its own means. In the case of re-regulation, the procedure adopted was ingeniously simple. The assertion that employment relationships emanate from freely negotiated contracts and should therefore be treated in accordance with the rules governing all contractual agreements was emphatically affirmed. All provisions resulting from the regulatory interventions of the state were in an equally categorical way assigned to the sphere of 'public law'.[55] The advantage was obvious: the parties' negotiations remained the contract's 'natural law'.[56] Hence any attempt to interfere with the employment relationship was, as before, evidently alien to the principles governing relations between individuals, and therefore had to be governed by the only possible justification, the police power of the state.[57] The *politeia* may have been forced to retreat from the market, yet it maintained the power to safeguard the 'public good' interpreted in an increasingly wide way. In short, the clear-cut distinction between the priority of the liberty of contract and the still rather exceptional use of police power restricted the regulatory activities of the state. Moreover, it above all suggested that despite the growing number of mandatory provisions nothing had in fact changed.

The scene was simultaneously set, in particular by courts and lawyers in France, Italy, and Germany, for a further means of adaptation, equally inherent in the existing regulatory system, yet definitely more flexible. The explicitly acknowledged duty of the contracting parties to respect 'good morals'[58] or the 'ordre public'[59] was slowly and unobtrusively reinterpreted. A decidedly broader understanding of both notions allowed social and economic considerations along the lines of the interventionist policies of the state to be included.[60] Besides, a new, additional aspect of the 'ordre public', the 'ordre public social', permitted corrective interventions to be combined with

---

[55] See P. Durand and R. Jaussaud, *Traité de droit du travail*, vol. i (Paris, 1947), 250 f.
[56] Ibid. 226.   [57] See also Bürge, *Privatrecht*, 483 f.
[58] See, for instance, art. 138 of the German Civil Code.
[59] See, for instance, art. 6 of the French Civil Code.
[60] See K. Simitis, *Gute Sitten und ordre public* (Marburg, 1960), 64 f., 162 f.

the right of those who had concluded collective agreements to improve the mandatory standards provided by the state.[61] Both approaches developed into an ideal way to fit interventionist regulations into well-known and generally accepted traditional rules. The reaction to re-corporation was infinitely more complicated, if only because none of the existing schemes was applicable to collective activities. They could neither be simply subsumed under the normal agreements initiated and concluded by individuals, nor was it possible to qualify them as part of state action. Moreover, as long as collective activities were penalized, to reflect on their implications for the regulation of conditions of work was senseless. Hence, in order to acknowledge and contain the interference of the 'new model' unions as a regulatory means, a policy explicitly outlawing collective activities had first to be given up. The English 'immunities' doctrine is as characteristic of this phase as the slow and cumbersome revision of the criminal law on the Continent.[62]

Hugo Sinzheimer's famous expression[63] 'collective autonomy' describes the next move. The individual's 'natural' liberty of contract was complemented and supplemented by an equally 'natural' right of the unions to negotiate conditions of employment. 'Collective laissez-faire' thus became a regulatory principle as self-evident as 'individual laissez-faire' had earlier been.[64] Once more, therefore, a procedure hardly compatible with the predominance of individual contracts was brought into line by being linked to a perfectly familiar principle. 'Individual' and 'collective' autonomy henceforth appeared as two aspects of one concept, the supremacy of state-free self-regulation.

To clarify the argument, it should be pointed out that 'collective agreements' are certainly accords, but not necessarily

[61] See G. Lyon-Caen, J. Pélissier, and A. Supiot, *Droit du travail* (18th edn., Paris, 1996), 54 f., 97.

[62] See Wedderburn, *Worker*, 520 f.; B. Simpson, 'Trade Union Immunities', in R. Lewis, *Labour Law in Britain* (Oxford, 1986), 161–94, 161 f.; Jacobs, 'Collective Self-Regulation', 200, 211.

[63] See H. Sinzheimer, *Ein Arbeitstarifgesetz* (Munich, 1916), 50 f.; id., *Arbeitsrecht und Arbeiterbewegung* (Berlin, 1927), 7.

[64] O. Kahn-Freund, 'Labour Law', in M. Ginsberg (ed.), *Law and Opinion in England in the Twentieth Century* (London, 1959), 215–63, 224; see also R. Lewis, 'Collective Labour Law', in Bain, *Industrial Relations*, 361–92, 366 f.; W. McCarthy, 'The Rise and Fall of Collective Laissez-Faire', in id. (ed.), *Legal Intervention in Industrial Relations* (Oxford, 1992), 1–78, 1 f.

'contracts'.[65] Significantly enough, continental lawyers for a long time experienced serious difficulties whenever they attempted to qualify collective agreements as contracts in the traditional sense, mainly because of their most salient feature, the 'normative' or at least binding effect of the provisions regulating the conditions of employment.[66] In addition, what for continental lawyers appeared to be ultimately a problem of coherence and purity of the contract concept was for British lawyers a question of principle. To regard collective agreements as contracts even in a broader sense would have meant abandoning the very aspect that in the eyes of both unions and lawyers made the British approach unique: the existence and acknowledgement of an extra-legal regulation that deliberately distances itself from the normal contractual rules.[67] However, what really matters is not whether in the end collective agreements are largely treated as contracts, as for instance in continental laws as well as in the United States,[68] but the common conviction that all such accords are legitimized by the 'collective autonomy' of the employees. It is this belief that illustrates the uniqueness of the agreements and justifies their integration into a system of rules relying on the priority of freely negotiated rights and duties. Therefore, collective bargaining operates against a well-known background and reproduces, though in a very different form, a customary regulation. However, at the same time collective autonomy marks, more than any other feature of the collective accords, another equally important implication of their recognition: the start of their instrumentalization.[69] Exactly as in the case of the individual contracts, 'autonomy', in other words, does not signal the end of all state interventions. It merely indicates an intentional and therefore reversible abstention.

[65] See esp. O. Kahn-Freund, *Labour and the Law*, ed. P. Davies and M. Freedland (3rd edn., London, 1983), 154 f.
[66] See, for instance, H. Sinzheimer, *Grundzüge des Arbeitsrechts* (2nd edn., Jena, 1927), 273 f.; Durand and Jaussaud, *Traité*, 129 f.
[67] See esp. O. Kahn-Freund, 'Collective Agreements under War Legislation', *Modern Law Review*, 6 (1943), 112–43, 143; id., *Labour and the Law*, 177 f.; Lord Wedderburn, 'Otto Kahn-Freund and British Labour Law', in id., R. Lewis, and J. Clark, *Labour Law and Industrial Relations: Building on Kahn-Freund* (Oxford, 1983), 29–82, 40: 'the root principle of British labour law'; Wedderburn, *Worker*, 8, 320; id., *Employment Rights in Britain and Europe* (London, 1991), 106 f.; Lewis, 'Collective Labour Law', 366; McCarthy, 'Rise', 4 f.
[68] Above, nn. 65, 66; H. H. Wellington, *Labor and the Legal Process* (New Haven, 1968), 90 f.
[69] See Simitis, 'Juridification', 104 f.

V

These admittedly rather general remarks must be linked to three caveats in order to avoid misunderstandings. First, regulatory maxims may have radically changed. The result was never a consistent application of the categorically affirmed liberty of contract and the no less emphatically proclaimed freedom of industry. Legal systems are not clear-cut constructs that can simply be exchanged. They grow out of the pre-existing order and are therefore always a combination of newly developed and remaining or slowly reinterpreted old concepts.[70] Second, the regulatory maxims may have transcended national borders. Their application was, however, at all times determined by the historical, political, and economic context typical of each country. The acknowledgement of the freedom of industry in France,[71] long delayed despite the early declarations, is a no less characteristic example than the extremely ambivalent understanding of this same principle in Germany culminating in its instrumentalization for the justification of cartels.[72]

Third, there is inevitably a striking contrast between a comparative micro-historical approach focusing on the implementation of specific rules, and an equally comparative legal analysis addressing the principles of particular systems. The first documents contradictions and deficiencies by uncovering the difficulties as well as the limits of the implementation and thus stresses the discrepancy between the regulatory ambition and the living law. The latter pictures a largely fictional world. Both the freedom of industry and the liberty of contract reflect visions and are inherently utopian. It would nevertheless be mistaken to conclude from the inadequacies of the implementation that the principles

---

[70] See also D. Sugarman, 'Law, Economy and the State in England, 1750–1914: Some Major Issues', in id. (ed.), *Legality, Ideology and the State* (London, 1983), 213–66, esp. 242: 'In fact the evidence is clear that the *"laissez-faire"* and state interventionism were not polar opposites but rather, different sides of the same coin: both co-existed in nineteenth century England.' Rückert, ' "Frei" und "sozial" ', esp. 281 f.

[71] See esp. M. David, 'L'Évolution historique des conseils de prud'hommes en France', *Droit social*, 2 (1974), 3–21, at 3 f.; Bürge, *Privatrecht*, 307 f.; Rogowski and Tooze, 'Arbeitskonfliktlösung', 321 f.

[72] Above, n. 17; B. Vogel, *Allgemeine Gewerbefreiheit: Die Reformpolitik des preußischen Staatskanzlers Hardenberg (1810–1820)* (Göttingen, 1983), 137 f.; K. H. Kaufhold, 'Gewerbefreiheit und gewerbliche Entwicklung in Deutschland im 19. Jahrhundert', *Blätter für deutsche Landesgeschichte*, 118 (1982), 73–114, 73.

are irrelevant. Their impact can, however, strange as it may at first seem, be measured only by their negative consequences, the everyday implications of a 'freely' established employment relationship as well as an ever more complex re-regulation and re-corporation. Irrespective of their specific motives, the statutes aiming for a progressive shortening of working hours, a lessening of health and safety risks, and continuous improvements in training, as well as the corresponding collectively agreed conditions of employment, mark the stages along the employee's journey from 'persona miserabilis'[73] to a self-reliant individual. However paradoxical it may therefore sound, the very principles that made labour a commodity, and so established and consolidated the employees' subordination, set in motion a development that ushered in the preconditions for restoring their autonomy.

As long as these provisos are taken into account it is both convincing and correct to state that neither the quest for a system of rules governed by the liberty of contract and the freedom of industry nor the reactions to its consequences are typical or even unique features of a particular national law. On the contrary, none of these developments can really be understood unless the ever present insistence on the uniqueness, for whatever grounds, of the various national laws is abandoned. A comparative analysis intentionally going beyond the frontiers of a purely formal collection of statutes and decisions, especially if based on a thorough examination of the economic and political background, is thus both an antidote against an often historicist sublimation of the differences between national laws and a constant reminder that they are ultimately no more than alternative answers to common questions. It is in exactly this sense that the comparison is an indispensable tool for a better understanding of any national approach.

---

[73] M. Rood, 'Labour Law in the 21st Century', in Lord Wedderburn, M. Rood, G. Lyon-Caen, W. Däubler, and P. van der Heijden, *Labour Law in the Post-Industrial Era* (Aldershot, 1994), 83–92, 89.

9

Industrial Tribunals and the Establishment of a Kind of Common Law of Labour in Nineteenth-Century France

ALAIN COTTEREAU

Industrial tribunals (*conseils de prud'hommes*) are a little-known French institution, not merely in international comparative social history but even in French social history. There are many reasons for this lack of interest, starting with a wide variety of ideological rejections. The distrust of the law once prevalent among working-class and Marxist movements in France consigned to oblivion a device of social relations based on the ideal of justice and conciliation. The mainstream of economic liberalism also avoided taking an interest in an institution for regulating social relations whose success did not fit into the *laissez-faire* framework. The traditions of paternalism likewise took no interest in it, because mediators belonging to the *notables* were ruled out by the fact that employer and worker *prud'hommes* were appointed by direct election. However, the most decisive reasons for the under-appreciation of industrial tribunals were not external. From the outset, they were linked to the very mechanics of the institution's functioning. The fact is that during the nineteenth century, the operation and success of industrial tribunals required them to occupy a unique position, separate and distinct from both public institutions and private arrangements; the device, based on individual conciliation of conflicts, mobilized the opinions of the occupational milieux of employers and workers and invited them to work out a collective consensus while eschewing publicity and overt collective representation. Following this original logic of limited publicity, a kind of customary or common law, never formulated in terms of principle, administered on a day-to-day basis, was established and maintained on the margins of, and occasionally in conflict with, the prevailing system of French law. This exclusion from the national public sphere formed part of the system of industrial-tribunal law, which helps to explain why, until recently, so little interest was taken in it.

The originality of the status of this labour law dispensed by the industrial tribunals leads me to refer in my title to 'a kind of common law'. My use of the Anglo-Saxon term is provocative and must clearly not be taken too literally. But it does draw attention to certain features of the establishment of this labour law, far removed from the kind of *légicentrisme* that had been in place in France since the Revolution and closer to a typically English kind of law as seen through continental eyes: a law constituted essentially by judicial decisions, developing on a case-by-case basis, rationalizing itself by using precedents, and appealing more to common sense and the sense of justice than to the interpretation of statutory texts when it came to justifying its legislative activity.

This essay will outline the content and operation of this French labour law by drawing a comparison with English employment law during the same period, the first two-thirds of the nineteenth century. On the French side, the essay draws on studies carried out over the last fifteen years of industrial-tribunal records and various other records, often unknown or unclassified at the time when they were studied. There are few publications based on examination of actual decisions of industrial tribunals. As a result, the evidence cannot, so far as France is concerned, be supplied in terms of detailed references to published works and available sources.[1] By contrast, as regards comparison with England, I

---

[1] Where this essay does not refer to a particular source or publication, it is based on my investigations of the records of industrial tribunals. The chief publications are as follows: a general outline of the institution of the industrial tribunal and of the investigation is given in Alain Cottereau, 'Justice et injustice ordinaire sur les lieux de travail d'après les audiences prud'homales (1806–1866)', *Le Mouvement social*, 141 (Oct.–Dec. 1987), 25–61. Since then, research has widened to include some fifteen industrial tribunals and has brought to light fresh records, though without altering the broad lines laid down in 1987. This special issue of *Le Mouvement social* includes two other articles based on first-hand research: Paul Delsalle, 'Tisserands et fabricants chez les prud'hommes dans la région de Lille-Roubaix-Tourcoing (1810–1848)', 61–80, and Heinz-Gerhard Haupt, 'Les Employés lyonnais devant le conseil de prud'hommes du commerce (1910–1914)', 81–100, as well as articles by jurists based on secondary legal sources. A contribution in A. Cottereau and P. Ladrière, *Pouvoir et légitimité: Figures de l'espace public* (Paris, 1992), focusing on the 'public sphere' (*espace public*, *Öffentlichkeit*) also throws some light on industrial tribunals. A more specialist publication, Alain Cottereau, 'L'Embauche et la vie normative des métiers durant les deux premiers tiers du XIXe siècle français', *Les Cahiers des relations professionelles*, 10 (Feb.

rely on published social history and reports in the *Parliamentary Papers*.

Comparing the two legal systems in the field of labour law brings out a major contrast: whereas in England, until the reforms of 1867 to 1875, the statutes governing employment reinforced the classification of workers as servants, the contrary was the case in France. From 1789, jurisdiction solemnly drew a strict distinction between the employment of workers for a specific job, known as *louage d'ouvrage*, on the one hand, and the hiring of domestic servants or casual labourers for service, known as *louage de service*, on the other. From 1866, however, an inversion in case law and doctrine took place in France, tending to lessen the distinction between *louage d'ouvrage* and *louage de service*, whereas at the same time, England was beginning to question its 'master and servant' legislation. This development is well known for England, but less so as regards France. The next section will therefore summarize the main features of developments in France.

The French Revolution and the liberty of workers

In 1789, French jurisdiction was characterized by a constant ambiguity giving rise to conflict: wage-earners, that is, manual or skilled workers or craftsmen working 'pour compte d'autri', were sometimes treated as 'lessors of labour' (*locateurs d'ouvrage*), in positions of legitimate commercial reciprocity with their employers, and sometimes as servants, subject to obligations of subordination that ruled out legitimate reciprocal bargaining. Historians of the Second Empire and the Third Republic, echoed by historians of labour law, mainly stressed the legal obligations of subordination implicit in the regulatory decisions of the king and the courts.[2]

1995), 47–71, studies a segment of labour law governed by industrial tribunals, *marchandage* or face-to-face bargaining. An essay in English, Alain Cottereau, 'The Fate of "Fabriques Collectives" in the Industrial World: The Examples of the Silk Industries of Lyons and London, 1800–1850', in C. Sabel and J. Zeitlin (eds.), *Worlds of Possibilities: Flexibility and Mass Production in Western Industrialisation* (Cambridge, 1997), 75–152, compares the economic regulation exercised by the Lyon industrial tribunals with the deregulation exercised during the same period in London's silk trade.

[2] This has been pointed out by the best known of the founders of labour history, Émile Levasseur, *Histoire des classes ouvrières en France depuis la conquête de Jules César jusqu'à la Révolution* (Paris, 1859).

However, a recent study, the first to have taken a close look at eighteenth-century legal debates about labour and to have taken into account the views expressed by parties to litigation, has demonstrated the extreme instability and conflicting nature of the norms put forward throughout the eighteenth century.[3] In that diversity, one thing that stands out is the constant opposition between, on the one hand, the legitimacy of the freedom of workers, insisted on by journeymen and occasionally upheld by some workers and employers, and on the other hand the necessity of submission of *service*, periodic attempts to impose which were made by coalitions of employers. They were usually backed in this by the higher echelons of the judiciary and the administration, whereas local magistrates were more inclined to compromise or to recognize workers' demands as legitimate.

That legitimacy, commonly embodied in negotiating practices at the workplace, found a framework of expression in the invocation of natural law against positive law. 'We are not slaves' ('Nous ne sommes pas des esclaves'), was a recurring theme. This referred to the Latin term which did not distinguish between servant and slave, bypassing the secular distinctions of status established between slavery, voluntary servitude, and domestic service. The invocation of natural law was not so much an appeal to a specific doctrinal content as an act of autonomy of judgement, indicating a competence to criticize the soundness of positive law in the name of higher principles, common to all humanity. Such criticisms also invoked a common law (*droit commun*) or a law of nations (*droit des gens*), though without considering their technical legal significance, instead giving them more or less the same significance as a critical appeal to the common principles of humanity.

This historical background is crucial to understanding the emancipatory power of the French Revolution in the field of labour law. The declaration of the rights of man, the proclamation of the principles of political and civil liberty, the abolition of all kinds of corporative regulation, the famous *Loi Le Chapelier* did not simply enshrine 'economic freedoms' such as were dear to classical economists and equally dear to the old clichés of the 'bourgeois Revolution'. These upheavals were experienced intensely as a real emancipation of the workers, as a triumph of good old causes, and as the establishment of a real ability to nego-

---

[3] Michael Sonenscher, *Work and Wages: Natural Law, Politics and the Eighteenth-Century French Trades* (Cambridge, 1989).

tiate on an equal footing with employers. It was not simply a question of new formal civil rights but of actually achieved possibilities, which were used on a massive scale. It was what in the everyday language of the day was called a 'revolution of manners' ('une révolution des mœurs').

This aspect of the emancipation of workers found little expression in legal texts or in declarations of new rights. To appreciate it, local judicial decisions before and after 1789 must be examined and placed in the context of industrial relations. The *tabula rasa* of the former statutory regulations then takes on a very precise significance in each local history. In the case of the Lyon silk industry, for example, the abolition of the old regulations and the industry's old jurisdictions led to a new system of relations between merchants, master-workers (*maîtres-ouvriers*), journeymen, and apprentices. Everywhere, the removal of the statutory restrictions on leaving jobs and changing employers was used as a fresh opportunity to negotiate working conditions and pay on an equal footing: periods of notice before leaving or dismissal became strictly reciprocal, and the permanent threat of leaving for more favourable conditions of remuneration enabled master workers and journeymen to keep up with the most favourable tariff scales (*cours de façon*).[4]

There is a great deal of evidence for this 'revolution of manners'. Among the most remarkable sources are the reports and petitions of employers between 1794 and 1804, when it was necessary, following the Reign of Terror, to build or rebuild an industrial order on the basis of new principles. The many letters, petitions, and memoranda sent by manufacturers and their associations to local or national authorities all note a new climate in labour relations, whether as a matter for regret or as something simply to be accepted: the spirit of liberty affecting all social relations left its mark on the workplace and ruled out any possibility of a return to the old rules of submission. The most vivid descriptions come from manufacturers demanding just such a return to the earlier regulation of labour. Drawing a disastrous picture of their 'impotence' in the face of the 'spirit of liberty' affecting workers, they asked for the support of the authorities in order to re-establish the old regulations and customs and thus 'to restore subordination'. Employer petitions even pointed out that a

---

[4] A more detailed analysis of these changes in Lyon before and after the Revolution may be found in Cottereau, 'The Fate of "Fabriques Collectives"'.

manufacturer merely mentioning the ancient customs of hiring and dismissal faced the threat of physical violence.[5]

The arguments and anecdotes related in all these petitions highlight the contrast between the old limitations on workers' freedom to quit and the new situation that had been in place since 1790. In a variety of languages ranging from approval to disapproval, they explain how former jurisdictions of control, entrusted with upholding obedience, had restricted individual bargaining, while the new system, on the contrary, gave free rein to discussion on an equal footing. Some, for instance, described how workers indulged in 'blackmail', threatening to quit their jobs if their employers did not revise their conditions of work and pay in line with this or that competitor. However, other employers, and with them the commercial courts and advisory authorities (*bureaux consultatifs* having replaced chambers of commerce during the Revolution), tended to hold that these instances of alleged 'blackmail' by workers should not be regarded as insubordination but as the legitimate exercise of the new liberty. Government and police authorities adopted this position. The few exceptions, mainly on the part of the police, seeking to suppress insubordinate behaviour on the strength of denunciations by employers in the spirit of pre-revolutionary paternalist supervision, were invariably rejected by the judicial and administrative hierarchy.

The example of the livret ouvrier *and freedom to leave*

A good illustration of the new climate of worker freedom may be seen in the discussions about reintroducing the *livret ouvrier* and subsequently in the case law implementing it. What is called *livret*

[5] For example, a petition from the weaving manufacturers of Rouen (July, 1804, Archives Départementales de Seine Maritime 10 M 4) talks about the workers' spirit of liberty and their habit of switching employers as soon as conditions or the price no longer suited them, all in the name of new principles of liberty as opposed to the regulations of the *ancien régime*. The petitioners demanded a return to those old regulations, to restrictions on the right to quit, and to penal sanctions. They did not obtain satisfaction, and neither did large numbers of petitioners throughout France. All these demands to restrict workers' freedom to change jobs were opposed by the successive governments of the Directory, the Consulate, and the Empire on the basis of the new, intangible principles of liberty, implying reciprocity of negotiations and sanctions. There are many files of this kind in local, departmental, and national record offices, classified either chronologically or according to commercial and judicial topics. Others are scattered in the files of various branches in the Archives Nationales, series F 12 for the periods concerned.

ouvrier in France was a document whose origins lay in various statutory regulations and judicial decisions of the *ancien régime*: in most manufacturing districts, no worker could leave an employer unless he had a 'ticket of leave' (*billet de congé*) from the employer, certifying that he had met his obligations and was not in debt. The different local statutory regulations modified this rule and laid down the periods of notice (which were often obligatory for workers only, or were longer for workers than for employers). In many instances, the local regulations stipulated that the 'ticket of leave' had to state why the worker was leaving, or even assess his conduct and 'habits' (*mœurs*) for the information of his next employer.[6] Between 1794 and 1803 there was some discussion as to whether these regulations should be re-established. Remarkably, there was a broad consensus, not only among workers but also among employers and government authorities, against reintroducing them.

Instead, a body of legislation put in place in 1803–4 provided for a *livret* (that is, a single booklet of various certificates of discharge) based on very different foundations. First, it transformed the *livret* from a document of supervision delegated by the authorities to the employers into a document required by private contractual law and designed to record certain aspects of the labour contract, just as commercial law stipulated that ledgers contain certain entries and record certain transactions. The *livret* had to certify an engagement for a specific job and its completion (*quittance*), or to acknowledge that the worker had not yet paid off advances received on wages, and that this debt remained to be deducted from future wages by the new employer, within limits compatible with workers' presumably low levels of solvency. The private law character stressed by legislators and jurisdiction meant

---

[6] As an illustration, one article from the 'Regulations and Statutes' of the Elbeuf wool trade, dated 19 Apr. 1667, is quoted here. It covers the obligatory nature of moral investigation and indicates the lack of symmetry in terms of giving notice: 'XXIV. A weaver may not quit his master until the piece of work with which he has dressed his loom has been completed, and in this connection he shall be obliged to notify his master when setting the piece up. And if the worker owes anything to his master, the person for whom he is going to work shall have a duty to inform himself regarding the life and habits of the said worker and the reason why he left the said master. The new master shall be obliged to pay what the said worker owes to the master he has left, as also in respect of what he owes for mistakes made in his work. Nor may the master dismiss a worker without 24 hours' notice.' Other articles stipulate that 'physical coercion' may be used to force workers who have quit without leave or without 'just cause' to return to their masters.

that the *livret* was separate from any considerations of public order. This character was expressed mainly in the fact that it no longer contained a repressive element, unlike the ticket of leave regulations under the *ancien régime*. Henceforth non-observance of *livret* legislation was punished neither by prison, nor fine, nor obligation to return to the employer. Breaches of contract were liable only to damages and interest, payable to the injured party, whether employer or worker. Industrial-tribunal decisions show, in fact, that damages and interest were paid at least as frequently to workers as to employers in the early days of implementation of these rules: workers wishing to leave their employment, for example, for better pay, and whose *livrets* were withheld by their employers without sufficient, proven cause, commonly had their *livrets* restored by industrial tribunals, together with compensation for lost time and wages.[7]

Secondly, the rules and subsequently the judicial decisions concerning registration of debts in fact operated according to the spirit of the promoters of the new civil law, giving rise not to measures restricting changes of employment but on the contrary to measures facilitating mobility. Registering debts in the *livret* was an arrangement that made it possible for a worker to change employers before he had paid off the advances received in respect of

[7] For more information about *livrets*, see Cottereau, 'Justice et injustice' and id., 'The Fate of "Fabriques Collectives"', which gives a detailed example of a judgment in which a *livret* was restored to a (female) factory worker with damages and interest (pp. 26–9). It is particularly important to stress the liberal operation of *livret* legislation, because from the beginning of the Third Republic it gave rise to some extremely imaginative historical writing: ultra-individualist, anti-reformist jurists (notably Marc Sauzet, 'Le Livret obligatoire des ouvriers', *Revue critique de droit et de jurisprudence* (1890), 21–30; and id., 'Essai historique sur la législation industrielle de la France', *Revue d'économie politique* (1892), 353–6, 890–930, 1097–136) sought to demonstrate, from the 1880s on, that there had been a continuity of 'interventionism' and police discretion between pre- and post-revolutionary legislations, particularly with regard to labour law and the *livret*. The works of Sauzet contained many such false and ill-founded assertions in terms of historiographical and legal documentation. For instance, he put forward the theory of a continuity between the *ancien régime*'s 'ticket of leave' (*billet de congé*) and the *livret* introduced in 1803, playing with anachronistic meanings of the old French notion of *police* and arguing that if penal sanctions had not been abolished irrevocably under the Revolution. His dogmatic statements masked a total ignorance of local judicial decisions. There would be no need to mention this author had he not unfortunately been often repeated without critical examination in French academic traditions of legal history. As a result, English authors who accepted these traditions at face value were led astray on key points of comparison: they thought they could establish a similarity between English employment law and alleged French restrictions on freedom to quit during the period 1800 to 1870.

wages, tools, or workshop equipment.[8] Whereas the old common law would allow the employer to retain a worker who was in debt by exerting economic pressure, the jurisdiction concerning *livrets* allowed debts to be circulated from employer to employer. When a worker who was in debt wished to change employers, whether he worked at home or in a factory, he could ask for his debt to be registered. That meant that the new employer became responsible for reimbursing the previous employer by deduction from the worker's future wages up to a limit of one-eighth. The worker thereby found his negotiating strength increased, and the employer had a relative guarantee of reimbursement, enabling him to take out a loan for workshop heads and to finance the recruiting, tooling, and equipping of workshops.

The *livret* now functioned as a kind of register of bills of discount on work and became the instrument of a free credit arrangement for workers and their workshops. It gave those who held it the opportunity to obtain free advances, guaranteed simply by their future work for successive future employers, on the strength of their *livret* and with possible backing from industrial tribunals. In the event of non-reimbursement, there were no penal sanctions or punitive constraints, unlike the sanctions of commercial law. Workers who could not repay did not repay, with no other dissuasive effect than some difficulty in obtaining credit again from the same employers in times of economic downturn. Granted, the arrangement inevitably gave rise to 'abuses': workers used the system to obtain multiple advances without repaying them, and employers tended despite everything to use debts to keep their workers. But industrial tribunals and justices of the peace appear to have curbed such abuses with some success, according to retrospective parliamentary inquiries carried out in 1848–50.

Thirdly, industrial tribunals and justices of the peace banned any kind of assessment of the person or conduct of *livret* holders. The *livret* was to contain no more than what was required by law:

---

[8] The laws created an obligation on the part of employers to allow workers in debt to leave when the initiative for terminating or modifying the terms of hire came from the employer. By contrast, in law the employer could demand prior repayment when the termination or modification was requested by the worker. However, most industrial-tribunal decisions applied the rule of freedom to quit before repayment without seeking to establish where the initiative originated.

attestation of hire and, where appropriate, of deferred reimbursement. This point was of great symbolic importance because it demonstrated a certain continuity of the revolutionary spirit of civil equality in the law of employment contract. In contrast to the norms current under the *ancien régime*, here was judicial confirmation that moral paternalism had been outlawed.[9] Employers tried hard to restore the custom of recording assessments of good or bad conduct on tickets of leave, but all the industrial tribunals studied made a point of rigorously and solemnly condemning any such record: employers were not entitled to restrict their workers' freedom to re-enter employment, no matter what the reasons for their dismissal had been. A new employer must have no official knowledge of the moral assessments of the employer whose service a worker had just left.

Contrasts in French and English jurisdiction (1790–1870)

In the domain of laws and judicial decisions concerning the right to leave employment, there is thus a complete contrast between France and England in the period 1789 to 1875. In England, the tradition of criminal punishment for breach of contract (up to three months' imprisonment) when servants left their masters without observing the rules actually gained in strength and scope at the same time as in France breaking the contract of employment was radically and definitively decriminalized by the Revolution.[10] The contrast is even more striking when we look at how, in each country, employment law in particular fits into the more general context of penalties for debt. In England, as Atiyah points out, the penalty, and particularly imprisonment for breach of

---

[9] The records of industrial tribunals usually include, for the early period of their operation, a number of cases of moral assessments of workers in their *livrets*. In every instance examined, without a single exception, this practice was repudiated, and negative assessments prompted severe condemnation of employers. In these cases the *livret* which contained the negative assessment was replaced, and damages and interest were awarded to the worker. The judicial hierarchy supported such decisions, and the government authorities who had the model *livrets* printed also drew attention to this rule. On the subject of the judicial outlawing of this kind of moral paternalism, covering the First Empire and the Restoration as well, see the detailed case study at the beginning of Alain Cottereau, '"Esprit public" et capacité de juger', in id. and Ladrière, *Pouvoir et légitimité*, 239–73.

[10] See the essay by Douglas Hay in this volume, which provides evidence for the English case.

contract, was not very different from imprisonment for debt generally, at least until the middle of the nineteenth century.[11] Furthermore, for several decades after that, English law appears to have upheld a moral view of poverty as a symptom of guilt, since it continued to punish the economic failures of the most indigent.[12] It was still possible for worker delegates to hold such views in 1866, for certain working-class members of the Select Committee on Master and Servant did not dare imagine or suggest the complete abolition of criminal sanctions for unpaid debts.[13]

From a comparative point of view, this moral vision is all the more striking for never having become as prevalent in France, where economic misfortune generally commanded respect and compassion.[14] In France, a threefold distinction operated at the level of jurisdiction throughout the nineteenth century, but to the advantage of the poorest: following the vacillations in revolutionary generosity, the reorganization of penalties for debt under the First Empire reserved the severest sanctions, including imprisonment, for cases under commercial law alone, that is to say, solely for speculative professional transactions, and excluding non-speculative professional transactions, among which were classed wage-earning activities; secondly, 'private' debts (as opposed to 'commercial' debts) were punished less severely, in accordance with the general rules of ordinary law; and finally, in this context the special system of workers' debts was generally thought of as an exceptional right in favour of workers.

Detailed comparison of the contents of the two case laws does not lessen the contrast; quite the opposite.[15] The testimony of the

[11] P. S. Atiyah, *The Rise and Fall of Freedom of Contract* (Oxford, 1979), 90. See also the essay by Paul Johnson in this volume.

[12] Paul Johnson, 'Small Debts and Economic Distress in England and Wales, 1857–1913', *Economic History Review*, 46 (1993), 65–87.

[13] *PP* 1866 (449), xiii, Dronfield, 799–800, Normansell, 948–52, Williams, 1106, 1152, Odger, 1987.

[14] Alain Cottereau, 'Providence ou prévoyance? Les "Prises en charge" de la santé des ouvriers, au cours des XIXe siècle britannique et français', *Prévenir*, 19 (2nd semester, 1989), 21–51.

[15] The comparison is limited, however, by the paucity of publications available in Britain on the actual implementation of the laws of master and servant, and on the texts and contexts of local judgments for the period concerned. Basically, the sources used were the *Parliamentary Papers* on the subject, with their lists of cases (*PP* 1865 (370), viii to *PP* 1875 (171), lxii concerning *Contracts of Service* or *Labour Laws*) and certain parliamentary investigations

shoemaker Odger, a London workers' representative, provides an interesting framework for comparison. Rather than focusing on abuses likely to be exceptional, it describes a habitual difficulty in utilizing the law to the advantage of workers:

As it affects my own trade . . . I would observe that the Act [on Masters and Servants, 1823] is almost inoperative.

—From what cause?—For this reason, I believe that the breaches of contract occur more frequently on account of the conduct of masters than on account of the conduct of men; our work . . . is all piece-work, and frequently an employer bargains to give out work; but when we go for the work he only gives us a part of it, and we cannot go on with the work; say, for instance, he gives us the leather to make the bottoms, but he does not give us the uppers, and the man has the work by him, and cannot proceed with it; it has been ruled in a case many years since in the City, that the contract commenced by the fact of the work having been given out; but still I never knew of but one case where a workman summoned the master for a breach; but invariably they wait until the master is prepared to give out the uppers, and when they get them they go on with their work; I have known a man wait about, sometimes nine or ten days, and from that to a fortnight before he could get all the things necessary to go on with his work; well, of course, under such circumstances, if the men were to be continually summoning the masters, we should have the most abominable amount of ill feeling, and everything else that could be conceived of as bad, and men prefer to make the best of it, and wait to their uppers, and when they get them go on with the work, or go somewhere else and try to get a pair from some other employer. That creates the difficulty at once, because if he should get a pair from another employer to make, then the other employer might say 'I will give you some more work as you seem to be slack'. Should the man under these circumstances keep the first employer's work out longer than the eight days allowed by law, he would be amenable to consequences of breach of contracts.

giving occasional examples of appeals to the courts (*PP* 1824 (51), v, *Artisans, Tools and Machinery Exportation* . . . [Joseph Hume] . . . , *PP* 1825 (414, 437), iv, *Combination of workmen* . . . , 1818 i, *PP* 1818, *Report from Committee on Silk* . . . , i, ii, iii, *PP*, (HL), 1823, clvi. 57, *Minutes of evidence . . . persons employed in the manufacture of silk*. For a point of departure see Daphne Simon, 'Master and Servant', in John Saville (ed.), *Democracy and the Labour Movement* (London, 1954), 160–201. In addition, see John Styles, 'Embezzlement, Industry and the Law in England, 1500–1800', in M. Berg, P. Hudson, and M. Sonenscher (eds.), *Manufacture in Town and Country before the Factory* (Cambridge, 1983); D. C. Woods, 'The Operation of the Master and Servants Act in the Black Country, 1858–1875', *Midland History*, 7 (1982), 93–113; Norma Landau, *The Justices of the Peace, 1679–1760* (Berkeley, 1984); Robert J. Steinfeld, *The Invention of Free Labour: The Employment Relation in English and American Law and Culture, 1350–1870* (Chapel Hill, NC, 1991); and the essays by Douglas Hay and Willibald Steinmetz in this volume.

—Then, what is the result: frequent prosecutions on either side?—No: they seldom, if ever, occur.[16]

In France, on the other hand, in home-working as well as in workshop or factory labour, worker summonses for non-observance of contract were very frequent, as were worker summonses generally, in every domain of employment for a specific job (*louage d'ouvrage*). In the case of home-working, local courts allowed workers to enforce verbal promises received, and they awarded damages and interest to punish delays on the part of entrepreneurs more severely than delays on the part of workers, deeming the former to be in most circumstances less excusable than the latter. Here is an example from the Lyon silk industry, very ordinary in local terms but chosen here for the striking contrast it presents with regard to Odger's testimony. In line with usual judicial practice, time lost through the fault of merchants was indemnified, as were the costs of adapting hand looms to the particular features of the pieces of cloth promised, costs that industrial tribunals made sure were compensated for by further orders for work, on penalty of damages and interest. The following record of an industrial tribunal session was made by *L'Écho de la fabrique*, a master workers' newspaper that was in the process of establishing itself as a journal reporting extensively on judicial decisions:

Master Giraud [a workshop head] is suing Mister Napoly [a manufacturer] for the sum of 144 francs in respect of a large number of days lost through the fault of his [i.e. Mister Napoly's] employees. He states that, being on the point of settling, because at the time he found more lucrative work, he was promised, if he wanted to continue making the thing that he was working on, three pieces of 60 ells each; and notwithstanding this promise he received only one of them and was refused the others.

Mister Napoly's response is to the effect that he no longer wishes to employ this worker because of his conduct, and states that he does not recall his promise of three pieces, given, he says, that he had only two to manufacture and was unable to promise more; but he nevertheless acknowledges that he was very slow in providing the first piece and has caused the worker to lose several days between that time and this; he thinks he has compensated for this, either by raising the price of handkerchiefs from 75 c. to 80 c., or by an increase of 10 c. on the penultimate piece and 20 c. on the last one.

[16] Odger, *PP* 1866 (449), xiii, Nos. 1809–10.

Giraud replies that the 20 c. increase is wrong; that it is clear that the figures have been redone. Never, he says, did I ask for more than 90 c. per handkerchief; this increase, entered as a bonus, was made purely with the intention of proving to the court that I had received satisfaction for the days lost. I constantly paid my worker at the rate of 80 c. for the first pieces and 90 c. for the last; so the price according to tariff was certainly not for meeting my expenses for time lost. I am now refused work because I have committed the great crime in the eyes of these gentle-men of saying I had been paid at 90 c. to a master who manufactures the same article at a cost of 80 c. That is why I am being refused the pieces I had been promised. But I wish to bring proceedings against Mister Napoly as guilty of forgery in private correspondence for having redone my figures without my consent.

After lengthy deliberation, the board sentenced Mister Napoly to pay an indemnity of 20 francs to Master Giraud.[17]

We see here two logics leading to opposite solutions: on the English side, as a result of a logic of industrial subordination, the judgement of entrepreneurs on the proper use of time was accepted without further enquiry. So far as French industrial tri-bunals were concerned, a concern for equity in individual bar-gaining led them to compensate for inequalities of economic situation through procedures of genuine reciprocity in bargain-ing, a reciprocity that in this case implied taking into account time lost as a result of the manufacturer's management of affairs. The same logical dualism is capable of explaining conflicting opera-tions of the burden of proof in disputes over verbal promises. Daphne Simon writes: 'while the courts readily assumed that wages were due, they also assumed that the wages had been paid unless the servant could show otherwise', and she cites a case,

---

[17] *L'Écho de la fabrique*, 10 (10 Mar. 1833), 80. The master-worker's argument as reported concerns an entry in his 'account book' (a document required by law, distinct from the *livret*, the *livre de compte* was kept in duplicate, one with the merchant, the other in the pos-session of the master-worker). The merchant had entered a bonus after the event in the account book in order to avoid acknowledging an increase in the making-up price (*prix de façon*), i.e. an increase in the rate at which he had the type of cloth in question woven. The manœuvre was designed to avoid giving rise to negotiated demands for price increases. But the industrial tribunal repudiated it, condemning the manufacturer at the same time as it granted the request for compensation for time lost. Note that the master-worker paid a worker to make up the piece. Since the custom sanctioned by industrial tribunals was always to give a fixed proportion of the *prix de façon* as wages for journeymen, and since journeymen were in the habit of checking making-up rates in the books of master workers, it followed that the journeyman's wage here provided proof of the making-up rate agreed in advance and corroborated the accusation of forgery of documents brought by the master worker against the merchant.

reported in the 1837 edition of Burns's handbook for justices of the peace:

A case tried some time back at the Guildhall which was an action by a workman at a sugar refiner's: a witness proved that the plaintiff had worked there for more than two years, but Lord Abbott said that he should direct the jury to presume that men employed in that way were regularly paid every Saturday night unless some evidence was given on the part of the plaintiff to satisfy the jury that the plaintiff had in point of fact never been paid; and as no such evidence was produced the plaintiff was nonsuited.[18]

In French industrial tribunals, the arguments and presumptions rested on quite different foundations. The system of proofs was derived from the traditions of commercial law, as interpreted by commercial courts. Manufacturers and merchants had obligations to keep regular accounts, and these obligations were sanctioned in the commercial courts by systematically giving the benefit of the doubt to the opposing party where accounts were lacking. When these rules were transferred to industrial tribunals, they were adapted to the unequal conditions of employers and workers by a similar logic of compensation: only employers were obliged to keep regular accounts; workers' demands in respect of payment due were systematically met if employers' account books, if necessary after expert appraisal, failed to prove otherwise.

The concern for fairness in negotiations might thus go so far as judicial decisions correcting and compensating for inequalities of economic situation. In the same spirit, rules had become established concerning the restitution of materials entrusted to homeworkers. Whereas in England, statutes and case law remained repressive, sometimes going so far as to establish a presumption of theft if restitutions were late or deficient, French legislation, which before the Revolution had been as repressive as English law, took a very different course after the Revolution, following some initial hesitation. Under the First Empire, demands from employers and even from members of industrial tribunals proposed deploying police searches against pilfering and embezzlement, but such preventive and repressive measures were rejected in the name of safeguarding civil liberties. Industrial tribunals then established precedents on which employers and workers could

[18] Simon, 'Master and Servant', 163.

agree. The tribunals went so far as to grant workers a 'right of retention', that is, the right to keep materials entrusted to them as security in case their wages were paid late, or not at all. Emergency industrial-tribunal hearings then served to produce amicable agreements to get things moving again when home-workers had refused to go on working.

The distinction between louage d'ouvrage *and*
louage de service *in France, compared with the unitary English
doctrine on 'master and servant'*

In France, industrial tribunals, justices of the peace, and commercial courts saw the employment of workers as conferring an obligation to deliver a particular result. Workers had the duty to produce a material product following the *règles de l'art* (rules of responsibility embedded in professional skill). Only the 'hiring of services' (*louage de service*), a term that did not apply to workers, by nature implied submission to the master's orders. In England, jurisdiction seems always to have regarded the employment of workers as an undertaking to obey, whatever the legal justification for this: customs and statutes of varying degrees of age, then new statutes of the nineteenth century, functional justifications of good industrial management, and theories of the implicit contract of obedience as formulated, for example, by the 1837 edition of Burns's handbook: 'The servant impliedly contracts to obey the lawful and reasonable orders of his master within the scope of the services contracted for.'[19]

In France, it is above all examination of local jurisdiction rather than legal doctrines or national jurisdiction that makes it possible to identify the distinction between employment for a particular job (*louage d'ouvrage*), and the relation of subordination implied in any 'hiring for services' (*louage de service*). It could be pointed out, however, that these differences in practice also corresponded to differences in doctrine that have now been forgotten but were present in most French handbooks of civil and commercial law between 1804 and 1870. Moreover, they were occasionally referred to in decisions of the *Cour de Cassation*. The technical vocabulary went back to the traditional terms *prix-fait* (since the sixteenth century, the French translation of *locatio conductio operis*) or *louage*

[19] Quoted by Simon, ibid. 163-4.

d'ouvrage. The authors of these handbooks connect these 'made-price' contracts with subcontractor undertakings, and more generally with all undertakings to manufacture a specific article, whereas service undertakings are of a different nature. The industrial jobs of day labourers (*journaliers*), unlike the industrial jobs of workers (*ouvriers*), were comparable to domestic service and other service relationships precisely to the extent to which they involved being placed at the disposal of the master's will, with no possibility of discussing and assessing the tasks to be carried out. Moreover, the legal distinction between 'worker' and 'day labourer' echoed an obvious social distinction in the industrial milieu: industrial workers looked down on industrial day labourers, seeing them as domestic servants or valets in subjection to their masters and considering, as did the courts, that they had relinquished their independence. Statistically, day labourers accounted for some 10 per cent of industrial wage-earners at the end of the Second Empire, and are not to be confused with the far larger British category of the unskilled.

The difference in the legal status of *journaliers* and *ouvriers* was particularly pronounced in the rules of evidence in force between 1803 and 1868; article 1781 of the Civil Code stated that 'the master's statement is believed in respect of the quota of wages; in respect of payment of the previous year's wages; and in respect of advances given for the current year'. Jurisdiction, with very few exceptions, deemed this article to apply to domestic servants and day labourers, but not to workers. It has already been shown that the tradition of commercial rules of evidence placed the burden of proving that workers' wages had been paid on employers alone.

A further illustration of the duality between *louage d'ouvrage* and the subordination implied by *louage de service* is the lengthy opposition put up by industrial tribunals to workshop rules (*règlements d'atelier*). When employers posted up factory rules and demanded obedience to their agents' orders, industrial tribunals almost invariably objected to the contractual fiction according to which the worker who had entered a workshop was deemed to be aware of and to have accepted these rules. The tribunals confined themselves to the lawfulness of a contractual reality, taking it upon themselves to verify, case by case, the reality of the supposed agreement and objecting to any rule that did not seem to them to be fair on the grounds that, where unfair rules were present, there could not have been a totally free agreement. Moreover, they placed a higher, compulsory value on local customs recognized in the trade or occupation.

It was only later, from the 1860s to the 1880s, that a change in judicial practice occurred, accompanied by a change in legal doctrines. The judicial hierarchy, followed by a section of the employers and their organizations, launched an initiative to have it considered that every time a worker entered into a contract of employment, he thereby undertook to obey the employer's orders. Railway companies rather than the manufacturing sector took the lead in this campaign. Doctrine soon accepted the idea that when the worker entered into a contract of employment, this was an undertaking 'of industrial service'. An equivalence was established between 'industrial-service hiring' and the new expression 'labour contract' (*contrat de travail*).[20]

From the 1880s on, this doctrine gained acceptance in the courts, starting from the top of the judicial hierarchy. It subsequently spread down the hierarchy, more by way of authority than conviction, when appeals were lodged against industrial tribunals and justices of the peace. From a comparative viewpoint, it was only then that French employment law moved closer to English law. From this point in time, the French worker once again became a kind of 'servant', an idea that was totally incompatible with the emancipation brought about by the Revolution. To make up for the constraints of submission, workers became the object of protective legislation and supported legal union representation. In England, on the other hand, the convergence resulted from a process of liberalization: penal sanctions for breach of contract were abolished, completing the development towards a purely contractual justification of master–servant relations.[21]

---

[20] Several aspects of this change, notably, as regards workshop regulations, are described in Cottereau, 'Justice et injustice', 55–8. The first occurrence of the term *contrat de travail* that I have been able to trace dates from 1885.

[21] A profound comparative misunderstanding was spread on the basis of a myth that took root in France under the Third Republic: republican writers on labour law pretended to themselves and persuaded others that 'service hiring' was a category of the Civil Code that had applied to the employment of workers from the outset. The comparative considerations of Otto Kahn-Freund, 'Blackstone's Neglected Child: The Contract of Employment', in *Law Quarterly Review*, 93 (Oct. 1977), 508–28, for example, were led astray by the French authors in whom he had placed his faith. Post-revolutionary authors using the work of Pothier — Robert-J. Pothier, *Traité du contrat de louage, selon les règles tant du for de la conscience que du for extérieur* (Paris, 1764); id., *Traité des contrats de louage maritimes* (Paris,

*Workers' sense of justice and its institutional
treatment in France and England*

As the comparison is explored more deeply, a broader question
arises: what relationships were established between sense of
justice, legitimacy, and legal systems? A key to comparison has
already been suggested: the institution of the industrial tribunal
was able to establish and harness views of justice shared by elected
representatives of employers and workers without going down
the usual road of public representation. The contrast is particularly noticeable with English trade unions and their recognition
in nineteenth-century England.

If we take as our point of departure the 1820s, the decade that,
in England, saw simultaneously the extension of penal sanctions
in the administration of the master and servant laws, the abolition of the last statutory regulations concerning labour, and the
liberalization of trade union law, we find a pattern of perfect
inverse symmetry between face-to-face negotiation and collective
negotiation by public representatives. In France, collective negotiation by public delegation was prohibited and punished, while
face-to-face negotiation was protected, encouraged, and judicially
regulated in favour of workers; in England, face-to-face negotiation, which was already strategically weaker than in France,
because of the demographic and economic conditions of industrialization in England, was subject to overt judicial intervention,
inequitably favouring employers, whereas collective adjustments,
traditionally practised in a dialectic with the law and local magistrates, were encouraged by law in the name of a liberalism that
admitted collective representation on a voluntary basis.

To understand the extent of the contrast, it is important first of
all not to underestimate the institutional reality and success of
appeals to industrial tribunals.[22] Unlike the usual kind of judicial

1769)—were more precise than Kahn-Freund thinks, and deliberately modified Pothier's
doctrine.

[22] For more details on the success of industrial tribunals, see Cottereau, 'Justice et injustice'. There is still a need to assess and compare the success of French justices of the peace
with that of the industrial tribunals, a task which French historiography has not yet performed. My trawls through the records of justices of the peace suggest a far greater variety
of practices, with some cases looking more paternalistic, others more repressive, and lastly
many cases that take their cue from industrial-tribunal precedents in the name of equity
and protection of the weak.

appeal, reference to an industrial tribunal was neither a declaration of hostility nor a transfer to a remote and superior world of the law, likely to hand down arbitration. Nor is this the paternalistic system of English justices of the peace (although comparisons are possible, at best, with popular magistrates, who had the reputation of being particularly fair).[23] Unlike the corporative, municipal courts of *ancien régime* France, the institution of the industrial tribunal was based on conciliation rather than on arbitration. Between the two, the philosophical gulf was complete: arbitration was compatible with a 'paternal justice' that gave notables an arbitrary power of peacemaking in the name of their superior understanding and lofty social position; conciliation, on the other hand, presupposed that the parties in disagreement had been invited by their industrial-tribunal advisers to re-evaluate their position themselves until a solution was found that was acceptable to all points of view in attendance. It presupposed a capacity for judgement on the part of workers as well as on the part of employers, under institutional conditions organized accordingly: industrial tribunals did not have an overall 'employer majority' up until 1848, as has too often been written. They were composed under a kind of tax-based internal suffrage in worker milieux as well as in employer milieux. But above all they nearly always operated on the idea that a consensus of justice should be reached, not just among tribunal members but also among the parties who came before them. This consensus was always aimed for and frequently achieved. It was simultaneously symbolized and organized by 'special boards' of conciliation, an initial stage at which between 80 and 100 per cent of disputes registered were settled: such boards comprised one employer and one worker, whereas organs of conciliation under the *ancien régime*, which had

---

[23] See also C. R. Dobson, *Masters and Journeymen: A Prehistory of Industrial Relations* (London, 1980), and Landau, *Justices of the Peace*. Gail Malmgreen, *Silk Town: Industry and Culture in Macclesfield, 1750–1835* (Hull, 1985), is the only monograph that allowed me to draw comparisons between the records of silk factory industrial tribunals and judgments of local courts in the same branch in England during the same period. The few scraps of information she provides (particularly on pp. 40–1), on the basis of the notebook of a local magistrate with a reputation for fairness, show that the causes of litigation and judicial arguments were similar and that the number of appeals in relation to the population was quite high, though still a long way below the level of French appeals to industrial tribunals. There was approximately one worker appeal to two employer appeals, which seems a surprisingly high proportion for England, whereas in France worker appeals were generally far more numerous than appeals by employers.

been appealed to much less frequently and had been much more controversial, had usually consisted only of masters.

The system of face-to-face conciliation, wrongly termed 'individual', had an important collective significance. It fostered an ongoing debate within occupational circles and gave rise to real systems of unwritten rules, managed on a day-to-day basis under the supervision of the whole of the milieu concerned. Take the example of *tarifs de façon* in Lyon, which were more or less equivalent to 'piece-rates'. From their very first sessions (January 1807), the industrial tribunals of Lyon laid down a scale of prices, which was printed like the 'lists' of the Spitalfields Acts system. The lists were periodically updated until 1831, when a newly negotiated update was repudiated by the government; the people of Lyon were told, after a section of employers complained, that the new rates could not have compulsory but only moral status. This repudiation triggered the famous first revolt of the *Canuts*. Here a key feature emerges, over and above many analogies with the lists negotiated by trade unions: in England, we find around the same time that the moral power of a joint agreement, with the active support of the unions, was expressed in the cases involving the least conflict, through actual respect for the settlements negotiated, without either judicial or executive backing.

In Lyon, as throughout France, respect for the rules could not be viewed in this way. A new system was established there from 1832 on, typical of how the country's industrial-tribunal regulations operated until the 1860s. Despite the withdrawal of the official scale, the *Canuts* had in part gained their case. If there was no list of compulsory prices, there was a semi-official system of reference prices, known as *le cours*, that industrial tribunals supported and helped to gain acceptance for. In conciliation, and even in judgment, they pronounced a wage increase wherever the agreed price was deemed insufficient. This was in flagrant contradiction to official liberalism and doctrines of civil law (though it was not inconsistent with commercial law). The notables of Lyon, like factory owners in many other French towns and cities, spoke a dual language: smooth operation of industrial relations had its local rules, but for reasons of efficiency it was important not to expose these to 'public opinion' (that is, to the national public sphere of the period). It was a kind of secret system that could survive only in so far as the notables who ran it achieved sufficient credibility and discipline among their peers to avoid appeals to the hierarchy of the courts.

If one had today to find a nineteenth-century English expression for the consensual practices of industrial tribunals, it would be by inverting a recurring theme of the skilled workmen of the period who protested against 'unprincipled competition': the regulations of the industrial tribunals worked towards '*principled competition*'. It might also be pertinent to see here some kinship with Thompson's moral economy, revisited in 1991, provided that that notion is not reduced to a strictly working-class point of view but enlarged into a more complex dialectic of recognition and legitimacy. The regulations of the industrial tribunals could then be considered as a different historical case in which political economy and equity interpenetrate in a way that is incomprehensible in the light of classical economic theory, for reasons similar to the opaqueness of moral economy.

In England during the period 1820 to 1870, areas of initiative to prevent, expose, or correct unprincipled competition had to do with a topology of the public sphere very different from that of the French public sphere.[24] Beyond what the Webbs, in *Industrial Democracy*, in an excessively managerial, evolutionist way, called the different methods of legal enactment, of collective bargaining, etc., there possibly operated, at a deeper level, a different system of the sense of justice, of publicity, and of power to intervene, a system common to the whole of English political life. To the French reader, a striking symptom of this different system is the use that English workers made of such terms as 'legal (illegal) men, lawful men, fair men' about workers who respected or failed to respect the rules laid down by the unions[25]—rules that were sometimes established by joint negotiation, but also rules that were unilaterally drawn up, in opposition to and in a state of declared war with government, judicial, and/or employer legality. In the latter case, the terms 'legal (illegal) men, lawful men' would have been untranslatable and incomprehensible in France at the time.[26]

---

[24] The term 'public sphere' draws both on the Habermas tradition (see the Preface to Jürgen Habermas, *Strukturwandel der Öffentlichkeit* (17th edn., Frankfurt and Main, 1990), 11–50) and on Hannah Arendt, *The Human Condition* (Chicago, 1958).

[25] The terms are taken from *PP* 1824 (51), v, *Artisans* . . . , and from E. P. Thompson and E. Yeo, *The Unknown Mayhew* (London 1973).

[26] 'Incomprehensible' only gradually, from the 1820s on. Previously, under the *ancien régime* and at the beginning of the Revolution, French worker assemblies had also had their

In the most comparable situations, when French worker collectives secretly imposed rules of negotiation and working conditions, they did not claim to have any independent legal force. Except in highly exceptional circumstances of overt, organized conflict, they did not have procedures of assembly and debate that were sufficiently open (clandestinely or publicly) to allow them subsequently to claim to be speaking for a duly established collective interest. Yet where there was a shared conviction of the justice of the case, an attempt began to gain recognition from local magistrates and the more accessible employers. This tactic frequently appears to have been successful.[27] When it failed, the occupational milieu concerned did not in consequence become subdivided into legal men (or legal shop) and illegal men. Semantically, there were not two legalities. On the one hand there was a legitimacy, a conviction of justice regarding the principles for which respect had to be secured. On the other hand there was an occupational milieu, employers and workers, that had to be convinced and improved, if necessary by appealing to 'the' law, redressing its misinterpretations and altering its pronouncements where these would lead to unfair practices.

In other words, the processes and areas in which the gap between legitimacy and legality occurs are not the same. In England at the time of the Chartist crisis, the first expansion of the electorate, and the miscarriages of the judicial system, the law became more remote from the citizen, and the state attracted more expectations and thus gave rise to more disappointments. If

own apparatus for drawing up rules, and they used the same vocabulary as that used in national procedures of judicial, legislative, or administrative deliberation. Examples of extensions are found during the first half of the 19th century, but they become increasingly rare.

[27] The reality of these successes is not easy to establish in the present state of historiography. There is a need for investigations reconstructing the normative life of occupational milieux, recognitions and repudiations of rules in different economic climates, which means going beyond the confines of heroic, detective, or management approaches to occupational conflicts. Police or court records, which generally give accounts of setbacks and violent confrontations, nevertheless carry traces of these searches for recognition. Frequently, researchers report that worker delegates arrested on the occasion of conflicts were astonished to be treated as criminals when what they were doing was pursuing a moral struggle for fair working conditions. Whether such disappointments were sincere or the historian suspects them of having been feigned for the purpose of defending the interested parties does not alter the conclusion that may be drawn here regarding the normative polarization of the sphere in which they were situated: tactical opportuneness presupposes a plausibility and admissibility that it makes sense to display.

self-help redistributed collective irresponsibilities, radical movements of workers for their part raised the search for answers to
the injustices of industrialization to the level of national debate,
and made a government issue of it. In this context, universalist
exasperation and sensitivity to class discrimination went hand in
hand. In the case of England, however, the tension between universalist legitimacy and class particularisms did not stop at the
symbolic life of justifications, and that is a big difference from the
situation in France at the same period. In England incompatible
grounds for legitimacy organized themselves, both as worker logics
and as dominant-class logics. The discriminations contained in
master and servant law and workers' sense of justice complemented and underpinned each other.

In contrast, the regulations of French industrial tribunals from
the beginning of the century to the 1860s represented a different
way of dealing with the tension between legitimacy and legality,
between universalist justice and class particularities. In France, no
one renounced the universal recognition of *le bon droit*, neither the
workers with regard to employers and the authorities, nor the
authorities and employers with regard to workers. The historical
experience of industrial tribunals shows how the public sphere
was established in France under the Revolution, and was then
curbed without being crushed during successive regimes from the
First Empire to the Second Empire. To be sure, a chronic fear of
mobs, demagogy, and public demonstrations notoriously caused
bans or restrictions on press freedom and freedom of assembly.
But the corollary of this locking of doors at the national level was
the emergence of local public spheres. Not merely spheres of
expression of opinion but spheres of deliberation: here local
authorities, both administrative and judicial, remained under the
control of local citizens; they were obliged to secure recognition
of the validity of their actions from a multitude of moral constraints, however appointed. In the legal domain, the invention of
a common law of industrial tribunals constituted an original
response to these requirements.

10

Master and Servant in England
Using the Law in the Eighteenth and Nineteenth Centuries

DOUGLAS HAY

Introduction

'Private law' in English usage means the civil law, 'those relations between individuals with which the State is not directly concerned', but such definitions concede, however reluctantly, that issues of public policy always arise that involve the state.[1] A central issue of public policy for most regimes is that of sustaining, stabilizing, explicating, and defending existing social relations in conditions of great social inequality. In the workplace, in England, the law that did so was termed, well into the twentieth century, 'the law of master and servant'.

This large corpus of law was based on medieval, Tudor, and Stuart legislation, reinforced in the eighteenth and nineteenth centuries by new enactments, and glossed in a large number of reported cases. The servants described and circumscribed by master and servant law constituted a large and variable class of people. The old terms servant, servant in husbandry, covenant servant, servant on a general hiring, recur in statute, case law, and court records. The unwritten, verbal 'general hiring' of the 'servant in husbandry', usually at Michaelmas, for a year, was the root category, derived from the Statute of Artificers and Apprentices (5 Eliz. I c. 4, 1562), and refined in the case law.

Other forms of service were fitted into the regime from the beginning, embedded in case law, occasionally modified, extended, or confirmed by statute. There was apprenticeship, with substantially similar requirements, but within the framework

[1] Earl Jowitt, *Dictionary of English Law* (London, 1959), tit. 'Law', from which the quotation comes. The research for this essay was supported by the Social Sciences and Humanities Research Council of Canada, and assisted by Chris Frank and Doug Harris.

of indentured service and instruction for a period of years. 'Covenant' servants were similarly engaged for longer than the year envisaged by the law of general hirings, but for adult occupations and with wages and other conditions instead of apprenticeship obligations. Both came within the jurisdiction of the same courts as did servants in husbandry. Many of the terms of the general hiring on verbal or written contract were extended by Parliament and the judges and magisterial practice to skilled workers in a wide variety of other trades, and indeed (for much of these centuries) to unskilled labourers working by the day or week, and to pieceworkers, and to domestic servants, and even to tradesmen contracting for particular jobs. Thus the coverage of 'master and servant' was very wide, but shifting over time in both definition and enforcement; several of the categories mentioned came to be excluded from the ambit of some of the statutes. Although the theoretical coverage of the law at any particular time can be determined, the numbers involved are conjectural. We can say that a large but unknown proportion (probably a majority) of working people fell under this body of law in the eighteenth and nineteenth centuries.

For those governed by it, the law defined much of the nature of employment. There were modifications of detail, sometimes significant detail, but a broadly similar model was in force over much of the period. There was the obligation for the servant to work faithfully, diligently, and obediently; for the master to maintain the servant in sickness and pay wages when due; for a quarter's notice on either side. There emerged clearly in the nineteenth century the legal doctrine of the 'entire' or complete contract, by which all wages could be forfeited if all the work contracted for was not completed. (There were continuing exceptions based on custom, as in London, where a month's notice sufficed.) The servant could sue in higher courts for unpaid wages (highly unlikely) but the judges had also given summary judgment to justices of the peace or other magistrates, which is where servants customarily turned for cheap law, and legislation through the eighteenth and nineteenth centuries confirmed and extended the practice. A substantial body of legislation gave similar summary remedies to masters for absenteeism, misbehaviour, unfinished or shoddy work, or failing to enter on contracted work. Masters' remedies were a combination of penal and pecuniary sanctions: imprisonment of the servant for one to three months for breach of contract, possibly with a whipping; and/or a proportional loss (abatement) of wages; or the termination of the contract and, as we have seen, possible loss of all wages.[2]

The provision of penal sanctions for breach by the servant, but not the master, became the most contentious part of the law. The worker in breach was often treated as a criminal; the master rarely was. Employment contracts were associated with criminality, unlike other agreements. In an 1813 case in which the owner of a carding mill tried to use the terms of a century-old statute in a claim against a clothier, the Lord Chief Justice objected. 'The penal provisions of this act shew strongly that it is not applicable to the adjustment of debts between parties of equal rank in trade: the person who shall refuse . . . to pay the costs and damages adjudged against him, is liable to be committed to the county gaol or house of correction.'[3] Equally fundamental was the fact, already mentioned, that this body of law was enforced almost entirely in summary hearings before propertied laymen: borough magistrates and county justices of the peace. Only in the nineteenth century do professional paid (stipendiary) magistrates begin to act outside London, and there are not many of them.

In mentioning these remedies I have made an elision from the terms of the Statute of Artificers (which mentions only one month's imprisonment and no orders for wages) to the case law and to a number of statutes, dating largely from the early to mid-eighteenth century, which provided for longer incarceration, in the midst of a host of terms defining lawful practices in a range of stated occupations, some from the great Statute, others not.[4] Such statutes not only covered breaches by the worker, but 'regulated the trade' with clauses dealing with apprenticeship, maximum (and sometimes minimum) wages and wage-setting, combination, embezzlement of materials, and indeed any of the common

---

[2] On the statutes see below.

[3] *R.* v. *Heywood* (1813), 1 M. & S. 624, at 628, a rare instance of equality in 13 Geo. I c. 23 s. 5. Penal sanctions for breach by the master were enacted explicitly in 1844, when masters of ships could be imprisoned for refusal to pay seamen's wages (7 and 8 Vic. c. 112). After 1848, other masters refusing to obey a justice's order for wages could be imprisoned on failure of distress (11 and 12 Vic. c. 43). In 1851 mistreatment of apprentices became punishable by imprisonment (14 and 15 Vic. c. 11). The only earlier instances of penal sanctions against masters of which I am aware were offences against public policy: paying excess wages, as in 5 Eliz. c. 4 (1562) and 7 Geo. I st. 1 c. 13.

[4] See below, n. 35.

points of conflict in particular trades. That conflict could be between masters and journeymen, or between those who had served a full apprenticeship and those who had not, or between large capitalists who wanted to hire the latter in opposition to small masters who wanted the older structures of the trade respected.[5] All such clauses depended on the Statute of 1562 for the interpretative structure, often the spirit, and sometimes direct inspiration. For London tailors, for example, it was an offence to refuse to enter a contract, if one was not employed, by an enactment of 1720, a recapitulation of the enforced labour clauses of the great Statute.[6]

The term servant, then, was ambiguous in both legal and demotic usage. The classic, paradigm instance of the 'servant in husbandry' turns out not to have been paradigmatic at all, and assuming that it was leads easily to the genetic fallacy, the assumption that a putative origin explains the later development. I shall return to the importance of diversity in master and servant law in England, and the social and economic origins of the diversity. Here, let me simply emphasize that justices of the peace, high court judges, and the general public all used the term 'servant' with a series of overlapping connotations, and probably had done so for centuries.

Occasionally (and increasingly) this bothered the high court judges, and they inconvenienced everyone else by trying to nail the term down, sometimes amplifying it, sometimes narrowing its import for particular kinds of cases.[7] But in general, in the eighteenth and nineteenth centuries, the answer to the question of who was the servant envisaged by the law of master and servant was given by the magistrates entrusted with the summary administration of the law. We must look in the jails, and in justices' hear-

[5] For the general context, see D. Hay and N. Rogers, *English Society in the Eighteenth Century: Shuttles and Swords* (Oxford, 1997), chs. 6–9.

[6] 7 Geo. I st. 1 c. 13.

[7] The few instances of case law mentioned in this paper are dealt with in greater detail in D. Hay, 'English Judges, Images of Service, and the Nature of Empire', paper to the joint meeting of the Law and Society Association and Research Committee on Sociology of Law, Glasgow, 10 July 1996, and in forthcoming work. See also Daphne Simon, 'Master and Servant', in John Saville (ed.), *Democracy and the Labour Movement* (London, 1956); Karen Orren, *Belated Feudalism: Labor, the Law, and Liberal Development in the United States* (Cambridge, 1991); Robert J. Steinfeld, *The Invention of Free Labor: The Employment Relation in English and American Law and Culture, 1350–1870* (Chapel Hill, NC, 1991); and Christopher Tomlins, *Law, Labor, and Ideology in the Early American Republic* (Cambridge, 1993).

ings, to see who servants and masters were, and the use they made of this distinctive body of law.[8]

In this essay I present some preliminary evidence suggesting a change in the nature of summary justice, including the use of the penal sanctions, between 1750 and 1850. Unenforced law may still generate social meanings, but it is less likely to do so than law which brings people before courts. My argument is that from the mid-eighteenth to the mid-nineteenth century, the law as it was applied became more identified with the interests of employers. Imprisonment became more common, and harsher, and in general outcomes became more favourable to employers; the advantages of the law for servants diminished, and remedies against masters became more difficult for them to use.[9]

In constructing this (or any) argument about the use of the law there are two large problems: the specific and often local nature of the law, and the incompleteness with which its enforcement was recorded. The specific and local nature of the law was based on the fact that its precise terms were often defined, by statute, for particular trades, but how both statute and case law were enforced depended also on the structure of local industry and indeed on 'the custom of the trade', which had the force of law when recognized in the high courts.[10] The remedies that the law gave to both masters and servants were therefore embodied in local, often highly specific legal cultures, which legitimized their claims. Such bodies of law were not static. In the eighteenth century they were the product of trade organization, social structure, legislation, and continual renegotiation. Because they differed from region to region, even from parish to parish in some cases, the way in which

---

[8] This chapter presents some early findings from a study of the legislation, case law, enforcement, and political significance of master and servant law in England between 1660 and 1875. It forms part of a larger project on master and servant law in the British Empire: see Douglas Hay and Paul Craven, 'Master and Servant in England and the Empire: A Comparative Study', *Labour/Le Travail*, 31 (spring 1993), 175–84; Paul Craven and Douglas Hay, 'The Criminalization of "Free" Labour: Master and Servant in Comparative perspective', *Slavery and Abolition*, 15/2 (Aug. 1994), 71–101, and in Paul E. Lovejoy and Nicholas Rogers (eds.), *Unfree Labour in the Development of the Atlantic World* (London, 1995); Paul Craven and Douglas Hay, 'Computer Applications in Comparative Historical Research: The Master and Servant Project at York University, Canada', *History and Computing*, 7/1 (1995).

[9] Although important issues surrounded the status of apprentice, and the justices were much involved with them, in what follows it has not been necessary to distinguish them from other workers, except where noted.

[10] See below.

the law was used, what law was used, how often it was formally enforced, differed greatly. We can see that variability in the national statistics after 1858, but it undoubtedly characterized the eighteenth-century use of the law as well. Unfortunately our records of the pre-statistical period are very uneven, and rarely directly comparable; even after 1858 the national statistics are often misleading. Our inferences about the variations of local practice must be based on scattered and often idiosyncratic sources.

Before the 1850s we have widespread local evidence, but no national statistics; before the 1790s the evidence for most parts of the country is even thinner. Broadly speaking, we can assess enforcement from three sources: the records of justices (sitting alone and, increasingly from the early nineteenth century, in petty sessions); the registers of houses of correction and other prisons and jails where they distinguish master and servant offences; and contemporary statistical series, notably the annual parliamentary returns of summary convictions from the late 1850s. Each provides details about different aspects of enforcement, making long secular trends a matter of argument, but comparisons of some points are possible across all three sources. It is worth noting that the cases that appear in the Law Reports are highly unrepresentative, in many ways, and especially as guides to enforcement, although important for an understanding of both judicial thinking and political conflict.

The work of the justices, 1700–1825

Because master and servant hearings were overwhelmingly summary rather than in courts of record, they are only preserved by the rare survival of the personal notebooks of some conscientious justices who recorded their cases, or where (usually not before the nineteenth century) records of petty sessions and borough courts are preserved. There was enormous variability in the diligence of justices: typically, a handful of men did as much business as a hundred of their less active colleagues. The few records of justices' activity must therefore be interpreted with caution.

Some eighteenth-century JPs' notebooks show very little adjudication of employment disputes. A busy Kent justice living near Chatham, Gabriel Walters, who acted in over 300 cases of official business in a period of twenty-four months, dealt with only five disputes between masters and servants.[11] William Brockman, another Kent justice, dealt with about eight cases a year, a fifth of his total business.[12] Ralph Drake Brockman, a Kent justice in the 1770s, dealt with an average of nine cases a year, a third of which were master and servant disputes.[13] In Kent there was also a steady run of such cases at petty sessions, where more than one justice sat; where the records survive, the numbers are comparable for those recorded by single justices.[14]

Such variations in activity are found everywhere in the country, because of the enormous differences in social and occupational geography, and in individual justices' zeal. When we look more closely at the work of five individual magistrates who left fuller records we can begin to discern some patterns. Devereaux Edgar was an active Suffolk JP in parishes just north-west of Ipswich for a number of years between 1700 and 1716. In most years he recorded about 200 instances of legal business: committals, examinations, warrants, etc.[15] About 10 per cent of his entries involved labour disputes brought before him by masters or servants: in these years he dealt with over 300 such cases. About half (149) were complaints by masters, usually against servants who had deserted (89 cases) or misbehaved (25). But almost as many cases (121) were brought by servants against their masters for unpaid wages (117 cases), mistreatment (9), or to ratify a mutually agreed parting (8). Almost all the cases involved farmers and their servants, with a few disputes brought by rural tradesmen like blacksmiths or bricklayers, and by gentlemen.

In the cases brought by masters we know that in over 10 per cent of the cases Edgar committed the servant to the house of correction (17 cases). Probably a high proportion of the proceedings for desertion resulted in the return of the servant to work, with the threat of prison in the background. In the case of servants bringing complaints for non-payment of wages, he made

[11] Norma Landau, *The Justices of the Peace, 1679–1760* (Berkeley, 1984), 177.

[12] Ibid. 178.   [13] Ibid. 178, 195.

[14] Ibid. 222, 224–5. See also 247 for evidence of the continuing concern of some Kent justices for wage regulation as late as 1732.

[15] Suffolk RO, qS 347.96, vol. i.

wage orders in almost every case (113). Masters and servants, then, used his services in about equal numbers, and probably when there was a high expectation of success, although Edgar does not record the outcome of most cases.

The notebook of William Hunt, who was a justice in the heart of rural Wiltshire in the 1740s, does provide that information. He recorded almost 600 acts of a wide variety that he performed as a 'single justice' over a period of five years, a high level of activity for a rural magistrate. Yet in that time Hunt, administering the law in a deeply agricultural setting, heard only seventeen complaints under the master and servant statutes, a third the number Edgar in Suffolk would have expected. Five were brought by masters: against a thatcher, a labourer, and two farm servants for leaving work without leave, and one woman for working for a new master without giving notice to the first.[16] Some of these cases came before Hunt on summons, some on a warrant of arrest, but in all the dispute was resolved by the servant returning to the master, usually by agreement, and sometimes paying the cost of the proceedings or the time lost to the master. All these cases took place before the Act of 1747 (which extended imprisonment) came into effect, but imprisonment was none the less an option in each; it is notable that that was not the course taken.[17] More often, Hunt was the recourse of turned-out or unpaid servants. He noted a dozen cases, probably all of them brought by farm labourers or servants in husbandry, in each of which he ordered payment or the parties agreed after the servant obtained a summons or warrant from Hunt. The sums ranged from 1s. to £1 1s.; in one case a labourer who complained of unpaid wages and clothes held by the master who dismissed him was admitted again to his service.[18]

Thus the statutes were by no means a dead letter, but the number of cases in a few rural parishes, if they were overwhelmingly agricultural, was usually small. In rural Wiltshire, in the 1740s, the penal clauses of the Master and Servant Acts were

---

[16] *The Justicing Notebook of William Hunt 1744–1749*, ed. Elizabeth Crittall (Devizes, 1982), entries 211, 247, 259, 310, 376, 417.

[17] On the statutory basis for imprisonment, see below.

[18] *Justicing Notebook of William Hunt*, entries 102, 246, 250, 251, 323, 345, 385, 386, 423, 433, 440, 463. One other case, entries 451 and 453, was a dispute within a family, ultimately dismissed. Cases for unpaid wages of course were often ways of trying cases of unfair dismissal, an issue on which the justices had an extensive but changing separate jurisdiction.

hardly used at all against workers, and summary justice was used twice as often by servants seeking the payment of their wages. Imprisonment was never necessary: the justice was able to secure agreement between the parties (although the threat of imprisonment was undoubtedly part of the equation).

To explain the evident differences between these examples from Suffolk and Wiltshire (more masters' cases and greater use of imprisonment by the justice in Suffolk) requires detailed local work. The explanations may be a more attractive market for labour in the area of Ipswich (encouraging desertion), the convenience of a house of correction there (and another was built at Woodbridge in these years), or a range of other factors that influenced the local culture of labour relations (some of them discussed below).[19]

The activity of Richard Wyatt, a justice of Chertsey in Surrey, dates from the 1760s and 1770s, and has some new elements. He charged 2s. for orders, and 1s. for the copy served.[20] Of some 224 cases of all kinds over nine years, there were four complaints by masters, three of them for quitting without notice or without consent, and one for disorderly conduct. Two of the four accused servants were imprisoned. One was an iron worker in a works at Weybridge, committed to the house of correction for a month, but subsequently released, as Wyatt ruefully noted, 'upon a writ of habeas corpus, no adjudication appearing on the mittimus which is necessary to be inserted in all committments upon penal statutes'.[21] In the same period, eleven workers came before Wyatt to begin legal proceedings for unpaid wages (sometimes also alleging violence by their employers).[22] Almost all of these were servants in husbandry under a general (yearly) hiring, but a few were men employed on piecework, such as broom-making or brickmaking. The willingness of magistrates to hear pay claims by pieceworkers, and by men in a wide range of industrial trades not explicitly mentioned

[19] On the active building programme for houses of correction at the beginning of the 18th century, and the specific case of Woodbridge, see Joanna Innes, 'Prisons for the Poor: English Bridewells, 1555–1800', in Francis Snyder and Douglas Hay (eds.), *Labour, Law and Crime: An Historical Perspective* (London, 1987), 80.

[20] *Deposition Book of Richard Wyatt, JP, 1767–1776*, ed. Elizabeth Silverthorne, Surrey Record Society 30 (Guildford, 1978), 1.

[21] Ibid., pp. vii, ix, and entries 86, 108–10, 121, 215.

[22] Entries 70, 84, 118–19, 120, 130–1, 161, 168, 178, 181, 301, 309. No outcomes are noted.

in the statutes, was paralleled, for the eighteenth century and at times in the nineteenth, by sanction for the practice in the high courts.

In the same years Sir Thomas Ward was an active magistrate in rural Northamptonshire, and here we begin to see a marked contrast to the largely agricultural pattern described above.[23] First, master and servant business bulked much larger in his caseload: about 25 per cent of the business for which he charged a fee, compared to the 10 per cent of Edgar's work, 7 per cent of Wyatt's hearings, and the mere 3 per cent of Hunt's in rural Wiltshire. The reason is suggested by the occupations: 11 masters were farmers (and another 6 'Mr.'), but 13 were weavers or woolcombers.[24] There was a similar proportion of textile workers among the servants. The setting was still rural, but Ward was dealing with a clientele found in many parts of the countryside in the eighteenth century. Rural production was the dominant form of industry. Parishes where the putting-out system and/or artisanal home production produced cloth, nails, scythes, or the hundreds of other products were populous, lively places where men and women in the trade had many reasons to appeal to a country gentleman justice of the peace as an adjudicator. Whereas a justice like Hunt heard mainly wage and leaving-service cases, Ward also dealt with charges of neglecting work, refusing work, leaving work unfinished, misbehaviour, and embezzlement brought by masters. Most cases brought by servants were still for wages (or pay for piecework), but also for mistreatment and wrongs to apprentices. Although servants brought most cases, the ratio was not so high as in the Hunt and Wyatt diaries: 37 of 66 cases. Unfortunately Ward's diary does not give outcomes of the hearings (it is a record of process issued) but it does tell us that he issued a mittimus to commit a worker to bridewell on only one occasion. Ward charged fees of 1s., usually, compared to Wyatt's 2s.: for most poor labourers this represented about a day's wages.

Finally, a magistrate in an almost entirely industrial setting. Macclesfield in Cheshire was one of the most important sites of silk-weaving outside London, the trade having been established there since the 1740s. We have the record of one active borough

---

[23] Based on 1767 and 1768 cases: twenty-nine master plaintiffs, thirty-seven servant plaintiffs.

[24] And seven other trades.

justice in the 1820s, Thomas Allen.[25] By then the town had a
population of almost 18,000, and there were said to be 10,000 silk
weavers working there (presumably the estimate includes those in
some nearby parishes.) Wages were 11s. a week for an average of
sixty-two hours' work making ribbons, squares, shawls, and handkerchiefs.[26] In one year (April 1823 to March 1824) Allen dealt with
100 master and servant cases, out of about 1,000 hearings of all
kinds. (The ratio is lower than Ward's because borough magistrates dealt with a much larger number of petty thefts, and public
order offences, than rural justices.) Masters brought 60 of the
cases, servants (including apprentices) 40. Apart from the predominance of masters as plaintiffs, the patterns are similar to
those in Ward's industrial parish a half-century before: the masters
complaining largely of servants who were absent or leaving service
(40), or not completing work in time (13). Most of the servants'
complaints were for wages (35 cases).

Allen's notes suggest how cases were decided, and the pattern
is similar to that in other sources. About 42 per cent of cases with
known outcomes were 'settled': the parties, aided by the magistrate, came to an agreement that did not require him to make an
order. Where an order was made, servants won in 53 per cent of
the cases they brought (92 per cent if settled cases are included);
masters won in 59 per cent of their cases (94 per cent if settled
cases are included).[27] In other words, both masters and servants
had substantial success in Allen's court, both in making settlements, and in winning where a settlement was not possible.
Indeed, it is often the case that either party might have brought
the case before the court, since disputes in such summary hearings, over the entire period, often revolved around a common set
of facts: dispute about quality of work, dispute about wages, or
both, with one party able to bring charges of disobedience, poor
work, or absenteeism, and the other party able to bring charges
of being turned off, or unpaid wages. This interlocking nature of
master and servant disputes makes generalizations about the
behaviour of employers, or workers, derived solely from summary

---

[25] Notebook of Thomas Allen, JP and Mayor, 5 Mar. 1823 to 24 June 1825, Cheshire
RO, D 4655. The volume was rebound at some time, with signatures misplaced; the pages
have been reordered chronologically for the following account.
[26] Census of 1821, *PP* 1822, xv. 35–6; Dorothy Sylvester, *A History of Cheshire* (London,
1971), 87–90.
[27] Servant plaintiffs: win 19, lose 3, settle 14. Master plaintiffs: win 30, lose 3, settle 18.

statistics, often misleading in a jurisdiction (like England) where both can have recourse to the law.

Of course, litigants choose to act only where there is a reasonable chance of success. And we should not assume that Allen was seen to be giving satisfaction to both sides of the trade equally often. An important reason was a new emphasis on imprisonment, caused partly by the predominance of master plaintiffs, partly by willingness to use the most drastic part of the law. Committals to the house of correction were made in 8 per cent of cases (13 per cent of those brought by masters). The charges were for leaving service, leaving work unfinished, absenteeism, being a disorderly apprentice. The sentences were one month (3 cases) or three months (5 cases) in prison. The 'settlement' of masters' complaints against servants was made in the shadow of the prison, and it is highly likely that many conformed to the pattern seen so often, and emphasized in all accounts of the nineteenth-century law: forced return to work, usually with the comment that the master 'forgave' the offender. And it is clear that the silkmasters of Macclesfield were more actively using the law than the farmers of rural parishes in the eighteenth century.

The pattern of magisterial activity in the first half of the nineteenth century, during a period of very rapid population growth and concentrating industrial production, can be traced in detail in a much larger number of petty sessions and other records than exist for the eighteenth.[28] Greater activity by masters, a greater recourse to the more penal sanctions, appears to be common in the petty sessions records I have examined for the nineteenth century. By the mid-nineteenth century, with more highly organized petty sessions (several justices sitting together for the regular transaction of business), bigger jails, more stipendiary magistrates and policemen to assist them, and regular reporting of such cases in the press, the taint of criminality ran through master and servant proceedings from the initiation of process. Servants were almost always brought before the court on arrest warrants, in custody; masters were almost always summoned. Petty sessions registers begin servants' cases with the words 'brought up in custody', and the defendant is usually referred to as 'the prisoner', the language of the criminal courts.[29] In rural petty sessions,

[28] I am currently working on a large sample of such records.
[29] e.g. Berkeley (Gloucs.) petty sessions 1866–71, Gloucs. RO, PS/BE M1/1.

where the participants were almost all farmers and farm servants, it appears from my work to date that there had been significant change from the eighteenth century in the distribution of cases. There are fewer claims for wages. In some areas the business of the magistrates is dominated by the penal proceedings brought by masters; young servants are often committed to prison for very minor offences. But some of these patterns can also be inferred from more continuous runs of records available in some parts of the country: the registers of houses of correction.

The evidence of penal sanctions

Most of the explicitly penal legislation was enacted in the eighteenth century, and only consolidated thereafter. The Statute of Artificers, which was the general governing statute for judges and for Parliament until the early nineteenth century, provided imprisonment, fine, or loss of wages for leaving work, misbehaviour by the worker, and a few other offences. It justified a practice which often had little more specific content.[30] We have convincing evidence that a very expansive attitude to their own powers, not often restrained by the high court judges, probably informed magistrates in the ensuing centuries, or at least by the beginning of the eighteenth century. The erection of houses of correction in the late sixteenth and early seventeenth centuries provided means of enforcing the penal sanction more systematically.[31] Where statutory justification was sought, in the seventeenth and early eighteenth centuries it was undoubtedly found in the very wide received interpretation of the words 'idle and disorderly' in 7 James I c. 4.[32]

The early eighteenth-century practice, at least in London, was for committals to the house of correction of runaway, absent,

---

[30] Although Shoemaker's suggestion that it emphasized private resolutions seems doubtful; the words 'according to the equity of the case' were to become common as a description of the *kind* of lawfully binding adjudication lay judges could employ; Robert B. Shoemaker, *Prosecution and Punishment: Petty Crime and the Law in London and Rural Middlesex c.1660–1725* (Cambridge, 1991), 83.

[31] Innes, 'Prisons for the Poor', 42–122.

[32] Shoemaker, *Prosecution and Punishment*, 37–9, 54–5. In this it was a counterpart to the wide interpretation of 'servant' and of the wage-setting clauses of the Statute of Artificers, for the benefit of the servant: Hay, 'English Judges'.

recalcitrant, or rude servants to be short but severe. Almost three-quarters of committals were for less than two weeks; about half of those committed were whipped and put to hard labour.[33] The chastened servant or apprentice was then released to her or his master; new misbehaviour meant a return to the house of correction. In Middlesex and Westminster, essentially London (outside the City), 7 per cent of all committals in 1663–4, 1690–3, and 1721 were for master and servant offences. In 1721 they amounted to 56 out of a sample total of 711 committals for a wide variety of petty offences.[34] But, to reiterate, they were committals made under the heading of idle and disorderly behaviour.

Then between 1720 and 1792, ten Acts of Parliament specifically provided imprisonment for leaving work and/or misbehaviour.[35] Two of the four earliest ones, in the 1720s, marked an important departure: two and three months in the house of correction, rather than the traditional maximum of one month derived from one of the clauses in the Statute of Artificers.[36] Moreover, almost all the eighteenth-century master and servant statutes introduced significant new language: all but one[37] specified that the imprisonment was to be with 'hard labour'; and two, an important Act of 1747 and another of 1792, introduced with Proclamation Society backing, added that the prisoner, once in the house of correction at hard labour, was 'to be corrected', that is, whipped.[38]

Some of these statutes were clearly responses to the increasing activity of the high courts, notably King's Bench, in scrutinizing justices' committals and convictions.[39] It can be argued that in many respects these Acts put on a firm statutory base what had

---

[33] Shoemaker, *Prosecution and Punishment*, 174–5, 188–9. My survey of early 18th-century provincial houses of correction shows (so far) very few committals, but the sources are extremely patchy.

[34] Ibid. 89, table 2.

[35] 9 Geo. I c. 27 (1722); 12 Geo. I c. 34 (1725); 7 Geo. I st. 1 c. 13 (1726); 2 Geo. II c. 36 (1729); 13 Geo. II c. 8 (1740); 20 Geo. II c. 19 (1747); 22 Geo. II c. 27 (1749); 6 Geo. III c. 25 (1766); 17 Geo. III c. 56 (1777); 32 Geo. III c. 57 (1792).

[36] 12 Geo. I c. 34 (1725, woollen trade); 7 Geo. I st. 1 c. 13 (1726, tailors).

[37] 6 Geo. III c. 25 (1766).

[38] 20 Geo. II c. 19 (1747); 32 Geo. III c. 57 (1792). The society was named after, and intended to implement the reforms of, a proclamation by George III against vice and immorality, 1787. The proclamation itself was the product of moral entrepreneurship.

[39] Hay, 'English Judges'.

formerly been possible informally when justices' actions were less likely to be reviewed by the high courts. But the cumulative effect of enactment, combined with the cumulative effect of the provision of new places of incarceration, produced a real change: from being a place of quick if painful correction (hard labour and a whipping), houses of correction became places where sentences were much longer, and where the words 'hard labour' (and, possibly, 'correction') were also transformed.

The sentences of a week or two characteristic of London in the early eighteenth century can be contrasted with those of houses of correction in industrial and agricultural regions of the provinces 100 years later, where the average sentence passed, and served, was about a month for most master and servant offences (absconding, absence, refusing to work, neglecting work, disorderly apprentices), although individual sentences ranged from one week to three months. For the offence of refusing to enter into work on an agreed contract, the average sentence served was two weeks.[40]

It is probable that rates of imprisonment for breach of contract were in part dependent on the relationship between the number of places in a house of correction or jail, and the demand. An instance is Gloucestershire, where the importance of the woollen industry made the penal provisions of the statutes of considerable importance. John Howard's survey of the Gloucestershire bridewells in the 1770s found that fewer than 100 prisoners a year had been held in all of them, and given their state it is highly unlikely that so many could have been accommodated.[41] (Only a proportion of these, it will be seen below, would have been master and servant offences.) From 1791 the four new houses of correction in that county had 160 separate cells, and an average annual rate of committals of 242.[42] While the number of imprisoned workers in the eighteenth century may (or may not) have been limited by the capacity of the very insecure and unhealthy bridewells, that was certainly not the case in the early nineteenth century. Gloucestershire was over-equipped: up to 1807, the four

---

[40] Calendars which show all committals (rather than simply how many prisoners were incarcerated at the times the courts sat), where they survive, are our most complete source.

[41] John Howard, *State of the Prisons* (London, 1780), 44–5, 325–7.

[42] J. R. S. Whiting, *Prison Reform in Gloucestershire 1776–1820: A Study of the Work of Sir George Onesiphorus Paul* (London, 1975), 105, 234.

new houses of correction never had more than half their cells occupied.

Sir George Onesiphorus Paul, the justice of the peace who was architect of the new system in Gloucestershire, argued in that year that a further crucial influence on the numbers committed was the distance of the bridewell from the committing magistrate's residence. Using the example of a magistrate punishing an apprentice who slept away from home, he suggested that a sentence of fourteen days' detention would only be passed if the bridewell was nearby. If it were 40 miles away, involving expense and delay in getting the apprentice back to work, the magistrate would choose a different penalty. Paul pointed out that most committals were from parishes relatively near the bridewells.[43]

The Gloucestershire bridewells began filling up, however, in the ensuing decades, and a high proportion of those imprisoned were workers in breach. In seventeen years between 1790 and 1810, they amounted to 835, which was 32 per cent of all cases, and an average of 49 a year.[44] The increase in the numbers imprisoned in an agricultural region of Gloucestershire to 1828 was about twenty times greater than what might be expected from population growth;[45] a similar pattern can be seen in Staffordshire (Fig. 1). In that rapidly industrializing county (including the Potteries and much of the emerging Black Country), between 1792 and 1814, 930 men and women were incarcerated under master and servant statutes, an average of 40 a year, and 39 per cent of all cases resulting in incarceration in the house of correction.[46] Between 1792 and 1798 master and servant cases in Staffordshire never accounted for more than a third of the incarcerations in the bridewell, and often for far fewer, and the total number ranged

[43] Ibid. 106. Paul also deplored the fact that magistrates in the Forest of Dean, near Gloucester city, continued to commit cases properly meant for houses of correction to the county prison there. These observations suggest that a comparison of committals per capita has not much meaning, unless for small jurisdictions close to houses of correction. It also may account for some of the variation in the decisions and sentences found in the notebooks of different magistrates in different parts of any given county, as well as different parts of the country.

[44] Gloucs. RO, Q/Gli 16/2, Q/Gn4.

[45] For the reasons cited in the previous paragraph, the population at risk cannot be accurately estimated, but the county population increased by 51% between 1801 and 1831: Phyllis Deane and W. A. Cole, *British Economic Growth 1688–1959* (Cambridge, 1969), table 24, 103.

[46] Staffs. RO, D(W) 1723/1, 2.

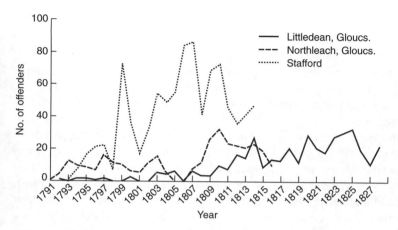

FIGURE I. Master and servant offenders imprisoned, Staffordshire and Gloucestershire, 1791–1828

between 2 and 23 a year. A marked change in 1799, 73 cases, or almost 60 per cent of the total, was thus unusual, but it also was the beginning of a longer period of generally higher totals, in which every year except 1801 was higher than all the years before 1799, often by a large margin.

Analysis of the published mid-nineteenth-century Staffordshire statistics has shown that in broad terms, the use of master and servant increased during periods of strong economic growth, and greatly declined in periods of depression.[47] Although the economic indicators for the late eighteenth and early nineteenth centuries are less complete, the same pattern appears to hold, especially if individual trades are considered. (In the Midlands, for example, war stimulated the iron and depressed the pottery industries.[48]) Preliminary analysis also suggests that areas with concentrations of particularly high-wage industries with a multiplicity of shops (notably in the Black Country) showed most use of master and servant.

How far the detailed evidence modifies the conclusions drawn by Simon in her pioneering article about the typical employer using

[47] D. C. Woods, 'The Operation of the Master and Servants Act in the Black Country 1858–1875', *Midland History*, 7 (1982), 93–115; see also below.
[48] D. Hay, 'War, Dearth and Theft in the Eighteenth Century: The Record of the English Courts', *Past and Present*, 95 (May 1982), 136–7.

master and servant (marginal men in small shops) in the mid-nineteenth century remains to be seen; at the least, the evidence suggests a more complex picture. There does seem to be a strong similarity to the use of master and servant in early twentieth-century Africa: the use of the law in circumstances where low-wage employers were trying to prevent the siphoning off of labour by high-wage employers.[49] The Midlands was an area of high wages in many of the new industries, but also of small workshops where there were probably large numbers of marginal employers, competing against precisely such high-wage competition. The contract of employment is, like all contracts, an attempt to limit the constant reallocation of resources in a free market, limiting that freedom for other ends, notably the security of existing contracts. Workers' interest in unilaterally ending disadvantageous contracts to make better ones is one of the problems that the law of master and servant (or the damages of more ordinary contract law) is designed to limit. One can expect recourse to the law where the economic inducements to breach, *and* the damage caused by breach to the first employer, are high. Where employers are able to agree on fixing wages, there will be less need to resort to legal compulsion: the compulsion of wage labour will act equally beneficially (assuming equal costs) for all employers. But where employers actively compete against each other then we can expect a lot of prosecutions. Many employers, of different sizes and economies of scale, can be expected to produce a pattern of high prosecutions. Those prosecutions will tend to occur in high-wage years, that is, years where there is insufficient labour (particularly skilled labour) to supply all employers at a low wage. But there will be different, sometimes contradictory, cycles for different industries.

Changes in lengths of sentences provide another long-term comparison. In the seventeenth and early eighteenth centuries, 60 per cent of the Middlesex and Westminster workers in the house of correction had sentences of less than two weeks. A hundred years later in Staffordshire, only 7 per cent of all sentences were this short; the average length was over forty days, the most common sentence was one month, and there were many of two and three months, reflecting the penalties enacted in the eighteenth-century statutes. (To keep our perspective, we should note

[49] See the studies in a forthcoming volume, edited by Paul Craven and myself, dealing with the use of master and servant throughout the British Empire.

that the average length of sentence for petty larceny was six months, and for an unwed mother, 10.3 months.) But something else had also changed. At the beginning of the eighteenth century most of the imprisoned servants in London were also whipped. By the early nineteenth century, at least in Staffordshire, no such sentences are recorded. It also appears that few were whipped in at least some other parts of the country in both the early eighteenth and early nineteenth centuries. The very full notebook of Edgar cites only three cases, one of them an incorrigible apprentice of 11 years of age; in Gloucestershire, the house of correction records record only one adult whipped (for embezzlement, not breach of contract) and several apprentices, again juveniles, for running away.[50]

Yet we know that in some places, in some circumstances, whipping was used in a most exemplary way. It was provided for in the general statute of 1747, under the rubric 'correction'.[51] That statute was judicially explained in a case which made abundantly clear how much it was still part of the law; how much whipping was actually used needs further local study.

Hoseason was a prosecution of a Norfolk JP of that name who had heard and decided the case of one of his own servants under the 1747 Act. His bailiff brought before him a labourer of 18 named Generel Batterbee who worked on Hoseason's farm, and Hoseason convicted him for misconduct and refusal to do his work. Batterbee had been in the midst of his dinner after a morning of loading wheat, and refused to cut short his hour's rest at the demand of the bailiff. The bailiff kicked and punched him, knocked him down, kicked him while on the ground. The servant went to Hoseason (whether as his magistrate or employer is unclear) to complain. Hoseason struck him in the face and immediately made out the warrant for his committal to the house of correction for one month at hard labour, and to be whipped at its conclusion.[52] Before the month expired a neighbouring gentleman appealed to Hoseason (on behalf of Batterbee's father) to have the labourer discharged without the whipping, and commented that 'the law will not allow a Man to act as a Judge in Cases in

---

[50] Above, nn. 17, 46, 48.
[51] 20 Geo. II c. 19. Craven and Hay, 'The Criminalization of "Free" Labour', 86–7, is in error on this point.
[52] *R.* v. *Hoseason*, 14 East 605; Battersby in the report.

which he is interested', a common sentiment (and an echo of Lord Mansfield). Hoseason was unrepentant:

My warrant does not of course express one third of the complaints made against him for frequent disobedience of orders, neglect of duty, contempt to his master, etc etc. for which he had been frequently called before me, and admonished without effect. At the time this last complaint was made to me upon oath, there was no other magistrate in Marshland, and I felt it my indispensable duty conscientiously so to punish him. Feeling I have done my duty, I never shall regret having committed him to Swaffham Gaol to be corrected for a month.

Nor did he, as it turned out. Batterbee served his month, and before release was whipped twenty lashes on his bare back, with a cat of three cords; he was 'severely whipped and was much cut and bruised'.[53] In his judgment (largely devoted to an analysis of just which statute justified whipping, a point of confusion) the Lord Chief Justice criticized Hoseason, saying, 'it was a most abusive interpretation of the law for a man to erect himself as a criminal judge over the servants on his own farm for an offence against himself'. None the less, Lord Ellenborough concluded that the JP acted from an 'error of judgement' rather than 'any bad motive' and he refused to grant a rule for an information against him. He made no comment on the appropriateness of the penalty to the offence.[54] We do know that he was enthusiastic about the virtues of imprisonment: in another case he had observed that the 1747 Act gave 'masters an easy method of correcting trifling misdemeanours and ill behaviour in their workmen and labourers'.

How common whipping was as an ultimate deterrent, and whether it increased in the early nineteenth century, remains to be shown. It is clear that imprisonment became more important. The huge increase in custodial capacity of the English state, both in county prisons and in houses of correction, as well as penitentiaries, has been remarked by many historians of the period 1790 to 1850. The opening of a large number of local prisons in England and Wales greatly increased the options of magistrates to make commitals in master and servant cases. Perhaps less atten-

---

[53] D. Hay, 'Patronage, Paternalism, and Welfare: Masters, Workers, and Magistrates in Eighteenth-Century England', *International Labor and Working-Class History*, 53 (Spring 1998), 40–5.

[54] Rule discharged, defendant to pay costs.

tion has been directed to their use for short-term sentences of workers, but contemporaries were often quite clear about it. Bedford's second new prison, opened in 1820, was built to accommodate the usual range of petty offenders, but the second category mentioned, after poachers, was 'servants in husbandry and other labourers for misbehaviour in their employment'.[55]

If the legislating of longer sentences in the mid-eighteenth century, and the provision of more cells in the late eighteenth century, both increased the bite of the penal legislation, so too did changes in the organization of prison and house of correction discipline. Hard labour, prescribed by most of the new eighteenth-century statutes, became transformed by the length of sentences, but also, eventually, by the development of treadmills and other more organized punishments in the third and fourth decades of the nineteenth century, replacing the haphazard provision of work that Joanna Innes has shown characterized the early modern workhouse.[56]

In these circumstances older workers as well as younger ones found themselves serving sentences in particularly humiliating conditions. Although the great majority of prisoners were young men and women, the laws were by no means limited to younger workers and apprentices (Fig. 2). Women constituted 15 per cent of committals to prison on master and servant offences, and were the majority of those identified as cotton workers or 'servants', which usually meant servants in agricultural labour: general labour, dairy work, and so forth. There was a marked periodicity in prosecutions for some offences, notably running away, being absent, absconding from service. Fig. 3 reflects regional variations and the lack of winter work in agriculture and sometimes in industry (due to weather conditions), the greater demands made by farm labour around harvest time when their bargaining position was best (July, August), and the fact that so many annual hirings concluded and began in October, leading to prosecutions when servants abandoned oppressive masters early in the contract, when few wages were owing.[57]

[55] Beds. RO, Q/S rolls 1820/69.   [56] Innes, 'Prisons for the Poor'.
[57] 'When the spring of the year came and labour bore a high price . . . a great number of agricultural labourers found themselves in consequence the inmates of a gaol because they attempted to break their contracts with their masters.' Simon, 'Master and Servant', 191, citing Hansard. Fig. 3 suggests the crucial period was harvest.

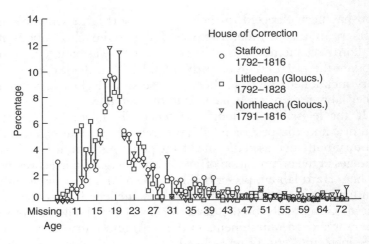

FIGURE 2. Age of master and servant convicts, Staffordshire and Gloucestershire

Diversity

There was always much regional distinctiveness in the direct use of master and servant law, as we see from the evidence of the justices' notebooks and petty sessions, as well as the mid-nineteenth-century statistics. Diversity, but not a simple pattern of differences between large geographical areas. There were some such large areas, some of them enduring into the twentieth century: hiring fairs in east Yorkshire, for example, continued to place adolescent farm servants, as horsetrainers, within a structure of legal expectations still largely defined by the tradition and terms of the general hiring.[58] But the principal variations in master and servant law in practice, a diversity that sometimes almost seems to ignore the unifying force of legal decision in the high courts, arose from the unique structures of different trades, and the sometimes co-variant, sometimes independently determined, nature of the magisterial bench.

In places like Macclesfield, or anywhere a trade was still organized in the eighteenth and early nineteenth centuries within an older structure of legislated protections, mutual adjustments, and

[58] Stephen Caunce, *Amongst Farm Horses: The Horselads of East Yorkshire* (Stroud, 1991).

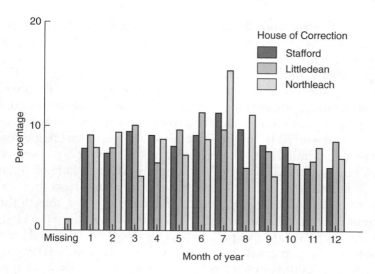

FIGURE 3. Month of master and servant offence

negotiation between masters and men, the adjudication of their disputes took on a different flavour. Such structures continued in several important silk-weaving centres: Coventry, because (it has been argued) common lands encircling the town prevented expansion and dilution of the trade; London because riot and sabotage were easy to conduct and difficult to repress, and Parliament bought peace by giving workers and small masters much of what they wanted, and large mercers had to accede. The justices in Spitalfields in London administered a complex system of wage-rates disguised as piece-rates, given the force of law by parliamentary sanction, until well into the nineteenth century. In other centres, outside the so-called 'Spitalfields Acts', it none the less appears that magisterial activity was largely the ratification of understandings that obtained throughout the trade.

The silk industry, of course, was a highly specialized craft, but one point that must be made in considering the diversity of experience of master and servant law is that dozens of trades in England had their own version of the law.[59] That is, a set of values,

[59] Marc W. Steinburg, 'The Dialogue of Struggle: The Contest over Ideological Boundaries in the Case of London Silk Weavers in the Early Nineteenth Century', *Social Science History*, 18/4 (winter 1994), 505–41.

claims, negotiated positions, *distinctive to the trade, and called the custom of the trade*, both shaped and was shaped by the statute and case law. Tudor and Stuart legislation in the woollen industry created expectations, for example, about apprenticeship, about fair working, and about fair wages. Those expectations determined what conflicts, what issues, would come before magistrates considering unpaid wages, unfair dismissal, incompetent weaving, or unfinished work. The force of such expectations, given greater resonance (or diminished) by legislation got by riot or by lobbying, was great in part because of its antiquity. Perhaps half of adult male labour was primarily agricultural in about 1700, but the figure understates the importance of industrial work, due to the extent of women's work and dual occupations, well into the eighteenth century. And this pattern was very old. Social and labour historians have pushed the history of large-scale industrial production, in putting-out networks to home-workers, or in artisan home production, back further and further into the seventeenth, sixteenth, fifteenth centuries. It was the antiquity of trade custom which gave it so much force in the eighteenth century, in a society that until about 1800 valued antiquity, particularly as a source of law.

The destruction of the traditional claims recognized by local legal cultures around particular trades is a large story that cannot be recapitulated here, but its main elements are the legislative and judicial erasure of apprenticeship, wage-fixing, protection from new machinery, and most of the other most-cherished parts of the larger 'law of master and servant' that operated in the interests of skilled and semi-skilled labour.[60] That change took place between about 1770 and 1820, with an acceleration in the first decades of the nineteenth century. The new perception of master and servant law, in terms of complaints from workers, is consequent upon these changes.

Collective protest and master and servant

It may be in these years also that master and servant law came increasingly to be identified with the suppression of trade union

---

[60] For a survey see Hay and Rogers, *English Society*, chs. 6–9.

activity. Most accounts of master and servant law quote a contemporary argument by Gravener Henson and George White on the usefulness of the laws in breaking strikes. Because in many trades the work was never fully completed, the result of a strike was a prosecution for leaving work unfinished. They expressly compared the effects of master and servant law to the far more notorious Combination Acts:

Very few prosecutions have been made to effect under the Combination Acts, but hundreds have been made under this law, and the labourer or workman can never be free, unless this law is modified. The Combination Act is nothing: it is the law which regards the finishing of work which masters employ to harass and keep down the wages of their workpeople; unless this is modified nothing is done, and by repealing the Combination Acts you leave the workman in ninety-nine cases out of a hundred in the same state you found him—at the mercy of his master.[61]

It was also easy for the master to prosecute on the grounds of being absent from service, general 'misconduct', and other offences under the Acts. Obviously the tactic was limited by the size of the strike. During a colliers' strike on Tyneside in 1765, a correspondent of the Earl of Northumberland explained why the 1747 statute had not been used:

this is very well, where two or three or a dozen men desert their service, and has been many times properly executed with good Effect, but where there is a general Combination of all the Pitmen to the Number of 4,000, how can this measure take Effect? in the first place it is difficult to be executed as to seizing the men, and even if they should not make a formidable Resistance which scarce can be presumed, a few only can be taken, for upon the Face of the thing it is obvious that the whole persons guilty can not be secured, so the punishment of probably twenty or forty by a month's confinement in a House of Correction, does not carry with it the least Appearance of Terror so as to induce the remaining Part of so large a Number to submit, and these men that should be so confined would be treated as Martyrs for the good Cause, and be supported and caressed, and at the end of the time brought home in Triumph, so no good effect would arise.[62]

---

[61] *A Few Remarks on the State of the Laws, at Present in Existence for Regulating Masters and Work-People* (1823), 51. This passage does not appear in the revision: George White, *A Digest of All the Laws Respecting Masters and Work People* (London, 1824).

[62] SP Dom. (George III), vol. iv; quoted in J. L. Hammond and Barbara Hammond, *The Skilled Labourer*, ed. John Rule (London, 1975), 12.

TABLE I. *Multiple committals,*[a] *master and servant cases, Stafford house of correction,* *1792–1814*

Offence	No. of persons committed		
	5–10	3–4	2
Refuse to work		2	4
Refuse to perform contract	1		1
Leaving service	1	1	1
Absent from service		4	12
Absconding	1	10	24
Neglecting work		3	7
[Combination]		1	
[Embezzlement]	1		
Total multiple committals	4	21	49
(Total number committed)	28	66	98

Note: Total single committals: 738.

  [a] Same occupation, same magistrate, same or adjacent days.

But such massive solidarity was (as always) the exception. The use of the Master and Servant Acts to break smaller strikes was undoubtedly common. Such cases typically surface in the court or prison records in the form of several convictions by the same magistrate, on the same or succeeding days, of men with the same occupation. Using those criteria,[63] Table I shows the number of multiple prosecutions in the Staffordshire committals. Thus between 10 and 21 per cent of those committed probably arrived in jail as a result of a collective dispute, according to the criteria used.[64] This was almost certainly the case with the eight miners whom Justice Sneyd committed for a month in March 1797 (all were 'very quiet and orderly' in the house of correction) for leaving service; or the four potters committed by the Reverend

  [63] The result may be to miss some strikes, since strikers may have been committed several days apart, or by different magistrates, or men with different occupational descriptions may be in the same strike; on the other hand, many of these committals may represent no more than a master deciding to take action against several men at once, under more ordinary circumstances. This is particularly likely to be the case when only two are committed.

  [64] The higher figure if a committal of two men is considered to be a labour dispute. See n. 63 above.

Justice Powys in 1807 (one on 20 April, three more on 25 April) for absconding (they too were 'orderly', two for two months, two for one month). But of course it is quite possible that a much higher percentage of those incarcerated were leaders of strikes, or at least men victimized to make a salutary example for others; an unknown proportion of 'single committals' must fall into this category.[65]

One other approach to this question of the 'collective' versus the 'individualized' uses of master and servant law for employers using the penal clauses is to compare the incidence of multiple committals to all committals for different occupations. It is remarkably high for colliers, men noted for their solidarity and successful strikes (not least because they could disappear underground when pursued by troops). It is moderately high for potters (many in the trade were very skilled men), and for a number of other trades in which workers with special skills ranked high in the hierarchy of labour, and attempted to maintain their position in these years.[66] It was very low for labourers and servants in husbandry. The last two, one unskilled and the second a mixture of unskilled and semi-skilled workers in low-wage occupations, were very unlikely to strike, and the small proportions of collective committals in those trades, and large numbers of single committals, suggests that employers used the law against such men as an individual discipline. What was probably the largest group of industrial workers in Staffordshire, nailers, are notable for very few prosecutions (thirteen), and nil collective ones. These were among the poorest workers in an industrial trade, and many were for the most part self-employed, buying rod iron as they could afford it, and selling the product to nailmasters. There may, therefore, have been few in a contractual master–servant relationship; in any case, the chronic oversupply of labour in the trade made it unlikely that any master would be bothered to try to enforce a contract with an unsatisfactory worker.[67]

One final, remarkable fact about prosecutions under these statutes can be seen in the house of correction statistics. In these

[65] For an example about which there can be no doubt, see the case of the single carpenter committed for the offence of combination, below.

[66] E. P. Thompson, *The Making of the English Working Class* (Harmondsworth, 1968), 553, notes cotton-spinners, calico-printers, among others.

[67] In this sample, 4 were prosecuted for embezzling iron, 7 for neglecting or being absent from work, and 1 for refusing to obey his master.

twenty-two years, when over 900 men and women were prosecuted for master and servant offences, many of them in the course
of collective struggles with their employers, only seven men were
summarily convicted for the actual offence of 'combination'.
Three of these were hatters, prosecuted in 1795, under 17 George
III c. 55 (1777).[68] The other four appear to be the only men convicted on the Combination Act of 1800 in the fourteen years after
its passage. One was a carpenter, sentenced by a JP to one month,
but released after two weeks; another was a collier committed by
two JPs for two calendar months but released after less than two
weeks; the remaining two were both colliers sent to the house of
correction by the same two JPs (Clare and Haden), 'For unlawfully attending Meetings held for the purpose of obtaining an
advance of wages & for prevailing on divers Colliers to leave their
employment against the form [of the statute]'. They were committed for three calendar months but were released after thirty-
seven days.

There is, then, overwhelming evidence from this Staffordshire
source to substantiate the observation of Gravener Henson and
George White that the Combination Acts were much less important to workers than the master and servant laws. M. D. George
made that contrast to support her argument that the Combination Act of 1800 was entirely unimportant.[69] E. P. Thompson
showed that Henson and White in fact argued that the Combination Act of 1800 was 'a tremendous millstone round the necks
of the local artisan, which has depressed and debased him to the
earth'.[70] But citing contemporary opinion in these matters, particularly the language of political pamphlets, is probably in the
end not very useful as a guide to actual practice; and, as Thompson has argued, the symbolic significance of the Combination Act
of 1800 was great. In any case, Henson and White went on, for

---

[68] Providing for three months' imprisonment on conviction before two JPs, which is the
circumstance in this case. They were released after a month. On this legislation, see John
Orth, 'English Combination Acts of the Eighteenth Century', *Law and History Review*, 5/1
(spring 1987), 192.

[69] M. D. George, 'The Combination Acts', *Economic History Review*, 1st ser. 6 (1935–6),
175.

[70] Thompson, *Making*, 555; the passage appears in White's 1824 edn. at 89. In a critique
of George's influential article, Orth shows that George, arguing for the unimportance of
the Act, ignored this passage, and cited only another asserting that the Combination Act
was no threat to the travelling trades with houses of call: John V. Orth, 'The English Combination Laws Reconsidered', in Snyder and Hay (eds.), *Labour, Law and Crime*, 134.

reasons we have seen, to describe the Master and Servant Act of 1766 (6 Geo. III c. 25) as 'the most cruel, unjust, and oppressive statute in the code'.[71]

Why was the Combination Act of 1800 used so seldom in Staffordshire?[72] Undoubtedly because master and servant was flexible, easily used, and in most cases the offence would be much easier to prove than combination.[73] There was an appeal to quarter sessions under the Combination Act of 1800; there was no appeal in case of committal under the statutes of 1747 and 1766.[74] There is also the possibility that the petitioning campaign against the 1799 Act, and the immense resentment over the passage of both it and the 1800 Act, so weakened their legitimacy that employers and magistrates found them likely to worsen disputes rather than cure them.[75] Master and servant prosecutions, in contrast, were based on statutes many decades old, statutes which were not recent innovations and which, unlike the Combination Acts, offered workers a *quid pro quo* of some value in the form of proceedings for wages and, until the early decades of the nineteenth century, some protection against arbitrary discharge by a master on his own authority. The only advantage the Combination Act purported to offer workers was the chance to prosecute masters for combination, a meaningless clause that was unenforceable and nugatory.

An increasing inequality?

The greatest politicization of master and servant takes place in the years after 1820, and apparently accompanied harsher enforcement of the penal provisions.[76] The change seems to have been most pronounced between about 1830 and 1850. This development toward a more employer-oriented law was not limited to

---

[71] White, *Digest*, 94.

[72] It may have been used more often to accuse rather than convict: one report from the west of England in 1802 suggests that magistrates in search of sedition used the pretext of a hearing to examine 'suspected persons' on oath: Thompson, *Making*, 551.

[73] Ibid. 553 on the difficulties.

[74] Ibid. for a contemporary comment on the difficulties appeals posed to employers; above, n. 35.

[75] Thompson suggests some other reasons: ibid. 552.

[76] The following paragraphs are based on unpublished work.

industrial areas. Scattered soundings in petty sessions registers from deeply rural areas also show a degree of punitiveness, and use of the law by employers rather than workers, that sharply contrasts with the balanced paternalism of eighteenth-century country gentlemen justices. It is not uncommon in the mid-nineteenth century to find servant girls prosecuted by farmers for not milking the cow, or otherwise neglecting work, and not only being brought up before the magistrates from custody, but returned to the prison to serve seven or fourteen days.

After the turn of the century there are also increasing complaints about the difficulty of using the summary procedure for recovery of wages. Even in the eighteenth century commentators noted difficulties in using the 1747 statute:

> This statute is extremely inconvenient for the recovery of the wages of servants or labourers by allowing the space of *twenty-one* days after the order of payment, thereof, before distress can be made, which gives the Master time to make away with his effects, and particularly in the case of haymakers and artificers, having finished their work, and removing to a distant part, to be obliged to wait three weeks, and possibly not receive their wages at last, is troublesome and vexatious, and makes many poor labourers go home without their wages, or accept an iniquitous composition. Therefore the distress ought to be immediate, upon refusal to pay according to the order.[77]

This kind of 'iniquitous composition' was noted in some of the case law. Problems like these were probably most often circumvented when a magistrate could impose, through his social prestige and local influence, practical rather than purely legal solutions. Thus Devereaux Edgar, the Suffolk magistrate active near Ipswich between 1700 and 1716, noted that in instances of complaints by servants 'against masters present and masters lately gone from, the first by misusage either in diet or beating and the latter from not paying of their wages when gone away' he did not always grant warrants. His motive, he said, was to save the complaining servant the cost: instead of a warrant, he wrote a note to the master asking that he do justice. He added that a further advantage to the servant was that it avoided the disgrace of arrest

---

[77] 20 Geo. II c. 19, Burn's *Observations*, 288, as quoted in John Huntingford, *Laws of Masters and Servants Considered* (London, 1790), 92. Huntingford was secretary of the Society for Encouragement and Encrease of Good Servants.

for the master, a disgrace which led often to revenge at a later date.

If this practice was at all general, it suggests that the ratio of wage cases to discipline cases may be even higher for the eighteenth century than I have suggested. But it is also a reminder that when a JP was a gentleman, in a social structure that gave him real authority and a credible if partial role as paternalist, a note from the justice might well be effective, without the need for further enforcement proceedings.

A century later, however, sharp complaints are heard about the difficulties in using the legislation to assist workers in getting unpaid wages:

there is redress, by summoning the master before the magistrate, but he may refuse to come forward, and supposing he does come forward, they may order payment of the sum agreed for, and he may refuse paying the sum. On refusal, they may grant a warrant, and after granting the warrant, he may appeal to the sessions, then it becomes so expensive, I am not able to follow him there, or few poor workmen I believe.

Q. When you are so treated, do you apply to the magistrate, or do you rest contented with the loss?—We generally rest contented with the loss, knowing the expence would be too heavy for us to follow.[78]

As magistrates were increasingly likely to be employers in the same trade, and as masters used lawyers to make points such as these, resolutions that a country gentleman might have imposed in a spirit of paternalism (or simple dislike of men in trade) were less and less likely.

Longer trends

We know something of the broad outlines of enforcement in the period after 1854, and especially after 1858, when statistical series become available, and work by Daphne Simon, David Woods, and others has shown its dimensions.[79] Briefly, there continues to be

---

[78] Thomas Thorpe, weaver, examined by Mundell, lawyer: *Hansard* 1802–3, viii. 896–7. I owe this reference to Ramneek Pooni. The appeal to quarter sessions allowed to masters in wage disputes (until 1823) was explicitly denied to workers who had been committed to the house of correction. Acts of 1747, 1766; 4 Geo. IV c. 34 s. 5.

[79] Simon, 'Master and Servant', and Woods, 'The Operation of the Master and Servants Act'.

strong evidence of diversity in a very disproportionate use of the penal clauses of master and servant (and probably of master and servant by master plaintiffs, in general) in certain counties and boroughs: Staffordshire (Walsall, Wolverhampton, the Potteries) and Sheffield in Yorkshire are among them. Certain trades, coal mining and potting and the small metal trades, to be found in those areas were particularly likely to generate prosecutions. There is also some evidence of a continuing increase in unequal impact of the law. The current estimates we have for the use of the penal parts of the law for the 1860s suggest that where it was most used, workers brought less than 20 per cent of claims, and masters brought at least 80 per cent. Moreover, probably 20 per cent of all prosecutions by masters not only resulted in conviction, but in imprisonment.[80] If so, there thus had been the growth, in parts of the country most actively organized by trade unions, of a sharp imbalance in the impact of what, in earlier periods, had been a body of law legitimized by the remedies it offered to workers as well as employers. But before considering why the law appears increasingly so sharply tilted toward the employer by the nineteenth century, I want to return to the issue of diversity in meaning, and in enforcement, over the longer period.

The connections between the early nineteenth-century use of master and servant and its significance in the 'statistical period' from the 1850s to 1870s are still largely unexplored. There are problems with the nineteenth-century returns that can only be resolved by very detailed local work in archival materials.[81] They conflate proceedings brought by masters with those brought by servants; they are itemized by administrative units that are often combinations of very different regional economies and different groups of trades; they do not identify, for such units, the outcomes of summary hearings of master and servant cases. Finally, I believe that they are quite incomplete because of how the returns were prepared, and incomplete in different ways in different places. That said, they suggest some distinctive patterns.

First, a unique Parliamentary Return of numbers in one house

---

[80] Woods identified 13.4% of prosecutions as brought by servants from the accounts in one newspaper; the figure for imprisonment in the 1860s is derived from the parliamentary statistics and my preliminary analysis of part of a larger sample of local sources.

[81] I am currently collating a wide sample of petty sessions records with the published statistics.

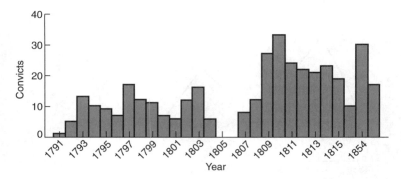

FIGURE 4. Northleach (Gloucestershire) prisoners, master and servant offences, 1791–1816 and 1854–5

of correction ties the nineteenth-century statistics to a house of correction register (see Fig. 4). It suggests that the great increase in master and servant imprisonments stabilized for the first half of the nineteenth century: the numbers in one (only partly used) house of correction in Gloucestershire are about the same in the mid-1850s as in the first two decades of the nineteenth century.

Secondly, an apparent great increase in summary hearings of master and servant cases in the last years before repeal in 1875, a point made by a number of historians, may be in part spurious.[82] In absolute terms there was certainly growth, but a more useful gauge of relative importance of master and servant hearings is a comparison with summary criminal prosecutions for all offences, of which master and servant always represented less than 3 per cent. Fig. 5 shows that the peak years of 1872 and 1873 (a period of booming employment) were no greater, in proportional terms, than the earlier peak of 1860, and that there is no upward trend overall. The greater numbers of prosecutions in the early 1870s were part of a general increase in the use of summary powers before justices, and probably reflect increased policing, more stipendiary magistrates, and other administrative and systemic changes in enforcement of all penal law, rather than a change in attitudes to the use of master and servant law. Of course, the

---

[82] e.g. Simon, 'Master and Servant', 190 n. 1, who attributes it to the exceptional boom, and hence large numbers of workmen employed, in 1872.

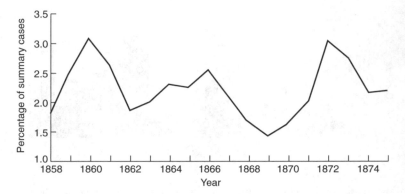

FIGURE 5. Master and servant cases as a percentage of reported summary cases, England and Wales

statistical evidence of a growth in absolute numbers contributed to the pressures to change the law.[83]

The great number of master and servant cases in Staffordshire, Lancashire, Yorkshire, and several other counties has always been remarked. In these cases it is clear that the law bulked larger in the caseload of magistrates than in other counties. Yet there is no correlation of master and servant cases simply with the industrial areas in which union militancy generated most protest about the law (and generated much of the statistical record, as employers used master and servant law against strikes and other work stoppages). Berkshire and Staffordshire were very different counties in the nineteenth century, but both benches made much use of master and servant, in terms of total caseload, although at different times (Fig. 6).

A comparison of the most deeply agricultural and most deeply industrial areas of England in the later nineteenth century, again in terms of the percentage of summary cases of all kinds that master and servant cases represented, shows a similar relative importance in magistrate's caseloads (Fig. 7). It also shows a difference in their periodicity, which is replicated across jurisdictions. The influence of the business cycle, noted in several studies, is part, but not all, of the explanation, and its influence is not a simple one.

[83] A question I consider elsewhere.

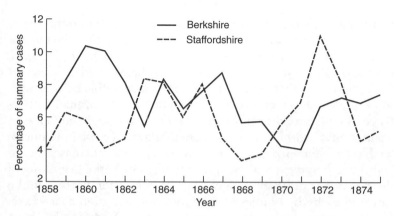

FIGURE 6. Master and servant as percentage of all summary cases, Berkshire and Staffordshire

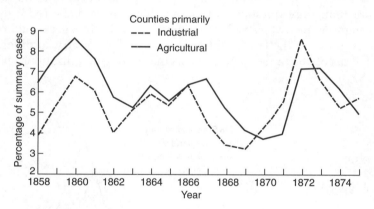

FIGURE 7. Master and servant prosecutions in industrial and agricultural regions of heavy enforcement

Note: Counties included are those with high proportional rates, and more than 1,500 prosecutions; see text.

Some of the influences determining these patterns are suggested when we compare the patterns of an industrializing with a de-industrializing county. Taking two of the counties for which earlier statistical information also exists (in the form of house of correction registers), we can make some longer-range comparisons also. Staffordshire was one of the heartlands of the nineteenth-century Industrial Revolution, in both the Potteries and the Black Country. Gloucestershire, on the other hand, had an ancient textile industry that survived into the nineteenth century, with some cycles of prosperity, but of increasingly marginal importance. Those broad trends can be seen in the slight increase in trend in Staffordshire, and the more marked decrease in Gloucestershire, of the percentage of master and servant cases heard before the magistrates of each county (Fig. 8). At the beginning of the statistical era (1858) such cases were twice as important in the caseload of both counties as they were in the nation as a whole. By 1875 they were even more important in Staffordshire, but from the late 1860s Gloucestershire echoed the lower national pattern almost exactly, and from the early 1860s its pattern bore very little relationship to that of the more industrialized county.

These very impressionistic uses of the national statistics do no more than raise questions, questions that can be answered only through detailed work in local archival records. The great differences in use of the law in different parts of the country, in different areas of the same county, means that most generalizations will

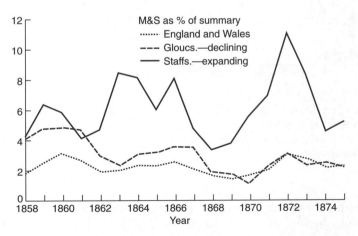

FIGURE 8. Industrial change and master and servant prosecutions, Staffordshire and Gloucestershire

be unsafe until the texture, incidence, and outcomes of prosecutions in a large sample of places and times are established. But the patterns of the nineteenth century in many ways do appear to replicate structures of conflict, paternalism, and accommodation also found in the eighteenth, even if other evidence suggests that a paternalist administration of the law by gentlemen justices of the peace was, by the middle of the nineteenth century, largely in the past.

Conclusion

This essay has presented some preliminary findings on the incidence and variations of the use of master and servant law in eighteenth- and nineteenth-century England. For the purposes of the argument I have largely ignored the great changes in statute and case law over the period, the changing nature of trade union organization and its use of the law, the rise of factory production, and its contribution to legal change. Significant changes in local government, the administration of justice, and the role of lawyers have also, for the most part, been ignored. All of these are important for understanding the political significance of master and servant law, as well as its practical application.

It is difficult, however, to assess those changes without a fuller understanding of how important the law was in the daily relations of capital, labour, and the local state. We have seen that master and servant law constituted a large part of the activity of the most active justices in many parts of the country; that the history of the law's penal sanctions is intimately related to the history of prisons and crime and trade union organization and the nature of the bench in the nineteenth century; and that all generalizations about the significance and incidence of its remedies must take account of an enormous variability in its application, according to region, trade, and the state of the economy.

Further work will explore all those connections, but even in the state of our present knowledge, it seems clear that between about 1750 and 1850 there was a marked change in the application of the law. Sentences became longer, and were increasingly likely to be served in the prisons and jails of the new carceral regime prescribed by reformers of criminal punishments. Between about

Was there a De-juridification of Individual Employment Relations in Britain?

WILLIBALD STEINMETZ

Introduction

The desire to be left alone by the law has been described as 'an instinct that is fundamental to British industrial relations'.[1] Even in animal life, however, instincts have a history, and in human history so-called fundamental 'instincts' may be of recent origin and may change quickly. With respect to the British labour movement's supposed instinctive aversion to the law, it is far from obvious when, how, and, above all, why it should have developed. Most accounts have seen legislative and judicial attacks on trade unions as the crucial factor. Much less attention has been paid to individual employees who tried to make use of the law in ordinary employment disputes. Yet there are good reasons to assume that such day-to-day encounters before British courts of law did much to instil into workers that fundamental distrust of judges and lawyers which in the long run led to an 'instinct' to avoid legal solutions altogether. The following paragraphs set out to explore some aspects of this supposition by concentrating on employees' experiences in English magistrates' courts and county courts between 1850 and the early 1920s.

Unequal treatment of workers had been a deeply engrained feature of English law since Elizabethan times, but there are signs of a marked aggravation in the early decades of the nineteenth century. Parallel to the criminalization of combinations between workmen, the old master and servant laws were gradually stripped of paternalistic features. By an Act of 1823 various older statutes

[1] K. W. Wedderburn, *The Worker and the Law* (2nd edn., Harmondsworth, 1971), 13.

were consolidated into an instrument to punish all sorts of employees who had gone on strike or otherwise broken their contracts. In addition, judges elaborated the common law of conspiracy to put a further check on trade union activities.[2] And as is shown by Douglas Hay in this volume, it was during the same period that justices of the peace came to adopt a harsher attitude towards labourers than in the eighteenth century. After all that the emerging working class could not but see the law as becoming increasingly unfair.

Starting from such a position it is no wonder that in most conventional accounts the legal history of labour in the second half of the nineteenth century appears to have been driven by efforts to get the repressive laws removed from the statute book and to eliminate the judiciary as far as possible from interfering with trade disputes. Unfair treatment is declared to have been the main stumbling block which stood between labour and the law. Many reform proposals by labour leaders indeed followed the guidelines advocated by the radical tailor Francis Place in the early 1820s: 'Repeal every troublesome and vexatious enactment, and enact very little in their place. Leave workmen and their employers as much as possible at liberty to make their own bargains in their own way.'[3] After prolonged campaigns and numerous setbacks— so the classical story continues—success finally came with the labour legislation of the 1870s and 1906. The story of these Acts is well known.[4] They made breaches of contract by individual workmen a matter of civil jurisdiction only and freed trade unions and their members from criminal prosecution or being sued under the common law of tort for certain acts committed during trade disputes, such as peaceful picketing, persuading others to join a strike, and thereby disturbing the trade or business of some other person.

[2] Cf. J. V. Orth, *Combination and Conspiracy: A Legal History of Trade Unionism, 1721–1906* (Oxford, 1991), 34–41 and 99–106. There is evidence that judges were more lenient up to 1850 and that common law inventiveness against trade unions only set in on a massive scale after that date; see Michael Lobban, 'Strikers and the Law, 1825–1851', in Peter Birks (ed.), *The Life of the Law* (London, 1993), 211–33.

[3] Quoted in E. P. Thompson, *The Making of the English Working Class* (Harmondsworth, 1984), 567.

[4] See Orth, *Combination*, and also Jonathan Spain, 'Trade Unionists, Gladstonian Liberals and the Labour Law Reforms of 1875', in Eugenio F. Biagini and Alastair J. Reid (eds.), *Currents of Radicalism: Popular Radicalism, Organised Labour and Party Politics in Britain, 1850–1914* (Cambridge, 1991), 109–33.

One might expect that since that time, after the stumbling blocks of unequal treatment had been removed, friendlier intercourse between labour and the law would have been possible. Yet it appears that mutual alienation had by then already reached such dimensions that British trade unions saw in the defence of their far-reaching legal immunities the most important or even the unique goal of their legal policies. Various attempts have been made in the 1970s and 1980s to circumscribe the procedures of collective bargaining by legislation, but no government, not even that of Margaret Thatcher, has been able or willing to break the voluntary structure of British industrial relations. Individual working conditions, too, remain among the least regulated in Europe, and the industrial tribunals established in 1971 have as yet not made such an impact and are not so fully appreciated that their existence in the present form seems to be assured.[5] While there has been an unprecedented number of statutes on employment in the last thirty years, it seems doubtful whether the result can be called progressive juridification. Many recent laws in fact aimed at deregulation and thus rather strengthened the opposite tendency.[6] The 'instinct' of avoiding legal solutions to conflicts between employers and employees whenever possible still seems to be very much alive. Such is, in brief words, the classic account of labour's relations with the law in nineteenth- and twentieth-century Britain.

This essay does not challenge the general thrust of this narrative. Nor will an entirely new argument be put in its place. Yet from a comparative perspective the above account gives rise to questions. Unequal treatment of workers and legal repression of trade unions were not unique to Britain. After the reforms of the 1870s occurrences of this kind were probably even less pronounced here than in Germany or France at the same time. In

[5] For a critical voice see, for example, the *Evening Standard*, 13 July 1994, p. 9: 'There are occasions when employees are dismissed unfairly and it is right that there should be some mechanism to deal with these abuses. But perhaps it is time we tightened up the criteria under which cases can be brought. . . . The Government should now consider setting up an inquiry into the workings of unfair dismissal tribunals. If the growing public perception of them as wasteful is sustained, the whole apparatus should be reformed, if not entirely scrapped.'

[6] Cf. (arguing against Spiros Simitis): Jon Clark and Lord Wedderburn, 'Juridification—a Universal Trend? The British Experience in Labor Law', in Gunther Teubner (ed.), *Juridification of Social Spheres: A Comparative Analysis in the Areas of Labor, Corporate, Antitrust and Social Welfare Law* (Berlin, 1987), 163–90.

any case, hostile judges and experiences of inequality before the law were common everywhere. As such these are not sufficient reasons why there should have been a special British path, why employment relations should have been withdrawn from the sphere of the law to such an extent. Other explanations have mainly hinged on the ideological outlook of the British working-class élite during the Victorian age—its affinity with middle-class values such as self-help, individualism, and freedom of contract. This could indeed be responsible for the reticence displayed by many labour spokesmen towards compulsory legislation. Chronological factors have also been put forward as reasons, particularly the fact that in Britain the emergence of an autonomous trade union movement, proud of its own traditions and achievements, preceded the formation of a political labour party and dictated its agenda, whereas in Germany for instance the development went the opposite way.[7]

All these explanations however, though plausible, seem to be too far removed from the day-to-day decisions of employers and employees to be entirely satisfactory. Whether people use courts of law in ordinary disputes does not usually depend on ideological considerations or faith in traditions. Much more important are immediate expectations of success, and these are founded on first-hand experiences of past cases. Knowledge of the actual working of the law is decisive, and this is transmitted locally, by friends, relatives, colleagues, local newspapers, trade journals, solicitors, or legal advice bureaux. It is thus at the lowest level of the justice system, at the level of the inferior courts and (if possible) the pre-trial stages, that an enquiry into the reasons for the (alleged) decreasing significance of the law in employment relations should start.

There is, however, not much to start with. Compared to spectacular and well-publicized cases on trade union rights, such as Taff Vale and the Osborne case, very little has been written on individual employment disputes in the period between the 1850s and the 1920s. Of particular interest would be the practice in cases of wrongful dismissal, unpaid salary or wages, deductions and

---

[7] See John Breuilly, 'Civil Society and the Labour Movement, Class Relations and the Law: A Comparison between Germany and England', in Jürgen Kocka (ed.), *Arbeiter und Bürger im 19. Jahrhundert: Varianten ihres Verhältnisses im europäischen Vergleich* (Munich, 1986), 287–318.

spoilt work, breaches of contract or of work rules, liability for accidents, and workmen's compensation, to name the most important categories. Apart from jurisdiction on accidents, on which some studies exist,[8] we do not even know how many of these cases were dealt with in the inferior courts, where most of them were finally decided. It is unclear who exactly brought these cases and whether the chances of winning were evenly distributed or whether unequal treatment was the rule. Almost no research has been done on disputes between individual employers and employees inside and outside British courtrooms after the reforms of 1875. Until this is done much of what has been said on possible reasons for alienation between the working class and the legal community must remain speculation. Whether the British experience in that respect was really exceptional compared to that of continental European states and whether there has indeed been de-juridification not only of collective but also of individual labour relations is an open question.

Justices of the peace and the unreformed
master and servant law

The operation of master and servant law before 1875 has been studied by a number of scholars. There is no doubt that the law itself was inequitable. Under the Act of 1823 servants in husbandry and workers in all sorts of industries could be prosecuted in summary proceedings and punished with up to three months' imprisonment with hard labour if they absented themselves from work without notice or neglected to fulfil their work or were found guilty of 'any other misconduct or misdemeanor in the execution thereof'.[9] These expressions gave magistrates wide discretion and made it relatively easy for employers to prove that a breach of contract had taken place. By comparison, masters were treated leniently. First of all breach of contract by an employer was considered a civil offence only. Moreover, the instances that gave the

---

[8] P. W. J. Bartrip and S. B. Burman, *The Wounded Soldiers of Industry: Industrial Compensation Policy 1833–1897* (Oxford, 1983); P. W. J. Bartrip, *Workmen's Compensation in Twentieth Century Britain: Law, History and Social Policy* (Aldershot, 1987); for the genesis of workmen's compensation legislation see also E. P. Hennock, *British Social Reform and German Precedents: The Case of Social Insurance 1880–1914* (Oxford, 1987), 39–105.

[9] 4 Geo. IV c. 34 (1823), s. 3.

servant a right to sue his master before a magistrate were more narrowly defined and more difficult to prove. A servant could only claim wages owing if he had left because the master had been excessively cruel, or if the master had failed to pay what was due or had dismissed the servant before the end of his term. In the latter cases the maximum claim allowed in a magistrates' court was £10. If higher amounts were owing or if the servant wanted additional damages for wrongful dismissal, he had to go to the county court.[10] By the end of the 1850s even middle-class observers agreed that this Act as it stood was objectionable because it violated the 'principle of equality which ought to pervade our laws'.[11]

Apart from the law itself being discriminatory in substance and procedure, its administration lay in the hands of people who more often than not were themselves employers. While landed gentlemen and the clergy continued to fill the benches in agricultural districts, more and more coal owners, ironmasters, and textile manufacturers were appointed justices in the industrial regions from the 1840s.[12] These were also the areas where the law was most thoroughly implemented. Particularly notorious was the Black Country.[13] Even if the new magistrates as individuals did not wilfully bend the law, they naturally defined terms like 'neglect' or 'misconduct' according to their own conceptions and used their discretion in admitting witnesses and interpreting the evidence. The mere fact that employers sat in judgment upon cases in which their own class and their own trade were affected made accusations of class bias inevitable and contributed to politicizing the issue on a national level. Trade unions, especially the

[10] Before 1846 the only option left in such cases was to bring an action at common law in the superior courts.

[11] A. Edgar, 'On the Jurisdiction of Justices of the Peace in Disputes between Employers and Employed Arising from Breach of Contract', *Transactions of the National Association for the Promotion of Social Science 1859* (London, 1860), 687–90, 690.

[12] In 1854 more than 50% of the Staffordshire magistracy were coal- and ironmasters, whereas twenty years earlier a majority had still been clergymen and landowners. See Roger Swift, 'The English Urban Magistracy and the Administration of Justice during the Early Nineteenth Century: Wolverhampton 1815–1860', *Midland History*, 17 (1992), 75–92, 83. For the late Victorian period see Hartmut Berghoff, *Englische Unternehmer 1870–1914: Eine Kollektivbiographie führender Wirtschaftsbürger in Birmingham, Bristol und Manchester* (Göttingen, 1991), 163–9.

[13] D. C. Woods, 'The Operation of the Master and Servants Act in the Black Country, 1858–1875', *Midland History*, 7 (1982), 93–115. On regional diversity in implementation see also Douglas Hay in this volume.

miners, engaged skilled lawyers like W. P. Roberts, the 'miners' attorney', who represented workers in court.[14] They managed to expose the unfairness inherent in the law and took care that obvious acts of injustice received publicity and were brought to the attention of the authorities.

In the early 1860s, when the campaign for a reform of the Master and Servant Act got under way, the radical and trade union press, papers like the *Beehive* and the *Glasgow Sentinel*, abounded with reports on such abuses. These in turn supplied much of the evidence submitted by union leaders to the select committee which led to a first reform of the law in 1867. Historians, too, have mainly relied on these statements and reports of scandalous miscarriages of justice when describing practice under the Act of 1823.[15] Yet sources reflecting employers' views confirm the impression of a fundamental imbalance in the law and its application. Case reports in trade journals (which were usually friendly to employers) are in some respects an even more interesting source. Their purpose was to inform readers about the day-to-day normality of the law. In endeavouring to portray the law as impartial these reports—unwittingly—highlight the subtle legal and procedural devices which prevented employees from exploiting to the full the few potentially favourable provisions which the law had to offer. Some cases reported in the columns of the *Colliery Guardian* of 1858 may serve as examples.

A contentious issue between coal owners and pitmen was safety. Of particular importance for workers was the question of under what circumstances they could lawfully refuse to enter a pit deemed to be unsafe. In theory it was a valid defence for workers accused of breach of contract to say that there had been danger to life or limb, for example because of firedamp or insufficient fencing or signalling equipment. The problem, however, began when they had to prove that a serious danger to life or health had really existed. Unspecified assertions by a workman at a colliery near Darlington 'that he had been set to work in an unfit place' or by a pitman in one of the Earl of Durham's collieries 'that the air in the pit did not agree with him' were brushed aside and did

---

[14] See Raymond Challinor, *A Radical Lawyer in Victorian England: W. P. Roberts and the Struggle for Workers' Rights* (London, 1990).
[15] See the valuable study by Daphne Simon, 'Master and Servant', in John Saville (ed.), *Democracy and the Labour Movement: Essays in Honour of Dona Torr* (London, 1954), 160–200.

not protect these workers from being sent to prison for a fortnight or a month.[16] If matters of opinion such as dangerous roofs or bad air were the moot points, virtually the only chance workers had was to secure the support of independent expert witnesses *before* they decided to abstain from work. Once a case had been brought to court it was too late to demand the attendance of the government inspector. This was tried by Francis Clark, William Bird, and James Saunders who were charged by a butty collier at Walsall with having left their employment. Even the fact that the 'doggy', a man named Parkes, 'admitted that the pit was "rather dampy", especially during the heat of the day,' did not help their case: 'The mayor said, the bench wished to deal as leniently as possible with the men, and committed each of them to prison for seven days.'[17] Only when visible defects in safety equipment had occurred, which could not well be concealed by the owner or his agents, was there a chance of getting away without punishment, as in the case of William Fearnley and James Metcalf who were tried before Colonel Smyth at the Wakefield petty sessions:

Colonel Smyth: Well, what is the reason you left your work without giving notice?—Fearnley: Because they have broken these rules (handing a copy to the Bench). If you look at the 23rd rule you will see that the lamps ought all to be locked. The lamp given to me was not locked.— In answer to Colonel Smyth, the bottom steward acknowledged that the lamp was not locked; but said, at the time to which the defendant referred, the pit was perfectly safe.—Fearnley: The lamp was not locked; neither had it a shield, and I left the pit because my life was in danger. . . . Colonel Smyth (to the defendants): In this case the magistrates think you had right grounds for leaving. The case is dismissed.[18]

Lucky escapes like these were an exception, and it might have been an advantage for the workers in this case that the interrogating chairman was not an employer but an army officer.

The 'rules' spoken of by the defendant Fearnley in the last case were another object of constant quarrel. By the Mines Act of 1855 coal owners had the duty to establish special rules for the guidance of workmen in collieries.[19] The rules had to be submitted to the Secretary of State for approval, and the employers had to

---

[16] *Colliery Guardian*, 30 Jan. 1858, p. 74; ibid. 25 Sept. 1858, p. 200.
[17] Ibid. 1 May 1858, p. 281.   [18] Ibid. 2 Oct. 1858, p. 216.
[19] 18 and 19 Vic. c. 108 (1855), s. 5.

make sure that they were made known to the workers. Where this had been done, they were considered part of individual employment contracts. Inspectors of coal mines supervised the observance of these provisions and could take proceedings in magistrates' courts against failing employers.

In addition to safety regulations many rules contained clauses as to notice. These created contractual obligations for both sides, and as the correspondent for Yorkshire in the *Colliery Guardian* pointed out, they were 'perfectly reciprocal; for the master, on the one hand, gives the workman a fortnight's notice before dismissal; and the latter, on the other hand, is expected to do the same.'[20] In breach of contract cases the rules now determined the controversial issue of periods of notice, a point which earlier on had to be decided by ascertaining the 'custom' of the trade in the respective region. The replacement of unwritten and therefore uncertain 'customs' by certain rules might have been considered an advantage for both parties, but in fact the employers gained more. They were, within the limits allowed by the state, the sole authors of the rules and they could also, again by respecting the procedures prescribed by the law, change them from time to time. It was different with 'customs'. These had been the result of informal negotiations at the workplace. In times of economic upturn they could gradually change through practice in favour of workmen, in times of crisis the then established 'custom' could be defended—at least for a while—by appealing to courts. In a way, the uncertainty of 'customs' gave workers the chance to participate in settling their working conditions. The rules to a large extent excluded them from this process. That is why workers tried again and again, but mostly without success, to contest the validity of the rules as part of their individual contracts. A typical claim was that they had not signed the rules when entering employment and were thus not bound by them. More than a dozen different cases were heard on this point before the justices at Wakefield, and according to the report in the *Colliery Guardian*, the men had 'retained for their defence "the collier's attorney-general" for the West Yorkshire district (Mr. Fearns, of Leeds), whose forensic ability and legal ingenuity have been exerted in their favour. But the justices have held that when the delivery of the rules was

---

[20] *Colliery Guardian*, 6 Feb. 1858, p. 89.

proved, and service commenced under them (although no contract had been signed), the collier was as firmly bound by those rules as if he had signed a written contract.' And the report further informed the readers that in order to bring home the point, several convictions had taken place and some delinquents had been committed to prison. 'This seems to have had the desired effect, for, judging from the colliers' conduct lately, they have received a salutary lesson.'[21] Other typical, but equally unsuccessful, defences were that the rules had not been posted up in places where they could be seen, or that they had not been read out to those who could not read.

One might expect that at least the general safety provisions in the Mines Acts, supplemented by the individual colliery's rules, were considered an advantage by workers. But here as well the practice turned out to be unsatisfactory from their point of view. Whereas miners were prosecuted directly in countless cases by employers or their agents for offences against safety regulations (bearing lucifer matches, smoking pipes, opening lamps in the pit, using improper signals, and the like), the coal owners themselves, if they had disregarded the Act or the rules, could not be sued in the same way, that is, directly by their workmen. For workers who were endangered by unsafe equipment or practices in the pits the proper procedure was to complain to the inspector of coal mines who then, after visiting the colliery, would prosecute the contravening employer in the magistrate's court. Thus, with regard to safety the Act and the rules created no mutually enforceable contractual obligations and no equality of procedure.

The result was not only that workers were often defendants under an Act whose declared intention had been their protection, but also that the punishments they received were disproportionately hard compared to those imposed on employers. For example, a coal proprietor who was charged by the inspector before the Bolton police court 'for working a mine at Burnden without a proper signal from the surface to the bottom of the shaft' was released from paying a fine on his pledge that he would 'fix a signal satisfactory to the inspector', and on a second charge 'for neglecting to sufficiently ventilate the mine' the magistrates contented themselves with a fine of £1.[22] On the other hand, an engineman

[21] *Colliery Guardian*, 6 Feb. 1858, p. 89.   [22] Ibid. 22 May 1858, p. 330.

at a colliery near Wakefield was sentenced to a month's imprisonment and hard labour for 'not using the particular caution requisite', as prescribed by the rules, when handling a signal, whereby a man was killed. This sentence was given despite a verdict of 'accidentally killed' at the inquest and although the solicitor for the defence had called witnesses who stated that the signals were out of order when the accident happened and that the accused had told the manager days before.[23]

While the Mines Act had thus given employers additional means to discipline and punish workers through summary proceedings, the workers themselves had gained almost no positive rights in return.[24] Under these circumstances it is quite understandable that miners were cautious when further regulatory legislation was advocated. In other regulated branches of industry, particularly those where the Factory Acts applied, the balance was less one-sided. The Factory Acts by definition made employers the prime targets of prosecution. But here too it happened that the factory owners managed in a significant number of cases to shift responsibilities onto overlookers or operatives or others.[25] And, what is perhaps more important, breaches of the Factory Acts by employers gave workmen and workwomen no direct claim against the owner and certainly no right to consider their contract at an end.[26] The situation was slightly different again in branches in which piecework or outwork were the dominant forms of production, as in the worsted, leather, and hosiery industries. Here various Acts, some dating from the eighteenth century, against 'embezzlements' of materials or 'neglect' to finish pieces enabled employers to keep their workers in submission even in those cases where the provisions of the Master and Servant Act were insufficient for the purpose.[27] The situation in these branches resembled that of the coal mines. Whereas employers could make creative use of the interplay between the Master and Servant Act and other regulatory statutes, employees had almost no chance to do

---

[23] Ibid. 22 May 1858, p. 329.
[24] The Mines Act of 1860 however permitted them to elect a checkweighman.
[25] Cf. Robert Gray, *The Factory Question and Industrial England, 1830–1860* (Cambridge, 1996), 170–5.
[26] On the disjunction between protective legislation and law of contract generally see Otto Kahn-Freund, 'A Note on Status and Contract in British Labour Law', *Modern Law Review*, 30 (1967), 635–44.
[27] 17 Geo. III c. 56 (1777); 6 and 7 Vic. c. 40 (1843).

the same when claiming rights for themselves. For them these laws were considered to be unconnected with each other. This even applied to the Truck Act. Under this law employees could indeed prosecute their employers in person (although for obvious reasons they seldom availed themselves of the opportunity), yet even a conviction of the employer had no bearing on the employment contract as such. It continued to exist, and payment in truck was no excuse for breach of contract on the part of the employee. W. P. Roberts, the miners' attorney, was aware of this injustice when he asserted 'as a matter of law, that where the law gives protection to a contract, and one party refuses to grant that protection, the contract is broken',[28] but in the case at hand, as in all other cases, the magistrates (and English law in general) did not accept this proposition and kept the protective parts of labour legislation strictly separate from those parts of the law (common law and statute) bearing on contract.

Previous to the reform of 1867 then, the magistrates' courts offered little which would make them attractive to employees. Between 1857 and 1867 there were on average 9,900 prosecutions per year under the Master and Servant Act and 5,800 convictions.[29] In a huge majority of these cases workers appeared as defendants—estimates lie between 80 and 90 per cent.[30] And even where they were in fact complainants, the methods of interrogation and cross-examination often pushed them into the role of defendant in the course of the trial, so much so that sometimes even the reporters got confused and called them 'defendants' while at the beginning of their report they had correctly spoken of 'complainants'.[31]

---

[28] Quoted in Challinor, *A Radical Lawyer*, 215.

[29] Simon, 'Master and Servant', 186; Woods, 'The Operation of the Master and Servants Act', 97, gives an average figure of 9,000 prosecutions per year between 1858 and 1867. Cf. also Douglas Hay's essay in this volume, especially his warning that the official statistics in the *Parliamentary Papers*, on which the numbers given are based, may be incomplete and therefore misleading.

[30] The official statistics on 'Offences relating to servants, apprentices, or masters' do not differentiate between servants as plaintiffs and as defendants. On the basis of a sample of reported cases in local newspapers of the Black Country, Woods, 'The Operation of the Master and Servants Act', 102, found that between 1858 and 1875 on average 13.4% of cases were initiated by workers.

[31] *Colliery Guardian*, 6 Mar. 1858, p. 151. Cf. also ibid. 11 Sept. 1858, p. 167. Here the reporter frankly admits that 'from the way in which business is done in this court it is difficult to tell how a case is going on, or who is the party complaining even'.

The operation of the law after the reform of 1867

The reformed Master and Servant Act of 1867 did little to change the substance of the law. In particular, the interplay described above between the Master and Servant Act and other regulatory statutes for various industries remained untouched. However, at least the clauses regarding procedure were now strictly reciprocal, and in theory both sides, employees as well as employers, were threatened with fines of up to £20 or imprisonment for up to three months in case of non-payment or if the magistrate found that their misconduct or ill-treatment had been 'of an aggravated Character'.[32] The 1867 Act thus established formal equality by extending penal sanctions to employers instead of abolishing them for servants. In practice however employers were highly unlikely to be convicted for offences of an 'aggravated character': in the five years between 1868 and 1872 only six convictions of employers under this section of the Act were recorded in England and Wales, the sentence in each case having been seven days' imprisonment; in the period between 1 January 1873 and 1 April 1874 one employer was sentenced to one month in prison. In the same periods the total figures for employed were 495 and 141 respectively.[33] The main feature of the Act of 1867 was the enormous amount of discretion vested in the magistrates: they could now either annul the contract or award damages or abate wages or impose a fine or send the offender to prison. This latitude, combined with the unchanged social composition of the magistracy, gave workers little reason to hope that they would now be dealt with more fairly.

The quantitative evidence available in the judicial statistics is inconclusive as to who used the law and with what success. Only overall figures are given. In the first years after the passage of the 1867 Act prosecutions went down to a low of 7,385 in 1869, but that was followed by a notable upsurge in the early 1870s. The peak was reached in 1872 with 17,082 cases resulting in 10,359 convictions. After that year the figures began to go down again.[34]

---

[32] 30 and 31 Vic. c. 141 (1867), ss. 9, 11, 14.

[33] Return of the Number of Convictions ... under the Fourteenth Section of 'The Master and Servants Act, 1867', *PP* 1873, liv (386) and 1874, liv (360).

[34] Woods, 'The Operation of the Master and Servants Act', 97–9; Simon, 'Master and Servant', 186.

Daphne Simon and D. C. Woods have attributed the sudden growth in absolute numbers to the economic boom of the early 1870s leading to greater trade union militancy and prompting more workers to leave their employment for more favourable conditions. This in turn would have driven more employers to prosecute. But Simon has also pointed out that in relation to the numbers of persons employed the incidence of prosecution was not significantly higher in the boom years than before. And Douglas Hay, when comparing the figures of prosecutions under the Master and Servant Act with those of summary criminal prosecutions in general, also relativizes the importance of the temporary upsurge.[35] Thus in the long run, particularly if developments after 1875 are taken into account, what really needs to be explained is the decreasing use of the Master and Servant Act after the reforms rather than the short-term peak in the early 1870s.

Daphne Simon has given several reasons for the long-term decline: first the tendency in many industries to employ workers with shorter periods of notice which would naturally reduce the number of prosecutions for breach of contract; second the growing efficiency of craft unions in disciplining members and persuading them to avoid leaving without notice; third the gradual squeezing out of the market of small masters who apparently had been more eager to use the Act.[36] The local study by Woods has thrown some doubts on the last point.[37] More detailed surveys of regions or specific industries may further differentiate the picture. What is more important however is that Simon (like others who have written on the subject) addresses only half of the question. While she explains reasonably well why employers might have lost interest in prosecuting workmen under the Act, she does not look at the other side. She does not even ask why employees in turn should not have complained more often. This one-sided view seems to result from an *ex post facto* perspective. It is as if twentieth-century historians have been so dazzled by the anti-legal sentiments displayed by trade unions and the working class in later decades that they have lost sight of the possibility that

[35] Woods, 'The Operation of the Master and Servants Act', 98; Simon, 'Master and Servant', 186 and 190 n. 1; Hay, pp. 259–60.
[36] Simon, 'Master and Servant', 190–5.
[37] Woods, 'The Operation of the Master and Servants Act', 110–13.

workers in the 1870s and 1880s might have thought differently. After all, from the workers' point of view the reforms of 1867 and 1875 could be seen as steps forward. The new enactments transformed master and servant law into an essentially civil matter, they established reciprocity of sanctions, and they defined possible claims in a more equitable way, now allowing both sides to appeal to court 'wherever any Question, Difference, or Dispute shall arise as to the Rights or Liabilities of either of the Parties'.[38] Such a broad definition might have induced workmen to bring all sorts of claims which prior to the reform had no chance at all of being heard. It is not unreasonable to assume that the new laws raised expectations among employees in the first place, and that workmen only began to turn away from the law again when their initial hopes were disappointed.

Case reports in the *Colliery Guardian* and other papers for the year 1870 throw some light on experiences which might have produced disappointment. To look at employers first, they were able to use the law in very much the same way as before, leaving workers little chance to escape. In the iron industry the owners sometimes availed themselves of the new opportunity of demanding compensation for losses sustained through workmen neglecting their work or absenting themselves.[39] In the majority of breach of contract cases magistrates now imposed fines, usually in the range between a few shillings and a few pounds and costs. As imprisonment had become an exceptional punishment, employers seem to have had fewer scruples in pressing charges against larger numbers of workmen, thus letting more of them feel the force of the law.[40] For workers, having to pay sums the equivalent of a week's wages, whether as compensation or fine, was in many cases as harsh a punishment as imprisonment. In addition, employers still could resort to prosecution under special colliery rules in order to achieve a prison sentence for serious neglect

[38] 30 and 31 Vic. c. 141 (1867), s. 4. Apart from this general clause the same section still enumerated several specific claims. In 1875 only a general clause remained. Claims were now allowed in 'any dispute between an employer and a workman arising out of or incidental to their relation as such' (38 and 39 Vic. c. 90 s. 3).

[39] Cf. *Colliery Guardian*, 4 Nov. 1879, p. 495, 'Prosecution against an Ironworker'; ibid. 22 July 1870, p. 95, 'Breach of Contract'.

[40] Cf. ibid. 14 Jan. 1870, p. 41, 'Colliers and Ten Per Cent'; ibid. 11. Mar. 1870, pp. 257 and 263, 'Ironworkers' Dispute at Middlesbrough'; ibid. 28 Oct. 1870, p. 474, 'Puddlers Charged with Neglect of Work'. Group prosecutions like these might be an explanation for steep rises in the number of cases from one year to another.

or misconduct.[41] If the reports are a fair reflection of real proceedings, employers' complaints were generally dealt with in a straightforward manner. Unless urged to do so by workmen's lawyers magistrates rarely enquired more deeply into the facts presented to them by employers and they never doubted their own capacity to adjudicate when employers brought a matter before them.

It was quite different when workmen appeared as complainants. Then magistrates were all too ready to listen to technical objections that would allow them to dismiss a case, or they would even of their own accord plead incompetence to judge the question at issue. For example, in a wage case at Darlington the bench accepted the objection that the complaining iron worker, Ebenezer Jones, had made the mistake of summoning the person who had engaged him and not his real employer (that is, the owner whom he had most probably never seen).[42] The intricate relations of subordination and subcontracting in coal and iron works often made it difficult for workers to know who in law was to be called their 'master' and who therefore had to be made liable. Jones's case was thus lost on a technical point. The same happened in the case of W. Pallister, a metal wheeler, who contrary to the printed rules of the firm had only received a week's notice and 'now claimed 26s, the equivalent for one week's labourer's wages'. In this case the bench, without even waiting for the defending solicitor's examination of witnesses, 'decided that they had no jurisdiction in the matter; the question of the 26s, was one of compensation, and therefore it should be tried in the county court'.[43] This was a clear misjudgment since the law of 1867 expressly allowed magistrates to settle a dispute by awarding damages or compensation.[44] In another case at Pontypool in which a man named Parfitt sued a contractor under the Ebbw Vale Company 'for some £2 odd' the justices, although admitting that the complainant might have a good case, took into consideration the firm's lawyer's 'suggestion that the amount due might be found to exceed £5' and said 'that the case had better be taken to the county court, and that they should decline to adjudicate

---

[41] Cf. *Colliery Guardian*, 18 Nov. 1870, p. 557, 'Serious Neglect at a Colliery'.

[42] *Darlington and Stockton Times*, 1 Jan. 1870, p. 3, 'Darlington Borough Police Court'.

[43] Ibid. 19 Mar. 1870, p. 3, 'Darlington County Police Court'.

[44] 30 and 31 Vic. c. 141 (1867), s. 4.

upon it'.[45] Here again, justice was denied under a technical pretext, for in other cases, and certainly when employers demanded damages, complainants were allowed to reduce their claims to nominal sums.[46] If despite such pitfalls complaining employees managed to win their case (something they rarely achieved without being helped by a lawyer), they still faced the possibility of finding their awards reduced by the magistrate almost as a matter of routine in consideration of some defence or counter-claim mounted by the opposite side.[47] Worse things could follow if a vindictive employer was able to use some other statute against a worker who had successfully fought a claim against him. Pieceworkers in the shoe and hosiery industries in particular suffered this fate, such as, for instance, one James Wilson, a Northamptonshire shoemaker, who was sentenced to one month's imprisonment for 'embezzling' leather entrusted to him only two days after he had won 3s. 6d. wages for work done.[48]

The evidence of the reported cases shows that workers certainly tried to assert what they conceived to be their rights under the Act of 1867. Even assistant labourers and young lads, groups who prior to the reform had not figured as plaintiffs in the columns of newspapers, now came forward with demands against their 'masters' who, of course, in all other respects were treated as 'servants'.[49] From the reports it appears that the chances of assistant labourers of succeeding were usually not better, but also not worse, than those of all other employees. In a way, assistants had less to fear from the law, because their superiors, themselves workers, would only exceptionally be able or willing to prosecute them in turn. On the other hand, for the more skilled workers the prospect of being torn between two status groups by means of a law which otherwise often proved to be extremely difficult to use

---

[45] *Colliery Guardian*, 21 Jan. 1870, p. 67, 'The Mining Customs of Monmouthshire'.

[46] Cf. ibid. 2 Dec. 1870, p. 606, 'Masters and Workmen'. This was a case of an employee (Adams) accepting £5 although he had originally demanded £10; under the law of 1867 damages were limited to £5.

[47] Cf. ibid. 30 Dec. 1870, p. 720, 'A Breach of Contract at Middlesbrough'; *Builder*, 26 Feb. 1870, p. 12, 'Wages in Manchester'.

[48] *Northampton Mercury*, 30 Apr. 1870, p. 6, 'Northampton Borough Petty Sessions'.

[49] Cf. *Darlington and Stockton Times*, 12 Feb. 1870, p. 3, 'Darlington Borough Police Court'; *Colliery Guardian*, 6 May 1870, pp. 471 f., 'Boy Labour in Collieries'; ibid. 9 Dec. 1870, p. 637, 'Can a Colliery Proprietor Impose Fines upon his Workmen?'.

with profit might have added to the sense of frustration which fuelled the campaign for a further reform.

Magistrates' practice under the Employers and Workmen Act of 1875

The major innovation brought by the legislation of 1875 was to repeal the Act of 1867 and finally to do away with all criminal sanctions in cases of breach of contract with a few exceptions involving apprentices, workers in public utilities (gas and water), and cases where the foreseeable consequences were danger to human life, serious bodily harm, or destruction of valuable property.[50] Furthermore, the procedure in master and servant cases before courts of summary jurisdiction was in all respects assimilated to that in county courts. This can be seen as the legislator's response to the criticism levelled by trade unions against the unfair (or at least uneven) practices of magistrates, especially the lay justices of the peace. That a curb on the discretion of magistrates was one, if not the principal, intention of the law known as the 'Employers and Workmen Act, 1875' is clearly expressed in its full title: 'An Act to enlarge the powers of County Courts in respect of disputes between Employers and Workmen, and to give other Courts a limited civil jurisdiction in respect of such disputes.'

Under the new Act magistrates no longer had the option of imposing fines or prison sentences, and all sums payable under the order of the court were considered a civil debt which could only be enforced according to the provisions of the Debtors Act of 1869.[51] Although this could still mean imprisonment for those unable or unwilling to pay, as is explained by Paul Johnson in this volume, employers who wished to achieve this effect had to take several procedural steps, and many may have regarded this as too troublesome. The law thus became less interesting to those employers who had primarily been attracted by its swift action and penal aspects. For workmen, on the other hand, the new law contained no provision which accorded them any positive right or claim which they had not had before. Moreover, in many places

[50] 38 and 39 Vic. c. 86 (Conspiracy and Protection of Property Act, 1875), ss. 4, 5 and 17; 38 and 39 Vic. c. 90 (Employers and Workmen Act, 1875), ss. 4, 6, and 9.
[51] 38 and 39 Vic. c. 90 (1875), s. 9.

magistrates had by this time so far discredited themselves in the eyes of organized labour that confidence in their impartiality was seriously disturbed. For neither side did the Act give any strong incentives to make more use of courts of summary jurisdiction.

This is also the obvious conclusion to be drawn from the judicial statistics. As already indicated the total number of cases dealt with by magistrates under the Act of 1875 was decreasing, going down to only 5,508 in 1879 and being on average around 6,600 per year from the late 1870s to the First World War. Whether this decrease was compensated for by more cases being transferred to the county courts, as envisaged by the law, is unclear. The county court statistics do not differentiate by nature of claims. What is clear, however, is that it took the public and even the authorities a considerable time to realize that summary master and servant jurisdiction was no longer a criminal matter. The statisticians themselves took more than seventeen years to adapt their tables and terminology to the text of the law.[52] Up to and including 1892 the civil proceedings under the Employers and Workmen Act were still subsumed under 'Offences Punishable by Justices' and accordingly the results were counted in the columns 'discharged', 'convicted', 'number committed', 'fined', and 'other punishment'. Particularly puzzling is the fact that a considerable number of people always appears as 'fined', for example 681 (out of 5,125 'convicted') in the year 1889, although the law knew nothing of 'fines'. Only from 1893 were cases under the Act subsumed under the heading 'Proceedings in Quasi-criminal Matters' (which strictly speaking was still incorrect) and the figures given were for 'applications' and 'orders'—unfortunately with no further details as to who applied and the kind of orders made. The enumeration of proceedings by police district was also discontinued from 1893. As in the pre-reform period, the official figures disclose neither who used the Act, nor, in particular, whether more employees appealed to justices and more successfully.

The evidence of reported cases in trade journals and the general press is too sketchy to serve as a substitute for the lack of statistics on these points. None the less certain broad trends are

---

[52] See Report of the Committee on the Judicial Statistics, *PP* 1895, cviii, esp. 18 ff. Returns from 1893 onwards were standardized on the calendar year; hitherto they had been based on the year ending 30 Sept. There were also alterations in the enumeration of offences.

discernible from samples I have been able to gather for a number of years between 1875 and the early 1920s. First of all newspaper reports of course reflect the interests of those who wrote and published them, as well as the (supposed) preoccupations of their readers. From this point of view employment disputes in magistrates' courts undoubtedly lost much of the news value and dramatic quality they had possessed during the preceding years of political agitation. While cases under the Employers and Workmen Act and collateral laws still received a good deal of attention in the early 1880s, reports became less frequent and less comprehensive in the following decades, interrupted only by short revivals of interest at times of industrial unrest, for example, the years 1911–12. Reporting on master and servant cases in the press virtually came to a standstill during the First World War and did not resume afterwards on any scale comparable to that of the pre-war years. This development can be interpreted in two ways which are not necessarily mutually exclusive. On the one hand it may simply reflect and parallel the actual fall in numbers of disputes dealt with. On the other hand it could be seen as an indication that by the 1890s or so these cases had become a matter of routine, like jurisdiction on motoring offences today, where under normal circumstances no difficult points of law arose and no scandalous irregularities occurred. This was, for instance, the opinion of George Howell who, in 1895, summed up twenty years' experience under the new labour laws as follows: 'in many cases the poor man can now act for himself in most ordinary cases of dispute as to wages, breaches of labour contracts, and the like. Courts of law under these Acts will not refuse justice simply because the poor man pleads his own case.'[53] According to this opinion one would expect unequal treatment and barriers created by class prejudice and language to have disappeared from court practice.

It is difficult to verify Howell's optimistic assertion on the basis of published reports precisely because these uncomplicated cases of workmen suing without any assistance, if they ever existed, were unlikely to be reported. Only few cases in the papers reflect the image of the poor man pleading his own case, and even here we cannot be sure that these persons had not received legal advice from a poor man's lawyer, a charity, or a trade union. In fact, the

---

[53] George Howell, *Handy Book of the Labour Laws* (3rd edn., London, 1895), p. x.

cases coming closest to Howell's ideal of an unaided complainant getting a fair hearing did not involve poor men, but poor women. For example a female fieldhand who sued a farmer before the Epsom magistrates for 6s. wages was vigorously assisted by the chairman of the bench. The farmer had detained 2s. wages per week as a kind of security that the pickers would finish their work properly and return the baskets. Speaking against the farmer's foreman and solicitor who defended the rule as a practical necessity the chairman condemned this system in strong words: 'They would make a little fortune out of these poor persons.' When the solicitor remarked that the fieldhands had agreed to the rule the chairman asked for signatures, although he well knew that oral contracts were as valid as written ones. In the end the woman received her 6s. and costs. 'The result was received with applause in Court, which was immediately suppressed.'[54] From many reports it appears that towards the end of the nineteenth century justices no longer hesitated to question more systematically the allegations of employers, something they had rarely done in the mid-Victorian period. London police court stipendiaries in particular seem to have felt an obligation to act as advocates for poor and ignorant litigants.[55] They did not do this out of mere sympathy, but as a conscious attempt to establish equality in procedure. Not all justices, of course, made as much of an effort as Mr Hutton, the stipendiary of Greenwich police court, who conducted the wage case of one Thomas Jordan, journeyman baker, as if he were his solicitor. The judge guided his 'client' through tricky questions during the interrogation and fought off a counterclaim brought by the opposing lawyer, a Mr Eves, who was solicitor to the London Master Bakers' Protection Society. At the beginning of the case Mr Hutton expressly justified his course and appealed to the professional honour of his counterpart when he stated that here they had a complainant 'who might be an ignorant man, whilst on the other hand they had Mr Eves, a very skilled lawyer, and he was glad to see him, for no doubt he would be able to render the court material assistance in the hearing of the case'.[56]

---

[54] *Women's Industrial News*, Aug. 1896, p. 4.

[55] In London this attitude of police court judges had a tradition reaching back to the mid-century, cf. Jennifer Davis, 'A Poor Man's System of Justice: The London Police Courts in the Second Half of the Nineteenth Century', *Historical Journal*, 27 (1984), 309–35.

[56] *Bakers' Record*, 29 Nov. 1912, p. 10 and 6 Dec. 1912, p. 5.

Such a commitment to fair proceedings on the part of magistrates was perhaps exceptional in 1912. On the other hand, examples of justices openly displaying class prejudices were by this time also on the retreat. They still existed, however, in industrial regions where employers who belonged to the same trade filled the benches. Thus in a case at Walsall, which turned on the custom of paying 'calf' (that is, advances for work given out) in the iron industry of that town, the magistrate used his position to give the complaining manufacturer, a Mr Martin, a lesson in business management. 'Mr. S. B. Wheway (magistrate) said he had abolished the "calf" system in his own works, and he advised Mr Martin to find out how much his own men owed him on it, and then stop so much per week till matters were level.' Needless to say that in this case the defending workman had to pay the full amount claimed, £1 10s. and costs.[57] Despite such differences in attitude it can be said that on the whole regional variations in court practice diminished between 1875 and the First World War. For workmen much still depended on where they lived and before whom they had to plead, but case reports show that most magistrates at least tried to listen to both sides and began to take workers' complaints as seriously as those of employers.

What has been said so far applies above all to employment disputes between individuals acting on their own. Among the reported cases only about one-half belong to this category. Most of these were brought by employers against one or a few workpeople in their firms. Employees who appeared without apparently being backed by someone else were often women, errand boys, apprentices, shop assistants, carters, agricultural labourers, piece- and outworkers, and generally all those working in occupations in which unions were weak or non-existent. These kinds of cases most frequently occurred in rural areas, small market towns, and in London.

In industrial regions and in cases where skilled workers were involved the reports often reveal, sometimes quite openly, that the worker was supported by a trade union or that the case was in fact a 'test case' in which the individual workman had been put forward by a union. Matters typically dealt with in such test cases were 'customs of the trade' pertaining to periods of notice or

[57] *Ironmonger*, 20 Jan. 1912, p. 156.

modes of payment, alleged breaches of collective agreements, and refusals by employers to recognize trade union rules which they allegedly had observed before. Judicial disputes about 'customs' of course had a long tradition in skilled trades, but with the extension of unionism they became ubiquitous. The legal status of collective agreements had also occasionally occupied magistrates in earlier times, but here again unions now tried more persistently to enforce them through the courts. Litigation on the ground that employers had disregarded trade union rules was a relatively new phenomenon; this issue did not appear in newspaper columns before the 1890s.

The crucial issue for the complaining party in cases which concerned collective agreements or union rules was to prove that the other side had agreed to be bound by them and was still so bound at the moment when the dispute occurred. With respect to trade union rules the burden of proof was high. It was not sufficient to say that employers had for some time run their business in accordance with them; actual consent had to be shown. Thus in a carpenter's application about 'grinding money' before the Thames police court the magistrate, Mr Mead, did not even allow the master to be summoned on this ground:

Mr. Mead: Did you agree with your master to pay that?
The Applicant: No, but every builder does it; it is in our rules.
Mr. Mead: I don't care about your rules. They have nothing to do with him if he did not agree to them. Before you can have a summons you will have to prove that.[58]

In principle the same reasoning was still valid after the First World War when employers tried to get rid of the arrangements for closed shops to which they had submitted during wartime. For example in 1923, in a test case arising out of the non-unionist issue before the Pontypool magistrates, colliery owners summoned fifty-two miners for breach of contract and claimed 26s. damages from each. The miners had gone on strike because the employers had refused to help the miners' leaders to get non-unionist men to join the union. The magistrates did not accept the miners' solicitor's defence that 'the owners had for twenty years recognized the custom of "show cards" and given assistance in getting all

---

[58] *Manchester Unity Operative Bricklayers' Monthly Trade Report,* 48 (Jan. 1906), 16.

workmen to join the Federation'. The fact was that the owners had adopted a change of policy two years before and now no longer felt bound to help the union. This was sufficient to decide the case against the miners.[59] Trade union rules, even if they had been observed for a considerable time, did not gain the more dignified status of established trade customs, which in the eyes of the law created an implied contract unless stipulations to the contrary had been made.

The legal status of collective agreements resembled that of union rules. If one side declared it was no longer bound by the agreement, this meant that the agreement was at an end. The critical question was whether previous notification was necessary. On this point, the decisions of magistrates were uneven. Workers were expected to give the usual period of notice before they could stop working under the agreed conditions. Even if they were honestly under the impression that the employer had broken the terms of the agreement, the only safe course for them was to give notice. In a case in 1882 before Nottingham magistrates fifty-seven men were summoned for breach of contract. Their solicitor's defence was 'that the agreement which the colliery manager made with them at the close of the strike had not been kept', but the bench decided 'that the breach of agreement was not such as to warrant the men leaving their employment'. Each man had to pay 10s., that is, much less than had been asked for by the colliery company, which is an indication that the bench was not entirely sure about its decision.[60] In a similar case in 1912 the stipendiary at Burslem said 'although the defendants might conscientiously have believed that they had a grievance, they were not justified in absenting themselves from work as they did. They could have legalised their action by giving in their notices to terminate their engagements.' Here the men had to pay the full amount claimed.[61] Employers could sometimes get away with not applying the terms of a collective agreement to individual contracts, although they were under moral pressure from their associations to keep such agreements. In a case before Croydon police court a member of the Operative Bricklayers' Society claimed an additional halfpenny

[59] *The Times*, 12 Mar. 1923, p. 9. The Miners' Federation gave notice of appeal in this case, but I have found no traces of an appeal case actually having taking place.

[60] *Capital and Labour*, 20 Dec. 1882, p. 535.

[61] *Brick and Pottery Trades Journal*, 1 June 1912, p. 283.

wages for 148 hours he had worked within a certain radius where
$10\frac{1}{2}d$. had to be paid, but he had started to work at 10*d*. per hour
having been wrongfully told by the foreman that the building site
was just outside that radius. The attention of the union and the
Master Builders' Association had been called to the matter, but,
as the Association's Journal remarked, 'rather than concede
the halfpenny the defendants resigned from the association'. The
foreman denied that the radius had been mentioned when the
complainant started work. 'The Bench were divided in opinion,
and by a majority the summons was dismissed.'[62] Here again magistrates seem to have been uncertain how exactly to draw the
boundary between individual freedom of contract and limitations
imposed by a collective agreement. In general, wherever such grey
areas existed in law, magistrates usually treated employers more
favourably than employees. Inequality thus remained a problem
when the law was unclear.

Cases turning on 'customs' posed less difficulties in terms of
law. In principle, so long as nothing else was stipulated individually or by properly displayed work rules, customs were always recognized as implied parts of contracts. None the less the outcome
of disputes on customs was extremely hard to predict. In these
cases nearly everything depended on questions of fact. Therefore
the statements of witnesses as to whether the custom existed and
what exactly it was were decisive. When it came to the evaluation
of witnesses' credibility however, magistrates almost invariably
gave more weight to the assertions of one single employer or
manager than to those of several workers. For example, in a bricklayer's case about an overtime rate before Lambeth police court,
it was deemed sufficient that the employer against whom the
action had been brought and his brother said that they did not
recognize the custom. The magistrate decided against the bricklayer 'on the ground that, to be a trade custom, there must be no
exception; or, to use his own words, it should be universal in the
trade'.[63] This might have been an extreme case, and the trade
union secretary who reported it might have omitted something
from the magistrate's reasoning, yet the general point that employers enjoyed a credibility bonus is undeniable. Costs were another
critical point in cases in which unions were involved. For

---

[62] *Master Builder and Associations Journal*, 7 Feb. 1912, p. 21.

[63] *Operative Bricklayers Society's Trade Circular & General Reporter*, 415 (Jan. 1896), 18.

organized workers it was certainly an advantage that most trade unions, at least the bigger ones, had developed some sort of procedure for giving legal advice and practical help. Many cases, for example that of the bricklayer claiming one additional halfpenny per hour, would never have been brought without a union undertaking to bear the costs. Some magistrates on the other hand seem to have regarded this as an unfair advantage or even as undue interference. There was a tendency (how widespread it was is difficult to establish) of not allowing costs to workers who had gained their case with the aid of a union.[64] As with the assessment of witnesses' evidence here was another area where magistrates could and did use their discretion in a one-sided manner.

While many cases involving trade unions, whether on the complainant's or the defendant's side, could still be described as individual employment disputes, this cannot be said of another category of cases which after 1875 appeared more often in the press reports: mass summonses. These were used by both sides as an additional weapon in the course of collective conflicts. Examples have already been mentioned. Employers, particularly coal owners in the north-eastern coalfields, often summoned dozens and sometimes several hundreds of workers for breach of contract. In times of labour unrest, for instance during the coal miners' strikes of 1912, the majority of these cases resulted in all workers having to pay damages, except those who could prove by a doctor's certificate that they had been ill, and those who could point to other extenuating circumstances.[65] Sometimes the employers contented themselves with the payment of costs and nominal damages on the workmen's promise to return to work.[66] On other, rarer occasions magistrates' courts operated as a kind of clearing agency where a dispute was solved by a settlement out of court after the arguments had been exchanged.[67] In all of these cases the law proved to be an effective symbolic force in the hands

[64] See, for example, the report of a machine manager's case in *Print: A Journal for Printing-House Employés of All Grades and Departments*, 15 June 1896, p. 3.

[65] Cf. *Colliery Guardian*, 26 July 1912, p. 184 (a case of 64 workmen at Durham); ibid. 23 Aug. 1912, p. 387 (a case of 318 hewers at Gateshead).

[66] Cf. ibid. 18 Aug. 1882, p. 267, 'The Brancepeth Dispute' (a case of 500 colliers at Durham); ibid. 21 Feb. 1896, p. 366, 'Miners Summoned for Leaving Work' (a case of 392 miners at South Shields).

[67] See, for example, *Labour Gazette*, June 1893, p. 42 (a case of 187 coal miners at Castle Eden).

of colliery owners. Trade unions tried to apply the same tactics of mass summonses against employers. If clear proofs of contract could be given, there was a chance of success, as in a case at Aberavon, south Wales, where workers had been dismissed at twenty-four hours' notice, although a contract book had been signed which provided for a period of fourteen days.[68] On the other hand, if the claims were based only on customs or rules, the outcome was usually unfavourable to workers. Thus in June 1893, at Birkenhead, '174 dock labourers claimed 2s. each damages for waiting to be paid, and 2s. for working during meal times, according to the rules of the Union. The Deputy Stipendiary dismissed the claim, holding that there was no proof of a contract, or that the Union rules had been adopted.'[69]

Mass summonses like these transformed the magistrates' courts into instruments of collective industrial action, a function which had certainly not been contemplated on that scale by the legislator at the time when the Employers and Workmen Act had been drawn up. From the statistical point of view these mass summonses create an uncertainty. It is unclear whether they were counted as one application only, or whether each summons was counted individually. If the latter was true, the decrease after 1875 in numbers of 'real' individual cases would actually be much more pronounced than it is anyway. The fact that in most years up to 1892 Durham county heads the list in the statistics and that this was the region where most mass summonses occurred is a strong indication that they were indeed counted as so many individual cases. The statistical figures for 'real' individual disputes would thus in all probability have to be corrected downwards by another 1,000 or 2,000 per year. That in turn would make the task of explaining the decrease in litigation even more difficult. Why was it that individual employers and employees made less and less use of the magistrates' courts to settle their disputes? After all, it has been shown that gross inequalities of treatment were on the whole diminishing, while the chances of individual employees of getting a fair hearing had become better. Experiences of unfair treatment alone cannot account for the change.

Two explanations which do not necessarily contradict each other offer themselves. First, the fall in numbers of applications

---

[68] *Colliery Guardian*, 9 Aug. 1912, p. 284, 'Notes from South Wales'.
[69] *Labour Gazette*, July 1893, p. 63.

may be due to a change in the behaviour of employers. As has been said, they had reason for losing interest in suing before justices. If that could be proved, it would mean that workers actually complained more often in magistrates' courts than before 1875, or that the number of workmen's complaints had at least remained more or less stable. The reformed labour laws could then indeed be seen as having brought about a (limited) improvement in employees' chances of claiming rights through judicial action. George Howell's optimistic statement would turn out to be true.

The second explanation would point to the jurisdictional and institutional shortcomings of magistrates' courts. This explanation works on the assumption that the ratio between employers' and workmen's complaints did not change significantly after 1875 and that both groups simultaneously turned away (or were turned away) from these courts. As an institution the magistrates' courts were ill equipped to solve employment disputes. The press reports reveal and sometimes expressly state that hearings of individual labour cases often took many hours, and the processing of mass summonses usually took at least a whole day. These proceedings impeded the main business of justices which was to deal with petty crime. It is well known that magistrates and London police court judges in particular were always in a hurry. They normally had to rush through more than 100 criminal cases, school board prosecutions, and civil applications such as licences etc. per day, most of it routine business.[70] No wonder they got impatient when claimants or solicitors raised complex points about trade customs, implied contracts, collective agreements, trade union rules, and the like—issues which required many witnesses to be heard and a special knowledge which ordinary justices did not normally possess, except when they happened to be employers themselves (which, of course, was reason enough for workers to avoid them whenever possible). Furthermore, as has been shown, these were issues where the law itself was far from clear and many grey zones existed. The outcome of proceedings was thus highly unpredictable, which for both sides was certainly no encouragement to risk judicial action. Even if justices had the best intentions of being just and fair, their situation was often not such that they

---

[70] Cf. Hugh R. P. Gamon, *The London Police Court To-day & To-morrow* (London, 1907), 101.

could deliver what was expected of them. Magistrates themselves seem to have regarded employment disputes as an alien and disturbing element in their practice. Complainants were often asked why they had appeared before them rather than go to the county court. Low costs and the hope of getting a quick settlement were the usual answers.[71] But applicants often did not get what they wanted. They were refused a summons on some more or less dubious legal ground and sent away to another institution of whose existence many might not have heard before: the county court. A telling example is communicated by Thomas Holmes, a London police court missionary, in 1900:

Recently a small boy, not twelve, applied at the North London Police Court for a summons. The magistrate asked him why he required a summons. 'For wages, sir.' 'But surely you go to school?' the magistrate said. Yes, he did go to school, but he was errand-boy at nights and all day on Saturdays, and earned two shillings a week. It was Saturday morning, and he had gone to his work, but found another boy, a wholetimer, in his place. His master had not given him notice, so he claimed a week's pay in lieu of it. The magistrate gravely told him that he was 'not a workman within the meaning of the Act,' and that he would have to take out a summons at the County Court, and off to the County Court the little fellow trudged.[72]

How fellows like this errand boy and employees generally fared when they appeared in a county court to claim wages or damages against their employers has never been studied. In fact, county courts are rarely mentioned in historical works on labour law, except those which deal with employers' liability and workmen's compensation. The following paragraphs can only present some preliminary findings from an ongoing research project on this topic.

Employers and employees in county courts

The county courts were created in 1846 all over England and Wales to facilitate the collection of small debts. A unitary system thus replaced the 'legal pluralism' of local courts of requests which previous to 1846 had served that purpose. The law and

---

[71] Cf. ibid. 55 f.
[72] Thomas Holmes, *Pictures and Problems from London Police Courts* (London, 1900), 110.

procedure adopted in the county courts were essentially the same as in the common law courts at Westminster, though somewhat simplified. As a consequence civil jurisdiction in England became more uniform, but also less flexible. The county courts offered less room for consideration of local customs and the needs of special industries. Procedures of mediation and conciliation which had formed part of judicial practice in many old local courts were also sidelined.[73] Yet contemporary criticisms along these lines rarely informed the debates within the legal community or the legislature. From the administrative point of view the new institution proved to be a success. The county courts were self-supporting, bringing in about as much in fees as it cost to pay the judges and other personnel and maintain the buildings. Not least for this reason the jurisdiction of the new courts was considerably extended.[74] Initially, in 1846, they were competent for all personal actions (with a few exceptions) where the debt or damage claimed did not exceed £20. Only four years later the limit was raised to £50, and in 1903 it was raised again to £100. Besides the extension of pecuniary limits various other jurisdictions (recovery of tenements, ejectments, equity, admiralty, bancruptcy) were 'pitchforked' onto the county courts.[75] Among the newly acquired functions two were particularly important for employees: cases under the Employers' Liability Act of 1880 and under the Workmen's Compensation Acts of 1897 and 1906.

The working classes, however, were not those for whom the county courts had been designed in the first place. On the contrary, as has been made clear by Gerry Rubin and Paul Johnson, labourers appeared in most cases as defendants. The main beneficiaries of the county court system were small businessmen who needed a speedy means to bring their debtors to book. Judging from the statistical figures the businessmen plaintiffs were satisfied with the new courts. The total number of plaints entered rose quickly from about 500,000 per year at the beginning of their existence to over one million per year from the late 1870s to the First

[73] On this aspect see H. W. Arthurs, 'Without the Law': Administrative Justice and Legal Pluralism in Nineteenth-Century England (Toronto, 1985), 42 f.

[74] For the stages of county court reform and the debates surrounding them see Brian Abel-Smith and Robert Stevens, Lawyers and the Courts: A Sociological Study of the English Legal System 1750–1965 (London, 1967), 32–7, 80–4, 90–3.

[75] Cf. M. D. Chalmers, 'The County Court System', Law Quarterly Review, 9 (1887), 1–13, 1; Charles Cautherley, 'The County Court System', Law Quarterly Review, 28 (1891), 346–53.

World War.[76] Throughout this period more than 90 per cent of claims were for sums below £20, and the majority of demands always concerned unpaid bills of all kinds.[77] Plaintiffs were most often local shopkeepers and dealers; particularly notorious were the tallymen.[78] Others were providers of services: doctors, money-lenders, music teachers, plumbers, painters, and the like, also land-lords, and in later years local gas and water works, and telephone companies. Plaintiffs were successful in more than 95 per cent of the cases leading to a judgment, and the defendants, who usually belonged to the poorer sections of the working class, were ordered to pay the amount claimed and costs. Imprisonment was still pos-sible if they could not or would not pay.

At first sight such a debt-enforcing machinery offered little to the poorer class of working men and women who, as consumers, were almost permanently indebted to local tradespeople and therefore most likely to be summoned. On the other hand, as ser-vants or workers they could become creditors themselves and might have looked to the county courts for redress. There was nothing in the law which prevented them from suing their employ-ers in these courts even for the most trivial sums. In theory employees' claims were treated like all other demands for civil debts or damages. Such claims could be for wages or salary earned, for work and labour done, for wages in lieu of notice in case of wrongful dismissal, or for other breaches of contract such as, for example, failing to engage someone despite having promised to do so. Like all other plaintiffs an employee, whether domestic servant, manual labourer, salaried clerk, or otherwise employed, could have a plaint entered by the registrar and thereby cause a summons to be issued. The scale of entering fees started at 1s. for claims up to £1 and went up to £1 for claims above £20. The fees to be advanced were thus relatively higher for small claimants than for those who sued for large sums. If the defen-dant chose to pay into court what was demanded (including the

---

[76] On this see Paul Johnson, 'Small Debts and Economic Distress in England and Wales, 1857–1913', *Economic History Review*, 46 (1993), 65–87, and the essay by the same author in this volume.

[77] Cf. Gerry R. Rubin, 'Debtors, Creditors and the County Courts, 1846–1914: Some Source Material', *Journal of Legal History*, 17 (1996), 73–81, 73.

[78] Gerry R. Rubin, 'Law, Poverty and Imprisonment for Debt, 1869–1914', in Gerry R. Rubin and David Sugarman (eds.), *Law, Economy and Society, 1750–1914* (Abingdon, 1984), 241–99; and id., 'The County Courts and the Tally Trade, 1846–1914', ibid. 321–48.

costs of entering the plaint) before hearing, the dispute was at an end. If he chose to defend, a hearing fee became due at the end of the trial. This had to be paid by the losing party, in addition to costs allowed by the court to the winner. Hearing fees were arranged on a similar scale, starting at 2s. for claims up to £1 and going up to £2 for claims above £20. County court fees were thus quite high compared to those in the magistrates' courts; for the little boy who claimed 2s. in lieu of notice they were certainly prohibitive, unless he found someone else to advance the sum for him.[79] Advocate's fees were not allowed in proceedings under £2, except by special order of the judge; they were further limited to 10s. in actions below £5 and to 15s. in actions below £20.[80] These limitations made the financial risk of losing a small wage claim at least calculable; on the other hand, they made it difficult for poorer litigants to employ solicitors themselves, as real costs would nearly always be higher than those allowed by the court. Proceedings *in forma pauperis* or a poor persons' procedure were not available in county courts until 1949.[81] While financial barriers were thus considerable, those who could afford the risk had the advantage of having their case heard by a professional judge, who had to be a barrister of at least seven years' standing. For all employees subject to the Master and Servant Acts, complaining before a county court could be a means of avoiding justices of the peace who might be of the same class as their employers.

To what extent employees were able to make use of the county courts is hard to establish. The official statistics are silent on the point since they do not specify the nature of causes, let alone occupations of litigants. We have to turn to the patchy evidence of the original plaint and minute books and to published reports in order to get a rough idea. The plaint and minute books were kept in more or less the same manner everywhere.[82] They are arranged

[79] Francis K. Munton, the secretary of the Law Society's Committee on County Courts, called the fees 'scandalously high'; see id., 'County Court Reform', *Law Quarterly Review*, 5 (1889), 134–9, 138.

[80] Cf. Arthurs, '*Without the Law*', 44 n. 196; Chalmers, 'County Court System', 8.

[81] Cf. Richard I. Morgan, 'The Introduction of Civil Legal Aid in England and Wales, 1914–1949', *Twentieth Century British History*, 5 (1994), 38–76.

[82] Rubin, 'Debtors', 77, erroneously states that the surviving records which had been preserved in the AK series of the PRO 'were apparently sent back to the county courts' themselves. My own checks have shown that these records were transferred to the respective county record offices and can be consulted there. Some archives possess additional (mostly unlisted) county court records which have never made their way to the PRO.

in tabular form and always state names of litigants, the matter in dispute (usually spelt out in just one or two words such as 'goods sold', 'medical attendance', 'rent', etc.), dates of hearing, appearance of litigants and solicitors, and finally details on judgments, orders of the court, fees, and costs. Particulars of occupations and places of residence are given only in a few early plaint books of the 1850s and 1860s, and again in most books from the 1890s onwards. Actions under the Employers' Liability Act appear on separate pages after 1880, and some Workmen's Compensation files have survived for various courts. Apart from the accident cases there is one type of entry, the claim for 'wages' or 'salary', which surely points to an employer–employee conflict. Certain other entries, especially if combined with details of occupations, can also be so identified, for example:

1 Nov. 1872: Alfred Marshall (default) v. William Harris the elder (person, attorney Mr. Wilson); [Claim:] loss of service of Wm. Harris junr. through breach of covenant, £21; [Judgment/order of court:] struck out, £2 10s. 8d. costs, 8th inst.[83]

2 Dec. 1872: Cornelius Daley (person, attorney Mr. Wilson) v. Charles Ross (person, attorney Mr. Wood); [Claim:] Damages for that the deft. by his foreman employed plt. for a job & in consequence of deft. not supplying a barge the plt. has sustained loss, 6s. 3d.; [Judgment/order of court:] Deft., 2s. costs, on 16th instant, hearing fee 2s.[84]

2–3 Dec. 1850: Ann Gibbons (by attorney) v. Christopher Morgan (def. service proved); [Claim:] Work done as a schoolmistress and materials provided, board & lodging provided and money paid, £20 2s. 8d.; [Judgment/order of Court:] Plt. £20 2s. 8d., £5 18s. 4d. costs, by instalments of one pound per month, attorney allowed.[85]

15 Oct. 1919: William Ford, Maidstone, Dentist, v. Sydney Walter Waldby, Maidstone, dentists Mechanic; [Claim:] Damages and Injunction, £50; Withdrawn.[86]

A problem is created by the entries 'work done' and 'labour' which appear quite frequently in all plaint books. These entries no doubt

---

[83] London Metropolitan Archives, CCT/AK15/6, Bow county court, Minute Book, 1872–3, No. 5595. My quotations are not arranged in the same order as in the books.
[84] Ibid., No. 6582.
[85] Centre for Kentish Studies, Maidstone county court, Plaint and Minute Book, Oct. 1849—Mar. 1851 (not listed), No. C 1213.
[86] Centre for Kentish Studies, Maidstone county court, Plaint and Minute Book, Ordinary Summonses, Aug. 1918—Feb. 1920 (not listed), No. Y 552. This was most probably a plaint based on a so-called 'radius agreement', whereby an employee agrees not to set up his own business within a certain radius of the business of his employer.

refer in many cases to a single piece of work or an occasional service rendered, such as the making of a coat, the repair of a broken pipe, or the unloading of a ship. This kind of work done by a self-employed artisan or an independent contractor would not normally be described as arising out of an employment relationship. On the other hand the same entries can also refer to piecework on a regular basis or to the short-term agreement of a casual labourer. When a miner sues a colliery owner for £1 'work and labour' or a labourer a quarrymaster for £11 'work and labour', one can certainly see these cases as employment disputes, even in strict legal terms.[87] However, as long as entries are unaccompanied by details of occupation, the question must remain undecided. This, and other uncertainties created by the scarcity of information and irregular bookkeeping, make an exact count of all employer–employee disputes for particular courts and periods impossible. What can be done is to give minimum figures, counting only the 'certain' cases. These are essentially those in which the words 'wages' or 'salary' or 'wrongful dismissal' (very rare) appear or where other unambiguous terms indicate an employment dispute. A survey of selected plaint books on these guidelines yields the following figures (not including employers' liability and workmen's compensation cases):

Bow county court (east London) (ordinary summonses)[88]

29 Aug. 1861–7 Feb. 1862: 66 out of 4,381 cases = 1.50 per cent
1 Nov. 1872–18 Apr. 1873: 60 out of 4,053 cases = 1.48 per cent
30 Dec. 1881–22 May 1882: 71 out of 4,497 cases = 1.57 per cent
23 Feb. 1912–22 May 1912: 49 out of 3,355 cases = 1.46 per cent

Kingston (upon Thames) county court (default summonses)[89]

26 Sept. 1912–26 July 1917: 40 out of 2,501 cases = 1.60 per cent

Guildford county court (ordinary summonses)[90]

19 May 1898–20 Jan. 1899: 14 out of 923 cases = 1.51 per cent
21 July 1911–7 Mar. 1912: 8 out of 913 cases = 0.87 per cent
3 May 1923–3 Apr. 1924: 15 out of 754 cases = 1.98 per cent

---

[87] Tyne and Wear Archives Service, Newcastle, 2160/1/2, Gateshead county court, Plaint Book, 1869–70, Nos. W 1038 and X 476.

[88] London Metropolitan Archives, CCT/AK15/5, CCT/AK15/6, CCT/AK15/7, CCT/AK15/10.

[89] Surrey County RO, Kingston, 3545/6.

[90] Ibid. 3544/1, 3544/2, 3544/3 (formerly AK 47/2, AK 47/4, AK 47/6).

Dorking county court (ordinary summonses)[91]
    1 Jan. 1852–20 Sept. 1856: 14 out of 541 cases   = 2.58 per cent
    11 March 1896–19 July 1899: 15 out of 1,125 cases = 1.33 per cent
    9 Dec. 1913–1 Dec. 1922: 6 out of 1,010 cases   = 0.59 per cent

Maidstone county court (ordinary summonses)[92]
    2 Oct. 1849–3–4 Mar. 1851: 13 out of 1,353 cases = 0.96 per cent
    1 Sept. 1868–12 Apr. 1869: 13 out of 1,315 cases   = 0.98 per cent
    13 June 1877–14 Jan. 1878: 10 out of 1,171 cases   = 0.85 per cent
    19 Oct. 1898–21 June 1899: 6 out of 1,577 cases   = 0.38 per cent
    19 Jan. 1910–21 Sept. 1910: 5 out of 1,740 cases   = 0.30 per cent
    9 Aug. 1918–11 Feb. 1920: 21 out of 1,319 cases   = 1.76 per cent

(West) Hartlepool county court (ordinary summonses)[93]
    15 June 1857–8 Mar. 1858: 17 out of 1,452 cases   = 1.17 per cent
    8 Oct. 1875–9 June 1876: 7 out of 1,461 cases   = 0.47 per cent
    8 Apr. 1910–21 Oct. 1910: 5 out of 1,553 cases   = 0.32 per cent
    6 June 1919–20 Aug. 1920: 1 out of 1,640 cases   = 0.06 per cent

Gateshead county court (ordinary summonses)[94]
    29 Mar. 1862–13 July 1863: 21 out of 2,752 cases = 0.76 per cent
    12 Aug. 1868–8 July 1870: 40 out of 4,928 cases = 0.81 per cent
    19 Jan. 1897–5 Dec. 1897: 10 out of 1,518 cases = 0.65 per cent
    17 Apr. 1907–8 Oct. 1907: 3 out of 1,513 cases = 0.20 per cent

Walsall county court (ordinary summonses)[95]
    10 Nov. 1909–11 Feb. 1910: 6 out of 2,336 cases = 0.25 per cent

Even on the basis of this sketchy evidence some provisional conclusions are possible. First, it is obvious that employment disputes
(other than those arising from accidents) were only of marginal
importance in the county courts. None the less, if one considers
that from the 1870s onwards on average a million plaints per year
were processed in the county courts, even percentages of around
1 per cent would yield a number of 10,000 employer–employee
cases per year. That is about as many as were dealt with in the
magistrates' courts under the master and servant laws. In the
busier county courts where workloads of 200 cases per sitting were
not unusual, one could expect about two employment disputes

[91] Ibid. 615/- (temporary list).
[92] Centre for Kentish Studies, Maidstone, Records of Maidstone county court (not listed).
[93] Cleveland County Archives, Middlesbrough, AK 19/1, AK 19/3, AK 19/9, AK 19/11.
[94] Tyne and Wear Archives Service, Newcastle, Acc. Nos. 2160/1/1, 2160/1/2, 2160/2/1, 2160/2/4, 2160/2/5.
[95] Walsall Local History Centre, AK 28/1.

each court day. A general awareness that such disputes were a regular part of county court business can therefore be assumed—the more so since cases in which a local employer appeared as defendant were likely to receive some attention in the press.

A second finding suggested by the above figures concerns changes of use over time. Figures show a noticeable fall in the percentage of wage claims, dismissal cases, etc. for all county courts observed. While the decrease set in at different dates, the process was well under way everywhere in the 1890s and went on in most places at least until the end of the First World War. This decline parallels the downward trend of employer–employee litigation in magistrates' courts and is just as difficult to explain. There were no drastic legislative changes with respect to county court practice which could account for the change. Other explanations must therefore be sought, and here the evidence of the plaint and minute books can give useful hints. One development in particular catches the eye and may be part of the answer. Around the turn of the century many dealers and companies seem to have adopted a policy of chasing their debtors systematically and *en masse*, thus driving up the figures of plaints for 'goods sold' and services such as 'gas supplied', 'water supplied', 'medical attendance', 'advertising', etc. For example, at Gateshead on 22 May 1907, there were 297 ordinary summonses of which 126 alone had been issued for one Gavin Hamilton, draper, against his debtors, and almost all the remaining plaints came from just a handful of other people.[96] This was no exception. Tailors, grocers, or furniture dealers took such mass actions at regular intervals. During winter and autumn, coal merchants were busy plaintiffs, particularly in the north of England. During spring and summer, especially in the south-east, the water works did the same.[97] It is obvious that court business must have been clogged by these kinds of mass summonses. As a consequence, individual plaintiffs with small claims were increasingly marginalized. Other proceedings which, perhaps, consumed even more time than the mass summonses were actions under the Employers' Liability and

---

[96] Tyne and Wear Archives Service, Newcastle, 2160/2/5, Gateshead county court, Plaint and Minute Book B, 1907.

[97] See, for example, entries for 13 Apr. 1910 and 13 July 1910, Maidstone county court, Plaint and Minute Book B, Jan.–Sept. 1910, Centre for Kentish Studies, Maidstone (not listed).

Workmen's Compensation Acts. Here too, large sums and powerful groups (trade unions, employers' associations, and above all insurance companies) were involved. Dealing with accidents became the most important function of county courts in the eyes of industrial workers and trade unions. Ironically, by focusing on this aspect of county court business, the labour movement itself may have contributed to the marginalization of those individual, often unorganized, employees who needed a hearing for their small wage claims.

A third, as yet more provisional, conclusion to be deduced from the above figures concerns regional differences in the use of the county courts. The plaint books suggest that individual employment disputes on wages, dismissal, etc. were a more common occurrence in the county courts of London and the suburban south-east than in the industrialized areas of the Midlands and the north (with predominantly rural areas coming somewhere in between).

This finding needs of course to be confirmed by further research on original plaint books, yet even from the evidence I have seen there is one explanation which suggests itself. Among employees suing in county courts certain occupations were over-represented, most notably domestic service and other jobs in the third sector—of low skill as well as highly qualified ones. These occupations were more frequent in London and its suburban environment than in the working-class dominated towns of the north. The data for Kingston-upon-Thames may serve as an example.[98] In 1913 there were 755 default summonses at Kingston, of which 23 (=3.04 per cent) were for wages. The occupations and gender of plaintiffs and defendants in these cases were as follows.

Kingston (upon Thames) county court, 1913
chauffeur (m.) v. car proprietor (m.)
temporary cook (f.) v. married woman (f.)
steward (m.) v. caterer and hon. secretary of County Club (m.)
fishmonger's assistant (m.) v. fishmonger (m.)
motor mechanic (m.) v. motor engineer (m.)
spinster (f.) v. hotel keeper (m.)
hairdresser (m.) v. hairdresser (m.)
spinster (f.) v. doctors of medicine (m.)

[98] Surrey County RO, Kingston, 3545/6, Kingston county court, Plaint and Minute Book C, Default Actions, 1912–17.

domestic servant (f.) v. male (m.)
ditto
vaccination officer (m.) v. Kingston Board of Guardians
cook (f.) v. widow, lady (f.)
charwoman (f.) v. confectioner (m.)
milk carrier (m.) v. dairy farmers (firm)
nurse housemaid (f.) v. male, independent (m.)
hosier (m.) v. vaccination officer (m.)
domestic (f.) v. gentleman (m.)
house parlour maid (f.) v. widow (f.)
general servant (f.) v. spinster, independent (f.)
domestic servant (f.) v. gentleman (m.)
commercial traveller (m.) v. Everbrite Polish Co. Ltd. (firm)
general servant (f.) v. gentleman (m.)
ditto

More than half of plaintiffs were female servants, and nearly all
male plaintiffs were occupied in some sort of service industry. This
is certainly an extreme example, but the general point is supported
by the evidence of other plaint books and published case reports.
Somewhat pointedly one could say that the county courts served
as the labour courts for the third sector and salaried employees in
industry, whereas the magistrates dealt with the industrial workforce. However, an important temporal reservation must be made
with regard to this statement. Until at least the early 1870s industrial workers and agricultural labourers formed a significant group
among male plaintiffs (or defendants) in the county courts. In
industrial and rural areas these two groups were even in the
majority. This is shown, for instance, by findings for Dorking
(1852–6) and Gateshead (1869–70).[99] In both courts female plaintiffs were in the minority: 4 out of 14 plaintiffs in Dorking and
only 4 out of 27 in Gateshead. The occupations of male litigants
were as follows:

Dorking county court, 1852–6
ostler v. innkeeper
labourer v. farmer
ditto
labourers v. general dealer

---

[99] Surrey County RO, Kingston, Dorking county court, Plaint Book, 1852–6 (temporary list 615/-); Tyne and Wear Archives Service, Newcastle, 2160/1/2, Gateshead county
court, Plaint Book, 1869–70.

labourer v. farmer
ironfounder v. ironfounder
labourer v. builder
ditto
labourer v. gentleman ('Esquire')
labourers v. farmer

Gateshead county court, 1869–70
pitman v. viewer
professor of music v. churchwarden
labourer v. plasterer
pitman v. under viewer
ditto
gentleman v. farmer
mason v. joiner
miner v. colliery owner
shackle maker v. foreman at chain department
miner v. colliery owner
labourer v. mill furnaceman
labourer v. labourer
tarnish maker's assistant v. paint, colour, and tarnish manufacturers
ditto
labourer v. carpenter
labourer v. mason
pitman v. under viewer
wagonman v. coal merchant
labourer v. quarrymaster
labourer v. contractor
brickmaker v. brick manufacturer
brickmaker v. iron manufacturers
cartman v. contractor

These lists contradict Daphne Simon's assumption that 'workmen must have been quite unaware that such a course [i.e. suing in a county court] was open to them'.[100] Press reports from the 1850s to the early 1870s provide further evidence that industrial as well as agricultural labourers made use of the county courts in order to evade the concurrent jurisdiction of magistrates—not always without success.[101] By the late 1890s, however, the occupational

---

[100] Simon, 'Master and Servant', 161.

[101] Cf. *Darlington and Stockton Times*, 16. Apr. 1870, p. 3, 'Dispute amongst Ironworkers at Darlington'; *Northampton Mercury*, 17. Dec. 1870, p. 3 (agricultural labourers suing in Daventry county court); *County Courts Chronicle*, 2 Aug. 1858, pp. 181 f. (agricultural labourer suing in Shrewsbury).

and gender structure of litigants had changed significantly. To take the same two courts as examples again: in Gateshead (1897) 7 out of 10 plaintiffs were now female servants.[102] And in Dorking (1896–9), while women were still in the minority (4 out of 15), almost all male litigants now belonged to the local world of shop-keepers and services (butchers, grocers, gardening, carting, gas works).[103]

If these findings can be substantiated, we would have an additional clue to explaining the downward trend in the use of county courts for employment matters. The decline could then be shown to be due to manual labourers turning their back on these courts at some time after the early 1870s. Possible reasons can at present only be guessed at. One thing at least is certain: the Employers and Workmen Act of 1875, which had professedly been enacted 'to enlarge the powers of County Courts in respect of disputes between Employers and Workmen', did nothing to make these courts more attractive to the latter. On the contrary, manual labourers seem to have deserted the county courts, but whether in consequence of changes brought about by the Act or for other reasons remains an open question. On the face of it the Act contained no provision which was detrimental to workers, except perhaps the new power of the judge to 'adjust and set off' mutual claims between the parties.[104] Under the old county court procedure an employer had to give notice of a special defence, if he wished to assert a counter-claim against a workman who had annoyed him by taking him to court. Yet it seems doubtful that such a slight alteration in procedure should have had the effect of ousting workers from the county courts.

A look at the outcome of proceedings helps to describe what happened, but is still inconclusive with regard to reasons for the decline. In cases leading to a judgment the success rate of complaining employees was somewhere in the range of 45 to 65 per cent.[105] The rate was much lower than for plaintiffs in general who

---

[102] Tyne and Wear Archives Service, Newcastle, 2160/2/4, Gateshead county court, Plaint and Minute Book B, 1897.

[103] Surrey County RO, Kingston, Dorking county court, Plaint Book A, 1896–9 (temporary list 615/-).

[104] 38 and 39 Vic. c. 90 (1875), s. 3.

[105] This is based on a sample of published case reports and the entries in plaint and minute books. I have been able to gather 396 cases covering the period 1849–1924 which were initiated by employees and where the outcome was a judgment (excluding employers' liability and workmen's compensation actions). Of these cases 219, that is 55.30%, were decided in favour of the plaintiffs.

consistently obtained favourable judgments in more than 95 per cent of decided cases. As to variations over time, employees' chances of winning seem to have been relatively bad in the early 1870s, rather good between the 1880s and the turn of the century, particularly bad in the last years before the First World War, and somewhat better again from about 1916 onwards. These statements must be taken with caution. The evidence is too sparse to allow for breakdowns into shorter periods or categories of litigants. On the whole, however, it can be said that variations in success rates were not such that employees' litigational behaviour was likely to be influenced by that factor.

Not all county court summonses resulted in a hearing and a judgment. In fact the proportion of plaints which were settled without proceedings in court was always quite high. At the beginning of the statistical age, in the late 1850s, more than half of all cases were so disposed of; in the following decades the rate went down to 35 per cent by the middle of the 1890s and then remained stable until 1914. Minute book entries which refer to pre-trial solutions are 'struck out', 'withdrawn', 'not served', and 'paid'. For obvious reasons this aspect of (extra-)judicial reality was hardly ever mentioned in the press, and the entries in the books only hint at what might have been going on between the parties to the dispute. However, it is striking that more and more employer–employee disputes were settled (or abandoned) in this way. Although the evidence of the minute books is scarce, a clear trend towards avoiding hearings and judgments is discernible, especially when compared with the inverse general trend (see Table 1). The figures show that in the mid-Victorian period employers and employees were more likely to fight to the bitter end than other plaintiffs and defendants. After 1900, by contrast, employers and employees displayed a much less litigious attitude than others. In cases where only small sums were at stake, the issue was now very

TABLE 1. *County courts (1846–1925), causes between employees and employers (percentages determined by judgment and disposed of otherwise)*

	Plaints	Judgments	Otherwise disposed of
1846–75	179	103 (57.5%)	76 (42.5%)
1876–1900	127	59 (46.5%)	68 (53.5%)
1901–25	132	51 (38.6%)	81 (61.4%)

often a settlement out of court. This could take various forms. Either the party complained against, usually the employer, 'paid' the amount demanded into court and thus avoided further trouble; or the plaintiff, usually the servant, abandoned the case which was then 'struck out'; or both parties came to an arrangement which led to the summons being 'withdrawn'. Why employers acted in that way is easy to understand, and legal advice books repeatedly made the point that by fighting a case they had much to lose and little to gain, except perhaps the 'doubtful honour of settling a new point of law in the County Court'.[106] The motivations of servants are more difficult to explain, but for them as well a calculation of possible gains and losses must often have resulted in not pressing a claim. Besides fees and costs it was the uncertainty of the outcome which made employment litigation in county courts a risky affair. Once a case came up for hearing and lawyers had been engaged, which was not at all uncommon, proceedings inevitably took on the confrontational stance prescribed by the written and unwritten rules of British court practice. Various factors then contributed to making the outcome unpredictable. First of all, in employment disputes much revolved round questions of fact and opinion. Who had said what about wages, specific duties, half-holidays, periods of notice at the moment of engagement? Who had done what to provoke the quarrel, and did it justify dismissal? Was there a custom of the trade, and was it or was it not known to the parties? County court judges hardly ever had the time to listen to mutual incriminations and contradictory assertions on such points. Throughout the Victorian period and particularly in the smaller and more remote courts ordinary wage and dismissal cases were decided as soon as the judge thought he had heard enough, and had made up his mind whom he wanted to believe. Many county court judges did not refrain from expressing strong personal views, and they also found ways around applying statutory rules or common law precedents too strictly if these were found to oppose what they conceived to be justice. This latitude could turn out to the advantage or disadvantage of complaining servants, depending on the individual judge's opinions. For example, as early as the 1850s not all judges were prepared to apply the harsh doctrine that a servant who had been rightfully

---

[106] *The Home Counsellor*, by A Barrister-at-Law (London, n.d. [post-1938]), 233.

dismissed forfeited all wages he had earned until dismissal; yet this was the law of the land, even if it meant that the servant lost several months' or half a year's wages.[107] On the other hand, there were county court judges who enforced this rule without hesitation, and as late as 1911 it was stated in the *County Courts Chronicle* to be valid, although by then with some expression of doubt as to its justice.[108] Despite attempts by the Lord Chancellor's office to bring about greater consistency, idiosyncratic administration of law in county courts continued to be a problem right into the twentieth century.[109]

Many employees' cases were undoubtedly disposed of in such a rough and ready manner. Waywardness was not advisable, however, in cases which raised a new legal point, or where lawyers were present who might threaten an appeal. In such cases judges showed a cautious attitude and preferred to adjourn hearings if time was short or if they needed advice themselves. This created delay and additional costs which an individual workman could ill afford. From press reports it appears that many small claims which were prolonged like this had in fact been initiated by trade unions. Unions used county courts in the same way as magistrates' courts. Both tribunals were occupied with test cases in order to ascertain 'customs' of the trade concerning payment, periods of notice, or specific ways of effectuating work. County court judges had to deal with similar difficulties regarding evidence, burdens of proof, and the bearings of customs on individual contracts. Additional problems were created by the fact that litigants in county courts, other than those appearing before magistrates, came from a wider range of occupations and often belonged to the middle rank or higher echelons of employees. Questions of status and appropriateness therefore made up a large part of arguments in county courts.

For instance, if someone had been engaged as a second pas-

---

[107] See, for example, *Northampton Mercury*, 18 Dec. 1858, 'Lutterworth' (*Bailey v. Spencer*). *County Courts Chronicle, County Court Reports*, 1 Apr. 1859, pp. 35 f. (*Smith v. Jefforth*). In this case the judge argued that plaintiff was a 'menial servant' and as such entitled to recover wages earned, although he had been engaged as a 'general farm servant' for a year.

[108] *County Courts Chronicle*, 1 Nov. 1858, pp. 247 f. (*Grist v. Nankivell*). Ibid. 1 June 1911, p. 124.

[109] See Pat Polden, 'Judicial Independence and Executive Responsibilities: The Lord Chancellor's Department and the County Court Judges, 1846–1971', *Anglo-American Law Review*, 25 (1996), 1–38 and 133–62.

trycook in a bakery, could he be required to make bread and more generally to make himself useful by doing cleaning work etc., or was this an unreasonable demand? This question had to be decided by Judge Cluer of Clerkenwell county court and he was of opinion that the plaintiff had a right to refuse: 'No doubt, had he been asked politely to assist in making bread, he might have done so, but he stood on his dignity and did not do so, not being part of his work.'[110] In another case, which came before Shoreditch county court a few months later, the same judge had to decide what constituted 'a reasonable notice for a factory superintendent in the boot trade'. The plaintiff himself thought that he should have had three months. The secretary of another firm who had been called as a witness stated that in his opinion it was customary for a 'manager in the position of the plaintiff, if paid by the week', to receive a week's notice only. The plaintiff's solicitor objected that this would be a very bad custom, since even a 'clerk in the City would be served better than that'—obviously implying that a factory superintendent was entitled to more than a clerk. Judge Cluer considered solomonically that a month's notice was appropriate, which in this case meant that the plaintiff had lost.[111] It is obvious that in this kind of demarcation dispute legal arguments in the strict sense were of little use. The principal task of the judge consisted in not upsetting the complicated social and occupational hierarchies which local businesses needed in order to function. Legal reasonings could rarely be decisive in such matters; they only served to justify decisions which had been reached otherwise, by common sense and by a more or less careful enquiry into what decent thinking people of both sides in the business were prepared to tolerate.

From the litigants' point of view the main problem with this aspect of county court justice was neither 'unequal' law nor class-prejudiced judges, but simply the fact that for the most common employment disputes, no firm legal ground was available on which judges, lawyers, and their clients alike could stand. Insecurity of outcome was the consequence, and it was this which most probably made extra-legal arrangements appear more attractive whenever they were achievable. None the less workers, salaried

[110] *Baker's Record*, 17 May 1912, p. 7, 'A Refusal Justified' (*Gregory v. Beale Ltd.*).
[111] *Boot & Shoe Trades Journal*, 13 Dec. 1912, p. 537, 'Browett v. Wright's Tackless Footwear Co.'

employees, and above all domestic servants continued to make use of the county courts, and there is no way of knowing how often the mere threat of bringing the matter before this tribunal induced employers to acquiesce in an 'amicable' settlement.

In the eyes of manual workers county courts gained a new lease of life after 1897/1906 when they were given exclusive jurisdiction in workmen's compensation cases. Contrary to the trend in other employment disputes, the use of courts rapidly increased in this particular field of law. In the last years before the Great War about 8,000 cases per year were settled in court and about 20,000 memoranda of out-of-court agreements were registered.[112] Despite all uncertainties created by the notorious phrase 'accident arising out of and in the course of the employment', the statute at last provided a clear legal basis for dealing with injuries received at work, without any need to prove the negligence of particular persons, and without running the risk of falling under the even more notorious doctrine of 'common employment'. More importantly perhaps, the statute established a procedure which allowed for pre-trial arrangements which after registration had to be supervised and enforced by the court. A huge majority of cases was always disposed of in that way. In disputed cases the judge acted as arbitrator, and the parties, in order to mark the difference, were called 'applicants' and 'respondents'. Although the complexity of the statute made it necessary for applicants to employ solicitors in almost all but the most clear-cut cases, the formula as a whole seems to have been attractive to them. In the majority of cases the judge merely sanctioned agreements made outside the court or during proceedings. Only if one of the parties insisted did proceedings take the adversarial course otherwise typical of the British legal system. Under such conditions individual county court judges were able to gain a great deal of credit even among those radical trade unionists who otherwise did not hesitate to condemn the whole system as class jurisdiction. One of these highly reputed county court judges was Judge French, of Bow county court in the East End of London, who died in 1902, shortly

---

[112] See the figures in Bartrip, *Workmen's Compensation*, 20–2, 68 f. During and after the war figures for litigation went down (for explanations see ibid. 133 ff.), but the number of memoranda registered remained stable. The statistics for 1936 show 4,482 applications dealt with in court and 20,815 memoranda registered. See Sir Arnold Wilson and Hermann Levy, *Workmen's Compensation* (London, 1939), 314.

after the Taff Vale judgment had brought the conflict between organized labour and the legal community to a climax. An obituary in the *Dockers' Record*, the journal of Ben Tillet's Dockers' Union, described him as one who had managed to combine law and justice in his judicial practice:

We believe him to have done more than any other Judge to command a belief in and respect for the law among the toilers, who have too often great grounds for believing that class prejudice taint even what should be honest and unimpeccable judgments. While the law has lost a great exponent, the poor, and justice itself, have lost a great friend.[113]

Conclusion

The findings of the preceding survey result in a paradox. On the one hand, it can be argued that from the 1870s to the 1920s unequal treatment of employees before lower courts of civil jurisdiction in Britain was—on the whole—diminishing. Asymmetries in the norms themselves were either removed by statute or gradually fell into disuse in judicial practice; obvious instances of class-biased magistrates and county court judges became an exception through better supervision and public vigilance; and access to legal advice and practical help was available to many (though not all) employees belonging to a union. All in all, the system became more just towards employees. Yet, on the other hand, there are strong indications that during the same period fewer and fewer employees tried to make use of the inferior civil courts to seek redress against their employers, except for workmen's compensation. Employees turned away from judicial solutions, although their chances of getting a fair hearing when bringing a case had improved. Despite a significant progress in substantive justice there was de-juridification of individual employment relations.

Some of the above findings need further empirical research to be established beyond doubt. But the overall trends seem to be clear enough. How can the paradox of decreasing use of the courts while at the same time the law and the legal community became more sympathetic to the claims of employees be explained?

[113] *Dockers' Record*, 7 (Aug. 1902), 2.

First, one could point to the parallel development of collective *laissez-faire* as a possible reason: the spectacular growth of the unions in terms of membership and bargaining power would have made it unnecessary for British employees to sue their employers individually. But, as has been shown, through the whole period a large proportion of claims (other than workmen's compensation) were brought by persons employed in trades or occupations in which unions were weak anyway and strikes difficult to organize. Why should these unaffiliated employees, who were left on the margins of collective bargaining, have relinquished the chance to appeal to a magistrate or a county court judge? Union growth cannot account for this. Moreover, many unions, and especially the powerful ones, maintained legal departments to help individual members who had difficulties with their employers. Fighting a case in court on behalf of such a member was certainly not the first option, but it was a course which even smaller unions were ready to take if necessary. And it was an option which naturally offered itself in all cases where more vigorous collective action could not be justified. More and stronger unions meant more legal departments, and this might have led—all other conditions remaining equal—to *more* wage and dismissal cases being fought instead of fewer. Many unions, however, seem to have concentrated all their efforts on workmen's compensation cases and let other disputes settle themselves. Unless one assumes that individual members in the 1920s really had fewer grievances against their employers than in 1870 or in 1890—grievances, that is, which would not require a strike or other massive threat—the retreat of unions, as well as unorganized employees, from legal action still needs to be explained.

The example of workmen's compensation indicates where an answer to the paradox might lie. Here a statutory enactment, which explicitly excluded common law considerations, made the outcome more predictable than in those cases where everything turned on the interpretation of some doubtful local trade custom, as in dismissal cases, or where all depended on judges' reasoning about uncertain concepts such as 'implied contract', 'restraint of trade', 'common employment', or 'public policy'. Procedural devices gave employees additional security that their interests would be protected against over-zealous insurance agents who might talk them into accepting lump sum payments which

12

Master and Servant Law and Constitutional Rights in the United States during the Nineteenth Century

A Domain-Specific Analysis

KAREN ORREN

The connection between master and servant law and the US Constitution is not well understood. As a historical matter, it is evident that the legal reordering of workplace relations in the modern era was accomplished only through a profound adjustment in the structures of American government. In retrospect, the lines of stress—the role of the states, the prerogatives of the judicial branch, the reception of English common law—are clear enough. How the pieces fit together as a going concern is another question. Examining the impact of the dual system of courts on the progress of workers' equality would no doubt show meaningful variation. But in some areas, like picketing, state courts decided more favourably to labour than federal courts; in other areas, like jury trial, it was the reverse. It is impossible to tell the story of late nineteenth-century collective action in the United States without the courts' overturning of statutes. Yet trade union parry and judicial thrust closely paralleled that of England, which lacked this constitutional practice. To observe that constitutional jurisprudence deferred to common law according to a standard of 'status quo neutrality' is valid as far as it goes.[1] But it begs the question of what elements composed the status quo, and by what principles they were organized.

Nineteenth-century commentary on the Constitution sheds scarcely more light. Mirroring the document itself, *antebellum* treatises like Story's and Smith's take account of other aspects of civil society—religion, property, commerce, slavery—but not master

---

[1] The phrase is from Cass Sunstein, *The Partial Constitution* (Cambridge, Mass., 1993), ch. 3.

and servant.[2] Thomas Cooley's *Constitutional Limitations*, published in 1868 and generally regarded as the single most influential legal writing of the era, gives master and servant a brief paragraph in passing, on another topic (habeas corpus).[3] Cooley's later volume, *General Principles of Constitutional Law*, published in 1880, has a short section on 'Employment' that names the liberty to hire out one's labour among 'the first and highest of all civil rights', denies that state legislatures may prohibit the employment of any state resident, and declares the exclusion of women and children from hazardous workplaces to be constitutionally permissible.[4]

As might be expected, this sequence registers increasing industrialization over the century. Cooley's 1880 text, without saying so, points as well to the trade union assault under way upon the existing master and servant regime. Chinese labourers were recruited as workers and strikebreakers on the railroads, and unions had pressed for laws to prevent their hiring; laws to restrict employment of women and children were aimed at (among other things) business strategies to undercut union membership and wages. The resolution of these conflicts, like the resolution of other labour-related conflicts in the following decades, would occasion important constitutional changes. But again, the causation is oblique; the changes brought on—here, in the plenary powers of Congress and the processes of constitutional amendment—had nothing particular to do with relations of master and servant.

To end the stand-off between historical entanglement and conceptual disregard it will be necessary to devise a method that relates constitutional *structures* to workplace *relations*, and not just in circumstances of breakdown and reconstruction but as they operated normally, which in this volume of essays means as they were presented in nineteenth-century courtrooms. The task entails a certain leeway with established terminology and periodization. As a first effort, the sections below—Rights, Domains, Officers, Authority—enlist (largely) familiar ideas in (some) unaccustomed usages, in order to reframe (mostly) well-rehearsed episodes.

---

[2] Joseph Story, *Commentaries on the Constitution of the United States*, 3 vols. (Boston, 1833); E. Fitch Smith, *Commentaries on Statutes and Constitutional Laws* (Albany, NY, 1848).

[3] Thomas M. Cooley, *A Treatise on the Constitutional Limitations which Rest upon the Legislative Power of the States of the American Union* (Boston, 1868), 340–41.

[4] Thomas M. Cooley, *The General Principles of Constitutional Law in the United States of America* (Boston, 1880), 231–2.

Rights

There is no stronger motivating theme in American constitutional history than rights. The US Constitution is saturated by rights—arising from the text itself; enumerated in the first ten amendments; and after the Civil War, in the thirteenth, fourteenth, and fifteenth amendments. Rights, constitutional and otherwise, are the switches in the system of legal provision. Their off-or-on status determines the passage from what is punished to what is protected, from what is demanded to what is provided—or, more precisely, what will be weighed in the balance by those with the authority, that is to say with the right, to decide. Located throughout the diverse stations of governance, sometimes proceeding under the banner of 'discretion', rights establish the order of precedence, from the highest state officers to the least privileged inhabitants and all points in between.

For this analysis, what is intriguing is how little practical difference constitutional rights seem to have made in the master and servant relation, regulated during the nineteenth century under common law essentially as it had been under English law for hundreds of years, or on the arduous efforts of workers to bring about change. Even if it be added that common law rights were 'constitutionalized' in American law, treated as 'vested', or by other doctrinal means made constitutionally enforceable, this still does not explain how it was that constitutional rights that were expressly provided in socially unqualified terms afforded employees less protection than their employers. Yet that this was the case is unambiguous on the historical record. Nor will it be sufficient to observe that common law rights 'trumped' constitutional rights. For then the question becomes, by what reasoning?

The first link in any chain of explanation will be found in the characteristic of common law systems that rights of every kind function legally only at the point that they give rise to actions—suits for redress accepted as valid in courts of law. This was true in nineteenth-century American law, notwithstanding the affirmative statement of specific guarantees in both federal and state constitutions. In the master and servant relation, both parties had actions—though servants had far fewer. Servants' rights effectively boiled down to suits for wages, either for the amount due 'on the contract' or for the contract's breach, for which damages could be awarded. Against these actions, masters had several defences. For example, masters might rely on the doctrine of the 'entire contract', providing that no wages need be paid until an entire job or period contracted for was completed; or masters might claim their own right to fire an employee for any legal reason, including reasons not known when the worker was dismissed.

The core of masters' rights consisted in the normally self-executing ones of hiring and firing and managing the workplace. These gave rise to suits against any outsider who interfered, the most important of which was the action of enticement, a suit at common law against persons interfering with a servant's continued employment or industry. In its own name or some other, such as interference in contract, packaged often as the requisite illegal means or end within suits for criminal conspiracy, enticement was present in virtually every litigation that involved trade union organizing, beginning with the cordwainers' strikes at the start of the century straight through to the consumer boycotts at the end. Moreover, when legislators passed protective statutes to restrict masters' discretion in various ways, the masters' rights against outside interference gave rise to actions—for equity injunctions and damage actions against state officers as well as for appeals from lower court judgments—that ensured against overly zealous enforcement.

In their defence, workers claimed constitutional rights to free speech and assembly and, when they were faced with injunctions and charges of criminal contempt, the right to jury trial. Later in the century especially, workers also claimed rights to contract freely for their labour and to compete against others for economic gain. These claims were regularly brushed aside by the judges who finally heard them; *People* v. *Melvin*, *Walker* v. *Cronin*, *In re Debs* are a few of the famous instances that come to mind.[5] Brushed aside is not an unfair description. Earlier I spoke of precedence: judges did not take seriously the idea that the servant's constitutional rights might be legitimately interposed against, let alone take precedence to, the uncontested common law rights of the master.

[5] *People* v. *Melvin* is reprinted in John R. Commons et al., *A Documentary History of American Industrial Society* (New York, 1958), iii. 278 (English conspiracy laws repugnant to equal rights enshrined in American constitutions); 107 Mass. 555 (1871) (non-defamatory speech); 158 US 564 (1895) (jury trial).

By contrast, as a rule of procedure, rights under the US Constitution did not give rise—directly, that is—to legal actions. With the exception of the circumstance of their arrest, when citizens might avail themselves of habeas corpus or post-conviction appeals to make constitutional claims, constitutional issues were most often raised in the course of civil suits against public officers, actions available at law for damages and at equity for injunctions. These suits required that plaintiffs first allege a traditional common law violation, like assault or trespass; when the officer defended his behaviour on grounds of duty, the plaintiff would counter that what occurred was *ultra vires*, performed under a statute or order that was unconstitutional for the reasons argued. Workers, however, were seldom situated to use the law in this way. While there were no doubt public officers in the thousands who, in an objective sense, violated workers' constitutional rights, there seldom would have been the required common law injury, nor in the calculable dollar amounts necessary for federal jurisdiction. Labour organizations, being in many cases unincorporated, could not have sued in their own name.

But even without these barriers, there was little incentive to sue when it was plain how very narrow was the range of constitutional claims that might be successfully pressed. On several occasions the Supreme Court had announced that federal rights did not apply to official actions taken under the authority of states, the setting where master and servant conflict almost always happened. The earliest and most important decision was in 1833, when the Supreme Court refused to find protection in the fifth amendment's 'takings clause' against the destruction of a private wharf's profitability as a result of a city's construction of public works.[6] Another time was in 1848 when, in answer to claims made by a Rhode Island insurgent seeking a wider state franchise, the Court said the Constitution's guarantee of a republican form of government in article IV was satisfied by the seating of a state's representatives in national councils.[7]

After the Civil War, federal rights protections remained elusive despite the expansive language of the fourteenth amendment. As is well known, this was accomplished in the first instance by the Court's severely limiting the rights of non-African Americans that

---

[6] *Barron v. Baltimore*, 32 US 243.   [7] *Luther v. Borden*, 48 US 1.

must be respected by states under the amendment's 'privileges and immunities' clause.[8] Any idea that servants might sue their masters for rights violations in connection with their employment was foreclosed by the Court's further limiting the amendment to 'state action'.[9] The impact of the Court's holdings on the amendment's 'due process' clause was to maintain rights under the employment contract just as they were; indeed, it was under the jurisprudence of 'due process' that enticement donned its constitutional clothes, as 'liberty of contract'.

The diverse auspices of these narrowings indicates the breadth of their theoretical underpinnings. Workers' disadvantage (and that of other aspiring rightsholders) did not hinge on a particular political regime or commercial outlook. The first decision, *Barron v. Baltimore*, was authored by Chief Justice Marshall, high priest of vested rights and advocate of national power; the second, *Luther v. Borden*, by Chief Justice Roger Taney, friend of legislative power and states' rights; the fourteenth amendment decisions followed the lead of Justice Samuel Miller, proponent of regulating business 'affected with the public interest' under the police power of the states. When, in a separate line of cases, the Supreme Court barred federal jurisdiction over civil suits against state officers based on the eleventh amendment, it did so on behalf of the authority of state legislators over the claims of state bondholders.

None of the above restrictions, of course, would have prevented state judges from adopting a more generous position than their federal counterparts by implementing rights in their own constitutions that paralleled federal guarantees. With regard to freedom of speech, for instance, Cooley writes in *Constitutional Limitations* how 'with jealous care of what is almost universally regarded a sacred right' each state by its constitution intended a 'shield of protection to the free expression of opinion in every part of the land'.[10] In fact, soon into the twentieth century, a few states (three) would become so jealous that their judiciaries would no longer agree to enjoin the union printing and distribution of information about strikes and boycotts—though leaving open the possibility of damage suits in the event of demonstrable injuries.[11]

---

[8] Slaughter-House Cases, 63 US 36 (1873).
[9] Civil Rights Cases, 109 US 53 (1883).   [10] Cooley, *Constitutional Limitations*, 414.
[11] One federal circuit also refused to enjoin persuasion by way of pamphleting and picketing. See *Allis Chalmers Co. v. Iron Molders*, 166 Fed. 45 (1908).

In the meantime, even the most intrepid of state judges flinched in the presence of the master's right against enticement. In *Vegelahn* v. *Guntner*, the Massachusetts case in which Oliver Wendell Holmes, Jr. dissented from the majority's order to end a picket line with his famous defence of striking workers' right to engage in the 'free struggle for life', Holmes reported to his brethren: 'There was some evidence of persuasion to break existing contracts. I ruled this was unlawful, and should be enjoined.'[12]

Domains

For insight into the everywhere-and-nowhere quality of constitutional rights as they affected nineteenth-century master and servant law, it will be useful to consult those who thought systematically about rights at the time. The most detailed and influential treatment of rights until the work of Terry and Holmes at the century's end was written by Jeremy Bentham. Bentham posited a 'universal law of liberty: a boundless expanse in which the several efficient laws appear as so many spots . . . or material bodies scattered over the immensity of space'. Within that space there existed what Bentham called 'legal powers', exceptions to the general duty not to harm others or to affect their interests adversely:

When the law exempts a man from punishment in case of his dealing with your person in a manner that either stands a chance or is certain of being disagreeable to you, it thereby confers on him a power: it gives him a power over you; a power over your person. Now this is what it may find necessary to do for various purposes: for the sake of providing for the discharge of the several functions of the husband, the parent, the guardian, the master, the judge, the military officer, and the sovereign: . . . These powers then form so many exceptions to the general rule that no man has the right to meddle with the person of another.[13]

Bentham's discussion advances our own in several important ways. In the first place, he makes no distinction between 'public' and 'private' rights to meddle, as might correspond to a

---

[12] 167 Mass. 92 (1896).

[13] Jeremy Bentham, *Of Laws in General*, ed. H. Hart (London, 1970), 200–1. See generally, Joseph William Singer, 'The Legal Rights Debate in Analytical Jurisprudence from Bentham to Hohfeld', *Wisconsin Law Review*, 1982 (1982), 975–1059.

distinction between 'constitutional' and 'common law' rights. More to the point, the powerholders Bentham enumerates are not distinguished according to their 'public' or 'private' position in government or society. And although Bentham's use of 'powers' corresponds to current (twentieth-century) usage of the word powers—rather than 'rights'—to refer to government authority and official discretion as if these were distinct categories, in his presentation it is in the nature of powers that they entail rights; here they entail the 'right' to meddle with the person of another, a right that is denied ordinary people upon pain of legal punishment. In this respect, Bentham's analysis of rights accords with the one suggested above, that is, rights as switches—in this case, 'on' for powerholders, 'off' for others.

Among the powerholders Bentham names, attention will be drawn immediately to the category of master, and after that, judge. Notice as well that nowhere in sight is that representative figure of Bentham's era, the 'man of commerce'—the entrepreneur, the commercial banker, the budding industrialist, the improving landowner. Now, obviously Bentham realized that social functions in real life overlap one another, that the budding industrialist was also a master, just as a judge was also a parent, and so on. What the omission signals is the historical fact that by the time this was written, not long after Americans adopted the Bill of Rights, 'men of commerce' were thought to inhabit the boundless expanse of liberty Bentham projects, whereas the exceptions he names inhabited legally regulated domains of personal hierarchy. The market activities of contracting and competing, even of purposely driving each other into poverty, were considered by Bentham and his contemporaries to be the epitome of liberty, while analogous harmful behaviour in other domains was still proscribed as illegal.

This division, between commerce and other relations, was mirrored at the level of government institutions. The displacement by parliamentary statutes of the older common law rules regulating commerce, alongside religious toleration which, like commerce, was likewise placed under legislative oversight, had been the specific programme that accompanied the proposition of rights by Locke and other (pre-)liberals and that was later incorporated by Blackstone and systematized by Bentham. Thus, another missing powerholder from Bentham's list is the legislator. Like his champion, the man of commerce, and unlike the judge and the sovereign (which in America would correspond to the executive), the legislator was conceived to operate non-hierarchically, being responsible to the people in all their ranks in the way that the man of commerce was responsible to the market.[14]

It is important that the distinction between the liberal ideology of rights, stated in universals, and actual institutional arrangements over time—the distinction underlying Bentham's own between liberty and 'powers'—be kept firmly in mind. On the one hand, to the extent that these rights described what was *legally* real, they contemplated those modifications in social and government regulation, prior to the nineteenth century, described above. When all but one of the American states formally received English common law and statutes as of some fixed date—the adoption of the state constitution, for example, or the US Constitution or the settlement of the colony—into their own legal systems, they grafted onto their own polities the legislative governance of commerce (and also of religion, which most of them quickly eschewed), along with those common law hierarchies that were left intact. The resulting distribution of rights, including Bentham's 'exceptions', became in nineteenth-century parlance 'vested'. On the other hand, to the extent that these same rights were promoted in universal terms, based on theories of nature or the rights of man, they maintained their *ideological* force as universals. In post-colonial America they cast a long political shadow; they were, as Abraham Lincoln would describe them, a 'standard maxim', expressed in constitutions and social movements over successive decades.

The truism that any legal system proceeds by both ideals and legal provision takes on special meaning in light of a distribution of rights in which specific social or governmental domains are purposeful exceptions to general rules. One ideal immediately thrown into doubt is the rule that the provision of rights will

---

[14] Bentham distinguishes the British corporate sovereign of Kings, Lords, and Commons, which emits only legislation and would be excepted from 'sovereign' here, from the persons of kings and executives who issue administrative orders and regulations. See *Of Laws in General*, 6–7. It is still possible that in the passage quoted he meant by 'sovereign', 'King in Parliament'; however, we know from his other writings that he was disinclined unduly to credit claims of parliamentary sovereignty. On this point, see Karen Orren, 'Labor Regulation and Constitutional Theory in the United States and England', *Political Theory*, 22 (1994), 98–123; at 114–15.

proceed by general rules, including such apparently fundamental rules that judges will follow precedents and will implement procedures with some measure of uniformity across society when making their decisions. From time to time, constitutional scholars have supplemented predominantly legal interpretations of judicial decision-making, focused on evolving streams of doctrine over time, with structural ones, according to which judges are understood to decide cases according to logics dictated by the purpose and array of particular institutions (e.g. presidency, Congress) or by the political commitments of historical periods (e.g. founding, post-Civil War, New Deal).[15]

A different structural interpretation may best capture the domain-specific allocation of constitutional rights in the nineteenth century. Such an interpretation would separately align master and servant law, extending in time from the founding period to the 1930s, against legal relations in other domains, notably commerce, but also family relations, slavery, relations among government officials, and other relevant areas. This would permit the observation of disparities and convergences of constitutional rights, as well as of legal doctrines—'vested rights', 'interference in contract', 'class legislation', and so on—that bear on their 'off-on' positions at various historical junctures. It would also draw attention to constitutional (or other) features that affect the separation and generality of endowments, for example the division of authority between national and state governments and among government branches at each level.

At the very least, one benefit of such a domain-specific analysis should be to quell the indignation with which scholars have sometimes viewed the administration of master and servant law.[16] The fact that workers and not businessmen were punished for interfering in contracts; that the law promoted business combinations while forbidding labour combinations; that judges did not endorse

---

[15] See for example, Charles Black, *Structure and Relationship in Constitutional Law* (Baton Rouge, La., 1969); and Bruce Ackerman, *We the People: Foundations* (Cambridge, Mass., 1991).

[16] See for example Haggai Hurvitz, 'American Labor Law and the Doctrine of Entrepreneurial Property Rights: Boycotts, Courts, and the Juridical Reorientation of 1886–1895', *Industrial Relations Law Journal*, 8 (1986), 307–61; and Ellen M. Kelman, 'American Labor Law and Legal Formalism: How "Legal Logic" Shaped and Vitiated the Rights of American Workers', *St John's Law Review*, 58 (1983), 1–68. The same ground is surveyed in William Forbath, 'The Shaping of the American Labor Movement', *Harvard Law Review*, 102 (1989), 1109–256, 1202 ff.

laissez-faire in situations of industrial conflict: the breakdown of these distinctions would eventually occur through workers' collective action that undermined not the logical consistency but the *descriptive* authority of the workplace as a separable domain. But for the time being, rights remained the default position, not only for employees but for other similarly subordinated persons.

A second implication of distinguishing domains bears on the alleged 'transformation' of the masters' property to include a number of new privileges protecting them against trade unions, and the irregular standards by which it occurred.[17] If the presumption is that judges administered rights according to precedent, then the alterations noticed are justly regarded as a deviation from some otherwise prevalent norm. But if judges read the constitution and laws structurally, in terms of rationales prescribed for particular domains, then the transformation was unremarkable. The adjustment of the master's property rights to include the operations of 'business'; the stretching of 'trespass' to cover any interruption of these; the free-wheeling resort to equity to forestall multiplying varieties of illegal duress: all evidenced consistency in doctrine rather than vagueness or confusion.

This structural interpretation is different from an interpretation based on class. Much of the weight in the argument that late nineteenth-century constitutional law was class-biased rests on the substantive due process decisions that struck down pro-labour statutes and punished collective actions, based on a doctrine of 'liberty of contract' under the fourteenth amendment. Here too, 'liberty of contract' was enabling and expansive in the case of employers, restricting and confined in the case of workers. But, importantly, the doctrine of 'liberty of contract' was domain-specific, as a practical matter seldom applied outside the relation of master and servant. Moreover, it coexisted with a vigorous doctrine of state police powers, exerted over business practices of all kinds, including pricing; far more of these regulations were upheld by American courts than were struck down.[18] For the historical reasons suggested, only the rights of masters—not of businessmen—held sway.

---

[17] The *locus classicus* of this argument is Morton J. Horwitz, *The Transformation of American Law, 1780–1860* (Cambridge, Mass., 1977).

[18] Frank R. Strong, *Substantive Due Process of Law: A Dichotomy of Sense and Nonsense* (Durham, NC, 1986), 273–92.

Officers

In fact, structural readings of nineteenth-century law are common in legal scholarship, even if they are not always referred to exactly that way. One reading emphasizes 'classical jurisprudence', formal rules enforced by nineteenth-century judges to order a world imagined as intersecting threads of political relations—citizen to citizen, citizen to state, legislature to judiciary, federal government to state. A different structural reading, seen in recent labour history scholarship, describes the law's treatment of the workplace as a jurisdiction, a cognate realm of legislation and enforcement.[19] An inadequacy of the first reading mentioned is its abstraction—as Morton Horwitz has said, the suggestion that the rules enforced were indeterminately 'flippable', from the service of one interest to its opposite.[20] The second idea, the workplace as a jurisdiction, is more concrete, rooted in actual social organization; but jurisdiction is too passive and uninflected a construct to depict the busy and variegated landscape of nineteenth-century constitutional rights.

Our own proposal so far, of legal domains, is subject to similar criticism. The delineation of separate domains leaves rights and relations among them unspecified; absent any principle of action attached, the notion of domains is as inert an idea as jurisdictions. The analysis, therefore, requires a further step that follows on Bentham's treatment of 'powers', which is that persons occupying positions favoured in law as exceptions to general rules of personal liberty be identified as officers—persons authorized by law to act within designated domains, without regard to constitutional or other rights of subordinates that might validly be asserted in other settings. This step imposes no undue abstraction on what is well established empirically: officers are presumed to exercise the privileges of their positions and to seek legal vindication when resisted. It also underscores the superior rights of husbands,

---

[19] These readings, respectively, will be found in Duncan Kennedy, 'Toward a Historical Understanding of Legal Consciousness: The Case of Classical Legal Thought in America', *Research in Law and Society*, 3 (1980), 3–24 and Karen Orren, *Belated Feudalism: Labor, the Law, and Liberal Development in the United States* (Cambridge, 1991). Also see, on jurisdiction, Robert J. Steinfeld, *The Invention of Free Labor: The Employment Relation in English and American Law and Culture, 1350–1870* (Durham, NC, 1991).

[20] Morton J. Horwitz, 'Santa Clara Revisited: The Development of Corporate Theory', *West Virginia Law Review*, 88 (1985), 173–224, 176.

masters, judges, and others while allowing for judges, for instance, to take precedence over masters and husbands when the latter enter the domain of the courts.

At first impression this use of 'officers' may seem inapposite, and I will defend it historically. As an analytic device, however, it demands no more than the favouring of the authoritative attributes of office—the duties officers were legally expected to perform and which established the terms of their accountability— over the administrative attributes—the details of how officers acquired and lost their jobs and how they were paid. It also substitutes the condition of state sanction, the backing of officers' actions by enforceable law, for the division between 'public' and 'private'.[21] By this method the structures of constitutional authority convert to components of action and motivation that may be juxtaposed and calibrated against officers (and for that matter, non-officers) whose rights derive, in whole or in part, from other legal sources.

Historical support for officeholding as an organizing conception may be found, first of all, in situations where the word 'officer' is used conventionally to describe what are treated in law as parallel relations. Consider for example the doctrine according to which the diverse authority of royal administrators was organized for purposes of assessing the legality of oversight by other officers, including judges. This doctrine proceeded on a distinction between 'judicial' actions, performed according to the officer's discretion and enjoyed as a right, without interference or oversight by others; and 'ministerial' actions, performed as a matter of duty and obligation, subject to review by other appropriate officers.[22] In so many words, this same doctrine was applied in the nineteenth century to the relations between 'officers' and stockholders in business corporations. To be sure, the application was a lenient one. When members of boards of directors were 'clothed with a discretion', they were not held legally liable for damages flowing from an exercise of judgement, however erroneous; with regard to their 'ministerial' duties, suits would be entertained only upon

---

[21] Elsewhere I have referred to the 'powers' named by Bentham as 'state-sanctioned martinets'. 'The Union Officer before and after the Wagner Act', Industrial Relations Research Association, *Proceedings of the Forty-Eighth Annual Meeting* (1996), 388–95.

[22] See Karen Orren, 'The Work of Government: Recovering the Discourse of Office in *Marbury v. Madison*', *Studies in American Political Development*, 8 (1994), 60–80.

a showing of gross negligence, non-attendance, and fraud.[23] The important point is that the law considered both sorts of 'officers' in the same frame.

Likewise, writs of *quo warranto* and the doctrine of *ultra vires*, relied on traditionally to enquire into the authority of state officeholders, were applied to officers of corporations.[24] With writs, the connections spread out. Habeas corpus, along with *certiorari* and *mandamus*, the chief writs relied upon to implement constitutional rights in nineteenth-century American courts, stemmed directly from those writs used to correct misappropriations of authority by medieval officeholders in the royal courts. Habeas corpus allowed one officer to question another concerning the legality of a prisoner's custody. Although today associated only with judges, habeas was available more widely in the nineteenth century for purposes of regaining custody of persons in the suitors' rightful charge. This use was familiar before the Civil War, most notoriously as it was employed by slaveholders to recapture their fugitive slaves. But leading law treatises of the post-bellum period continued to consider the rights of ordinary masters, alongside husbands, parents, guardians, schoolteachers, and bailers—in our terms, other officers—as they might (or might not) avail themselves of the writ.[25]

Masters in particular enjoyed a historical affinity with government officers through property owners' traditional rights ('office') of holding court for the various persons employed on their lands. These rights, of 'jurisdiction', lingered on, for instance in the privilege of modern masters to assess fines on their employees for infractions of the work routine. The 'relative servitude' of the medieval serf as Maitland described him, a free man against everyone except his lord, becomes the 'relative liberty' of the nineteenth-century servant as we have described him, a rightsholder

---

[23] See Herbert Hovenkamp, 'The Classical Corporation in American Legal Thought', *Georgetown Law Journal*, 76 (1978), 1593–689, at 1667–8.

[24] Ibid. 1662–7, 1669–72.

[25] Cf. Cooley, *Constitutional Limitations*, 341; and Rollin C. Hurd, *A Treatise on the Writ of Habeas Corpus* (Albany, NY, 1858; 1871), bk. 1, ch. 3. By the late 19th century, the habeas writ was available to masters only to recover their apprentices. In the United States, employees were not legally held to specific performance on their contracts. However, the custodial spirit of the masters' power continued to be expressed in courts' ordering workers back to their employment during labour strikes, a practice that was not ended by the Supreme Court until 1894 (*Arthur v. Oakes*, 63 Fed. 310).

except as it affected the rights of his master.[26] Such reverberations, however, would have only antiquarian interest did they not figure actively in nineteenth-century legal consciousness, and especially *outside* the regulation of master and servant, where, after all, they might be anticipated.

On this score as well, evidence is ample and found in surprising places. Thus, in his important section on the police powers of the states in *Constitutional Limitations*, Cooley suggests an exchangeability between public and private functionaries when he approvingly cites a well-known decision by Judge Isaac Redfield requiring that a railroad build fences and assume liability for damages caused by the running of trains, even though no provision for these duties was made in the company's charter: the police power 'resided primarily and ultimately in the legislature'; but 'in the absence of legislative control, the corporations themselves exercise [the police power] over their operatives, and to some extent over all who do business with them, or come on their grounds, through their general statutes, and by their officers'.[27]

Or for another evoking of the same parallel structure, with direct relevance to the rights and vulnerabilities of masters: in his chapter on 'Freedom of Speech', Cooley considers the constitutional status of criticisms made of public officeholders and candidates and concludes that such speech is protected against libel actions even if it leads to a person's subsequent dismissal or nonselection. The rule was subject only to the qualification that the remonstrance must be addressed to an officer or body that the citizen believes is 'an authority possessing power in the premises'. In support of this tenet, Cooley notes: 'a complaint to a master, charging a servant with a dishonest act which had been imputed to the complaining party, has also been held privileged.' This precedent appears with others concerning postmasters and a Secretary of War.[28]

Authority

That judges associated discretion above all other characteristics with the position of master is readily demonstrated in their

---

[26] Orren, *Belated Feudalism*, 91–102.   [27] Cooley, *Constitutional Limitations*, 575.
[28] Ibid. 434.

decisions on workers' collective action. Thus in *State* v. *Glidden*: 'the strikers' purpose was to deprive the Carrington Publishing Company of its liberty to carry on its business in its own way.'[29] In *Barr* v. *Essex*: the foundation of commercial enterprise depends on investors anticipating they 'will be able to control their affairs according to their own ideas'.[30] In *Cœur d'Alene*: if the workers' designs be carried to 'their logical conclusion, the owner of property would lose its control and management'.[31] In *Hopkins* v. *Oxley Stave*: defendant workers intended to compel persons 'to submit to the dictation of others the management of their private business affairs'.[32]

Their own complex authority—within the federal system, in relation to their state legislatures and to Congress, inside their judicial hierarchies—would have made judges among American officeholders the first to appreciate infringements on discretion, including infringements from below. Here is Justice Brewer's opinion, denying that Eugene Debs's imprisonment for criminal contempt violated his right to jury trial. 'The power of a court to make an order carries with it the equal power to punish for disobedience of that order . . . To submit the question of disobedience to another tribunal, be it jury or another court, would operate to deprive the proceeding of half its efficiency.'[33]

The fellow-feeling between judges and masters has been arguably better documented than understood. My claim is that by arraying the diverse stations of constitutional authority, broadly considered, as offices, not as metaphors but as frameworks of motivation and decision, I can more cogently explain the provision and non-provision of constitutional rights. With that in mind, let us revisit a conundrum of the nineteenth-century master and servant law, the non-enforcement of statutes providing maximum working hours that were *not* struck down as unconstitutional. Their nullity has been attributed variously to weak enforcement machinery, contractual exception clauses, and sheer interpretative perversity. While not inconsistent with these, our analysis offers an explanation that goes, if you will, constitutionally deeper.

United States v. *Martin*, decided in 1876, concerned a fireman-labourer in the steam plant at the United States Naval Academy

---

[29] 55 Conn. 46 (1887), at 71.   [30] 53 Eq. Dick Ch. 101 (1894), at 113.
[31] 51 Fed. Rep. 260 (1892), at 263.   [32] 83 Fed. Rep. 912 (1897), at 917.
[33] *In re Debs*, 158 US 564, at 594.

who sued for overtime pay for the hundreds of twelve-hour days he had worked after Congress had passed an Act in 1868 declaring 'eight hours shall constitute a day's work for all laborers, workmen, and mechanics employed by or on behalf of the government of the United States'. The Court dismissed the petition, deciding Martin had no right of action. The legislation was 'in the nature of a direction from a principal to his agent, that eight hours is deemed to be a proper length of time for a day's labor, and that his contracts shall be based upon that theory. It is a matter between the principal and his agent, in which a third party has no interest.'[34]

Now, the fact that *United States* v. *Martin* concerned public employment rather than private might have been expected to limit the holding's impact. The members of Congress and the officers of the Naval Academy were, it must be conceded, officers officially, and for that reason legitimately denoted as principal and agent. Therefore it is instructive that this became a leading case, followed in disputes arising from state statutes that provided maximum hours in private employment, and with the same legal effect, that is, the judges' treatment of these statutes as advisory— though now between the legislature as principal and the master as agent—and their denial that the employee had any actionable claim.[35] To complete this inter-office circle, the private cases reappear in arguments as precedents concerning government officers.[36]

The hours-statutes opinions, true to the period, are infused by the rhetoric of free contract. They extol the employees' new liberty over 'control of their time' alongside the 'option' to work longer. But more revealing still for our interpretation is judges' repeated insistence on those constraints of the workplace that are independent of the parties' will, a sheer consequence of the position—the structure—both were in. 'The printing of photographs, the work of bringing them out and retouching must greatly depend on the character of the weather, as sunlight is one of the essential elements.'[37] The hours of a public boatman 'necessarily depend . . . upon the action of the wind and tide, causes which

[34] 94 US 400 (1876), at 404.
[35] *Grisell* v. *Noel Brothers Flour, Feed Company*, 9 Ind. App. 251 (1893).
[36] See, for example, *Rush et al.* v. US, 33 Ct. Cl. 417, 428 (1898).
[37] *Schurr* v. *Savigny*, 85 Minn. 144 (1891), 147.

would often prolong those hours beyond the control of either party to the contract'.[38] Against a carpenter's claim, the court poses the extreme inconvenience 'if after the work was done and accepted either party could insist on an inquiry whether more or less than ten hours a day had been worked'.[39]

Shades of Justice Brewer quoted in *In re Debs* above; shades of the railroad-receiver cases, grandiosity now seen to be something more than smug identification with magnates. Here is Brewer again, in a receiver case, mingling virtue with blunt necessity in dismissing as 'trivial' a workman's claim of improper discharge:

It has cost over $30,000,000 to build this road of 1,300 miles, and the men whose money built it, the men who put their money into the building of the road so as to furnish work and support to-day to the 3,000 or 4,000 men employed along its line, have not during the last year received a dollar. Now, is it not fair and but common justice that they should have something, and that the earnings should not be all turned in one direction to lift up the wages of laboring men? . . . There is not one of you that if you started a business of your own would not do just as the officers of this company are doing.[40]

The maximum hours statutes left employees, if anything, worse off. Liberty of contract presumed a new duty: if an employee was unsure about hours 'it was his duty to have so informed his employers, so they could have considered that question before entering an agreement'; a worker unwilling to work more than ten or eight hours had the 'duty, at the end of eight hours' work on the first day', to inform his employers.[41] As usual, the workers' liberty redounded to the master's privilege. The statutory cases routinely set out the workers' liberty of contract, and the abasement entailed in any 'tutelage' of that, and proceeded to explain how it was that the master therefore could also not be restrained—according to a rule of mutuality; or on the reasoning that labour equals property, and vice versa.[42] Such arguments may well have had special appeal as the number of businesses taking on the form

---

[38] *McCarthy v. Mayor*, 96 NY Rep. 27 (1884), 33.

[39] *Brooks v. Cotton*, 48 NH 50 (1868), 51.

[40] *Frank v. Denver & R. G. Ry. Co.*, 23 F. 757 (1885), at 758.

[41] *Helphenstine v. Hartig*, 15 Ind. App. 172 (1892), at 176. Also see *Luske v. Hotchkiss*, 37 Conn. 219 (1870).

[42] See *Godcharles v. Wigeman*, 113 Pa. 431 (1886); *State v. Goodwill*, 33 W. Va. 179 (1889); *Ritchie v. People*, 115 Ill. 98 (1895); and *Johnson v. Goodyear Mining*, 127 Cal. 4 (1899).

of state-chartered corporations greatly increased.[43] In any case, seldom was the master's 'due process' upheld on its own legs.

The hours statutes remind us, finally, that liberty of contract must be located not only in the masters' domain, but in the judges'. The protection of rights, of persons and property, was the specific basis upon which the authority of the judiciary, the least institutionally secure among the constitutional branches, entirely dependent on legislatures for its workaday operations, had been stabilized. The restriction of constitutional rights under the fourteenth amendment; the self-denying doctrine of sovereign immunity; the 'police power' that promoted legislatures over courts and that would not be dislodged by the Supreme Court until early in the century: all expressed the outlook of a post-war Republican party still ambiguous about national power and especially ambiguous about national judicial power.

The fluidity of officers' authority in the nineteenth century and the crossfire in which judges—in this case state judges—found themselves may be illustrated with a decision by the Supreme Court of Colorado in 1899. The occasion was a habeas corpus appeal by a mining company officer convicted for violating a state statute that provided for an eight-hour day for various mining industry employees. Four years earlier, this same Colorado court had struck down a virtually identical version of the same statute; since then, however, the US Supreme Court had upheld a similar Utah statute as a valid exercise of the state's police power.[44]

The Colorado court was unmoved. It declaimed the state legislature's 'defiance . . . against [its] solemn decision'. Tempted to follow the rule of *stare decisis* and affirm 'our previous announcements', but cognizant of the important principles at stake, the court's opinion offered a full-dress review of both state and federal authority on the issue at bar, concluding that the statute was an unwarrantable infringement on 'the right of both the employer and employee in making contracts'. The fourteenth amendment had not changed the rights of citizens under state law. Whether a given act of a state legislature violated the federal constitution was for justices of the United States Supreme Court (in our perspective, their right) to decide, and their decision would bind all other

---

[43] See *State* v. *Brown & Sharp Mfg.*, 18 RI 16 (1892); *State* v. *Peel Splint Coal Co.*, 36 W. Va. 802 (1983); *Leep* v. *Railway Co.* 58 Ark. 407 (1894).

[44] *Holden* v. *Hardy*, 169 US 366 (1898).

tribunals; whether or not a state law was valid under a state's constitution was to be decided by the supreme court judges of that
state, and their decision was equally binding. The court ordered
the prisoner released.

Shortly into the new century, in an institutional comeback
already signalled by the embrace of national executive authority
in *In re Debs*, the US Supreme Court would assert itself, first against
the police powers of the states in *Lochner v. New York* and, three
years later, against the powers of the United States Congress in
Adair v. United States. Each of these landmark decisions had as its
subject matter the rights of master and servant.[45] In recent years,
scholars have argued that the tenacious hold of the doctrine of
liberty of contract over labour law in the United States was an
artefact of the unique constitutional power of American judges.[46]
In the analysis offered here, liberty of contract, and the rigours
of nineteenth-century master and servant law, far from being
artefacts of American judges' constitutional power, emerge as its
premiss.

Conclusions

Did the participants in the nineteenth-century drama of master
and servant perceive the distribution of rights as it is described
above? Ours is an overview; contemporaries would not have
spoken of switches and domains. But basically, the answer is yes.
Officers of every degree well understood their prerogatives and
those of their counterparts and rivals; workers saw constitutional
rights for the nullity and promise they were.

To the extent that the analysis is successful, the assimilation of
rightsholders—superiors and subordinates, public and private—
within a continuous system of legal provision and non-provision

---

[45] *In re Debs*, 158 US 564, had held that the Attorney General of the United States had
standing to seek an injunction against the Pullman strikers, based on no statute or injury
to property; *Lochner v. New York*, 198 US 45 (1905), struck down a ten-hour law for bakers;
Adair v. US, 208 US 161 (1908), struck down a federal statute prohibiting 'yellow dog' contracts in interstate commerce. (These were contracts requiring workers to refrain from
union membership as a condition of employment.)

[46] Victoria Hattam, *Labor Visions and State Power: The Origins of Business Unionism in the
United States* (Princeton, 1993); and Forbath, 'The Shaping of the American Labor
Movement'.

has important implications for the study of both master and servant law and American constitutionalism. The first implication is for the usual disconnection between these two, which is, in a word, untenable. The core constitutional principle of rights is not comprehensible except in the presence of non-constitutional forms of regulation that activate rights in concrete situations. Moreover, what are conventionally seen as purely structural features of the constitution—judicial review and dual courts and the force of statutes, for example—are now seen to be integral to the network of rights that organizes the system as a whole.

Another implication is for the place of master and servant law and its eventual overturning in American constitutional history. The famous *Carolene Products* footnote, which in 1938 announced the Supreme Court's new dedication to civil rights and liberties in the wake of the demise of liberty of contract, has been singled out for its 'clairvoyance' about the Court's agenda for the next half-century.[47] Our analysis suggests that this train of events, if not a *necessity*, was at least a more forcefully logical and non-opportunistic one than is sometimes presented. Without the removal of the many 'exceptions' to the rules of personal liberty provided in common law to masters and others, there was only scant freedom of speech or assembly or jury trial to protect. With their removal, the overriding accomplishment of the American labour movement, the 'rights revolution' that followed was all but foreordained.

As a last point, it is worth underscoring the fact that the distribution of rights in the United States, during the nineteenth century and otherwise, is a normative expression of the complicated skein of legally enforcible privileges that ties officers to one another and to the citizenry. This system has been schematized above, rather than thoroughly traced out, something that would need to be done for any particular episode in history. It is possible that a strong case can be made for the proposition that by the mid-twentieth century the categories 'officers' and 'non-officers', even as analytically defined, corresponded more closely to a division between 'government' and 'citizens', 'public' and 'private', and 'powers' and 'rights' than was the case 100 years earlier. What

---

[47] See, for example, David P. Currie, *The Constitution in the Supreme Court: The Second Century, 1888–1986* (Chicago, 1990), 244. The footnote is n. 4 in *United States v. Carolene Products Co.*, 304 US 144 (1938), 152–3.

Part IV
LANDLORDS AND TENANTS

13

Urban House Tenure and Litigation in Nineteenth-Century Britain

DAVID ENGLANDER

Nowhere has the assertion of social rights encountered greater resistance than in respect of rental tenures. Landlords and property owners appear to have bucked the trend towards greater social protection that was so distinctive a feature of advanced industrial society in the generation before the First World War. Tenants of rental properties were largely unaffected by the growth of collective authority and the extension of public support beyond the protection of political and juridical rights. Rent regulation remained a private affair. In the relationship of landlord and tenant dwellings were let in accordance with the rules of property and contract. The burden of rent and the poverty of rent payers were not considered. The landlord as the owner of the dwelling could fix rentals at a figure of his or her choosing. Where a tenant declined to pay the rent, the landlord was empowered to distrain upon his goods and evict the defaulter. Upon expiry of the lease the landlord could resume possession of his property and refuse to renew the lease for any or no reason. The competition between landlords was supposed to protect the tenant against the imposition of extortionate rents.

There was little correspondence between theory and practice. The rental market was not a free market. The difficulties tenants experienced in securing complete information of competitive offers, the custom in many communities of terminating leases and moving on one particular day a year, the segregation of immigrant and income groups in certain localities, had created semi-monopolistic conditions. The rental market was characterized by inequalities, frictions, and lagging adjustments in which the lower income groups in the big cities were provided with substandard housing at a relatively high cost, in defiance of legally prescribed standards of sanitation and safety. The law of landlord and tenant was feudal in origin and framed to protect property owners against deficient tenants. From Henry III to Queen Victoria measures were enacted to create an effective and efficient means of distraint and eviction. The right of distress, aptly described as 'one of the few survivals of self-help in modern legal systems', empowered the landlord to enter the property of a defaulter, impound his or her goods, and, if the rent remained unpaid, sell the goods and satisfy his claim for rent out of the proceeds.[1] Violence to secure entry was prohibited but, once inside, the law sanctioned the use of force and also gave the landlord extraordinary powers of forced entry into the homes of others to seize goods and chattels that had been unlawfully secreted to escape seizure for arrears of rent. Comparable provision respecting the landlord's security for his rent was embodied in Scots law.[2]

Eviction, by contrast, required the sanction of the courts. Having by experience found it detrimental to peace and order to allow landlords to turn out their refractory tenants by force, legislators took steps to place the rights and processes of eviction under the control of the courts. Landlords seeking to recover possession were required to advise the tenant of the termination of the tenure, either on the grounds that the period of tenure had expired or by failure of the tenant to meet his obligations, accompanied by a written notice to quit. In the event that the tenant failed to deliver possession within a reasonable time, the landlord had perforce to warn the tenant of his intention to apply to the courts for an order of ejectment.

The proprietor's position was formidable. The rights of the landlord pre-empted those of all other creditors. The privileged position which the landlord occupied was underwritten not only by exceptional powers of distress, but also by the enactment of new laws. The Small Tenements Recovery Act, 1838, one of the most significant but barely noticed pieces of early Victorian legislation, provided for a cheap and expeditious means of summary eviction for owners of working-class houses. The hitherto protracted and expensive procedure was simplified, abbreviated, and reduced in cost. Once an order had been granted, the weekly tenant had around four weeks to surrender the property prior to

[1] Quotation from A. C. Jacobs, 'Landlord and Tenant', in E. R. A. Seligman (ed.), *Encyclopaedia of the Social Sciences*, 15 vols. (New York, 1933), ix. 146 (*b*).

[2] David Englander, *Landlord and Tenant in Urban Britain, 1838–1918* (Oxford, 1983), 30.

the forcible ejectment of himself, his family, and their possessions. Scottish landlords, too, found the legislature sympathetic towards their claims for an ever more summary form of eviction, the House-Letting and Rating Act of 1911 providing for the ejectment of defaulters within forty-eight hours! These powers were used extensively. Warrants for eviction in late Victorian London were in the ratio of 1 to every 1,818 inhabitants; in New York (metropolitan area) the ratio was 1 to every 92 inhabitants; in Glasgow the ratio was 1 to every 54 inhabitants.[3]

Intervention into the relationship of landlord and tenant was generally on behalf of the former rather than the latter. Such reforms as were introduced were more concerned with questions of order and authority rather than with the redefinition of an unjust relationship. Apart from legislation to protect goods belonging to subtenants and other occupants from indiscriminate distress, measures were introduced to bring the broker and his myrmidons under the control of the courts. Until the passage of the Law of Distress Amendment Act of 1888, there was practically no remedy against the oppressive acts of brokers and their men. Thereafter no one could act as a broker or bailiff without a licence from the county court. Tumult and disorder may well have diminished in consequence, although breaches of the peace continued to be provoked by the misconduct of bailiffs and their assistants. The common law right of the landlord to seize, without legal process, the personal chattels of his tenants for non-payment of rent was not otherwise affected. There was nothing in English or Scottish law that was comparable with the German Civil Code which gave tenants the right to sue for damages or reduce rents unilaterally if repairs etc. were not made in reasonable time.[4]

The relationship between landlord and tenant was unequal and always potentially oppressive. The landlord, fortified by the courts and constabulary, was well placed to control those required to purchase his services. How did landlords use their authority? Uniformity of practice should not be assumed. The possession of power is one thing; its exercise is another. Even in an asymmetrical relationship there was scope for considerable diversity. The rental market, as I hope to show, relied upon negotiation and

---

[3] Ratios derived from data presented ibid., and from Richard H. Chused's contribution to this volume.

[4] See the contribution by Tilman Repgen in this volume, pp. 397–9.

compromise as well as crude coercion. The concentration upon legal and market relationships should not, however, obscure the importance of the parties as social actors with particular value systems that were not always consistent with the idea that the allocation of house space should be determined entirely by the level of demand.

The following account proceeds from a brief review of recent research to an examination of urban tenurial relationships in the late nineteenth and early twentieth centuries. The focus is upon the situation of the working-class tenant. The middle classes, though often at odds with their landlords—particularly in respect of commercial and business properties—were largely unaffected by the legal and economic relations that are discussed in the essay below. Its aims are to explore the nature of the rent contract and the ways in which the contracting parties interacted with one another. Attention is fixed upon the dynamics of the landlord–tenant relationship, upon the available strategies and the circumstances of their application, and upon the shifts and adjustments that informed the process of negotiation. Litigation in this context, it will be seen, was more likely to enforce obligations than to establish or protect rights. Its importance lay in the realm of political theatre and personal defence strategies rather than in the substance of judicial decision-making.

Rental tenure: recent research

The conflicts generated by the operation of the rental market have in recent years begun to attract scholarly attention. Historians of housing have started to widen the focus of their studies to capture more than the welfare and social policy aspects of public housing. The development of the relationship between private landlords and their tenants has, for example, been presented as critical in the evolution of social housing in France, while in Britain the structure of urban landlordism and its relative political weakness have been identified as equally central to the emergence of owner-occupation as the predominant form of housing tenure.[5] By con-

---

[5] Roger-Henri Guerrand, *Propriétaires et locataires: Les Origines du logement social en France, 1850–1914* (Paris, 1987); M. J. Daunton, *A Property Owning Democracy: Housing in Britain* (London, 1987).

trast, scholars who are primarily interested in tenancy reform, and its implications for the shaping of public policy, have given priority to the growth of working-class housing reform pressure groups and the emergence of tenants' movements both in Europe and in the anglophone world. The exploration of these movements has been the subject of several detailed studies. Their origins, membership, growth, and character have been documented and their implications assessed. Approaches vary. Rent strikes have been studied in relation to the creation of a new strategic repertoire of collective action, an innovation in the forms of labour protest with an important bearing on the theoretical issues concerning the class-consciousness of urban workers.[6] The study of conflicts between landlords and tenants, it is further suggested, not only supplies insights into the problems of worker mobilization and action, but also takes us towards a better understanding of popular attitudes towards housing reform in general, even though the resultant conclusions are sometimes divergent.[7] The need to locate such differences within a broader perspective has not only been recognized but is beginning to find expression in the attempt to set the social history of house tenure within a more explicitly comparative framework.[8]

Rent strikes and tenants' movements inevitably direct attention towards the spatial relations of classes. Although the connection between the urban environment and the incidence of social conflict remains uncertain, there is now a growing body of research which pinpoints an association between worker radicalism and the character of the local community. Particular emphasis has been given to the ways in which the growth of neighbourhood organization and the network of relationships it sustained served to

[6] See Bert Moorhouse, Mary Wilson, and Chris Chamberlain, 'Rent Strikes: Direct Action and the Working Class', in Ralph Miliband and John Savile (eds.), *The Socialist Register* (London, 1972), 133–56; Steven Shifferes, 'Tenants' Struggles in the 1930s', MA dissertation (University of Warwick, 1975); Ronald Lawson (ed.), *The Tenant Movement in New York City, 1904–1984* (New Brunswick, NJ, 1985).

[7] Contrast, for example, the dissimilarities in working-class attitudes towards housing reform derived from their study of urban tenant movements in different national settings by Englander, *Landlord and Tenant*, and Susanna Magri, 'Le Mouvement des locataires à Paris et dans sa banlieue, 1919–1925', *Le Mouvement social*, 137 (1986), 55–76.

[8] See, in particular, Terry Robert Grigg, 'Landlord and Tenant Relations, Melbourne 1860–1980', Ph.D. thesis (La Trobe University, Melbourne, 1994). See, too, the introduction in M. J. Daunton (ed.), *Housing the Workers: A Comparative Perspective, 1850–1914* (Leicester, 1990), and the conclusion in Colin G. Pooley (ed.), *Housing Strategies in Europe, 1880–1930* (Leicester, 1992).

extend work-based solidarities and reinforce class identities. Experiences shared among friends and neighbours in pubs and clubs, factories and workshops, streets and localities, were critical in the formation and transmission of the popular traditions on which labour mobilization depended. The greater durability of radicalism among Parisian tenants after the First World War, or, indeed, the implantation of post-war communism, are sometimes cited as an expression of a new community consciousness.[9] In Britain, too, the importance of residential solidarities in enlarging the possibilities for collective action have also found recognition. The transformation of urban space, the separation of housing and labour markets, and the creation of class-segregated residential neighbourhoods in which working people created new institutions and new social and cultural relationships, it is argued, supplied the basis for the reconstruction of closely integrated and relatively autonomous communities in which class loyalties and collective capacities were pronounced.[10] The disposition towards tenant radicalism, it is sometimes suggested, was greater in these communities than elsewhere. Even so, we may wonder why, in view of the wholesale reorganization of spatial relations in nineteenth-century British cities, rent agitation and tenant community mobilization were not more widespread. In short, why was tenant radicalism so limited? Is it possible that urban working-class communities were less cohesive than their social geography might indicate? Is it possible, too, that legal and economic relationships served to discourage collective action and constrain tenants rather than provoke protest and movements for reform? The following essay will consider both possibilities. It will be suggested that the individualizing tendencies of the rental market militated against organized resistance particularly in working-class neighbourhoods

[9] Magri, 'Le Mouvement des locataires à Paris'. On social bases of worker radicalism, see G. Jacquemet, *Belleville au XIXe siècle* (Paris, 1984), and T. Stovall, *The Rise of the Paris Red Belt* (Los Angeles, 1990); also discussion in G. Noiriel, *Workers in French Society in the 19th and 20th Centuries* (New York, 1990), 42–5.

[10] On urban transformation see R. Lawton, 'The Population of Liverpool in the Mid-Nineteenth Century', *Transactions of the Historical Society of Lancashire and Cheshire*, 197 (1955), 93–4; R. M. Prichard, *Housing and the Spatial Structure of the City* (Cambridge, 1976); James Vance, Jr., 'Housing the Worker: Determinative and Contingent Ties in Nineteenth-Century Birmingham', *Economic Geography*, 43 (1967), 95–127; Gareth Stedman Jones, *Outcast London: A Study in the Relationship between Classes in Victorian England* (Oxford, 1971). Note, too, the observations of J. E. Cronin, 'Coping with Labour, 1918–26', in id. and Jonathan Schneer (eds.), *Social Conflict and Political Order in Modern Britain* (London, 1982), 123–5.

which were often less socially homogeneous than is sometimes imagined.

The sources available are fragmentary and on the whole unsatisfactory. Landlords and tenants have left few records from which their relationship might be reconstructed. Press reports, periodical publications, parliamentary and local inquiries, though they provide some insights into their everyday dealings, are all too often muddied by the public debates on questions of housing reform and urban improvement to which they were originally addressed. Court proceedings, usually well covered in the 'police intelligence' columns of local newspapers, invariably represent the parties in their most antagonistic phase. To the best of my knowledge, historians in Britain have not, as yet, located a wealth of documentation comparable with the business records of local estate agents which Terry Grigg has used so effectively in his study of housing management strategies in the private sector in Melbourne, Australia.[11] Contemporary social investigation, though not exclusively concerned with the tenurial relations, did collect considerable information on matters pertaining to rental properties. Charles Booth's comprehensive survey of life and labour in the metropolis included substantial material on housing, rents, and landord–tenant relations. Booth's street survey of east London, undertaken in connection with the measurement of poverty, also recorded the social characteristics of the population, its living standards, lifestyle, ethnic composition, and territorial location. That information, once confined to Booth's unpublished notebooks, has recently become more widely available and forms the basis of the following discussion.[12]

Collective action: problems and prospects

Landlords and their agents, in London as in Paris, were rarely presented as anything but odious creatures. In the cartoons of

[11] Grigg, 'Landlord and Tenant Relations', ch. 5. On housing management issues in urban Britain, see in general Englander, *Landlord and Tenant*, and M. J. Daunton, *House and Home in the Victorian City: Working Class Housing, 1850–1914* (London, 1983), chs. 6–7.

[12] All the London street references given below are accessible by name in Rosemary O'Day, Judith Ford, and David Englander (eds.), *Charles Booth's Poverty Notebooks: A Calendar for the Computer* (CD-Rom, 1997). Henceforward, for references to street names given in the body of the text please refer to this CD-Rom.

Daumier or in the plays of Shaw, the rent collector was represented as a hateful person, a heartless and avaricious grinder of
the faces of the poor. Property owners in such accounts were not
participants in a socially benign form of investment, but a parasitical and malignant influence upon the virtuous and hardpressed householder. Many no doubt were. Rental properties that
were unfit for human habitation when let were a commonplace
of Victorian social observation. The tenants of such properties
seemed equally unworthy. Tenurial issues, indeed, were frequently
defined in terms of the alleged character defects and antisocial
conduct of the low-income householder. 'Some of my readers',
the author of a popular legal manual remarked, 'may think,
perhaps, that I insist on this point at a length quite too tiresome.
But let them consider the conduct of many occupiers of dwellings
in England, and they will not be at all surprised to hear that one
has the greatest difficulty in the world to convince many people
that they have no right to damage the house they live in. Don't
you know many householders who think nothing of driving a lot
of nails into the doors of their houses, who knock pieces of plaster
out of the walls, cut up the woodwork to suit their own convenience, and commit a variety of other wasteful acts?' The taking
of doors, banisters, fences, and floorboards for firewood was
regularly reported as characteristic of the worst class of tenant.[13]
Children were represented as being even more vicious than the
parents. In this discourse, the destructive classes were invariably
minors, hacking away at stair-rails, carving their names on
window sills, smashing down doors, and employing knives, boots,
and diverse means of self-expression. Landlords hated and feared
them, and discriminated against households that included them.[14]
Respectable people, above all working-class tenants, did not identify with these residual elements nor with the coercive powers that
were upheld as necessary for their control. Nothing, it seemed,
provided more ample confirmation of the necessity for the legal
privileges possessed by the landlord, than the ruffianly conduct of
the lowest class of householder. Low-income tenants of this sort

[13] See, for example, Ernest Street, Mile End Old Town, and Cottage Street, Poplar,
Charles Booth's Poverty Notebooks. Quotation from *Cassell's Family Lawyer, Being a Popular Exposition of the Civil Law of Great Britain*, 3 vols., special edn. (London, n.d.), i. 134.

[14] See, for example, Queen's Place, Stutfield Street, St George's-in-the-East; and also
Columbia Square, Bethnal Green, *Charles Booth's Poverty Notebooks*.

were considered to be as much the agents as the victims of their fearful condition. Incapable of improvement, such people were as menacing as the properties in which they were resident.

The situation of the Irish gave particular cause for concern. All that was negative and fearful about city life found expression in contemporary representations of Irish areas of settlement. Irish communities were identified as dirty, disreputable, and dangerous. Filth was a distinctive feature. Rook Street, Poplar, for example, with an all-Irish population, was noted for its drunkenness, poverty, and dirt where 'children could be seen running about naked playing in the gutter'. Nearby in Sophia Street lived a similar population described as 'literally the scum of the town'.[15] With dirt went disorder. Rent collecting in such quarters was considered both dangerous and disagreeable in consequence of the lawlessness of the occupants. 'Irish attacks of broom and poker' and vicious assaults were said to be commonplace within what were perceived as volatile and ill-policed communities. Areas like the Fenian Barracks—the very name signified danger and disloyalty—were a nightmare. This group of streets, situated near the Limehouse Cut, Booth was told, 'sent more police to hospital than any other block in London'. The men who lived there, said his informant, 'are not human; they are wild beasts'. On which Booth commented: 'But being Irish they are at least human to this extent, that if one of their number is taken by the police a rescue is attempted.'[16] The Irish, indeed, set a standard below which civilization ceased. The description of Kinnear Dwellings as unlettable due to the Irish presence gave vent to more than a deeply rooted tradition of intolerance.[17] It also expressed widely held fears of unrest, violence, and disorder that were given currency by the revision of property rights, once held inviolable, in response to the Irish Land Campaign. John Ruskin, who owned several rental properties in Marylebone, wondered—only half jocularly—whether an urban Rent War might not be long in the making. 'I know I have the right to keep anybody from living in them unless they pay me', he told readers of *Fors Clavigera*; 'only suppose some day the Irish faith, that people ought to be

---

[15] See, too, Wartons Place, Stepney, and Franklin Street, Bromley by Bow, *Charles Booth's Poverty Notebooks.*

[16] Charles Booth, *Life and Labour of the People in London*, 17 vols., Religious Influences Series (London, 1903), i. 47.

[17] See Bakers Alley, Bromley by Bow, *Charles Booth's Poverty Notebooks.*

lodged for nothing, should become an English one also—where
would my money be?'[18]

Persistent fears which do not with hindsight appear realistic
should not, however, be dismissed as no more than an expression
of the overwrought and febrile imagination of the propertied
classes. The myths, images, and stereotype representations of
urban tenurial relations, as several scholars have noted, served to
mobilize public opinion in favour of some policies and against
others and possessed a dynamism that compelled a response from
those interested in public policy.[19] The idea of a concerted and
possibly violent campaign to restrict the rights of urban landlords
was not, however, entirely fanciful. Parisian tenants had in the
spring of 1848 organized a large-scale co-ordinated refusal to pay
rents which was with difficulty suppressed. The social policies of
the Commune—rent control, and a three-year moratorium on
debt repayments—were not only prompted by collective tenant
action, but again underscored the plastic quality of so-called inviolable property rights.[20] But whereas the influence of the French
example remains to be established, that of the Irish is incontrovertible.[21] Irish land legislation and the methods applied to contain
it suggested possibilities for comparable action to a nascent socialist movement that was in search of a popular constituency.

In Paris and in London the housing crisis of the 1880s presented
opportunities for popular mobilization which socialists found
intriguing. Rumours of rent strikes, petitions, and organized vig-
ilantism circulated widely. Marxists in both capitals considered the
case for a rents agitation particularly promising. In the spring of
1881 the Paris police chief reported the formation of 'revolutionary committees' to conduct an urban rent war against landlords;
in the winter the Democratic Federation announced that 'it had
taken up the question of Fair Rents in London and intend to carry
out a vigorous agitation for Rental and Sanitary Reform'. Tenants'

---

[18] John Ruskin, *Fors Clavigera: Letters to the Workmen and Labourers of Great Britain*, 10 vols.
(Orpington, 1895), i, letter 4, 1 Apr. 1871, p. 12. On Cabinet expressions of similar anxieties, see J. L. Hammond, *Gladstone and the Irish Nation* (London, 1938), 93.

[19] See J. A. Yelling, *Slums and Slum Clearance in Victorian London* (London, 1986).

[20] Michelle Perrot, 'Les Ouvriers, l'habitat et la ville au XIXe siècle', in *La Question du
logement et le mouvement ouvrier français* (Paris, 1981), 23.

[21] The influence of the French example may not have been lost on English radicalism.
As Royden Harrison has shown, the doings of the Communards were monitored closely
by workers and sympathizers on this side of the Channel. See *The English Defence of the
Commune* (London, 1973).

leagues were to be formed, action co-ordinated to resist the levying of distress, and public space reserved for the registration of protest. Street theatre was to include dramatic demonstrations of the evicted and related performances to create and inform opinion. The authorities received a good deal of evidence of the growing unrest among working people and there was much loose talk of 'Plans of Campaign' and 'No Rent' strikes, most of it of little consequence. Socialists in Paris quickly fell out among themselves. Socialists in London found tenants fearful and resistant. The most substantial attempt to organize tenants was abandoned after four months because, as one of the organizers explained, 'they found that they were becoming the persecutors of those they wished to benefit as when pressure was put on the landlords to improve their premises, they either evicted the tenants or put an extra amount on the rent'.[22]

The idea of the rent strike as an instrument of mass radicalization, however, continued to engage certain elements of the libertarian left. Parisian anarchists formed flying squads to assist absconding tenants and composed stirring marches to urge them on. London anarchists issued landlords with blood-curdling notices and cultivated a rent-free lifestyle. In both cities unpopular landlords were burned in effigy.[23] The effect of all this was negligible. Property owners were not intimidated and tenants not inspired. There was no metropolitan equivalent of the agrarian radicalism that transformed Irish land tenure. Collective resistance remained exceptional. Tenant grievances were not readily translatable into public issues. There was no debate on tenancy reform. Tenant claims continued to be marginalized by the stereotypical representations of the dominant proprietorial interest groups and perhaps by a labour movement which, on the basis of such unpromising experiences, found no pressing need to rethink its bias in favour of workplace organization. Tenants, in short, were left to shift for themselves.[24]

[22] Englander, *Landlord and Tenant*, 103–5; Ann-Louis Shapiro, *Housing the Poor of Paris, 1850–1902* (Madison, 1985), 113–15.

[23] Shapiro, *Housing the Poor*, 114; Roger Magraw, *A History of the French Working Class*, 2 vols. (Oxford, 1992), ii. 34; Englander, *Landlord and Tenant*, 104; Little Collingwood Street, Bethnal Green, *Charles Booth's Poverty Notebooks*.

[24] In this respect Londoners were more persistent than Parisians, who only returned to the problems of tenant organization shortly before the outbreak of the First World War. See Magri, 'Le Mouvement des locataires à Paris'.

Fragmentation and the operation of the rental market

Landlords included men and women, some whose incomes were supplemented by rent from a few houses and those with extensive portfolios of rental properties. The latter, though, were exceptional. Rental property ownership seems to have been widely diffused throughout the middle classes. Most landlords were small-scale investors drawn from members of the professions, shopkeepers, publicans, contractors, and retired persons. Properties were held in small units. Individual proprietors generally held less than half a dozen properties.[25] London displayed a greater range and variety of holdings than anywhere else. The metropolitan mosaic included aristocratic and corporate ground landlords, small and substantial freeholders, and large numbers of leaseholders. The diversified pattern of rental property ownership implied considerable variation in tenants' experiences. Some landlords lived locally and personally collected their weekly rents; others preferred to delegate authority to professional agents who worked on commission. The multiformity of management practices was likewise pronounced.

The relationship between landlord and tenant was not only unequal; it was often very confusing. In multi-occupied houses landlords sometimes tried to avoid the cost of employing an agent by devolving responsibility for the collection of rents upon one tenant who, for a small consideration or special privilege, became liable for the rents from the various sublessees.[26] Role confusion, division, and cleavage were, moreover, sustained by disputes over the sharing of space and amenities. 'Both exasperated families live on the edge of bitter feud', wrote Maud Pember Reeves of terraced accommodation in Lambeth where the upstairs tenants were forced to pass through both the rooms of the lower tenants whenever they left or entered the house. Washing facilities in particular were a source of dissension. 'Differences which result in "not speaking"', she observed, 'often begin over the copper.'[27]

[25] N. Morgan and M. J. Daunton, 'Landlords in Glasgow: A Study of 1900', *Business History*, 25 (1983), 264–81; B. Elliot, D. Macrone, and V. Skelton, 'Property and Politics in Edinburgh, 1875–1975', in J. Garrard (ed.), *The Middle Class in Politics* (Farnborough, 1978), 99–109; and see references in Englander, *Landlord and Tenant*, 51–2.

[26] See, for example, Prices Court, Bethnal Green, *Charles Booth's Poverty Notebooks*; Maud Pember Reeves, *Round about a pound a week* (London, 1913), 29–30, 37–8.

[27] Pember Reeves, *Round about a pound a Week*, 32–3.

The divisive effects of the free market in rental property did not only affect the poorest elements of the population. Those who were able to often took advantage of the market, either to reduce living costs or to secure better value for money. The high level of residential mobility among working-class tenants in part represented the search for cheaper and better accommodation rather than the restless instability noted by middle-class observers. In urban Scotland, where inflexible house-letting arrangements prevented a similar expression of consumer preferences, tension between landlord and tenant ran high. The sense of frustration that arose from the discrepancy between fixed long-term tenancies and short-term contracts of employment was absent from tenurial relations in England and Wales where landlords were rather more market-responsive and housing management practices more varied.[28]

Between landlord and tenant in urban Scotland there stood a class of professional managers responsible for the regulation and control of tenants, rent collection and property maintenance, and the payment of insurance and local taxation. Estate agents appear to have been used less extensively for the management of working-class housing in English cities. The repertoire of proprietorial practices in London, for example, served to balkanize and isolate tenants. As in the labour market, so in the rental market, differentials exerted a negative influence upon the formation of residential solidarities. The averages with which historians must of necessity operate cover a wide area in which significant variations are too often concealed. At street level, however, it was the absence of uniformity which contemporaries found noteworthy. The social homogeneity said to be characteristic of occupational communities is not always apparent in Booth's London. Brook Street, Stepney, for example, was in terms of occupation and residence extremely mixed. Apart from shopkeepers, its householders included a coffee house keeper, cooper, tailor, glazier, stevedore, casual labourer, publican, old clothes dealer, bootmaker, sailmaker, packer, ballastman, street seller, butcher, char, ratcatcher, and female old clothes dealer. Fuller Street, Bethnal Green, too, contained enormous distinctions. 'This street', wrote Booth's

---

[28] A detailed examination of the Scottish tenurial system will be found in Englander, *Landlord and Tenant*, ch. 8.

assistant, 'runs from Bethnal Green Road to Hare Street. The two ends of the street are a great contrast, the north part (lower numbers) being nice houses—some nearly new—& inhabited by people in resp. & comf. circs. The south end (higher numbers) contains some exceedingly bad houses . . . old, dark, dilapidated, & filthy, & crowded with a wretchedly poor & low lot, mostly thieves. These houses have about 6 rooms & 2 cellars (sometimes inhabited).' The basis for social solidarity in streets in which neighbours were rarely workmates, and in which income differences were pronounced and cultural distinctions wide, may well have derived from the need for the creation of shared survival strategies.[29] Neighbourliness, however, was constrained by the influence of the rental housing market which remained a principal source of division and insecurity.

Booth's analysis of London street by street disclosed striking dissimilarities in the rental value of similar properties on the same street or in adjacent streets. Even within so-called mean streets, informants reported considerable variety in the rents obtained. Brook Street, Stepney, with its mixed population, displayed anything but the dull uniformity represented by the image of the mean street. The size of houses was as varied as the population, ranging from three to eight or nine rooms with rents from 6s. to 16s. per week and sublet single rooms at 2s. 6d. to 3s. each. High Street, Poplar, was equally distinctive 'Very varied class of houses', wrote Booth's assistant. 'Scarcely six consecutive houses alike. Some old fashioned wooden-fronted houses. Private houses let out from 7/6 to about 18/- & shops from 12/- to 25/- per week . . . Very mixed people. From professionals to poor labouring peoples.' In Collingwood Street, by contrast, there was less social differentiation, but rents on four-roomed properties ranged from 5s. 6d. to 7s. 6d.[30] Next-door neighbours might not only pay different rents to the same landlord; they might also be beholden in different measure.

The preference for weekly over annual tenancies gave landlords in working-class London greater flexibility than their compeers on Clydeside in the adjustment of rent levels. Property owners and their agents, when required to raise rents, seem to

---

[29] See Ellen Ross, 'Survival Networks: Women's Neighbourhood Sharing in London before World War I', *History Workshop Journal*, 15 (1983), 4–27.

[30] See, too, Corfield Street, Stepney, *Charles Booth's Poverty Notebooks*.

have preferred to proceed by a strategy of phased or creeping rent increases that preserved differentials and so limited the emergence of an untoward uniformity from which collective resistance might be borne. The widespread opposition provoked by the universal increases made necessary by the revised rating arrangements of 1867–8, disclosed the dangers of rapid large-scale changes and may well have served to moderate the pace and extent of subsequent movements.[31] In New Castle Street, Whitechapel, Booth's informants not only recorded enormous variation in rents: six or seven rooms for 12s. 6d. (Nos. 1–11); four for 7s. or 8s. in Nos. 12 and 13; six rooms for 12s. in No. 15; four rooms and kitchen for 10s. in No. 28—but also found that changes were introduced gradually. 'Old rents are raised when tenants are changed from 8/- to 10/- 10/- to 12/- or more even 16/-.' In some cases, too, rents were graduated in accordance with the length of the tenancy—from 6s. to 10s. in Northampton Street, Stepney— again posing a formidable barrier to concerted action on the part of tenants.

The rent contract, as the above suggests, was more personal and less visible than the labour contract. Landlords, so far from the monsters of popular representation, were a motley crew influenced in varying degrees by ideas of rational economic calculation in dealings with their tenants. Some, by conviction or temperament, managed their properties with great severity. In Egleton Road, Bromley by Bow, for example, tenants were turned out if the rent was a week in arrears. So exacting was the landlord that children from this street were excused attendance at school because their boots had been pawned for rent. In Scottish cities, where housing management operated within an extremely authoritarian framework, weekly tenants in arrears were more likely to be evicted and sold up than in England. In Glasgow, for example, the coercive tradition was so strong that landlords declined to allow arrears to accumulate during severe periods of unemployment in spite of a sharp rise in the proportion of unlet houses.[32] Elsewhere, considerations of economy were outweighed by want of information rather than more punitive priorities. As Grigg has shown in his study of Port Melbourne, landlords and

---

[31] On the unrest among working-class tenants caused by the shift to compounding, see Englander, *Landlord and Tenant*, chs. 5–6.
[32] Ibid. 30–1.

their agents often declined to negotiate lower rent levels even when it made little economic sense to refuse.[33]

In general, though, landlords in urban England exercised a fine discrimination in their dealings with weekly tenants. Much depended on the state of the housing market. Its characteristic long cycles of boom and slump implied periodic shifts in the balance of advantage between landlords and tenants. When houses were scarce landlords could pick and choose to whom they would let. When vacancies were high tenants might please themselves. Market movements, though, did not obviate the need for judgement. Tenants who looked after the property and were punctual with the rent, or at the very least made no attempt to default on payment, were generally regarded as a creditworthy risk during hard times. To retain these valued clients landlords often allowed arrears to mount up during the winter when trade was slow for repayment the following summer when work was more plentiful. It was this elasticity with regard to rent which outweighed all other considerations among casual workers. The quality of housing in nearby model dwellings may have been superior, even affordable, but so long as the management regime took no account of the seasonality of employment, such accommodation lay beyond the reach of the casual poor for whom local credit connections—with shopkeepers as well as landlords—were the staff of life. Tenants, who lived dangerously close to the precipice, were as likely as not to feel beholden to lenient landlords rather than outraged by the wretched accommodation they were forced to accept. Landlords and their agents understood their fears and conducted themselves accordingly. Thus rents were commonly raised on a change of tenancy. Long-standing and reliable tenants, exempted from rent increases, minimized market adjustments and secured to the landlord an uninterrupted flow of income.

The bond of debt that united landlord and tenant sometimes snapped. It was those on the lowest of incomes who were most likely to make the break. The collection of rent might in the worst circumstances then descend into a war as in Whitethorn Street, Poplar, whose transient population rarely acknowledged their obligations, or in Butlers Buildings, Bethnal Green, which Booth's informants described as 'a wretched dirty Court' full of destitute

---

[33] On the unequal distribution of information among market participants, see the illuminating discussion in Grigg, 'Landlord and Tenant Relations', 140–5.

Jews, who 'pay 3/- rent when they like'. In general, two strategies were readily available to would-be defaulters: absconding or intimidation. The first, the moonlight flit, brought about the immediate termination of a stressful relationship and an escape from debt. Its downside was the consequent loss of a clean rent book, widely accepted as a character reference, and the possibility of the loss of a vital credit connection if compelled to remove from the locality. Intimidation, the second strategy, might be expressed through threatening conduct, litigation, and malicious damage to property. Singly, or in combination, all imposed financial penalties upon house owners. The tenant might in the first place threaten to turn informer and involve the local health authorities in order to persuade errant landlords to become more amenable. If the landlord remained obdurate, the tenant might begin vexatious litigation to improve his bargaining power. The scope here depended upon the character of the court and its procedures. Among lower-income tenants in Scotland, as I have shown elsewhere, the latter was much the preferred option.[34] By such means the eviction process was delayed, landlord losses increased, and the opportunity for the application of further pressure was created. The period between the service of notice to quit and the execution of a warrant for ejectment was, in urban Britain, the most favourable moment for vandalizing house property. Landlords knew it and made much of it both to justify and protect their special privileges. Tenants, in seeking to strengthen their negotiating position by threatened and actual malicious damage, sometimes prevented forcible ejectment, but in doing so fortified arguments for the preservation and extension of the landlord's special remedies.

The strategies outlined above expressed both the despair and isolation of those at the very bottom of the rental market. Beyond their poverty little is known about them. Householders in more stable tenures did not identify with their stratagems, at least in public. The idea, frequently advanced by property owner interests, that the coercive powers of the landlord were reserved for the discipline and control of the vicious and dissolute touched upon widely held status anxieties and worked against the construction of broader solidarities. Nomads circulating around inner

---

[34] Englander, *Landlord and Tenant*, ch. 3.

city areas of intense housing stress to whom were attributed all the characteristics of the urban degenerate were not considered members of a mobilizable community. Transients, without traditions rooted in trades or in stable neighbourhood networks, they lacked both the material and cultural resources that made for concerted political action. The collective capacities of the more settled population, however, were not much greater. The neighbourboods analysed by Ross for late Victorian London were not only self-regarding or at any rate defensive in character, they were less homogeneous than might be supposed. Neighbourhoods, though capable of collective assistance, were not cell-like units awaiting activation. Neighbours, in nineteenth-century London, as in eighteenth-century Paris, offered temporary accommodation as families shot the moon, obstructed bailiffs, even engaged in ritualized expressions of defiance, but rarely united for a concerted campaign over rents and repairs.[35] The rental market in fact generated spatial and social tensions, encouraged division and fragmentation, and, in large part, immobilized tenants to a degree that was much greater than is sometimes imagined.

Conclusion

The legal relationship of landlord and tenant posed formidable obstacles to the formation of effective tenants' associations in nineteenth-century Britain. The law gave the landlord exceptional remedies for securing the rent. The tenant, by contrast, was denied rights but loaded with duties. Apart from the coercive legal framework, the structure of property ownership and multiplicity of management strategies limited the scope for collective action. Unequal though it was, the relationship between landlord and tenant was not, however, uncontested. Negotiation and compromise were constant. Landlord strategies found expression in public discourse and in individualizing initiatives both of which served to fragment and disable tenants. For low-income tenants the personalization of the relationship was central to the creation of a viable survival strategy. Nevertheless, it was an unsatisfactory relationship in which 'the capacities of the parties to meet each other's expectations so rarely coincided that tension and suspicion were

---

[35] Ross, 'Survival Networks', 6, 18; David Garrioch, *Neighbourhood and Community in Paris, 1740–1790* (Cambridge, 1986), 44–5, 50–1; Grigg, 'Landlord and Tenant Relations', 112.

to remain perennial factors'.[36] Landlords in the main possessed superior resources to smother conflict and retain the advantage. Collective resistance generally occurred when the burden of rent payments rose dramatically and was compressed in time and space. Universal rent increases imposed on whole streets or neighbourhoods provoked such responses in English cities, and it was the universality of Scottish property management policies which seems to have encouraged the higher level of organized tenant resistance on Clydeside in the generation before the First World War. The resort to litigation, a characteristic feature of such contests, must be seen as part of the repertoire of protest, a means to dramatize conflict and focus public attention, rather than the pursuit of a legal remedy. Until 1915 the law provided no such remedy. The introduction of statutory tenancies in that year, in response to the unrest produced by the uniform imposition of rent increases in centres of armament manufacture, constitutes a turning point in the development of tenurial relations. The Rent Act of 1915 fixed rents at the pre-war standard.

The national emergency created by the First World War transformed the bargaining power of the householder as producer and consumer. Tenants in Britain, particularly working-class wives who invariably represented the household in everyday dealings with landlords and their agents, seized the opportunity to reinvent themselves, assume a new patriotic identity, and broaden the terms of the debate on tenurial relations to encompass the rights of tenants rather than the powers of landlords. In this redefined discourse landlords rather than tenants became the wreckers, not of property, but of the war effort. Landlords, by their selfish action in raising rents and evicting soldiers' dependants, were represented as acting in a manner that was prejudicial to war production and troop morale. The government accepted the claim that tenants had rights that ought to be protected.

How, though, does the British experience compare with that of other countries? The origins and development of rent regulation between the wars still awaits its historian.[37] The studies of French,

---

[36] Grigg, 'Landlord and Tenant Relations', 93.

[37] For the contours, see E. L. Schaub, 'The Regulation of Rentals during the War Period', *Journal of Political Economy*, 28 (1920), 1–36, and the surveys undertaken by the International Labour Office, *European Housing Problems since the War, 1914–1923, Housing Situation in the United States*, and *Housing Policy in Europe*, Studies and Reports, ser. G, Nos. 1–3 (Geneva, 1924–30).

German, and American tenants included in this volume, however, underscore the point that there was no unilinear movement towards rent regulation. Nevertheless, the most significant extension of governmental intervention into urban housing was a war-related development, and one, moreover, that touched non-belligerent nations as well as those countries that were at war. The French in 1914 led the way with a moratorium on rents not unlike that introduced in previous national emergencies, to be followed by the introduction of rent control legislation in Great Britain, New South Wales, and Russia in 1915. Italian tenants secured a partial moratorium in 1916 while protective legislation was introduced in the Netherlands, Switzerland, Sweden, and Germany in 1917. By the close of the fighting most European countries had laws restricting rents and evictions. The conditions which made rent control necessary during the war became more acute in its aftermath, prompting new measures in India, the Latin American states, and the United States.

The system of rent control varied from country to country. In some countries it took no account of income and military service; in others it was selective. Sometimes protection embraced buildings rather than persons and sometimes it was area-specific. The progress and persistence was equally varied, being determined by the extent of monetary inflation and problems of post-war adjustment, the political programmes of governments, the severity of the effects of war, the difficulties of the transition to peace, and the political power of tenants. The latter, we have seen, was considerable.

The agitation that produced rent control was sustained thereafter by an equally vigorous popular campaign to enforce the law and extend its scope. In Britain, as in France, new areas of expertise were developed in order to police exceptionally complex measures of rent regulation and persuade tenants to overcome their suspicions of the legal process. In both countries, too, the tenants' movement sought to act simultaneously as an advisory service and as a pressure group concerned to widen the basis of rent regulation and strengthen tenurial rights. As in France, the post-war housing shortage and the widespread feeling of insecurity it engendered fuelled a campaign that was as much concerned with improved security of tenure as with the prevention of rent increases. By 1924, the British Parliament had enacted legislation affecting rents on at least five occasions, and restrictions were more extensive than ever. The limits of rental were doubled in 1919 and trebled the following year with the result that there were something like 500,000 more houses under control in 1920 than there had been five years earlier.[38]

The exposure of abuse and recovery of illegal increases, the major preoccupation of tenants' associations up and down the country, served to mobilize opinion in favour of the retention of rent regulation as a permanent feature of post-war housing policy. Special measures for the composition of differences, comparable with the commissions of arbitration that were established in France, or the special courts that were created in certain parts of the United States of America, encountered fierce opposition in Britain. Although favoured by enlightened opinion within local government and the judiciary as a means of reducing tension and thereby smoothing the path towards gradual de-control, tenancy courts were unacceptable to landlords who regarded them as a dangerous form of socialism.[39] Ironically, it was the obduracy of British proprietors, as much as the agitation of their tenants, that helped to sustain opinion in favour of continued statutory protection.

---

[38] *Report of Inter-departmental Committee on the Rent Restrictions Acts*, PP 1930–1, xvii. 15–20.
[39] See Englander, *Landlord and Tenant*, 312–15.

14

Landlords, Tenants, and the Law
Paris, 1850–1920

Susanna Magri

French historians have paid little attention to relations between landlords and tenants and how they were regulated by the state during the nineteenth century and in the first half of the twentieth century. The subject is touched on, admittedly, in many works which deal mainly with Paris. Various socio-economic studies have looked at the evolution of housing conditions and rents, the latter being considered in terms of capitalist profit, income, or expenditure.[1] Social history has regarded landlords as an element of the bourgeoisie and tenants as workers. This category of tenant has benefited at the expense of the rest from what is a very full history of the working class, the revival of which has led to investigation of forms of private life as well as of sociability and collective action.[2] And studies dealing with government policy in the area of working-class housing have examined demands and conflicts, seeking to define the involvement of tenants in the origin and development of such policy.[3] However, no work has taken landlord–tenant relations as its specific subject, let alone the use that landlords and tenants made of the law, although there is a large

---

A modified version of this essay has been published as 'Les Propriétaires, les locataires, la loi: Jalons pour une analyse sociologique des rapports de location, Paris 1850–1920', *Revue Française de sociologie*, 37 (1996), 397–418.

[1] Michel Lescure, *Les Banques, l'État, le marché immobilier en France à l'époque contemporaine, 1820–1940* (Paris, 1982); Christian Topalov, *Le Logement en France: Histoire d'une marchandise impossible* (Paris, 1987); Adeline Daumard, *Maisons de Paris et propriétaires parisiens, 1809–1880* (Paris, 1965); Françoise Marnata, *Les Loyers des bourgeois de Paris, 1860–1958* (Paris, 1961).

[2] Adeline Daumard, *Les Bourgeois de Paris au XIXᵉ siècle* (Paris, 1970). On the subject of working-class history, see two pioneering works: Michelle Perrot, *Les Ouvriers en grève, France (1871–1890)* (Paris, 1974), and Yves Lequin, *Les Ouvriers de la région lyonnaise (1848–1914)* (Lyon, 1977).

[3] Roger-H. Guerrand, *Les Origines du logement social en France* (Paris, 1967); Jean-Paul Flamand, *Loger le peuple: Essai sur l'histoire du logement social* (Paris, 1989).

body of contemporary literature on an exchange relation that was regarded as 'problematic' even before it became the target of a highly controversial policy of rent control.

To tackle such a subject involves using judicial records—a difficult undertaking made even more difficult by the fact that, even when the information is there, it is not always easily accessible. For example, details of disputes between landlords and tenants brought before the Parisian courts are available only where those disputes were dealt with as ordinary controversies, in which case the documents are widely scattered among the body of judgments preserved. Conversely, documents relating to special interventions by the judicial authorities following the Franco-Prussian War and during and after the First World War occupy a separate place in the archives but fail to provide adequate information: the records give the judge's ruling but neither his arguments nor those put forward by the opposing parties, though these are essential if the respective positions of those parties and what was at issue in the dispute are to be reconstructed. Consequently, researchers have fallen back on other sources, notably police records, which made it possible to study the tenant movements that emerged during 'critical' periods such as cost-of-living crises, wars, and the aftermath of wars.[4]

This essay draws on these works and on the findings of social history mentioned earlier. It sets out to show that the social relation that places landlords over against tenants varies with the positions that the two parties occupy in social space; and that because of this it also varies in time, changing according to the economic circumstances that influence those positions, threatening them or transforming them. What is at issue in this exchange relation is bound up with the social positions of landlords and tenants. Thus on the one hand, as a source of income, the object of the lease plays a part in determining the standard of living and the social future of the lessor, but that influence varies with the composition and size of the lessor's total resources—here the large landlord is distinguished from the small, the person whose prop-

---

[4] Susanna Magri, 'Le Mouvement des locataires à Paris et dans sa banlieue, 1919–1925', *Le Mouvement social*, 137 (Oct.–Dec. 1986), 55–76; Jean-Louis Robert, 'Ouvriers et mouvement ouvrier parisiens pendant la Grande Guerre et l'immédiat après guerre', doctoral thesis (University of Paris I, 1989).

erty constitutes only part of his wealth from the *rentier* or person who lives from his property, and all of them from the wage-earner who sublets his dwelling. On the other hand, the lease object represents an expense and a use value locating the lessee in commercial (shop), domestic (dwelling), or urban (the city) spaces that are organized into social hierarchies. In controlling access to the resources of the city in terms of jobs, clienteles, consumer goods of all kinds, and social relations, this situation plays a key role so far as the user is concerned in preserving acquired social position and in the way this develops. However, it is itself dependent on the means users have at their disposal for living, and in a broader sense on the resources they owe to their social position. Landlords and tenants thus bring to their relationship interests that are different but not necessarily opposed. If the social future of both is at stake, it is so unequally, their presence in a given segment of the property market being constrained to an extent that varies with the nature and size of the resources commanded by each. Antagonism would therefore enter into the relationship only in so far as the pretensions of one side threatened or challenged the positions and plans of the other. It would reach a climax in periods of crisis, possibly threatening to shatter social harmonies. Such a situation would make government intervention inevitable.

This essay is limited to Paris, on which by far the most work has been done. It will first take stock of the terms and conditions of the tenancy relation fixed by law in the nineteenth and early twentieth centuries, before the implementation, from 1918 onwards, of special legislation governing those terms and conditions. In the process, the characteristics of the populations concerned, landlords on the one hand and tenants on the other, will be outlined in order to highlight their internal heterogeneity. Once it has been established, on the basis of this analysis, what was at stake in a conflict of interests at normal times and what its origins were, two periods when exceptional economic circumstances meant that the conflict was publicly expressed, the cost-of-living crisis of 1910–11 and the First World War, will be examined. These situations brought together the conditions under which special legislation governing tenancy emerged in place of the general rules which had applied hitherto.

Landlords and tenants in nineteenth-century Paris

The regulations governing the renting of dwellings and shops in nineteenth-century Paris were fixed by the *Code Napoléon* and by custom as enshrined in jurisdiction. These regulations themselves revealed the diversity of an exchange relation that, depending on the use of premises—domestic, commercial, or industrial—and the amount of rent, placed two populations, tenants and landlords, each of which presented deep internal social differences, in opposition with each other.

One of the forms of renting property was the lease (*bail*), which in normal contemporary usage described a written contract with a set lifetime.[5] A document drawn up in the presence of a notary or private witnesses, the lease usually related to premises which commanded a high rent: in excess of 1,500 francs per annum under the Second Empire (1852–70), and 2,000 francs in the early years of the twentieth century. Commercial rents were generally twice as high as domestic ones.[6] Consequently, leases governed the renting of large apartments as well as businesses of a certain size. This brought together people from the same bourgeois milieu, often both landlords, for in Paris it was not unusual for property owners, exploiting their estates as a whole, to be themselves living in rented accommodation.[7]

However, the bourgeois in his apartment and the wealthy tradesman in his shop did not have the same obligations in relation to the landlord. The first had only to provide the landlord with security in the shape of personal property to a value at least equivalent to the annual rent, while the second was obliged by custom to put down a cash deposit equal to six months' rent. This advantage on the part of the lessors of commercial premises offended the business logic favoured by the lessees, who were unhappy to see their cash deposit producing interest only for the

[5] Louis Delanoue, *Guide-manuel des propriétaires et locataires de bâtiments* (Paris, n.d. [mid-19th century]), 12.

[6] In the new buildings in Haussmann's rue de Rivoli, apartments could be rented for 5,000–6,000 francs, shops for 10,000–15,000 francs; see Jeanne Gaillard, *Paris, la ville, 1852–1870* (Paris, 1977), 90. Alexandre Weill, *Paris inhabitable: Ce que tout le monde pense des loyers de Paris et que personne ne dit* (Paris, 1860), 41, quotes rents for commercial leases of 20,000–80,000 francs per annum.

[7] In 1897, 39% were in this position, according to a recent study by Marc H. Choko, 'Investment or Family Home? Housing Ownership in Paris at the Turn of the Twentieth Century', *Journal of Urban History*, 23 (1997), 531–68.

landlord. And the same logic prompted tradesmen and artisans to rebel against a second prerogative of the landlord: safeguarded by law against his tenant going bankrupt, the landlord was in fact the first creditor to be reimbursed, having the right to seize the bankrupt's goods to a value equal to the total amount of rent due throughout the lifetime of the lease.[8]

In other words, within the bourgeois world, the real-estate exchange relation could involve a certain conflict of interests. Riddled with exceptions to the rules normally governing commercial relations, it revealed the landlord as 'sovereign':

our manners respectfully salute the landlord as a sovereign who gives up his property and takes it back; today allows you to enjoy it to his advantage, and tomorrow replaces you, in the absence of a bilateral provision; decrees, orders, settles, rules, holds, retains, and stops only before compulsory purchase for reasons of public utility.[9]

That 'bilateral provision', a mutual obligation between two parties, bound the landlord to his tenant throughout the term of the lease. It certainly did not prevent the landlord, on expiry of the lease, from asking for a higher rent and if necessary obtaining it on penalty of notice to quit. This was the case especially at periods when real estate enjoyed high value, as at the time of Haussmann's major renovation of Paris. Rents soared in the 'better districts', and where sites were at all desirable—shops on the right bank, for example—tenants conformed to the pretensions of lessors, though not without some protest. Tradesmen's spokesmen, for example, called upon the government to put an end to the 'privileges' of this very 'particular' type of businessman, to appoint special tribunals of 'wise men' (*prud'hommes*) to regulate their conduct, and to take steps to ensure that supply matched demand by abolishing tax relief on unlet buildings, and by investing in the railways in such a way as to expand the property market.[10]

Meanwhile, business flourished under the Second Empire, and paying high rents was not an insurmountable problem. As Jeanne Gaillard stresses: 'Trade and industry appear sufficiently prosperous to bear the increases, leases are periodically reviewed with no

---

[8] Delanoue, *Guide-manuel*, 24–5.
[9] Auguste Luchet, *Les Mœurs aujourd'hui* (Paris, 1854), 144–5.
[10] Weill, *Paris inhabitable*, 44–7.

obvious recriminations on the part of tenants.'[11] Even after 1871, in fact, the wealthy bourgeoisie experienced no major obstacles in fulfilling its requirements for housing or business premises. Haussmann's redesigned capital enlarged and improved the body of real estate available, increasing the scope of choice. Where central quarters had been little affected by the town-planning work, as was the case on the left bank of the Seine, they could now be abandoned for the new districts—to the west for the bourgeoisie of the right bank, to the south for those of the left bank. Rents there were certainly high, and made higher by this exodus, but the benefits of residing there were greater, as it became possible to avoid rubbing shoulders with the working classes.[12] The construction of handsome apartment buildings went on more or less continuously after 1871 until the overproduction crisis of the early 1900s. The Parisian bourgeoisie found their rents increasing less rapidly than did the working classes, with increases slowing down markedly after the turn of the century.[13]

Wealthy tenants did not, as a rule, deal directly with their landlords. From the Second Empire onwards, a new type of landlord became established in Paris, alongside the small investor who put his savings into real estate. Businessmen, occasionally members of the nobility, and construction or insurance companies generally held a considerable amount of property—the record in 1897 being forty-two apartment buildings owned by the Pereire banking family. Whether private individuals or corporate owners, they placed their property in the hands of a managing agent.[14] The renting of property was thus treated as a business, and the possibility of friction was further reduced by the fact that the agreement was enshrined in a written contract. Occasions for litigation were limited: apart from the rent, they included the quality of the premises (repairs incumbent on the landlord, work carried out by the tenant) and services (notably heating), as revealed by sampling the records of the justice of the peace of the sixteenth *arrondissement*.[15] The situation was quite different with regard to the less luxurious accommodation of the middle classes and in working-class tenements.

---

[11] Gaillard, *Paris, la ville*, 128.   [12] Ibid. 43–6, 90–1.

[13] Topalov, *Le Logement en France*, 128–34.

[14] Gaillard, *Paris, la ville*, 121–7; Choko, 'Investment or Family Home?'

[15] Archives de Paris, D 16 III.

In most Parisian housing, it was not a lease (*bail*) that linked land-lord and tenant but a simple written or verbal rent agreement. This was of indeterminate duration, subject to local custom, and com-monly known as a *location*. The dates when the rent was due, the periods of notice, and the forms of appeal open to the parties varied in such agreements according to the category of rent involved.

Thus although the rent was in all cases payable quarterly in equal instalments, where the annual rent was under 400 francs it was not payable on the same day as under agreements where the annual rent was more than 400 francs. In the former case, the tenant was granted a 'period of grace' of one week, the 'term' being due on the 8th; in the latter, it was due on the 15th. It was the same with periods of notice, these being six weeks and three months respectively for dwellings and six months for bus-iness premises and shops, whatever the rent. In the event of non-fulfilment of the agreement, tenants and landlords applied to different courts, depending on the amount of rent involved. Thus default of payment by the tenant could have different conse-quences. If the two parties had come to a prior arrangement, the judge in emergency session usually granted a further period of grace and no procedural difference depending on the amount of rent was made. Otherwise, the landlord resorted directly to seizure of his tenant's furniture and chattels. To make it enforceable, the seizure had to be validated: the competent judicial authority was the justice of the peace where the rent did not exceed 600 francs, and the tribunal of first instance (*tribunal de première instance*) where it was above that figure. When the landlord wanted to get rid of a recalcitrant tenant, he was guaranteed a swift procedure in the case of 'minor' *locations*, with justices of the peace holding special sessions on dates of payment—the 8th where the rent did not exceed 400 francs, the 15th where it lay between 400 and 600 francs. The tenant was summoned as a matter of urgency, and judgment was handed down and enforced on the same day. Where higher rents were concerned, however, the landlord had to appeal to the judge in emergency session, who ordered the tenant to be summoned by the bailiff, and then decided on eviction.[16]

The inequality of condition expressed in the amount of rent was also reflected in prodecures for regulating tenancies. To rent

---

[16] Delanoue, *Guide-manuel*, 11–25, and *Petit memento du propriétaire à Paris* (Paris, 1909), 3, 8.

accommodation for 400 francs or less meant, in the Paris of the second half of the nineteenth century, being exempt from tax, which in the eyes of contemporaries was tantamount to being included among the poor. To pay between 400 and 600 francs meant escaping from that situation, certainly, but only just, particularly when at the end of the century the threshold for tax exemption was raised to 500 francs.[17] Membership of the world of poverty was thus signified not only by the bareness or mediocrity of one's accommodation but also by being obliged to settle one's 'term' earlier than wealthy tenants, to pass through the streets with a handcart loaded with furniture on a different day from that which saw the discreet removals of the bourgeoisie, by being relegated to the lowest level of the judicial hierarchy, appearing before a justice of the peace who officiated closest to the people—all signs that reinforced the frontier between two social worlds.

Yet neither world was homogeneous. Historians have concentrated on the major social contrasts; they have paid less attention to the more subtle distinctions that help us to understand the different facets of social inequality as they evolved. Local customs that were compatible with the condition of some were a source of difficulty for others, but the border between what was tolerable and what intolerable was a shifting one and did not always coincide with the major social cleavages. This was the case with the custom that insisted on rent for domestic accommodation being paid quarterly, with nothing in advance, the furniture serving as security. Contemporaries saw this as the reason for the widespread acrimony directed at landlords:

Paid only four times yearly, [rent] has the fault of representing a comparatively substantial sum each time: it has the further fault of being, at the moment when it is paid, the price of something enjoyed in the past; consequently, one pays it with reluctance, regretting that one is giving so much, all at once, to a single individual.[18]

However, this method of payment appears to have suited those who enjoyed incomes that, if not large, were at least regular enough to set aside a portion for the rent each quarter day, people

[17] The exemption granted in Paris concerned the personal property contribution, the rate of which varied with the amount of rent, and the fixed-rate tax for removal of household waste.
[18] Victor Bellet, *Les Propriétaires et les loyers à Paris* (Paris, 1857), 51.

like civil servants or public-sector workers who had the advantage
of being paid monthly. They would not pay 'in desolation' or even
grudgingly except when the rent went up, forcing them to sacri-
fice any surplus or move into a smaller dwelling.[19] There was a
recurrent problem, on the other hand, for those with irregular
incomes. The majority of workers were in this position. Whether
they were on piecework or paid by the day, their incomes were
rarely fixed and were always paid more frequently than monthly.
Nevertheless, the kind of budget management that made it possible to meet such a quarterly outlay was not unknown among
workers, who were accustomed to short-term methods of saving.[20]
A greater obstacle was the frequency of interruptions to employment. A clandestine move then became inevitable—the 'moonlight flit'—to avoid rent day and seizure, or following eviction.

If the landlord was 'hated' in working-class circles, it was mostly
because of his intransigence in collecting the rent, which the pre-
cariousness of resources made intolerable. Every rent increase
made him a 'vulture', a popular nickname coined in 1806 but still
current a century later.[21] It is significant in this connection that
complaints by workers—collected, admittedly, in periods of crisis
(1867, 1884)—rarely concerned the method of payment of rent.
Only employers stressed the inconvenience of that, while at the
same time insisting for their part, too, that rents in Paris were too
expensive, periodically emptying the pockets of the workers.[22]
At least the workers only paid for their housing retrospectively:
the system was generally regarded as fair, and it was one they
demanded for their workshops. Thus home-workers joined
wealthy tradesmen in calling for the abolition of rent paid in
advance without interest, pointing out that the fruit of their
labours was collected only on delivery of the finished product.[23]

---

[19] Luchet, *Les Mœurs aujourd'hui*, 146–7.

[20] Alain Cottereau, 'Prévoyance des uns, imprévoyance des autres: Questions sur les
cultures ouvrières face aux principes de l'assurance mutuelle au XIXe siècle', *Prévenir*, 9
(May 1984), 57–68.

[21] Michelle Perrot, 'Les Ouvriers, l'habitat et la ville au XIXe siècle', in *La Question du
logement et le mouvement ouvrier français* (Paris, 1981), 21–2.

[22] The complaints of workers are reported by Gaillard, *Paris, la ville*, 128–9, for 1867 and
by Perrot, 'Les Ouvriers, l'habitat et la ville au XIXe siècle', 28–9, for 1884. On the opinion
of industrialists, see Denis Poulot, *Le Sublime ou le travailleur comme il est en 1870 et ce qu'il peut
être* [1872], new edn., introd. Alain Cottereau (Paris, 1980), 146–7.

[23] This demand was put forward by the *tabletiers* (makers of fancy articles of ebony, ivory,
bone, etc. and inlaid ware) in 1867. See Gaillard, *Paris, la ville*, 129.

For most tenants and landlords of domestic accommodation, therefore, the amount of the rent rather than the method of payment was the bone of contention. For everyone, however, the importance of the amount of rent they paid depended on their social condition as much as on their plans for the future. A few hypotheses will now be outlined. The works of Adeline Daumard have demonstrated that the ownership of property among bourgeois circles grew during the nineteenth century, both as a source of enrichment and as a way of consolidating positions achieved. This increase is confirmed by an analysis of the distribution of such property in 1897. Ninety-five per cent of all owners of buildings were private individuals. Of these, 2.8 per cent owned more than four buildings, and only 0.2 per cent more than ten. The average was close to two buildings per individual.[24] This large number of owners of one or two buildings did not, of course, constitute a homogeneous category. The income from their property varied according to the quality of the building and how it had been acquired, and its place in the resources of each individual depended on his social position.

From the Second Empire onwards, many new buildings located in the centre or west of Paris guaranteed well-to-do landlords—merchants and industrialists, professionals, civil servants, and high-level employees—tenants with sufficient income and social status for the risk of non-payment to have been very small. If vacancies were more numerous in such properties than in popular tenements, they tended to be brief and infrequent.[25] Rent increases, which might be steep outside periods of crisis, enriched such landlords, especially when they had inherited their property or purchased it with profits from their businesses.[26] Tolerated by tenants who had consolidated their bourgeois status, such increases were borne less well by those who had not yet succeeded in doing so, possibly leading to difficulties that might force them into moving. The uncertainty surrounding most middle-class professionals in the second half of the century, many of whom never progressed beyond mediocre positions, probably accounts for the

---

[24] Choko, 'Investment or Family Home?'

[25] After the middle of the century, there were only three periods when vacancies in 'bourgeois' apartment buildings increased: 1884–6, 1892–6, and 1902–5. See Topalov, *Le Logement en France*, 123–7.

[26] Adeline Daumard, *Les Bourgeois et la bourgeoisie en France depuis 1815* (Paris, 1991), 201–3.

fairly high level of residential mobility among them.[27] It is conceivable that, apart from moves connected with increasing family size, moving house was related to social trajectory: success as well as failure are reflected in the kind of dwelling a person lives in, and the former depends on it if success requires joining an elevated social milieu.[28]

However, proprietors of buildings were not always wealthy. According to Adeline Daumard, in 1875–80 'the added *arrondissements* had taken over from old Paris, and it was only there that the less well-off bourgeoisie could continue to have access to property'.[29] On the outskirts of Paris and especially in the working-class districts to the east, big property owners certainly existed—in 1897, the second biggest in order of size of holding owned thirty-nine buildings in the twentieth and twelfth *arrondissements*.[30] But the ordinary property owners were artisans and shopkeepers, employees or lower-income professionals, widows of modest independent means, or retired businesspeople, each owning one or two apartment houses of little value which were let to the many workers, small shopkeepers, and employees who lived in these districts. This stock of buildings, consisting in the main of one- or two-roomed apartments without any conveniences, tended to become more diverse towards the end of the century as a result of town-planning operations extending to the east of Paris. More expensive dwellings appeared, and there were fewer less expensive ones, a development that led to a general increase in rents.[31]

At between 200 francs (the highest rent for a pauper in 1869) and 600 francs, sometimes more, the rent for such dwellings was a real stake for landlords and tenants alike. In many cases, landlords were able to own buildings only by going into debt. Artisans and shopkeepers took out a mortgage: the operation was successful only if business was otherwise good and the rents guaranteed more than the repayments.[32] For such landlords the real risk was outstanding rent payments. These particularly threatened the small landlord's lifestyle if his property was his only source of

[27] Ibid. 110.
[28] Christophe Charle, *Histoire sociale de la France au XIXᵉ siècle* (Paris, 1991), 180–227, and Jean-Luc Pinol, *Les Mobilités dans la grande ville: Lyon fin XIXᵉ–début XXᵉ siècle* (Paris, 1991).
[29] Daumard, *Maisons de Paris*, 241.
[30] Choko, 'Investment or Family Home?'
[31] Topalov, *Le Logement en France*, 128–34.
[32] Daumard, *Les Bourgeois de Paris au XIXᵉ siècle*, 272–3.

income. For tenants, rent increases could present a twofold problem. By absorbing a growing proportion of their budgets, a rent increase might force tenants to cut back on essentials or, worse, go into debt, thus destroying their chances of improving their condition in the short or medium term.[33] But a high cost of living might also deny a tenant access to accommodation suitable for the needs of a growing family, and become an obstacle to the tenant going about his business when this was associated with the district. It is known that at the turn of the century workers had to leave Paris to have larger dwellings, though it was 'with great reluctance' that they made for the suburbs, so great was their attachment to the city.[34] Home-workers, particularly women employed by the Paris fashion industry, preferred to live in over-crowded conditions in dilapidated housing rather than live away from the centre under the Second Empire. Later, when they were pushed out of the centre, they were reluctant to leave the outlying *arrondissements*. The tailor/dressmaker and the small shop-keeper, whose clientele was in the city, were obliged to put up with rent increases for the same reasons: reduced margins and possible seizure of goods as a result of non-payment of rent ruined any hope of emerging from the condition of wage-earner.[35]

Thus a conflict of interests between landlords and tenants existed both in working-class tenements and in bourgeois apartment buildings. In both cases, the question of rent was a bone of contention whenever it reduced people's chances of social success or social mobility. However, while the occupants of tenements risked being plunged deeper into poverty, the residents of bourgeois apartment buildings merely stood to have their average standard of living reduced. This inequality was enhanced by the inequality of access to housing and its use. The constraints imposed by landlords and the 'abuses' perpetrated by them and their concierges nourished a swelling stream of pamphlets in the nineteenth century that reinforced the idea of a shared 'agony' of tenants in Paris. It is true that, on applying to rent, most tenants

[33] See Perrot, 'Les Ouvriers, l'habitat et la ville au XIXe siècle', and on employees Charle, *Histoire sociale de la France au XIXe siècle*, 187–93.

[34] On the reluctance of workers to move to the suburbs, see Alain Faure (ed.), *Les premiers banlieusards: Aux origines des banlieues de Paris, 1860–1940* (Paris, 1991); on the subject of attachment to the city, see Perrot, 'Les Ouvriers, l'habitat et la ville au XIXe siècle'.

[35] On this instability, see Heinz-Gerhard Haupt and Philippe Vigier (eds.), 'L'Atelier et la boutique', *Le Mouvement social*, 108 (July–Sept. 1979).

placed themselves in the power of a landlord who checked the value of their furniture, enquired into the stability of their employment and the standard of their morals, and in the 1880s refused children and dogs.[36] Custom also required that the arrangement be sealed by payment of a *denier à Dieu* (a 'shilling for God') to the 'porter' of the bourgeois apartment building or the 'concierge' of the popular tenement, with the landlord occasionally demanding (illegally, in the case of residential accommodation) a quarter's rent in advance. Once installed, every tenant was policed by the concierge—responsible, it is true, for the security of the building.[37] Tenants were at the mercy of the concierge's indiscretions, and could suffer harassment. Finally, no one was spared the risk of arbitrary eviction, however much notice was given.

Such practices could undoubtedly poison the existence of the bourgeois tenant, who nevertheless was not without recourse, particularly against the concierge.[38] But these practices became increasingly harsh towards the other end of the social scale, prompting more vigorous, even violent reactions. For example, where children were refused, it was usually working-class families that were affected, because they tended to be larger: the collective complaint of workers in this connection, in 1867 as well as in the early 1880s, expressed a level of individual exasperation that is documented by accounts in the press.[39] In a generally tight market, outrages against poor tenants tended to be the rule, such as excessive demands as regards the *denier à Dieu*, offensive distrust, and indiscreet investigation of the resources of the applicant for accommodation. District networks of familiarity no doubt enabled some to avoid this, but local solidarities left 'strangers' without protection. Once a place had been rented, daily surveillance and calls to order poisoned relations between a landlord who, whether he collected the rent himself or through his concierge, was often, in the anxious run-up to each rent day, to

---

[36] Georges Piart, *Locataires et propriétaires: Étude sociale sur les abus de la propriété à l'égard de la location* (Paris, 1882).

[37] *Étude parisienne: Les Concierges défendus par un concierge. Types de locataires* (Paris, 1890).

[38] A large body of case law from the Seine tribunal and the justices of the peace of the Seine *département* since the beginning of the 19th century defines the obligations of porters. See Delanoue, *Guide-manuel*, 126–7.

[39] On the subject of joint complaints, see Gaillard, *Paris, la ville*, 128–9; acts of violence reported in the press are cited by Piart, *Locataires et propriétaires*, 9–13.

be found on the premises,[40] and a tenant jealously guarding the remnant of freedom he still had, and which had to be vigorously defended at work. This was probably one of the most potent sources of conflict in working-class tenements: the relationship of dominance that became established there was particularly tense because it recalled the situation at work, it was coupled with physical proximity, and, the land*lord* being in many cases a land-*lady*, it reversed the hierarchical positions normally occupied by the sexes.[41]

Faced with abuses of power on the part of the landlord and the concierge, poor tenants only exceptionally resorted to legal action. The judge would intervene where there was a serious dispute, whether verbal or physical, at the invitation of the landlord, who was invariably the victim. He was often in the position of plain-tiff, whether for eviction or seizure. Such humiliating proceedings, however, were usually not taken against bourgeois tenants. The response of working-class tenants in such a situation was usually flight or collective defence. In the early part of the twentieth century, such defence tended to be put up by organizations which first came into being during the cost-of-living crisis of 1910–11, and were then revived between 1914 and 1918. During the First World War relations between tenants and landlords were medi-ated by their respective organizations and the role of the courts changed as a result of the advent of government intervention.

Collective movements and emergence of legislation governing rents

For the working classes of Paris, 1905 marked the beginning of a period of crisis: a rise in the cost of living which reduced the pur-chasing power of wages between 1905 and 1913, tension in the

---

[40] In 1897, the poorest quarters of east Paris shared with the wealthy western quarters the highest proportions of landlords living in the building they owned—in the former case, a tenement; in the latter, a private house. See Choko, 'Investment or Family Home?'

[41] The highest proportions of widows living in the buildings they owned were found in the working-class districts of east and south Paris (ibid.). Sampling of the official records for the years 1914–18 tends to show that, in these districts as well as in the working-class communities in the suburbs, 'disturbances' and 'insults' directed against a resident proprietor often concerned a woman. Notable examples are the cases brought before the magistrates in Saint-Ouen in 1914 (Archives de Seine–Saint-Denis, Saint-Ouen 4 U8) and in the eleventh *arrondissement* (Archives de Paris, D 8 U1, 104).

market for rented accommodation reflected in a drop in the number of vacancies, and a particularly sharp increase in rents in 1911 as a result of the re-evaluation carried out by property owners following the decennial tax investigation into rental values. It was during this period that the proportion of working-class household budgets devoted to rent, higher in Paris than elsewhere during the nineteenth century, reached a peak of 24 per cent, according to the French Department of National Statistics.[42]

The disturbances provoked by the price explosion of 1910–11 were about more than simply rents.[43] However, rents did form the target of a specific movement of protest and collective defence reminiscent of, but also different from, the demonstrations triggered by the rent increases of 1881–4. Noisy gatherings attempting to prevent evictions, street processions by families with large numbers of children in search of somewhere to live, but also temporary lodgings in apartment buildings provided by philanthropic members of the bourgeoisie: such images, as exposed by the press, bear witness not only to working-class agitation but also to its new legitimacy. Another novelty was the setting up of a Tenants' Union, which in 1912 boasted 3,500 members and was well established in the more working-class districts of Paris and its suburbs. Inspired by libertarians but also from now on by revolutionary syndicalists, it restored the old socialist demand of a government 'tax on rents' to the political agenda, and accompanied the fight against evictions every inch of the way with catchphrases drawn directly from popular fears: workers' furniture should not be liable to seizure, the outlawing of verbal notice to quit, and guarantees for large families.[44]

The government made no direct response to these movements, and they received little support from the Socialist opposition, which was busy getting a law through Parliament to authorize the municipal construction of low-cost housing. The passage of this piece of social legislation on 23 December 1912 seems to have been favoured by the economic crisis, whereas neither the CGT

---

[42] On the general cost-of-living crisis, see Michelle Perrot, 'Les Classes populaires urbaines', in Fernand Braudel and Ernest Labrousse (eds.), *Histoire économique et sociale de la France* (Paris, 1979), iv. 490–501.

[43] Jean-Marie Flonneau, 'La Crise de vie chère et les syndicats, 1910–1914', *Le Mouvement social*, 72 (July–Oct. 1970), 58–76.

[44] Perrot, 'Les Ouvriers, l'habitat et la ville au XIXe siècle', 24–5; Magri, 'Le Mouvement des locataires à Paris', 57, 59, 64.

(*Confédération Générale du Travail*) nor the Tenants' Union, which disappeared by 1913, mobilized on this front. Historians have shown that this lack of interest does not reflect any indifference on the part of members of the working class to comfortable living conditions. The desire for a decent place to live, which the better-off among them now defined as a suburb offering the healthiness of the countryside and already inhabited by the middle classes, went hand in hand with a demand for independence guaranteed by self-governing co-operatives without philanthropic patronage. In other words, rented low-cost housing units, whether built by private individuals or local authorities, with their barrack-like appearance and strict rules, presented little attraction.[45]

The situation changed with the First World War, when government intervened in tenancy relations right from the outbreak of hostilities. As in 1870, it authorized the suspension of payment of rents, the measure forming part of a general moratorium introduced in August 1914 to cover all commercial exchanges. The initial consensus regarding the measure broke down as soon as the German advance had been contained, but the compulsory moratorium was retained for men on active service as well as for 'small' tenants in accommodation for which the rent was below 600 francs (77 per cent of households in Paris and 84 per cent in the suburbs in 1915), and shops or workshops where the rent was below 2,500 francs. As early as 1915, the large number of units involved raised the question of liquidation of the debt, and Parliament was asked to look at this. The trade unions, which favoured releasing tenants from their debts, argued about the criteria, while the rapidly reconstituted Tenants' Union called for it for all with immediate effect, reviving the popular demand met earlier by the Commune.[46] Despite pressure from all sides, the government put off a final decision: it extended the moratorium for three months at a time until the end of hostilities, and did not ask the legislator to decide about liquidating the debt until 1918.[47] This policy of procrastination was dictated by fear of tearing the social

---

[45] A. Faure, 'Paris, le peuple, la banlieue', in id. (ed.), *Les premiers banlieusards*, 103–220; Magri, 'Le Mouvement des locataires à Paris', 66, 72–3.

[46] The precise chronology of the measures passed by the Republican Assembly and the Commune is found in Guerrand, *Les Origines du logement social en France*, 183–201.

[47] I analyse this policy in detail, comparing it with that of the British and German governments, in S. Magri, 'Housing', in Jay Winter and Jean-Louis Robert (eds.), *Capital Cities at War: Paris, London, Berlin 1914–1919* (Cambridge, 1997), 374–418.

fabric, which had to be maintained for the purpose of waging war. The government received warning in 1915 of an increase in 'antagonism between owners and landlords on the one hand and tenants on the other',[48] which was being used by the intransigent, Socialist-inspired Tenants' Union. Property owners, particularly the smaller ones, started organizing in November 1914 to demand a return to ordinary law. Failing to obtain this, they called for the abolition of the compulsory moratorium for small tenants not on active service, which would enable owners to question in court a tenant's inability to pay.[49] But they carried too little weight, measured against the importance of what was at stake politically, and all they achieved was a moratorium on their own mortgage repayments. The mass of small tenants, on the other hand, finally had an old grievance met in that they were allowed to retain their accommodation when it became temporarily impossible for them to pay the rent. However, the effects of the moratorium created highly unequal situations among tenants, occasionally blurring the usual lines of social cleavage.

Above all, a fresh division now appeared between women and men. Women left on their own experienced a deterioration in their housing conditions. While protected by the moratorium, the widows of the employees, teachers, shopkeepers, and professionals who constituted a large proportion of the soldiers at the front nevertheless found themselves forced to move into cheaper accommodation by the sudden drop in their incomes. Women refugees from the occupied regions or women working for the war effort could afford only a hotel room or furnished accommodation on which, in a seller's market, landlords made sure they got a good return.[50] So far as men were concerned, the dividing lines were not necessarily between workers and tenants of higher social strata. Thus Parisian workers recalled to Paris in August 1915 to work in armaments factories were able to move back into their

[48] According to a 1915 report from the chief of the Paris police, cited by Jean-Jacques Becker, *Les Français dans la Grande Guerre* (Paris, 1980), 127.

[49] Archives Nationales, Ministry of Justice, BB 30 1536, 'Protestations'.

[50] The number of hotel rooms and hastily furnished rooms grew in the Paris urban region during the First World War. From 1916 the number of people living in them increased not only in industrial districts but also in lower-middle-class residential districts. See Magri, 'Housing'. Study of the press and sampling of the records of the Paris magistrates' courts suggest that evictions of women with children from such accommodation were relatively frequent.

homes, while their provincial or foreign fellow-workers were consigned to furnished rooms or even army barracks. Still, as skilled
workers drawing good wages, though the purchasing power of
those wages declined as the war drew on, such men had no reason
to envy the employees and civil servants who were sent to the front
and whose families were not always able to retain the accommodation they had occupied in 1914, or those who, posted to their
offices, did not always benefit from the compulsory moratorium
because of their fixed salaries, though these were little higher than
the best workers' incomes.[51] Making savings at the expense of the
landlord, workers were all the more determined to obtain release
from payment of their debt as such release was the only way in
which, after the war, they would be able to retain the advantage
gained.

The Law of 9 March 1918 'concerning the modifications
made to leases as a result of the state of war' only partially
paved the way to a return to regularity. Above all, it corrected
(at the expense of landlords) the most glaring wrongs resulting
from the war by compulsorily releasing 'small' tenants who had
been on active service and recipients of social security benefits
from paying their debt. But it authorized landlords to claim what
was due to them from all other beneficiaries of the moratorium. Thus owners were once again able to take proceedings against recalcitrant tenants. Commissions of arbitration
were set up for the purpose, modelled on those created by the
Versailles Assembly in 1871. Consisting of two representatives of
tenants and two of landlords selected from a list drawn up by
the City Council, they were presided over by a justice of the
peace, who had the casting vote. Such commissions were in operation by July 1918, and a year later they had dealt with nearly
220,000 cases for the city of Paris alone, representing 30 per cent
of tenancy relations below 500 francs per annum. This reveals the
scope of the conflict that had flared up again in the working-class
milieu. The acuteness of that conflict is demonstrated by the fact
that 'reconciliations' formed a minority in the final settlements
arrived at by the commissions (43 per cent in 1918 and again in
1919).[52]

[51] Magri, 'Housing'.
[52] Ibid.

Analysis of the tenants' movement in the key period 1918 to 1920 shows the changes that the war wrought in this conflict. However, it cannot replace a study of direct confrontations before the commissions of arbitration, which would reveal at least the outcome of the judgments handed down.[53] The scope of the movement is itself indicative of the determination of small tenants to stand up for themselves. The Tenants' Union in the Seine *département* numbered 46,000 members in 1918, increasing to 70,000 in 1919, and local meetings in the predominantly working-class *arrondissements* (eleventh, thirteenth, and eighteenth) were regularly attended by between 2,000 and 3,000 people. Women and families were the main protagonists in this collective defence, but the militants organizing local sections were recruited from the male world of direct-action syndicalism, particularly among the now unemployed war-industry workers whom landlords no doubt frequently summoned before the commissions of arbitration. Indeed, it was against these landlords that the militants directed their attentions, calling for a boycott and organizing resistance to the eviction of tenants who failed to fulfil the conditions of the sentences imposed on them. The figure of the 'rapacious' land-lord aided and abetted by the courts reappeared, 'taxation' of rents returned to the agenda as an urgent political demand, and the Tenants' Union hounded the 'vultures' who attempted to impose rent increases.[54] However, the return of these slogans cannot obscure the reversal of positions of strength that had been brought about by the reorientation of government policy in this domain.

Hardly indemnified by the Law of 9 March 1918, and in most cases deprived of their profits, landlords threatened rent increases and mass evictions even before peace was restored. In a period of extreme economic and social instability, the government opted for conservative measures: leases which had been extended since 1914 were re-extended to October 1921; releases granted in March 1918 were extended until April 1920; all rents were frozen by the Law of 23 October 1919 concerning 'illicit speculation'. Balance in the property market remaining out of reach, lease extension and

---

[53] Research undertaken at the Archives de Paris has not so far revealed the records of proceedings of these commissions, whereas those of the commissions of arbitration of 1871 are preserved there. A more thorough search will therefore need to be made.

[54] Magri, 'Le Mouvement des locataires à Paris', 64–70.

rent control were continued in stages throughout the 1920s and, ultimately, throughout the entire inter-war period. This policy reversed the relations that landlords and tenants had had with the courts: the law tied the hands of the landlords while tenants were now able to appeal to the judge to have the law upheld. As a result, the nature of popular demands was transformed. A 'secure home' was now claimed as a right, and any increase in the rent was resisted as illegitimate, unless warranted by repairs and renovations. Eventually, even having the local authority build rented accommodation was accepted as an essential weapon in the fight against housing shortages. Tenants' relations with the law were also changed by the way in which government policy was implemented. A complex body of regulations, obscure to the layman and including a reduction in the number of categories of premises to which the law applied, involved frequent recourse to the courts: it led to a familiarization with the language and nuances of the law hitherto unknown in working-class circles. It completely transformed the function of the Tenants' Union, whose role as legal adviser and interpreter of the legislation grew, enhancing its standing in working-class districts.[55]

Conclusion

In preparing the ground for an analysis of relations between landlords and tenants in the nineteenth century, this essay has attempted to show how important it is to look more closely at the unequal relationship in which these two parties stood to the law, and at the authorities responsible for making and implementing it. This essay has drawn attention to the fact that the social effects of a law are revealed not only in the change in material conditions that it brings about, but also in the change in the rights that the agents whom it affects perceive and assert in dealings with the legal authorities, for it is very largely through this medium that the material changes themselves come about.

In the process, two points of method have been implicitly touched upon. On the one hand, to grasp what is at stake in the

[55] Magri, 'Le Mouvement des locataires à Paris'.

tenancy relationship involves more than simply analysing protest movements. Historiography has already shown that protests and the mobilization to which they give rise make sense only in the light of the arrangements and practices peculiar to the group concerned. Thus it is essential to grasp the internal diversity of the working class in terms of origin, occupation, spatial stability, and individual and family way of life if we are to understand the meaning of demands in which these elements are usually articulated.[56] However, one aspect is often overlooked. If 'the character of the working class' is to be, as Jacques Rancière puts it, 'in permanent transition',[57] the analysis must take account of the trajectories that may be traced within it. Protest, whether individual or collective, is never the expression of a demand determined solely by the present situation; it is also determined by a plan reaching into possible futures. This is, of course, true of all the groups that face one another in the social relationship under investigation. There is a lack, in France, of studies of landlords considered both as a composite social group and as an organized group asserting its interests over against tenants.

On the other hand, to understand the social reality of the relationship between landlords and tenants, even in terms of just one of its sociological aspects, involves looking at the variations of that relationship throughout the social hierarchy. The relationships that form within working-class tenements make sense only when compared with the relations governing transactions in the nearby apartment buildings of the lower middle class, and the more or less distant ones inhabited by the affluent classes. This kind of comparative analysis will bring out clearly the social inequality that, as we have seen, is implicit in the very norms governing the property transactions. But by outlining the social space of the positions occupied by landlords and tenants in their interrelationship we can become aware not only of the inequalities implicit in that interrelationship at any one time, but also of the dynamics of the practices that cause it to evolve. For example, working-class practices to avoid the constraints of renting are certainly consistent with the particular way of life of that social group;

---

[56] This avenue was opened up in France by Perrot, *Les Ouvriers en grève*.

[57] Jacques Rancière, *La Nuit des prolétaires* (Paris, 1981), 40.

15

Tenancy in Germany between 1871 and 1914

Norms and Reality

TILMAN REPGEN

The housing situation in German towns, as well as the labour question, formed a central part of the 'social question' throughout the nineteenth century. In urban areas about 90 per cent of the population lived in flats.[1] Tenancy law was therefore of considerable social importance. This essay aims to show, by using some examples, how private law dealt with the *Wohnungsfrage* (housing question).[2] Literature at the turn of the century certainly did not ignore the issue of whether tenancy law had any influence on the *Wohnungsfrage*. Opinions which were influenced by Social Democratic thought considered the legal system to be a consequence of economic conditions. They ignored the fact that private law, as a binding norm, also affects the economy. Conservative authors also underrated the importance of private tenancy law and preferred public law solutions, such as changing building regulations.[3] But there were voices that emphasized the importance of private tenancy law. In this context, the town councillor of Frankfurt, Karl Flesch, deserves special mention. He made

[1] Clemens Wischermann, *Wohnen in Hamburg vor dem Ersten Weltkrieg* (Münster, 1983), 147, 214. He computed the following statistical data concerning the sharing of rented flats: Berlin, 1895: 92.4%; 1910: 93.5%; Frankfurt, 1900: 84.1%; 1910: 86.2%; Hamburg, 1895: 89.9%; 1910: 92.6%. See Hans J. Teuteberg and Clemens Wischermann (eds.), *Wohnalltag in Deutschland 1850–1914: Bilder—Daten—Dokumente* (Münster, 1985), 89.

[2] It is not clear who coined the term 'Wohnungsfrage'. An early example of its use is in a publication by Victor Aimé Huber, 'Die Wohnungsfrage in Frankreich und England', *Zeitschrift des Central-Vereins in Preußen für das Wohl der arbeitenden Klassen*, 2 (1860), 3–37 and 3 (1861), 123–96. On Huber cf. Ernst Engel, *Die moderne Wohnungsnoth: Signatur, Ursachen und Abhülfe* (Leipzig, 1873), 1 f. Wischermann, *Wohnen in Hamburg*, 6 writes that 'since' Wilhelm Adolph Lette, the problem had been designated as 'Wohnungsfrage'. This is a little inexact, because Lette's work was not published until 1866.

[3] Cf. Teuteberg and Wischermann (eds.), *Wohnalltag in Deutschland*, 155–65.

important statements on the *Wohnungsfrage* in the *Verein für Sozialpolitik* (Association for Social Policy) as well as in the *Verein für Armenpflege und Wohltätigkeit* (Association for Relief of the Poor and Charity).[4] This essay investigates private law rather than public law aspects of tenancy for two reasons. First, as Flesch pointed out, it is of great significance for everyday life, and secondly, a number of studies have recently been published on public aspects such as housing policy and rent controls.[5]

Before some characteristic problems of tenancy are dealt with, it will be necessary to describe briefly actual housing conditions in the Kaiserreich. The following examination of the legal situation will focus on the time before the First World War. Home-building collapsed as a result of the war, which soon produced economic and legal hardship. The situation was comparable to earlier conditions, but not similar to them. In December 1914, for example, the *Einigungsämter* were created. At first these offices intended only to mediate between tenants and landlords, but they did not have any authority to decide conflicts. This changed with the *Verordnung zum Schutze der Mieter* of 26 July 1917, a decree for the protection of tenants which granted the *Einigungsämter* permission to overrule terminations by landlords of rental agreements. In contrast to the time before the First World War, wartime decrees tended to address private law problems using administrative law.[6] As this way of addressing the housing problem deviated from former approaches, this essay will be restricted to the Kaiserreich before the First World War. This could be called the age of private law. During the war and the Weimar Republic the

[4] Karl Flesch and Paul Zirndorfer, 'Das Mietrecht in Deutschland', in *Verein für Socialpolitik* (ed.), *Neue Untersuchungen über die Wohnungsfrage in Deutschland und im Ausland*, vol. i/2 (Leipzig, 1901), 277–308, 319; Karl Flesch, 'Die Wohnungsnoth vom Standpunkte der Armenpflege', *Schriften des Vereins für Armenpflege und Wohlthätigkeit*, 6 (Leipzig, 1888), 121–72.

[5] Wischermann, *Wohnen in Hamburg*; Karl Christian Führer, *Mieter, Hausbesitzer, Staat und Wohnungsmarkt: Wohnungsmangel und Wohnungszwangswirtschaft in Deutschland 1914–1960* (Stuttgart, 1995); Gerhard Neumeier, *München um 1900: Wohnen und Arbeiten, Familie und Haushalt, Stadtteile und Sozialstrukturen, Hausbesitzer und Fabrikarbeiter, Demographie und Mobilität—Studien zur Sozial- und Wirtschaftsgeschichte einer deutschen Großstadt vor dem Ersten Weltkrieg* (Frankfurt am Main, 1995). Cf. also the works listed in n. 7.

[6] On developments since the First World War see: Hans-Günther Pergande and Jürgen Pergande, 'Die Gesetzgebung auf dem Gebiete des Wohnungswesens und des Städtebaues', in *50 Jahre im Dienste der Bau- und Wohnungswirtschaft: Deutsche Bau- und Bodenbank Aktiengesellschaft 1923–1973* (Frankfurt am Main, 1973); Jürgen Sonnenschein, 'Der Mietvertrag über Wohnraum zwischen Vertragsfreiheit und staatlicher Reglementierung', *Deutsche Wohnungswirtschaft* (1992), 193–9.

borderline between private and public law as far as tenancy was concerned became less distinct. Tenancy law in Germany has never quite recovered from public law interventions. The result is a mixed bag of public and private law regulations. At times of economic crisis, public law interventions have generally been stronger. This does not mean that private tenancy law lost all its functions, but in many areas it was superseded, as the example of rent fixing shows. This applied, more or less, to tenants from all social groups.

Actual housing conditions

From the middle of the nineteenth century people interested in these matters began to collect statistics on the housing situation in Germany. They included politicians, especially at local level, and academics who had come together, for instance, in the Association for Social Policy. The relevant historical and economic studies make extensive use of these statistics.[7] Unfortunately these statistics were not collected in a uniform way.[8] The explanation for the different, sometimes even contradictory figures, is to be found in the political purpose for which they were collected. Thus in 1904,

---

[7] From the vast literature the following examples are named here: Ulrich Blumenroth, *Deutsche Wohnungspolitik seit der Reichsgründung* (Münster, 1975); Sylvia Brander, *Wohnungspolitik als Sozialpolitik: Theoretische Konzepte und praktische Ansätze in Deutschland bis zum Ersten Weltkrieg* (Berlin, 1984); Johann Friedrich Geist and Klaus Kürvers, *Das Berliner Mietshaus 1862–1945* (Munich, 1984)—the volume contains many documents of the history of the notorious Berlin tenement house 'Meyer's-Hof'; Elisabeth Gransche and Franz Rothenbacher, 'Wohnbedingungen in der zweiten Hälfte des 19. Jahrhunderts', *Geschichte und Gesellschaft*, 14 (1988), 64–95; Thomas Hafner, *Kollektive Wohnreformen im Deutschen Kaiserreich 1871–1918* (Stuttgart, 1988); Neumeier, *München um 1900*; Teuteberg and Wischermann (eds.), *Wohnalltag in Deutschland*, which contains many sources, especially some important contemporary reports about daily life; Wischermann, *Wohnen in Hamburg*—perhaps the best work for an initial orientation; Clemens Zimmermann, *Von der Wohnungsfrage zur Wohnungspolitik: Die Reformbewegung in Deutschland 1845–1914* (Göttingen, 1991). (I am very grateful to Prof. Günther Schulz for useful references.)

[8] One example: according to Wilhelm Treue, *Gesellschaft, Wirtschaft und Technik Deutschlands im 19. Jahrhundert* (9th edn., Stuttgart, 1970; repr. 1979), 378, in 1871 about 64% of the population of the German Reich lived in rural areas. In 1910 the figure was still 40%. By contrast Zimmermann, *Von der Wohnungsfrage zur Wohnungspolitik*, 79, uses the following figures: in 1870: about 95% rural population; in 1910: 78.7% rural population. The housing statistics of the Kaiserreich were made by the local authorities, which led to great differences. A set of central housing statistics was not established until after the First World War. In the official statistics the social conditions were not mentioned, so that assumptions about social classes did not find a statistical proof; Wischermann, *Wohnen in Hamburg*, 7, 10.

at the height of the discussion of housing conditions, the first
General German Housing Congress was held in Frankfurt am
Main. This provided a forum for the reformers. In a lecture
Ludwig Pohle, a sociologist, argued that despite all complaints,
actual housing conditions in Germany had improved, not
declined, over recent decades. The reformers found this argument
provocative. Many regarded it as biased, and rejected it. Albert
Südekum, an SPD deputy in the *Reichstag*, interjected that he had
not attended this congress in order to be in a landlords' association.[9] The distrust expressed here was not totally unjustified. At
that time, too, statistics could be massaged for political purposes.
This essay will therefore primarily be based on significant individual cases which illustrate the housing situation.

At the time in question, a population explosion was taking
place. Between 1871 and 1910, for example, the population of
Hamburg grew by a factor of four to nearly a million people.[10]
During the same period the population in Berlin increased by a
factor of eighteen.[11] As in the 1870s, home-building did not
expand with the urban population, and the situation in the cities
deteriorated sharply. The co-operative self-help projects of the
1860s proved inadequate, which provoked calls for state intervention.[12] In his opening speech to the Association for Social Policy
Gustav Schmoller advocated 'a strong supreme power, standing
above egoistic class interests, giving norms, leading the administration with a fair hand, supporting the weak, lifting the inferior
classes'.[13]

The key words tenement building, rent levels, moving house,
and unhealthy conditions capture the main points of criticism
concerning the state of housing in the Kaiserreich. The urban
lower and middle classes normally lived in multiple dwellings,

---

[9] Cf. Wischermann, *Wohnen in Hamburg*, 1 f.

[10] Ibid. 5, 56 ff. The phenomenon of urbanization was not restricted to Germany
as some figures from France and Russia show. All refer to 1850 and 1890: Paris
1,000,000/2,200,000; Marseilles 195,000/360,000; Moscow 365,000/612,000; St
Petersburg 458,000/877,000. Cf. Heinz Hürten, in Reinhard Elze and Konrad Repgen
(eds.), *Studienbuch Geschichte*, ii (3rd edn., Stuttgart, 1994), 433. Between 1871 and 1891 the
population of the German Reich grew by approximately 7 million, and by 1910 it had
grown by a further 15 million. Cf. Hafner, *Kollektive Wohnreformen*, 35 f.

[11] Treue, *Gesellschaft, Wirtschaft und Technik*, 378.

[12] Wischermann, *Wohnen in Hamburg*, 20 f.; 49 ff. on the development of the German co-
operative building societies; Engel, *Wohnungsnoth*, contains a contemporary criticism.

[13] *Ständiger Ausschuß* (ed.), *Verhandlungen der Eisenacher Versammlung zur Besprechung der socialen
Frage am 6. und 7. Oktober 1872* (Leipzig, 1873), 4.

often in the notorious tenement blocks, which were large buildings on relatively small sites, five storeys high, and containing
thirty to fifty flats. Many 'flats' were in reality only bedsitters.
Cellars and lofts were mostly inhabited. Perhaps the most infa-
mous tenement house in Germany was Meyer's-Hof in Berlin-
Wedding, built in 1874. It was certainly an extreme, but a clear
example.[14] On an area of 40 by 150 metres were crowded no fewer
than seven five-storey buildings. In the six inner courtyards and
also in the buildings all kinds of trades were practised, from a coal
merchant's and a bathing establishment to a butcher's shop. For
a time as many as 2,000 people lived on this site.

At that time the rents were considered unbearably high almost
everywhere. As early as 1868 the statistician Hermann Schwabe
had found a connection between rents and income. He stated that
'the poorer someone is, the higher is the proportion of his income
which goes on rent'.[15] For salaries below 1,000 *Taler* those who
earned less than 325 *Taler* spent an average of 24.1 per cent of
their income on rent (approximately 78 *Taler*), while those who
earned more than 925 *Taler* spent an average of 17.42 per cent
(approximately 161 *Taler*) on rent. Similar results can be found for
salaries above 1,000 *Taler:* those who earned 1,100 *Taler* spent an
average of 27.55 per cent (approximately 303 *Taler*) on rent, while
someone who earned 10,800 *Taler* spent an average of 9.09 per
cent (approximately 981 *Taler*) on rent.[16] Between 1861 and 1910
the average rent nearly doubled from approximately 400 to almost
800 *Mark*. The level of 1910 had already been reached once
before, in the 1870s, just after the foundation of the Kaiserreich.[17]
At least for Hamburg it is possible to demonstrate that the average
rent, especially for low wage-earners, rose out of all proportion to
earnings.[18]

[14] For a detailed documentation see Geist and Kürvers, *Das Berliner Mietshaus 1862–1945*.

[15] Hermann Schwabe, 'Das Verhältnis von Miethe und Einkommen in Berlin', *Berlin und seine Entwickelung: Gemeindekalender und städtisches Jahrbuch*, 2 (1868), 266.

[16] All data from Schwabe, ibid.

[17] Cf. Wischermann, in Teuteberg and Wischermann (eds.), *Wohnalltag in Deutschland*, 145.

[18] Cf. the statistics of the state of Hamburg in 1904 in Teuteberg and Wischermann (eds.), *Wohnalltag in Deutschland*, 146. Examples of household expenditures in Otto Leixner, *1888 bis 1891: Soziale Briefe aus Berlin. Mit besonderer Berücksichtigung sozialdemokratischer Strömungen* (Berlin, 1891), 166–200; and Rosa Kempf, *Das Leben der jungen Fabrikmädchen in München: Die soziale und wirtschaftliche Lage ihrer Familie, ihr Berufsleben und ihre persönlichen Verhältnisse. Nach statistischen Erhebungen dargestellt an der Lage von 270 Fabrikarbeiterinnen im Alter von 14 bis 18 Jahren* (Leipzig, 1911), 177–81. Cf. Teuteberg and Wischermann (eds.), *Wohnalltag in Deutschland*, 149–51 and 322–4.

Any description of housing conditions would be incomplete without a reference to the large fluctuations in the housing market. Contemporaries described the urban population as leading a downright nomadic life.[19] Various reasons for this can be mentioned: termination of the rental agreement by the landlord in order to raise the rent, transfer or change of employment, family or economic changes. Some figures illustrate the frequency of changes of residence. In Hamburg a total of 396,473 people moved in 1893; that is, 66.2 per cent of the population.[20] In 1900 the number was 421,547 people or 59.8 per cent, and in 1912, 651,112 people or 65.9 per cent. Taking into consideration that people traditionally moved only on 1 May or 1 November, on the religious holidays of Ascension Day and St Martin's Day,[21] the nomadic image becomes a reality.[22] These moves caused great distress. Not only did they disturb social relations within the neighbourhood, but since tenants usually stayed for only a short time, their arrangements were always provisional. It was not worth paying for interior decoration because they would soon move again anyway. Added to this was the loss of time and money, because each move cost on average approximately 4 per cent of the annual rent.[23] The *Augsburger Allgemeine Zeitung* published a report on a moving day at Easter, on 1 April 1872:

For eight days nearly half of Berlin has been full of hectic activity because of the dreadful change of flats. This moving day has left only few houses unaffected. . . . In a building with sixteen tenants only one stayed, and that thanks only to his acceptance of an enormous rise in rent. Nowadays neither the extremely high costs nor the unavoidable damage to the furniture are the worst aspect of a move in Berlin, but

[19]   Engel, *Wohnungsnoth*, 6 (in a quotation from a book by Bernhard Friedmann of 1857), 25, 65; Hermann Schwabe, 'Das Nomadenthum in der Berliner Bevölkerung', *Berliner städtisches Jahrbuch für Volkswirthschaft und Statistik* (Berlin, 1874), 29–37.

[20]   In this context 'moves' means those within the city as well as those into the city. The data is based on Wischermann, *Wohnen in Hamburg*, 471.

[21]   Ibid. 228.

[22]   Between 1888 and 1912 within the cities of more than 50,000 inhabitants an average of 30% to 35% of the population moved each year; moves into and out of the cities are not included. Cf. Teuteberg and Wischermann (eds.), *Wohnalltag in Deutschland*, 116f. The highest statistical moving rate is reported for the city of Essen in 1900—the credibility of these data may be questioned. In this year 91.59% of the population are said to have moved, cf. Brander, *Wohnungspolitik*, 108.

[23]   At least this is claimed by Engel, *Wohnungsnoth*, 12.

the continuous disturbance of the family peace and the difficulty of quickly establishing a new home caused by the shortage of flats. . . . Seldom does the tenant find his new flat empty when he arrives there with his belongings . . . Many families this time suffered the misfortune of having left their old flat with bag and baggage, without gaining access to their new flat . . . According to a rough estimate the number of people who were left homeless in this way is about 1,200 to 1,500 heads . . . Many fathers have built poor board cabins on the outskirts of the town, where they are awaiting better days with their families.[24]

Although large, comfortable flats were available during the second half of the nineteenth century, there was a serious housing shortage. Relatively small flats (one to three rooms) were often occupied by several families. In Berlin around 1905, an average of 1.9 persons lived in one room; in Chemnitz and Breslau the figure was 1.5.[25] It was common to put in subtenants to help pay the high rents. Especially in industrial areas these people were often *Schlafgänger*, which meant that they rented a bed, sometimes only for certain hours. In Berlin, Munich, Hamburg, and Frankfurt am Main between 1871 and 1910 *Schlafgänger* made up about 25 per cent of the total population.[26] In spite of the high rents, flats were often unhealthily cold, dark, damp, and insanitary. In 1885 only 7 per cent of all flats in Hamburg had a bathroom;[27] in Berlin at the same time the number was 4 per cent; but by 1910, it had risen to 14 per cent.[28] Cellars and lofts were occupied, although not adequately converted. In Berlin in 1871 10.8 per cent of all flats were in the basement; in 1910 the number was still 3.3 per cent. For Hamburg the figures were 5.9 per cent in 1871 and 4.9 per cent in 1910.[29] A description of a basement flat in Hamburg can be found in a newspaper report from the late 1880s:

One should only have a look at the cellars, so-called 'Hinterkeller', in

---

[24] Cited from ibid. 3 f.; the report on Berlin is followed by a similar one about conditions in Vienna, which were not better (p. 6). As early as 1857 Bernhard Friedmann claimed that the people of Vienna had lost the feeling of being settled.

[25] Wischermann, *Wohnen in Hamburg*, 406. Contemporaries used the expression 'überwohnen', e.g. E. Pfersche, 'Das Mietrecht in Österreich', in *Verein für Socialpolitik* (ed.), *Neue Untersuchungen über die Wohnungsfrage in Deutschland und im Ausland*, i/2. 321–36.

[26] For detailed data see Teuteberg and Wischermann (eds.), *Wohnalltag in Deutschland*, 317.

[27] Wischermann, *Wohnen in Hamburg*, 337.

[28] Siegfried Ascher, *Die Wohnungsmiethen in Berlin von 1880–1910* (Berlin, 1918), 109, published in Teuteberg and Wischermann (eds.), *Wohnalltag in Deutschland*, 141.

[29] All data from Wischermann, in Teuteberg and Wischermann (eds.), *Wohnalltag in Deutschland*, 230.

some streets! In utter darkness, a dozen steps downwards, a room almost entirely below street level! Thick ice on the walls! Such a place, which will never be touched by a beam of sunlight, costs 120 Marks rent a year![30]

These examples may be enough to provide a first impression. Did the private law not offer tenants protection against frequent forced moves? Did tenants not have contractual rights to inhabitable flats? Tenants were dependent on landlords economically as well as legally. Therefore it must be asked how the *legal* relationship between tenants and landlords was constructed.

The following sections will focus on three typical problems of tenancy law, which clearly mirror the social conflicts: (1) sale breaks tenancy; (2) termination of contract; (3) unhealthy housing and the landlord's liability for material defects. I will first comment on the situation in written law, before examining whether the legal provisions corresponded to the actual situation.

Tenancy: the situation according to written law

Until 1 January 1900 there was no homogeneous private law in the Kaiserreich.[31] Many smaller German states were governed by Roman common law, which was in part applied directly, and in part subsidiarily. In most parts of Prussia the law in force was the Prussian General Code (*Allgemeines Landrecht, ALR*). Some areas of the Rhine Province were under French law, whereas in Baden a slightly revised version of the French *Code civil* was in force. The Saxon *Bürgerliches Gesetzbuch* of 1865 must also be mentioned. The Jutish, Danish, and Frisian laws only covered small territories. The innumerable special norms of *Land* laws will not be mentioned. Not until 1900 did the German Civil Code, the *Bürgerliches Gesetzbuch* (*BGB*), at last homogenize the legal situation. From the social point of view, the *BGB*'s provisions for tenancy were an improvement, especially those concerning termination of contract where there was a risk to health, and those about the security of possession in the case of the sale of a site.

---

[30] Cited from K. Schneider, *Das Wohnungsmietrecht und seine sociale Reform* (Leipzig, 1893), 56 n. 1.

[31] The *Deutsche Rechts- und Gerichts-Karte*, by Franz Winterstein (Kassel, 1896) offers a good survey.

Many legal enactments belonging to public law were intended to improve housing conditions. They are disregarded here, because the subject of this essay is the private law. The same applies to the initiative to create a uniform housing law for the whole of Germany (*Reichswohnungsgesetz*), which ultimately failed.[32]

1. *Sale breaks tenancy.* If a landlord transfers a flat to someone else, the question arises as to whether the new proprietor is permitted to expel the tenant from the lodging or whether he has to tolerate his staying. This question, which initially may appear abstract and theoretical, gains practical relevance whenever houses become objects of speculative investment. Before the First World War land prices in German cities shot up. Therefore, house owners who wanted to speculate were interested in whether, in case of sale, the old tenancy was ended and it was possible for them to come to a new, more lucrative agreement. Therefore it seems natural that at this point during the development of the new Civil Code a vigorous debate started. Despite this debate the question was not really important, because tenancy agreements offered landlords different ways of getting tenants out of their properties. But because of the political dimension, the question is worth considering as it shows the different points of view very clearly.

Under Roman common law the tenant's legal position in this respect was rather weak. The tenant had no right to security of possession and could take action against the landlord only under the terms of the contract. Such action was limited to damages.[33] The tenant could be expelled by the new purchaser.[34] The rule 'sale breaks tenancy' was valid. It derived from D. 19.2.25.1, which says that the vendor of land should ensure that the tenant or lease-holder could continue to use the property as stipulated. If the

[32] See Zimmermann, *Von der Wohnungsfrage zur Wohnungspolitik*, 208–24; Brander, *Wohnungspolitik*, 176–85; Wischermann, *Wohnen in Hamburg*, 23, 84. On the purposes of the *Verein Reichswohnungsgesetz*, Karl von Mangoldt (ed.), *Der Verein Reichs-Wohnungsgesetz und seine Vorschläge* (Frankfurt am Main, 1898), 35–7, published in Teuteberg and Wischermann (eds.), *Wohnalltag in Deutschland*, 393.

[33] On the situation in ancient Roman law see Max Kaser, *Das römische Privatrecht*, I, § 132 (2nd edn., Munich, 1971), 562 ff.; Bernhard Jüttner, *Zur Geschichte des Grundsatzes 'Kauf bricht Miete'* (Düsseldorf, 1960), 20–32.

[34] Bernhard Windscheid, *Lehrbuch des Pandektenrechts* (6th edn., Frankfurt am Main, 1887), § 400 n. 7; the exceptions to this rule, which were developed during the Middle Ages originating from C. 4.65.9, were not taken notice of in the 19th century: cf. Eltjo Johannes Hidde Schrage, 'Zur mittelalterlichen Geschichte des Grundsatzes "Kauf bricht Miete"', in id. (ed.), *Römisches Recht im Mittelalter* (Darmstadt, 1985), 281–97.

tenant was prevented from doing so, the Digest granted him an
actio ex conducto, which gave him the right to claim damages. C.
4.65.9 was even more favourable to the purchaser: 'The purchaser
of real estate is not obliged to continue the lease or tenancy, if he
did not buy the property under this condition.'

The courts applying Roman common law made an effort to
improve the position of the tenant. For example, the highest court
of appeal in the kingdom of Saxony, located in Dresden (*Oberappellationsgericht*), granted the tenant a period of time before he had
to give up possession.[35] Another remedy for the tenant was the
legal device by which the vendor and purchaser concluded a contract for the benefit of a third party (that is, the tenant). If the
vendor and the purchaser had agreed to continue the tenancy, and
the purchaser later wanted to force the tenant to move, the tenant
had the right to his own claim under the terms of this contract,
although he was not actually a party to it.[36] Basically, the Roman
common law privileged the free market in houses over the interests of the tenant.

By contrast, under the Prussian *ALR* the legal situation was
more favourable to the tenant. Tenancy was constructed as a real
right, because the tenant was a 'real' possessor of the rented property (I. 7, §§ 1 and 3 *ALR*). Possession had the character of a real
right in the *ALR* (I. 21, § 2). This was important for the tenant as
I. 21, § 3 *ALR* specified: 'The obligation to allow the obligee [i.e.
the tenant] to exercise his real right passes to the new proprietor
of the encumbered property.' The consequence of this was that
the tenant had complete security of possession, and so it can be
said that the principle 'sale does not break tenancy' applied in the
Prussian General Code.

The French *Code civil*, which was in force in the Rhineland and
with some modifications in Baden, had the same effect as the
Prussian *ALR*, even though tenancy was not defined as a real right.

[35] *Oberappellationsgericht* Dresden, judgment of 1 Jan. 1853, *Seuffert's Archiv*, 8 (1855) (repr.
1867), No. 42, 379.
[36] *Appellationsgericht* Celle, judgment of 23 May 1868 (3rd division), *Seuffert's Archiv*, 25
(1871) (repr. 1870 [!]), No. 102, 917 f.; *Appellationsgericht* Celle, judgment of 2 Oct. 1872 (2nd
division), *Seuffert's Archiv*, 28 (1873) (repr. 1872 [!]), No. 22, 499 f.; *Appellationsgericht* Celle,
judgment of 1 May 1877 (1st division), *Seuffert's Archiv*, 32 (1877), No. 318, 415 f.; in the same
sense Joseph Unger, 'Verträge zu Gunsten Dritter', *Jherings Jahrbücher für die Dogmatik des
heutigen römischen und deutschen Privatrechts*, 10 (1871), 21 n. 25; Rudolf von Jhering, 'Passive
Wirkungen der Rechte: Ein Beitrag zur Theorie der Rechte', *Jherings Jahrbücher*, 10 (1871),
568 n. 219; against it: Windscheid, *Pandekten*, § 400 n. 7, 534.

Art. 1743 *CC* protected the tenant if the contract fulfilled specific formal conditions.[37] The Saxon Civil Code followed the Roman law tradition concerning the principle 'sale breaks tenancy' (§ 1225 *SächsBGB*). The tenant could obtain a temporary postponement of the ending of his rental agreement when a sale took place.[38] The purchaser could only terminate the contract immediately after a certain period of time had elapsed. Furthermore, the former landlord had to pay damages in case of eviction (§ 1222 *SächsBGB*).

The *BGB* ultimately accepted the principle of 'sale does not break tenancy' (§ 571), after a vigorous debate on the first draft, which had preferred the contrary. The summary of the critical remarks on this question by the *Reichsjustizamt* (Department of Justice) fills thirty-four pages. Considerations of social policy caused the legal draftsmen to take the tenants' position.[39] The main arguments were that frequent changes of residence increased poverty, encouraged speculation and the charging of usurious rent, cost time and money, and disturbed families' peace. It was believed that a claim for damages could not compensate for these disadvantages. Therefore § 571. I *BGB* ruled that in the case of a sale, the purchaser replaced the landlord with respect to the tenancy.

2. *Termination of contract and protection against eviction.* In times of speculation in real estate landowners have an interest in being able to terminate a tenancy quickly so that they can sell unencumbered property without loss of time. This wish on the part of the landlord contrasts with the interests of the tenant in staying in the flat at the lowest possible rates.[40]

---

[37] Carl Crome, *Handbuch des französischen Civilrechts*, vol. ii (8th edn., Freiburg, 1894), 565–7.

[38] Friedrich Albert Wengler and H. A. Brachmann, *Das Bürgerliche Gesetzbuch für das Königreich Sachsen nach den hierzu ergangenen Entscheidungen der Spruchbehörden erläutert und unter Berücksichtigung der neueren Gesetzgebung* (Leipzig, 1878), § 1222 n. 1.

[39] Under the pressure of the vigorous debate, the German Department of Justice, which was gaining increasing influence over the preparing of the code, opted for the principle of 'sale does not break tenancy'. The 'preliminary commission' had therefore prepared a proposal along these lines, which was accepted without difficulty by the second commission and the *Reichstag*. For details see Hans Schulte-Nölke, *Das Reichsjustizamt und die Entstehung des Bürgerlichen Gesetzbuchs* (Frankfurt am Main, 1995), 316 f.

[40] Historical developments are well researched by Udo Wolter, *Mietrechtlicher Bestandsschutz: Historische Entwicklung seit 1800 und geltendes Wohnraum-Kündigungsschutzrecht* (Frankfurt am Main, 1984).

The routine termination of an unlimited tenancy was permitted everywhere within a specified period of time. A condition of a routine termination under Roman common law was that a certain period of notice was required, the length of which depended on local practice.[41] Under *ALR* I. 21, § 340 a tenancy which was unlimited in time ended with a notice to quit (*Aufkündigung*). This gave the tenant three months before he had to give up possession. It was an advantage for the tenant that the termination had to fulfil certain formal requirements in order to be valid.[42] But the level of security offered by periods of notice was often counteracted by standard form contracts, which allowed for termination without notice in many cases.[43] The *Code civil* strictly followed the Roman common law, except that contracts had to be terminated by a court.[44] The Saxon *BGB* also allowed for routine termination within a specified period of time. The length of the period depended on the amount of rent (§ 1215). This criterion was both new and surprising in a social respect, because the tenants of bad, small, and therefore cheaper flats were less protected than the tenants of bigger and therefore more expensive flats. The cut-off point was a rent of 50 *Taler* per year. The period of notice matched the frequency at which rent was paid (§ 1215 s. 3).

A landlord who wished to evict a tenant with immediate effect could do so only if he had a valid reason. The various legal codes spelt out several specific reasons for lawful termination without notice. In addition, the courts recognized a general catch-all clause allowing termination without notice for 'an important reason'. Moreover, it was possible to stipulate further specific reasons for immediate termination in the rent agreement. One of the reasons prescribed by law was the tenant defaulting on the rent. The various legal systems differ with respect to the length of time arrears were tolerated. Under Roman common law the tenant had to be in arrears with the rent for two whole years.[45] Under Prussian law, two months' arrears was sufficient (I. 21, § 398 *ALR*). The same applied to Saxony with regard to § 1220

---

[41] Windscheid, *Pandekten*, § 402, 546.

[42] Heinrich Dernburg, *Lehrbuch des preußischen Privatrechts und der Privatrechtsnormen des Reiches*, vol. ii (Halle, 1878), § 172, 420; *Obertribunal* Berlin, judgment of 6 May 1848, *Entscheidungen des Königlichen Geheimen Ober-Tribunals*, 16 (1848), 43–51.

[43] Wolter, *Bestandsschutz*, 32.   [44] Crome, *Handbuch*, § 349, 559 ff.

[45] D. 19.2.54.1; 19.2.56; Windscheid, *Pandekten*, § 402, 547.

SächsBGB. The *BGB* (§ 554)[46] made the position of the tenant even worse as he could now be given notice even before he had missed two complete payments.

Other typical reasons for termination without notice were misuse of the rented property, the need for major repairs, unforeseen personal use (Roman common law[47]), forced sale (I. 21, §§ 350 ff. *ALR*), bankruptcy of the tenant (§ 1220 *SächsBGB*), and the tenant's death (I. 21, §§ 366 ff. *ALR*; § 569 *BGB*). In addition to these legal grounds, the courts recognized termination without notice for serious reasons. This general clause made it possible to end the tenancy if the relationship of trust between landlord and tenant had broken down. Thus in 1918 the highest German court (*Reichsgericht*) ruled that a lessor or landlord could terminate the contract without notice if quarrels between him and the tenant made a continuation of the contract impossible. In the case in question the lessee had insulted the lessor, who was a priest, and had attacked him with a pitchfork.[48] A decision by the Prussian *Obertribunal*[49] in Berlin, which started the development of a rule which favoured the tenant, is of some importance. After the reason for the termination had occurred the landlord was allowed to exercise his right of terminating the contract only within the short period of time which it would take to deliver the termination.[50] With reference to our question it is essential that other reasons for immediate termination could be defined by contractual agreement. Some examples will be considered later.

3. *Unhealthy housing and the landlord's liability for material defects.* This section will explore legal questions which resulted from inadequate standards of building and hygiene. In Berlin in 1892 more

[46] The old version of § 554 *BGB* said that: (1) the landlord can terminate the contract without observing a set period of notice if the tenant is in default with the rent or parts of the rent twice in succession. The termination is not allowed if the tenant pays the landlord before he gives notice of the termination. (2) The termination is void if the tenant freed himself of his debt by set-off and if he declared the set-off immediately after the termination of the contract.

[47] Windscheid, *Pandekten*, § 402, 547.

[48] *Reichsgericht*, judgment of 13 Dec. 1918, *Entscheidungen des Reichsgerichts in Zivilsachen*, 94 (1919), 234–6.

[49] *Obertribunal* Berlin, judgment of 2 Mar. 1866, *Striethorst (Archiv für Rechtsfälle . . . des Königlichen Ober-Tribunals)*, 62 (1867), 184–8.

[50] *Reichsgericht*, judgment of 6 Dec. 1901, *Juristische Wochenschrift* (1902), 69; in the same sense already for the Prussian law: *Reichsgericht*, judgment of 5 Jan. 1898, *Juristische Wochenschrift* (1898), No. 10, 111, and restrictively (the obligee has to have a sufficient time for reflection): *Reichsgericht*, judgment of 13 Apr. 1897, *Juristische Wochenschrift* (1897), No. 16, 272.

than 100,000 people lived in damp, dark cellars.[51] Damp new flats were regularly rented out until they were dry, and this practice was called 'living dry'. Poor people lived in the damp flat for a slightly reduced rent and dried it with their own heating. It was common knowledge that this was unhealthy. Apart from over-crowding, lack of light and dampness were the main points of contemporary criticism, followed by insanitary facilities.[52]

It is in the nature of tenancy that the landlord grants the tenant the use of the rented property. This presupposes that the property is suitable for use. But is a cellar without a window and with ice on the walls suitable for living in? In less obvious cases the distinction becomes more difficult. It is not just the definition of 'suitability' which causes problems, but also the question of the legal consequences. Can the tenant withdraw from the contract? Will the rent be reduced? Is there a claim for damages because of non-performance? In short, the legal question is: what constitutes a defect and what consequences does it have?

Under Roman common law the landlord was responsible for the suitability of the rented property. If he could not deliver possession, for instance because the house belonged to someone else, he was liable to pay damages. The same applied where later use became impossible through a fault of the landlord.[53] The land-lord was obliged to keep the rented property in a suitable condition.[54] If the accommodation posed a real risk to the tenant's health and safety, he could withdraw from the contract.[55] This right to withdraw was interpreted restrictively. The tenant had to allow the landlord an extension of time for improvement. This rule was invalid only if the defect could not be repaired at all, or could not be repaired in time.[56] By law the landlord had to bear

---

[51] Rudolph Eberstadt, 'Berliner Communalreform', *Preußische Jahrbücher*, 70 (1892), 577–610, here 578.

[52] Cf. the accounts by Teuteberg and Wischermann (eds.), *Wohnalltag in Deutschland*, 220 ff.

[53] Windscheid, *Pandekten*, § 400, 532. In case of impossibility of performance not caused by the fault of the landlord, both sides will be free similar to § 323 *BGB*.

[54] *Reichsgericht*, judgment of 19 Oct. 1880 (3rd division), *Seuffert's Archiv*, 36 (1881), No. 118, 168 f.; Windscheid, *Pandekten*, § 400, 532.

[55] *Reichsgericht* (cf. n. 54), 168.

[56] *Oberlandesgericht* Cassel, judgment of 4 Dec. 1888, *Seuffert's Archiv*, 47 (1892), No. 23, 38 f. In the case in question bugs could be eliminated by spreading acid on the floors and walls, scraping out and surfacing the cracks, putting on new paint and new wallpaper within three days, so that the court denied the tenant's right to withdraw from the contract.

maintenance costs. If a fault occurred, the tenant could at least partly reduce the rent.[57] Damages for non-performance were only due if the landlord had concealed the defect or assured the tenant of its absence.

The tenant's knowledge of the defect was significant. Such knowledge pointed to a tacit waiver of the enforcement of his claims against the landlord, which was the starting point for a regime comparatively unfavourable to tenants.[58] The Roman law derived this rule from a Digest fragment which specified that the landlord did not owe the tenant any damages if he had rented a house defective from the beginning and therefore only had himself to blame (D. 39.2.13.6).

In 1884 the following case came before the *Oberlandesgericht* Hamburg. The defendant lived in a damp flat, which had been assessed as unhealthy and unsuitable for occupation by a doctor. The defendant, a woman, had rescinded the contract, but the plaintiff wanted to continue the contract and won. Although the court admitted that the flat was objectively unsuitable for occupation for reasons of health, they nevertheless argued that as such damp rooms were commonly inhabited, there was no defect which justified a rescission.[59] This practice perpetuated miserable housing conditions. As the defective flats were inhabited the definition of a fault depended on custom, and the threshold of the concept of defect was very high. In practice the Roman common law offered no effective help. Furthermore, the landlord was not liable for initial defects if they were recognizable. In accordance with the *Reichsgericht*,[60] the *Oberlandesgericht* Hamburg said that the conclusion of a contract which involved a defective matter was to be interpreted as a tacit waiver of the warranty claim.

The *Oberlandesgericht* Brunswick went even further than the court in Hamburg. It decided in 1880 that perfection could not always be expected. In bigger cities, the court said, flats which

---

[57] Windscheid, *Pandekten*, § 400, 532; *Oberappellationsgericht* Cassel, judgment of 11 Oct. 1849, *Seuffert's Archiv*, 8 (1855) (repr. 1867), no. 252, 489.

[58] *Reichsgericht*, judgment of 19 Oct. 1880, *Seuffert's Archiv*, 36 (1881), No. 115, 164 f. The rule is deduced from D. 39.2.13.6 and D. 21.1.48.4.

[59] *Oberlandesgericht* Hamburg, judgment of 25 Mar. 1884, *Seuffert's Archiv* (1884), No. 297, 403–5.

[60] *Reichsgericht*, judgment of 19 Oct. 1880 (3rd division), *Seuffert's Archiv*, 36 (1881), No. 115, 164–5.

were situated in overpopulated, dark streets did not meet even low requirements in most respects; nevertheless they were rented. These circumstances were to be taken into consideration in dealing with the question of what was acceptable.[61] As these uninhabitable flats were nevertheless inhabited, in poorer districts rented accommodation did not have to meet even the lowest requirements. The *BGB* reacted to this failure by creating § 544, which grants the tenant a mandatory right to terminate without notice, whether or not he was aware that the rented property contained risks for his health. The Roman common law thus stated that first, the landlord had to keep the rented property in appropriate condition at his own expense. Second, defects were a reason for reducing the rent. Third, damages for non-performance were owed only if the defect had been fraudulently concealed or if the rented property lacked an essential feature that had been promised. Fourth, all these rights were void, however, if the tenant had been aware of the initial defect. This last rule was generally interpreted to the disadvantage of the tenant.

Under the Prussian General Code (*ALR*) the tenant was entitled to the ordinary use of the rented property (I. 21, §§ 270f.). Even if the tenant knew of defects at the time of concluding the contract, the landlord had to hand over the rented property free of defects (I. 21, § 272).[62] The landlord was obliged to maintain the rented property during the whole period of the tenancy (I. 21, § 291). If the landlord did not meet these requirements the tenant had the following rights (I. 21, § 273): (1) he could withdraw from the contract.[63] (2) He could demand renovation and could even remove initial defects without notice at the expense of the landlord.[64] (3) He could claim damages if the landlord was responsible for the defect.[65]

A judgment dating from 1875 by the *Obertribunal* in Berlin, which

---

[61] *Oberlandesgericht* Brunswick, judgment of 26 Nov. 1880, *Seuffert's Archiv*, 36 (1881), No. 191, 283–5.

[62] Dernburg, *Preußisches Privatrecht*, § 168, 404. The rule was not applicable if a group of assets was rented 'in the bulk', which means without any specification (I. 21, §§ 275 ff.). Dernburg, *Preußisches Privatrecht*, 401.

[63] Dernburg, *Preußisches Privatrecht* (cf. n. 42), § 168, 405. Parallel to D. 19.2.24.4.

[64] But he had to give notice of subsequent faults, I. 21, § 365 *ALR*.

[65] The necessity of fault is derived from I. 5, § 360. Dernburg, *Preußisches Privatrecht*, § 168, 406.

was the highest court of appeal in Prussia, may serve as an example of jurisdiction under the *ALR*, which was somewhat more favourable to the tenant than the Roman common law.[66] The tenant had rented a flat in an unfinished house. He did not move in because of defects, but withdrew from the contract according to I. 21, § 273 *ALR* and additionally claimed damages. In the end his action was dismissed only on the technical ground that he had not sufficiently specified his damage.[67] The court said that when the code mentioned compensation *or* withdrawal from the contract, it did not mean an alternative, but an enumeration of rights that could be claimed *cumulatively*, because the tenant's situation required that he be able to look for different and suitable accommodation. The court decided in favour of the tenant in three respects: (1) damages and withdrawal from the contract were permitted cumulatively. (2) It was assumed that the landlord was at fault.[68] (3) The action was not entirely dismissed, but the tenant was given the chance to substantiate his damage later.

The French *Code civil* (art. 1721) and the Saxon *BGB* (§§ 1198, 1213, 1221) both allowed the tenant to reduce the rent, to claim damages, and withdraw from the contract if the rented property had any defects.[69] The landlord's liability for initial defects was excluded if the tenant had been aware of them.[70]

According to the German *BGB*, which is still in force today, the landlord had to let the property in a condition suitable for the use the parties had agreed upon and keep it that way (§ 536 *BGB*). The suitability depended on the mutual agreement and could not be defined objectively. In interpreting the contract, local practice had to be taken into consideration.[71] In case the property was defective, for example because of excessively fuming stoves,

---

[66] *Obertribunal* Berlin, judgment of 28 May 1875, *Striethorst (Archiv für Rechtsfälle . . . des Königlichen Obertribunals)*, 94 (1876), 29 ff.

[67] *Obertribunal* Berlin (cf. n. 66), 32.

[68] The landlord of an unfinished house had a warranty of quality of the house.

[69] Crome, *Handbuch*, § 346, 545 f.; Friedrich Albert Wengler, *Der Miethvertrag nach königlich sächsischem Rechte* (2nd edn., Leipzig, 1891), § 11, 76–90.

[70] Crome, *Handbuch*, § 346, 545 n. 4; Wengler, *Der Miethvertrag*, §11, 76–90.

[71] Hermann Brückner, *Die Miete von Wohnungen und anderen Räumen nach dem Bürgerlichen Gesetzbuche* (Leipzig, 1900), 43; Max Mittelstein, *Die Miete nach dem Rechte des Deutschen Reiches* (2nd edn., Berlin, 1909), § 31, 144.

leaking gas mains, dampness, or dry rot, or indirectly because of noise, smell, or because of a police order prohibiting the use of the house,[72] the tenant could demand the removal of the defect (§§ 536, 537). Further, the law allowed for a reduction in rent for the time of the impairment (§ 537). Finally, a claim for damages could replace these rights (§ 538).

In contrast to the wording of § 538 *BGB*,[73] case law and literature soon developed a construction which allowed the tenant to reduce rent and claim damages cumulatively. Originally it was common belief that § 538 *BGB* contained a *facultas alternativa*. If the tenant opted for a reduction in rent, he had chosen between reduction and damages, and lost the chance of an action for damages.[74] This result seemed to be unfair, because often the tenant discovered defects whose removal he could have demanded only after the reduction. Therefore the interpretation was accepted that for any defects which were not covered by the reduction, damages could be demanded in spite of a former reduction according to § 538 *BGB*. It only had to be recognized that the reduction could be considered as a part of damages.[75] Concerning the damage claim the law differentiates with respect to the fault. In case of an initial defect the landlord had a liability even if the defect was not his fault. In case of a subsequent defect, however, he was liable for damages only if he was responsible for the defect. Finally, the tenant could terminate the contract without notice because of the landlord's failure to grant contractual use, but only after the lapse of a reasonable extension granted to the landlord (§ 542 *BGB*).

All these rights of the tenant were void if he knew of the defects at the time of the conclusion of the contract, or did not know of them because of his own gross negligence (§ 539 *BGB*). This rule did not apply if the landlord concealed the defect fraudulently or

---

[72] The examples by Oskar Niendorff, *Mietrecht nach dem Bürgerlichen Gesetzbuch: Handbuch für Juristen, Hauswirte und Mieter* (10th edn., Berlin, 1914), § 21, 137.

[73] The old version of the first subparagraph of the article read: where a defect as described in § 537 is in existence at the time of the conclusion of the contract or occurs later because of a circumstance for which the landlord is responsible, or if the landlord is in default with the removal of the defect, the tenant can demand damages for non-performance *instead of* claiming the rights described in § 537.

[74] *Oberlandesgericht* Kassel, judgment of 26 Nov. 1903, *Die Rechtsprechung der Oberlandesgerichte auf dem Gebiete des Civilrechts*, 7 (1903), 467.

[75] *Reichsgericht*, judgment of 3 July 1908, *Juristische Wochenschrift* (1908), No. 10, 549f.; Mittelstein, *Die Miete*, § 35, 178; Niendorff, *Mietrecht*, § 20, 5b, 136.

guaranteed its absence, or if the tenant accepted the property subject to certain provisos (§§ 539, 460, 464 *BGB*). The renting of a flat which was not in good condition and had been inspected by the tenant did not invalidate the landlord's obligation to let the property in good order.[76] As a last resort § 544 *BGB* provided that tenants could terminate without notice if the flat posed a considerable, objective risk to the tenant's health. This even applied to cases in which the tenant had explicitly waived this right in the contract.

This norm is remarkable, because it was introduced in the *BGB* for reasons of social policy, although the *Reichsjustizamt* had tried to leave explosive questions of this nature out of consideration if possible.[77] Anton Menger was the first to ask for a norm like § 544 *BGB* in his famous criticism in *Das bürgerliche Recht und die besitzlosen Volksklassen*.[78] The preliminary commission of the *Reichsjustizamt*, which prepared the hearings of the second commission, had taken up Menger's idea and worked out a corresponding clause. It is interesting that the minutes inform us of the social motivation of the draftsmen:

The following was taken into consideration: The norm [i.e. § 530 of the preliminary draft, corresponding to the later § 544 *BGB*] contains a fair limitation of the freedom of contract caused by social and humane motivations, which is quite compatible with the principles of the private law. The right to have notice of defects which put the tenant's health at risk, is an inalienable right of the individual. It must not be excluded where the tenant knows about the defect, because the tenant is often ignorant of the bad influence the defect has on his health and the extent of his ability to sustain the risk.[79]

To sum up, the tenant's situation in all aspects of law except for some shades of meaning did not look too bad. The landlord always had to provide a suitable property and to bear the maintenance costs. In case he did not meet his obligations, the tenant had the right to terminate the contract. Furthermore, he could generally reduce the rent and claim damages.

---

[76] See e.g. Mittelstein, *Die Miete*, § 31, 144 n. 6.

[77] On the politics of the *Reichsjustizamt*: Schulte-Nölke, *Das Reichsjustizamt*, 312–15.

[78] (Tübingen, 1890), 185–7.

[79] *Protokolle Reichsjustizamt*, 453 f., in Horst Heinrich Jakobs and Werner Schubert, *Die Beratung des Bürgerlichen Gesetzbuchs in systematischer Zusammenstellung der unveröffentlichten Quellen: Recht der Schuldverhältnisse II, §§ 433–651* (Berlin, 1980), 460.

Reality: the use of the law by landlords and tenants

Although there is no disputing the balance of the legal norms, it remains to be examined whether judicial and extra-judicial practice corresponded to the written legal system. Some aspects of judicial practice are reflected by the judgments mentioned in the previous section. But this is only one part of a larger whole.

If we ask how tenancy was constructed in reality, limitations are soon reached. In contrast to the actual housing conditions no statistical records about the practice of the courts are available. Therefore it would be speculation to say that, for instance, most lawsuits concerned actions for possession. Contemporary surveys of this kind are not known, and whether the material in the archives is sufficient for a reliable survey is at least doubtful. Published decisions are an obvious source. In contrast to Anglo-American law, in Germany it neither is nor was customary to make statements about names and personal data in the published decisions. This information was given only if it was relevant to the decision. Nor can we answer the question of whether case law in favour of the tenant may be explained by the fact that most judges were tenants themselves and therefore biased. It is not possible to ascertain how many judges lived in rented flats, even though it is probable that most did, because approximately 90 per cent of the urban population lived in rented accommodation. In any case, this would not be sufficient evidence of bias. To conclude this would mean ignoring the specific way of thinking imparted by a legal education, which teaches the individual to abstract from his personal convictions. Without idealizing the situation we must be careful about assuming a conflict of interests from personal involvement. Typical cases, from which tendencies and patterns of argument can be derived, can provide evidence of the legal reality. Apart from the judgments, contracts, usually written, are the most important source for the reality concerning tenancy. Contracts, however, have to be read in conjunction with legal treatises and case law, which interpreted them.

All over the German Kaiserreich the tenant law regulations with few exceptions, like termination because of health risks, were *dispositiv* which means that parties to the contract could opt out of the regulations given by law. To achieve this landlords normally used standard form contracts, which, to put it plainly, ascribed only duties to the tenant and only rights to the landlord.[80]

As a rule the standard form contracts were designed by local associations of property owners (*Haus- und Grundbesitzervereine*). In 1832 the first of these associations was founded in Hamburg. One of its first official acts was to draw up a list containing the names of all tenants who had once dodged the landlord's lien by moving out secretly. The members of the association were advised not to let a flat to such tenants. In 1879 the *Centralverband deutscher Haus- und Grundbesitzervereine* was founded in Dresden with its registered office in Berlin and by 1912 approximately 800 local associations had joined this central association.[81] In 1899 the central association issued a standard form contract in Elberfeld[82] which all local associations were instructed to use as a model. The tenants, on the other hand, were not so well organized. Not until 1900 was a national organization of tenants' associations formed, the *Bund Deutscher Mietervereine e.V.*[83]

The landlords' associations, which were better organized, were able to enforce their standard form contracts almost everywhere. In 1893 the *Haus- und Grundbesitzerverein* in Hamburg distributed 40,000 copies of the form. By 1900 the number had even risen to 106,000, and in the following years it lay between 50,000 and 80,000. On the basis of this data Wischermann suggests that in Hamburg 80 to 90 per cent of all rental contracts used these forms.[84] This estimate seems quite realistic. It is confirmed by contemporary sources for different cities. In 1911, for example, the *Landgericht* in Munich said in a judgment to which we shall return that it was practically impossible to rent a flat in Munich if you were not willing to sign the standard form issued by the *Haus- und*

---

[80] That tallies with the contemporary estimation in the literature: Fritz Stier-Somlo, *Unser Mietrechtsverhältnis und seine Reform* (Göttingen, 1902), 10; Brückner, *Miete*, 165; Friedrich Endemann, *Einführung in das Studium des Bürgerlichen Gesetzbuchs: Lehrbuch des bürgerlichen Rechts*, i: *Einleitung—Allgemeiner Theil—Recht der Schuldverhältnisse* (5th edn., Berlin, 1899), § 8, 34 n. 2; § 168, 753 n. 2; Josef Kohler, 'Bürgerliches Recht', in *Enzyklopädie der Rechtswissenschaft in systematischer Bearbeitung*, founded by Franz von Holtzendorff, ed. Josef Kohler, vol. ii (7th edn., Munich, 1914), 1–191, here 111; Engel, *Wohnungsnoth*, 102; Paul Eltzbacher, *Großberliner Mietverträge* (Berlin, 1913), 6; Niendorff, *Mietrecht*, § 33, 246 f.; Rudolf Breuer, *Das deutsche Wohnungsmietrecht nach den Formularverträgen der Vermietervereine*, doctoral dissertation (Heidelberg, 1914), 1 f., 15, 71; cf. the judgment of the *Landgericht* Munich I from 13 Jan. 1911, see below n. 115.

[81] Wischermann, *Wohnen in Hamburg*, 220.

[82] Published in Brückner, *Miete*, 162 ff.; cf. Stier-Somlo, *Unser Mietrechtsverhältnis*, 11 f.

[83] Wischermann, *Wohnen in Hamburg*, 221.   [84] Ibid. 222.

Grundbesitzerverein.[85] In 1903 the Bonn civil lawyer Konrad Cosack wrote: 'in many cities the landlords are accustomed to use printed forms for the conclusion of rental agreements. These forms contain many clauses in their favour; a tenant is defenceless against this, because he cannot find a landlord who does without the form.'[86] At the turn of the century the standard form contracts were the actual legal instrument most frequently used to create a dependency of the tenants on the landlords.[87] This may be illustrated by some examples concerning the three areas of conflict already discussed earlier: sale breaks tenancy, termination, and unhealthy housing.

As to the problem of continuing a rental agreement after a change of proprietors, even § 571 *BGB*, which had been inserted into the *BGB* for reasons of social policy, and by which the former landlord could be made liable for damages caused by the new proprietor, was considered *dispositiv*. By means of the standard forms it was often agreed that if the house was sold the tenant had to leave it without any compensation six weeks after receiving written notice.[88]

As to termination, the *BGB*, like the other bodies of law examined here, provided a number of reasons which had to be given if a rent agreement was to be terminated without notice. Nevertheless it was undisputed that more reasons for termination could be agreed upon in the contract. The background to this was the legislator's deliberate decision in favour of freedom of contract. This is shown in the minutes of the commission and the *Reichstag*. Different political parties introduced motions proposing that a norm, which could invalidate the agreement of reasons for termination, be inserted into the Code.[89] Hermann Struckmann, who acted as commissioner of the *Bundesrat* in the *Reichstag* and considerably influenced the majority, granted that the core of

---

[85] See below, n. 115.

[86] Konrad Cosack, *Lehrbuch des deutschen bürgerlichen Rechts*, vol. i (4th edn., Jena, 1903), 479.

[87] For a summary of the contents of the standard form contracts see Breuer, *Wohnungsmietrecht*. The work is based on sixty different standard form contracts of *Haus- und Grundbesitzervereine* in Germany.

[88] Niendorff, *Mietrecht*, § 40, 299; similarly Endemann, *Lehrbuch*, § 168, 753 n. 2; Breuer, *Wohnungsmietrecht*, 67 with reference to Altona (§ 20), Düsseldorf (§ 17), and Elberfeld (§ 13).

[89] Cf. the motions put by Frohme and Stadthagen during the meeting of the commission on 7 Mar. 1896 and of the Social Democrats in the plenum, Jakobs and Schubert, *Recht der Schuldverhältnisse II*, 614–15.

these motions was sensible with regard to conditions in Berlin. But he pointed out that such a far-reaching limitation of the freedom of contract was unsuitable for the diversity of life.[90]

Often the right to terminate the contract without notice was linked to offences against the house rules, which were always made part of the agreement. Paragraph 6 of a Berlin standard form contract of about 1910 contained the following rule: 'Standing and sitting around as well as children playing in or at the flat doors, in the yards, staircases and halls is forbidden.'[91] Given the number of children who lived in the crowded flats, there was probably not a single family which had not offended against this rule at least once. In the same form § 11 granted the landlord the right to terminate the contract without notice in case of a violation of § 6. A Berlin standard form contract from about forty years earlier contained the following rule: 'It is forbidden to quarrel, to make any music, to sing, to slam the doors; children are not to yell and servants are not to make any superfluous noise in the house and in the yard. It is not permitted under any circumstances to walk around on the stairs and in the halls wearing clogs or wooden slippers.'[92]

The purpose of these clauses was to have the tenant in one's hand. The landlords were able to terminate the contracts as they wished, because some flimsy reason for termination could always be found, be it only that the tenant had carried something smelly out of his flat before 10 p.m., that he had hung his quilt out of the window to air it, or that he had not replaced a broken windowpane immediately.[93] The limited number of reasons for termination in the written code was vastly extended by these contractual agreements, to the disadvantage of the tenant.

As to liability for material defects and unhealthy conditions, we have seen that in all systems of written law before and including the *BGB* the landlord was liable for the suitability of the rented property. Renovation, rent reduction, and damages were the ordinary consequences of defects. This distribution of the burden was

---

[90] Heller's report on the meeting of 7 Mar. 1896, ibid. 614–15.

[91] § 6 No. 4, standard form contract of Schönhausen, published in Eltzbacher, *Großberliner Mietverträge*, 7–12.

[92] § 9 No. 17, 'Berliner Mietvertrag der 70er Jahre', published in Engel, *Wohnungsnoth*, 100.

[93] § 6 No. 5 (garbage); § 6 No. 7 (beds); § 4 V (windowpane), standard form contract of Schönhausen (cf. n. 91).

perverted by these standard form contracts. For example, under § 4 of the Berlin standard form contract mentioned above,[94] the tenant had to acknowledge that the rooms met the contractual requirements.[95] Even initial defects did not give the tenant a claim against the landlord for warranty. The exclusion, however, was not to apply to those defects which made it impossible to use the rented property at all.[96] The tenant had to keep the premises in a suitable state and was responsible for all damage.[97] According to § 7 the landlord was permitted to 'enter each room at any time even during the absence of the tenant' and 'to remove the damage found without notice at the tenant's expense'.

In considering these problems we must bear in mind that housing standards were considerably below levels which would be regarded as tolerable today. In those days conditions were called faultless which nowadays would lead to a considerable rent reduction. For example, people who lived in one of the privileged households equipped with central heating[98] could not count on not freezing during the winter. The forms specified that the temperature in the living rooms had to be 13°Réaumur (approximately 16°C or 61°F) between 8 a.m. and 10 p.m.[99]

There were some critical voices in the scholarly literature as early as the 1870s, and they increased in number at the turn of the century, but the attitude of the courts seems to be of special importance. For the whole period under discussion it can be shown that the courts did not treat the relationship of landlord and tenant impartially. They often interpreted the standard form contracts in favour of tenants. Scholarly literature, which tended to favour the tenant,[100] served as a model for the courts' inter-

[94] Cf. n. 91.
[95] Breuer, *Wohnungsmietrecht*, 22, reported that those clauses were usual in almost all standard form contracts. People rented 'as is'.
[96] *Landgericht* Berlin I, 37 S 157/02, quoted by Niendorff, *Mietrecht*, 132.
[97] § 4, standard form contract of Schönhausen, cf. n. 91. An untypical exception to the rule is a form contract from Hamburg which was distributed there in the 1880s, specifying that the landlord had to bear the maintenance costs. § 2 Gieschen, Hamburg, 1884, published in Teuteberg and Wischermann (eds.), *Wohnalltag in Deutschland*, 117.
[98] In around 1910 only 2% of the Berlin households belonged to this category, Ascher, *Wohnungsmiethen*, 109, published in Teuteberg and Wischermann (eds.), *Wohnalltag in Deutschland*, 141.
[99] § 2, standard form contract of Düsseldorf, cf. Breuer, *Wohnungsmietrecht*, 22.
[100] Contemporary literature already noticed that tendency: Niendorff, *Mietrecht*, § 33, 247; Breuer, *Wohnungsmietrecht*, 15; also see Burkhard Ostermann, 'Richterliche Kontrolle vorformulierter Mietverträge um 1900', *Zeitschrift für Miet- und Raumrecht* (1992), 370f.

pretation of standard form contracts or supported it. For example, Niendorff's tenancy handbook wrote as follows on interpreting the house rules: 'The house rule is to be interpreted strictly, and in case of doubt in the manner which is the least troublesome for the tenant.'[101] Thus the host of reasons for termination without notice was at least reduced to a certain degree provided, of course, that the tenant was prepared to litigate. If, for example, the house rule forbade standing *and* sitting around in front of the doors, standing around alone was not affected by the contract.[102] 'The injunction against hanging laundry or other items out of the window is only violated if the item hangs over the window-sill completely and the landlord would be liable in case it fell out. It is not enough if quilts lie in the window and only stick out a foot.'[103]

The authors of the *BGB* considered the judicial interpretation of contracts to be the real instrument for checking contracts. The greatest possible freedom of contract should be granted by the law. The *BGB*'s fundamental decision can be demonstrated by reference to a number of discussions on tenancy.[104] Following a Social Democratic motion in the plenum of the *Reichstag*, § 553 *BGB* limited the *landlord's* right to terminate without notice, even when the tenant used the property in a manner contrary to the terms of the tenancy, to those cases in which the landlord's position was 'severely' ('in erheblichem Maße') infringed.[105] A vigorous debate had preceded this motion during the meeting of the commission, where the 'vexatious and extortionate Berlin forms' were given as a reason for the demand for the right of termination to be restricted. Struckmann had replied that the courts were able to interpret the contracts in good faith so that they did not have a vexatious effect.[106] Thus the authors of the draft code were not inclined to state intervention motivated by social policy. The decision of the *Reichstag* in § 553 *BGB* was of special importance for judicial practice because the criterion of the severity of the violation of the law was applied analogously to those additional reasons for termination which had been

---

[101] Niendorff, *Mietrecht*, § 33, 250 and § 16, 89. Similarly, Mittelstein, *Die Miete*, § 31, 147.
[102] Niendorff, *Mietrecht*, § 33, 251.   [103] Ibid., § 33, 251.
[104] Besides the following discussion see above, n. 89.
[105] Cf. Jakobs and Schubert, *Recht der Schuldverhältnisse II*, 498.
[106] Cf. ibid. 497–8.

stipulated by contract.[107] This fulfilled the intentions of the legislator.

By referring to some characteristic judgments concerning the termination of contract and warranty, the final part of this essay will show that case law in principle tended to arrive at decisions in favour of the tenant. The purpose of this account is to demonstrate how the courts used their interpretation to check the contracts in line with the expectations of the legislator.

The *Obertribunal* in Berlin had to decide the following case in 1874.[108] The contested rental contract contained a clause saying that offences against the house rules could be a reason for termination without notice. The standard form contract signed by both parties read: 'Pots containing malodorous substances must not be carried outside before . . . o'clock in the evening and have to be well covered.' The gap in the form, which was left open for the exact time, was not filled in. A maid—the problems of the *Wohnungsfrage* were not restricted to the lower classes—had taken such substances to the backyard one morning in an open bucket. Thereupon the landlord had terminated the contract. The *Revision* (appeal on the question of law only) led to a final dismissal of the action. Of all possible interpretations of the clause mentioned above, the court of appeal, dealing with appeals on questions of law, chose the one most favourable for the tenant. As the parties had not filled in a certain time, the questionable clause had not been agreed upon at all. The *Kammergericht*, the Berlin court of appeal dealing with questions of fact and law, which had previously decided this case, at second instance, had interpreted the contract in such a way as to save its legal force as much as possible. It had said that the parties had at least agreed that the substances mentioned were only to be carried outside in the evening. The *Obertribunal*, by contrast, said that if such had been intended, the words 'before' and 'o'clock' would have been crossed out. If in individual parts of a standard form contract the necessary handwritten additions were missing, the complete rule would not form part of the agreement.[109]

---

[107] *Reichsgericht*, judgment of 22 Jan. 1904, *Juristische Wochenschrift* (1904), 139 f., No. 4; Brückner, *Miete*, 61 f.; Mittelstein, *Die Miete*, § 27, 124.

[108] *Obertribunal* Berlin, judgment of 9 Feb. 1874 (3rd division), in *Striethorst* (*Archiv für Rechtsfälle . . . des Königlichen Obertribunals*), 91 (1875), 85–9.

[109] *Obertribunal* Berlin (cf. n. 108), 86 f. The landlord lobbies learned from this judgment: e.g. in the Schönhauser form it was not necessary to fill in the time in question by handwriting (cf. § 6 No. 5).

In the same judgment the *Obertribunal* set up another important principle in favour of the tenant. In the case in question the landlord had terminated the contract four months after the tenant had fallen into arrears with his rent. The court considered the interim continuation of the contract a tacit declaration of the continuation of the tenancy. Acting in good faith, the landlord had no right to leave the tenant in doubt about whether he wanted to terminate the contract, but he had to give a declaration immediately.[110] This view made its way into case law.[111]

A constant quarrel between landlords and tenants concerned laundry. Almost all house rules forbade washing clothes in the flat,[112] and this applied in a case which the *Reichsgericht* had to decide in its first year.[113] The court said that the tenant, acting in good faith, had not wanted to commit himself to doing something unusual, such as postponing the children's laundry until washing day. It had therefore been the intention of the parties for the prohibition to refer only to 'major' laundering, which meant the laundry of the whole family taking a longer period of time. But 'lesser' laundering for immediate use was allowed. The *Reichsgericht* classified the washing of five shirts, several kitchen-towels, shirt-collars, some children's clothes, and aprons as 'lesser' laundering. The rigorous prohibition against laundering in the house rule was restricted by the *Reichsgericht*'s judgment to a more acceptable level. But these issues continued to be a source of conflict. Twenty years later the *Landgericht* of Berlin considered it a valid reason for termination that a maid had washed her own skirt and petticoat together with the 'lesser' laundry.[114]

The third example of judges amending standard form contracts is a judgment by the *Landgericht* of Munich in 1911.[115] The disputing parties had signed a standard form contract which provided

---

[110] *Obertribunal* Berlin (cf. n. 108), 88.

[111] Cf. *Obertribunal* Berlin, judgment of 2 Mar. 1866, in *Striethorst (Archiv für Rechtsfälle . . . des Königlichen Obertribunals)*, 63 (1867), 184–8; *Reichsgericht*, judgment of 11 May 1887, in *Die Praxis des Reichsgerichts in Civilsachen*, 4 (1887), 203 f.; *Reichsgericht*, judgment of 13 Apr. 1897, *Juristische Wochenschrift* (1897), No. 16, 272—the *Reichsgericht* toned down the rule mentioned by introducing a period of reflection on whether one wants to terminate. *Reichsgericht*, judgment of 5 Jan. 1898, *Juristische Wochenschrift* (1898), No. 10, 111; *Reichsgericht*, judgment of 6 Dec. 1901, *Juristische Wochenschrift* (1902), 69.

[112] Cf. evidence in Breuer, *Wohnungsmietrecht*, 23 f.

[113] *Reichsgericht*, judgment of 28 Nov. 1879, in Niendorff, *Mietrecht*, § 33, 254.

[114] *Landgericht* Berlin I, judgment of 25 Nov. 1899, quoted by Niendorff, *Mietrecht*, § 33, 254.

[115] *Landgericht* Munich I, judgment of 13 Jan. 1911, *Deutsche Juristenzeitung* (1911), cols. 461 f. as well as a more detailed report in *Seufferts Blätter für Rechtsanwendung*, 76 (1911), 217–20.

that the tenant had to pay a fee ('housing damage') of 10 per cent of one year's rent if he terminated earlier than two years after signing the contract. The tenant moved out after nine months. Therefore the landlord, as plaintiff, demanded the payment of the 'housing-damage' fee, but he lost the action because the court considered the clause mentioned unconscionable and therefore void according to § 138. I *BGB*.[116] The purpose of the 'housing-damage' fee was to complicate the tenant's right to terminate the contract, said the court. Because of the monopolistic position of the landlords, who almost all used such forms, the use of such clauses was unconscionable. The *Landgericht* clearly realized the problematical consequences of the fact that the written legal norms were *dispositiv*. The judges explained that the legal norms could be adapted in each individual case. Generally, however, the norms were to be expressions of a typical balance of interests. If, therefore, the courts detected a continuous deviation from the legal idea, they had to ask themselves whether this deviation was just. If the difference served as an abuse by landlords of their economic dominance, this was not an expression of contractual freedom, but of its improper use, the prevention of which was the purpose of § 138 *BGB*.[117] In this case the court did not exercise control by interpreting the contract itself, but by using the general clause of § 138. I *BGB*, which says that a legal transaction contrary to public policy is void. The court had based its opinion on scholarly opinions. Endemann said very clearly that standard form contracts which unilaterally violated the rules of the *BGB* were against good morals. He wrote:

The judge will have the duty, according to the power granted to him, to make sure that respect for the well balanced system of the *BGB* will also be preserved in regard to the standard form contracts. A contract is against public policy if its contents are pressed upon the tenant, exploiting the local housing shortage.[118]

Conclusion

During the Kaiserreich the actual housing situation in the German cities was deplorable for most sections of the population.

---

[116] 'Ein Rechtsgeschäft, das gegen die guten Sitten verstößt, ist nichtig.'
[117] *Landgericht* Munich I (cf. n. 115).   [118] Endemann, *Lehrbuch*, § 168, 753 n. 2.

The standard of housing improved only slowly until after the First World War. All in all, private tenancy law did nothing to ameliorate these conditions. It is true that according to the written law the tenant's position was not so bad, as, for example, the protection against eviction as well as the warranty show. If the written norms had been implemented with a firm hand, some abuses would not have survived. But contemporary private law doctrine did not have as high a regard for state intervention as it did for the preservation of freedom of contract. This opinion is the key to the correct understanding of the conflict of interests between landlords and tenants. Freedom of contract made it possible to avoid the legal model. From our point of view the landlords, whose economic position was usually superior, fully exploited this option. The tenants became completely dependent on the landlords, so that the legal reality was highly disadvantageous for the tenant—so long at least as there was a shortage of affordable housing. In the fast-growing and overcrowded German cities before 1914 this was almost always the case. Nevertheless it can be said for the whole period under examination here that the courts made an effort to break the one-sidedness of the standard form contracts and to find balanced rules. A scholarly literature motivated by considerations of social policy supported this trend.

The success of this case law cannot be measured clearly. It was always directly effective only in individual cases. Looking back, we can see that it has gained enormous importance. The origins of consumer protection, which we take for granted in today's private law, lie in the disputes about the burning social issues of the Kaiserreich. One of these issues was tenancy. In retrospect, the judicial control of contract in particular proved to be an effective social element in the reality of tenancy law.

16
Landlord–Tenant Courts in New York City at the Turn of the Twentieth Century

Richard H. Chused

Introduction

Save for the monthly ritual of paying rent, landlords and tenants in late nineteenth-century New York City most often met each other during eviction proceedings. Thousands of tenants from immigrant neighbourhoods and tenement house districts were summoned to court each year to learn if their failure to pay rent would lead the judge to order their immediate ouster or give them a few days to pay their rent.[1] Other outcomes were unlikely. Henry Howland, an attorney of the time, provided one picture of the judicial scene:

When court opens, the room is crowded with lawyers, litigants, some of whom plead their own causes, witnesses, and unhappy tenants, and in the lower East-Side districts the experience appeals to more senses than that of sight. In the dispossess cases the woman of the family generally appears, dragging a child by the hand, and carrying a babe in the arms, for sympathetic reasons. Failing offspring of tender age, a child is not infrequently borrowed from a neighbor. 'Mrs. Pasquale,' or 'Mrs. Reilly,' says the judge, 'why don't you pay your rent?' and then interrupts the eloquent flow in answer to so intricate a question by saying, 'I'll give you until Monday, or the marshal will put you out.'[2]

---

[1] According to William McLoughlin, in 'Evictions in New York's Tenement Houses', *Arena*, 7 (1892), 48–57, 5,450 dispossess warrants issued from the district covering the Lower East Side between Oct. 1891 and Sept. 1892. This number is almost surely much smaller than the number of cases actually filed. A significant number of the disputes were probably resolved before the warrant stage. Another 6,100 warrants were issued from the court in a neighbouring district; 29,720 came from all the landlord–tenant courts in New York City. If each evicted family had five people—a quite conservative estimate—about 150,000 people were ordered out of their homes in the 1891–2 period.

[2] Henry E. Howland, 'The Practice of the Law in New York', *Century Magazine*, 62 (1901), 803–25. The presence of women may not have been merely for sympathy. Fathers,

While Howland evinced little sympathy for the plight of tenants, his little story confirms that tenants failing to pay their rent could only beg for a bit more time to find some cash or another place to live before the constabulary showed them to the door. The quality of the tenant's housing was irrelevant. Broken promises by landlords to make repairs were of no concern. Neither the length of a tenant's stay nor the plight of children was germane. Time to restore financial solvency was not provided. The scope of a commercial tenant's investment in the property was immaterial. The illegality of the tenement apartment building's construction or use was of no moment. Publicly provided housing to take in those ousted from their privately owned apartments did not exist.[3] The streets beckoned.

During the same year Howland's article describing landlord–tenant courts appeared in print, the New York state legislature adopted the Tenement House Act of 1901[4]—the culmination of a major, long-term effort by Progressive reformers to ban the construction of poor-quality apartment buildings.[5] The coexistence of a major Progressive Era housing reform movement and a landlord–tenant court evicting thousands of persons each year from poor-quality tenement houses seems anomalous to this late twentieth-century mind. This essay will tell the story of how such apparently contradictory streams of legal events occurred simultaneously.

The legal part of the tale has three parts. First, some knowledge of nineteenth-century American landlord–tenant law is a

husbands, brothers, or sons may well have been out working for the funds needed to pay the rent. The frequency of borrowed baby appearances is unknown. But if the men in the family were off working, it is hardly surprising that babies would show up in court.

[3] The United States has never had a programme of publicly funded housing construction as broad as those commonly available in Europe. For some of the history of American public housing programmes and the problems associated with their servicing only the lower classes, see Lawrence Friedman, 'Public Housing and the Poor: An Overview', *California Law Review*, 54 (1966), 642–69.

[4] Laws of NY, ch. 334 (1901).

[5] A review of some of the Tenement House Act history may be found in Lawrence Friedman and Michael J. Spector, 'Tenement House Legislation in Wisconsin: Reform and Reaction', *American Journal of Legal History*, 9 (1965), 41–63. The classic histories of the tenement reforms include Robert DeForest and Lawrence Veiller (eds.), *The Tenement House Problem* (New York, 1903); Lawrence Veiller, 'The Housing Problem in American Cities', *Annals of the American Academy of Political and Social Sciences*, 25 (1905), 248–72; Roy Lubove, *The Progressives and the Slums: Tenement House Reform in New York City 1890–1917* (Westport., Conn., 1962); Steven Andrachek, 'Housing in the United States: 1890–1929', in Gertrude Fish (ed.), *The Story of Housing* (New York, 1979), 123–76.

prerequisite to understanding the reforms of the Progressive Era. The arrival of speedy eviction remedies before the Civil War dramatically altered the shape of residential leaseholds. Second, some changes did occur in landlord–tenant law during the decades surrounding the turn of the twentieth century. The constructive eviction doctrine evolved to allow a few more tenants to leave their abodes without further obligation to pay their rent. Tort remedies also expanded, providing some relief in situations where tenants were injured by their landlords' failure to obey newly enacted building codes or tenement house acts. But none of these changes had any impact on the operation of the summary dispossess remedy. And, as already mentioned, Tenement House Acts began to appear near the end of the nineteenth century.

The final and most important part of the story involves the limited vision of the Progressive Era. A number of its reform societies, public service groups, and other organizations were anxious to improve the quality of urban life in America. Reviewing the history of these reform movements—describing their middle- and upper-class roots and commenting on their ethnic and racial biases—will impart a sense of the circumscribed imagination of the Progressive Era and help us understand why the reforms of that time left the summary dispossess process untouched and impoverished tenants without legal remedies.[6]

Summary dispossess statutes and early American landlord–tenant law

Nineteenth-century residential leasehold disputes commonly occurred in three situations. First, landlords sought to evict tenants who were living on the property but not paying rent. Second, landlords sued for unpaid rent from tenants who had given up possession of the property. And third, tenants who were injured while using rented property sometimes sued their landlords for damages.[7]

---

[6] Parts of this story, especially the use of speedy procedures against poor defendants, are remarkably similar to the tale told by Paul Johnson in 'Creditors, Debtors, and the Law in Victorian and Edwardian England', another essay in this volume.

[7] These same three situations still arise today, though they are now handled in somewhat different ways from a century ago. Despite all of the recent reforms, however, landlords are still usually able speedily to get rid of their non-paying tenants.

Most states handled all three situations according to a standard vision of American landlord–tenant law.[8] The vision rested upon an English tenurial notion that in return for authority to use land, a tenant agreed to pay rent, to maintain the land, and to return the land when the lease expired. It was a simple contract exchanging the right to possession for some form of payment in cash or kind. The landlord's obligations were fulfilled upon transfer of possession to the tenant. Once that transfer was complete, the tenant was obligated to pay the rent and return the land to the landlord at the termination of the lease. The standard leasehold was envisioned as giving almost complete control over the use of the rented property to the tenant for the length of the lease.[9] If the tenant vacated the land before the end of the lease, the obligation to pay rent, therefore, did not end. The landlord transferred the entire rental term and was under no obligation to take it back.[10] Similarly, if a tenant was injured while in possession of rented land, the landlord was not responsible. Tenants were obligated to keep the land safe for their own use and occupancy. And, of course, if the tenant did not pay rent, the landlord could reclaim possession.

The simplicity of this legal relationship was re-emphasized by nineteenth-century civil procedure in the United States. Procedural norms, also based in many ways on English precedents, were often as single minded as the standard lease. If someone had a legal problem, they filed a writ about that problem and litigated the issue. There were certain defences to each kind of writ, but merger of claims and parties, and the use of counter-claims, was

---

[8] For material on the 19th-century history of American residential landlord–tenant law, see John Humbach, 'The Common-Law Conception of Leasing: Mitigation, Habitability, and Dependence of Covenants', *Washington University Law Quarterly*, 60 (1983), 1213–90; Sarajane Love, 'Landlord's Remedies when the Tenant Abandons: Property, Contract and Leases', *Kansas Law Review*, 30 (1982), 533–70; Mary Ann Glendon, 'The Transformation of American Landlord–Tenant Law', *Boston College Law Review*, 23 (1982), 503–76; Richard Chused, 'Contemporary Dilemmas of the Javins Defense: A Note on the Need for Procedural Reform in Landlord–Tenant Law', *Georgetown Law Journal*, 67 (1979), 1385–403; Stephen Siegel, 'Is the Modern Lease a Contract of a Conveyance? A Historical Inquiry', *Journal of Urban Law*, 52 (1978), 649–87.

[9] In many ways this vision was false. If, for example, rent was paid in kind, the landlord might take large portions of the tenant's crops. The terms of the lease could easily leave a tenant as a virtual servant of the landlord.

[10] The common law rules went so far as to hold a tenant responsible for rent even after the building was destroyed by fire, storm, or other natural cause. That result was altered by statute in New York in 1860. Laws of NY, ch. 345 (13 Apr. 1860).

unknown.[11] Thus, when landlords sought to evict tenants for non-payment of rent, the tenant could not respond by asserting that the leased property was not good for farming. Or when tenants not in possession were sued for rent they had not paid before their departure from the land, they could not usually assert that they had left the premises after suffering an injury caused by the landlord's negligent behaviour.

Together the land lease and the writ system established a legal regime in which suits against tenants for either possession or unpaid rent were quite separate from each other and from suits for breaches of other contracts. If a written lease contained contractual terms on matters other than the possession for rent exchange of a standard rental, the additional contractual terms were not thought of as part of the lease. Disputes over these other contracts were handled separately from controversies over the lease. The lease was both substantively and procedurally independent of other contractual terms. Indeed, that independence of contracts (usually called 'covenants' in traditional cases) idea governed not only the law of leases but much of nineteenth-century contract law. Since different covenants in a lease were said to be independent, breach of one covenant could not be defended by claiming that the other side breached a different covenant. Thus a suit for unpaid rent was defendable only by a claim of accord and satisfaction (payment), constructive eviction (an action by the landlord so disturbing to the tenant's right to possess the property that the rent for land exchange was deemed void), or perhaps fraud in the inducement (fraud that induced the tenant to agree to a contract he would otherwise have eschewed).

For tenants, the most serious consequence of this vision of landlord–tenant law was the ability of landlords speedily to evict non-paying tenants. Indeed, American practice 'purified' the early English law by getting rid of many impediments to the eviction of defaulting tenants. Early in the nineteenth century, for example, New York landlords seeking possession of rented property

---

[11] Today, plaintiffs may join all their claims against the defendant in the same case and must join those arising out of the same facts. Defendants may respond to a plaintiff's case by asserting all available claims against the plaintiff. Claims arising out of the facts giving rise to the plaintiff's case must be asserted. In most cases, all the parties involved in the claims may be joined in the same case. This sort of wide-open litigation process was unknown for most of the 19th century. Serious reforms did not arise until the Federal Rules of Civil Procedure were adopted in 1938.

pursued ejectment claims modelled on a British statutory antecedent.[12] When rent was at least six months in arrears and the landlord had reserved in the lease a right to re-enter the property, the landlord could sue in ejectment for possession of the property. This version of the ejectment remedy arose in an agricultural world where many leases were in writing and most lasted for a term of years. Leasehold arrangements formed the backbone of much of early English property law and embodied a large set of cultural norms and interlocking chains of human relationships. In such a world it made sense to provide for a six-month waiting period before ejectment could occur. Removal of a tenant from the tenurial chain could cause a drastic change in social status and class. It served to protect not only the lower classes, but also those in the upper ranks of society who fell upon hard times.

This system could not last long in New York. By the early nineteenth century, New York City had a large number of residential tenants. Many of them were immigrants occupying apartments or houses under oral, periodic leases that could be terminated on a month's notice. Use of the ejectment process made it quite difficult to evict those tenants not paying their rent. Landlords using oral leases could not always prove they had reserved a right to re-enter the premises. The six-month grace period seemed too long in urban periodic tenancy cases. Evicting a tenant usually did not have major cultural repercussions. In 1820, the General Assembly rewrote the eviction statute, allowing a tenant to be summarily removed if he held over past the end of the term or defaulted in the payment of rent. This statute not only did away with the six-month waiting period, but shifted the proceedings to a different court for speedier action. In a rent default case, the landlord had to show that the rent was due, that he had reserved a right to re-enter the property, and that he had served a written demand for the rent at least three days before filing the judicial proceeding.[13]

In an 1840 report, the New York Senate claimed that the 1820 statute was motivated by two concerns:

[12] 4 Geo. II c. 28 (1731). For some of the early history, see *Michaels* v. *Fishel*, 169 NY 381, 62 NE 425 (1902).

[13] Laws of the State of New York, ch. 194, at 176 (13 Apr. 1820). At least one court decision also imposed a requirement that there be insufficient personal property available on the premises for distress (self-help seizure by the landlord) to satisfy the rent due. *Oakley* v. *Schoonmaker*, 15 NY [Wendell] 1226 (1837). It is not clear when this notion fell into disuse.

the difficulty of enforcing payment of rent in the city, which was likely to operate with great severity upon the poor, because it would drive lessors to exact security for rent indiscriminately; and 2d. The difficulty of obtaining possession of demised premises after the lease had expired.[14]

The second claim rings true. The earlier statute had left landlords seeking possession from holdover tenants to the sloth and technicalities of the ejectment proceeding. As New York City grew and the number of commercial and residential tenants increased, building owners' dissatisfaction with the tenant removal process grew. At some point landlords were going to demand and the legislature was going to create a speedier way of removing tenants who were overstaying their welcome. However, the claim by the 1840 authors of the Senate Report that the changes in nonpayment proceedings were designed to protect poor tenants is more difficult to understand. It may reflect an honest reconstruction of the General Assembly's motivations in 1820. It is not illogical to expect that landlords would seek larger security deposits from tenants if it was difficult to remove them when they failed to pay their rent. But the statements of sympathy for the poor may also have been generated by the bad times extant after the Panic of 1837, the starting point for one of the major economic downturns in America's history. Regardless of the 1840 report's accuracy, however, it was not surprising that fast-paced urban developments in New York City forced the legislature to repeal the six-month grace period in the ejectment law for those failing to pay their rent. Those owning leased buildings in the quickly growing environs of lower Manhattan Island were not going to sit on their hands while tenants occupied their premises rent free for long periods of time. Indeed, landlords drafted the 1820 Act and nursed it to passage.[15]

Save for the passage of a few minor amendments, the basic structure of the 1820 summary dispossess statute remained intact for approximately 150 years.[16] The paucity of amendments and the short-lived nature of the single ameliorative change adopted

[14] Documents of the Senate of New York, Report No. 65, at 9 (1840).

[15] Ibid.

[16] The summary dispossess statutes were routinely re-enacted each time the state legislature recodified New York law. See, e.g., 3 George Bliss, *The New York Civil Procedure Code as it is January 1st, 1895*, vol. iii at 2612–43 (1895). Significant changes in the summary dispossess process did not come until about 1970 when state courts all over the nation began

in the nineteenth century attests to the widespread assumption that speedy evictions were needed to ensure the development of New York City. The single change involved the adoption in 1840 of an amendment banning use of the summary process against any tenant with more than five years left to run on a lease.[17] Some business interests complained that it was unfair summarily to evict tenants occupying premises under long-term leases for failure to pay small amounts of rent after they had made significant capital improvements. The bad economic times following the Panic of 1837 generated sympathy for their position. Indeed, a great deal of debtor protection legislation was enacted all over the United States during the 1840s.[18] Protection of long-term, mostly commercial tenants fit neatly into that mould.[19]

Enactment of this change did not occur without controversy. Landlords lobbied against the reforms, complaining that they should not be forced to bear the economic losses of their tenants. The state Senate, in rebuffing such claims, commented:

It is worthy of remark that the English statutes, from which our statutes on this subject were substantially derived, were devised and enacted by a legislative body in which the tenantry of the country had almost literally no representation. In the House of Peers, the whole body were landlords, and in the House of Commons, the landed interest greatly predominated over all others; and having thus the legislative power, this favored class would naturally omit nothing, in making laws so nearly affecting its own interests. Yet in our legislation we have apparently gone far beyond the English law in providing remedies for landlords.[20]

to allow tenants to raise certain defences in summary dispossess proceedings if there were health and safety code violations in their apartments. The most famous of these cases is *Javins* v. *First National Realty Corp.*, 428 F. 2d 1071 (1970). *Javins* began to be followed in New York almost immediately. See, e.g., *Amanuensis, Ltd.* v. *Brown*, 318 NYS 2d 311, 65 Misc. 2d 15 (1971); *Steinberg* v. *Carreras*, 344 NYS 2d 136, 74 Misc. 2d 32 (1973).

[17] Laws of New York, ch. 162, at 119 (25 Apr. 1840).

[18] Bankruptcy legislation, foreclosure regulations, exemptions of certain sorts of property from attachment by creditors, abolition of imprisonment for debt, and Married Women's Property Acts were the most common sorts of enactments. See Richard Chused, 'Married Women's Property Law: 1800–1850', *Georgetown Law Journal*, 71 (1983), 1359–425, at 1402–4; Peter J. Coleman, *Debtors and Creditors in America: Insolvency, Imprisonment for Debt, and Bankruptcy, 1607–1900* (Madison, 1974).

[19] The structure of landlord–tenant law was the subject of debate at the New York State Constitutional Convention in 1846 and in several sessions of the state legislature during the 1840s. The high point of tenant-oriented reform measures in the period was the abolition of the remedy of distress for rents in 1846. Laws of NY, ch. 274 (1846).

[20] Report No. 65, n. 14 above, at 11.

Legislative sympathy for tenants did not last long. When the summary dispossess statute was re-enacted in 1849 during better economic times, the requirement that landlords use the old eject-ment procedure for getting rid of long-term tenants was removed.[21]

Later amendments only added to the list of settings in which the summary process could be used. Getting rid of bawdy houses after soldiers returned home from the Civil War was the object of the legislation adopted in 1868.[22] Five years later, the summary dispossess process was made available to evict lessees using a premises for any 'illegal trade, manufacture or other business'.[23] This provision was rarely used.[24] Indeed, tenement houses were teeming with sweat shops and small industrial establishments by the end of the century. Licensing schemes were established in a weak attempt to control them. Not until the Triangle Shirt Waist factory fire in 1911 did New York begin seriously to attack the unsafe working conditions of many labouring in the tenements and lofts of New York.

New York was far from alone in establishing speedy eviction procedures during the nineteenth century. While it was the first state to enact a summary dispossess remedy, states commonly adopted such schemes.[25] Indeed, adoption of summary dispossess statutes fit nicely into the American vision of landlord–tenant law in the nineteenth century. The speedy process met the need for a particular form of relief for landlords and was naturally separate from other claims that tenants might have against their landlords. In a simple, formalistic legal world this all made some sense. It allowed landlords to use oral, month-to-month leases without seriously disturbing the ability of landlords to rid themselves of unwanted tenants. The investment and speculative aims of landlords were easily protected. There was no need for

---

[21] Laws of NY, ch. 193, at 291 (3 Apr. 1849).

[22] Ibid., ch. 764, at 1724 (9 May 1868).

[23] Ibid., ch. 583, at 895 (22 May 1873).

[24] There is only one reported case on the provision. It held that the summary process was available only when the illegal activity was actually occurring. Once the illegal activity ceased, the landlord was left to pursue ejectment. *Shaw* v. *McCarty*, 63 How. Prac. 286 (Com. Pleas 1882).

[25] Many states adopted summary eviction remedies prior to 1850. Ohio enacted a statute in 1831, followed by Georgia in 1833, Massachusetts in 1841, Tennessee in 1842, Indiana in 1843, Illinois in 1845, Michigan in 1846, Texas in 1848, and California in 1850. The best summary of the 20th-century statutes may be found in American Law Institute, *Restatement (Second) of Property* (Philadelphia, 1977), §12.1, Statutory Note, at pp. 399–406.

tenement house owners to rely upon onerous contractual terms, like those used in Germany,[26] to control the use of their land.

Reform and the Progressive Era

One might expect that in an industrial nation full of ghastly urban problems, this standard, formalized vision of landlord–tenant law would fall apart, that development of large-scale urban reform movements during the Progressive Era would lead to the creation of legal fora more sympathetic to the needs of those living in tenement houses and apartments. This did not happen. The first clue that landlord–tenant courts were going to be relatively immune from change appeared in the 1840s in New York with the adoption of procedural reforms in the Field Code. The Field Codes were the first attempt to remove some of the writ system's baggage, to simplify pleading by allowing multiple claims and parties in the same case.[27] But these civil procedure reforms had no impact on summary dispossess proceedings. Indeed, summary dispossess statutes proliferated around the country while Field Codes were being adopted. The legal system did not find it anomalous that an array of defences and counter-claims were available in virtually every procedural context except summary dispossess courts until the 1960s.

The first major changes in the nineteenth-century American vision of landlord–tenant law were generated by enactment of housing and building codes in New York. Major tenement house laws were adopted in 1894 and 1901. Other changes followed, as scandals erupted over lack of maintenance of tenements by

---

[26] Cf. the essay by Tilman Repgen in this volume.

[27] For more on the Field Codes, see Robert Bone, 'Mapping the Boundaries of a Dispute: Conceptions of Ideal Lawsuit Structure from the Field Code to the Federal Rules', *Columbia Law Review*, 89 (1989), 1–118; Stephen Subrin, 'David Dudley Field and the Field Code: A Historical Analysis of an Earlier Procedural Vision', *Law and History Review*, 6 (1988), 311–73. Many judges resisted the reforms of the Field Codes, insisting that pleadings read much like the old writs to pass muster. Earth-shaking procedural change did not occur in the United States until the Federal Rules of Civil Procedure were promulgated in 1938 and then copied by many state court systems. Those reforms clearly allowed multiple claims and parties, set up fairly simple rules for the filing of counter-claims, and began the final dissolution of separate courts of law and equity in most states.

famous persons and religious organizations,[28] fires killed people in their apartments and in sweat shops buried in the tenement districts, and rent strikes popped up in the slums.[29] Jacob Riis published his famous muckraking book *How the Other Half Lives* in 1890. The General Assembly's Tenement House Committee produced a massive report during the 1895 session of the state legislature, describing in detail the conditions in tenement houses and exploring the ownership of large numbers of tenement houses by the Trinity Church.[30] For the most part enforcement of the new standards was accomplished by setting up bureaucracies and establishing criminal penalties for violations of new codes, not by making changes in the summary dispossess proceeding or in other areas of landlord–tenant law. But two areas of landlord–tenant law—tort liability of landlords and constructive eviction law— were significantly influenced by the burgeoning Progressive Era reforms.

As the legislatures in New York state and New York City began to adopt housing and building codes after the turn of the twentieth century, courts used the new codes as a basis for redefining the duties owed by landlords to their tenants who were injured on the premises. By 1925, injured tenants were no longer limited to recovery only in cases where the common areas, like hallways, were dangerous.[31] The courts referred to the new building and housing codes as sources of law for defining the contours of landlord responsibility.[32] The change in approach was quite gradual.

---

[28] In 1894 a scandal broke when it was revealed that the Trinity Church Corporation owned a number of rental buildings that were in deplorable condition. See, e.g., 'Old Trinity Shanties', *New York Times* (15 Dec. 1894), one of a series of articles about the controversy.

[29] There was a significant surge of rent strikes in 1904 in response to widespread rent increases. See, e.g., Archibald Hill, 'The Rental Agitation on the East Side', *Charities Review*, 12 (16 Apr. 1904), 396–8.

[30] Report of the Tenement House Committee, NY Assembly Documents, 18th Sess., No. 37 (1895).

[31] Under the standard American vision of landlord–tenant law, landlords were not responsible for injuries occurring on property rented by tenants. But in apartment buildings, tenants rented only their own living quarters. Common areas, like hallways, were under the control of landlords. Even before the Progressive Era, the courts had ruled that landlords were responsible for defects in common areas. Otherwise, landlords were no more responsible to tenants for defects in their apartments than sellers of real property were to their buyers. *Jaffe* v. *Harteau*, 56 NY 398 (1874); *Schwartz* v. *Apple*, 48 NYS 253 (1897).

[32] The first cases indicating a change in rules involved falls in hallways because of bad lighting. Although the falls were in common areas and therefore could have been decided by recourse to standard common law rules, the courts looked to the tenement house legislation as a source of law for defining the landlord's duty of care. *Ziegler* v. *Brennan*,

It was not applied in a case involving injuries inside a tenant's apartment until 1922.[33] These changes, however, did not have much of an impact on the day-to-day life of most tenants. Cases with damages that were large enough to make it worth a lawyer's time to take on the dispute were not common.[34] And the redefinitions of landlords' duty of care to tenants for tort purposes did not translate into any limitations on the landlord's right summarily to dispossess a tenant not paying rent.

At about the same time as these tort decisions began to appear, contract law was undergoing some significant changes, particularly in commercial transactions. The New York Court of Appeals rendered a famous series of opinions in the early twentieth century affirming the validity of a variety of commercial contracts and treating them as unified deals with dependent, rather than independent, covenants. The court helped restructure remedy theories to account for the multiplicity of ways in which such unified contracts might be breached and recognized the importance of commercial customs and expectations in the development of contract law.[35]

But the law of residential leases did not respond in the same way. The idea of independent covenants continued influencing landlord–tenant law long after it was dead in the rest of contract law. The only modification that occurred was a slight easing in the strictures of constructive eviction law. In the early

---

78 NYS 342 (1902); *Gillick* v. *Jackson*, 83 NYS 29 (1903); *Bornstein* v. *Faden*, 133 NYS 608 (1912).

[33] Under the old rules, a ceiling collapse inside an apartment did not provide the basis for tort liability. *Schwartz* v. *Apple*, 48 NYS 253 (1897); *Kushes* v. *Ginsburg*, 91 NYS 216 (1904). That rule was changed in a famous opinion written by Judge Benjamin Cardozo in *Altz* v. *Leiberson*, 233 NY 16 (1922). *Altz* was also a fallen ceiling case.

[34] Lawyers handling tort cases worked then, as they do now, on a contingency fee basis. If they won the case, they got a share of the proceeds. If they lost, they went away empty handed. It therefore was unlikely that a lawyer would take a case that involved only a small amount of damages. Lawyers taking eviction cases were paid on an hourly rather than contingent fee basis. It obviously was difficult for tenants sued for possession to pay lawyers. Only with the advent of legal service programmes for the poor in the 1960s did tenants begin to show up in landlord–tenant courts with lawyers. Today, many tenants are represented by law students given the right to handle certain sorts of cases under the supervision of a member of the bar.

[35] See, e.g., two famous opinions by Justice Benjamin Cardozo: *Wood* v. *Lucy, Lady Duff-Gordon*, 222 NY 88, 118 NE 214 (1917); *Sun Printing and Publishing Ass'n* v. *Remington Paper and Power Co., Inc.*, 235 NY 338, 139 N.E. 470 (1923). For commentary, see Arthur Corbin, 'Mr. Justice Cardozo and the Law of Contracts', *Columbia Law Review*, 39 (1939), 56–87; Walter Pratt, 'Contract Law at the Turn of the Century', *South Carolina Law Review*, 39 (1988), 415–64.

cases, a tenant moving out of an apartment could use the constructive eviction defence in an action for unpaid rent brought by a landlord only if the tenant's departure was justified by an intentional act of the landlord depriving the tenant of possession.[36] Late in the nineteenth century, health and safety code requirements began to have an impact on constructive eviction rules.

The narrow quality of the changes made in constructive eviction law is demonstrated by some of the early cases involving faulty plumbing systems that allowed sewer gas to seep into apartments.[37] In a couple of cases decided in the 1890s, the New York Court of Appeals eased constructive eviction rules to a less subjective standard.[38] Rather than looking to the nature of the landlord's intent or actions, the courts began to pay attention to the practical difficulties of using a place for its intended purpose. Even with the eased rules, however, constructive eviction was a risky adventure for tenants. If they guessed wrong and moved out without paying the landlord, they were stuck with a rent obligation. If they guessed wrong and stayed, they had to use and pay for an inadequate apartment. Furthermore, most tenants sued for rent lost even after constructive eviction rules were changed. It was still difficult for tenants to prove that they had moved out because the premises were uninhabitable.[39] Landlord violations of new public health and safety codes that did not render an apartment unlivable provided no basis for tenant relief when a landlord sued for rent. Nor did claims that landlords had breached an express promise to make repairs. The action for rent still was said

[36] *Edgerton v. Page*, 14 How. Prac. 116 (1856). Fraud, in addition to an actual ouster, might provide the necessary intentional action. *Wallace v. Lent*, 29 How. Prac. 289 (1865). In one case ouster was found after the landlord turned off the water supply. *West Side Savings Bank v. Newton*, 57 How. Prac. 152 (Ct. App. 1879). But damp conditions, vermin, or noxious smells did not suffice. *Truesdell v. Booth*, 4 Hun. 100 (1875).

[37] The first breakthrough case involved a public health order to clear out sewer gas. The tenants successfully claimed constructive eviction when they moved out and were sued for rent. *Bradley v. Nestor*, 67 How. Prac. 76 (Com. Pleas 1884). See also *Thalheimer v. Lempert*, 1 NYS 470 (1888). There were also cases going the other way. *Franklin v. Brown*, 118 NY 110 (1889); *Dexter v. King*, 8 NYS 489 (1890).

[38] *Tallman v. Murphy*, 120 NY 345, 24 NE 716 (1890); *Sully v. Schmitt*, 147 NY 248 (1895). Lower court opinions then took over, gradually extending constructive eviction rules to include services like heating, sewers, and water.

[39] For an early case refusing to find a constructive eviction even though the landlord was under Health Department orders to fix the sewer system, see *Dexter v. King*, 8 NYS 489 (1890). In a later case, *Sherman v. Ludin*, 79 App. Div. 37 (1903), the tenant lost a constructive eviction claim because the defects in the apartment existed and were known to the tenant when he moved in. That sort of result renders the defence useless in most cases.

to involve a covenant independent of any other covenant a tenant might have with the landlord. Tenants were relegated to bringing a separate case if the landlord breached a clause in the lease unrelated to the exchange of possession for rent.

And, of course, none of these changes was of any use in the summary dispossess context. Because tenants in dispossess actions had not moved out, constructive eviction was not helpful.[40] The changes in public health and safety standards did not lead to the creation of any new defences for tenants seeking to avoid eviction in a summary dispossess case. Even if they had a separate contract case against their landlord for breaking some promise, those issues could not be raised in the possession action. They might eventually win such a separate action, but the outcome of the dispossess case would long since have put them on the street. And that of course is the dilemma. Why did reform of rent and possession law lag so far behind change in other areas, such as tort law and basic contract law? Why could tenants not claim that landlords had a duty to make repairs and that if they breached that duty, raise that breach defensively in a dispossess action? Why were landlords running tenement houses in violation of public health and safety codes given routine access to the summary dispossess remedy?

The Progressive Era reformers

The Charity Organization Society (COS) of the City of New York published its Fifteenth Annual Report in 1897. On the front cover of that report, the editors inserted two slogans.

We have no right to make our alms a temptation to the poor; and it is a dangerous, though easy, thing to teach a man that he can live without work.

To put one family beyond the need of charity is more useful than to tide twenty over into next week's misery.

These two little aphorisms betray a deep sense that charity must be carefully bestowed, that only the worthy poor deserve assistance, and that most of the lower classes are lazy and undeserv-

---

[40] By definition, constructive eviction was a defence to an action for rent brought against a tenant not in possession.

ing. These sentiments became quite overt in the body of an article in the 1897 Report of the Society, authored by Harold Kelsey Estabrook, the Special Agent on an Investigation of Dispossessed Tenants. Estabrook used the summary dispossess courts as a source for finding charity clients and got deeply involved in the way the judges decided how much time to give tenants to pay their rent before they could be evicted. He bragged that the court normally took quite seriously the recommendation of the COS as to whether the tenants should be given as much as five days to pay the rent before they were thrown out. Despite this narrow legal context—whether to evict after zero or up to five days—Estabrook was perfectly prepared to make stark judgements about whether tenants deserved a smidgen of extra time. And he never claimed that tenants' rental obligations should be reduced or eliminated when landlords violated state or city housing codes.

He wrote:

I am not ready to urge landlords in general to be either more strict or more lenient; for, though only from 30 per cent. to 40 per cent. of the families investigated were in need of either relief or time, and though probably not more than 10 per cent. more of them were doing all they should to pay their rent, yet the dispossessed tenants—we must always remember—belong, most of them, to a lower class—a less honest and less energetic class—than most tenants who never or very seldom are dispossessed. For the good of landlords and tenants alike, more than half of those dispossessed probably should have been dispossessed more promptly; but of tenants not dispossessed, I believe that many more than half are doing all they can to pay their rent promptly, and should not be dispossessed. Often I would urge a landlord to be more strict—as, for example, when he allows a young couple, both able to work but often drinking, to live six months in his house after paying only one month's rent, and then dispossesses them because they quarrel with the housekeeper; but, often, too, I would urge a landlord to be more lenient, as when he dispossesses a family of whom no one is working and some are ill, and who have paid rent to him regularly for eight years until this month.[41]

Estabrook's sense that 'dispossessed tenants . . . belong . . . to a lower class—a less honest and less energetic class—than most

[41] Harold Kelsey Estabrook, 'Report of the Special Agent on an Investigation of Dispossessed Tenants', in *15th Annual Report, Charity Organization Society of the City of New York* (New York, 1897), 44–53, at 51.

tenants' was certainly not unusual in late nineteenth-century America.[42] While the idea that only the worthy poor deserved either welfare or charity had been around since the days of the English and colonial American Poor Laws, many in the middle and upper classes, including many claiming to be reformers, developed particularly virulent attitudes about lower-class persons in the post-Civil War United States.

Attitudes about race and ethnicity played central roles in framing the Progressive Era culture. Whatever optimism might have existed right after the Civil War that freed slaves could be quickly integrated into the general culture had totally dissipated by the turn of the century. Indeed, racism was boldly proclaimed as appropriate in many quarters. The Jim Crow system of segregation was in full flower.[43] The Ku-Klux-Klan was a powerful political movement; lynching reached its high point in this era.[44] Restrictive covenant schemes blossomed in the first two decades of the twentieth century, barring sale or rental of housing to African Americans in many areas.[45] Even the women's suffrage movement adopted a strategy that agitated for the vote while implicitly, and in some cases explicitly, supporting a variety of schemes to bar voting by minority persons of either gender.[46]

Racial and class animosities were certainly not new features of American culture that emerged suddenly after the Civil War. But a number of factors brought attitudes about ethnicity and poverty to a fever pitch during the Progressive Era. Shifts in scientific, cultural, and legal understandings merged with demographic factors, including emancipation of the slaves and their entry into the employment market, huge waves of immigration, and movement

[42] Another example of this sentiment appeared in an article by Dr Arnold Eilvart, 'An Attempt to Give Justice', *Charities Review*, 3 (1894), 343–51. This is ostensibly a much more radical article than Estabrook's. Eilvart came from a union background and was urging that tenants organize into groups to pursue remedies with housing authorities. Although he believed that tenants were educable, he ascribed the problems in tenement houses to three causes—the rapacity and indolence of landlords, the neglect of officials, and 'the selfishness of dirty tenants'.

[43] See the classic book, C. Vann Woodward, *The Strange Career of Jim Crow* (New York, 1966).

[44] See Jacquelyn Dowd Hall, *Revolt against Chivalry: Jessie Daniel Ames and the Campaign against Lynching* (New York, 1979).

[45] See Garrett Power, 'Apartheid Baltimore Style: The Residential Segregation Ordinances of 1910–1913', *Maryland Law Review*, 42 (1982), 289–328; Clement Vose, *Caucasians Only: The Supreme Court, the NAACP, and the Restrictive Covenant Cases* (New York, 1959).

[46] Sara Evans, *Born for Liberty: A History of Women in America* (New York, 1989), 152–6.

of people to cities, to create fear and consternation among large segments of the native-born white population. Those fears made it impossible for many reformers to see the 'clients' of the summary dispossess court as worthy of sympathy and understanding.

Darwinism provided a convenient intellectual cover for American domestic racism. It had enormous influence on American culture. Trust in scientific progress was a byword of the time. Advances in public health and the development of electricity, telegraphs, telephones, pumped water plumbing and sewer systems, photography, sound recordings, and automobiles created great faith in the possibilities of human ingenuity. When Darwinism arrived as scientific truth, it confirmed in the minds of many that native-born white Americans came from superior stock. The widespread acceptance of evolutionary theory allowed for easy categorization of people as higher or lower on the development ladder.

In such an environment many immigrants arriving during the Progressive Era were criticized as unworthies. Though thirst for industrial labour drew millions to American shores, desperate attempts were made to ban entry of unworthy men and women. What was wanted was families. Relying on family solidarity, many thought, was the only way to stem the immigrant tide of male miscreants and female prostitutes pouring onto American shores.[47] By the 1920s, immigrants from some nations were wanted more than from others. Large numbers of Germans or other northern Europeans were welcomed, while entry of disfavoured groups like Italians and Jews was restrained. Estabrook's statement that 'dispossessed tenants . . . belong . . . to a lower class—a less honest and less energetic class—than most tenants' was standard fare. Indeed it was a relatively mild form of ethnic divisiveness when compared to the statements of non-progressives like those belonging to the Ku-Klux-Klan or lynching African Americans on false charges of raping white women. Sentiments like those of Estabrook allowed little room for empathy with the plight of impoverished tenement house occupants. Landlord–tenant court reform was simply not on the agenda of charity workers willing to condemn their own clientele.

---

[47] Kitty Calavita, *U.S. Immigration Law and the Control of Labor: 1820–1924* (London, 1984); Bina Kalola, 'Immigration Laws and Immigrant Women: 1885–1924' (1996) (student paper on file with author).

Estabrook's casework approach to the salvation of those impoverished families competent enough to escape moral decay did not
speak for the entire Progressive movement. Indeed, Edward
Devine, a Professor of Social Economy and secretary of the New
York Charity Organization Society from 1896 to 1912, produced a
stream of works contesting the Society's preoccupation with the
links between personal immorality and poverty. As Paul Boyer
noted some time ago, Devine dismissed as a 'halfway explanation'
the belief that immorality caused poverty, even though such notions
were 'thoroughly interwoven into a vast quantity of literature and
into almost the whole of our charitable tradition'. Boyer wrote:

> The causes of destitution, he [Devine] declared, were 'economic, social,
> transitional, measurable, [and] manageable'; the urban vice and
> immorality that so distressed middle-class social workers were 'more
> largely the results of social environment than of defective character.'
> Charity organizations, he concluded firmly, should shift from 'arbitrary
> and artificial' efforts at individual uplift to a broader program of envi-
> ronmental change.[48]

Positive environmentalism—the idea that changing surroundings will change behaviour—dominated a significant segment of
the Progressive reform community. Followers eschewed the worst
excesses of the Progressive moralists and Darwinian racists. They
looked for guidance to those scientific advances in public health,
sanitation, and social science that supported the ability of any
group of persons to make moral progress when living in supportive and healthy surroundings. This movement was especially
influential in the housing and architectural worlds. Those supporting tenement house reforms believed strongly that better
access to air and light would improve both the physical and moral
health of the occupants. Their reports were filled with data on
disease and death rates in various sorts of housing environments.
The City Beautiful Movement in the architectural world grew out
of a similar belief structure. Based in significant ways on the work
of Frederick Law Olmstead, who designed Central Park in the
1850s, architects began to structure housing complexes as part of
a larger ecological whole. In a somewhat romantic effort to recapture memories of a more bucolic and morally pure rural past, site

[48] Paul Boyer, *Urban Masses and Moral Order in America, 1820–1920* (Cambridge, Mass.,
1978), at 69–70.

planning and landscape architecture became important parts of urban planning. In 1878, the journal *Plumber and Sanitary Engineer* announced a competition for a model tenement design. The contest drew wide publicity and a number of entries. Many of the ideas suggested in this contest were later codified in Tenement House Acts.[49] And, of course, the zoning movement was heavily influenced by the positive environmental movement of the early twentieth century. New York City adopted the nation's first zoning ordinance in 1916.

Though ostensibly less hostile to immigrants and African Americans, the positive environmentalists were no more interested in landlord–tenant courts than the more punitive, Darwinian sectors of the Progressive community. Their movement fought against family-by-family assistance programmes, searching instead for ways to alter the contours of the larger urban environment. Major legislative initiatives, public health campaigns, water and sewer construction programmes, revision of architectural practices, adoption of health, building and fire codes, and enactment of zoning schemes made up their agenda. Their concern for physical and moral improvements was motivated as much by a desire to protect middle-class notions of polite urbanity as it was by any charitable instincts toward the less well-off. Native-born whites were attracted to Tenement House Acts designed to reduce disease and crime in cities. Zoning, perhaps the crowning achievement of the positive environmentalists, made sense to otherwise conservative Americans because it allowed government to protect middle-class residential neighbourhoods from encroachment by 'disfavored' uses.[50]

The legal culture of the time was as divided as the broader Progressive community. It was an epoch in which debates between conservative, classical legal theorists and reform-minded realists were in full flower. Despite the vigour of the jurisprudential debates, landlord–tenant courts were not of concern to either side. Classical legal theory found a home in late nineteenth-century

[49] Lubove, *Progressives and the Slums*, at 28–32.

[50] It is difficult to understand why the quite conservative Supreme Court of the 1920s approved zoning, see *Village of Euclid v. Ambler Realty Co.*, 272 US 365 (1926), in an opinion written by Justice Sutherland, later an arch-enemy of the New Deal, without knowing that zoning was pushed by the Hoover administration, widely approved by middle-class community groups, and framed in ways that guaranteed the protection of well-heeled residential communities.

American legal culture. The post-Civil War debates over the status of freed slaves gave new credence to the importance of contract theory. The right of African Americans to contract for their labour made the market a central part of the post-war meaning of 'liberty'. Industrialists used the same language for their own free market purposes, urging that freedom of contract was a necessary feature of the capitalist age.[51]

Adherents of classical legal theory, in its purist form, opined that law was a science, that legal rules could be derived from a few universal principles. They argued that it was impossible to find a definition of the public good that all could agree to. The best way to ensure that each person would be able to obtain his own vision of the good was to prevent government from interfering with private ordering. The purpose of the law was fairly straightforward: to protect private property and contract from interference by government authority. The result was a ruthless form of equality. Of necessity, all men had the right to contract freely. Each was in that sense a juridical equal. There was no sympathy for class distinctions, poverty, or language difficulties. Those who fell by the wayside were either inferior beings or responsible for their own plight. In theory any tenant could write clauses into leases to make various covenants dependent rather than independent or to create certain tenant rights if landlords failed to make repairs. The routine failure of tenants to do so was simply part of the free market. In this view, landlord–tenant courts were the highest form of social ordering. The failure of tenants to pay their rent only meant that the courts' primary obligation was to insure that the leasehold contracts were enforced. Classical legal theorists had no more interest in allowing tenants to defend eviction actions than they did in allowing legislatures to regulate the content of the labour contract.[52] Their approach to legal issues and widespread influence in late nineteenth- and early twentieth-century legal circles represented a high water mark for the importance of contracts and markets in the defining of legal obligations.[53]

---

[51] A nice example of this sort of rhetoric may be found in William Howard Taft, 'The Right of Private Property', *Michigan Law Journal*, 3 (1894), 215–33. For some history of classical legal thought, see Thomas Grey, 'Langdell's Orthodoxy', *University of Pittsburgh Law Review*, 45 (1983), 1–53.

[52] See, e.g., *Lochner* v. *New York*, 198 US 45 (1905); *Adkins* v. *Children's Hospital*, 261 US 525 (1923).

[53] For more on classical legal theory, see Gary Peller, 'The Metaphysics of American Law', *California Law Review*, 73 (1985), 1151–290, at 1191–219; Grey, 'Langdell's Orthodoxy'.

But what about the Realists? Why did they not take up the summary dispossess issue? They were highly critical of the classical notion that law could be derived from a small set of universally agreed-upon principles. Law was a political, not a scientific undertaking. Property and contract law were not the province of private preference, but the by-product of public policy-making. Courts should not be protectors of private preferences, but administrators of legislative will and purveyors of fairness. Their job was not to impose a certain vision of economic power upon the body politic, but to allow legislatures to resolve important public questions.

The early Realists[54] were much like the positive environmentalists. They too looked to the social sciences for guidance. Their goal was to restructure the economy of the nation, especially the labour market. The Realists, like the positive environmentalists, had a bias towards legislative action.[55] That bias arose out of hostility to classical judges who invalidated a large number of state reform initiatives, as well as a belief that broad legislative change was the best hope for the nation. It was possible, the Realists thought, to change the environment in which people lived and worked. Indeed, it was necessary to change that environment in order to improve the quality of life for most people. And so the Realists, along with many Progressives, supported minimum wages laws, restrictions on child labour, protective labour legislation, union organizing, tenement house reforms, and zoning laws.

Roscoe Pound, for example, wrote one of the earliest Realist critiques of classical legal contract theory during the tenement house era.[56] He described his concerns with invalidation of labour legislation by classical jurists, blaming the rise of classical legal

[54] For a summary of the Realist movement, see Joseph Singer, 'Legal Realism Now', *California Law Review*, 76 (1988), 465–544; Note, 'Formalist and Instrumentalist Legal Reasoning and Legal Theory', *California Law Review*, 73 (1985), 119–57.

[55] Realists, of course, were eventually appointed to the bench. Some of them, such as Justice Cardozo, engaged in significant reforms of the common law. But the larger goal, not fully accomplished until the New Deal era, was to give legislative reformers room to operate.

[56] Roscoe Pound, 'Liberty of Contract', *Yale LJ* 18 (1909), 454–87. Many of the themes taken up by Pound became the focus of work by later well-known Realists. See, for example, Robert Hale, 'Bargaining, Duress, and Economic Liberty', *Columbia Law Review*, 43 (1943), 603–28; Morris Cohen, 'The Basis of Contract', *Harvard Law Review*, 46 (1933), 553–92; Robert Hale, 'Coercion and Distribution in a Supposedly Non-coercive State', *Political Science Quarterly*, 38 (1923), 470–94.

thought on individualistic conceptions of justice that exaggerated the importance of property and contract, the training of judges and lawyers in eighteenth-century legal philosophy and natural law theory, and reliance on theories of general application instead of realistic concern for the situations and facts underlying the adoption of remedial statutes. Pound complained that the courts were bent on barring the legislature from 'bringing about any real equality in labor-bargainings, even though thereby strikes and disorders may be obviated'.[57] His focus, like that of most Realists, was on the labour market. And his cure was to allow legislatures to investigate the facts and enact new workplace regulations.

In hindsight, it is not surprising that eviction courts did not garner much Realist attention. Both the emancipation of the slaves and the rise of larg-scale industrial production after the Civil War made the workplace the central focus of attention for politicians, economists, and lawyers. Since use of public funds to construct decent housing was unthinkable in late nineteenth-century America, the underlying problems in the housing market were unlikely to be altered without increasing the wealth of tenement house occupants. Labour market reform, adoption of minimum wage laws, and support for unions was therefore a high priority. The most that could be done in housing was to fix some of the more egregious health problems and protect middle- and upper-class neighbourhoods from the depredations of urban blight. The focus of reformers on tenement house construction, parks, and zoning was the logical result.

Finally, the Realists, like most of the rest of the body politic, were affected by ethnic and racial attitudes. Although the structure of Realist beliefs certainly led them to focus on large-scale legislative initiatives, they, like many Progressives, were heavily influenced by the routine racism and nativism of the day.[58] Zoning schemes, for example, were routinely framed as ways of protecting the livability of neighbourhoods full of single family housing. Tenement houses were often described as potential nuisances to less dense residential communities. Indeed that nuisance rationale formed the backbone of Justice Sutherland's opinion in *Village*

---

[57] Pound, 'Liberty of Contract', at 481.
[58] Who, for example, can forget Justice Holmes's famous statement that three generations of imbeciles are enough in *Buck* v. *Bell*, 274 US 200 (1927)?

of Euclid v. *Ambler Realty Company*,[59] the Supreme Court decision affirming the constitutionality of zoning.

Epilogue

There is reason to believe that the sea change in racial attitudes between the 1920s and the Vietnam War era had much to do with the eventual reform of landlord–tenant courts and eviction law in the 1960s and 1970s. These recent reforms occurred during an unusual moment in American history. International criticism of segregation by newly independent third world nations and the emergence of a number of charismatic leaders in the African American community set the stage for the civil rights era. The post-Second World War economic boom in the United States generated both very high expectations that all Americans could be successful and reduction in fear among lower-class whites that ending segregation would also end their employment. Many whites came to believe that the time for segregation had passed. The result was the creation of a powerful coalition of forces— intellectuals, labour unions, civil rights groups, many important political organizations, and a number of businesses—interested in the problems of race and poverty. Ironically this high water mark of concern about remedying racial injustice arose at the very time that poverty was a less significant problem than it had been during any other moment in American history.[60] The plight of those in the underclass became highly visible while most of the nation basked in economic security.

The result was a wave of programmes to end poverty—welfare reforms, housing construction programmes, subsidies for organizing indigenous community groups, legal services for the poor, urban renewal, and a host of other programmes. This reform movement viewed impoverishment not as a flaw, but as a problem. Believers claimed money was available in both the government and private sectors to relieve the suffering of the poor. This movement did not limit itself to large-scale structural changes wrought by legislative action. It reached down into poor communities

[59] 272 US 365 (1926).
[60] See, e.g., Edward Rabin, 'The Revolution in Residential Landlord–Tenant Law: Causes and Consequences', *Cornell Law Review*, 69 (1984), 517–84.

themselves, urged agitation, and noticed the contradictions inherent in landlords being able easily to get rid of tenants living in substandard buildings. It was, in short, a moment in which the poor were not blamed for their own impoverishment and race was not a total barrier to the creation of coalitions among groups in the lower class. Those three factors—a glance at racial understanding, a momentary empathy with the poor among many in the middle and upper classes, and a window in which alliances among lower-class white and African American groups were possible—made reform of landlord–tenant courts possible in the 1960s and 1970s. The absence of these factors among Progressive reformers had made the same reforms impossible at the beginning of the twentieth century.

Part V

PRODUCERS AND CONSUMERS

17

Usury in France in the Nineteenth Century

FABIEN VALENTE

Within the relations betweeen private law and social inequality the question of usury in nineteenth-century France touches upon a number of areas. The prohibitions on lending money at interest and on credit have first of all a moral dimension. The falling into debt of the most disadvantaged groups in society made credit appear immoral to them. Social policy legislation in this context was also preoccupied with morality. But it is above all economic development and the constraints it produces that determine the relations between creditors and debtors. That is why the following account of usury legislation in France and its application must be placed into the wider context of relations between producers and consumers. The object of this essay is to study how laws responded to economic developments on the one hand, and how economic behaviour was shaped by laws on the other. Professor Batbie was alluding to this when he wrote in 1866: 'Since Turgot's *Mémoire* and the letters of Bentham, the history of usury is entirely contained in the facts and in the laws.'[1] In France, what is called the 'great' nineteenth century is marked by the Industrial Revolution. Having begun in England in the eighteenth century, industrialization did not cross the Channel until after 1815. The new forms of capitalism were characterized by the spectacular growth of huge industrial and commercial enterprises as well as by the rise of banking and insurance.

As to the laws, some years before the Industrial Revolution France had experienced the legal and social revolution of 1789, which had swept away what is conventionally termed the 'old law', the legal system that had made a principle of banning money-lending at interest. Indeed, canon law as well as royal edicts[2]

---

[1] A. Batbie, *Mélanges d'économie politique* (Paris, 1866), 75.
[2] Edicts of 1567, of 1510 (art. 65), of Blois, 1579 (art. 202).

and civil jurisdiction prohibited usury, pronounced usurious agreements null and void, and punished usurers severely. Jews, who were not subject to canon law, and Lombards were unaffected by this ban. Under the old legal system, then, lending at interest and usury were synonymous. However, the Church soon realized that it must soften its position and lift the ban on lending at interest where this was justified; hence a certain number of exceptions was allowed. These mainly concerned forfeiture clauses (*commissoria lex*), stipulation of a penalty for late payment, loans on a piece of land, manual exchange with transfer of substance, the case of risk for the capital lent, and the commercial company.

Criticized by French lawyers as harmful to trade, the ban on lending at interest was lifted by the Constituent Assembly. The Law of 3–12 October 1789 laid down that in future anyone would be at liberty to lend money at interest within the confines of the legal rate: 'The National Assembly has decreed that all private individuals, corporate bodies, and communities and people in mortmain may in future lend money at fixed term, stipulating interest in accordance with the rate fixed by law, without intending to make any change to the customs of commerce.' The Law of 3 October 1789 fixed the legal rate at 5 per cent for civil purposes, based on the rate of government stock current at the time of the Revolution. For commercial purposes, no figure was fixed, and interest depended on circumstances of time and place. It was thus for the courts to assess, in accordance with commercial custom, whether interest was usurious and, if so, to order that an appropriate amount be deducted from the capital.

With the revolutionary law, the definition of usury assumed its modern form: to exceed the permitted legal rate was considered usurious. To uphold the credit of the revolutionary government's *assignats* or promissory notes, the Convention banned the trade in coin by the Law of 11 April 1795. It lifted that ban with the Law of 28 April 1795 but reimposed it on 24 May of the same year. This situation remained in place until 23 July 1796. This last law of the eighteenth century concerning lending at interest comprised three relatively brief articles which proclaimed freedom of contract.[3] According to the ruling of the *Cour de Cassation* (the

---

[3] Art. 1: 'From the date of promulgation of the present law, every citizen shall be free to contract as he sees fit; the obligations to which he has subscribed shall be performed in the terms and values stipulated.' Art. 2: 'No one may refuse his payment in orders at the

Supreme Court of Appeal),[4] this law was intended to abolish the limitation on interest by repealing the restrictive Law of 3–12 October 1789.

The complete abolition of legal regulation gave rise to serious abuses. Those who were drafting the new Civil Code were therefore asked to put an end to this situation. At the beginning of the nineteenth century, during the preparation of the Civil Code, the question of freedom of usury clearly arose when the paragraph concerning moneylending was discussed in the Council of State. The principle of a legal rate of interest was eventually adopted by the authors of the Civil Code, but the fixing of that rate was deferred for subsequent legislation.[5] The code was meant to last, and the authors did not wish to include in it a figure that was apt to vary with the economic circumstances of each period.

Jurisdiction, however, interpreted the system set out in the Civil Code as that of the total freedom proclaimed by the decree of 23 July 1796. There was thus no legal prohibition, either against usury or against compound interest.[6] However, the hope of the authors of the Civil Code, which was to 'restrain greed with the brake of shame'[7] by simply requiring the rate of interest to be set down in writing, was largely disappointed, and as during the Convention there were many abuses.

Thus the history of lending at interest in nineteenth-century France was to open with some initial regulation that quickly came into conflict with the reality (part 1), and to close on the eve of the twentieth century with the probably unintentional elimination of legislation on usury (part 2).

---

rate of the date and place at which payment shall be made.' Art. 3: 'Any legal provisions running counter to the present law are repealed.'

[4] Judgment of 5 Oct. 1813; Batbie, *Mélanges*, 77.

[5] Art. 1907 of the Civil Code: 'Interest is legal or conventional. Legal interest is fixed by law. Conventional interest may be in excess of legal interest whenever the law does not forbid this. The rate of conventional interest must be fixed in writing.'

[6] See *Cour de Cassation* (*Cass.*), 20 Feb. 1810 (*S.*=J.-B. Sirey, *Recueil général des lois et arrêts*, 10.2.205); *Cass.*, 16 Nov. 1813 (*CN=Collection nouvelle* (L. M. Devilleneuve and A. A. Carette, *Recueil général des lois et arrêts . . . rédigé à partir de l'ancien Recueil général des lois et des arrêts fondé par M. Sirey, 1791–1830, revu et complété, 1840–1843*) 4.1.466). However, it was decided that usurious interest levied before the 1807 law should be set off against the capital; see Rennes, 20 June 1817 (*CN* 5.2.295).

[7] J. Gauffre, 'Essai sur une tendance actuelle à l'unification du droit civil et du droit commercial', dissertation (Montpellier, 1898), 63.

Initial regulation put to the test of the facts

In the first decade of the nineteenth century, the Law of 3 September 1807 (the Law on the Maximum) stipulated the rate of legal interest and fixed a ceiling for conventional interest. According to article 1907 *Code civil*, legal interest meant the rate fixed by law, and conventional interest meant the rate fixed by the contractual parties in writing. Although debated with passion for three-quarters of a century and supplemented by the Law of 19 December 1850, the 1807 law was soon subjected to major limitations. These restrictions were as much the result of legislative measures as of judicial decisions that substantially reduced the applicability of the Law on the Maximum.

The Law of 3 September 1807 was introduced by Napoleon against the advice of his Minister of Finance, Mollien. It was intended as a remedy for the excesses of usury, and was undoubtedly linked with the promulgation of the Commercial Code in 1807, which Bonaparte had had drafted in an attempt to end the chaos resulting from a wave of bankruptcies. The period from October 1805 to July 1807 had in fact witnessed a major financial crisis, followed by an industrial crisis. Although these were chiefly confined to Paris, affecting only the Exchequer, big business, and the top of the banking world, the general lack of confidence as a result of the war led to a slowing down of currency circulation and a rise in the cost of credit, then to the progressive paralysis of trade and industry. The victory of Austerlitz on 2 December 1805 ended the financial crisis, but the climate of industrial unease persisted until 1807.

When looking at the beginning of the Napoleonic regime another fact must be taken into consideration. The Church's prohibition on lending at interest for Catholics had led Jews to specialize in the trade of moneylending. In the first years of the Napoleonic regime the amount of money owed to Jews was particularly high, especially in the east of France. In Alsace there were riots in 1805–6: the Christian debtors of the Jews demanded moratoriums, a reduction of their debts, or at least a reduction in the interest rates that applied to their loans. These problems were brought to Napoleon's attention by the prefects, but the most notable consequence was the *décret infâme* of 17 March 1808. This decree created an exception to the ordinary law by subjecting the

Jews to certain formalities by which they had to prove the validity of their claims against their debtors.

In this situation the Law of 3 September 1807 laid down that conventional interest might not exceed 5 per cent for civil purposes and 6 per cent for commercial purposes. The rate of legal interest was fixed at the same figure. Article 3 of the law continued: 'When it is shown that the conventional loan has been made at a rate in excess of that fixed by article 1, the lender shall be sentenced by the court to which the dispute has been submitted to repay such excess, if he has received it, or to suffer a reduction of the principal of the loan, and he may even, if there is occasion, be sent for trial by the criminal court, where he will be judged in accordance with the following article.' The fourth and final article stipulated: 'Any person who has been warned against indulging habitually in usury shall be brought before the criminal court and in this case sentenced to a fine that may not exceed one-half of the capital he has loaned usuriously. If it emerges from the trial that there has been a fraud on the part of the lender, he shall be sentenced not only to the said fine but also to a term of imprisonment not exceeding two years.'

This law was fiercely attacked by political economists, who objected on principle that money was a commodity and that trading in money was a business like any other. These economists desired the greatest possible measure of freedom for commercial transactions. They argued that the price of money should rise or fall according to the needs of the moment, like that of all natural or industrial products, and they concluded that the law should no more impose a maximum rate of interest on money than it fixed a maximum price for any goods forming the object of trade.

The earliest judicial decisions bearing on the 1807 law concerned the conditions of its application in time and space. Thus it was decided in 1809 that the Law of 3 September 1807 fixing the rate of interest at 5 per cent for civil purposes was not applicable to interest arising out of earlier contracts, even if such interest had been accruing since the code.[8] Similarly, the *Cour de Cassation* later ruled that interest stipulated in a contract prior to the Law of 3 September 1807 must be paid at the rate fixed by agreement, even where that rate was higher than the one laid

[8] Brussels, 24 May 1809 (*S.* 10.2.567); *Cass.*, 21 June 1825 (*S.* 26.1.301).

down by the law, with no distinction between interest due before and interest due since its promulgation.[9] Regarding application of the Law on the Maximum in space, the appeal court in Bordeaux decided that when two Frenchmen had agreed in a foreign country where they were domiciled on interest above 5 per cent, if the law of the place of contract allowed, then the agreement was enforceable in France, the Law of 3 September 1807 notwithstanding. In that case, it was thus not the law of the place of execution that governed the stipulation of conventional interest.[10]

A second field of conflicts to be decided by the courts was cases of concealed usury. Thus the *Cour de Cassation* laid down in 1829 that usury did not simply consist in collecting the usurious interest stipulated; it consisted in the mere stipulation of such interest. It followed that the offence of usury was perpetrated by the simple fact of the borrower putting his signature to a usurious obligation and that obligation being handed back to the lender. According to this interpretation of the law, it mattered little that, after proceedings had been instituted, the parties to the contract had reduced the interest to the legal rate.[11]

Doctrine considered sales with right of repurchase (*ventes à réméré*) to be particularly suspect as a means of concealing usury. In order to combat fraud, the appeal court in Riom decided that judges could state according to the presumptions and facts of the case that a contract of sale was feigned and served no other purpose than to cover usurious occurrences.[12] In another case, it was decided that the sale of moveables for an undiscussed price as a condition of the loan and with the intention of masking the collection of usurious interest must be annulled as constituting an instance of usury.[13] In another example, the Colmar appeal court decided that, although annulment for reason of tort was not provided for in the exchange contract, a real-estate exchange contract could and should be annulled if its sole object had been to cover up and disguise a usurious transaction.[14]

Judges were also required to pronounce on the matter of assignments of claims. The Agen appeal court decided that, although under the terms of article 1694 of the Civil Code claims could be transferred for a sum less than the amount of the claim, it did not

[9] *Cass.*, 15 Nov. 1836 (*S.* 31.1.939).
[10] Bordeaux, 26 Jan. 1831 (*S.* 31.2.178).
[11] *Cass.*, 8 May 1829 (*S.* 30.1.347).
[12] Riom, 20 Mar. 1822 (*CN* 7.2.46).
[13] Paris, 7 Feb. 1835 (*S.* 35.2.139).
[14] Colmar, 25 Mar. 1823 (*S.* 35.2.159).

follow that such a transfer necessarily ruled out usury. Thus the person who, in accepting the transfer of a claim for a price less than the sum transferred, secured a guarantee that the claim would be paid in full was guilty of usury. In this case the assignee was obliged to restore to the assigner what he had received from the transferred debtor over and above the actual price of the assignment.[15]

The matter of the contract of settlement of annuities was also brought before the courts. The *Cour de Cassation* decided in 1846 that the Law of 3 September 1807, which had fixed the rate of interest, applied not only to loan contracts but also to contracts settling an annuity, and that it did so even where the annuity was settled in kind rather than money.[16]

Jurisdiction also considered certain gifts as constituting usuries prohibited by law. The appeal court in Bordeaux ruled that, when an act of borrowing was followed by a donation made by the borrower in favour of the lender, and described as being in consideration of services rendered, if the circumstances were such as to suggest that that donation had been a condition of the loan, it merged with the initial contract to form an indivisible entity. If as a result the lender had gained in this agreement an advantage greater than the legal interest on the sum loaned, the agreement was null and void in respect of the surplus.[17]

As well as defining the main instances of concealed usury, jurisdiction had to define the characteristics of the criminal offence of usury and occasionally fraud, which constituted an aggravating circumstance of the offence of usury, as laid down by article 4 of the 1807 law. It has already been mentioned that usury was a criminal offence only in so far as it was habitual in the person practising it. This principle was confirmed by the *Cour de Cassation* in 1811: collecting excessive interest was not enough to establish the criminal offence of usury; the accused must be convicted of indulging in usury habitually.[18] For example, in 1826 the *Cour de Cassation* ruled that for usury to be called habitual it was sufficient that several successive usurious loans had been made to the same person.[19] In another case, it was considered sufficient that the usurious loans had been made to at least two people.[20]

[15] Agen, 28 Jan. 1824 (*CN* 7.2.307).
[17] Bordeaux, 17 Dec. 1827 (*S.* 28.2.65).
[19] *Cass.*, 4 Mar. 1826 (*S.* 26.1.361).

[16] *Cass.*, 26 Aug. 1846 (*S.* 47.1.113).
[18] *Cass.*, 22 Nov. 1811 (*S.* 12.1.88).
[20] *Cass.*, 24 Dec. 1825 (*CN* 8.1.246).

To give judges the greatest possible latitude in combating usury, the *Cour de Cassation* decided that the evidence of witnesses should be widely admitted in the matter, even in cases involving sums above 150 francs.[21] In terms of procedure, the criminal offence of usury opened the way for actions initiated by the Public Prosecutor. However, it was specified by the courts that the victim of usurious transactions could neither act by way of direct summons against the usurer nor bring a civil action within the criminal proceedings instituted by the Public Prosecutor. The victim could only bring his action separately before civil jurisdiction.[22]

Despite the evidence that French courts were able to work with the Law of 3 September 1807, a number of exceptions point to the difficulty of applying it consistently. From the outset, it was always considered that the 1807 law left untouched the special decrees of 24 Thermidor XII (11 August 1804) and 8 Thermidor XIII (27 July 1805), which gave pawnshop managers the right freely to fix interest rates on the loans they granted. What had been a recognized exception since 1807 was finally confirmed by the Law of 24 June 1851.

During the political and economic crisis of 1814, application of the 1807 law was temporarily suspended in France. The war, the military defeats, the general political situation, and the lack of confidence among the business class led to the progressive collapse of trading relations with Germany, northern Europe, Spain, and Portugal. There was a wave of bankruptcies in Paris, and in 1814 the crisis deepened with a rise in unemployment. Following Napoleon's surrender on 1 April 1814, the recovery took until the spring of 1816 to mature.

A third instance where the law did not apply was in the French colonies, where interest rates were generally free. In Algeria, for example, the ordinance of 7 December 1835 (suspended in 1848, restored in the following year, and finally confirmed by a Law of 27 April 1881) declared any agreement on interest rates to be lawful for civil and commercial purposes alike.

Partly because it was considered ineffective in combating usury,

---

[21] *Cass.*, 18 Feb. 1829 (S. 29.1.96); *Cass.*, 13 Feb. 1880 (*Jurisprudence du XIX* siècle (1880 vol.), pt. 1, 485).
[22] See *Cass.*, 3 Feb. 1809 (S. 9.1.206); *Cass.*, 8 Mar. 1838 (S. 38.1.361); Bordeaux, 12 July 1837 (S. 38.1.361).

but partly also for political reasons, the 1807 law was amended by the Law of 19 December 1850, which introduced heavier penalties. In the first place, the 1850 law provided that the borrower could, as a matter of right ('de plein droit'), set off interest in excess of the legal rate against the capital, whereas according to the Law of 3 September 1807, victims of usury had needed a court sentence before making such a deduction. Secondly, the penalty for habitual usury, which could only be a fine under the 1807 law, now consisted of a term of imprisonment from six days to six months. Finally, in the event of repetition of the offence (in which case even an isolated incident was sufficient), the courts had to apply the maximum penalty and could as much as double it. These provisions provoked fierce criticism from those who advocated freedom in the matter of moneylending. Once again, the legislator had not listened to them.

A first indication that the legislator took a more liberal line and reacted to economic needs was the Law of 10 June 1857 which authorized the Bank of France to raise its discount rate and the rate of interest on its advances above 6 per cent where necessary. Indeed, the business recovery had pushed the discount rate of the Bank of France up to 9 per cent. This had been held at 4 per cent from 1 February 1820, then raised to 5 per cent in January 1847 and to 6 per cent in 1855–6. Once again, the 1807 law found itself in conflict with reality. In general, the Bank of France did not receive the effects of small merchants because these did not have the kind of reputation that would make it possible for their solvency to be assessed. They were therefore obliged to go to bankers who advanced them money and subsequently arranged for the Bank of France to discount the bills that carried their own signature. However, if those bankers were having to pay 9 per cent to the Bank of France, they were not going to be satisfied with interest at 6 per cent on the advances they had made to small merchants. Doing violence to the 1807 law was the only way to enable people to escape from this impasse. Consequently, the Law of 10 June 1857, while retaining the 5 per cent rate for civil purposes, set commercial loans free.

For their part, legal doctrine and jurisdiction also admitted a certain number of exceptions to the 1807 law. Thus the law was held to be inapplicable to aleatory money loans, to loans on bottomry, to loans of moveables other than sums of money (loans of produce or loans of securities), and money debts having a cause unconnected with the loan, such as the credit sale stipulating interest for the vendor, the amount carried forward, exchange, and discount. Numerous judicial decisions illustrate these different exceptions and the difficulty of consistently applying the Law on the Maximum.

In the first place, a judgment handed down by the *Cour de Cassation* on 13 August 1845 can be cited. This decided that, when a loan was accompanied by aleatory circumstances placing the lender at risk of specific losses, and when the interest stipulated was also lower than the legal rate, the compensatory donation to the lender of assets that, added to the interest stipulated, exceeded the legal rate did not constitute concealed usury but was an aleatory, lump-sum compensation for the potential losses to which he had been exposed.[23]

As regards loans of moveables, the *Cour de Cassation* decided on 8 March 1865 that the Law of 3 September 1807 could not be applied to shares or industrial bonds.[24] Similarly, the transfer, on a loan basis, of shares or industrial bonds on the condition that the borrower must return the shares themselves or their value on the due date did not constitute a loan of money within the meaning of the Law of 3 September 1807; it followed that the rules governing the rate of interest could not be applied to such a loan.[25]

It is known that the exchange contract and banking transactions gave rise to profits that were analogous to interest but were not regarded as usurious by legal experts and in practice. Such profits were discount, exchange, and commission. The banker who performed one of these transactions was not thereby making a loan; all he was doing was purchasing a claim with a greater or lesser degree of surety. The *Cour de Cassation* decided in 1828 that the Law of 3 September 1807 could not be applied to discount or to negotiations involving commercial assets. For example, the banker negotiating or discounting assets for a third party was entitled to collect, on top of the legal rate of interest, a discount and commission to be fixed by agreement between the parties.[26] It was

---

[23] *Cass.*, 15 Aug. 1845 (*S.* 45.1.714).
[24] *Cass.*, 8 Mar. 1865 (*Jurisprudence du XIX* siècle (1865 vol.), pt. 1, 17).
[25] Paris, 12 Dec. 1863 (*Jurisprudence du XIX* siècle (1863 vol.), pt. 2, 21).
[26] *Cass.*, 4 Feb. 1828 (*S.* 28.1.99).

likewise decided that a right of commission could, in addition to legal interest, be granted by a borrower to his lender, in the same way as it could be granted to others, apart from the lender, as an administration fee: in no way was this a usurious charge.[27] It was also decided that the discount and commission fees levied by bankers, irrespective of legal interest, could not be deemed usurious if charged in conformity with commercial custom and if the banking transactions were not fictitious.[28] Nevertheless, the field of banking transactions remained the terrain where most usury occurred. This is why, despite the dominant case law on the subject, certain decisions (minority decisions, admittedly) recalled the existence of the 1807 law.[29]

Given these deviations in case law from the original intent of the law of 1807, it was surprising how long the Law on the Maximum remained on the statute book. The fact is that from 1871 to 1884 the average number of convictions under that law had gone down to fifteen per annum. It was not until 1886 that France, too, took the liberal road, at a time when most foreign legal systems had already come out in favour of freedom of interest rates.

New legislation undermined by judicial
decisions and economic reality

With the Law of 12 January 1886, French legislation returned to revolutionary law, that is, to the Law of 3 October 1789. However, application of this liberal system had the unintentional effect of decriminalizing usury. As will be shown, this consequence of the 1886 law, unforeseen by the legislator, stemmed from the lack of definition of the features making it possible to distinguish between a civil loan and a commercial loan.

In bringing itself into line with the majority of foreign legal systems, French law went back to the system of freedom of interest rates. This principle had already been adopted by Brazil in

---

[27] Cass., 7 May 1844 (S. 45.1.53).

[28] Grenoble, 16 Feb. 1836 (S. 37.2.361). For further special cases on banking transactions creating exceptions to the 1807 law see: Paris, 18 Jan. 1839 (S. 39.2.262); Cass., 8 Nov. 1825 (S. 27.1.84); Cass., 2 Aug. 1878 (*Jurisprudence du XIX* siècle (1878 vol.), pt. 1, 480).

[29] For examples of such minority decisions see: Montpellier, 13 Aug. 1853 (S. 53.2.469); Metz, 31 Dec. 1825 (CN 8.2.170); id., Cass., 24 Dec. 1825 (CN 8.1.246); Cass., 21 July 1847 (S. 47.1.797). See also, in this sense: Cass., 8 Apr. 1825 (S. 25.1.358); Cass., 26 Aug. 1825 (S. 25.1.360).

1832, by the UK, Portugal, and Tuscany in 1833, by Spain in 1838, by Denmark in 1855, by Norway, Piedmont, and the Netherlands in 1857, by Sweden in 1864, by Belgium and Italy in 1865, by Prussia and Bavaria in 1866 and 1867, and by Austria and Hungary in 1868. It was extended to the whole of Germany in 1871 and to Alsace-Lorraine in 1872. Finally, some of the Swiss cantons and the United States of America also rejected any regulation of conventional interest. In Britain the radical reform begun in 1818 with a House of Commons resolution, continued in 1833, and interrupted between 1837 and 1851 by provisional legislation was finally completed on 10 August 1854 by a statute of Queen Victoria that repealed all the laws relating to usury and fixing a legal rate of interest. In Germany, a law of 1880 punished anyone who abused the needs and inexperience of a borrower to stipulate excessive rates of interest.

In France, the liberal movement obtained the abolition of maximum interest rates in commercial transactions. The republican leaders included powerful businessmen who advocated economic liberalism. For example, Léon Say, an associate of the Rothschilds, was Minister of Finance for most of that time. The bourgeoisie who had supported the regime of Louis Philippe, and who came around to supporting the Republic after 1873, also hoped that the Republic would take note of their interests. For these reasons, republican leaders tried to reassure the business community and to satisfy them by stimulating the economy. In 1884, Jules Ferry claimed: 'As far as I am concerned, there is no such thing as an illegitimate profit.'

The single article of the French Law of 12 January 1886 stated: 'The Laws of 3 September 1807 and 19 December 1850, in their provisions relating to conventional interest, are repealed for commercial purposes; for civil purposes, they remain in effect.' This distinction was easily explained in the legislator's mind. Merchants, being more in touch with the ways of commerce, could do without the protection of the law, whereas it would have been dangerous to grant the same freedom to less experienced people—country landowners, for instance. With this single article, the legislator gave the courts a decisive and delicate role in the application of the 1886 law. The problems might be further aggravated in cases of usury where loans were made by a French person to a foreigner.

An initial question confronted judges: was the Law of 12 January 1886 retroactive? For civil purposes, article 2 of the Civil Code was quite clear: the law disposes only in respect of the future; it has no retroactive effect. This principle was confirmed by jurisdiction.[30] For criminal purposes, on the other hand, article 4 of the Penal Code admitted the principle of non-retroactivity only when the law in question created a new penalty or increased an existing penalty. It therefore had to be admitted that the 1886 law did possess a retroactive character for criminal purposes. It followed that the usurer who had committed usurious acts prior to 1886 which the law no longer touched on could not now have those acts challenged, from the moment the law was promulgated.

The chief question concerned the consequences of the 1886 law with a view to determining where usury was present. The distinction between a civil loan and a commercial loan was thus crucial, and it was one that the legislator left to the courts to make. The courts then had no alternative but to refer to general law, that is, the Commercial Code, to find out whether a loan was civil or commercial. However, the 1807 code was no clearer in its definition of the domain of commercial law. The authors of the code had not in fact declared themselves as between the objective view, according to which commercial law was the law of acts of commerce, and the subjective view, which held that commercial law was the law of merchants (*commerçants*). Article 1 of the Commercial Code defined merchants as 'those who performed acts of commerce and made doing so their habitual occupation'. Furthermore, articles 632 and 633 of the Code listed the main acts of commerce without ever defining the notion. Articles 632 and 633 stated: 'The law deems an act of commerce to be any purchase of produce and commodities for resale . . . any banking transaction . . . any obligation between dealers, merchants, and bankers, and finally, bills of exchange in general.'

It is clear from these articles that all loans that constituted banking transactions, all loans represented by bills of exchange, etc., were commercial transactions, loans made for commercial purposes. However, in order for commercial law to be applicable, the transaction had to have the character of an act of commerce for both the parties concerned. But the act of commerce indicated

---

[30] Besançon, 21 Apr. 1886 (*Jurisprudence du XIX* siècle* (1887 vol.), pt. 2, 202).

in articles 632 and 633 of the Code might also be mixed, that is, it might be part act of commerce and part civil act. An example would be a non-merchant borrowing a sum of money from a banker in order to provide for the needs of his family. When an act of commerce was mixed, it was in principle necessary to apply civil law to the part in respect of which the act was civil and to apply commercial law to the other. Under the 1807 law, this question had been controversial. Two solutions offered themselves to judges. The first lay in considering that it was the nature of the borrower's action that should determine whether the loan was civil or commercial and whether the rate of interest was or was not restricted, and that by virtue of the theory of the accessory the borrower's capacity as merchant led to the presumption of an act of commerce on his part. Only a small number of isolated decisions admitted this first solution. The argument of this opinion was that interest represented the risks of loss of the capital sum. In this sense, it was judged that the courts were invested with the power to strip an ostensibly commercial transaction of its visible forms and decide that, under the guise of a discount or exchange transaction, what had actually been accomplished was a civil loan.[31]

The second solution, which was the one generally adopted by jurisdiction, consisted on the contrary of deeming a loan to be commercial whenever the lender was a merchant. This was in effect a return to the case law that had formed under the 1807 law, which was confirmed by decisions taken in the wake of the Law of 12 January 1886. For example, it was decided that a merchant making a commercial loan, particularly a banker opening a current account for a private individual, might stipulate the legal rate of interest for commercial purposes even where the borrower was not a merchant, and that such a stipulation of interest was not usurious.[32] The argument of this opinion was twofold: on the one hand, in practical terms the banking business would become impossible if, for every transaction, the banker had to consider the destination of the funds lent to him; on the other hand, interest

[31] See Montpellier, 13 Aug. 1853 (S. 53.2.469); id., Agen, 12 May 1853 (S. 53.2.273); id., Agen, 19 July 1854 (S. 54.2.593). Later, Cass., 20 Jan. 1888 (Jurisprudence du XIXᵉ siècle (1889 vol.), pt. 1, 281); Cass., 9 Nov. 1888 (Jurisprudence du XIXᵉ siècle (1889 vol.), pt. 1, 393).

[32] Bourges, 14 Feb. 1854 (S. 54.2.531); id., Cass., 11 Mar. 1856 (S. 56.1.729); id., Cass., 27 Feb. 1864 (S. 64.1.341). See also Cass., 28 Apr. 1869 (S. 1869.1.306); Cass., 10 Jan. 1870 (S. 70.1.57 and 59).

represented not only the risk of loss of the capital sum but also the loss of enjoyment of the money parted with.

However, this doctrine led to an irregular consequence that certain decisions attempted to correct. When a loan was made for the commercial needs of the borrower, if the lender was not a merchant the loan was described as civil and interest on it restricted to 5 per cent. For example, two isolated decisions of the *Cour de Cassation* suggested that the nature of the loan should be determined by the occupation of the lender, and if the lender was not a merchant by that of the borrower.[33] The principle nevertheless remained that the loan must be commercial, irrespective of the destination of the money, when the lender was a merchant.

What was the position with regard to loans made by a French person to a foreigner? Despite the fact that, as we have seen, many countries had taken the liberal road before France, most foreign legal systems were not like that of France. While some countries had abolished any limitation of interest rates, others had kept the limitation but chosen a different maximum rate from that obtaining in France. This gave rise to the following question: in loans made by a French person to a foreigner, was it possible, for civil purposes, for a rate of interest above 5 per cent to be stipulated, whether tacitly or expressly, without risk of the lender being prosecuted for usury? Here, two hypotheses needed to be distinguished.

The first hypothesis was that when usury was committed outside France by French lenders or against foreign borrowers, French justice could take no action. Indeed, in the former case, under the terms of the Law of 17 June 1866 amending the Code of Criminal Procedure, instances of usury committed by French persons abroad were not punishable in France unless they were also punished by the foreign law concerned.[34] In the latter case, if the usurious act had been committed in a country that admitted freedom of interest rates by a foreign lender dealing with a French

---

[33] *Cass.*, 18 Feb. 1836 (*S.* 36.1.940); *Cass.*, 7 May 1845 (*S.* 45.1.644).

[34] The Law of 17 June 1866 further required four conditions before prosecutions could occur: it was necessary that the accused should not have proved that he had already been tried abroad; it was necessary that the action should be instituted at the request of the Public Prosecutor; it was necessary that a complaint by the injured party or a denunciation to the French authorities by the authorities of the country where the offence had been committed should have preceded the prosecution; lastly, it was necessary that the accused should be back in France.

borrower, French justice was again powerless to act by virtue of the rule *locus regit actum*.

The second hypothesis was that when an instance of usury took place in France and one of the parties was French and the other foreign, the fact of habitually lending above the French legal rate, that is, at the legal interest of a foreign law higher than the French legal rate, did not constitute the offence of usury, except in case of fraud. Indeed, under the terms of article 1134 of the Civil Code, legally constituted agreements took the place of law for those who had made them. Article 3 of the same code, stipulating that police and security laws were binding on everyone who lived in the territory, and article 6, stipulating that private agreements might not depart from the laws concerning public order and good morals, did not apply in connection with loans at interest, for the 1807 law was considered by most judicial decisions to be a law of relative rather than absolute public order.

For example, a judgment handed down by the Rouen appeal court on 12 July 1889 decided that as the rate of 12 per cent was authorized in the Republic of Ecuador, that rate was lawful even for a loan made in France to a company with its registered office in Guayaquil.[35] A judgment handed down by the *Cour de Cassation* on 19 February 1890 confirmed this decision by saying that the opening of a credit account requested abroad by a trading company having its registered office there was not governed by French law so far as interest was concerned but by the law of the country where the trading company was established.[36]

It followed that there was only one case in which the offence of usury could exist in international law: when in France (or in a foreign country where usury was defined in the same way as in France) there was a stipulation of interest above 5 per cent between French persons and foreigners whose national law prohibited the stipulation of interest above 5 per cent as usurious. In that case, such an agreement was indeed unlawful and the rule *locus regit actum* could not be invoked, any more than could the fact that the foreigner intended to refer to his national law. Consequently, usury may be said to have become very rare in international law.

[35] Clunet, *Journal de droit international privé* (1890), 129.
[36] Ibid. 495.

The new statute of 1886 and the case law which referred to it had the effect of legalizing loans made by usurers. Indeed, the levying of interest in excess of the legal rate was subject to *peines correctionnelles* (penalties of more than five days' but less than five years' imprisonment) only where it was habitual (Law of 19 December 1850, art 2). This circumstance, which made it possible to punish high-interest lenders, was about to become their salvation, for by making money-dealing their chief occupation usurers incontestably assumed the occupation of merchant, applying articles 1 and 634, paragraph 4, of the Commercial Code. This occupation of merchant then enabled them to stipulate interest above the legal rate, with the result that the freedom of interest rates proclaimed for commercial purposes came to be indirectly exercised for civil purposes. Because of this, in late nineteenth-century France, the legislation concerning usury was virtually eliminated and usury no longer existed as an offence, since usurers were considered to be merchants who could no longer be prosecuted. From the civil standpoint, then, there remained only a single exception in which the penalties of the 1807 and 1850 laws were still applicable: the case of a person practising no specific trade who happened to lend a sum of money intended for a civil transaction at interest above 5 per cent.

However, these consequences of the 1886 law were to be tempered by a sudden turnaround in case law. Certain judgments, indeed, were to attribute a civil character to loans made by merchants where these were intended for a civil transaction.[37] There was thus a return to the principle whereby the civil or commercial character of the loan was determined by the use for which the sum loaned was intended, regardless of the occupation of the borrower. For example, the *Cour de Cassation* decided in 1888 that the advances on accruing terms made to state pensioners by the manager of a discount bank for pensions did not constitute commercial loans, given that the pensioners concerned were not merchants, that the transactions in question had nothing commercial about them, and that the very form of the contracts concluded was that of civil contracts.[38]

It was further decided that the Law of 12 January 1886, which

[37] See *Cass.*, 2 June and 9 Nov. 1888, and Lyon, 3 June 1889 (*S.* 89.1.393; 90.2.41); id., Paris, 10 Mar. 1896 (*Jurisprudence du XIXᵉ siècle* (1898 vol.), pt. 2, 486.

[38] See *Cass.*, 9 Nov. 1888 (*S.* 89.1.393).

had admitted freedom of conventional interest and subsequently abolished the penalties for usury for commercial purposes, could not be applied to loans made to a merchant who had signed promissory notes to the lender with the trade name of the company of which he was a member, when those loans had not been made with a view to his trade and served no other purpose than that of satisfying his taste for expenditure and settling his gambling debts. Thus, as regards applying the 1886 law, the judges responsible for preventing usury had the right and the duty to seek out, in the facts of the particular case, the civil or commercial character of loans, whatever the guises in which those loans had been dressed up and the forms in which they had been cast.[39]

It can thus be stated that, at the end of the nineteenth century, case law wavered between two well-defined theories for applying the system put in place by the Law of 12 January 1886. The probable explanation for such wavering was the persistent problem of how to distinguish civil from commercial loans.

The first theory deduced the commercial nature of the loan from the intended purpose of the money loaned, that is, from the type of act performed by the borrower. It was necessary that there should be an act of commerce on his part. While according to doctrine this theory was the one closest to the intention of the legislator, it was nevertheless rejected by case law as being detrimental to the non-merchant in need of a short-term loan.

The second theory characterized the civil or commercial nature of the loan by the occupation of the lender, and occasionally by that of the borrower. Further removed from the intention of the legislator, this theory was justified by doctrine with reference to Scaccia's adage: *Plus valet pecunia mercatoris quam pecunia non mercatoris.* The prevailing case law took its cue from this second theory as being more practical and as such apparently more in tune with real-life needs. This duality of doctrine, together with the waverings of case law, in reality showed that the 1886 law had failed to find a satisfactory solution to the problem of usury in France in the final years of the nineteenth century.

This legal criticism might be supplemented by one of an economic nature: the maximum legal interest rate of 5 per cent for civil purposes and the legal interest rate of 6 per cent for com-

---

[39] *Cass.*, 14 May 1886 (*Jurisprudence du XIX* siècle (1887 vol.), pt. 1, 345).

mercial purposes no longer corresponded to the state of the capital market, which had experienced a drop in interest rates. The legal rates were thus out of step with the real economic situation. Faced with the need to revise the legal rate, the Law of 7 April 1900 lowered the double rate of the law by one unit, but the imperfect system installed by the 1886 law was still there as the twentieth century dawned.

18

Defining the Common Good and Social Justice

Popular and Legal Concepts of *Wucher* in Germany from the 1860s to the 1920s

MARTIN H. GEYER

Introduction

Wucher, or usury, is an ambiguous and elusive term. It intermingles various meanings derived from popular, political, economic, and juridical language. However, the phenomenon itself always addresses a constellation of injustice and real or perceived social dependencies and inequalities. In the vernacular of German-speaking countries, the term *Wucher* had traditionally been tinged with moral outrage that was codified in more neutral terms in civil and criminal law. In common legal terminology, the term was used primarily to describe the potentially exploitative relationship between debtors and creditors and their respective interests. *Wucher* could be defined as a 'business, especially an interest-earning business, by which one increases one's capital in an illicit or at least dishonourable manner',[1] or as 'large, exploitative capital gains'.[2] However, towards the end of the nineteenth century, many German political economists broadened the narrow meaning of 'excessive interests'.[3] They interpreted *Wucher* as including the 'use of a de facto monopoly in economic life, in the hands of certain people, solely for their benefit and to the

---

[1] D. Sanders, *Handwörterbuch der deutschen Sprache*, 2 vols. (Leipzig, 1863, 1865), ii. 1666.

[2] Josef Hellauer, 'Über Wucher', dissertation (Linz, 1898), 51. For contemporary juridical efforts to define the subject, cf. Hermann Blodic, *Der Wucher und seine Gesetzgebung* (Vienna, 1892); Constantin Isopescul-Grecul, *Das Wucherstrafrecht in vergleichender dogmenhistorischer, dogmatischer und kriminalpolitischer Darstellung* (Tübingen, 1906).

[3] For a summary of the academic debates in Germany see Leopold Caro, *Der Wucher: Eine socialpolitische Studie* (Leipzig, 1893), 73 ff.; Kurt Peschke, 'Wucher', in *Handwörterbuch der Staatswissenschaften*, vol. viii (Jena, 1928), 1081–108.

detriment or even ruin of a third party'.[4] This definition referred to exploitative contractual relationships in general and had an inherent twist against concepts in law and economics that were ascribed to liberalism: 'Wucher is the opposite of freedom of contract; it is its anti-social exploitation.'[5]

Yet the term has also always possessed another dimension, peculiar to the German language. Contrary to the English term 'usury', the German word *Wucher* is firmly rooted in the idea of a paternalistic form of consumer protection. Terms such as *Kornwucher* or *Kriegswucher* referred to phenomena that eighteenth-century English people decried as 'profiteering', 'forestalling', and 'engrossing'. Such language was part of what E. P. Thompson called the 'moral economy'.[6] In addition to the relationship between debtors and creditors, *Wucher* can thus refer to the relationship between consumers and producers. Although this latter meaning became increasingly obsolete in the second half of the nineteenth century, it did not disappear altogether, especially in the vernacular. Like the resurgence of food riots, the rhetoric of *Wucher* reappeared after the turn of the century in strikingly political language during the debates over tariff policies and what the French called the 'vie chère' in the pre-war years. The consumer protest of the First World War was highly charged with attacks against 'profiteering' and *Wucher*.[7]

This brief sketch has already shown that the term *Wucher* depicts several very different types of phenomena with apparently little in common. A juridical analysis of the clause pertaining to

[4] August von Miaskowski, *Verhandlungen der am 28. und 29. September 1888 abgehaltenen Generalversammlung des Vereins für Socialpolitik*, Schriften des Vereins für Socialpolitik 38 (Leipzig, 1888), 7.

[5] Peschke, 'Wucher', 1082.

[6] Edward P. Thompson, 'The Moral Economy of the English Crowd in the Eighteenth Century', in id., *Customs in Common* (London, 1991), 185–258; for Germany see Manfred Gailus, 'Collective Estate Society, Moral Economy, and the Market', to appear in Cynthia Bouton, John Bohstedt, Manfred Gailus, and Martin H. Geyer (eds.), *The Politics of Provisions from the 18th to the 20th Century*.

[7] Christoph Nonn, *Verbraucherprotest und Parteiensystem im wilhelminischen Deutschland* (Düsseldorf, 1996); Paul R. Hanson, 'The "Vie Chère" Riots of 1911: Traditional Protests in Modern Garb', *Journal of Social History*, 21 (1987–8), 463–81; Martin H. Geyer, 'Teuerungsprotest und Teuerungsunruhen 1914–1923: Selbsthilfegesellschaft und Geldentwertung', in Manfred Gailus and Volkmann Heinrich (eds.), *Der Kampf um das tägliche Brot: Nahrungsmangel, Versorgungspolitik und Protest 1770–1990* (Opladen, 1994), 319–45; id., 'Teuerungsprotest, Konsumentenpolitik und soziale Gerechtigkeit während der Inflation: München 1920–1923', *Archiv für Sozialgeschichte*, 30 (1990), 181–215.

Wucher in the Civil Code (§ 138 *BGB*) and Penal Code (§ 302 *StGB*), for example, will not deal with the issue of *Mietwucher* (rack-rent) in the inter-war period because the latter term pertains to another area of law.[8] However, phenomena appearing different at first might actually have many things in common if one does not study them through the perspective of normative concepts. Hence the aim of this essay is not to study the development of the juridical codification of *Wucher*, but to examine the semantics of this word and the legal and social action prompted by the various uses of this term. Of particular interest here is the problem of administrative and judicial intervention in contractual relations. I will describe the fundamental tension between efforts to regulate by law something as opaque as *Wucher*, on the one hand, and popular perceptions of morality and social justice, on the other. The essay deals with what might well have been said at the time by individuals and social groups who dwelt on the injustices associated with *Wucher* and with what actually could be done through the existing laws to alleviate these perceived injustices. Thus this essay will demonstrate how the term was used in the popular, legal, and political discourse. It will be shown that the word lent itself to being used to legitimize a system of social protection and to define, if often vaguely, principles of the 'common good' by addressing a system of social and economic inequalities. This is of interest for two reasons. First, an examination of this issue reveals a vital, though rarely studied aspect of how the modern interventionist welfare state came into being. Second, and more precisely, the discourse on *Wucher* and the specific, albeit ever-changing use of the term illustrate an interesting aspect of the 'modification of private rights by reference to their social function, the restriction of legal powers by social ethics, and the retreat from the formalism of the classical private law system of the nineteenth century',[9] a development

---

[8] A good example is Markus Sickenberger, *Wucher als Wirtschaftsstraftat: Eine dogmatisch-empirische Untersuchung* (Freiburg, 1989). The author treats the inclusion of *Mietwucher* in the Civil Code in 1971 focusing narrowly on § 305 *BGB*, and thus missing most of the legal history of rack-rent.

[9] Franz Wieacker, *A History of Private Law in Europe, with Particular Reference to Germany*, trans. Tony Weir (Oxford, 1995), quotation at 427 f.; see also 431 ff. German text: 'Relativierung der Privatrechte durch ihre soziale Funktion, die sozialethische Bindung dieser Befugnisse und die Abkehr vom Formalismus des klassischen Privatrechtssystems des 19. Jahrhunderts', Franz Wieacker, *Privatrechtsgeschichte der Neuzeit unter besonderer Berücksichtigung der deutschen Entwicklung* (2nd edn., Göttingen, 1967), 539; see also 543 ff.; see also Knut

which redefined the ways in which people of unequal social and economic status could use the law. It will be argued that these changes in legal practice were rooted in a broader discourse about justice and the law in which the First World War marked a watershed.[10]

Contending with liberalism

Ever since the beginning of Western civilization, efforts to regulate interest rates in lending have reflected almost paradigmatically the ambiguities involved in coming to terms with money and the marketplace. Even though canon law, with its strict and unrelenting prohibition on demanding interest for loans ('pecunia pecuniam parere non potest'), had become perforated by the end of the Middle Ages and was replaced by state-administered maxima for interest rates, canon law's stigmatization of moneylenders and their supposedly pernicious impact on society had a long-lasting legacy, whose worse aspect was popular anti-Semitism.[11] The new political economy of the eighteenth century attacked publicly fixed maxima for interest rates as well as for food prices.[12] These restrictions were not only considered infringements on the free development of markets, but they were also thought to advantage certain groups over others. After the ill-fated efforts of the French Revolution, the ideas of economic liberalism quickly prevailed in the mid-nineteenth century. In most countries usury laws regulating interests for both private and commercial

Wolfgang Nörr, *Zwischen den Mühlsteinen: Eine Privatrechtsgeschichte der Weimarer Republik* (Tübingen, 1988), 12 ff.; Jan Schröder, 'Kollektivistische Theorien und Privatrecht in der Weimarer Republik am Beispiel der Vertragsfreiheit', in Knut W. Nörr, Bertram Schefold, and Friedrich Tenbruck (eds.), *Geisteswissenschaften zwischen Kaiserreich und Republik* (Stuttgart, 1994), 335–59.

[10] I have developed some ideas in my essay 'Recht, Gerechtigkeit und Gesetze: Reichsgerichtsrat Zeiler und die Inflation', *Zeitschrift für neuere Rechtsgeschichte*, 16 (1994), 349–72; Joachim Rückert, 'Richtertum als Organ des Rechtsgeistes: Die Weimarer Erfüllung einer alten Versuchung', in Nörr, Schefold, and Tenbruck (eds.), *Geisteswissenschaften*, 267–313.

[11] For a summary Hans-Jörg Gilomen, 'Wucher und Wirtschaft im Mittelalter', *Historische Zeitschrift*, 250 (1990), 265–301; Max Neumann, *Geschichte des Wuchers in Deutschland bis zur Begründung der heutigen Zinsgesetze 1654* (Halle, 1865).

[12] No study comparable to that by Muldrew Craig, 'Interpreting the Market: The Ethics of Credit and Community in Early Modern England', *Social History*, 18 (1993), 163–84, is available for Germany. See also Keith Tribe, *Governing Economy: The Reformation of German Economic Discourse, 1750–1840* (Cambridge, 1988); William M. Reddy, *Money and Liberty in Modern Europe: A Critique of Historical Understanding* (Cambridge, 1987).

loans were repealed one by one, starting in the late 1830s (with a notable delay on the part of France, as described by Fabien Valente in this volume). England took the lead here, starting with the liberalization of commercial credit. Even if these laws had long been circumvented or simply not enforced at the time of their repeal, they were nevertheless thought to have legally undermined the position of the creditors. Reform was not easy and often highly contested. In Prussia, the debate over the abolition of interest maxima dragged on for over two decades. Even though agrarian interests in the *Herrenhaus* (the First Chamber) were losing ground—in 1866 interest rates for loans not secured by mortgages were liberalized—they remained steadfast in their opposition to initiatives put forward by both the liberal majorities in the lower house and, just as importantly, the liberal, reform-oriented members of the state bureaucracy. However, in 1867, the liberals and the reforming bureaucrats prevailed, just as they had in other states such as England (1854), Spain (1856), the Netherlands (1857), Belgium (1865), Württemberg (1839), the main cantons of Switzerland (1855–1867), Saxony (1864), and the city of Frankfurt (1864). Austria followed suit in 1868 after a series of protracted political struggles.[13]

Despite some opposition to the politics of liberalization, the issue only came to a head when the economic boom of the 1860s bust in the following decade. The impact of the economic crisis, namely the tightening of credit, was felt particularly in agriculture, which for almost three decades was to experience falling prices for its products.[14] The resulting squeeze on profits was felt in an increasing burden of debt, the total value of which rose in proportion to the value of agricultural products. This situation was a powerful factor in mobilizing interest groups representing farmers as well as artisans who decried the financial distress that led to an increase in foreclosures and the ruin of their businesses.[15]

[13] For a summary of legislative reform see Karl von Lilienthal, 'Die Wuchergesetzgebung in Deutschland', *Jahrbücher für Nationalökonomie und Statistik*, NS 1 (1880), 140–61, 366–85; Peschke, 'Wucher', 1091 ff.; Caro, *Der Wucher*; Blodic, *Der Wucher*; Carl von Chorinsky, *Der Wucher in Österreich* (Vienna, 1877).

[14] See Hans Ulrich Wehler, *Deutsche Gesellschaftsgeschichte*, iii: *Von der 'Deutschen Doppelrevolution' bis zum Beginn des Ersten Weltkrieges, 1845–1914* (Munich, 1994), 39 ff., 100 ff.

[15] Ibid.; Hans Rosenberg, *Große Depression und Bismarckzeit* (Berlin, 1967); Shulamit Volkov, *The Rise of Popular Antimodernism in Germany: The Urban Master Artisans, 1873–1896* (Princeton, 1978), 172 ff.

The ideological confrontations that had been mounting during the debate over the policies of liberalization suddenly escalated sharply. *Wucher* became a highly politicized slogan, the use of which defined fundamental ideological positions. The term became part of a divisive political code. Critics argued that the abolition of the usury laws marked the victory of what was disrespectfully called *Manchesterliberalismus*.[16] In fact, the rhetoric of *Wucher* implied first and foremost an attack on liberalism. The programme of deregulation, whether it applied to the monetary arena or to the question of eliminating corporations of artisans, epitomized the ideal of the free circulation of goods, people, and ideas. In line with Bentham's argument of 1788, defenders of liberalism stressed that usury—like other phenomena which the state attempted to control by setting maxima—had been caused by the pernicious laws themselves, since these prevented the free flow of money; protection was based on privilege, prejudice, and an ill-conceived understanding of the public interest. The people supposedly protected by these laws were actually being victimized by them. If left solely to market forces, the price of money would cause usury to disappear as lenders asking for excessive interest would be forced to comply with the demands of the marketplace.[17]

Running parallel to this economic argument was a powerful juridical argument, pertaining particularly to issues involving the freedom of contract.[18] Contracts were not to be regulated by socially and politically defined standards of equity; the state should not be the arbiter of 'morality' (*Sittlichkeit*). Furthermore the freedom to enter into a contract was based on the idea of the free individual, responsible for himself. The construction of usury by the existing laws prior to liberal reform threatened both the principles of contractual freedom and contractual fidelity and thus the principle of *pacta sunt servanda* so fundamental to the

[16] Rudolf Walther, 'Exkurs: Wirtschaftlicher Liberalismus', *Geschichtliche Grundbegriffe: Historisches Lexikon zur politisch-sozialen Sprache in Deutschland*, vol. iii (Stuttgart, 1982), 787–815, 803 ff.

[17] The German debate had been sparked off in the 18th century largely by Jeremy Bentham's *Defense of Usury* (1787), translated and published as *Verteidigung des Wuchers* (Halle, 1788), and A.-R. J. Turgot, *Mémoire sur le prêt à interest et sur le commerce de fers* (Paris, 1789); see Caro, *Der Wucher*, 16 ff.

[18] See the widely noted speech by Levin Goldschmidt, *Verhandlungen des VI. Juristentages*, 1 (Berlin, 1867), 271 ff.; Wilhelm Endemann, *Die Bedeutung der Wucherlehre* (Berlin, 1866); for the background see Diethelm Klippel, *Politische Freiheit und Freiheitsrechte im deutschen Naturrecht des 18. Jahrhunderts* (Paderborn, 1976).

liberal concept of private law. Moreover, it also threatened concepts of an individualistic conception of the state. The setting of maxima for interests as well as for food prices was by definition a public regulation of economic activities. Finally, the pre-modern usury laws were equated with leniency towards debtors at the expense of creditors.

The issue of *Wucher*, reintroduced into public debate by opponents of eighteenth-century political economy, gave them a means of addressing the new political, social, and legal order, *as well as* the system of inequality existing between debtors and creditors. In other words, the rhetoric of *Wucher* re-emerged in the 1870s as a powerful weapon in the political arena. It was a weapon that could be used not only to contest economic and political liberalism, but also to question the effects of liberal reform on the relationship between debtors and creditors.

The first legislative initiatives in this backlash against the earlier policies of liberalization were proposed in the diet of the Austrian province of Galicia in 1874. The judicial committee of the diet painted a gloomy picture of the situation of the rural population and attacked what it considered to be the perniciousness of the liberal laws, claiming that these laws had entirely overlooked the state's responsibility to enforce certain moral standards.[19] The committee's evaluation started a protracted political struggle that was to have an important spillover effect, particularly in German-speaking regions. The eventual passage of usury laws in Galicia and the Bukovina in 1877 demonstrated, first, that a revision of liberal policy was indeed feasible and, second, that the acerbic political rhetoric of *Wucher* with its inherent anti-Semitism was spreading like wildfire and could be politically instrumentalized. Soon similar legislative initiatives were introduced in both the Prussian and Bavarian diets in 1879. In that same year, the Swiss canton of Solothurn actually put a usury law back on the books.[20] The pressure on the Reich to react similarly was also mounting. Things finally came to a head when a delegate of the Catholic Centre Party, Peter Reichensperger, a long-time advocate of usury laws,[21] proposed far-reaching legislation to define and combat usury. He was supported by sixty-nine fellow party members and

[19] Caro, *Der Wucher*, 40 ff., 176 ff.; Chorinsky, *Der Wucher*, 118 ff.   [20] Ibid. 45.
[21] Peter Reichensperger, *Gegen die Aufhebung der Zinswuchergesetze* (Berlin, 1860); id., *Die Zins- und Wucherfrage* (Berlin, 1879).

by the Conservatives. Reichensperger's bill imposed ceilings on interest rates, graduated according to the purpose of the loan, and also introduced civil law provisions that would have made it possible to annul any contract exceeding the prescribed maximum interest rate. This provision, which alone did much to limit the principle of freedom of contract, was supplemented by another provision that would have restricted the capacity of individuals to draw bills of exchange (*Wechselfähigkeit*). Soon afterwards, the Conservative deputies von Kleist-Retzow, von Flottwell, and Freiherr von Marschall submitted a bill that differed from Reichensperger's, not least by ignoring the issue of interest rate ceilings. This bill eventually provided the basis for the legislative draft that was adopted by the government early in 1880 and became law in May of the same year.[22]

More than anything else, the legislative initiative of 1879/80 must be seen as a fundamentally political gesture. For one thing, the established parties stirred up an issue propagated by unruly anti-Semites in order to use the widespread discontent among the rural and urban populations to broaden the electoral base of their support.[23] For another, *Wucher* rhetoric fitted in with the efforts of the political right to form a political alliance with the Catholic Centre Party.[24] Finally, the incorporation of the concept of *Wucher* into 'legislation designed to assist, protect, and reprimand'[25] ideologically complemented the often evoked concept of 'protection for the nation's labour' (*Schutz der nationalen Arbeit*), namely social insurance legislation and tariff policies, which were being hotly debated at the same time as the usury bills were introduced early in 1879.

Thus there are many good reasons to view the government's draft legislation of 1880 primarily as part of its efforts in coalition-building. Furthermore it might be argued that the new law did not have much of an impact. Although much of what was said in the

---

[22] A good summary is given by W. Henle, *Das Wuchergesetz vom 24.V.1880 und 19.VI.1893* (Munich, 1893); see also Drucksache No. 265: 'Bericht der XII. Kommission', *Verh. des Reichstages*, 4th legislative period, sess. II, vol. vi.

[23] Volkov, *The Rise of Popular Antimodernism*, 223 ff.

[24] Wehler, *Von der 'Deutschen Doppelrevolution'*, 990 ff.; Lothar Gall, *Bismarck: Der Weiße Revolutionär* (Frankfurt am Main, 1980), 590 (with regard to the protagonists of the usury laws of 1879).

[25] *Verh. des Reichstages*, 4th legislative period, sess. III, vol. i, 8 Apr. 1880, 564 (Reichensperger).

ensuing debate on this legislative proposal might have been little more than a smokescreen, the debate itself did indeed fundamentally challenge the prevailing legal positivism. At stake was the question of how to use the law to define social standards and then how to use these standards to shape the moral order of society.

The law and the 'common good'

One of the striking features of the debate surrounding the usury legislation was the appeal to the sentiments of the *Volk*, and to a supposedly prevailing feeling of righteousness, a *Volksbewußtsein*, that did not 'concur with (liberal) legislation'.[26] Reichensperger appealed to 'the sentiment of the people'. What needed to be expressed, he claimed, was that an 'internal, communal cause prevailed in the legislation'; law was to be a 'sword of justice' for the 'defence of the common good' (*Schutz des Gemeinwohls*).[27] As in many other fields, the advocates of using legislation contested the liberals' claim that they represented the people and that they spoke for the people. Reichensperger argued that the new legislative proposal would destroy the 'doctrinal chains under whose weight the German nation had suffered for all too long'. In much the same way, Kleist-Retzow viewed the new legislation as a victory over the 'power of moneyed interest', the *Geldmacht*, which had gained the 'prerogative' over royal power.[28]

This appeal to *Rechtsgefühl*, *Rechtsempfinden* (sense and feeling of justice), and *Volksgeist* (spirit of the people) was standard fare both in the contemporary literature on this topic and in the parliamentary debates in Germany and Austria. Even Eduard Lasker, the liberal champion against the earlier usury laws in the 1860s, grudgingly noted in 1880 that the initiators of this new legislation had 'satisfied a public and justified demand to stigmatize usury in legislation to the degree it deserves'.[29] If the wolves were 'howling for freedom', as the jurist Rudolf von Jhering noted, this was understandable; he added sarcastically that if the sheep, namely the liberals like Lasker, were joining them in raising their voices,

---

[26] Ibid. 573 (Kleist-Retzow).   [27] Ibid. 564, 567.   [28] Ibid. 563, 573.
[29] Ibid. 20 Apr. 1880, ii. 838. Following the fiery speech given by Kleist-Retzow, the Liberal Dreyer noted that Kleist-Retzow spoke as though there was still someone in the Reichstag who needed to be convinced. Ibid. 8 Apr. 1880, i. 574.

it only proved that they were indeed sheep.[30] In 1872 Jhering proclaimed the 'fight for justice against injustice' by warning that the
'people did not understand the law and the law did not understand the people'. With regard to the relationship between creditors and debtors he wrote apodictically: 'It is better to do glaring
injustice to a hundred creditors than possibly to treat one debtor
too harshly.'[31] Small wonder that the proponents of usury laws
claimed him as one of their own. Jhering was quoted as saying
that the freedom of contract and movement were nothing but a
'hunting license for thieves and pirates with the right to prey upon
all those who fall into their hands'.[32]

The excesses of the liberal law of contract were played up time
and again. By putting this political struggle in terms of a fight for
justice in the name of the people, these critics were addressing the
balance of power between creditors and debtors which supposedly disadvantaged the latter. Although no systematic surveys of
the problem were readily available for Germany at the time, the
cases of Galicia and Bukovina, where some data had been gathered, played a major role in the debates. The miserable state of
these two Austrian provinces seemed to corroborate the seemingly
endless number of individual stories and vivid depictions of
'usurers, bloodsuckers of the worst sort' preying on the rural
population.[33] Liberated from the fetters of law, it was argued,
these villains, the *Wucherer*, could go about their evil business in
the light of day; even if an individual judge might have been motivated to act against them, the courts had to allow the usurers to
pursue their legal claims against their victims. Horrifying allusions
to the 'enslavement of peasants'[34] and the population at large, to
usurers as parasites of the body social, and to the people at the
mercy of an omnipresent enemy were popular. A survey of 1,173
convictions for debt in Bukovina in the years 1876 and 1877 found
that the interest rates demanded had averaged about 33 per cent

[30] Jhering is quoted in Caro, *Der Wucher*, 50.

[31] Rudolf von Jhering, *Der Kampf ums Recht* (1878), ed. Hermann Klenner (Freiburg,
1991), 8, 15, 94. See also Fritz Loos and Hans-Ludwig Schreiber, 'Recht, Gerechtigkeit', in
Geschichtliche Grundbegriffe, v (Stuttgart, 1984), 231–311, at 296 ff.

[32] Theobald Rizy, 'Zur Wucherfrage: Rede, gehalten im österreichischen Herrenhause
am 3. Mai 1881', *Zeitschrift für das Privat- und öffentliche Recht der Gegenwart*, 8 (1881), 774–84,
at 780.

[33] *Verh. des Reichstages*, 4th legislative period, sess. II, vol. vi, 31 Apr. 1879 (Reichensperger).

[34] The term was originally used in 1874 by a Polish representative of the Galician diet
and was picked up by various authors; by 1893 Leopold Caro, *Der Wucher*, could argue that
it had almost become a 'household word' (p. 180).

per year; for the majority of debts of less than 100 *Gulden*—which actually made up almost half the cases—the interest rates were significantly higher.[35]

The persona of the usurer played an important role: he was described as an outsider who attempted 'to exploit those in dire straits for his own benefit with satanic cunning'.[36] The extensive surveys—unsatisfactory even by contemporary methodological standards—published by the *Verein für Sozialpolitik* in the 1880s are odd collections of sources on ruses. The narratives of social and economic conditions in various regions of Germany thrived on the supposed maliciousness of the usurer who preys on his ignorant victims. Seldom did these studies analyse rural credit relations; instead they judged usurers from an altogether moral perspective, generalizing in a grand narrative on the moral depravity of the moneylenders. The usurer was thought to be both a symptom and the cause of backwardness. Breaking the *Wucherer's* hold on the country was considered the prerequisite for modernizing society, and this could be achieved by introducing new credit facilities and promoting efficient agricultural estates.[37]

Research on anti-Semitism has often pointed to the connection between the construction of the figure of the *Wucherer* and the Jew, an issue which cannot be dealt with in greater detail here, yet which is of great importance.[38] The surveys mentioned above are a good example of this.[39] The appeal to the idea of community

[35] Julius Platterer, 'Der Wucher in der Bukovina' (1878), in id., *Kritische Beiträge zur Erkenntnis unserer sozialen Zustände und Theorien* (Basle, 1894) 317–70; material on Galicia is presented by Caro, *Der Wucher*, 176 ff.

[36] *Verh. des Reichstages*, 4th legislative period, sess. III, vol. i, 8 Apr. 1880, 573.

[37] *Bäuerliche Zustände in Deutschland*, Schriften des Vereins für Socialpolitik 22–4 (Leipzig, 1883); *Der Wucher auf dem Lande: Berichte und Gutachten, veröffentlicht vom Verein für Socialpolitik*, Schriften des Vereins für Socialpolitik 35 (Leipzig, 1888). Julius Platterer, 'Der Wucher und die Bauern in Deutschland' (1888), in id., *Kritische Beiträge zur Erkenntnis*, 395–423. For a contemporary critique see Julius Zuns, *Der Wucher auf dem Lande: Eine Kritik des Fragebogens* (Frankfurt am Main, 1880); Gottlieb Schnapper-Arndt, *Zur Methodologie socialer Enquèten* (Frankfurt am Main, 1888).

[38] M. Kayserling, *Der Wucher und das Judenthum* (Budapest, 1882) was concerned that debates on the reform of the usury laws would automatically spark off a debate on the role of Jews. A most perceptive study in this respect is James F. Harris, *The People Speak! Anti-Semitism and Emancipation in Nineteenth-Century Bavaria* (Ann Arbor, 1994).

[39] Platterer, 'Der Wucher und die Bauern', 387, summarized the survey as follows: 'Wherever this most terrible form of usury exists, the transaction of business follows a typical, traditional pattern; the issue of race comes to the fore and the businessman is a Jew.' German text: 'Überall, wo es diese schlimmste Art des Wuchers gibt, ist der Verlauf der Geschäfte ein ganz typisch-gleichmäßiger, traditioneller, es ist Rasse in Geschäft und der Geschäftsmann ist ein Jude.'

to be found in popular, academic, and parliamentary debates was accompanied by an express desire to be rid of the so-called 'foreign elements' in that community, to expel outsiders. This rhetoric, laced with stories of communal or individual misery, lent itself to creating the sense of an acute state of emergency, which required drastic action. Characteristic in this respect is the conservative political economist Albert Schäffle who claimed that 'movable capital was waging a war of annihilation against productive labour' and that this movable capital deserved to be 'thoroughly skinned once and for all'.[40] In the words of another author, it was the purpose of law to prevent the 'debilitation and marginalization of entire societal groups, to give the members of these groups living conditions that are both physically and mentally healthy at the expense of those individuals who gradually exhaust and use up the wealth'.[41] The need to deal with *Wucher* was a 'matter of life', not a matter of legalistic hairsplitting.[42] Law was to be derived from the experience of life in order to defend life and society. Law was to embody transpersonal, social criteria. Law was to be used, not least, to fulfil the state's responsibility to uphold public morality (*Sittlichkeit*). The criticism of liberalism as allegedly biased against social aims, the defence of the moral authority of the state, and the organic concepts of state and society, so prevalent among Catholics, converged in a curious way in the debates on *Wucher*.[43] At the core of all these complaints and legislative initiatives stood the appeal to material justice, which was based on ethical standards and, from a juridical point of view, antiformal norms.[44]

Both the government and the majority in the *Reichstag* were eager to separate the realm of the law clearly from that of popular rhetoric. The language of those who were to define usury juridi-

---

[40] In German: 'Er müsse aus dem "Pelz endlich und gründlich herausgeschüttelt" werden', cf. Albert Schäffle, *Deutsche Kern- und Zeitfragen* (Berlin, 1894), 304; see also Chorinsky, *Der Wucher*, 95 ff. Cf. Drucksache No. 265 (n. 20), 1602.

[41] Isopecul-Grecul, *Das Wucherstrafrecht*, p. vi.

[42] In his somewhat esoteric treatment of usury, Lorenz von Stein stated that it was necessary 'to avoid . . . purely theoretical discussions and to look at life as it really is', *Der Wucher und sein Recht: Ein Beitrag zum wirthschaftlichen und rechtlichen Leben unserer Zeit* (Vienna, 1880), 6.

[43] The authoritative statement of the Catholic view is by Hermann Ratzinger, *Sittliche Grundlagen der Volkswirtschaft* (Freiburg, 1881).

[44] See also Max Weber, *Wirtschaft und Gesellschaft: Grundriß der verstehenden Soziologie* (5th rev. edn., Tübingen, 1972), 507.

cally was conspicuously different. Notions of material justice were to be erased: fixing interest-rate maxima was thus out of the question, since, as it was stated perceptively, 'there exist neither national-economic, nor legal, nor ethnic reasons to subject these freedoms to restrictions'. Such maxima served neither the interests of the debtor nor the needs of financial transaction.[45]

A similar shift away from social standards can be seen with respect to the formal juridical definition of the offence. The Chancellor's son, Graf Herbert von Bismarck, who was an ardent proponent of interest-rate maxima (graduated according to whether the credit was for commercial or agricultural purposes), hit the nail on the head when he complained that once lawmakers neglected to set clear norms for what constituted usury, the law became 'individualized'.[46] His suspicion was corroborated by the twofold definition of the crime of usury: it had to be proven that the financial advantages were 'strikingly out of proportion to the services' rendered, and that there had been a 'continuous effort' on the part of the accused to exploit the 'dire straits, the inexperience, the lack of judgment or the considerably weak will' of the other party. In stressing the possible deficiencies of the plaintiff, this legal definition of usury narrowed down further the number and type of cases which could be brought to court.

Yet at the same time it is obvious that judges were to be granted a great deal of discretionary power in usury cases. After the free presentation of the evidence, it was to be left to the judge to evaluate each case on its own merits and according to the judge's individual authority, instead of along the guidelines laid down by a clearly defined set of norms.[47] In other words, judges were to be the medium through which individual cases were adjudicated without recourse to clearly defined standards. It was thought that their own daily experience of life in general would be close enough to that of the people for them to be capable of evaluating each individual case of usury according to a 'judicious interpretation of the law'.[48]

This reliance on judicial prerogative was a sensitive point in the

[45] Drucksache No. 265 (n. 20), 1600; see also the statements by Schelling on behalf of the government, *Verh. des Reichstages*, 4th legislative period, sess. III, vol. i, 8 Apr. 1880, 562 f.

[46] Ibid., vol. ii, 20 Apr. 1880, 829.   [47] Drucksache No. 265, 1603.

[48] Ibid. 1603 f.

government's proposed legislation, and one which received considerable attention for good reason. The idea of judicial independence was criticized not only by conservative critics such as von Bismarck who, unlike his colleagues from the Centre Party, mistrusted the 'people'. By replacing social standards (defined by maxima as he had demanded) with the court's judgments, Bismarck argued, lawmakers were inadmissibly overlaying the law with 'morality' of their own; furthermore, legislators were thereby surrendering their sovereignty to the judges.[49] Instead of furthering morality, others argued, the law would destroy the belief in law and justice once judges were left to rule on cases at their own discretion.[50] In light of later developments, these words are noteworthy.

In statistical terms, the adjudication of usury is a story quickly told. In 1882, 176 people were charged in 261 cases; in 1885, the figures had dropped to only 99 people in 131 cases, and the numbers remained at this level in the years that followed.[51] Remarkably, no other type of crime even came close to having such a large percentage of acquittals as usury. On a nationwide basis, the percentage of convictions decreased from 56.7 per cent to 37.4 per cent, whereas in the various individual regions they were significantly lower. With regard to Berlin, for example, where only 11.8 per cent of cases ended in conviction in 1885, one expert remarked that 'either the prosecutor's office was unduly resolute or the court was tremendously lenient in the proceedings'.[52]

These figures might be interpreted as meaning that *Wucher* was nothing short of a rhetorical construct used to define political and social morality. It was not the legal means to prosecute usury that were missing, but the opportunity and the will to apply them. Having stated this, however, it is important to point out that, despite the relatively small number of cases actually tried in court and ending in a conviction, social and political mobilization in rural areas, headed by the Catholic Centre Party, the Conservatives, and anti-Semites, constituted a way of negotiating

---

[49] *Verh. des Reichstages*, 4th legislative period, sess. III, vol. ii, 20 Apr. 1880, 829.

[50] Von Lilienthal, 'Die Wuchergesetzgebung', 382.

[51] Karl von Lilienthal, 'Der Wucher auf dem Lande', *Zeitschrift für die gesamte Strafrechtswissenschaft*, 8 (1888), 157–221, 157; in the following years this trend continued, see 'Gesetz betr. Ergänzung der Bestimmungen über den Wucher', Drucksache No. 70, *Verh. des Reichstages*, 8th legislative period, sess. II, vol. i.

[52] Von Lilienthal, 'Der Wucher auf dem Lande', 161.

the relationship between creditors and debtors outside the court-room. The law provided a means to put pressure on individuals who were identified with usurious practices.[53] The effectiveness of this pressure, as well as of the public resonance of individual trials, should certainly not be underestimated.[54]

Proponents of the usury laws argued that it was the inherent individualist construction of the law and its narrow focus on 'interest' that hindered its application. They referred to a long list of scams that had been discovered, for example, in the surveys published by the *Verein für Sozialpolitik*, namely *Viehwucher*, *Landwucher*, *Warenwucher* ('cattle usury', 'land usury', and charging 'exorbitant prices' for merchandise). In 1893 the laws were amended to include the criminalization of *Sach- oder Leistungswucher* (goods and services usury), which also covered legal transactions that were 'strikingly out of proportion to services rendered'.[55]

The intent of the new, expanded law as proposed by the government clearly aimed to give the debtor wider protection. Yet to the dismay of those propagating the amendment, the debates demonstrated that the language of morality, overwhelmingly appropriated by conservatives, was vulnerable to challenge. As early as 1880, one Social Democrat had argued that his party 'naturally' considered 'almost everything that represents personal profit in society today to be a type of usury'.[56] In the 1890s, the party orchestrated this theme much more forcefully: employment contracts should come under the usury laws since they often exhibited an 'exploitation of distress'.[57] As the debates on amendment in 1893 show, *Wucher* was interpreted as including a broad spectrum of exploitation. For example, some even claimed that the highly contested tariff policies possessed a 'usurious character';[58] not only was a finger pointed at property usury, the right of retention by landlords, and rack-rent, but also at the usurious

---

[53] Ibid. 216. [54] *Der Spieler- und Wucherer-Prozeß in Hannover* (2nd edn., Berlin, 1893).
[55] Cf. Henle, *Das Wuchergesetz*, 89 ff.

[56] *Verh. des Reichstages*, 4th legislative period, sess. III, vol. ii, 20 Apr. 1880, 837. 'Der Wucher als ökonomisches Übel ist nicht die Ursache, sondern die Folge und Wirkung unserer ungesunden Wirtschaftsverhältnisse', *Die Sozialdemokratie im Deutschen Reichstag: Tätigkeitsberichte und Wahlaufrufe aus den Jahren 1871 bis 1893* (Berlin, 1909), 226.

[57] *Verh. des Reichstages*, 8th legislative period, sess. II, vol. iii, 14 Apr. 1893, 1843 ff. (Stadthagen); cf. also Frohme, ibid., vol. i, 655 ff. Similar initiatives were launched by the Social Democrat Stadthagen during the debates on the Civil Code in 1896, cf. *Erste, zweite und dritte Berathung des Entwurfs eines Bürgerlichen Gesetzbuchs im Reichstage* (Berlin, 1896), 272 ff.

[58] *Verh. des Reichstages*, 8th legislative period, sess. II, i. 656.

dealings of industrial cartels, of the stock exchange, and even of theatre agents.[59] The Social Democrats called for people's courts (*Volksgerichte*) to guarantee that the law would be applied. They argued that the people knew all too well what usury was.[60] French Socialists undoubtedly shared these sentiments: the food riots of 1910 and 1911 caused by 'la vie chère' were replete with attacks on *accapareurs* and profiteers who needed to be punished.[61]

On many of these issues the Conservatives, representatives of the Centre Party, and Social Democrats did form an alliance, especially the latter two groups. If Social Democrats tended to stress economic and social equality and liberty, the first two groups focused on the moral role of the state which allowed for intervention into the private law system. By the 1890s, the term *Wucher* had become synonymous with the exploitation of 'national labour' and a means, although often disguised in different terms, to advance issues of social protection[62] and economic intervention.[63] But the issues that divided the parties are equally important: unlike the Conservatives and certain factions within the Centre Party who strove to protect the 'producers'—that is, artisans and farmers—the Social Democrats focused fully on the protection of 'consumers'. In their view, tariff policies were nothing but publicly licensed *Wucher*.[64] Furthermore, the issues of justice, and the morality of law, order, and society being addressed in the debates on usury were repeatedly intertwined with an equally important fault line, namely, the issue of anti-Semitism. During the parliamentary debates of 1893, anti-Semitism as a political code aligned the political right (including factions within the Centre Party) against the Social Democrats.[65]

---

[59] *Verh. des Reichstages*, 8th legislative period, sess. II, i. 656 ff.   [60] Ibid., iii. 1844.

[61] Cf. Hanson, 'The "Vie Chère" Riots'.

[62] The representative of the Centre Party, Hitze, characteristically put the argument as follows: 'Den Arbeitsvertrag, speziell in seinen wucherischen Formen zu treffen, war vor allem die Aufgabe des Arbeiterschutzes.' Cf. *Verh. des Reichstages*, 8th legislative period, sess. II, vol. i, 24 Jan. 1893, 660.

[63] The debates that led to the law of 1896 regulating the stock market are full of indirect and direct allusions to *Wucher*. Cf. R. Gerhard, *Wuchertum und Spekulation* (Leipzig, 1894); T. Fritsch, *Zwei Übel: Boden-Wucher und Börse* (2nd edn., Leipzig, 1894); for the parliamentary debates cf. the unsystematic description by Wolfgang Schulz, *Das deutsche Börsengesetz: Die Entstehungsgeschichte und wirtschaftlichen Auswirkungen des Börsengesetzes von 1896* (Frankfurt am Main, 1994).

[64] Nonn, *Verbraucherprotest*.

[65] *Verh. des Reichstages*, 8th legislative period, sess. II, i. 655 ff., iii. 61 ff., 1841 ff., 2053 ff.

Wucher *and consumer policies during the First World War*

In the debate on usury, as in many other aspects of social, political, and economic life, the First World War and its aftermath marked a fundamental turning point. Whereas legal codification in the pre-war period had drawn a distinct line between popular and juridical language, a fundamental realignment now occurred in the realm of legislative and state action, and judicial practice. The issue of *Wucher* suddenly lent itself to stipulating a system of transpersonal criteria by which the common good was defined, and to determining a level of state intervention that would hardly have been imaginable a few years earlier.

Because of shortages and steep price increases for food and soon for most other essentials of daily life, *Wucher* became one of the catchwords used by all social groups. To talk about *Wucher* meant to attack the deliberate exploitation of the grave economic circumstances by groups and individuals who either withheld goods for speculative reasons, charged 'unjustly' high prices, or drove up prices. Producers, that is, the agricultural interest groups which had lashed out against the 'capitalist creditors' before the war and which had initiated the usury laws, suddenly fell silent. Those groups that had complained about 'slavery' at the hands of creditors were now being accused by consumers of rapaciously exploiting the people, if not, as in the case of Germany, of being 'profiteers' who also tried to rid themselves of debt by taking advantage of inflation.[66]

Undoubtedly, the situation was aggravated in Germany and Austria by the fact that the pie of goods and income to be distributed had shrunk considerably since the war and that people in these two countries were much worse off than those in France or England.[67] The threat of hunger was perceived not only as a state of emergency but as an emergency of the state, which called for far-reaching intervention: 'Let provisions run short in the shops

---

[66] A wealth of information is given by Belinda Davis, 'Home Fires Burning: Politics, Identity and Food in World War I Berlin', dissertation (University of Michigan, 1992); Jean-Louis Robert et al., 'The Image of the Profiteer', in Jay Winter and Jean-Louis Robert (eds.), *Capital Cities at War: Paris, London, Berlin 1914–1919* (Cambridge, 1997), 104–32; for further references cf. also Geyer, 'Teuerungsprotest'.

[67] A good survey is given by Richard Wall and Jay Winter (eds.), *The Upheaval of War: Family, Work and Welfare in Europe 1914–1918* (Cambridge, 1988); Avner Offer, *The First World War: An Agrarian Interpretation* (Oxford, 1989).

for a single moment, and panic will spread and riot be imminent,'
a French author argued. 'A government desirous of maintaining
order, of keeping the national spirit of resistance unimpaired must
take measures in order to avoid such dangers.'[68] Moral outrage
against 'excessively' high prices, *Wucher*, and the profiteering of
small groups proved to be a tremendously powerful social and
political force. Public outrage led to the passage of war emergency
laws that intervened widely in the economy, going far beyond the
rudimentary policing powers that still existed in some countries
with respect to food prices.[69] This constellation, in conjunction
with the various degrees of pressure being exerted in these countries for social and political reform, made possible a critical renegotiation of rights and, in the end, a transformation of some
aspects of the private law system. The individualistic construct of
Wucher by nineteenth-century civil and criminal law was supplanted by vague and highly contested definitions of social justice.

Germany is a particularly good example in this respect.
Nowhere else did the government intervene so extensively into the
economy on behalf of the consumer (and fail so miserably,
perhaps with the exception of Austria) as in Germany.[70] Prices
became subject to public control, and major societal groups
wanted to have a hand in setting them. While the people tended
to decry almost any price increase as being usurious, a number of
laws and ordinances tried to establish a framework for what legally
constituted a 'reasonable' or 'just price', and for combating
'regrading', 'engrossing', and 'forestalling' (*Schleich- und Ketten-
handel*). This framework was expanded upon by local and regional
price-control and price-fixing committees and by precedents
set by court decisions. Price-control committees consisted of

---

[68] Michel Augé-Laribé, 'Agriculture', in id. and Pierre Pinot (eds.), *Agriculture and Food
Supply in France during the War* (New Haven, 1927), 1–154, 69. It is, in fact, striking how similar
was the legislation developed between 1914 and 1919 in France and Germany, as well as
in a non-combatant country such as Switzerland.

[69] For a survey of different countries cf. Peschke, 'Wucher', 1096 ff. The legal
justifications in Germany were § 3 of the Enabling Act of 4 Aug. 1914 and the law on the
state of siege, according to which prohibitions could be issued in the interest of securing
public order. Later reference was made to art. 48 of the Weimar constitution, cf. Max
Alsberg, *Preistreibereistrafrecht* (Leipzig, 1922), 1 ff.

[70] The best English summary of a vast literature is Gerald D. Feldman, *The Great Disorder: Politics, Economics, and Society in the German Inflation, 1914–1924* (New York, 1993), 59 ff.,
73 ff.; Davis, 'Home Fires Burning'; for the many organizational details cf. August Skalweit,
Die deutsche Ernährungswirtschaft (Stuttgart, 1927).

members of local or regional administrations and of corporate bodies representing groups such as merchants, producers, and consumers, that is, representatives of blue- and white-collar workers, civil servants, pensioners' organizations, and tenants' and housewives' organizations.

The rapidly expanding volume of consumer legislation sought to combat wartime usury (*Kriegswucher*) primarily by setting standards in a way that was distinctly different from the approach of the pre-war period. Whereas the earlier legislation had been centred around the individual victim and the offender, the new ordinances referred to the overall conditions of the market and prohibited 'excessive profits'. Once maximum prices had been introduced for most essential commodities, it was not difficult to determine what constituted 'excessive profit'. This development reflects most clearly how the earlier concept of criminalizing usury on a case-by-case basis was replaced by one in which the crime was defined by social and political criteria: maximum prices were the consumer's equivalent of maximum interest rates for producers.

The definition of excessive profit remained critically important, especially from 1920 when maximum prices for most goods, with the exception of bread, were abolished. Beleaguered by public protest and the threat of riots, the authorities repeatedly declared an emergency market situation (*Notmarktlage*) in order to combat *Wucher* during phases of the *Mark's* rapid decline after the war. In conjunction with the courts, the authorities took the liberty of defining what 'reasonable' prices were.

It is no wonder that such events soon produced a highly charged situation. In the press, in publicly distributed pamphlets, and in speeches, the authorities urged consumers to report 'excessive' and 'usurious' prices to them. In turn, farmers, artisans, and shop-keepers were up in arms because their economic freedoms were being infringed for the benefit of consumers. Equally important was that their business dealings were tainted with an aura of illegality and that they faced possible punishment, which they claimed—not unjustifiably—deprived them of such fundamental rights as those of property and due process of law. This is interesting not least because the radical rhetoric of *Wucher* before the First World War had called for extraordinary measures to combat the evil. At the end of the war, special courts (*Wuchergerichte*) with extensive powers were set up in Germany, as in many other countries including England.[71] Each court consisted of three judges and two jurors all of whom exercised their own discretion in determining the extent of the evidence heard; their decisions were binding and not contestable. Later, in 1920, property could be confiscated in the case of conviction.

These courts were established in response to public demands for far more drastic measures, such as 'public flogging' and 'hanging', which inflamed the fantasies of even highly respectable people. Although there were great regional variations in the number of usury cases, the incidence of usury was not a minor phenomenon. Whereas, since the 1890s, there had never been more than 150 cases of *Wucher* in the courts per year in the whole of Germany, by 1917 there were 1,538 successful prosecutions in Hamburg alone on the basis of the new laws. These led to the closure of 5,551 firms, custodial sentences totalling 12,208 days, and fines totalling 92,300 *Mark*.[72] By 1920, there were over 27,000 cases pending in the Reich; after a decline in 1921 and 1922, the number rose even higher in the year of hyperinflation.[73] Most of these cases were petty offences, and some of the convictions were politically expedient examples used to pacify the public. In other words, a great deal of symbolic politics was involved. However, this enraged those accused of *Wucher* even more, not least since it seemed to demonstrate not only how powerful consumers had become but also the cynical truism that the little fish were always caught while the big ones, namely industry and wholesalers, swam free.

The profiteering laws regulating prices for daily commodities proved to be short-lived; they were repealed in 1926 under circumstances that will be described later. They were outlived by another type of emergency war legislation, namely that of rent control. Although it might at first appear strange to view rent control within the context of *Wucher*, the parallels are quite obvious.[74] For one, the protection of tenants from *Auswucherung*,

[71] For initiatives in other countries cf. Peschke, 'Wucher', 1100; for Germany cf. Feldman, *The Great Disorder*, 73 ff.; Geyer, 'Konsumentenpolitik', 198 ff.

[72] Niall Ferguson, *Paper and Iron: Hamburg Business and German Politics in the Era of Inflation 1897–1927* (Cambridge, 1995), 132.

[73] *Mitteilung der Preisprüfungsstellen*, 6 (1921), 168; 8 (1923), 34.

[74] For the following cf. Richard Bessel, *Germany after the First World War* (Oxford, 1993), 166 ff.; Karl Christian Führer, *Mieter, Hausbesitzer, Staat und Wohnungsmarkt* (Stuttgart, 1995); Martin H. Geyer, 'Wohnungsnot und Wohnungszwangswirtschaft in München 1917 bis 1924', in Gerald D. Feldman et al. (eds.), *Die Anpassung an die Inflation* (Berlin, 1986), 127–62.

rack-renting, played an important part in public and political discourse. For another, the issue here was also to determine 'equitable prices' for rent, an issue that appealed to large sections of society. Setting such prices became an equally contested public issue following the war because soon rents were no longer freely negotiable in the marketplace. Before the war, the housing market had sometimes favoured landlords, sometimes the tenants, but traditionally had been defined to a large degree by a public consensus on what constituted a reasonable price for housing. Although there were apparently cases when the courts applied the usury clauses on individual rental contracts,[75] there is no indication that this was used to set uniform standards.

Scarcities in the housing market and the desire to protect tenants from excessive price increases led to the *Mieterschutzverordnungen* (Renter Protection Ordinances) of 26 July 1917 and September 1918, which were amended and extended by a host of local and state ordinances especially during the months of the revolution. In the years that followed, legislation at national level tried to establish more uniform legal regulations. Although local housing agencies had existed in many cities before the war, their function had been limited to mediating disputes between landlords and tenants and, more importantly, to monitoring standards of hygiene. Now the establishment of local housing agencies became obligatory, and the agencies gained substantial control over the rental market and rental prices.

The introduction of rent-control legislation deeply divided landlords and tenants, virtually undoing the pre-war power relationship described by Tilman Repgen in this volume. Again, this was anything but typical for Germany.[76] From 1914, and even more so from 1917, it became easier for tenants to challenge both rent increases and evictions, and during the revolutionary turmoil, many cities established control boards (*Ausschüsse für Mietpreisbildung*). Representing landlords, consumer groups, and members of local government, these boards acquired extensive powers because their discretionary decisions were (at least until 1923) incontestable in regular civil courts. Although these boards were constituted somewhat differently from the *Wucher* courts mentioned above, the

[75] Peschke, 'Wucher', 1093.
[76] See the contribution by Susanna Magri in this volume; Tyler Stovall, 'Sous les toits de Paris: The Working Class and the Paris Housing Crisis, 1914–1924', *Proceedings of the Annual Meeting of the Western Society for French History*, 14 (1987), 265–72.

similarities are striking. In 1918–19, private negotiations between landlords and tenants ceased almost completely; instead, the fixing of rents was transferred to the public arena. Even though no out-right socialization of housing occurred, strong public controls did remain in place, especially for rents. Under the *Reichsmietengesetz* (Reich Rental Law) of 1922, guidelines were set up for determining legally stipulated rents ('gesetzliche Miete'). Theoretically, landlords and tenants still had the freedom to negotiate rent. Yet in practice, the legally stipulated rents quickly became a sort of price ceiling, since tenants had the right to refuse to pay more. To landlords, this infringement on their property rights was socialism, pure and simple. By the time hyperinflation set in, rents were usually fixed at ridiculously low levels. Even though this trend was reversed when the economy stabilized in 1923–4, rent controls were maintained. Indeed, compared with the pre-war period, tenants enjoyed an unprecedented degree of protection and legal empowerment.

The courts, social justice, and the issue of equity

All these attempts to combat *Wucher* and to set 'reasonable', 'just', and 'equitable prices' had troubling repercussions. If, for example, consumers accused shopkeepers of *Wucher*, the latter complained in turn that the true villains were the wholesalers and the industries. Landlords complained that their tenants sublet rooms at excessive rents; but they themselves were to come under fire from other groups for paying off their mortgages cheaply during the period of hyperinflation, if not before. Almost every societal group could, and indeed did, claim to be the victim of *Wucher*.

To understand this phenomenon, it is necessary to examine the dynamics of inflation itself, which in 1922–3 developed into hyperinflation in Germany. The widespread destitution associated with the devaluation of money during and after the war is very important, but it was certainly not the only source of social disorder. Of far greater importance was the fact that inflation reversed a seemingly stable system of social inequality, whether between creditors and debtors (in the broad sense of the term, namely contractual relations), or between consumers and producers. Formal contracts, as well as informal social relations defined by custom, had to be renegotiated. Emergency laws enacted during the war and described above fundamentally changed the rules of the economic game and, as many observers argued at the time, contributed a good deal to creating the usury problems that they were meant to solve.

Each of these cases, in which one group or party to a contract accused another of *Wucher*, shows that the courts were left with the task of constructing formulas of social equity of their own. Understandably, the definitions of 'excessive profit' offered by the courts were unsatisfactory and highly contested. Yet such definitions of equity in the field of consumer protection influenced other areas of contractual relations. Even if formulas were seldom long-lasting, unequivocal, and viable, it was made clear time and again that the profits made by farmers, artisans, and shopkeepers were not to exceed the rises in income of groups such as civil servants. This also applied to the contracts being contested. Judges could be vehement on establishing such rules of justice.[77]

This development had far-reaching implications. Only by broadly interpreting the general clauses of the German Civil Code ('equity and good faith', the *clausula rebus sic stantibus*) could judges address the constant complaints of injustice. However, once formulas of 'equity' were introduced and left to be defined by judges, these formulas fundamentally redefined the traditional concepts of the rule of law. There was a clear 'shift from reason to morality'.[78] Moreover, judges abandoned the *laissez-faire* basis of contract and made contracts a means of guaranteeing vague, socially based concepts of equity.[79] The issue of justice and morality was a sharp wedge driven into established notions of private law. As Joachim Rückert has demonstrated in his study of the

[77] Geyer, 'Zeiler', 355 ff.; for the civil service pay that played an important role as a yardstick, cf. Andreas Kunz, 'Verteilungskampf oder Interessenkonsensus? Einkommensentwicklung und Sozialverhalten von Arbeitnehmergruppen in der Inflationszeit 1914 bis 1924', in Gerald D. Feldman et al. (eds.), *Die deutsche Inflation: Eine Zwischenbilanz* (Berlin, 1982), 345–84; id., *Civil Servants and the Politics of Inflation in Germany, 1914–1924* (Berlin, 1986), 77 ff.

[78] David B. Southern, 'The Impact of Inflation: Inflation, the Courts and Revaluation', in Richard Bessel and E. J. Feuchtwanger (eds.), *Social Change and Political Development in Weimar Germany* (London, 1981), 55–76, 59; for more details cf. Geyer, 'Zeiler', 358 ff.

[79] Michael L. Hughes, 'Private Equity, Social Inequity: German Judges React to Inflation 1914–1924', *Central European History*, 16 (1983), 76–94, 82; id., *Paying for the German Inflation* (Chapel Hill, NC, 1988).

language in which major court decisions were framed, judges appealed to the 'realities of life' as opposed to the mere 'rule of law'. The widening gap between 'justice' and 'law' had to be closed. The strong appeal to *Rechtsgefühl*, *Rechtsempfinden* (feeling and sense of justice), and *Volksgeist* (spirit of the people) is striking.[80]

A widely shared sentiment, especially in 1922–3, was that 'justice' could not be obtained through the 'law', that in fact 'injustice' would result from adhering to the law. Food rioters referred to the same issues, if for different reasons, as did grocers or landlords or judges, who, after all, were also consumers, landlords, tenants, or creditors. The rhetoric of 'justice' appealed strongly to sentiments of 'self-defence' and thus natural law; the belief that society was in a state in which 'every man must fend for himself' flourished among all societal groups. When some of the judges in the Reich courts clashed with the executive branch in 1923–4 by ruling in favour of the claims of impoverished creditors—arguing that the legal principle of '*Mark* = *Mark*' would have bankrupted creditors—the struggle was couched in terms of 'battling the law in the name of justice'.[81]

These controversial questions all but disappeared after the stabilization of the currency in the winter of 1923–4. 'Revaluation' (*Aufwertung*) of debts was just one hotly contested issue. A ruling by the Reich Court in November 1925 that a barber shop shave was to be considered a 'necessary everyday commodity' was equally symptomatic. The court thereby upheld the ruling of a lower court, which had punished a hairdresser for *Wucher* since, on the recommendation of his trade association, he had charged 30 *Pfennig* for a shave instead of 20 *Pfennig*, which the price-control committees considered to be an 'equitable price'.[82] Equally typical was the case of a business deal in which one party had signed a contractual agreement to purchase goods valued at 2,610 *Mark*, and, after having paid 2,000 *Mark*, refused to pay the rest of the money, claiming the original price was tantamount to *Wucher*, a claim the courts upheld.[83] Even more disturbing was the fact that the courts started to regulate interest rates, which skyrocketed to unprecedented levels in 1923–4 as a result of the policies of economic stabilization. The courts were responding to complaints

[80] Rückert, 'Richtertum', 297 ff. [81] Geyer, 'Zeiler', 363 ff.
[82] *Juristische Wochenschrift*, 55 (1926), 592 f. [83] Ibid. 26 (1927), 2723.

that usurious practices were widespread and that these should be curtailed. They therefore intervened in contractual relations between banks and their customers—a development quite inconceivable a decade earlier. The argument put forward was that money represented the 'bread of the economy', and that the usury laws of 1923, which had been extended to include 'services', should be applied. To lend money became a matter of 'regrading'. After all, it was argued, the aim of the usury laws had been to protect the general public against profit-seeking exploitation of hardship and to prevent an increase in the general cost of living. On 19 July 1926, the *Reichstag* repealed the war emergency laws, thereby pulling the rug from underneath the broadly interpreted definitions of the 'common good' used by some of the judges in their rulings.[84]

Summary

The Weimar constitution explicitly stated that 'freedom of contract' was to be guaranteed; yet in the same clause (§ 152) it forbade *Wucher* and declared legal transactions that transgressed the moral order (*gute Sitten*) to be null and void. Provisions from the criminal and civil codes were adopted almost literally. Yet the idea was 'to define the term *Wucher* more comprehensively and to declare such legal transactions illegal and thereby void'.[85] This vague wording fitted the general idea of the constitution that the freedom to dispose of property was subject to social restrictions. Transformed and concealed in the language of social policy and social justice in the public and political discourse, the term *Wucher* had become a means by which to order social life and tackle vital aspects of social inequality. Whereas the pre-war usury laws had addressed the critical balance of social power primarily between creditors and debtors, the debates and social conflicts over setting 'just and equitable prices' during the war

---

[84] For discussions of this important issue, see esp. Bernhard Hamelbeck, 'Zinswucher', ibid. 25 (1926), 233–7; Kurt Peschke, 'Zinswucher', ibid. 675–7; Peschke, 'Wucher', 1099. These initiatives must be seen in the context of efforts to lower prices, cf. Dieter Hertz-Eichenrode, *Wirtschaftskrise und Arbeitsbeschaffung: Konjunkturpolitik 1925/26 und die Grundlagen der Krisenpolitik Brünings* (Frankfurt am Main, 1982), 58 ff.

[85] Gerhard Anschütz, *Die Verfassung des Deutschen Reichs vom 11. August 1919: Ein Kommentar für Wissenschaft und Praxis in 4. Bearbeitung* (1933) (repr. Aalen, 1987), 703.

appealed to 'consumers' as an abstract group that needed and deserved legal protection.

In this context a private law construction of rights was superseded by a social, public type of law. In order to understand this, one must look at both structural and political developments. Before 1914, the rhetoric of *Wucher* had addressed a relatively static system of social inequality that could be sharply criticized but, on the basis of the existing laws, only marginally changed. In fact, the private law system was a bulwark against change because in a certain sense it kept the populist debates within manageable confines. The very arguments against an extensive legal interpretation of *Wucher*, namely the issues of freedom of contract and the inability to define moral standards and thereby justice, came to the fore after the outbreak of the war. The war created an emergency of the state that allowed for intervention in economic and social affairs to a degree hardly imaginable in the past. In addition, a seemingly *static system* of social inequality was becoming more fluid as a result of inflation and the interventionist war economy. Contractual and thus social relationships of all sorts had to be renegotiated under the worst of all circumstances, namely a declining gross national product, with the issues of 'social justice' and moral arguments creeping up on all fronts. Structurally, it might be argued that the individualistic, and, for that matter, liberal legal concept of *Wucher* was not adequate to solve the ubiquity of the social, economic, and political problems. Hence public intervention was necessary, and there were strong political pressures to intervene.

In the context of such change, the courts obtained tremendous discretionary power. Again, it is noteworthy how much the popular debates on *Wucher* in the pre-war period had lent themselves to creating enemies and developing a logic of intervention in order to safeguard morality and the authority of the state. In the face of such public criticism, the courts had to tackle the relationship between law and justice—so fundamental to the issue of *Wucher* before the war and so hotly debated in all walks of life since 1914. Whereas the earlier legal positivism had made great efforts to ensure that issues concerning morality and material justice were sealed off by the very idea of the rule of law—the codification of the usury laws in 1880 and 1893 exemplifies this well—these fundamental certainties on which the legal system was based had become increasingly questionable since the war. It has often been noted that judges expanded their discretionary powers in the light of this development, arguing (as did many other societal groups when justifying their actions) that they were attempting to reconcile justice and law. The reference to a *Volksrecht*, to be left to judges to interpret, is related to similar ideas voiced in the 1870s. In addition to the contested issue of the revaluation of debts, attempts to set interest rates in 1923–4 show not only how far judges were willing to go in defining standards of the 'common good' but also how far they had departed from nineteenth-century concepts of legal recourse.

The application of notions of justice and equity to the discussion of prices remained a critical issue in Germany, one that was addressed time and again by the courts, the parliament in its social policy, and, later, by Brüning in his rule by decree. The central task was to mend a social system in which the balance of power—both social and political—had been fundamentally disturbed.

19

Creditors, Debtors, and the Law in Victorian and Edwardian England

PAUL JOHNSON

In 1853 the granddaughter of the eminent English jurist Sir William Blackstone entered in her local county court a plaint for damages against Thomas Turner, agricultural labourer and part-time town crier of Wallingford in the county of Berkshire. Following an earlier legal dispute between Turner's brother William and Miss Blackstone over the rent of allotment gardens, in which the case against Blackstone had been dismissed, Thomas Turner was alleged to have assaulted Miss Blackstone as she left the court. According to the plaintiff, Turner 'thrust both his clenched fists' at her over the shoulder of another man, 'and struck at me three or four times close to my face. He did not touch me but was very close. . . . He also made use of some very opprobrious expressions unfit for any woman to hear. He said "D— your b— eyes you have robbed and swindled me of £30".'[1]

The initial reason for the resort to legal process by William Turner, and common to the great majority of cases pursued through the new county courts established in 1846, was an alleged contractual debt. Indeed, the legislation establishing this county court system, which rapidly came to dominate all other civil courts in terms of the volume of business conducted, was entitled 'An Act for the more easy Recovery of Small Debts and Demands in England'.[2] However, these courts also had jurisdiction in actions founded on tort, up to the value of £50, and it was on this basis that Miss Blackstone brought her case for damages against Thomas Turner. This case of *Blackstone* v. *Turner* is of significance for reasons other than the juridical ancestry of the plaintiff,

This essay is part of a larger research project on laws and markets in Victorian England, which has been supported by a British Academy Research Readership.

[1] *Berkshire Chronicle*, 16 July 1853.   [2] 9 and 10 Vic. c. 95.

because it illustrates some of the biases of court procedure and sentencing policy in these lowly civil courts.

Thomas Turner 'conscientiously, strongly and firmly' denied that the alleged offence of constructive assault had been committed, though he agreed his language had been unguarded. Blackstone called forth her maid, her land surveyor, a butcher, and a labourer as witnesses to the assault; Turner called a hotelier, two painters, and a bootmaker and his daughter (who also happened to be, respectively, his brother-in-law and niece), all of whom attested to the fact that they had not seen Turner raise his fists. Judge J. B. Parry, QC, had no doubt about Turner's guilt, since in his view 'if every person in that court had been called and said they did not see the defendant strike the plaintiff, it could not have countervailed the evidence of unimpeached witnesses'.[3]

This unequivocal verdict stood at odds with the evidence. Miss Blackstone had initially attempted a criminal action against Turner, and had taken out a summons for him to appear before the magistrates, but had been forced to abandon that course,[4] probably because of the flimsy nature of the case. One anonymous Wallingford JP noted in a letter to the *County Courts Chronicle* that there had been 'a great discrepancy of the evidence produced, and several credible witnesses swore positively that no assault had been committed'.[5] Why Judge Parry took such a one-sided view of the conflicting evidence is unclear, but the social pressures for him to do so must have been great. Miss Blackstone's brother William Seymour Blackstone was the Deputy Lieutenant for Berkshire, had been the Conservative MP for Wallingford for the twenty years from 1832, the family had the patronage of the Anglican living at Wallingford,[6] and according to Dod's *Electoral Facts* in 1853, 'the territorial and personal influence of Mr Blackstone and his family' remained considerable.[7]

We see in this verdict a clear favouring of the word of a person of standing above that of a labourer. This is perhaps not surprising; similar social biases in the evaluation of witnesses and the assessment of evidence were a powerful force in the shaping

[3] *Berkshire Chronicle*, 16 July 1853.   [4] Ibid.
[5] *County Courts Chronicle* (hereafter *CCC*), Sept. 1853, p. 120.
[6] M. Stenton, *Who's Who of British Members of Parliament*, i: *1832–1885* (Hassocks, 1976), 36.
[7] C. R. Dod, *Electoral Facts from 1832 to 1853* (London, 1853), 323.

of the Victorian criminal justice system.[8] What is more revealing here is the nature of the judgment and the way it was enforced by this minor civil court. Judge Parry awarded damages at the maximum sum of £50, plus full costs, to Miss Blackstone, and quite exceptionally ordered immediate execution of this award. Turner could not pay, and so his personal possessions were seized by the court bailiff; at sale they realized just £3 3s. Turner was then ordered by the court to pay off his debt at the rate of 6s. per month, which, in the words of the *County Courts Chronicle*, had the effect of 'alienating a considerable proportion of his weekly earnings for seventeen years prospectively, and subjecting him, in default of payment, to repeated monthly imprisonments during the whole of his future life'.[9] Turner defaulted on the first instalment, and in November he again appeared before Judge Parry, now owing £63 12s. 9d., a result of additional court charges.

In the previous month Turner had earned an average of 14s. 8d. per week, on which he attempted to maintain his wife and five dependent children aged between 18 months and 15 years. He had spent his savings of over £6 on legal expenses, and since the seizure and sale of his personal property the family had no possessions other than clothing and basic household goods. Nevertheless Judge Parry concluded that Turner had had the means to pay his instalment, and had wilfully refused to do so. Turner was sent to Abingdon Jail for thirty days for deliberate non-payment of a debt; his wife and family sought relief in the local workhouse. When William Church, 'a respectable tradesman of the town', rose in court with an offer to pay the instalment on behalf of Turner, he was 'ordered by the judge to sit down and remain silent'.[10]

The evident vindictiveness of Judge Parry's decision inspired the 'leading inhabitants and tradesmen' of Wallingford to send a deputation of protest, led by the mayor, to the Home Secretary, Lord Palmerston. They argued that, regardless of the merits of the verdict in the case of *Blackstone v. Turner*, the sentence was unjust in principle:

People of England with all their boasted privileges, could never live in a state of security if upon any trivial breach of the law, they might be

[8] Carolyn A. Conley, *The Unwritten Law: Criminal Justice in Victorian Kent* (New York, 1991).
[9] *CCC*, Jan. 1854, p. 4.   [10] *Berkshire Chronicle*, 19 Nov. 1853.

subjected to fines amounting to more than the whole of their property, or, in default of payment, to imprisonment during the whole of their lives.[11]

Palmerston was reported to have taken a prima-facie view that the case was one of great 'hardship and cruelty',[12] but as the *County Courts Chronicle* noted, this was 'a wrong without a remedy'.[13] The judge had acted strictly within the law, there was no right of appeal from the county court to a higher court, the Secretary of State had no power to interfere with the orders of a judge, and the royal prerogative did not extend to custody under civil process. Thomas Turner had received a sentence of virtual life imprisonment from a civil court because of non-payment of a debt incurred through an alleged minor verbal abuse of a middle-class woman.

The case of Thomas Turner was exceptional in its detail, but the imprisonment of small debtors by county court judges was common, both before and after the 1869 Act 'for the Abolition of Imprisonment for Debt'.[14] Yet large-scale debtors, those who had the financial status and presence of mind to petition for bankruptcy, could avoid the double jeopardy faced by Turner of a creditor imposing a substantial claim on his future income, and threatening imprisonment in the case of non-payment. Bankruptcy was intended to facilitate a rational distribution of assets to creditors, not saddle the debtor with long-term liabilities. By the 1870s the nature and extent of this legal discrimination was widely recognized. It was not just the radical political economist Leoni Levi who was noting the 'incongruity, if not injustice' in this system;[15] a leading article in *The Times* concluded that 'the law is really unfair and unequal. Under an appearance of justice to all classes, it presses hardly on some.'[16]

The differential treatment of what, almost oxymoronically, might be called 'rich' and 'poor' debtors appears to be at odds with both contemporary and modern interpretations of the rise of contract law in Victorian England. In his *Treatise on the Law of Contracts*, the legal theorist Charles Addison argued in 1847 that

[11] *Berkshire Chronicle*, 17 Dec. 1853.   [12] Ibid.   [13] *CCC*, Jan. 1854, p. 4.
[14] 32 and 33 Vic. c. 62.
[15] L. Levi, 'On the Abolition of Imprisonment for Debt', *Law Magazine and Review*, 3 (1847), 598.
[16] *The Times*, 27 Dec. 1879, reprinted in *County and Borough Prisons: Correspondence in the 'Times'* (London, 1880), 6.

'the law of contracts may justly indeed be said to be a universal law adapted to all times and races, and all places and circumstances, being founded upon those great and fundamental principles of right and wrong deduced from natural reason which are immutable and eternal'.[17] More recently, Patrick Atiyah has suggested that 'the period 1770–1870 saw the emergence of general principles of contract law closely associated with the development of the free market and the ideals of the political economists'.[18]

While general principles may characterize some elements of contract law in Victorian England, they do not seem to apply to the legal relationship between creditors and debtors. Despite three official inquiries into the working of the county courts and the imprisonment of small debtors between 1873 and 1909,[19] there was no move towards universalism in the law regulating the recovery of debts in the Victorian and Edwardian period. As well as suffering their poverty, the poor had to suffer an overtly prejudicial class bias in the one area of contract law that had direct and repeated bearing upon their lives.

In this essay I want to consider why small debtors received disproportionately harsh treatment as compared with bankrupts—in other words, why legal theory and legal practice were so consistently and enduringly at odds with each other. I will examine, in turn, four possible explanations for this discriminatory treatment: differences in the legislative basis of the separate debt recovery systems relating to bankruptcy and small debts, differences in their practical procedures, differences in the economic circumstances of the debtors, and differences in their social status. However, in order to provide some context for this discussion I will first present a brief outline of the development of the law relating to small debts and bankruptcy in Victorian England.

I

In 1846 a comprehensive system of county courts was established to supersede the idiosyncratic network of courts of requests

---

[17] Cited in P. S. Atiyah, *The Rise and Fall of Freedom of Contract* (Oxford, 1979), 400.
[18] Ibid. 398.
[19] *Select Committee on Imprisonment for Debt, PP* 1873, xv; *House of Lords Select Committee on the Debtors Act, PP* 1893–4 (HL), ix; *Select Committee on Debtors (Imprisonment), PP* 1909, vii.

through which civil actions for low value had hitherto been conducted.[20] The county courts had jurisdiction where the debt, damage, or demand claimed did not exceed £20, a limit raised to £50 in 1850 and to £100 in 1903.[21] This definition of 'small' was relative. In the 1850s few manual workers, even skilled artisans, could have earned more than £1 per week, a figure that may have doubled by the turn of the century,[22] so debts equal to a year's wage income could be pursued through these courts. In practice the sums owing were generally much less. Throughout the period 1847–1914 over 98 per cent of cases were for sums of less than £20, with an average amount owing of around £3,[23] and many claims were for less than the equivalent of a week's wages. Court records from both London and an industrial area of northeast England for 1910–11 show that half of all small debt cases were for sums owing of less than £1, and a quarter were for less than 10s.[24]

The county court system was an immediate success, at least in terms of the amount of business conducted. In the first quinquennium the yearly average of causes was 433,000, and by 1904 over 1.4 million plaints for recovery of debt were initiated in these courts. This may, in part, have reflected the accessibility of the courts. Despite their name, the county courts were not organized by administrative county, but instead the country was mapped out into sixty circuits encompassing over 500 court towns, chosen according to the Registrar General of Population's enumeration districts.[25] Court towns within each circuit had an average range of jurisdiction of 7 miles, which was considered a reasonable distance for a plaintiff or defendant to walk in order to attend a

---

[20] H. W. Arthurs, ' "Without the Law": Courts of Local and Special Jurisdiction in Nineteenth Century England', *Journal of Legal History*, 5 (1984), 130–49.

[21] Sir Thomas Snagge, *The Evolution of the County Court* (London, 1904), 14.

[22] C. H. Feinstein, 'New Estimates of Average Earnings in the United Kingdom, 1880–1913', *Economic History Review*, 43 (1990), 595–632.

[23] Aggregate statistics of court business are derived from the returns of the county courts, published annually in the *Judicial Statistics* volume of the *Parliamentary Papers*. See also H. Smith, 'The Resurgent County Court in Victorian Britain', *American Journal of Legal History*, 13 (1969), 126–38, at 128.

[24] West Hartlepool county court plaint book, 1910; Teesside Archives AK 19/9; Wandsworth county court, ordinary summons book B (1911); London Metropolitan Archives AK 21/1.

[25] Snagge, *Evolution*, 13. There were fifty-nine new county court circuits, plus the existing City of London court.

hearing.[26] Accessibility to the due process of law was a necessary requirement of a more general and commercial system of contract law, and in this sense at least, county courts fit with the rationalizing process noted by Atiyah.

However, a logical organizational structure does not guarantee the application of 'universal law', and in the case of recovery of debts in nineteenth-century England universality was undermined by the evolution of a quite separate but parallel legal system for the administration of bankruptcy. Although the substantive law of bankruptcy was in place in England by 1800, the nineteenth century saw successive attempts to improve the efficiency of bankruptcy administration.[27] Important legislative changes in 1831 and 1883 expanded the role of government in the management of bankrupt estates, although in the 1860s there was a short-lived reaction against 'officialism' and a return to creditor-managed administration. However, the basic principles of bankruptcy endured throughout the century. Traders, and from 1861 non-traders who owed substantial debts, could file a petition in bankruptcy. Debtors had to be fairly wealthy to go bankrupt, since a £10 fee was levied on bankruptcy petitions, but this could be a sound investment. Bankruptcy status protected the assets of the debtor from summary seizure by creditors, and safeguarded any future earnings from claims arising from previously acquired debts and liabilities.

The annual business of the bankruptcy courts was, relative to the county courts, minuscule in terms of number of cases, but significant in terms of sums owing. Up to 1860 there were between 1,100 and 2,000 cases annually, with losses averaging £4 million to £5 million a year. After the 1883 Bankruptcy Act, there were around 4,000 bankruptcies a year, with losses averaging £5 million—a not dissimilar figure to the more than £4 million of debts annually being pursued through the county courts in the Edwardian period. It should be noted that formal bankruptcy was not the only way of shedding debts; private arrangements between creditors and debtors appear to have been more numerous than formal bankruptcy proceedings at least until the 1880s, and the

[26] J. E. D. Bethune, Report to the Lord Chancellor on the formation of county court districts, 19 Dec. 1846. PRO, LCO 8/1 137401.

[27] The 19th-century reforms of bankruptcy law are covered in detail in V. Markham Lester, *Victorian Insolvency* (Oxford, 1995).

growth in the number of limited liability companies meant that by the end of the century company winding-up accounted for annual losses in the order of £20 million.[28]

However, it was not differences between county and bankruptcy courts in the average size of debt or number of cases heard which produced the accusations of unfairness, injustice, and class bias in the treatment of debtors. What concerned the critics was the relative viciousness of the county courts in exacting full payment from small debtors, and in imposing penal sentences on those who could not or would not pay. In the small debt courts, when a case was found for the plaintiff (and the chances of a case being found for the defendant were never better than 1 : 50, and usually nearer 1 : 100),[29] the debtor was required to pay 100 per cent of the sum owing. Since, almost by definition, small debtors had few assets, the requirement to pay off the debt in full was effectively a lien on future earnings. This contrasted with bankruptcy proceedings where the object was to distribute the bankrupt's remaining assets proportionately among the creditors on some pro-rata basis which seldom exceeded a payment of 10s. per £1 of debt, and to prevent creditors exercising a claim on the future earnings of the bankrupt. In the case of small debtors, past errors were to be redeemed by future virtue, while for bankrupts, past errors were to be written off.

The degree of financial discrimination against small debtors was striking, but it was not the primary justification for describing the legal system of debt recovery as 'class law'.[30] This epithet was used particularly to characterize the quite iniquitous system of imprisoning small debtors who failed to redeem their debt by paying up the sums due, and at the times specified by the court. Arrest on *mesne* process was abolished in 1838, and the Debtors Act of 1869, entitled 'An Act for the Abolition of Imprisonment for Debt', appeared to abolish arrest and imprisonment on final process,[31] but in practice, as Gerry Rubin has demonstrated

[28] Ibid. 240–6; 306–13.

[29] Paul Johnson, 'Small Debts and Economic Distress in England and Wales, 1857–1913', *Economic History Review*, 46 (1993), 67.

[30] Paul Johnson, 'Class Law in Victorian England', *Past and Present*, 141 (1993), 147–69; G. R. Rubin, 'Law, Poverty and Imprisonment for Debt, 1869–1914', in G. R. Rubin and David Sugarman (eds.), *Law, Economy and Society, 1750–1914* (Abingdon, 1984), 241–99, at 275–6.

[31] Arrest on final process had been abolished for debts of less than £20 in 1844, but in 1845 this liberalizing measure was reversed by a new Act which designated as fraudulent

in his pioneering analysis of this Act, several thousand people each year continued to be incarcerated for non-payment of small debts.

As well as being discriminatory, this retention of the power of committal over small debtors seems to run counter to the more general, rational, and market-oriented development of contract law in the Victorian period described by Atiyah. If the purpose of a legal system for the recovery of debt is to maximize the payments to creditors, it seems perverse to apply the sanction of imprisonment on the debtor, since this will almost of necessity prevent him acquiring or earning the means to pay. Imprisonment for debt signified the continuation of a pre-modern punitive sanction against the body of the debtor for his economic transgression. Bankruptcy proceedings, on the other hand, sought a rational distribution of economic loss among the creditors, on the principle they had all openly entered into contracts with the defaulting party, and had to accept the downside of market fluctuations and business failure.

II

Describing the difference in treatment of bankrupts and small debtors is easy; explaining it is more tricky, especially when we know that the prejudice the law expressed towards small debtors was widely recognized by contemporaries. Was the utilitarian pursuit of general legal principles, rational administration, and equal treatment nothing more than a rhetorical smokescreen to disguise blatant class prejudice, or should we look for a more complex and more subtle historical explanation? I believe that in most respects both the reforms to, and the operation of, the laws of bankruptcy and indebtedness were rational and equitable; that the outcomes should have been so diverse is a consequence of contemporary presumptions about economic psychology and moral worth. In order to make this case I will look in turn at the legislative basis and the practical procedures of the small debt

any debt contracted by an individual lacking any reasonable prospect of being able to pay; a condition which applied to most working-class debtors most of the time. Fraudulent debtors were not exempted from arrest on final process by the 1844 Act. See Rubin, 'Law', 244–9.

and bankruptcy systems, at the economic circumstances of the debtors, and at their social status.

Legislation. The intention of the 1846 Act which established the county courts was clear—to improve the efficiency of debt collection. Pursuit of debtors through the existing courts of request involved a number of hindrances which became increasingly burdensome as the scale and range of commercial activity expanded in the era of the penny post and the railway. The commissioners or judges who decided on cases in these courts were laymen (by the 1830s they had to be substantial property owners) with limited legal knowledge, and limited time to devote to hearings. More important, perhaps, the jurisdiction of the courts of request was geographically limited and judgments could not be enforced against defendants whose goods or persons lay beyond the court borders.

What the county courts provided, from 1847, was a comprehensive and standardized network of small claim courts, with common competences and rules of procedure. There was an official code of rules, common forms and scale of costs, judges were trained lawyers with seven years' standing at the bar (later raised to ten years), and they were assisted by registrars who required five years' standing as solicitors.[32] This professionalization of small debt recovery procedure was not restricted to the judiciary; lawyers also enhanced their status by obtaining a near monopoly of the right to represent litigants, to the exclusion of unqualified 'low attorneys'. The 1846 Act gave courts the power to refuse to hear any but the parties to a suit or their attorney or counsel. In practice this work was conducted by solicitors rather than barristers; there was no acknowledged county court bar, even in the largest towns.[33] There remained, however, some ambiguity about exactly who could speak on behalf of whom in court. Narrow application of the restrictive conditions of the 1846 Act[34] gave way to a recognition that working men might often be unable to attend a hearing and so should be allowed to be represented by a wife or other family member or even a 'friendly neighbour'.

[32] Snagge, *Evolution*, 12.

[33] Ibid. 23–4; David Sugarman, 'Simple Images and Complex Realities: English Lawyers and their Relationship to Business and Politics, 1750–1950', *Law and History Review*, 11 (fall 1993), 2: 257–301. See particularly p. 295.

[34] *CCC* 4 (Sept. 1847), 79.

Likewise employers could be represented by someone in their employment, for instance a bookkeeper, but judges attempted, not always successfully, to draw the line at 'the class of accountants and debt-collectors' because 'their function is not to represent absent parties'.[35]

H. W. Arthurs has written rather negatively of the way in which the 1846 legislation saw the final demise of local and communal justice and the rise of formalism and professionalism,[36] but in terms of rational administration on general principles, the county courts represented a positive step along the progressive path outlined by Atiyah. Greater legal formalism was a way of reducing the discretion of the courts and, as far as parties to any contract were concerned, of increasing the certainty of outcome. In economic terms, this contributed to an overall reduction in transaction costs, a factor identified by institutional economists as a key element in the development of the industrial economies in the nineteenth century.[37]

Victorian legislation on bankruptcy was similarly intended to improve efficiency and reduce costs; this has been analysed recently by Markham Lester. He sees this history as fitting very definitely into Atiyah's model of reform induced by classical economic ideals, even though the creation of the posts of official assignee by the 1831 Bankruptcy Act, and official receiver under the 1883 Act, do not conform to an absolutist interpretation of *laissez-faire* government.[38] The primary intention of these reforms was to promote a more efficient administration of bankrupt estates, and to maximize the dividends paid to creditors. Some legal regulation was required to ensure the rational distribution of assets among a multiplicity of competing claims from creditors, and to prevent bankrupts spiriting away any assets in their possession before administration of their estate could begin. There

---

[35] Comments of Judge Snagge in Halifax county court, on the question of unqualified practitioners. *CCC* 31 (Apr. 1888), 368. The fact that this opinion needed to be reiterated more than forty years after the establishment of the county courts indicates that the boundaries of professional competence between lawyers and other professionals or quasi-professionals remained contested throughout the Victorian period. See D. Sugarman, 'Qui colonise l'autre? Réflexions historiques sur les rapports entre le droit, les juristes et les comptables en Grande-Bretagne', *Droit et société*, 7 (1993), 169–82.

[36] Arthurs, 'Without the Law', 143–4.

[37] Douglass C. North, *Institutions, Institutional Change and Economic Performance* (Cambridge, 1990).

[38] Lester, *Insolvency*, 301–2.

were substantial differences of opinion, within both the commercial and legal communities, about how these goals could best be achieved, but little disagreement about the goals themselves.

Procedure. Legislative intent may not be translated into effective action. How rational, general, open, and efficient was the system of debt recovery in practice? Bankruptcy administration faced a particular procedural problem in the case of small estates—it was not worth the while of any individual creditor to expend time and effort administering the bankrupt's estate for a small share of the dividend, and collective supervision of private assignees was also often more trouble than it was worth. The result was erratic, sometimes irresponsible, and sometimes corrupt administration of bankrupt estates, yet consistent bankruptcy administration was a necessary feature of an efficient commercial society. Private interest was not sufficiently motivated to ensure the public good, and it was this failure of both individual and collective action in the case of small estates that motivated Lord Brougham to propose that an official assignee be appointed by the court to administer the bankrupt estate, and to draw appropriate compensation from the estate. This element of officialism was a key component of the 1831 Bankruptcy Act.

The introduction of official administration may have promoted the public good by imposing a more standardized and rational procedure for the distribution of assets to creditors, but the creditors themselves were far from convinced of the merits of the system. Lester has shown that the business community, although far from unanimous in its attitudes towards bankruptcy reform, was vociferous in its opposition to official administration. The principal complaint related to cost; the expenses of administration on average consumed one-third of the assets available for distribution in a bankrupt's estate.[39] Yet a return to creditor-managed bankruptcy in 1869 did nothing to reduce costs, and the 1883 Act which reimposed administration by official receivers for bankruptcies with assets under £300 failed to bring administration costs below 40 per cent of gross receipts in these smaller cases.[40]

The small debt courts, by comparison, were models of efficiency. The average debt was around £3, the cost of entering a plaint and issuing a summons for a claim of this sum was 4*s.*,

---

[39] Lester, *Insolvency*, 133.   [40] Ibid. 295.

followed by a further charge of 1s. for taking the admission if the case was admitted, or 6s. 9d. for a hearing. For a straightforward case of average value, therefore, costs represented around 8 per cent of the sum owing if settlement was achieved before a court hearing, and 18 per cent if the case came to court. Even if a case was pursued through to the issue and execution of a warrant of commitment, the additional fees amounted to only 1s. 2d. per £1 of debt, or a total cost of under 24 per cent of the average debt.[41]

Not only was the small debt recovery procedure cheap, it was also quick. The first stage was for the creditor to enter a plaint for recovery of the debt with the registrar of the court. This plaint gave the name and address of the alleged creditor and debtor and the nature and size of the alleged debt. A summons stating the substance of the action was then served on the defendant, giving the date of a court hearing, which was usually within four weeks of a plaint being entered. If the case came to court and a judgment was issued, it was up to the plaintiff to secure the compliance of the debtor. If the debtor could not or would not pay, the creditor could apply for a judgment summons to be issued, which obliged the debtor to attend court to explain why he had not paid as directed. If a defendant failed to attend a judgment summons hearing without notification of good cause, then a warrant for execution against goods owned, or for commitment to prison for up to six weeks, was issued against him. Few cases went this far; on average only 60 per cent of cases came to court, judgment summonses were issued in about 20 per cent of cases, warrants of commitment issued in about 7 per cent, and imprisonment enforced in less than 0.5 per cent of cases.

Universal accessibility to a uniform system of law had been one of the objectives in the establishment of the county courts, and simplicity of procedure was held to be an important element of accessibility. Particulars of claims were entered in straightforward language in the plaint book, parties were able to be witnesses in their own case, and judges were empowered to admit hearsay evidence about, for instance, a defendant's ability to pay. Compared with the complexity of bankruptcy administration, this was almost a model of plain man's law, although which plain man benefited

---

[41] Scale of Court Fees. *CCC*, Mar. 1855. See also *Select Committee on Imprisonment for Debt*, *PP* 1873, xv, q. 197 (evidence of Mr Henry Nicol, superintendent of county courts in the Treasury).

could depend on the outlook of the particular judge or registrar. In 1905 the President of the County Court Registrars' Association prompted a fervent exchange of opinion in the trade journal, the *County Courts Chronicle*, by stating in his presidential address that:

In the smaller class of cases, as they knew, they did not insist on the rules of evidence. No registrar who knew his business thought of insisting on the rules of evidence. He asked for the tradesman's books the very first thing, and, if the entries were properly made up and in order of date, that was taken as *prima facie* evidence in many cases to which, very rightly, a great deal of importance was attached.[42]

Yet this flexibility could equally work in the interests of the debtor. Courts had no resources to investigate the means of each defendant, and in determining the size and frequency of repayment instalments they typically took the unsubstantiated word of the defendant or his representative about how much could be afforded each week or month.

In the early days of the county courts some judges took informality and accessibility too far, at least in the eyes of the *County Courts Chronicle*. At Brentford county court in 1847, not only did the court sit in the back room of a public house, with large numbers of 'intoxicated and noisy' defendants present, but the judge, clerk, and high bailiff all sat at 'at a common lodging table, none of them being distinguished by any badge of office'.[43] The *Chronicle* remarked that judges should always appear in wig and gown, and clerks in robes, because 'it is a form in the administration of justice to which the public mind has become so familiarised that it will not associate the idea of equal dignity and importance to a Court that shows them not'.[44]

Concern about the public 'face' of justice, as represented by the theatre of court proceedings, recurred throughout the years up to 1914. In 1905 it was reported that Judge Edge had refused audience to an unrobed solicitor in his court, even though robing was a recommendation, not a requirement, of the Law Society; in an echo of the discussion almost sixty years earlier, it was suggested in the *County Courts Chronicle* that robing should be enforced 'to maintain the dignity of the legal profession'.[45] But the stage set

---

[42] *CCC*, July 1905, p. 175. See also correspondence in *CCC*, Aug. 1905, p. 203.
[43] *CCC*, Sept. 1847, p. 77.   [44] *CCC*, Oct. 1847, p. 88.
[45] *CCC*, May 1905, p. 123.

was as important as the costumes. After an extension of the jurisdiction of the county courts in 1903 the editor of the *Chronicle*
lamented the 'disgraceful accommodation at the metropolitan
county courts', and argued that their physical facilities should be
enhanced to match their increased importance. As in Brentford
in 1847, part of the concern was that the propriety of legal proceedings was being compromised by an association with common
drinking dens. In Westminster county court, of all places, it was
claimed that:

The registrars' court is about as large as a railway carriage, and situate
in a sort of passage; the robing-room is about the same size, and has no
adequate accommodation at all. There are no waiting rooms or proper
lavatories for suitors. Consultations must be held in the public street or
the public house. In the court, counsel, solicitors, witnesses and judge
are all huddled together in a miniature Black hole of Calcutta.[46]

But if the external status of the courts continued to be a cause for
concern, their rising professional status was a matter for some
self-congratulatory puffery; fifty years on from the foundation of
the county courts, the *Chronicle* could boast that of the twenty-nine
judges appointed in the previous six years, thirteen were QCs.[47]

There was no obvious sign of this growing legal formalism
crowding out the layman's direct access to the due process of law.
Whilst many traders used solicitors to represent them in court, in
a minority of cases working-class plaintiffs appeared in person to
pursue their claims for payment by lodgers or for repayment of
small loans.[48] It is unclear how far this use of the county courts
by working-class plaintiffs indicates a general acceptability of the
institution and the process of debt recovery. The enormous
number of cases annually processed by these courts must mean
that the experience of being 'county courted' was common among
manual workers, even though defendants failed to attend initial
hearings in around half of all cases that came to court. For those
who did attend a hearing (or, as was frequently the case, whose
wife attended the hearing), the experience of court procedure
must have been breathtaking; records of the West Hartlepool
court show that cases were heard and judgments dispensed at the
rate of one every eighty-five seconds.[49]

---

[46] *CCC*, Jan. 1905, pp. 3–4.   [47] *CCC*, Apr. 1897, p. 87.
[48] Johnson, 'Class Law', 166 n. 61.   [49] Johnson, 'Small Debts', 70.

If we compare bankruptcy and small debt procedure in terms of cost, speed, and accessibility, then it is small debt recovery in the county courts that most closely reflects a universal law responding to the novel needs of a commercial society.[50] It seems unlikely, therefore, that the widely perceived discriminatory nature of small debt enforcement can be attributed either to differences in the legislative basis or the procedural norms of the bankruptcy and small debt courts. Perhaps, then, the explanation lies in substantive differences in the economic circumstances of bankrupts and small debtors.

Economic circumstances. The majority of defendants in the small debt courts were male manual workers—in the small number of plaint books I have found in which occupation is recorded, over 90 per cent of defendants fall into this category, with around 5 per cent being dealers or traders of some sort. The plaintiffs were overwhelmingly local traders, with drapers usually heading the list, but with general dealers and grocers following closely behind.[51] In the bankruptcy courts, on the other hand, grocers, publicans, builders, and farmers constituted the largest categories of debtors, followed by bootmakers, tailors, drapers, butchers, and bankers.[52] In the main, therefore, bankrupts were shopkeepers and dealers who owed other traders, small debtors were working men who owed shopkeepers and dealers.

But this clear distinction by occupation becomes fuzzy when we attempt to distinguish by reference to the financial value of the debts. By the late Victorian and Edwardian period, between 30 and 40 per cent of bankruptcy estates had a gross asset value of under £25, with an average value of around £12. By comparison, in 1911 the average per capita value of working-class financial assets held across a broad array of saving and insurance institutions was around £11,[53] and a contemporary estimate put the average value at death of working-class estates in the period 1899 to 1904 at £16.[54] Around one-third of bankrupts, therefore, were indistinguishable from the majority of adult male manual workers

---

[50] Atiyah, *Rise and Fall*, 518–19.

[51] Johnson, 'Small Debts', 68.

[52] Lester, *Insolvency*, 314–15.

[53] Paul Johnson, *Saving and Spending: The Working-Class Economy in Britain 1870–1939* (Oxford, 1985), 205.

[54] L. G. Chiozza Money, *Riches and Poverty* (3rd edn., London, 1906), 51.

in terms of the value of their accumulated financial and non-financial assets.

If we examine the financial threshold of claims allowable in the county courts we also find no clear distinction between small debts and bankruptcy. In 1910, 70 per cent of bankrupt estates yielded gross assets of less than £100, which was the maximum threshold for action in the county courts. Of course the stated liabilities of bankrupts typically would have been over £100, but so too could be the liabilities of small debtors. Whereas in bankruptcy the claims of all creditors were pooled, in the county courts individual creditors pursued their claims independently, so a multiple debtor could face several simultaneous claims for recovery of debts each up to the value of £100. Although the legislation relating to recovery of debts appeared to establish a crisp distinction of scale between bankruptcy and small debt proceedings, in fact this was illusory.

Social status. What really distinguished the defendants in bankruptcy and small debt proceedings was their social status, and this mattered because of assumptions made by judges about the economic motivations of people of different social class. The majority of county court judges presented a consistent view, in both their judgments and their responses to official inquiries, that many working men defaulted on their debts quite deliberately, that this was an oppressive burden on honest traders, and that the power of imprisonment must be retained in order to extract due payment. A few examples must suffice.

In an open letter to Lord Palmerston, Home Secretary, in 1854, Judge Johnes of the Caernarvon county court could not have been more explicit in his beliefs about the rights and wrongs of plaintiffs and defendants:

Take a common case—a young man, without family, earning high wages as a miner or mechanic, contracts a debt of a few pounds with a small tradesman, who sues him and obtains judgement. To take out execution against the goods is futile because, though in one sense wealthy, the defendant probably has none worth levying on. His high wages are possibly squandered in taverns or secreted in such a way that they cannot be reached by the creditor . . . The defendants who thus evade and defy their creditors, are commonly men who are, in a pecuniary sense, much better off than the great majority of the professional men of this country—the wages they receive being commonly higher than the average remuneration of professional men, especially when we take into account the less refined mode in which they live . . . On the other hand, the creditors, whose confidence they abuse, generally belong to the poorest and most necessitous class of small retail dealers, a class who have no superfluous funds to spend in dubious litigation with knaves, and to whom legal redress, unless it be really cheap and accessible, is a mockery.[55]

Here we see, combined in one short comment, moral judgments about the fecklessness of manual workers and the integrity of small traders, together with a gross misrepresentation of the economic circumstances of working-class life.

Although Judge Johnes was more forthright and open in his opinions than many county court judges,[56] his views about the calculated dishonesty of working-class debtors were widely shared by his fellow judges. Judge Snagge, in Witney court in 1897, remarked that: 'A judgment summons is the only way in which a levy can be made effectually upon the pockets of the labouring man who has obtained credit and wishes to button up his pocket and does not wish to pay . . . They often say they will not pay, but do so cheerfully when they hear the clang of the prison door behind them.'[57] This sentiment was echoed by Judge Cadman at Dewsbury: 'There was undoubtedly a determination on the part of persons not to pay until the very last moment. Debtors in the past had been given every consideration, and tradesmen and other plaintiffs who had to pay for the goods they sued for in court were worthy of equal consideration.'[58] The fact that 99.5 per cent of defendants who had lost their cases paid up before the prison door closed behind them was taken to imply that the initial non-payment was, in many cases, wilful. It was also asserted that many of the initial purchases, particularly from itinerant traders or tallymen, were unnecessary fripperies, so the debtor was doubly unworthy.

Not all judges were as questioning of working-class intentions as Snagge and Cadman; there was always a diversity of opinions among the county court judiciary and more widely within the legal profession. The *Law Times* was adamant that fraudulent debtors constituted 'an insignificant minority' of cases coming to the county courts. The majority of debtors were 'poor persons to

---

[55] *CCC*, July 1854, p. 164.
[56] Judge Johnes was a frequent correspondent to the *County Courts Chronicle*.
[57] *CCC*, June 1897, p. 155.   [58] *CCC*, Feb. 1897, p. 35.

whom credit is often recklessly given, who benefit little by it, to whom debt is a calamity, whose "means" are so shadowy that evidence of them is most difficult to present in any satisfactory shape to a judicial tribunal'.[59] According to the progressive Judge E. A. Parry, between 1869 and 1914 the county courts had sent to prison over 300,000 people who were not guilty of any crime: 'they have been imprisoned mainly for poverty or, if you will, for improvidence.'[60] Nevertheless, the majority view of the judiciary presented to three separate select committees between 1873 and 1909 was that the ultimate sanction of imprisonment must be retained in order to force working men to honour contracts they had openly entered into with traders.

In bankruptcy proceedings, on the other hand, the legal system endorsed the view of traders and businessmen that unpaid debts were an unfortunate consequence of the inevitable uncertainties of the commercial world. In the eyes of small businessmen, bankruptcy statistics were

the saddest official figures published, for the statistics relating to Poor Law administration must of necessity relate to a very large number of people who have never made a legitimate attempt to keep themselves from want, and are not deserving of consideration, while the bankruptcy figures must include amongst the failures a large proportion of men and women who may have missed success by the merest chance, but who have honestly attempted to carve out a career for themselves.[61]

This was, of course, a specious argument when applied to the working-class debtors dragged through the county courts. In an age before extensive sickness and unemployment insurance, when most manual workers were hired and paid by the day or the week, it was almost certainly workers rather than traders who had least control of their economic circumstances, and who had least economic opportunity to be extravagant. Moreover, as the *Law Times* remarked, the treatment of small debtors was unequal in law, regardless of the underlying economic, social, and moral circumstances: 'If the theory of imprisoning for nonpayment of money which a court orders to be paid is the right one, there ought to be no distinction. Every money judgment in every court should be enforceable by commitment.'[62]

[59] *Law Times*, quoted in *CCC*, Mar. 1893, p. 60.
[60] E. A. Parry, *The Law and the Poor* (London, 1914), 57.
[61] *Trade Protection Journal*, Oct. 1907, p. 170. See also Lester, *Insolvency*, 136.
[62] *Law Times*, quoted in *CCC*, Mar. 1893, p. 60.

III

I set out to consider why small debtors received disproportionately harsh treatment as compared with bankrupts, and why the concept of a more general, commercial, and rational law of contract seemed not to emerge in the practice of debt recovery. What I have attempted to show is that in structure and procedure, both small debt recovery and bankruptcy administration did become more rational in the nineteenth century; this was particularly so in the recovery of small debts, where costs were low and action swift. But rational reform of both the small debt and bankruptcy systems did not produce similar outcomes.

In theory the different financial circumstances of bankrupts and small debtors might explain the divergence in outcomes. In practice, however, the financial circumstances of most bankrupts were not significantly different from those of many manual workers, so different outcomes cannot easily be explained by reference to objective economic criteria. What allowed lower-middle-class bankrupts to shed a large proportion of their debts was a legal presumption that they were worthy but unlucky traders who wished honestly to repay, to the best of their ability, debts often unwittingly incurred because of fluctuations in trading conditions. What led to the harsh and discriminatory treatment of small debtors was a judicial assumption that some significant proportion of them ended up in court because of a fundamental lack of desire and intention to honour debts they had willingly entered into. Of course these presumptions were seldom investigated; bankruptcy administrators sought to distribute assets, not uncover fraudulent intent; and in the county courts the judges, dealing with cases in little more than one minute each, had not the time, even if they had the inclination, to enquire into the motives and morals of the debtors. Despite the driving force of an autonomous legal rationalism in Victorian England, there remained considerable social inequality of legal outcomes for bankrupts and small debtors because of the deeply rooted belief among a majority of judges that the working classes were morally inferior.

20

The Action was outside the Courts

Consumer Injuries and the Uses of Contract in the United States, 1875–1945

EDWARD A. PURCELL, JR.

The legal history of personal injury claims in late nineteenth- and early twentieth-century America lies not only in the law of torts but equally, if not more importantly, in the law of contracts. The bulk of that history, moreover, lies not in formal judgments of courts but in private decisions of injury victims to waive, settle, or abandon their claims without judicial resolution. A major part of that out-of-court process, in turn, consisted not of freely bargained agreements that occurred randomly but rather of pressured settlements that were harvested systematically. To a large and insufficiently unexplored extent, the legal history of personal injury claims lies in the organized release-seeking practices of thousands upon thousands of corporate lawyers, doctors, and claim agents who secured quick and low-cost settlements in countless numbers of homes, streets, offices, roadways, factories, vehicles, and hospitals where injury victims and their families were found.

The years from the 1870s to the 1940s constituted a distinct period in the development of corporate settlement practices. During the last quarter of the nineteenth century, a rapid increase in commercially related accidents and the emergence of a plaintiffs' personal injury bar coincided with the nationalization of the economy and the rationalization of corporate management techniques to spur a systematic use of releases to pre-empt potential tort claims. By the end of the century the methodical and aggressive new practices were in widespread use. Then, in the early years of the twentieth century, continued expansion of the plaintiffs' personal injury bar and the growth of labour unions and consumer groups increased the de facto access of tort victims to counsel, while popular attitudes increasingly supported the idea that injured persons should be more fully compensated. Both courts and legislatures moved to strengthen the legal position of those who sought to sue corporate defendants. Beginning in the 1920s, the numbers of commercially related accidents declined, and insurance coverage expanded rapidly, spreading costs, bringing financial predictability, and decreasing the pressure on corporations to terminate adverse tort claims for the barest possible amounts. By the mid-twentieth century, corporate settlement practices—especially those of large insurance companies and their well-protected clients—had become increasingly bureaucratized and routinized. The result was to moderate some of the companies' most objectionable practices, raise the general level of compensation paid, and increase somewhat the regularity with which the de facto tort compensation system operated.

A consideration of corporate release-seeking practices highlights a major gap that has marked the history of personal injury litigation. From the turn of the century corporate spokespersons decried the work of 'ambulance chasers' and complained about a purported flood of frivolous and fraudulent claims.[1] Many lawyers and bar associations joined the attack, denouncing the 'abuses' fostered by contingent fee agreements and the ethical failures of personal injury attorneys. Similarly, much contemporary law and economics literature follows the same track, focusing on frivolous 'strike' and 'nuisance' suits.[2] While such commentary has raised important issues, it has also largely ignored significant elements of the de facto litigation and settlement process. One, for example, is the abusive tactics that corporations utilized. '[W]hen we are for the defendant', explained one corporate lawyer, 'nothing can start us.'[3] They delayed cases, raised frivolous defences, filed excessive motions and appeals, and tried numerous other similar tactics to compound plaintiffs' burdens and raise their costs. Another element often ignored is the fraudulent and unethical

---

[1] Edward A. Purcell, Jr., *Litigation and Inequality: Federal Diversity Jurisdiction in Industrial America, 1870–1958* (New York, 1992), 150–4 and sources cited therein.

[2] See, e.g., Lucien Arye Bebchuk, 'Suing Solely to Extract a Settlement Offer', *Journal of Legal Studies*, 17 (1988), 437–50.

[3] Quoted in Sol M. Linowitz, *The Betrayed Profession: Lawyering at the End of the Twentieth Century* (New York, 1992), 25. On the importance of building a litigation 'reputation', see, e.g., Samuel R. Gross and Kent D. Syverud, 'Getting to No: A Study of Settlement Negotiations and the Selection of Cases for Trial', *Michigan Law Review*, 90 (1991), 319–93.

behaviour of defendants. From 1889 to 1902, for example, the Metropolitan Street Railway Company of New York paid thousands of dollars in bribes to doctors, witnesses, court personnel, and police officers in order to defeat countless numbers of claimants. Eventually, after its practices were exposed, the company admitted that its legal department had been 'a perjury mill'.[4] A third such element, which this essay explores, is the methodical solicitation of inequitable out-of-court settlements. Indeed, corporate release-seeking practices helped stimulate— even necessitated—'ambulance chasing'. If plaintiffs' lawyers did not reach injury victims quickly, corporate agents would have their signatures on releases. No adequate understanding of the litigation and settlement process is possible without a consideration of such social factors.

Consumers and claiming

In the decades around the turn of the century industrial accidents caused approximately 35,000 deaths and almost 2 million injuries per year.[5] For 'consumers' as a growing and identifiable social group, injuries resulted from contacts with a nearly infinite variety of objects, products, vehicles, activities, and facilities. For half a century the railroads injured 5,000–10,000 passengers every year and annually caused the death of several hundred more.[6] In the decade from 1887 to 1896 streetcars in New York City averaged some 140 accidents per year, while in Boston trolley accidents rose from just over 200 in 1887 to more than 1,700 in 1900.[7] Other new urban services similarly caused untold numbers of accidents. Gas and electricity accounted for twenty-eight deaths in Boston in 1900, and gas alone caused 142 deaths in New York City ten years later.[8]

---

[4] *In re Robinson*, 136 NYS 548 (App. Div. 1st NY 1912), *affirmed* 103 NE 160 (Ct. App. NY 1913); New York State Bar Association, 'Report of Committee on Contingent Fees', *Proceedings of the Thirty-First Annual Meeting* (1908), 121.

[5] Lawrence M. Friedman, *A History of American Law* (2nd edn., New York, 1985), 482.

[6] United States Department of Commerce, Bureau of the Census, *Historical Statistics of the United States: Colonial Times to 1970* (Washington, 1975), pt. 2, 740.

[7] W. J. Clark, 'A Chapter of Accidents', *Street Railway Journal*, 13 (Oct. 1897), 667–70, 669; Robert A. Silverman, *Law and Urban Growth: Civil Litigation in the Boston Trial Courts, 1880–1900* (Princeton, 1981), 101.

[8] Silverman, *Law and Urban Growth*, 108; Randolph E. Bergstrom, *Courting Danger: Injury and Law in New York City, 1870–1910* (Ithaca, NY, 1992), 51.

Although the conditions of late nineteenth- and early twentieth-century life created literally millions of potential tort claims, the courts disposed of relatively few of them. Most never became lawsuits, and a majority of those that did were settled without final legal judgment. In one way or another, out-of-court resolutions accounted for more than 90 per cent of all potential tort claims and well over half of those that were filed in court.[9]

There are few reliable statistics, but it seems likely that, compared to injured workers, at least, consumers as a group converted a somewhat higher—though still relatively small—percentage of their potential claims into lawsuits and may have prosecuted a slightly higher percentage of those suits to judgment.[10] Consumers were generally free from the kinds of social and economic pressures that corporate employers used so effectively to discourage suits by their own employees,[11] and they often had little to lose and much to gain, especially if their injuries were serious and contingent fee arrangements allowed them counsel. Further, again as compared to injured workers, consumers occupied a more favoured legal position. They did not have to confront the daunting fellow-servant defence, and they could often avoid difficult evidentiary problems by invoking the doctrine of *res ipsa loquitur*. Finally, some consumers—principally passengers on elevators and escalators, amusement park rides, taxicabs, railroads, streetcars, and buses—enjoyed an especially favoured position. Common carriers owed them not merely the standard duty of 'reasonable care' but rather a much more rigorous duty of 'the highest care'. That higher standard meant that injured passengers could more commonly and economically prove the carriers' liability. Moreover, in the frequent cases that involved collisions, derailments, explosions, and other mechanical failures, carriers were deprived of two of their most powerful defences, contributory negligence and assumption of risk.

---

[9] Frank M. Munger, Jr., 'Miners and Lawyers: Law Practice and Class Conflict in Appalachia, 1872–1920', in Maureen Cain and Christine B. Harrington (eds.), *Lawyers in a Postmodern World: Translation and Transgression* (New York, 1994), 185–228, 210, 228 n. 42; Purcell, *Litigation and Inequality*, 32–3, 259–60.

[10] Lawrence M. Friedman, 'Civil Wrongs: Personal Injury Law in the Late 19th Century', *American Bar Foundation Research Journal* (1987), 351–77, 367.

[11] Social and economic vulnerability and the fear of employer retaliation made workers extremely reluctant to sue their employers for tort compensation. Munger, 'Miners and Lawyers', 209–11, 227 n. 40, 228 n. 43; Purcell, *Litigation and Inequality*, 37–42.

Corporate defendants: incentives and leverage

Whatever the exact percentage who brought suit, corporate defendants worked painstakingly to keep as many tort victims as possible out of court. A handbook for railroad accountants emphasized the importance of settling claims without judicial involvement. While a corporate legal staff handled a variety of problems, it explained, a 'very large part of its duty is to effect settlement of disputes outside of court,' especially in 'personal injury' cases.[12] A streetcar company announced bluntly that its policy was 'to settle all accident cases promptly, and never allow them to reach the courts if we can possibly prevent it'.[13]

Powerful economic incentives spurred corporate efforts to settle out of court. Potential tort claims threatened regular and substantial economic exposure.[14] Transportation companies, in particular, had compelling economic incentives to settle adverse claims. They tended to be involved in large numbers of personal injuries, and often their fault was clear and no legal defence available. In such cases out-of-court settlements constituted the best—and perhaps only—opportunity to resolve claims for relatively minimal amounts.[15] Further, railroad and streetcar companies were often under acute financial pressure, and they sought avidly to trim their variable costs wherever possible.

An additional economic incentive may also have inspired corporate settlement efforts. Some scholars have maintained that common law judges sought economically 'efficient' results. They maintain, that is, that the courts tended to hold defendants liable for negligence only when the 'costs' of preventing an injury were less than the 'costs' of the injury itself discounted by its likelihood of occurrence. If they are right, that common law dynamic created a compelling economic incentive for corporate defendants to press for minimal settlements. For, by holding down settlement amounts generally, they could help create and maintain a widespread perception that the 'costs' of injuries—a subjective, socially generated criterion—were and should be quite low. By

[12] J. Shirley Eaton, *Handbook of Railroad Expenses* (New York, 1913), 197–8.

[13] Quoted in Friedman, 'Civil Wrongs', at 371.

[14] See, e.g., M. L. Byers, *Economics of Railway Operation* (New York, 1908), 566–9; Eaton, *Handbook*, 81–83, 115–17, 187–91, 197–8.

[15] Friedman, 'Civil Wrongs', at 375; Bergstrom, *Courting Danger*, at 158–60.

minimizing the generally perceived 'costs' of injuries they could ensure that the applicable negligence formula would shrink the scope of their potential liability and thereby reduce the overall number of cases where the law would require them to pay damages.[16]

Driven to minimize the cost of claims, corporate defendants came quickly to recognize the advantages of out-of-court settlements. Most fundamental, they learned that such settlements could often be arranged easily and cheaply if accomplished immediately after an accident. Victims were frequently in no condition to negotiate knowingly or effectively. Often they were alone, in shock or pain, disoriented and frightened, and ignorant of both their legal options and the extent of their injuries. Above all, their immediate and overwhelming concern was to obtain proper medical treatment. The victim of a Santa Fe Railway collision, for example, who had received cuts, bruises, a broken leg, and a fractured skull, signed a release in the railroad's hospital four days after the accident. The victim 'did not seem to care' about 'the matter of dollars and cents', the agent who secured the agreement testified. 'All he wanted was to have proper care.'[17] Sometimes, injury victims were preoccupied with the condition of another member of their family who had also been injured. Sometimes, they were emotionally shaken but deeply relieved—and therefore pliable—because they had apparently not been injured more seriously. 'I was glad to save my life,' explained one injured worker who signed a release shortly after his injury.[18] An insurance company official acknowledged the obvious. 'In settling claims considerable money can be saved if done in the early stages before the case falls into the hands of an attorney.'[19]

While corporations held overwhelming advantages in dealing with accident victims immediately after their injury, they also had other advantages they could use against those who resisted settlement. First, corporations learned that most injury victims were unable to bear the burdens of litigation. If companies insisted on

---

[16] See, e.g., Richard A. Posner, 'A Theory of Negligence', *Journal of Legal Studies*, 1 (1972), 29. Cf. Bergstrom, *Courting Danger*, 167–96.

[17] *Atchison, Topeka & Santa Fe Railway Co. v. Cunningham*, 54 P. 1055, 1057 (Sup. Ct. Kan. 1898).

[18] United States House of Representatives, *Hearings before Subcommittee No. 4 of the Committee on the Judiciary of the House of Representatives*, 80 Cong., 1 sess. (1947), 72.

[19] Quoted in Roy Lubove, 'Workmen's Compensation and the Prerogatives of Voluntarism', *Labor History*, 8 (1967), 254, 260 n. 15.

their non-liability while making low settlement offers, they could compel injured individuals to choose between a quick, easy, and cost-free resolution and a risky, expensive, and protracted litigation. They knew that potential plaintiffs were balked by any number of practical obstacles: psychological inability to face confrontation, ignorance of the judicial system, fear of the company or its representatives, unfamiliarity with—or deep distrust of—lawyers, a desperate need for money to pay medical expenses and provide for their families, knowledge that attorneys' fees would consume much of any award they might win, the costs of retaining expert witnesses and locating and assuring the timely appearance of fact witnesses, the innumerable risks and uncertainties involved in litigation and trial, the costs and delays of the nearly inevitable appeal that would follow any plaintiff's victory, and, finally, the cumulating personal and family pressures that years of waiting for a final legal judgment could generate.[20] By the late nineteenth century corporate defendants had learned that those pressures would combine relentlessly to make most claimants falter and eventually succumb to discounted settlement offers. They understood, in short, the uses and forms of strategic cost imposition.[21]

Second, corporations also learned to use their economic leverage. They had relatively fixed legal costs and handled large numbers of cases and, consequently, were able to spread the higher costs of the relatively few cases they chose to litigate over the much larger number they settled. In contrast, individual claimants bore the entire cost of their litigations and had to pay for them out of whatever proceeds resulted from their single suit. Moreover, because corporate defendants had legal costs that were budgeted, relatively fixed, and spread over a large base, they were not subject to significant economic pressure by any action that an adversary might take in filing, litigating, trying, or appealing a

[20] See, e.g., Austin Sarat, 'Studying American Legal Culture: An Assessment of Survey Evidence', *Law and Society Review*, 11 (1977), 427–88, 436, 448–52, 464–5, 466–72; David M. Engel, 'Cases, Conflict, and Accommodation: Patterns of Legal Interaction in an American Community', *American Bar Foundation Research Journal* (1983), 803–74, 816–22, 851; Purcell, *Litigation and Inequality*, chs. 2 and 3.

[21] Kathleen Engelmann and Bradford Cornell, 'Measuring the Cost of Corporate Litigation: Five Case Studies', *Journal of Legal Studies*, 17 (1988), 377–99; Keith N. Hylton, 'Litigation Costs and the Economic Theory of Tort Law', *University of Miami Law Review*, 46 (1991), 111–48.

claim. Further, knowing that most claims would ultimately settle, they could generally be indifferent to the fate of any individual case,[22] a position that strengthened their resolve to stand firm on low settlement offers. Finally, their permanent legal staffs and substantially lowered per-case costs meant that corporate defendants could, when necessary, allocate extensive resources to litigate specific and troublesome disputes. That capability, in turn, enabled them to drive up the costs of those claimants who chose to litigate seriously—thereby devaluing their claims—and to increase their own chances of winning in court.[23] Corporations utilized, in short, the strategic advantages they held as the least costly litigators.

To obtain quick releases, corporate defendants organized special claims departments and retained networks of agents across the country. 'These cases constitute so regular and large a group, and are so nearly similar', explained a railroad accounting handbook, 'that they result in specialization with regular staffs to handle them.'[24] One of the first responsibilities of a corporate legal staff, announced a study of railroad economics, was '[t]he settling of claims for personal injury'.[25] A streetcar company explained that it instructed its agents to 'hunt up' injury victims, get in their 'good graces', and 'insist on paying [them] something' to get their signatures on releases.[26]

Those regular staffs and individual agents enjoyed wide discretion in conducting their operations. They had one clear goal—to obtain quick and inexpensive settlements—and one clear test of success—whether or not they got the desired releases. They could choose their tactics, adapt their approach to any situation, and

[22] Corporate attorneys would ensure the settlement—generously, if necessary—of suits that were legally or prudentially indefensible or that threatened to alter the law in an unfavourable direction. See, e.g., Wayne V. McIntosh, *The Appeal of Civil Law: A Political-Economic Analysis of Litigation* (Urbana, Ill. 1990), 146.

[23] See Stanton Wheeler, Bliss Cartwright, Robert A. Kagan, and Lawrence M. Friedman, 'Do the "Haves" Come Out Ahead? Winning and Losing in State Supreme Courts, 1870–1970', *Law and Society Review*, 21 (1987), 403–45, 439–40; McIntosh, *Appeal of Civil Law*, 146, 150–1. For defendants' legal/economic advantages, see Robert D. Cooter and Daniel L. Rubinfeld, 'Economic Analysis of Legal Disputes and their Resolution', *Journal of Economic Literature*, 27 (1989), 1067, 1073–4; Martin J. Bailey and Paul H. Rubin, 'A Positive Theory of Legal Change', *International Review of Law and Economics*, 14 (1994) 467–77.

[24] Eaton, *Handbook*, 197–8. Compare R. W. Kostal, *Law and English Railway Capitalism, 1825–1875* (Oxford, 1994), app., 373–88.

[25] Byers, *Economics of Railway Operation*, 566.

[26] Quoted in Friedman, 'Civil Wrongs', at 371.

rely on the fact that their statements would go unrecorded. Their positions gave them both the opportunity and incentive to pressure claimants immediately, vigorously, and tenaciously. Their employers profited from their successes and had little or no economic incentive to supervise them closely or to restrain their tactics. Individual tort claimants held no significance as regular customers or suppliers, and they seldom possessed any social or economic leverage against their corporate adversaries. Neither the companies nor their agents had any noticeable incentive to cultivate their goodwill. The companies devoted few resources to constrain their agents, and the agents quickly learned the most efficient methods available to bring in the largest number of settlements at the lowest possible cost.[27]

Practice

Reported release cases do not merely state the law. They also record something quite different: the operation of an alternative corporate legal process—massive, organized, profitable, and largely invisible to the public.[28] They reveal the companies' standard tactics, their frequent successes, and the substantial savings they reaped. They suggest, further, both the relative unimportance of substantive legal norms and the decisive importance of the

---

[27] Economic and rational choice theories support this conclusion. See, e.g., Cooter and Rubinfeld, 'Economic Analysis of Legal Disputes', 1078–86. See Carl Gersuny, *Work Hazards and Industrial Conflict* (Hanover, NH, 1981).

[28] There was an interesting split in the period's legal literature. Judges and practitioners frequently referred to organized and aggressive agent tactics, but the university law reviews were largely silent on the subject. Revealingly, when the law reviews discussed releases, they did so with an almost exclusive focus on matters of doctrine and 'logic'. Indeed, they directed most of their efforts to a critique of a single topic, the 'joint tortfeasors rule'. Obviously dysfunctional and unfair, the rule lent itself readily to a sharp doctrinal critique; e.g., note, *Harvard Law Review*, 28 (1915), 802–4; note, *Yale Law Journal*, 28 (1918), 90–1; *Michigan Law Review*, 18 (1920), 680–4. Only rarely, and well after the turn of the century, did the law reviews discuss the significance of organized corporate release practices: e.g., note, *University of Chicago Law Review*, 5 (1938), 455–63. This difference between the courts and the law reviews suggests, again, that legal 'formalism' was a relatively limited phenomenon, that the bench was generally sensitive to the law's social context, and that there was much less congruence than often assumed between the 'mentalities' of some 'high formalists' on the one hand (e.g. the discussion of releases in Samuel Willston, *The Law of Contracts*, vol. iii (New York, 1929), 3138–208) and large numbers of judges and practitioners on the other. See Edward A. Purcell, Jr., review of G. Edward White, *Justice Oliver Wendell Holmes*, *Journal of Southern History*, 61 (1995), 620, 622.

social characteristics of the parties in determining who received compensation and how much they received.

The single most obvious and important characteristic of corporate practices was the sheer speed with which claim agents acted. Repeatedly, the courts criticized their 'unseemly haste'.[29] Claim agents, declared a lawyers' magazine in 1905, 'fly with the wings of an eagle to the scene of the accident'.[30] The Vice-President of the American Electric Railway Association acknowledged that corporations sought 'the immediate settlement of accidents and damages'. Indeed, companies should provide their claims agents with a ready cash 'Working Fund', he advised, so that their agents could settle cases without having to 'wait until the regular check and voucher can be received'.[31] The railroads sometimes held trains in place until their claims agents arrived and secured the desired releases. One court, for example, criticized a railroad for

[h]olding the train, sending for a law agent to make a settlement before any medical or other attention was given [the injured person], and when she was suffering from [a concussion of the brain and spine], and, if conscious, giving her attention to her little, bleeding grandson.[32]

The railroads took injured passengers to company hospitals where their claim agents had ready access to them; they placed agents on board their trains to secure releases from them while they travelled; and they stationed agents in waiting at passengers' down-line transfer or destination points. Railroad, streetcar, taxicab, and bus companies took injured passengers to depots or company offices or tracked them to nearby hospitals or doctors' offices. Within days of accidents—sometimes hours—agents arrived at the doors of injured persons' homes or resting places seeking their signatures on releases. Immediate contact with injured persons and control of the post-injury situation was designed to exploit the uncertainty, confusion, and anguish that followed in the immediate wake of personal injuries. In 1908 the New York State Bar Association castigated

---

[29] e.g. *Chicago, Rock Island and Pacific Railway Co.* v. *Lewis*, 109 Ill. 120, 134 (1884).

[30] Editorial note, *Virginia Law Register*, 11 (1905), 843.

[31] Irville Augustus May, *Street Railway Accounting: A Manual of Operating Practice for Electric Railways* (New York, 1917), 253.

[32] *Southern Railway Co. in Kentucky* v. *Brewer*, 105 SW 160, 163 (Ct. App. Ky. 1907).

the practice, now become notorious, of unscrupulous agents of railroad corporations seeking out injured persons, and, through chicanery and fraud, obtaining from them, in the moment of their pain and suffering, releases on insufficient consideration.[33]

The releases that such victims signed were almost invariably for steeply discounted amounts, often for small or wholly token payments.

Incessant pressure was the second major characteristic of corporate settlement practices. Agents hounded potential claimants to sign releases. They pressured them with repeated visits to their hospitals and homes; they told them that they had to leave town and that there could be no settlement if the victims waited; and they persistently pressed them to sign releases regardless of their feelings, prior refusals, and uncertain medical conditions. 'The agent of the company who approached [an injured passenger] was notified by her nurses and attendants that she was not in a mental and physical condition to attend to any business', the Supreme Court of Georgia explained in one case, 'but he insisted on an interview or settlement.'[34] The Eighth Circuit described the case of an injured man in the hospital under the influence of narcotics:

Three or four days after the accident, while this [narcotics] treatment was going on, and while his arms were suspended over a rope stretched across his bed in order to relieve the pressure upon his injured spine, and when he was tortured and racked with physical pain (when not under the influence of opiates), the defendant's agents found their way into his sickroom, from which his friends and all others, save his nurses, had been excluded, by order of his physician.[35]

The Wisconsin Supreme Court described the actions of an agent who secured a release from a 66-year-old woman by making a number of false representations:

He succeeded in getting her to sign by high-pressure methods during a siege at her bedside in the hospital, from 7:30 to 9:30 p.m., within seventy-five hours after she had been injured. She was badly shocked,

---

[33] New York State Bar Association, 'Report of Committee on Contingent Fees', *Proceedings of the Thirty-First Annual Meeting* (1908), 103.

[34] *Smith v. Georgia Railroad & Banking Co.*, 62 SE 673, 674 (Sup. Ct. Ga. 1908).

[35] *Union Pacific Railway Co. v. Harris*, 63 F. 800, 803 (CCA 8th 1894), *affirmed* 158 US 326 (1895).

and grievously hurt, her hip was fractured, the pain was excruciating, she was dazed, confused, mortified, and embarrassed . . . While she was in an exhausted and distressed condition, packed in sand bags to keep her hip immobile, and racked with pain and under the influences of sedatives and hypnotics, the adjuster, whom she had never known, entered her room without her permission.[36]

Agents of one railroad secured a release by making the injured person's mark and having him touch the pen while he 'was lying in his bed, the morning after his foot had been amputated, under the influence of opiates'.[37] Another agent persuaded a doctor to suspend his examination and treatment of an injured passenger—who 'was suffering severe pain'—while he secured his signature on a release.[38] The Supreme Court of Pennsylvania found that another claimant 'was in the hospital, suffering from his injuries, and was unconscious, at the time it is alleged the release was signed by him'.[39]

The third major characteristic of corporate settlement practices was their methodical and often ruthless opportunism. Agents reached agreements not only with persons suffering great physical and emotional distress, but also with those who were elderly, illiterate, unable to speak or understand the English language, and under the influence of some type of drug or alcohol given as a painkiller. They attempted to deal with injured persons while they were alone, often trying to keep others out of the room while they obtained their signatures. Some succeeded in getting releases from parties with attorneys by dealing with them alone and without their attorneys' knowledge. One railroad treated a female passenger, gave her narcotics, and placed her on a train in a locked car with several of its agents.[40]

Claim agents used a variety of dubious techniques. They offered jobs with the company and promised to 'take care of' victims if their injuries proved more serious than they appeared. They tried to divide potential claimants and use them against one another. They apparently switched or misrepresented documents or altered

[36] *Allison v. Wm. Doerflinger Co.*, 242 NW 558, 561 (Sup. Ct. Wisc. 1932).
[37] *Jones v. Alabama & Vicksburg Railway Co.*, 16 So. 379, 380 (Sup. Ct. Miss. 1894).
[38] *Springfield Consolidated Railway Co. v. Picket*, 125 Ill. App. 519 (Ct. App. 3d Ill. 1906).
[39] *McCaw v. Union Traction Co.*, 54 A. 893, 895 (Sup. Ct. Pa. 1903).
[40] *St. Louis, Iron Mountain and Southern Railway Co. v. Phillips*, 66 F. 35, 37–8 (CCA 8th 1895).

the terms of the agreements they had negotiated when they presented written releases for signature. A street railway employee told an injured woman that 'she would be kicked off the car' unless she signed a release,[41] while a claim agent bought a victim six drinks in a bar before obtaining his signature.[42] Another agent used the captivating lure of, literally, a pile of money. He 'came to the meeting with a general release all prepared, except filling blanks, and with 100 $5 bills, which at some time during the negotiation were laid in a pile on the table before the [injured person]'.[43]

Again, claim agents quickly gathered and then used whatever relevant information they could discover. They interviewed doctors who had treated injured persons, apparently violating the patients' rights to confidentiality, and obtained valuable medical information that could help the company in future lawsuits. More immediately, they used such medical information directly, telling injured persons about their conversations and claiming that the victims' own doctors regarded their injuries as minor or temporary. Similarly, agents interviewed both victims and potential witnesses, obtaining additional information both to pressure claimants for settlements and to prepare for litigation. Together with regular company employees, they asked passengers to sign reports about the nature and cause of their injuries, securing potentially powerful admissions to undercut subsequent claims.

Their efforts, too, were comprehensive. They insisted on getting releases even from those who believed they had not been injured or who disclaimed any desire for compensation. The agents pressed them to accept token payments in order to cover possible injury to their clothing, parcels, or baggage; they insisted that they take small amounts of money to compensate for whatever 'expenses' or 'inconveniences' they might have suffered. Sometimes, the agents offered the money as a purported 'gift' or 'donation'. The signed agreements that they obtained in return proved invariably to be complete releases for claims of all varieties, including personal injuries. Frequently, such releases precluded subsequent suits by those who later realized or learned that they had, in fact, suffered significant injuries.

---

[41] *Dalmage* v. *Crow*, 49 NYS 1004 (City Ct. NY 1898).

[42] *Logue* v. *Philadelphia Rapid Transit Co.*, 78 Pa. Sup. Ct. 239 (Sup. Ct. Pa. 1922).

[43] *Barrett* v. *Lewiston, Brunswick & Bath Street Railway Co.*, 85 A. 306, 308 (Sup. Jud. Ct. Me. 1912).

A 1929 Texas case was both typical and revealing. In *Bankers' Health & Accident Co. of America* v. *Shadden*,[44] the court found that an agent's own testimony 'conclusively demonstrated' his fraudulent behaviour. He had preyed

upon a widow of limited education without training in matters of business, wholly unacquainted with the exclusions, inclusions, and highly technical phrases of an accident insurance policy, with practically no understanding or comprehension of the facts involved, or her legal rights thereunder, and over whom the clouds of bereavement, by reason of her husband's recent death, were still hovering.

Among other statements, the agent admitted telling the woman that he had studied the policy and that it simply did not cover her husband. He threatened that 'if you don't make a settlement with me, you are going to have to fight with my company and they are not going to pay you a dime'. He insisted further that 'if you go to an attorney with this, your attorney won't get enough of it to pay their [*sic*] fee'. Finally, as his emotional *coup de grâce*, he informed the grieving widow that 'where there is any doubt about an accident they remove the body from the grave and have it examined'.[45] Two aspects of the case are particularly significant. First, the agent testified freely about his tactics, evidencing his belief that they were wholly ordinary and legitimate. Second, he also testified that he had been a claim agent for twenty-six years.[46] Together, those two facts suggest that manipulative and unscrupulous practices were in common use and that they affected thousands upon thousands of victims whose claims never reached the courts.

Innumerable cases support those conclusions. It was a railroad's division superintendent, for example, who secured a release within eighteen hours of an accident by twice meeting with a woman who had a fractured shoulder blade and was in a state of shock.[47] An agent with fifteen years' experience secured the release of a woman's claims by bringing her husband's supervisor to the meeting where he negotiated the settlement. The supervisor, who 'had authority to retain or discharge' the husband, told the wife

[44] *Bankers' Health & Accident Co. of America* v. *Shadden*, 15 SW 2d 704 (Ct. Civ. App. Texas 1929).
[45] Ibid. at 706.   [46] Ibid.
[47] *Chicago, Rock Island and Pacific Railway Co.* v. *Lewis*, 109 Ill. 120 (Sup. Ct. Ill. 1884).

that 'it would be better for them to sign the release'.[48] Again, it was the 'chief special claim agent' of an insurance company who felt free to adopt an even more dramatic tactic. Trying to settle a $2,500 life insurance policy for $500, the agent left the attorney of the widow-beneficiary and, contrary to his promise, went directly to the woman's home. Alone with her, he used a series of false statements and threats to coerce a release.[49]

The fourth major characteristic of corporate settlement practices—especially of railroad and streetcar companies—was the maintenance of company hospitals and doctors. Claim agents sent or accompanied injured persons to company physicians and facilities, and in countless other cases company doctors turned up at the accident scene or, shortly thereafter, visited victims at their homes or hospitals. In some cases, even though injured persons had already received emergency medical care or were under treatment by their own physicians, the company doctors came to examine and treat them anyway.

The ready availability of medical care minimized victims' suffering and often prevented more serious injuries, but the benevolence was grounded in well-understood corporate interests. 'Medical and hospital service', a railroad accounting handbook explained, 'is of the nature of preventive measures to avoid when possible more serious injuries or fatalities with the consequent heavier damages.'[50] Company doctors were also superb discovery instruments. By conducting their own examination of victims, they prepared themselves to testify on the basis of first-hand knowledge and gained critical information that would otherwise have been unavailable to their companies prior to trial. Finally, and probably most important, by becoming the victims' physicians and tending their injuries, company doctors earned both their gratitude and their confidence. When they advised patients that their injuries were minor or temporary, they eased their worries and raised their hopes. When they supported, directly or indirectly, the constant importuning of the ever-present claim agents, they helped induce their patients to settle on the agents' terms.

The cases suggest that injured persons were often susceptible to

---

[48] *Peterson v. A. Guthrie & Co.*, 3 F. Supp. 136, 137 (DCWD Wash. 1933).

[49] *Harms v. Fidelity & Casualty Co. of New York*, 157 SW 1046, 1048, 1049 (Ct. App. Mo. 1913).

[50] Eaton, *Handbook*, 190.

the doctors' lead. Hurting, shocked, and distressed, they desperately wanted to believe that they would recover fully and that they would shortly be back about their lives as if nothing had happened. When company agents and doctors told them that their injuries were 'minor' and 'temporary', injury victims seized hungrily on such welcome news. Pressed to make decisions quickly, they often opted to accept the happy future that was promised, or at least dangled as a likelihood, and to go ahead and take the settlement offered.

In many cases company doctors participated in the effort to obtain releases from their patients. Sometimes they initiated negotiations themselves, informing patients that they were not seriously injured and urging them to settle quickly. Sometimes they introduced their patients to claim agents, and sometimes they merely advised them to go and see the agents. Sometimes, apparently when they were not formally company 'employees', they joined with claim agents to seek quick releases so that the company would pay for their services immediately. Such efforts nudged injury victims towards settlement and, in many cases, gave them the impression that accepting the agents' offer was the best—or only —option available.

While company doctors did not always encourage settlement, they were apparently expected never to discourage it. The Supreme Court of Kansas focused on some critical testimony. Several witnesses testified that the company doctor had told them that his patient had come 'within a hair's breadth of breaking his neck' and that he had 'intended to warn him against signing a release of the railroad company'. He had not done so, however, the doctor explained, because 'the claim agent was so near at hand that he had no chance'.[51]

The intrinsic conflict of interest that plagued company doctors repeatedly created situations that were at best ambiguous. Company doctors made mistaken diagnoses and rendered opinions that proved to be overly optimistic, and they apparently failed frequently to warn their patients about the dangers of future complications and disabilities. Even assuming their most scrupulous good faith, they regularly and directly advanced their companies' interests by the frequent support they gave for immediate settle-

---

[51] *Missouri Pacific Railway Co.* v. *Goodholm*, 60 P. 1066, 1068 (Sup. Ct. Kan. 1900).

ments. With surprising frequency, the courts found that company doctors had engaged in fraudulent behaviour and that they had purposely or recklessly misled their patients in order to obtain releases.

<h3 style="text-align:center">Social variations: gender and race in the
informal legal process</h3>

While company agents used a variety of tactics against injury victims, it seems likely that they were particularly effective in securing releases from women and especially from blacks.[52] The cases show that women were often subjected to some of the agents' most intrusive and manipulative tactics. In a collision that occurred around one or two in the morning, for example, agents of one railroad pressured an injured woman all night long while she 'was laboring under great nervous strain'. In addition to her own injuries, 'she was greatly distressed and excited' because '[h]er infant was injured about the head'. After hours of effort, the agents finally secured her signature on a release 'about day-break'.[53] The Supreme Court of Illinois described another female passenger who

was in her private room at the hotel, suffering at the time the most intense pain, was partly disrobed, and was being attended by a lady,—a casual acquaintance,—who had been applying liniment to her person, and was then combing her hair, when two strange men entered the room to secure her signature to the paper.[54]

Another railroad agent arrived at a widow's home less than two hours after she had viewed her husband's 'mutilated remains' which had been found 'scattered along the track, the hands at one place, the head at another, and the liver at another'. When she confessed to the agent that her 'one thought' was to have her husband's remains buried at his old home in another county, the agent immediately seized the opportunity. He told her that

[52] Cf. Ian Ayres and Peter Siegelman, 'Race and Gender Discrimination in Bargaining for a New Car', *American Economic Review*, 85/3 (1995), 304–21.

[53] *St. Louis, Iron Mountain & Southern Railway Co. v. Reilly*, 161 SW 1052, 1053 (Sup. Ct. Ark. 1913).

[54] *Chicago, Rock Island and Pacific Railway Co. v. Lewis*, 109 Ill. 120, 132 (Sup. Ct. Ill. 1884).

if she did not sign a release to the railroad company, she would have to bury her husband at her own expense; that he was in a hurry to get back and notify the undertaker; that it was too great expense to bury her husband at his old home; that the railroad company would do nothing towards burying her husband but would 'hands off' unless she would sign a release. He also stated that the railroad company was not liable to her.

All of the agent's statements, the Supreme Court of Georgia subsequently found, were false.[55]

If agents tried more often to bully and intimidate women, female claimants who subsequently took their claims to court sometimes received a particularly sympathetic hearing. The courts often showed solicitude for widows, and they appeared willing to give relatively heavy weight to the argument that women were not responsible for signing releases because they possessed little or no business experience. A Kentucky court affirmed a verdict for a female plaintiff on the ground, inter alia, that she 'had no male friend present to advise her' when she signed a release,[56] and the Supreme Court of North Dakota did the same for a woman who 'was away from her husband and without legal advice'.[57]

While gender sometimes won judicial sympathy for female plaintiffs, it often made no difference. Many women claimants received not a whit of special consideration. The courts often upheld the releases they contested, even when the circumstances were dubious. Although the nature of the evidence makes any conclusions tentative, it seems likely that claim agents frequently exploited the special vulnerabilities of female injury victims and that the courts remedied their abuses only erratically.

If women were relatively vulnerable to agent tactics, blacks suffered even more, especially in the South. First, as a practical matter, the opportunity for blacks to pursue tort claims was problematic and even dangerous. Repression, intimidation, and violence were integral parts of southern race relations; and blacks knew all too well the risk of offending whites for 'not knowing

[55] Hixon v. Georgia Southern & Florida Railway Co., 137 SE 260, 261 (Sup. Ct. Ga. 1927).
[56] Southern Railway Co. in Kentucky v. Brewer, 108 SW 936, 937 (Ct. App. Ky. 1908).
[57] Clark v. Northern Pacific Railway Co., 162 NW 406, 409 (Sup. Ct. ND 1917). See Barbara Y. Welke, 'Unreasonable Women: Gender and the Law of Accidental Injury, 1870–1920', Law and Social Inquiry, 19 (1994), 369–403.

their place'.[58] Filing an action that reflected badly on a local white—a small businessman, a corporate employee involved in the injury, or a claim agent responsible for settling the matter—could provoke social abuse, economic retaliation, or physical violence. Second, most blacks were relatively poor and uneducated, and they suffered as a group from high illiteracy rates. The inability of large numbers to read and write increased their vulnerability to white dishonesty. A black sharecropper who signed a highly disadvantageous contract remembered the lesson. '[I]f you didn't understand it', he explained, 'they just took advantage of your ignorance.'[59] Finally, most blacks looked on what they called 'the white folks' courthouse' with deep scepticism, if not outright hostility.[60] In many southern and border states blacks could not serve on juries, while black witnesses subjected themselves to unknown extra-legal dangers and, in any event, risked the cold disbelief of white juries.[61] There was also reason to believe that white juries would not award large judgments to black plaintiffs.[62] Further, in order to dare a court case blacks had little choice but to retain white attorneys. As one white southern attorney remarked: 'Negro lawyers do not get "good breaks" before white juries.'[63] Thus, hazarding a lawsuit would most likely require a black to trust a white attorney, as well as a white judge and white jury. Small wonder that in his classic study, *An American Dilemma*, Gunnar Myrdal concluded that as a practical matter most southern blacks were 'restricted to trying to settle things outside of court'.[64]

---

[58] 'To lodge a complaint against a white person was also to invite harassment and sometimes violence.' Leon F. Litwack, *Been in the Storm So Long: The Aftermath of Slavery* (New York, 1980), 285.

[59] Theodore Rosengarten, *All God's Dangers: The Life of Nate Shaw* (New York, 1975), 151. See David M. Katzman and William M. Tuttle, Jr. (eds.), *Plain Folk: The Life Stories of Undistinguished Americans* (Chicago, 1982), 157.

[60] Quoted in Gunnar Myrdal with the assistance of Richard Sterner and Arnold Rose, *An American Dilemma: The Negro Problem in Modern Democracy* (New York, 1944), at 537.

[61] Gilbert Thomas Stephenson, *Race Distinctions in American Law* (New York, 1910), 253–77; Myrdal, *American Dilemma*, 549–50; Litwack, *Been in the Storm So Long*, 287; Katzman and Tuttle, *Plain Folk*, 181.

[62] Maxwell Bloomfield, 'From Deference to Confrontation: The Early Black Lawyers of Galveston, Texas, 1895–1920', in Gerard W. Gawalt (ed.), *The New High Priests: Lawyers in Post-Civil War America* (Westport, Conn., 1984), 159.

[63] Quoted in John Dollard, *Caste and Class in a Southern Town* (1st pub. 1937; 3rd edn., Garden City, NY 1957), 262.

[64] Myrdal, *American Dilemma*, 528. Accord W. J. Cash, *The Mind of the South* (1st pub. 1941; New York, 1991), 120, 414.

Given those conditions, it seems almost certain that corporate claim agents, who lived on their ability to secure cut-rate releases, leaned frequently and heavily on the lever of race. 'Any white man can strike or beat a Negro, steal or destroy his property, cheat him in a transaction and even take his life, without much fear of legal reprisal,' Myrdal summarized. 'The minor forms of violence—cheating and striking—are a matter of everyday occurrence.'[65] Race relations, especially in the South, created an ideal context in which claim agents could ratchet up the social pressures they applied and secure drastically discounted settlements. When cornered by a white man and asked to sign an employment agreement, a southern black reported, '[w]e would have signed anything, just to get away'.[66]

Especially striking was the aftermath of a Seaboard Air Lines wreck in North Carolina in 1911. A special excursion train, scheduled for the annual outing of the St Joseph's African Methodist Episcopal Sunday School, carried 912 blacks packed into seven wooden coaches that had been designed to hold fifty people each. When the special crashed into a slow-moving freight, ten blacks were killed and another eighty-six injured, fifty-eight seriously. The Seaboard was clearly responsible for the wreck and had no legal defence to its passengers' claims. Immediately, the railroad dispatched agents to the scene, and a local paper reported that the resulting settlements ranged from $1 to $1,000.[67] Contemporaneously, a congressional study found that tort judgments for injured railroad workers averaged more than $900 in cases involving temporary injuries, $2,500 in death cases, and from $4,000 to $11,000 in permanent disability cases.[68] Apparently, therefore, the Seaboard's agents secured discounts of 80 to 90 per cent of the judgment value of the claims.

More revealing is the fact that the Seaboard's payments were low even compared to other out-of-court settlements. Such settlements, of course, were almost invariably lower than judgments, and the same congressional study found that they averaged approximately $70 for temporary injuries, $1,200 for both per-

[65] Myrdal, *American Dilemma*, 559.

[66] Hamilton Holt (ed.), *Life Stories of Undistinguished Americans as Told by Themselves* (New York, 1906), 191.

[67] Katie Letcher Lyle, *Scalded to Death by the Steam: Authentic Stories of Railroad Disasters and the Ballads that were Written about Them* (Chapel Hill, NC, 1991), 79–80.

[68] Sen. Doc. 338, 62 Cong., 2 sess. (1912), i. 131, 135, 139, 143.

manent partial disability and death claims, and just under $4,000 for claims of permanent total disability.[69] Two powerful forces, of course, helped keep those worker settlements relatively low: first, employers often threatened their employees with sanctions, including the loss of jobs, if they did not settle their claims readily; and, second, employers had a battery of special legal defences that made employee claims particularly unpromising.[70] The blacks injured and killed in the Seaboard wreck, in contrast, confronted neither of those compelling pressures and, indeed, occupied a commanding legal position because the railroad seemed clearly at fault. Regardless of those facts, however, the black passengers apparently settled for amounts significantly lower than those that the railroad workers obtained in their out-of-court agreements. Indeed, the blacks in the Seaboard wreck obtained much less than another group of passengers had received more than thirty years earlier. In 1880 the West Jersey Railroad settled forty claims on behalf of eighteen dead and twenty-two injured passengers for an average of $1,270 per claim, probably at least double or triple the average amount the blacks received.[71]

While the calculus of race placed black tort victims at a steep disadvantage, it did not invariably deny them justice. Conditions varied widely across the nation and even in the South, and the legal options available to blacks may have improved somewhat after the 1920s. Further, those known to be 'good blacks' and those who had white 'sponsors' were sometimes treated with benevolence. Those fortunate enough to obtain able white counsel and get into court—at least on claims with no 'racial' overtone—could sometimes succeed in winning relief. Indeed, black passengers injured on trains owned by foreign corporations probably had a relatively decent chance of prevailing. Reported release cases involving blacks—few in number—suggest that southern and border state courts would on occasion find in favour of blacks who seemed truly deserving, especially if they were old, severely injured, obviously overreached, and—perhaps—female.

The relatively small number of release cases involving blacks, however, together with the evidence of general racial repression

[69] Ibid. 131, 135, 139, 143.
[70] Purcell, *Litigation and Inequality*, 38–41, 72–82; Bergstrom, *Courting Danger*, 158–60.
[71] Robert B. Shaw, *A History of Railroad Accidents, Safety Precautions and Operating Practices* (2nd edn., [n. p.], Vail-Ballou Press, Inc., 1978), 422–3.

and discrimination, supports a simple conclusion. The overwhelming number of blacks settled their claims out of court,
received relatively low amounts of compensation, and dared challenge releases only rarely and only under unusually favourable
social circumstances. '[N]o one of us', recalled one southern
black, 'would have dared to dispute a white man's word.'[72]

Using legal rules: policing and counter-crafting behaviour

The pressure tactics of company agents and the minimal amounts
paid in settlements combined to make many judges deeply sceptical of releases signed shortly after accidents or in hurried circumstances. Frequently, they voided such agreements for fraud,
protecting claimants against many of the agents' most overt and
deceitful tactics. Given the need to prove 'intentional' misrepresentation and to meet a higher 'clear and convincing' standard of
proof, however, fraud was difficult to establish. Suspicious courts,
therefore, often turned to other theories to void dubious releases.

Increasingly, they used the doctrines of 'mistake' and 'mental
incompetence'. Both filled the middle ground where serious
doubts existed about an agent's actions but intentional misrepresentation had not clearly been shown. If misleading statements
had not been made intentionally, then they had necessarily been
made on the basis of an erroneous assumption of fact. In such
event, both parties were mistaken, and the intended agreement
had not been consummated. Similarly, if injured persons were not
able to act 'rationally', they lacked the mental competence to enter
into binding agreements. In either case, their contracts could be
set aside.

The irony, of course, was obvious. Corporate agents persistently sought out injury victims as soon as possible after accidents
and pressed them to sign releases immediately, regardless of their
physical and mental state and regardless of their ignorance about
their medical condition. The agents' goal was precisely to deal
with potential claimants while they were acutely vulnerable and
to pre-empt suits before they could become aware of the nature
of their injuries and obtain informed legal advice. Ignoring the

---

[72] Holt, *Life Stories of Undistinguished Americans*, 191.

essence of the social practice of corporate release-seeking, courts used fictitious concepts of 'mistake' and 'competence'—sporadically and erratically—to try to limit its overall operation. They drew essentially arbitrary lines to police the worst excesses of a social practice that flooded broadly beyond their control.

While the law provided some escape hatches for those who signed releases, it also provided corporate attorneys with powerful tools to defend many of their agents' most aggressive tactics. The 'mere concealment' rule, for example, was often useful. Since parties had a duty to read whatever agreements they signed, written releases were not voidable for fraud if agents 'merely' concealed the contents as opposed to fraudulently misrepresenting them. '[I]f by negligence and indifference to his own interests one permits himself to be overreached', explained one court, 'the law affords him no redress because his own conduct is blameworthy.'[73] Agents might succeed in securing legally binding agreements, in other words, even though the written document they presented contained terms that were different from those they had orally discussed or promised. If the injured person had an opportunity to read the agreement, the 'mere concealment' rule could salvage a release from a claim of fraud.

The 'statement of law' rule was equally serviceable. 'The law is presumed to be equally within the knowledge of all parties,' declared an Ohio court, upholding a contested release. 'The agent's opinion as to [the claimant's] legal rights, however strongly stated, was not a misrepresentation of a fact for the consideration of the jury.'[74] Thus, if agents couched their comments and exhortations in legal terms—the victim's 'fault', the company's non-liability, the legal significance of the alleged facts, or the elements that a claimant would have to prove if she went to court—they could stay within the law and probably ensure the validity of the releases they obtained.

There was an even more comprehensive rule—the 'opinion' rule—that was, understandably, of even greater utility. 'The true rule is that the mistake must relate to either a present or past fact or facts that are material to the contract of settlement', declared the Supreme Court of Nebraska, 'and not to an opinion as to future conditions as the result of present known facts.'[75] Artfully phrased, or at least testified to, statements about a victim's prognosis, the efficacy of the company's safety precautions, the weight due to the victim's testimony, the soundness of a doctor's evaluation, and other similar topics could be considered mere 'opinions' and, hence, insufficient to sustain a claim of fraud. The rule was especially serviceable in defending the optimistic prognoses of company doctors and the glowing assurances of their claim agents. 'A physician's diagnosis is necessarily a matter of opinion', wrote one court, 'except in cases where the ailment is external and visible.'[76] Though sensible in some contexts, the 'opinion' rule encouraged ambiguities to thrive where conflicts of interest inhered. The rule conferred a sweeping leeway on those whose statements served two masters, and it imposed heavy burdens on anyone who tried to challenge their craft. As long as agents cast their statements as opinions, they could hover in the grey, and their companies' attorneys could readily defend their actions.

Although courts often invoked the 'opinion' rule, they came increasingly to limit it after the turn of the century.[77] They seemed to grow more sensitive to the wiles of agents and the vulnerabilities of victims. 'The rule that a forecast of what will happen in the future is merely promissory, and not a statement of existing fact', explained the Supreme Court of Missouri in 1927, 'does not apply, where the matter involved is peculiarly within the speaker's knowledge.' The court upheld a ruling voiding a release because the 'agent was in better position to know the facts about [plaintiff's medical condition] than the plaintiff'.[78] Similarly, the courts seemed to become more willing to scrutinize records and find that statements of opinion actually contained misrepresented or concealed 'present facts' that company doctors knew or should have known. Such an interpretation allowed them to avoid the 'opinion' rule altogether. 'The gist of fraudulent misrepresentation is the producing of a false impression upon the mind of the other party', explained the Supreme Court of Oklahoma in 1913, 'and if this

[75] *Simpson* v. *Omaha & Council Bluffs Street Railway Co.*, 186 NW 1001, 1003 (Sup. Ct. Neb. 1922).

[76] *Denver and Rio Grande Railroad* v. *Ptolemy*, 169 P. 541, 542 (Sup. Ct. Colo. 1918).

[77] Compare, e.g., *Chicago and Northwestern Railway Co.* v. *Wilcox*, 116 F. 913, 919 (CCA 8th 1902) with *Great Northern Railway Co.* v. *Fowler*, 136 F. 118 (CCA 8th 1905).

[78] *State ex rel. St. Louis & San Francisco Railway Co.* v. *Daues*, 290 SW 425 (Sup. Ct. Mo. 1927).

result is actually accomplished the means of accomplishing it are immaterial.' Affirming a judgment for plaintiff, the court noted simply that the plaintiff was 'ignorant' and that 'the [company] physician had superior knowledge'.[79]

The courts increasingly recognized that experience, knowledge, and craft allowed agents to posture their behaviour and frame their statements in order to pressure victims to settle while at the same time avoiding any obvious, or at least provable, overreaching.[80] They knew, too, that such artfully ambiguous behaviour enabled company attorneys to characterize agents' actions in legally defensible ways and thereby to maintain the validity of the releases they secured. In the early twentieth century, by restricting such doctrines as the 'mere concealment' and 'opinion' rules, many judges began trying to limit the ability of agents to accomplish by art what the law condemned in principle.

The utility of releases and the scope of the informal legal process

As often as the courts voided releases, their decisions reached only a small percentage of the agreements that companies secured. The major social significance of corporate release practices did not occur in the frequent cases where courts voided agreements. Rather, their principal impact occurred in three other classes of cases where the releases prevailed.

The first was the large class of cases in which the courts did not void releases even though the record suggested pressured circumstances, agent overreaching, or a victim who had little or no understanding of his legal rights, medical condition, or the document presented. A New York appellate court refused to void a release signed the day after a streetcar accident by an 80-year-old man who had suffered a dislocated shoulder,[81] and the Supreme Court of New Jersey upheld a release for $100 signed by a passenger who had lost his arm while riding on a streetcar.[82]

---

[79] *St. Louis & San Francisco Railroad Co.* v. *Reed*, 132 P. 355, 357 (Sup. Ct. Okla. 1913).

[80] See, e.g., *Scheer* v. *Rockne Motors Corporation*, 68 F. 2d 942, 945 (CCA 2d 1934) (Hand, J.).

[81] *McLoughlin* v. *Syracuse Rapid Transit Railway Co.*, 101 NYS 196 (App. Div. 4th Dept. NY 1906).

[82] *Zdancewicz* v. *Burlington County Traction Co.*, 71 A. 123 (Sup. Ct. NJ 1908).

The law of releases, in other words, did not grind exceedingly small. '[C]ourts have shown a special disposition to sustain compromises of disputed claims', the New Hampshire Supreme Court declared in 1915, 'often without much regard to the injustice resulting.'[83] In *Spritzer* v. *Pennsylvania Railroad Co.*, for example, it was uncontested that plaintiff had been injured in a train wreck, thrown some 10 or 15 feet from the train, carried unconscious to a hospital, and placed on the floor on a stretcher in the company of approximately 100 other victims of the same wreck. The plaintiff testified that he awoke a couple of hours later 'in a kind of stupor', that he was 'cold because I was naked', and that he had 'a very terrible pain in my shoulder'. Finally, it was also uncontested that an agent approached the plaintiff while he was lying on the floor and, approximately three hours after the wreck, obtained a release. The Supreme Court of Pennsylvania upheld the agreement on the ground that the plaintiff had not set forth sufficient facts to show that he had been 'incompetent' when he signed it.[84]

The second class of cases where corporate release practices had their major social impact included those where the courts refused to void releases because the facts showed little or no evidence of culpable overreaching. Those cases revealed, instead, simply that the victims had acted most unwisely and—for whatever reason— had settled for inadequate compensation. In these cases it made no difference to the courts that the releases were signed within days or weeks of injury, that the victims were without knowledgeable advisers, that they might have been influenced by mistaken diagnoses of company doctors, that they were injured more severely than they had thought, or that they had probably had little or no real understanding of the documents they signed. The law protected releases that were free from certain identifiable— and properly proven—types of overreaching, regardless of the substantive unfairness of their terms or the gross inequality between the parties. In 1914, for example, the Supreme Court of Arkansas upheld a $10 release, signed two days after a train collision, and overturned a $2,500 jury verdict for a woman who had received permanent internal injuries. 'The settlement was an improvident one', the court acknowledged, 'but the plaintiff

---

[83] *McIsaac* v. *McMurray*, 93 A. 115, 118 (Sup. Ct. NH 1915).
[84] *Spritzer* v. *Pennsylvania Railroad Co.*, 75 A. 256, 257 (Sup. Ct. Pa. 1910).

entered into it in full possession of her senses and without the per-
petration of any trick or fraud.'[85]

The third class of cases where corporate release practices had
their major impact was the least visible but by far the largest and
most important. It was the class where the practice of organized
release seeking bore its true and most abundant harvest. It consisted of the vast and untold numbers of releases that were never
challenged in court and, hence, that never surfaced in the reported
'cases' or left traces in the judicial records. This third class was
founded on the beliefs of millions of tort victims that the releases
they signed had terminated any chance of legal recovery. The
major social impact of corporate settlement practices, in other
words, occurred outside the courts in a legal process that was
quick, effective, largely invisible, extremely profitable for the companies, and in every practical sense final and irremediable.

Exact measurement is impossible, but three basic facts suggest
the huge size of this third class. Millions of potential tort claims
arose every year; only a tiny percentage of them were resolved
judicially; and corporations maintained specialized departments
devoted to the goal of keeping adverse claims out of court. The
staggering disparity that existed between the number of potential
claims and the number of actual lawsuits establishes that the
number of out-of-court dispositions was huge, and the extensive
and methodical nature of corporate practices suggests that
their claims departments must have been highly successful in settling out of court the overwhelming number of claims against
them. Those claimants who did challenge releases in court, therefore, almost certainly constituted but a minute fraction of the
total number of tort victims who signed corporate settlement
agreements.

Those who signed releases were, of course, severely disadvantaged in any subsequent attempt to assert their original claim.
Before they could even attempt to present their case on the merits
they would have to convince a court to void the release. That
required them to establish fraud, mental incompetence, or mutual
mistake—all of which required a substantial legal and practical
effort. Equally important, they faced a series of procedural
obstacles designed to protect the integrity of releases. Many

---

[85] *Kansas City Southern Railway Co.* v. *Armstrong*, 171 SW 123, 125 (Sup. Ct. Ark. 1914).

jurisdictions required them to attack releases only in a separate suit in equity. That requirement imposed on them the burden of prosecuting two suits instead of one, a burden that increased their costs, delayed their action on the merits, and often deprived them of a jury on the critical questions at issue. Similarly, most courts held claimants to a particularly high standard of proof. The need to prevail by 'clear and convincing' evidence compounded claimants' problems of proof, warning them of the need to locate more and better witnesses and increasing their overall risk of ulti-mate failure. Finally, many courts required claimants to tender back to defendants the money paid pursuant to the releases. Though a seemingly minor procedural matter, the tender require-ment could impose significant hardships on poorer claimants, create a technical defence that could complicate or even bar their action, and, in some cases at least, prevent those who lacked funds from even getting into court.

That combination of legal and practical burdens undoubtedly discouraged large numbers of injured persons who came to regret their original settlements and belatedly considered the possibility of taking legal action. The major de facto function of releases, then, was not to block claims in court, but to dissuade claimants from ever attempting to seek relief in any court.

Conclusion: peering outside the courts

An examination of corporate settlement practices during the period from 1875 to 1945 suggests a number of conclusions. First, the release cases support the proposition that tort victims as a group received drastically discounted compensation for their injuries, that corporations extracted substantial benefits from the overall de facto process of claims disposition, and that the law allowed—and in some ways encouraged—those results. It would be impossible to quantify in any precise way the overall economic impact of this claims disposition process, and any complete accounting would have to include a range of discounting factors and a variety of other costs, including those unfairly or improp-erly imposed on corporate defendants. Still, the organization, numerical scope, and frequent ruthlessness of corporate settle-ment efforts suggest both that the methodical practice of release seeking constituted a highly effective way of minimizing overall corporate costs and, further, that in its direct economic impact on ordinary Americans the practice far overshadowed the importance of formal legal processes. The de facto system of corporate release seeking harmed tort victims seriously and benefited corporations substantially, and it rendered the common law tort system of the period highly inefficient.[86]

Second, the study of corporate settlement practices highlights the paradoxical and ambiguous nature of freedom of contract. A wondrous instrument of liberty, creativity, and material progress, contract was also a duplicitous and ruthless tool of coercion, oppression, and exploitation. Too often its proponents—like its detractors—saw only one side of its power. In the period from 1875 to 1945, largely congruent with the so-called '*Lochner* era', courts and commentators praised contract fervently, but they also began to recognize its oppressive uses and tried increasingly to limit them.

Third, the study also suggests more broadly that 'costs' are not only unavoidable burdens that occur in all human endeavours but also tools that are sought out, created, magnified, and—above all—used. 'Litigation' is neither an abstract nor wholly rule-bound process. Rather, it comprises an infinite variety of actions—legal and extra-legal as well—that clients and their attorneys take in order to pressure their adversaries to discount or abandon their claims. Corporate claim departments used the feared costs of litigation as a threat to persuade injured persons to discount or forsake their claims. They used the burdens of actual litigation to drive up the costs of pursuing those claims in order to serve the same purpose. They used releases to add new obstacles—economic and social—to the paths of tort victims who might subsequently be tempted to revive their claims. The study of litigation costs requires not only the study of generalized and economically inevitable 'transaction costs' but, more importantly, an examination of 'strategic and tactical costs'—the costs that lawyers discover, create, magnify, manipulate, and exploit.

Fourth, examination of corporate settlement practices shows

---

[86] See I. P. L. Png, 'Litigation, Liability, and Incentives for Care', *Journal of Public Economics*, 34 (1987), 61–85; A. Mitchell Polinsky, 'The Deterrent Effects of Settlements and Trials', *International Review of Law and Economics*, 8 (1988), 109; Hylton, 'Litigation Costs and the Economic Theory of Tort Law'.

that both empirical studies of judicial caseloads and analytic theories about the 'selection' of cases for litigation, settlement, and trial need to be deepened and contextualized. This study shows that the interests and practices of institutions and groups helped shape the contours of the out-of-court settlement process. Settlements did not occur randomly or accidentally. Rather, they had distinct patterns depending on the nature of the parties and the types of claims involved, and changing social factors were critical in shaping those patterns and determining their practical results.[87] Understanding the nature and distribution of judicial caseloads and the process by which cases were 'selected' for litigation or settlement requires an understanding of the social interests and institutions at work in any given historical period, not merely a logical analysis of timeless probabilities about the litigation options of abstracted 'plaintiffs' and 'defendants'.[88]

Fifth, the study of corporate settlement practices also shows that in some socio-legal contexts the ostensibly applicable substantive law may have little or no effect on the content of private agreements. In spite of the law's varied impact in other contexts, it had only an oblique and contingent relationship to the settlement agreements that corporate agents secured. Any study of the social or economic impact of legal rules, in other words, must examine both the extent to which various specific types of actors were able to avoid those rules as well as the extent to which they were able to use them in ways that went beyond their formal purposes. Legal rules were not self-executing, and in the great majority of disputes they were never judicially applied. Consequently, there is no a priori reason to assume that they determined, shaped, or even affected the out-of-court settlement of any individual case or any particular class of cases.[89]

Sixth, this study also highlights the fact that 'difficult' cases, 'ambiguous' situations, and 'disputed' facts do not always just

[87] See, e.g., the discussion of 'social litigation systems' in Purcell, *Litigation and Inequality*, 248–50.

[88] Barry Nalebuff, 'Credible Pretrial Negotiation', *Rand Journal of Economics*, 18 (1987), 197–210; Marc Galanter and Mia Cahill, '"Most Cases Settle": Judicial Promotion and Regulation of Settlements', *Stanford Law Review*, 46 (1994), 1339; John C. Harsanyi, 'Games with Incomplete Information', *American Economic Review*, 85 (1995), 291.

[89] e.g. Samuel R. Gross, 'The American Advantage: The Value of Inefficient Litigation', *Michigan Law Review*, 85 (1987), 734–57. Cf. Austin Sarat and Thomas R. Kearns, 'Beyond the Great Divide: Forms of Legal Scholarship and Everyday Life', in A. Sarat and T. R. Kearns (eds.), *Law in Everyday Life* (Ann Arbor, 1993), 21–61.

happen. Rather, they are often created and sometimes systematically cultivated. By seeking quick releases—by dealing with injured persons when they were alone, in pain, without counsel, under medication, and ignorant of the true extent of their injuries—corporate agents chose to operate in a grey area where ambiguities not only would abound by nature but could also thrive by design. By artfully crafting their behaviour and statements to remain arguably within the limits of certain legal rules—the 'opinion' rule or the 'mere concealment' rule, for example—they could ensure that their actions would be legally defensible, regardless of the calculated de facto pressures or misconceptions they generated. As organized and experienced parties, in other words, corporate agents learned to play in the grey, and their companies profited from the results.[90]

Finally, though this study only glances at the formal law, it suggests the amazing constitutive power of legal language and doctrine. The law of releases helped define and animate the ideology of the 'free' and 'rational' economic individual. In a context where organization, sophistication, and calculation confronted ignorance, confusion, desperation, and pain, the law presumed fairness, knowledge, capacity, and mutuality. Establishing those ideal qualities as 'normal', it required parties who would attack releases to prove by 'clear and convincing evidence' that their situations were aberrational. Absent such proof of fraud, the law forced them to speak of 'incompetence' and 'mistake' in situations where neither of those concepts fairly or realistically captured what had in truth occurred. Therein lay a powerful act of creation.

---

[90] Some statutes tried to restrict the use of releases. See, e.g., *Thorne v. Columbia Cab Co.*, 3 NYS 537 (City Ct. NY 1938).

Notes on Contributors

RICHARD H. CHUSED is a Professor of Law at Georgetown University Law Center in Washington, where he teaches property, copyright, family law, and legal history. His numerous writings include a property textbook, a history of legislative divorce, and articles on landlord–tenant law and Married Women's Property Acts. He is currently working on a history of gender and law in the United States.

RAYMOND COCKS is Professor of Law at Keele University. He has written on property law, legal history, legal education, and the legal profession. His publications include *Foundations of the Modern Bar* (1983), *Sir Henry Maine: A Study in Victorian Jurisprudence* (1988), (with others) *Planning for Affordable Housing* (1995), and 'Law Reform and the Use of Sources at the Public Record Office', *Journal of Legal History*, 16 (1995), 256–80.

ALAIN COTTEREAU, sociologist and historian, is senior researcher at the CNRS (Centre d'Étude des Mouvements Sociaux, École des Hautes Études en Sciences Sociales), Paris. His earlier works were on urban politics, history of hygiene, and various aspects of French labour history. More recently his research is concerned with relations between justice at the workplace, movements within the public sphere, and the history of industrial districts, with a particular focus on Franco-British comparisons. Among his publications are: *Pouvoir et légitimité*, ed. with P. Ladrière (1992), and articles on working conditions in the French and British textile industries.

DAVID ENGLANDER, Reader in History at the Open University, died on 7 April 1999 at the relatively young age of 49. His research interests included the history of social reform and investigation and aspects of urbanization. He co-founded the Charles Booth Centre. Among his many publications were *Landlord and Tenant in Urban Britain, 1838–1918* (1983), the standard monograph on the subject; (with R. O'Day) *Mr Charles Booth's Inquiry* (1993) and *Retrieved Riches* (1995); and his acclaimed *Poverty and Poor Law Reform in Britain: From Chadwick to Booth* (1998).

LAWRENCE M. FRIEDMAN is the Marion Rice Kirkwood Professor of Law, Stanford University, California. His main fields of interest are legal history and the study of law and society. His books include *A History of American Law* (2nd edn., 1985), *The Republic of Choice: Law, Authority and Culture* (1990), *Crime and Punishment in American History* (1993), and *The Horizontal Society* (1999).

UTE GERHARD is Professor of Sociology and Director of the Frankfurt Centre for Women's and Gender Studies. Her research interests are the history and theory of feminism, social policy, and women's encounters with the law. She is co-founder of *Feministische Studien* and co-editor of *L'Homme: Zeitschrift für feministische Geschichtswissenschaft*. Among her publications are *Verhältnisse und Verhinderungen: Frauenarbeit, Familie und Rechte der Frauen im 19. Jahrhundert* (1978) and *Gleichheit ohne Angleichung: Frauen im Recht* (1990), and she has edited *Frauen in der Geschichte des Rechts: Von der frühen Neuzeit bis zur Gegenwart* (1997).

MARTIN H. GEYER was Deputy Director of the German Historical Institute in Washington, and is now Professor of Modern History at the University of Munich. His research interests cover the history of social policy, inflation, and legal discourse. He is author of *Die Reichsknappschaft: Versicherungsreformen und Sozialpolitik im Bergbau, 1900–1945* (1987) and *Verkehrte Welt: Revolution, Inflation und Moderne: München 1919–1929* (1998).

JEAN-LOUIS HALPÉRIN is Professor of Legal History at the University of Dijon and a junior member of the Institut Universitaire de France. He has written on French revolutionary and nineteenth-century law. Among his publications are *L'Impossible Code civil* (1992) and *Histoire du droit privé français depuis 1804* (1996). He is also working on judicial history and lawyers.

DOUGLAS HAY is Professor at Osgoode Hall Law School, York University, Canada. He is editor and co-author of numerous works on the history of crime, labour law, and English society in the eighteenth and nineteenth centuries. He is also engaged in a project on the history of labour law in the British Empire. His most recent publication (with N. Rogers) is *Eighteenth-Century English Society: Shuttles and Swords* (1997).

PAUL JOHNSON is Professor of Economic History at the London School of Economics. His current research interests include the interaction of laws and markets in Victorian England, changes in the standard of living during the Industrial Revolution, and the economics and history of pensions systems. He is author of *Saving and Spending: The Working-Class Economy in Britain 1870–1939* (Oxford, 1985), *Ageing and Economic Welfare* (1992), and editor of *Twentieth-Century Britain: Economic, Social and Cultural Change* (1994).

SUSANNA MAGRI, sociologist, is Research Fellow at the research unit Cultures et Sociétés Urbaines (IRESCO-CNRS), Paris. She works on the comparative history of urban housing and housing policy. Recent publications include *Les Laboratoires de la réforme de l'habitation populaire en France:*

De la Société Française des Habitations à Bon Marché à la Section d'Hygiène Urbaine et Rurale du Musée Social, 1889–1909 (1995), and 'Housing', in J. Winter and J.-L. Robert (eds.), *Capital Cities at War: Paris, London, Berlin 1914–1919* (1997).

KAREN ORREN is Professor of Political Science at the University of California, Los Angeles. Her publications include *Belated Feudalism: Labor, the Law and Liberal Development in the United States* (1991). She is currently working on a developmental theory of the US Constitution.

EDWARD A. PURCELL, JR. is Professor of Law at New York Law School. He has practised law in New York City, and has taught both history and law. His research interests focus on American legal, cultural, and intellectual history, and his publications include *The Crisis of Democratic Theory: Scientific Naturalism and the Problem of Value* (1973) and *Litigation and Inequality: Federal Diversity Jurisdiction in Industrial America* (1992). His most recent book, *Brandeis and the Progressive Constitution: Erie, the Judicial Power, and the Politics of the Federal Courts in Twentieth-Century America*, will be published by Yale University Press.

TILMAN REPGEN is *Assistent* in the Law Faculty at the University of Cologne. His research interests are the history of Roman law in medieval and early modern Europe and the history of private law in the nineteenth and twentieth centuries. He is author of *Vertragstreue und Erfüllungszwang in der mittelalterlichen Rechtswissenschaft* (1994) and is currently working on a study of social aspects in the German Civil Code of 1900.

SPIROS SIMITIS is Professor of Labour Law, Civil Law, and Computer Science and Law at the University of Frankfurt. He is also Director of the Institute of Labour Law and of the Research Centre for Data Protection at Frankfurt. He has been Visiting Professor at Yale University since 1980 and at the University of Paris since 1993. His publications include works on labour law and industrial relations, anti-discrimination laws, data protection, and family law, especially children's rights.

WILLIBALD STEINMETZ has been Research Fellow at the German Historical Institute in London and is now a Deutsche Forschungsgemeinschaft scholar at the University of Bochum. His main fields of interest are the comparative history of political languages, intercultural transfers, and modern social and legal history. He is author of *Das Sagbare und das Machbare: Zum Wandel politischer Handlungsspielräume: England 1780–1867* (1993), and is currently preparing a study on the legal history of labour in nineteenth- and twentieth-century Britain and Germany.

FABIEN VALENTE is *Maître de conférences* at the University of Montpellier I where he teaches history of law. His main fields of interest are the history of commercial law and the history of justice. His main publications are: *Le Gestionnaire dans le 'Parfait Négociant' de Jacques Savary* (1992), *Une découverte récente: Le Projet de Code de commerce lyonnais de 1802* (1993), *Les Premiers Rudiments de l'enseignement de la gestion commerciale aux derniers siècles de l'Ancien Régime* (1995), *Les Débuts de la justice de paix dans le canton de Givors* (1997), and *Saint Augustin et la Juridiction épiscopale* (1998).

URSULA VOGEL is Senior Lecturer in the Department of Government, University of Manchester. Her research interests cover the political and legal thought of the Enlightenment, theories of citizenship, and feminist conceptions of rights. Publications include (with M. Moran) *The Frontiers of Citizenship* (1991), and a variety of articles on women's property rights, the institution of marriage, and ideas of community in German Romanticism. She is currently completing a book on marriage and the political order.

MONIKA WIENFORT was *Assistent* in the Faculty of History at Bielefeld University and is now a Deutsche Forschungsgemeinschaft scholar. Her main fields of interest are the history of legal institutions, the monarchy, and the middle classes in modern Europe. She is the author of *Monarchie in der bürgerlichen Gesellschaft: Deutschland und England von 1640–1848* (1993), and has written numerous articles on law and society in nineteenth-century Germany. She is currently preparing a book on the Prussian patrimonial courts.

Index

Index

Knatchbull, Sir Edward 54
Krupp, Alfred 193
Ku-Klux-Klan 426–7

labour
    commodification of 187, 190, 192, 194,
        202
    division within family 154
    father's right in children's 188–91
    husband's right in wife's 99, 143, 191
    opposed to 'capital' 468
    as property 330
    protection of 464
    sweated 419
    unfree 8
    see also contract; hours of work; piece-
        workers; home-workers
labour market 190, 210, 235
    entry of freed slaves into 426, 430
    focus on by 'realist' law reformers 431–
        2
    and rental market 349, 351–2, 367
    and use of master and servant law
        243–4, 278
labour movement 265–6, 333, 347
Labour Party 268
labour relations
    and constitutional rights (US) 313–34
    in countryside 85–6
    and law 181–202, 203–26, 227–64, 265–
        312
Lancashire 260
landlords
    as tenants 362
    blacklisting absconding tenants 401
    churches as 421
    economic behaviour of 351–2
    as elements of the bourgeoisie 359, 362
    exerting political pressure 417–18
    image of 343–4, 347, 367, 377
    liability for injuries of tenant 414, 421–
        2
    liability for repairs 364, 388, 394–9,
        403–4, 412, 423–4
    organizations 375, 384, 401–2
    as plaintiffs in English county courts
        295
    property rights infringed by public rent
        control 478
    property rights threatened by tenants'
        action 345–7
    social composition of 348, 360–1, 364,
        368–9

    see also eviction; housing; rent; tenancy
        law; tenants (urban)
landowners
    as debtors 448
    favoured by English law 163, 418
    as magistrates 270
    using the law 45–51, 54–63
    see also agricultural labourers; estate
        owners; farmers; peasants; tenants
        (rural)
languages 27, 28, 457
    of civil courts 497
    of community 111, 114, 117, 120–1
    of contractual individualism 95, 102,
        329–30, 430
    of criminal courts 238
    of equality 95
    of factory owners 223
    of fourteenth amendment to US
        Constitution 317–18
    of individual rights 111, 115
    of judicial statistics 283
    of 'justice' 480
    of the law 7–8, 69, 94, 101, 144, 378,
        457–9, 468–9, 473, 535
    of liberalism 7, 99
    of morality 471
    as obstacle in legal proceedings 430
    political 254, 458–9, 462
    popular 457–9, 468, 473
    prompting legal and social action 459–
        60
    reactionary 114
    of social policy and social justice 481
    of statutes 240
larceny, *see* theft
Lasker, Eduard 465
Laski, Harold 7
Latin America 356
law
    accessibility of 497, 499
    'in action' 28, 139, 171, 174–5, 201, 268,
        271
    autonomy of 7, 28, 156, 504
    avoidance of 22, 24, 223–4, 265, 267–9,
        279, 305–6, 308, 310–12, 534
    awareness of 62, 510–11, 527, 529, 535
    becoming more favourable to
        employees 310
    becoming more favourable to
        employers 231, 255, 258, 263–4
    defined as political undertaking 431
    defined as science 430